AGRICULTURAL BOTANY

CONVERSION TABLES

Length

1 inch=25·4 millimetres
12 inches=1 foot=30·48 centimetres
3 feet=1 yard=0·9144 metre

Area

1 sq. inch=6·416 sq. centimetres
144 sq. inches=1 sq. foot=929·034 sq. centimetres
9 sq. feet=1 sq. yard=0·8361 sq. metres
4,840 sq. yards=1 acre=4046·873 sq. metres

Weight

1 ounce (1 oz.)=28·352 grams
16 ounces=1 pound (1 lb.)=4·536 hectograms
14 pounds=1 stone=6·35 kilograms
28 pounds=1 quarter=12·7 kilograms
4 quarters=1 hundredweight (1 cwt.)=50·8 kilograms
20 hundredweights=1 ton=1·016 metric tons

Capacity

8 pints=1 gallon=4·54596 litres
8 gallons=1 bushel=36·37 litres

AGRICULTURAL BOTANY

by

N. T. GILL, B.Sc., Ph.D.

Head of the Biology Department, Harper Adams Agricultural
College, Newport, Salop

and

K. C. VEAR, M.Sc.

Head of the Botany Department, Seale Hayne Agricultural
College, Newton Abbot, Devon

GERALD DUCKWORTH & CO. LTD.
3 Henrietta Street, London, W.C.2

First published 1958
Second edition 1966

© N. T. Gill and K. C. Vear, 1966

Printed in Great Britain by Photolithography
Unwin Brothers Limited, Woking and London

PREFACE

AGRICULTURAL botany is a subject which has no clearly defined boundaries, and which necessarily merges into pure botany on the one hand, and into agronomy on the other. Its scope has in Britain been largely influenced by the late Professor John Percival's *Agricultural Botany*, and any textbook of the subject must owe a great debt to that classical work. The present authors gladly and gratefully acknowledge that debt, but their book is in no sense a revision or adaptation of 'Percival'. It is, rather, an attempt to cover, at an elementary level, as much as possible of the rather wide range of topics now commonly accepted as forming parts of the subject, and to bring together for the student's benefit some of the relevant information scattered through the literature of botany and agriculture. It has been envisaged as covering the main requirements of agricultural diploma and pass-degree students, but no attempt has been made to adhere rigidly to any set syllabus, and it is hoped that the book may also be of use to others.

Since the book has been primarily designed for British students the main emphasis has throughout been on the crops economically important in this country. To have confined attention to these alone would, however, have resulted in a very limited and disconnected picture, and related plants have therefore been included. The line between agricultural and horticultural crops is not always well defined, and it has been thought desirable to include brief references to the majority of plants grown as vegetable crops.

Some knowledge of elementary botany has been assumed, but a glossary of botanical terms has been included for the convenience of non-botanical readers. Since the book is not intended primarily for advanced students, no attempt has been made to give references to original publications except where the results of particular trials or experiments are being quoted, but relevant books suitable for further reading are listed at the end of each section of the book. In many cases these include full bibliographies, from which reference to original literature may be made.

It has been assumed that the majority of students who may use this book will be pursuing a systematic course at some centre for agricultural education and will receive direction in practical work in the laboratory and in the field. For this reason no detailed suggestions for practical work have been included here. The authors would, however, wish to emphasize the point that the study of crops and weeds in the field is an essential component of the science of agricultural botany, and students should take every opportunity to develop this study.

The authors have received much help, in preparing this book, from friends and colleagues, and to them they wish to express their deep sense of gratitude. In particular their thanks are due to Dr. Janet Maclagan, who has been responsible for the collection of specimens and the preparation of all the diagrams of weeds in Section III, and who also assisted with several of the text figures in other sections. In addition, Dr. Maclagan has read and re-read the manuscript at all stages and has made many helpful suggestions.

Our thanks are also due to Mr. J. G. Jenkinson, M.Sc., who has read various sections and made many valuable suggestions, to Mr. N. C. Preston, M.Sc., for helpful advice and criticism in relation to the section dealing with plant diseases, and to Mr. W. D. Burrell, B.Sc.(Agric.), to whom we are grateful for suggestions in relation to Section I.

We acknowledge, with thanks, permission to quote from the literature of the National Institute of Agricultural Botany kindly granted by the Director, Mr. F. R. Horne, M.A., N.D.A., N.D.D.(Hons.), to whom we are also grateful for certain advice relating to nomenclature of crops.

The authors owe a debt of gratitude to the authors of all the publications mentioned in the text and acknowledge these valuable sources of information. Finally, we must express our thanks to the owners of the copyright of illustrations reproduced in the text.

N. T. G.
K. C. V.

January, 1958

SECOND EDITION

The sections on the Seeds Regulations and on Herbicides have been revised; modern varieties of crop plants have been introduced and a few diagrams have been re-drawn. Numerous minor alterations and additions which had become necessary with the passage of time, have also been made.

February 1966

CONTENTS

Section One

PLANT-BREEDING AND CROP IMPROVEMENT

Section Two

CROPS

Section Three

FARM WEEDS

Agricultural Botany

Section Four

DISEASES OF FARM CROPS

Chapter I

INTRODUCTION

THE study of botany in relation to agriculture is concerned chiefly with the crops of the farm in health and in disease and with the weeds which in various ways may cause losses to the farmer. It is a specialized study of a small section of the plant kingdom. In order to view this section in relation to the rest of plant life on the earth, let us first consider a general classification which includes most types of plants.

FLOWERLESS PLANTS OR CRYPTOGAMS

Division	*Class*	*Examples*
Thallophyta	Algae	Soil algae, fresh-water algae, seaweeds
	Fungi (including bacteria)	Mildews, moulds, mushrooms
Bryophyta	Hepaticae	Liverworts
	Musci	Mosses
Pteridophyta	Lycopodineae	Club mosses, etc.
	Equisetineae	Horsetails, etc.
	Filicineae	True ferns

FLOWERING PLANTS OR PHANEROGAMS (SPERMATOPHYTA)

Gymnospermae	Coniferae	Pines, firs, etc.
Angiospermae	Dicotyledons	Potato, beet, oak
	Monocotyledons	Grasses, onions, palms

Some of the above groups of plants are of little practical interest to students of agriculture, and will not be considered further. The algae which live in the soil, together with certain soil-inhabiting fungi and bacteria, play an important role in the maintenance of fertile soil conditions. The fungi are of importance further in that they include many species which live as parasites on crops and produce diseases, such as rusts, blights and mildews. This role of the fungi is considered in more detail in Section IV.

Among the ferns is bracken, the control of which provides an important problem in British agriculture. Certain horsetails too may occur on farms, and some species have caused poisoning of farm livestock.

Gymnospermae include many valuable forest trees, but are of little direct agricultural interest. Some species may be planted on farms in the form of shelter belts, and yew is of interest as a common cause of poisoning of livestock.

The agricultural crops and most of the weeds are found in the last division, the Angiospermae.

ANGIOSPERMAE

This division consists of flowering plants in which the seed is enclosed within a fruit, in contrast with the Gymnospermae, in which the seed is exposed, usually between the scales of a cone.

Within the division there are two classes:

(*a*) *Dicotyledons*. This class contains plants which have two cotyledons in their seeds. The veins of their leaves are usually branched and form a network. The vascular tissues of their stems are present in the form of a single ring of vascular bundles or, in woody plants, a cylinder of xylem or wood separated from a ring of phloem or bast by cambium. The parts of their flowers are present usually in fours or fives or multiples of these numbers, rarely in threes.

(*b*) *Monocotyledons*. In this group the seeds contain a single cotyledon. The veins of the leaves are usually parallel to one another. The vascular bundles of the stem are scattered or arranged in more than one ring, and there is no cambium. The parts of the flower are usually in threes or multiples of three.

Families. Each of the above classes is further sub-divided into Families, in which groups of plants showing similar general floral and other characteristics, which suggest that they are related, are placed together under a family name. For example, the grasses and cereals all have a similar type of flower, all produce a grain (or caryopsis), and in addition all show similarities in their leaf structure and arrangement, and in their general growth habit. All grasses and cereals are therefore placed in the same family, the *Gramineae*, within the Monocotyledons. Families may be grouped together in varying numbers to form groups known as *Orders*. For example, the families Papaveraceae, Fumariaceae, Cruciferae and Resedaceae together form the order Rhoeadales.

The name of a family may indicate some common characteristic of the family, for example, Cruciferae—cross-bearers—refers to the cruciform arrangement of the four petals of the flowers; Leguminosae refers to the type of fruit, the legume, which is common to most members of this family. Other family names are based on the name of one of the genera (see below) contained within the family; for example, Rosaceae is the family containing the genus *Rosa*, and Chenopodiaceae includes the genus *Chenopodium*.

Genera. Each family is sub-divided into smaller natural groups known as *genera* (singular, *genus*). For example, wheats and barleys possess common characteristics which place them in the family Gramineae, but they are readily distinguishable from one another and are placed in separate genera, the wheats in the genus *Triticum* and the barleys in the genus *Hordeum*.

Species. Within each genus are still smaller groups of plants known as

2

species. For example, within the genus *Triticum* there are several different species of wheat, of which one might mention the bread wheat grown in the large wheat-growing areas of the world and the macaroni wheat grown in certain Continental countries.

Species are designated by a combination of the *generic* name, or name of the genus, and a *specific* name, or name of the species within the genus. Thus, bread wheat is known botanically as *Triticum aestivum* and macaroni wheat as *Triticum durum*. This binomial, or two-name, system was adopted by the Swedish scientist Linnaeus (1753), who described and named a large number of plant and animal species. Other species have been described and named by other people since Linnaeus, and in order to indicate the author of a particular name the whole or part of the name of the person who originally described and named the species may be added after the specific name of the plant. Thus the red clover species which was described and named by Linnaeus is fully styled *Trifolium pratense*, Linn. or *Trifolium pratense* L.

There is now an International Code of Botanical Nomenclature which gives directions with regard to the naming of plants. Under this code the earliest appropriate name normally has priority and, in some cases, names which have become widely recognized have had to be abandoned in favour of earlier ones. Some species named by an earlier authority have subsequently been transferred to a different, more appropriate, genus by a later worker. In such cases the authority for the new genus is required by the code to retain the old specific name and the authority for the specific name is indicated in brackets after that name. Thus the common chickweed was formerly known as *Alsine media* L., but is now named *Stellaria media* (L.), Vill.

The scientific, binomial system of nomenclature may appear to hold little interest for the practical farmer, yet it is important to the student for various reasons. Firstly, it assists towards an understanding of the relationships of plants, which often have some bearing on their agricultural characteristics. Secondly, the scientific names are of value because they are fixed and definite, unlike the so-called common English names, which may vary from one part of the country to another. For example, a very common pasture weed is known in various parts of the country as ragwort, ragweed, staggerwort, stinking billy, stinking weed, yellow-weed, etc. As a result of this diversity, a native of one area might not be understood in another area when referring to the weed by the name common in his own locality. The botanical name of the weed, *Senecio jacobaea*, on the other hand, is not only used by botanists in all parts of the country, but is also used internationally. A further complication in the use of common names is the fact that one common name may be used for different species in different areas—for example, the name lakeweed is used in some districts for the species *Polygonum amphibium*, whilst in other districts it is applied to the species *Polygonum persicaria* (also known as redshank or persicaria).

Because the scientific names are international they are of great value in connection with scientific communication between different nationalities, and students visiting other countries or reading the scientific literature of other countries will quickly discover the wider value of scientific names as opposed to the more local value of common English names.

Botanical Varieties. In botanical classifications some species are subdivided into groups known as varieties, and the separate varieties are given scientific names. For example, the species *Pisum sativum* includes the garden and field peas. On the basis of flower colour, field peas, which have coloured flowers, are distinguished as a botanical variety and named *Pisum sativum* var. *arvense*, whilst the garden pea with white flowers remains the type of the species *Pisum sativum*.

Other Botanical Groups. The main botanical groups, families, genera, species and varieties have been indicated above. Occasionally it is convenient to make other groups, for example, within a family genera may be grouped together under the name of *Tribes*. Sub-groups within the main groups are referred to as sub-families, sub-tribes, sub-genera, and sub-species.

FAMILIES OF THE ANGIOSPERMAE

The classification of Angiospermae is based largely upon the structure of the flowers, fruits and seeds; arrangement of the leaves and habit and anatomy of the plants are also involved. From a study of fossils and from other evidence it is possible to suggest that certain characteristics appeared early in the course of evolution.

The following list, adapted from Hutchinson,* indicates the characters which are thought to be more primitive as opposed to those believed to be of more recent origin:

1. In any individual family or genus trees are more primitive than herbs, and trees and shrubs than climbers.

2. Perennials appeared before biennials or annuals.

3. Land forms are more primitive than aquatic, epiphytic, saprophytic or parasitic forms.

4. The spiral arrangement of parts is earlier than opposite or whorled arrangements.

5. Simple leaves are usually more primitive than compound leaves.

6. Hermaphrodite flowers are earlier than unisexual flowers.

7. For unisexual flowers the monoecious habit is more primitive than the dioecious habit.

8. The solitary flower came before the inflorescence.

9. In flowers there is a general tendency towards the gradual reduction in the numbers of the various parts; thus the absence of petals is an advanced character.

10. Free petals are more primitive than united petals.

11. Regular (actinomorphic) flowers are more primitive than irregular (zygomorphic).

* J. Hutchinson, *British Flowering Plants*, 1948, Gawthorn.

4

12. The hypogynous condition is most primitive, then perigynous and finally epigynous.

13. Free stamens are earlier than united stamens.

14. Free carpels are more primitive than united carpels.

15. Endospermic seeds with a small embryo appeared earlier than non-endospermic seeds with a large embryo.

16. Simple fruits are more primitive than compound fruits, and as a rule capsules are earlier than drupes or berries.

The dicotyledons with their single ring of vascular bundles are considered to have evolved before the monocotyledons with their scattered vascular bundles. Within each of these two main groups the more primitive families generally possess many of the primitive characters listed above, whilst families considered to be more highly evolved show few of these characters and more of the characters considered to be advanced.

The buttercup (*Ranunculus acris*) with its regular, hypogynous flowers with free petals, numerous stamens, numerous free carpels and endospermic seeds, shows largely characters which are considered to be primitive. The buttercup family, Ranunculaceae, is considered to be one of the oldest, although in some classifications families containing largely trees and shrubs, and herbaceous species obviously related to them, are placed earlier than the Ranunculaceae, in which most species are herbaceous.

On comparing flowers of other families with the buttercup, it will be observed that certain modifications exist which are considered to be more recent in origin; for example, in the family Cruciferae the number of stamens is reduced, usually to 6, and the carpels are reduced to 2 and are united, also the seed is non-endospermic. Various families have evolved in various directions, and families cannot really be arranged in an evolutionary series. A correct picture of the relative positions of various families from an evolutionary point of view would be provided better by consideration of the branches of a tree spreading out from various levels in various directions and producing further branches. Any list of families therefore can only suggest their approximate relationships.

Families of Agricultural Interest

The families of flowering plants dealt with in Sections II and III represent only a small proportion of all families. The order in which they are arranged is designed to suggest their natural relationships and follows that adopted in *Flora of the British Isles* (Clapham, Tutin and Warburg).

Some families are of interest because they contain both crop and weed species. They appear therefore in Section II (Crops) and Section III (Weeds); other families appear in only one of these sections.

In the following key to the families, which is based on a few floral characteristics, most of the families appear in the order in which they are dealt with in the text; one or two exceptions to this order occur, owing to the limited number of characters considered in the key.

A. *Dicotyledons*

Sub-class I *Archichlamydeae*—in which the petals, when present, are free from each other (rarely united).

1. Flowers usually possessing both sepals and petals:

(*a*) Flowers hypogynous, with an apocarpous gynaecium:
Ranunculaceae, the buttercup family (p. 405).

(*b*) Flowers hypogynous, with a syncarpous gynaecium:
(i) Placentation of the ovules parietal.
Papaveraceae, the poppy family (pp. 109 and 410).
Fumariaceae, the fumitory family (p. 410).
Cruciferae, the cabbage and charlock family (pp. 109 and 411).
Violaceae, the violet family (p. 415).
(ii) Placentation of ovules free-central or basal.
Caryophyllaceae, the campion family (p. 416).
(iii) Placentation of ovules axile.
Linaceae, the linseed family (p. 142).
Geraniaceae, the cranesbill family (p. 420).

(*c*) Flowers perigynous:
Leguminosae, the bean family (pp. 147 and 423).

(*d*) Flowers perigynous to epigynous:
Rosaceae, the rose family (pp. 185 and 425).

(*e*) Flowers epigynous (ovary inferior):
Onagraceae, the willowherb family (p. 427).
Umbelliferae, the carrot and hemlock family (pp. 190 and 427).
Cucurbitaceae, the white bryony family (p. 431).

2. Flowers with a perianth usually of one whorl (or absent), usually sepaloid but sometimes petaloid:
Chenopodiaceae, the beet and fat hen family (pp. 130 and 419).
Euphorbiaceae, the spurge family (p. 431).
Polygonaceae, the buckwheat and dock family (pp. 196 and 431).
Urticaceae, the nettle family (p. 435).
Cannabinaceae, the hop family (p. 199).

Sub-class II *Metachlamydeae*—Petals united to form a tube; rarely free or absent. Families in this group are considered to be more highly evolved. Frequently they show a considerable degree of adaptation to secure pollination.

1. Flowers hypogynous:

(*a*) Corolla regular.
Primulaceae, the primrose family (p. 437).

Boraginaceae, the comfrey family (pp. 206 and 437).
Convolvulaceae, the convolvulus family (p. 439).
Solanaceae, the potato and deadly nightshade family (pp. 208 and 441).
Plantaginaceae (petals small, scale like), the plantain family (p. 451).

(*b*) Corolla irregular.
Scrophulariaceae, the foxglove family (p. 444).
Orobanchaceae, the broomrape family (p. 445).
Labiatae, the deadnettle family (p. 448).

2. Flowers epigynous:
Rubiaceae, the bedstraw family (p. 453).
Dipsacaceae, the teasel family (p. 219).
Compositae, the sunflower and thistle family (pp. 220 and 453).

B. *Monocotyledons*
1. Perianth present:
(*a*) Flowers hypogynous:
Liliaceae, the onion family (pp. 227 and 465).
Juncaceae, the rush family (p. 470).
(*b*) Flowers epigynous:
Iridaceae, the iris family (p. 472).
Dioscoreaceae, the black bryony family (p. 470).
2. Perianth absent or represented by small scales or bristles.
Araceae (perianth present in the genus *Acorus*), the arum family (p. 472).
Cyperaceae, the sedge family (p. 474).
Gramineae, the grass family (p. 228).

Within families some genera are more closely related than others as are some species within a genus. With the advance of the sciences of cytology and genetics since the beginning of the century much light has been thrown upon such relationships, and a greater knowledge of the evolution of species has been obtained. In Section I of this book the elements of genetics and cytology are considered, together with some of the applications of these sciences to the breeding of crop plants and to the elucidation of the means by which new types of plants arise naturally.

THE CLASSIFICATION OF CROP PLANTS

The increased knowledge of the origins of our cultivated plants, together with the new types of plants being produced by plant-breeders, provide difficulties in the application of a system of botanical classification and nomenclature developed originally for the description of naturally-occurring wild plants.

No problems occur in connection with the larger groups, families and tribes, and in most cases generic distinctions are also clear. In a few cases, however, fertile hybrids have developed from crosses involving different genera, e.g. bread wheat (p. 256); in such cases it is customary and convenient, if not strictly logical, to retain the name of one of these genera (*Triticum*) to which these plants were referred before their origin had been worked out.

The definition of species in cultivated plants presents more problems; many groups of crop plants, known or assumed to have originated in cultivation by hybridization or selection, are commonly described as species. Thus, taking wheats as an example, various so-called species are known to be the result of different crossings (p. 255). Percival reserved the term 'species' for those groups known as wild plants, using the term '*race*' for those known only in cultivation, but this usage has not become general. In some cases cultivated plants have been split into different species on single character differences; thus two-rowed, four-rowed and six-rowed barleys have been described as three distinct species, although they readily cross with the production of fully fertile offspring. Such multiplication of species appears undesirable, and in this book the cultivated barleys have been treated as one specific group, *Hordeum sativum*.

Within the species the problem becomes still more complicated. The botanical terms *sub-species* and *variety* are available, but are entirely inadequate to cover the great range of different forms found within many of the important crop species. In some cases, as, for example, in barleys, very elaborate classifications involving varieties, sub-varieties, sub-sub-varieties and other groups have been proposed. Such classifications usually involve purely arbitrary decisions as to which characters shall be used as the major distinctions, and may well result in the creation of a large number of specially named categories, to include rare types of negligible importance, whilst still not providing a satisfactory grouping of the commonly-grown agricultural forms. Further, when two types exist within a species, each with certain agricultural merits, it may be expected that, sooner or later, they will be crossed by a plant-breeder in an endeavour to produce a plant combining the advantages of both. Thus the multiplicity of types increases, and there is considerable justification for the view that in such groups 'systematics have been defeated by plant-breeding'. Such an attitude has been adopted in this book, and within the individual species no attempt has been made to give a full and systematic classification, with Latin-named categories. Usually the noncommittal term 'group' has been employed, in default of any satisfactory and generally accepted alternative, and the common English names employed, although where Latin varietal names exist, these are in many cases given for reference.

Agricultural Varieties and Strains. The term *variety* as commonly applied to agricultural plants is used in a sense which differs from its strictly botanical usage. For example, within the botanical variety *Pisum sativum* var. *arvense*, the field pea, there are several agricultural varieties. The term is normally applied to units smaller than the botanical variety, and units in which characters of agricultural importance may provide points of distinction—for example, in barleys, standing capacity of the straw, malting quality of the grain, resistance to frost and earliness of ripening provide important differences between agricultural varieties, such as Spratt-Archer, Pioneer and Kenia.

In crops which are normally reproduced vegetatively, such as potato, a clone (see p. 48) is normally known as a variety and the plants within the variety are alike in botanical and agricultural characters and are likely to remain so from year to year. In such varieties stability and uniformity can be expected.

In self-pollinated crops, such as barley and wheat, a variety is a reasonably definite unit, usually fairly uniform when released by the plant-breeder and likely to maintain its uniformity of type, with regard to major characters, for some generations, with but little effort on the part of the breeder or seed-producers. The uniformity and stability of such varieties is not so great, however, as in vegetatively propagated varieties; a certain amount of genetic variation is more likely to occur in time in sexually reproduced plants.

In cross-pollinated crops the term 'variety' is popularly applied to units the members of which are much less closely related and much more variable than the members of a vegetatively-propagated or a self-pollinated variety. In such units there is much less uniformity of botanical and agricultural characters between individual plants and a mean standard type for the variety is maintained from season to season only with considerable effort (see p. 67). These less stable, more variable cross-pollinated 'varieties' are often referred to as *strains*, and there is a tendency in some countries to reserve the term 'variety' for application to vegetatively-propagated and self-pollinated crops. There is as yet, however, little uniformity in the use of these terms, and 'strain' is often used to describe a smaller unit within a 'variety'. The problem of the definition of the terms 'variety' and 'strain' in relation to agricultural crops is further complicated by the popular use of 'strain' in relation to grasses and clovers, and 'variety' in relation to comparable units of other cross-pollinated crops, such as mangel and turnip. A further complication arises through the use of the term 'strain' in designating the various forms of a particular virus (see p. 584).

The term *cultivar* is now used internationally in scientific communications as a designation for varieties and strains of cultivated plants.

The use of the term 'strain' for herbage plants has been popularized in this country but the council of the National Institute of Agricultural Botany has endorsed the suggestion of an international body that 'variety' should be used for all agricultural crops. Thus the term 'strain' should eventually disappear in this connection.

The reader should be careful not to confuse the agricultural 'variety' and the botanical variety, and should bear in mind the distinctions drawn above between agricultural varieties of vegetatively-propagated, self-pollinated and cross-pollinated crops.

Section One

PLANT-BREEDING AND CROP IMPROVEMENT

Chapter II

PLANT-BREEDING: ART AND SCIENCE

THE early history of our cultivated farm crops is, in most cases, somewhat obscure. Clearly the earliest cultivated crops must have been obtained from wild plants which had been proved, by experience, to be suitable for the provision of food for man and his animals. Further development of cultivated crops would be brought about as a result of natural selection in which environmental factors acting upon the crops under cultivation resulted in the concentration of plants suited to the conditions and the elimination of others less well adapted. Some development may have resulted from the selection of plants, by observant cultivators, for the production of seed for the following crop. Such early attempts at crop improvement are likely to have consisted of mass selection of large numbers of plants, a method which has limited value in crop improvement, as will be seen later.

From the end of the seventeenth century onwards a more scientific interest was taken in crop improvement. At first methods of selection from existing crops were used, and these occasionally gave valuable results.

Differences between individual plants in a crop may be due to different environmental conditions or to inheritable characteristics. The differences due to environment are known as *fluctuations*, and selection of plants which are outstanding because of fluctuations does not produce any permanent improvement in the crop. Fluctuations are not inherited. When plants which show outstanding *hereditary variations* from the rest of the crop are selected crop improvement becomes possible.

In self-pollinated crops, such as the cereals wheat, oats and barley, the discovery and selection of a single plant showing hereditary qualities superior to those of the rest of the crop may give rise to a useful new variety. By this method of *single plant selection* notable new varieties of cereals were obtained about the middle of the nineteenth century by Shirreff and Le Couteur. By the same means, Victory oat, introduced in 1906, was obtained at the plant-breeding station at Svalöf in Sweden from a stock of an old Probsteier oat known as Milton. In more recent times Earl barley (introduced in 1947) was produced by single plant selection from the variety Spratt-Archer at the Cambridge Plant Breeding Institute.

Selection from existing crops, as a means of crop improvement, dates back into antiquity, but *hybridization*, or artificial crossing of plants in order to obtain new types from which improved varieties may be selected, is of more recent origin. One of the earliest plant-hybridizers was Thomas Andrew Knight, who, in England, about the middle of the eighteenth century, produced notable varieties of fruit and other crops, including wheat. Knight was followed towards the end of the nineteenth century by a number of notable plant-breeders who produced new varieties by means of hybridization. Among these pioneers may be mentioned Henri de Vilmorin working in France on wheat; John Garton in England on oats, barley and wheat; Wm. Farrer in Australia and A. P. Saunders in Canada on wheat.

The work of early hybridizers showed that after artificially crossing varieties of self-pollinated crops stable forms could be produced combining some characteristics of both parents. This result was achieved by selection for a number of generations from the progeny of the original cross. The breeders found, but could not explain, that there was uniformity in the first generation after crossing and variability in the offspring in subsequent generations. To these early workers the production of new varieties was an art based on observation and years of laborious selection and trial. Plant-breeding had not yet become a science.

MENDEL

A more scientific approach to the problems of plant-breeding and, incidentally, of animal breeding, became possible after the rediscovery of the published work of Gregor Mendel in 1900. Mendel, a monk in the monastery at Brünn in Austria (now Brno in Czechoslovakia), provided the foundations on which the present-day science of *genetics* (the study of heredity) has been built. Although Mendel's Laws of Inheritance have been modified as a result of later scientific investigation, it is worthwhile to repeat briefly an account of his work.

Mendel (1822-1884) published the results of his researches in 1865, but at the time they failed to receive the recognition which was their due. The rediscovery of the published work resulted from the discovery of similar facts by De Vries in Holland, Correns in Germany and von Tschermak in Austria.

The published account of Mendel's work dealt mainly with experiments on the hybridization of garden peas (*Pisum sativum*). Peas are normally self-pollinated; therefore, it is possible after artificially crossing two varieties to follow the inheritance of their characteristics in subsequent generations, produced by self-pollination, without any fear of complications due to fertilization by pollen from another plant. The garden pea was a useful species for this work because of the multiplicity of existing varieties showing contrasting characteristics the inheritance of which could readily be observed. For example, tall and short varieties could be crossed and the inheritance of height followed in subsequent generations. Similarly, smooth-seeded and wrinkled-seeded varieties provided a pair of characters the inheritance of which could readily be observed. It was by concentrating upon unit characters of this type, rather than upon the characteristics of the plant as a whole, that Mendel achieved a solution of the problem of inheritance which had baffled his predecessors.

(The garden pea was a fortunate choice because, as is now known, it is a diploid species, and therefore the complications which occur in the inheritance of characters in polyploid species (see p. 40) did not arise.)

SINGLE FACTOR CROSS

As an example of the type of experiment performed by Mendel, let us consider the results obtained when a tall variety of pea is crossed with a dwarf variety, taking into consideration only the question of height in the offspring. Seeds produced by such a cross will give rise to a generation of plants, known as the *first filial generation* (denoted briefly as F.1), all of which are tall.

When the F.1 tall plants are allowed to produce seed by their normal method of self-pollination, the seed will produce in the next generation (second filial generation or F.2) 75 per cent. tall plants and 25 per cent. dwarf plants (or 3 : 1). If the self-pollinated seed from each of these plants is harvested separately and grown in separate plots, it is found in the next generation (F.3) that the seed from all the dwarf plants produces only dwarf plants, i.e. breeds true for dwarfness, but of the original 75 per cent. tall plants only one-third (i.e. 25 per cent. of the total F.2 generation) will breed true for tallness, whilst two-thirds (50 per cent. of the original F.2 generation) will produce some tall and some dwarf plants. Thus the F.2 was made up of 25 per cent. true-breeding dwarf plants, 25 per cent. true-breeding tall plants and 50 per cent. tall plants not true-breeding. This result may be summarized thus:

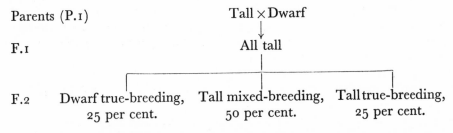

It will be observed that the dwarf character disappears in the F.1, but the tall character persists. The dwarf character is not completely lost, however, as it reappears in subsequent generations. In peas, therefore, dwarfness is said to be *recessive* and tallness *dominant*.

Mendel explained the results of the above and similar experiments by assuming that each plant carries two factors for height, one factor contributed by the male nucleus of the pollen grain (the male *gamete*), and one contributed by the egg nucleus (the female *gamete*) of the ovule. These two factors combined at fertilization, which resulted in the formation of the embryo from which the plant was grown. Thus the pure tall parent plant at the beginning of the experiment carries two factors for tallness which may be represented by the capital letters 'TT' and the pure dwarf parent carries two factors for dwarfness represented by the small letters 'tt'. *When these plants produce their reproductive cells, or gametes, the pairs of factors segregate,* so that each gamete contains only one factor of the original pair. Thus the gametes of the tall parent will carry a single factor for tallness 'T' and the gametes of the dwarf parent a single factor for dwarfness 't'. On crossing these two plants the gametes of the tall plant will contribute a factor for tallness and those of the dwarf plant a factor for dwarfness to the resulting seed. *The result will be the same whether the tall plant is used as the male parent or pollen-producer and the dwarf plant as the female parent or seed-producer or vice versa.*

Supposing that the tall parent contributes the pollen, the result of crossing the two plants may be expressed thus:

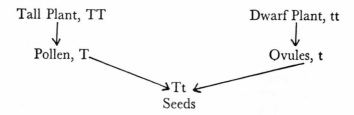

It will be seen that the seeds produced by the cross all carry a dominant factor 'T' and a recessive factor 't', and all will produce tall plants in the F.1 generation.

When the F.1 tall plants (Tt) produce their gametes *the pairs of factors 'Tt' segregate so that half the gametes receive a factor for tallness 'T' and half receive a factor for dwarfness 't'.* In other words, half the pollen grains produced will carry 'T', half will carry 't', and two types of ovules 'T' and 't' will also be produced in equal proportions. The possible offspring resulting from self-pollination of the F.1 plants (or from crossing them with one another) may be obtained thus:

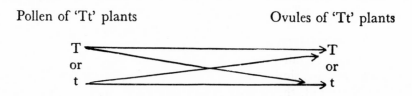

The arrows show how fertilization may occur between 'T' pollen and 'T' *or* 't' ovules, also between 't' pollen and 'T' *or* 't' ovules. Combining the letters as indicated by the arrows, we get the result:

14

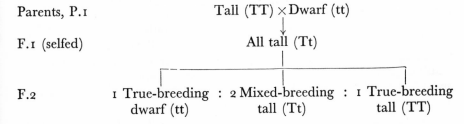

1, tt : 2, Tt : 1, TT

Or 25 per cent. tt : 50 per cent. Tt : 25 per cent. TT

(True-breeding dwarf) (Mixed-breeding tall) (True-breeding tall)

The complete results for the two generations may be summarized as follows:

Parents, P.1 Tall (TT) × Dwarf (tt)

F.1 (selfed) All tall (Tt)

F.2 1 True-breeding : 2 Mixed-breeding : 1 True-breeding
dwarf (tt) tall (Tt) tall (TT)

MENDELIAN RATIO

It should be noted that the *Mendelian Ratio* 1 : 2 : 1 in the F.2 is approached only when a large population of plants is being considered in this generation. If only four seeds were grown on to the F.2 all tall plants or all dwarf or the various possible proportions of the two might be obtained. When a large population of, say, 1,000 or more plants is considered the proportions are more nearly exact. This follows from the purely chance pairing of the two classes of pollen (T and t) with the two classes of ovule (T and t).

In just the same way, if two coins are tossed together a very large number of times and the results carefully noted, these will be found to approach very closely to the proportions 25 per cent. Two heads (HH) : 50 per cent. One head, One tail (HT) : 25 per cent. Two tails (TT) or 1 : 2 : 1. If the coins are tossed a small number of times, these proportions are much less likely to occur.

HOMOZYGOTE AND HETEROZYGOTE

The true-breeding dwarf and true-breeding tall plants each contain two similar factors for height 'tt' and 'TT' respectively. These plants are therefore each said to be *homozygous* (*homos*, alike) and are referred to as *homozygotes*. The mixed-breeding tall plants which contain two unlike factors (T and t), affecting the characteristic of height, are said to be *heterozygous* (*heteros*, different) and are called *heterozygotes*.

PHENOTYPE AND GENOTYPE

The two types of tall plants, i.e. homozygous tall (TT) and heterozygous tall (Tt) are similar in appearance in so far as height is concerned, both are tall, they are therefore said to be *phenotypically* alike or of the same *phenotype* (*phainein*, to appear). When judged on the unit factors, or *genes* as they are now called (see Chapter III), the two types of tall plants are different and they differ in their breeding potentialities.

They are therefore said to differ *genotypically* or to be different *genotypes* (*genos,* race or descent).

In the first generation (F.1) all the plants are alike phenotypically (Tall) and genotypically (Tt). Thus in this generation there is uniformity of material. In the second generation (F.2), and in subsequent generations, two phenotypes (tall and dwarf) and three genotypes (tt, Tt and TT) appear. Thus after the F.1 generation there is a variety of types.

TESTS FOR PURITY

Of the three different genotypes obtained in the F.2, only the one showing the recessive character, dwarfness, can be selected with certainty that it will be true-breeding. Because the plants are dwarf they must have the double dose of the recessive gene 't' and will therefore breed true. Of the tall plants the homozygous (TT) and the heterozygous (Tt) cannot be distinguished except by discovering what type of progeny they produce. Such a *progeny test* may be carried out in two ways. In the first method the seeds are harvested from each plant, the produce of each plant being kept separately, and later sown in separate plots. The seed produced by self-fertilization by the homozygous tall plants, will produce all tall plants, whilst that from the heterozygous tall plants will produce tall plants and dwarf plants again in the ratio 3 : 1.

The alternative method is to *back-cross* the tall plants to the pure recessive, i.e. to a dwarf plant. The seed produced from such a cross would give rise to all tall plants from the homozygous tall plants and to 50 per cent. tall and 50 per cent. dwarf from the heterozygous tall plants. The proportions in the latter cross result in the way shown below:

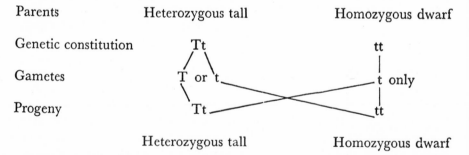

Because equal proportions of tall (Tt) and dwarf (tt) plants are produced by this cross, the chances of some dwarf plants being produced when only a small number of seeds is sown are greater than they would be if only a small number of seeds were sown after self-pollination of the heterozygous plants.

ALLELOMORPHIC PAIRS

Pairs of alternative factors, or genes, like those for tallness and dwarfness in peas, are called *allelomorphs* (*allelon,* of one another) or *allelomorphic pairs.* Other allelomorphic pairs in peas are the factors for smooth round seed and wrinkled seed, yellow cotyledons and green cotyledons, green unripe pod and yellow unripe pod. In each of these pairs the first-named is dominant. (It should be noted that seed shape and colour of the cotyledons are controlled by the genetic make-up of the embryo of the seed, which includes the cotyledons, not by that of the plant which bears the seed. Thus on fertilizing plants produced from homozygous wrinkled seed (rr) with pollen from a plant produced from homozygous round seed (RR) the resulting seed (Rr) would be round. In other words, the dominant seed shape develops immediately on formation of the seed after the cross-fertilization, whereas the other dominant characters, such as tallness, appear later when the F.1 plants are raised from the seed resulting from the cross.)

The genes of an allelomorphic pair are not always dominant and recessive to one another as were the pairs studied by Mendel in peas. In many cases the presence of both allelomorphs in a heterozygote produces a characteristic in between the two extremes. For example, in some species of flowering plants when red-flowered varieties are crossed with white-flowered varieties the heterozygous individuals obtained have pink flowers. In cases such as these the heterozygous plants can be recognized immediately by their intermediate characteristics. There is really no dominance of one factor over the other, but many writers describe this as *partial dominance* or *incomplete dominance*.

MULTIPLE CHARACTER CROSS

We have considered so far the inheritance of a single character in peas, i.e. height. Pea plants differ, however, in many more characters than that of height; for example, some have smooth round seeds, some wrinkled seeds; some have yellow cotyledons, some green cotyledons; some have green unripe pods and others yellow unripe pods, etc.

Having decided that each of these characters is controlled by a pair of factors (genes) which *segregate* when the gametes are formed, Mendel's next step was to consider how the various characters were inherited in relation to one another. As a result of his experiments he decided that the *different pairs of factors segregate independently of one another*. It is now known that this is not always true for other factors, as will be shown later (p. 30), but in the case of the characters considered by Mendel this did occur.

For example, if plants of a variety of pea which is tall and produces green pods are crossed with a variety of dwarf pea with yellow pods, the seeds produced will give rise to plants all of which are tall with green pods (F.1). When these F.1 plants are allowed to produce seed by self-pollination the seed so produced gives rise in the next generation (F.2) to four types of plant in the proportions 9 tall with green pods : 3 tall with yellow pods : 3 dwarf with green pods : 1 dwarf with yellow pods.

This result may be explained by assuming that the tall parent with green pods carries two genes for tallness and two genes for green pod. Similarly, the dwarf parent with yellow pods carries two genes for dwarfness and two genes for yellow pod. Because the F.1 progeny are all tall with green pods tallness and green pod must be dominant; therefore the genetic make-up of the original tall green-podded parent may be written thus, 'TTGG'. The dwarf, yellow-podded parent plant showing two recessive characters will have the genetic make-up 'ttgg'. When the pairs of genes segregate to produce gametes the tall, green-podded parent will produce gametes all carrying 'TG', whilst the dwarf, yellow-podded parent will produce gametes all carrying 'tg'. On cross-fertilization between these two plants the resulting seed will have the genetic constitution 'TtGg' and will produce all tall plants with green pods, thus:

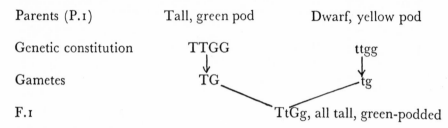

Parents (P.1)   Tall, green pod   Dwarf, yellow pod

Genetic constitution   TTGG   ttgg

Gametes   TG   tg

F.1   TtGg, all tall, green-podded

The tall, green-podded plants of the F.1 are heterozygous for tallness and heterozygous for green pods. The gametes produced by these plants must contain one gene controlling height and one gene controlling pod colour. Now, the 9 : 3 : 3 : 1 ratio obtained in the F.2 can only be explained on the assumption that the various genes are able to segregate independently of one another to produce four types of gamete, i.e. TG, Tg, tG, and tg in equal proportions. Thus in the F.1 plants there will be four types of pollen grain and four types of ovule, and any one type of pollen grain may fertilize any of the four types of ovule, thus:

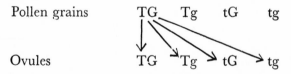

Pollen grains   TG   Tg   tG   tg

Ovules   TG   Tg   tG   tg

In this way four different combinations are obtained for each type of pollen grain and, as there are four different types of pollen grain, sixteen combinations result in all. The sixteen combinations are not all different, however. The proportions of the various types can be arrived at simply by the chequer-board method illustrated opposite.

Phenotypes. Remembering that tall and green pod are dominant, wherever T and G occur the plants will be tall with green pods; where one or the other is absent, the corresponding recessive will show. Thus it will be seen that in the F.2 there are four different phenotypes produced in the proportions shown on p. 19:

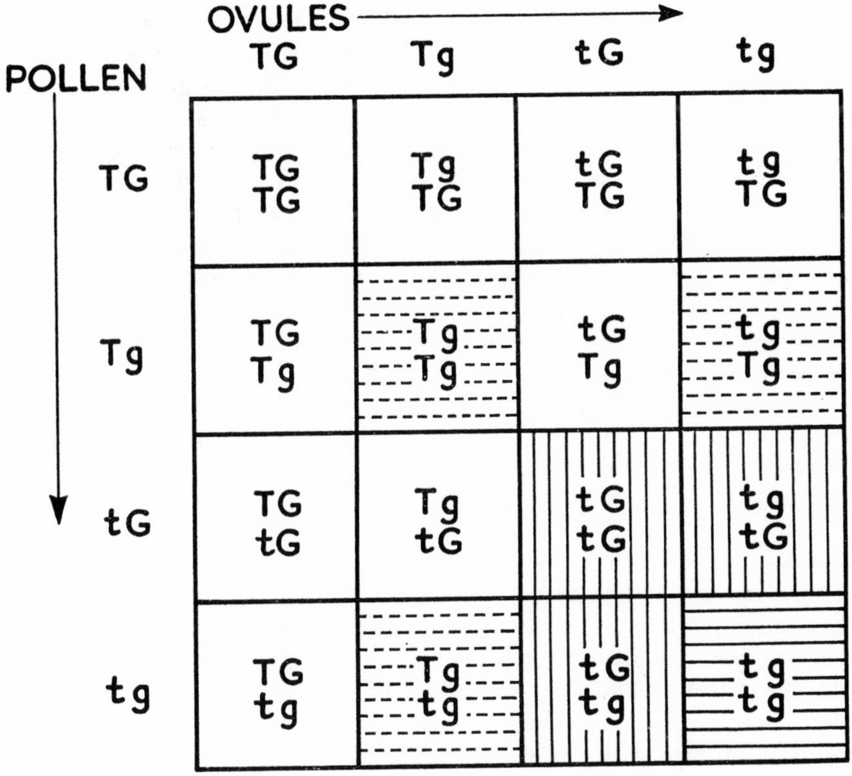

OVULES ⟶

POLLEN	TG	Tg	tG	tg
TG	TG TG	Tg TG	tG TG	tg TG
Tg	TG Tg	Tg Tg	tG Tg	tg Tg
tG	TG tG	Tg tG	tG tG	tg tG
tg	TG tg	Tg tg	tG tg	tg tg

9 Tall with green pods (unshaded in the diagram).
3 Tall with yellow pods (dotted in the diagram).
3 Dwarf with green pods (shaded vertically).
1 Dwarf with yellow pods (shaded horizontally).

Genotypes. Of the 9 tall, green-podded plants only one, TTGG, is homozygous, and therefore true-breeding, for both characters. Similarly in each group there is one which will breed true, being homozygous, for both characters represented. The rest of the plants are heterozygous for one or both characters, and therefore not true-breeding. The genotypes may be written down as follows:

1 (or 6¼ per cent.)   TTGG, i.e. homozygous tall, homozygous green pod.
1 (or 6¼ per cent.)   TTgg, i.e. homozygous tall, homozygous yellow pod.
1 (or 6¼ per cent.)   ttGG, i.e. homozygous dwarf, homozygous green pod.
1 (or 6¼ per cent.)   ttgg, i.e. homozygous dwarf, homozygous yellow pod.
2 (or 12½ per cent.) TTGg, i.e. homozygous tall, heterozygous green pod.
2 (or 12½ per cent.) TtGG, i.e. heterozygous tall, homozygous green pod.
2 (or 12½ per cent.) ttGg, i.e. homozygous dwarf, heterozygous green pod.
2 (or 12½ per cent.) Ttgg, i.e. heterozygous tall, homozygous yellow pod.
4 (or 25 per cent.)   TtGg, i.e. heterozygous tall, heterozygous green pod.

16 (100 per cent.)   Total.

It should be noted that the only one of the above types which can be selected, by eye, with certainty that it will breed true to type, is the one showing the two recessives dwarfness and yellow pods. As the two recessives show, its genetic make-up must be 'ttgg'. Where one or both of the dominant characters show it will be necessary to grow on for another generation, produced by self-pollination, or to back cross to the pure recessive (ttgg) in order to discover which plants are homozygous and which heterozygous. Thus TTGG, TtGG, TTGg and TtGg are all tall with green pods, and further test is needed in order to distinguish the various genotypes.

From the above example, it will be noticed that it is possible for characters existing in two separate varieties to be combined in a new variety. Here we began with tall plants with green pods and dwarf plants with yellow pods, and among the progeny in F.2 we have true-breeding plants which are tall with yellow pods (TTgg) and dwarf with green pods (ttGG).

INTERACTION OF GENES

Following the rediscovery of Mendel's work attempts were made to apply his theories to results obtained in breeding experiments with various types of plants and animals. It was quickly realized that inheritance did not always work quite so simply as was suggested by Mendel's experiments with peas. Whilst it was found that the Mendelian ratios could be obtained with certain crosses, different ratios appeared in other crosses, and Mendel's theories did not seem to apply. It was soon demonstrated, however, that interaction may take place between different pairs of genes, and on the basis of such *gene interaction* many of the apparent exceptions to Mendel's laws could be explained.

Gene interactions may be very complex and not easily elucidated. In the examples given below two simple gene interactions, which give rise to modifications of Mendel's original ratios, are described.

COMPLEMENTARY GENES

In studying inheritance of flower colour in sweet peas (*Lathyrus odoratus*) Bateson and Punnett found that purple was dominant to white. They also found that white varieties when self-pollinated bred true, and when white varieties were crossed they usually produced only white progeny. One cross between two white varieties, however, gave rise only to purple offspring in the F.1 generation. When these purple-flowered F.1 plants were self-pollinated they produced, in the F.2 generation, a ratio of 9 purple to 7 white-flowered plants. Of these, all the white-flowered plants, when self-pollinated, gave rise to white-flowered plants only. Whilst a few of the purple-flowered plants produced only purple offspring, others produced purple-flowered and white-flowered offspring in the ratio of 3 purple to 1 white or of 9 purple to 7 white.

These results may be explained by assuming that colour, in this species, is dependent upon the interaction of two pairs of genes. Purple colour depends upon the presence of two independent dominant genes P (purple) and C (colour). In the absence of one or both of these genes the flowers would be white. The 9 : 7 ratio in F.2 can be explained if one of the original white parents is assumed to have the genetic constitution CCpp and the other white parent variety the constitution ccPP. In each case the flower colour is white because C and P are not present together. The result of crossing these two varieties is shown below:

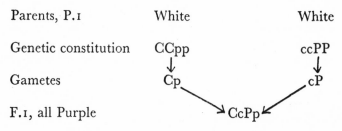

Parents, P.1	White	White
Genetic constitution	CCpp	ccPP
Gametes	Cp	cP
F.1, all Purple	CcPp	

When the F.1 plants produce their gametes four different types are obtained in equal proportions, i.e. CP, Cp, cP, and cp. The possible combinations resulting from self-pollination of the F.1 plants (or from crossing them among themselves) are illustrated in the following diagram:

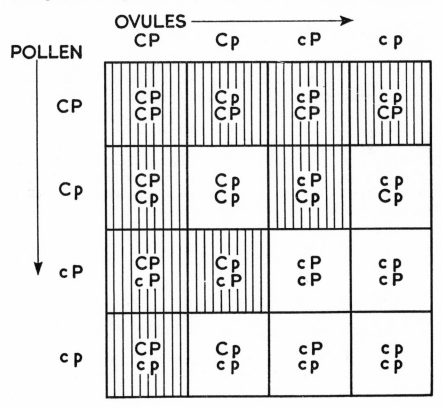

In the above diagram the shaded squares indicate purple-flowered plants, unshaded, white-flowered plants. Of the nine combinations which result in purple flowers only one is homozygous for both genes on which the appearance of purple flowers depends, i.e. CCPP, and this combination only will produce all purple-flowered offspring after self-fertilization. All other combinations producing purple-flowered plants will result in both purple-flowered and white-flowered offspring in the next generation, produced by self-pollination, as all are heterozygous for one or both of the pairs of genes concerned.

Genes which interact in the manner of the two genes 'C' and 'P' in the above example are called *complementary genes*; they are genes which together produce an effect which is distinct from the effects produced by any one of them separately.

EPISTASIS

Sometimes the effect of a particular gene may be masked by the presence of a different gene which is not its partner in an allelomorphic pair. This phenomenon is known as *epistasis*. The gene which masks the effect of another gene in this way is said to be *epistatic* (*epi*, upon; *stasis*, standing), whilst the gene which is masked is *hypostatic* (*hypo*, under; *stasis*, standing).

A simple illustration of this is found in the inheritance of fruit colour in summer squashes which belong to the vegetable marrow species *Cucurbita pepo*. Different varieties of these plants may have white, yellow or green fruits. White appears to be dominant to both yellow and green. Yellow, although apparently recessive to white, is dominant to green. Thus, green is recessive both to white and yellow.*

As a result of breeding experiments, it has been shown that fruit colour in these plants is controlled by two pairs of genes and that a single gene 'W' can not only dominate its own recessive 'w', but can hide the effect of the genes for yellow and green fruit colours. True-breeding white-fruited plants may be represented by WWYY or by WWyy. True-breeding yellow-fruited plants are represented by wwYY, and green-fruited plants by wwyy.

When homozygous white-fruited plants which are known to have the constitution WWYY are crossed with green-fruited plants (wwyy) all the F.1 plants are white-fruited as shown below:

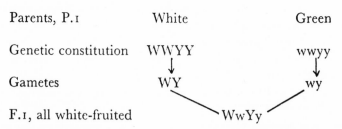

From these F.1 plants four types of gametes are possible, WY, Wy, wY, and wy, and when the F.1 plants are crossed among themselves

* Sinnott, E. W., and Durham, G. B. Inheritance in the summer squash. *Jour. Heredity*, 13, 1922.

an F.2 ratio of 12 white : 3 yellow : 1 green is obtained, as indicated in the following diagram:

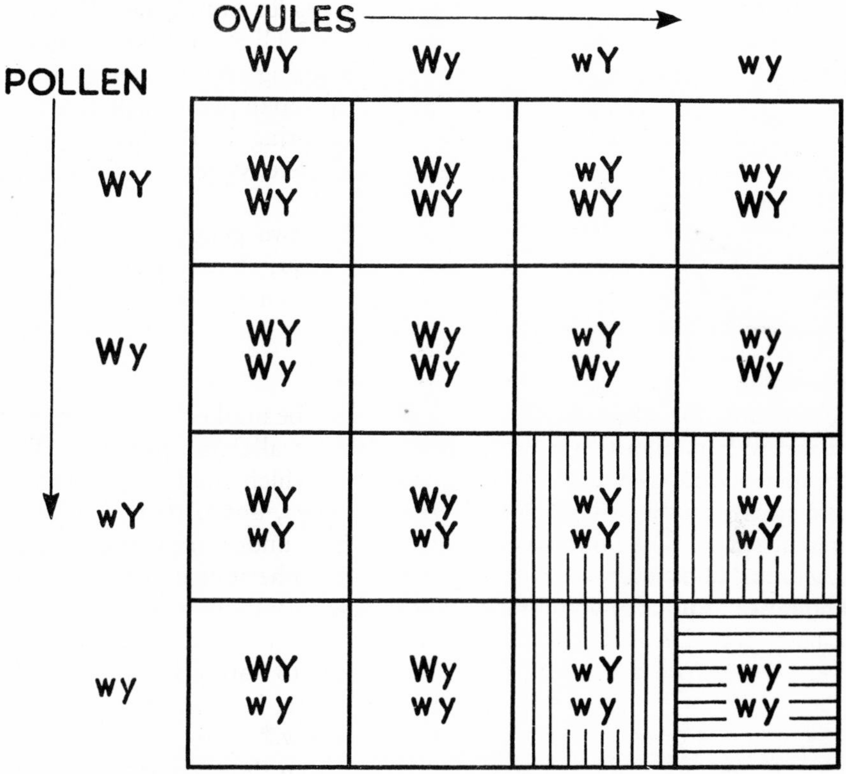

POLLEN	OVULES ⟶			
	WY	**Wy**	**wY**	**wy**
WY	WY WY	Wy WY	wY WY	wy WY
Wy	WY Wy	Wy Wy	wY Wy	wy Wy
wY	WY wY	Wy wY	wY wY	wy wY
wy	WY wy	Wy wy	wY wy	wy wy

Remembering that the gene 'W' is epistatic to 'Y' and dominant to 'w' and it therefore prevents the appearance of yellow or green, it will be seen that all 12 combinations in the white squares will produce white fruit. The 3 combinations in the vertically shaded squares, which include the dominant 'Y' but not 'W', will produce yellow fruit, and the one combination wwyy in the horizontally shaded square will produce green fruit as both 'W' and 'Y' are absent.

Above we have dealt with but two types of factor or gene interaction in order to demonstrate that results obtained in breeding cannot always be interpreted on a simple Mendelian basis (see also Linked Genes, Crossing Over, Cumulative Influence of Genes and the Gene Complex—Chapter III). Although such complications occur, it should be emphasized, however, that Mendel's conception of pairs of factors or genes segregating on formation of the gametes, and the formation of pairs again at fertilization, is fundamental to the understanding of heredity.

For a more complete knowledge of genetics it is necessary to know something of the science of *cytology*, or the study of cells. Some of the main points of interest in connection with that science are dealt with in the next chapter.

Chapter III

CHROMOSOMES, GENES AND PLANT-BREEDING

THE PHYSICAL BASIS OF INHERITANCE

FERTILIZATION, which results in the production of a new plant, consists essentially of the fusion of a male nucleus from the pollen grain and a female nucleus in the embryo sac. It is therefore to the nuclei that we must look for the means by which hereditary factors or genes are passed on from parent to offspring.

Every living cell of a plant body contains a nucleus and when a cell divides to produce two new cells the nucleus divides producing two nuclei, one for each daughter cell, by means of a process known as *mitosis*. When nuclei are about to divide they become modified into a number of more or less elongated structures called *chromosomes* (*chroma*, colour; *soma*, body: from the fact that they stain deeply in microscope preparations). The chromosomes are normally constant in number in all *somatic* or body cells of a plant and of other plants of the same species. The number of chromosomes present in the somatic cells of some species of crop plants is as follows:

Crop species	Chromosome number (*2n*)
Garden pea—*Pisum sativum*	14
Bread wheat—*Triticum aestivum*	42
Rye—*Secale cereale*	14
Barley—*Hordeum sativum*	14
Oats—*Avena sativa*	42
Cabbage—*Brassica oleracea*	18
Common turnip—*Brassica rapa*	20
Swede—*Brassica napus*	38
Potato—*Solanum tuberosum*	48
Red clover—*Trifolium pratense*	14
White clover—*Trifolium repens*	32
Linseed or flax—*Linum usitatissimum*	30
Beet and mangel—*Beta vulgaris*	18

Usually the number of chromosomes in somatic cells is an even one because the chromosomes are present in pairs. One of each pair has been derived from the male gamete and the other from the female gamete; these came together at fertilization. Such pairs of chromosomes are known as *homologous pairs* or *homologues*. It follows that the gametes possess, in their nuclei, half the number of chromosomes which occurs in the somatic cells resulting from their fusion. The somatic number of chromosomes is usually referred to as *2n* or *diploid* (*diploos*, double; *eidos*, likeness), the gametic number as *n* or *haploid* (*haploos*, single).

When the plant produces its gametes there is a halving of the number of chromosomes during the formation of gametic cells from somatic cells. Thus the pollen mother cells and the embryo sac mother cells each contain *2n* chromosomes, but they divide to produce cells with *n* chromosomes in their nuclei. This process of reduction division is called *meiosis*.

MITOSIS

The division of a somatic cell to form two new somatic cells, or mitosis, is illustrated in fig. 1. During the *prophase* (*pro*, before) the granular material

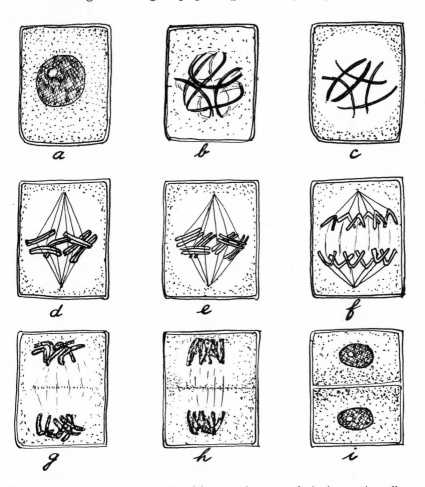

FIG. 1. Diagrammatic representation of the successive stages of mitosis. *a*, resting cell. *n*, nucleus. *b* and *c*, prophase. *d* and *e*, metaphase. *f* and *g*, anaphase. *h*, early telophase. *i*, two daughter cells.

of the nucleus is resolved into a number of protoplasmic threads which are the chromosomes. At this stage the chromosomes consist of double threads held together at some point along their length, known as the *centromere*. Each thread of the chromosome is known as a *chromatid*. The chromosomes twist spirally, shortening and thickening as they do so. The short thick chromosomes arrange themselves across the middle of the cell or *equatorial plate*. This is the *metaphase* (*meta*, beyond). At this stage protoplasmic threads radiating from the poles of the cell and connecting with the chromosomes may be seen. These form the so-called *spindle*. The chromatids now separate completely, forming two daughter chromosomes. At the *anaphase* (*ana*, back) the separate daughter chromosomes are driven along the spindle threads to the opposite poles of the cell. Thus two complete sets of chromosomes have been formed, and one set is now in each half of the cell. The chromosomes next lose their identity and join together to form two nuclei; this stage is called the *telophase* (*telos*, end). During this phase a cell wall forms across the equator of the spindle, thus separating the two daughter cells and mitosis is then complete.

MEIOSIS

Reduction division or meiosis differs from mitosis in that the division results in the formation of daughter nuclei (*haploid*) containing half the number of chromosomes contained in the nucleus of the mother cell (*diploid*).

The nucleus of the mother cell first becomes resolved into a number of long thin chromosomes which are often granular in appearance (fig. 2); the dense granules are known as *chromomeres*. When they first appear the chromomeres are not divided longitudinally. Homologous chromosomes are attracted to one another, and they pair off chromomere to chromomere, along their length. The pairs of chromosomes at the equator of the cell now coil around one another and contract, becoming short and thick. During this stage the chromosomes divide longitudinally, each chromosome forming two chromatids; each pair thus consists of four chromatids in all. Suddenly the homologous chromosomes appear to repel one another and the pairs fall apart. At first the chromatids of opposite chromosomes appear to stick together at some point or points as the chromosomes separate. As separation becomes complete, breaks occur at these points of attachment, and exchanges of corresponding sections of the chromatids take place between partners (fig. 3). These exchanges are called *chiasmata* (singular, *chiasma*). The process is known as *crossing over*.

The split chromosomes or *bivalents* now pass along the spindle threads to opposite ends of the cell. The chromosomes then split apart, as in mitosis, and separate to form four haploid sets. Cell walls develop at right angles dividing the cell into four. The chromosomes in each of the four cells now form a nucleus. The four new cells with haploid nuclei are the germ cells in which the gametes will be formed. In the case of the male germ cells each of the four develops into a pollen grain, whilst

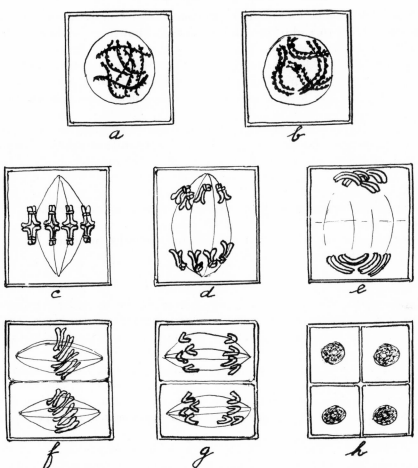

FIG. 2. Diagrammatic representation of meiosis. *a*, chromosomes appearing and *b*, pairing chromomere to chromomere. *c*, paired bivalents after completion of crossing over (see Fig. 3 below). *d* and *e*, first division; one bivalent of each pair going to each pole of the cell *f*, *g* and *h*, second division; bivalents split apart and the chromatids separate to form four nuclei.

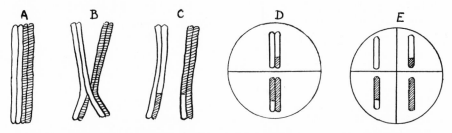

FIG. 3. Diagram of successive stages of crossing over between one pair of homologous chromosomes. In the example only one chiasma is shown. D and E show the ultimate distribution of the four chromatids in the four new cells.

27

in a developing ovule, usually, only one of the four cells develops, to produce an embryo sac; the other three disappear.

The points of importance in meiosis are:

1. Two nuclear divisions occur, but only one division of the chromosomes, thus resulting in a halving of the number of chromosomes.

2. Crossing over leads to an exchange of parts of the chromatids between paired homologous chromosomes.

3. The four chromatids (daughter chromosomes) of each original pair of chromosomes are finally distributed *at random* in the four resulting daughter cells.

CHROMOSOMES AND GENETICS

As a result of much experimental work, chiefly upon the small insect *Drosophila*, it is now known that the genes are arranged longitudinally along the chromosomes in much the same manner as beads on a string. The genes present together on a single chromosome are called *linked genes*, and they form a *linkage group*. When a chromosome divides into two at *mitosis*, one group of genes gives rise to two identical groups. Now, in somatic cells, the chromosomes are present in pairs, and homologous chromosomes carry genes of the same type in the same order. Thus, after mitosis each new cell which has received a full set of pairs of chromosomes (*2n*) will also have received a full set of paired genes, and the sets of genes in the two daughter cells will be the same as those of the original mother cell.

At *meiosis* the germ mother cells divide to give four cells, each containing one set of chromosomes, and therefore one set of genes. Fig. 4

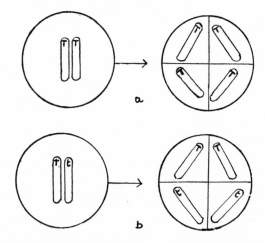

FIG. 4. Chromosomes and one pair of genes at meiosis.
a, homozygous. *b*, heterozygous.

shows what happens to a single homologous pair of chromosomes at meiosis, and to any single allelomorphic pair of genes carried by such a pair of chromosomes; (*a*) shows a pair homozygous (TT) for the genes under consideration—here four cells are produced each carrying the gene 'T'; (*b*) is heterozygous for the pair of genes being considered—in this case half of the four cells formed carry the dominant 'T', half carry the recessive 't', which conforms with the Mendelian assumption that half the gametes of a heterozygous individual would carry the dominant gene and half the recessive of a single pair.

Now let us consider what happens when the whole set of genes of a homologous pair of chromosomes is taken into account. Fig. 5 represents a pair of homologous chromosomes which are homozygous for all the gene pairs. In this case meiosis would result in four cells all receiving a chromosome carrying exactly the same set of genes, even if crossing over takes place. Fig. 6 shows a pair of homologous chromosomes in a plant which is heterozygous for the various characters represented on

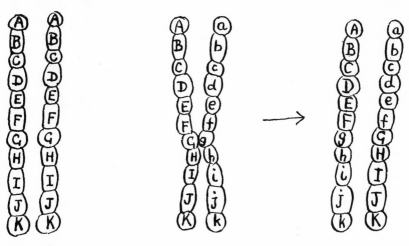

FIG. 5. A homologous pair of chromosomes showing linked genes. The pair are homozygous for all the genes represented.

FIG. 6. Crossing over between homologous chromosomes resulting in new combinations of genes.

the chromosomes. During meiosis crossing over will result in the redistribution of the various dominant and recessive genes. In fig. 6 only one chiasma is shown, but chiasmata may occur at more than one point along a single homologous pair of chromosomes and at different points in the corresponding homologous pairs in different mother cells. As, in addition, the different pairs of chromosomes in any mother cell segregate independently of one another, during meiosis, the parental genes are reshuffled and in a heterozygous individual many new combinations of genes arise in the gametes, differing from the combinations supplied by either parent. No gamete is likely to receive all the genes supplied by any one parent of the plant.

If we consider Mendel's results in relation to the chromosomes we see that when one allelomorphic pair of genes is considered, as shown in fig. 7, the results obtained are identical with those of Mendel. The homozygous dominant 'AA' crossed with the homozygous recessive 'aa' produces heterozygous individuals 'Aa' in the F.1 and these, on self-pollination, give rise to the Mendelian ratio 1AA : 2Aa : 1aa in F.2.

Now, when we consider the inheritance of two pairs of genes Mendel's results can be obtained if the genes under consideration are present on

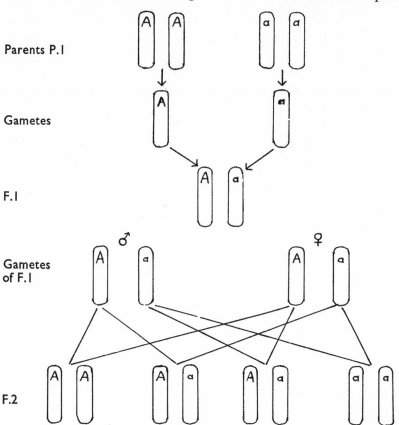

Parents P.1

Gametes

F.1

Gametes of F.1

F.2

Fig. 7. Inheritance of a single allelomorphic pair of genes.

separate chromosome pairs as shown in fig. 8. Here the plant carrying the dominant genes 'AA' and 'BB' on separate homologous chromosomes is crossed with a plant carrying the recessives 'aa' and 'bb' in the same way. The gametes produced will carry 'AB' and 'ab' respectively, and the F.1 of the cross will all carry 'Aa.Bb', each gene on a different chromosome. These chromosomes, by random assortment on formation of the gametes, can give rise to the four types of gamete 'AB', 'Ab', 'aB', 'ab' which is the requirement in order to obtain the 9 : 3 : 3 : 1 ratio in the F.2 (see p. 18).

If, however, 'A' and 'B' were located on the same homologous chromosomes and 'a' and 'b' were similarly located, and if they did not separate by crossing over during formation of the gametes (see fig. 9), the F.1 offspring would again carry 'Aa.Bb' but, because of linkage, the gametes produced by the F.1 plants would be of two kinds only, 'AB' and 'ab', so that the 9 : 3 : 3 : 1 ratio could not be produced in the F.2.

Thus, Mendel's second law can only hold when the different pairs of

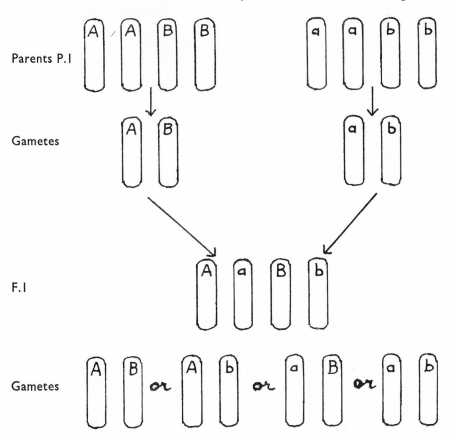

Fig. 8. Inheritance of two allelomorphic pairs of genes on separate homologous pairs of chromosomes.

genes under consideration are located on different homologous pairs of chromosomes. Where pairs of genes located on the same homologous chromosomes are being considered the ratio of the different types of progeny in the F.2 will vary with the amount of crossing over involving the two pairs of genes.

Where linked genes are widely separated, as for example 'A' and 'K' and 'a' and 'k' in fig. 6, crossing over is likely to result in the separation of these genes situated at the extremities of the chromosomes. Thus it would be possible to obtain four types of gamete 'AK', 'Ak', 'aK' and 'ag' (where these two pairs of genes only are being considered). Genes which are closely linked, like 'A' and 'B' and 'a' and 'b' in fig. 6, are less likely to be separated by crossing over. Some genes are so closely linked that they rarely, if ever, separate as a result of crossing over.

For some plants it has been possible to prepare *chromosome maps* indicating which genes are linked on a particular chromosome and their relative positions on the chromosome. Such maps are possible as a result

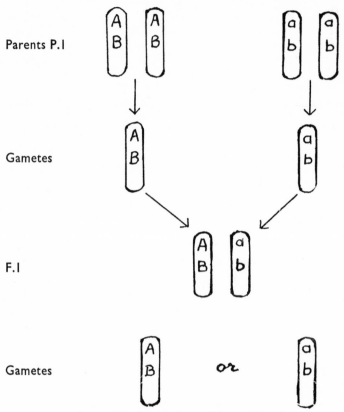

FIG. 9. Inheritance of two allelomorphic pairs of genes on the same homologous pair of chromosomes.

of complex series of breeding experiments associated with microscopic examination of the chromosomes.

STABILITY OF GENES

The genes are normally fairly stable, and a self-pollinating plant which is homozygous for all its major characters will give rise to progeny, generation after generation, resembling itself very closely. When two homozygous individuals showing different characters are successfully crossed the F.2 plants give rise to a great variety of offspring as the result of the re-shuffling of the chromosomes and the formation of new gene combinations during meiosis. Although new types of plants arise as a result of the new gene combinations, the genes themselves normally remain unchanged.

MUTATIONS

On rare occasions genes may change giving rise to new and unexpected variations in the plant. A variation resulting from some change in the genes is known as a *mutation* (*mutare*, to change). Mutation may affect a single gene and produce a change in a single character. Mutations affecting several genes or complete chromosomes may result in very marked changes in the characteristics of the individuals in which they occur. Mutations may involve a change in the number of genes or of the arrangement of one or more genes in relation to the rest of the genes on one or more chromosomes. A chromosome may be added or lost as a result of irregular separation of the pairs during meiosis or mitosis. Finally, the number of complete sets of chromosomes may be increased, giving rise to a special form of mutant individual known as a *polyploid*.

De Vries explained evolution on the basis of mutations occurring suddenly and producing new forms. Mutant forms which were well fitted to their environment would persist whilst other mutant forms which were not so well suited to their environment would die out.

Mutations may arise in any cell of the plant. Those arising in the gametes or in the fertilized egg will affect all cells of the resulting plant, including the gametes it will produce. The change would therefore be heritable. *Somatic* or *bud* mutations may develop in cells from which buds develop, such buds later giving rise to shoots showing new characteristics. Single mutant shoots may arise, in this way, on an otherwise normal plant. Bud mutations may or may not be heritable through the seed produced by the mutant shoots, depending on the depth to which the tissues of the shoot have mutated. If the epidermal layers only have been affected, by the change in the genes, the bud mutation would not affect the seed as the gametes are produced from sub-epidermal layers of cells. Bud mutations of this latter type may be perpetuated by vegetative reproduction. For example, mutations resulting in change of skin colour in potato tubers may give rise to new and distinctive forms which can be reproduced by means of the tubers (see *Chimaeras*, p. 49).

All mutations which affect the gametes are heritable. When mutant plants showing new heritable characters of value are obtained, these, if selected, may be used for breeding new crop types.

Mutations occur naturally at irregular and infrequent intervals in most species. They may result in the production of plants showing new characters which increase their value from the farmer's point of view. On the other hand, the mutation may result in characters which detract from the value of the plants. Some mutant genes, known as *lethals*, even result in the early death of plants when present in a homozygous condition. For example, recessive genes for lack of chlorophyll when occurring in a homozygous condition result in the production of seedlings which fail to form chlorophyll and, because of their inability to carry on photosynthesis, such seedlings die after the food stored in the seed has been exhausted. Such lethal genes can thus continue to exist only when present with a non-lethal partner in a heterozygous individual. Lethal effects may also result from the presence of defective chromosomes of which portions have been lost possibly during meiosis.

The exact causes of mutations under natural conditions are not fully understood. Mutations have, however, been induced artificially in a large number of plant species by means of various treatments, such as regulation of temperature, exposure to X-rays or to gamma-rays from some radio-active element such as cobalt, bombardment with neutrons in an atomic pile and by treatment with certain chemicals. Occasionally such mutant forms show promise of value in agriculture or horticulture, either directly or as breeding material for crossing with commercial varieties. The majority of mutant forms, on the other hand, are quite useless.

POLYPLOIDY

It has been mentioned, in the previous section, that hereditary changes may result from the increase in the number of complete sets of chromosomes. If 'x' is taken to represent the basic haploid number for a particular group of plants the diploid would carry '$2x$' chromosomes in its somatic cells. Plants may arise naturally which possess more than two sets of chromosomes in their somatic cells. Any multiple of sets of chromosomes greater than two is known as *polyploid*. If there are three sets of chromosomes present in the somatic cells ($3x$) the plant is called a *triploid*, i.e. a form of polyploid having three sets of chromosomes. *Tetraploids pentaploids, hexaploids, heptaploids* and *octaploids* contain 4, 5, 6, 7, and 8 sets of chromosomes in their somatic cells or $4x$, $5x$, $6x$, $7x$ and $8x$ respectively.

An examination of the chromosome complement of some of the species of the wheat genus *Triticum* will illustrate these facts. The basic chromosome number 'x' for this genus is 7, thus a diploid would have 14 ($2x$) chromosomes in its somatic cells. Now, when the chromosome numbers in the somatic cells of various species of *Triticum* are examined it is found that there are various multiples of 7, as shown in the following table:

Triticum species	Somatic chromosome number
T. aegilopoides. Wild small spelt . . .	14 ($2x$)
T. monococcum. Small spelt	14 ($2x$)
T. dicoccum. Two-grained spelt or emmer .	28 ($4x$)
T. durum. Macaroni wheat . . .	28 ($4x$)
T. turgidum. Rivet wheat	28 ($4x$)
T. compactum. Club wheat	42 ($6x$)
T. aestivum. Bread wheat	42 ($6x$)

The first two species in this table are diploids and the rest are polyploids, those with 28 chromosomes, or 4 sets of 7, being tetraploids, those with 42, or 6 sets of 7, being hexaploids. Thus the modern bread wheat

T. aestivum would appear to have originated as a result of an increase, in some way, of the number of sets of chromosomes during the course of evolution. The probable means of increase is discussed in Chapter XV.

Similarly, other cultivated crops of today are polyploids, for example the cultivated potato *Solanum tuberosum*, 48 chromosomes, is a tetraploid ($x = 12$) and the common oat *Avena sativa*, 42 chromosomes, is a hexaploid ($x = 7$).

On the other hand, many cultivated crops still possess the diploid number of chromosomes, for example barley, *Hordeum sativum*, and rye, *Secale cereale*, are both diploids with 14 chromosomes. Sugar beet, *Beta vulgaris*, 18 (2×9) and red clover, *Trifolium pratense* 14 (2×7) are further examples.

Two types of polyploidy are recognized (see fig. 10).

(1) A tetraploid may arise by the doubling of the chromosomes of a normal diploid individual; the new type thus produced is called an *autotetraploid* (*autos*, self). Autotetraploids have been known to occur in nature in a number of species—for example, in the weed thorn apple (*Datura stramonium*, *2n*, 24) forms with 48 chromosomes have been found.

(2) Doubling of the chromosomes may occur after two species have been crossed (either naturally or artificially). In this case the two sets of chromosomes to be doubled are of different origin and type. A tetraploid produced in this way is known as an *allotetraploid* (*allos*, other or different). Allotetraploids are also known as *amphidiploids* (*amphi*, both; *diploos*, double). The swede (*Brassica napus*, *2n*, 38) is thought to be an allo-tetraploid (amphidiploid) resulting from a cross between the cabbage species (*Brassica oleracea*, *2n*, 18) and the common turnip (*Brassica rapa*, *2n*, 20). To such a cross the cabbage gametes would contribute 9 chromosomes and the turnip gametes would contribute 10, giving a total of 19. The chromosome number was then doubled, giving a total of 38, of which 20 originated from the turnip parent and 18 from the cabbage parent. Alternatively, the same result would be achieved if the two species produced diploid gametes and diploid eggs of one were fertilized by diploid pollen of the other.

The general terms *autopolyploid* and *allopolyploid* are used to denote any polyploid of the two types respectively.

An autotetraploid is often larger and more vigorous than the original diploid type, but usually it is not markedly different in appearance. There is, however, often a lowering of fertility in autotetraploids. The reduction of fertility is explained by the fact that there are now two identical sets of allelomorphic pairs of chromosomes, and during meiosis the chromosome pairs of each set are attracted to one another. Two pairs of chromosomes become involved together in chiasma formation and irregularities are liable to occur which result in the formation of infertile gametes.

Allotetraploids (or amphidiploids) are usually intermediate in general characteristics between the two parents and there is usually a higher

35

degree of fertility than in autotetraploids. The higher fertility depends upon the fact that in this type the pairs of chromosomes of different parental origin form chiasmata independently and meiosis proceeds along normal lines.

Polyploids result from irregularities in cell division. Reduction division may fail to occur during gamete formation, resulting in the production

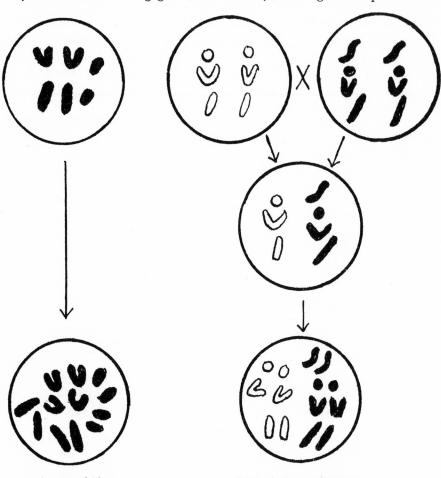

Autotetraploid   Allotetraploid or Amphidiploid

FIG. 10. Diagrammatic representation of *Left* the formation of an autotetraploid and *Right* the formation of an allotetraploid by doubling the chromosome number after hybridization.

of diploid gametes instead of the usual haploid. If the diploid ($2x$) gametes are fertilized by a normal haploid (x) gamete a triploid ($3x$) would be produced. When two diploid gametes fertilize one another a tetraploid ($4x$) results. Alternatively, the irregularity in cell division may occur soon after fertilization; for example, in a normal diploid zygote the chromosomes divide, but the cell may fail to divide, thus producing a cell with twice the normal number of chromosomes. If cell division then occurs normally the tetraploid cell will give rise to a tetraploid embryo. Finally, multiplication of the chromosome sets may occur, in a similar way, in somatic cells of an adult plant; buds produced from the resulting polyploid cells would give rise to polyploid shoots, whilst other shoots produced from diploid cells on the same plant would be normal diploids.

Infertility of Triploids

In triploids (*3x*) there is an odd set of chromosomes, and thus regular pairing of chromosomes at meiosis cannot occur. As a result of this, triploids are usually highly or completely sterile. A similar effect occurs in pentaploids and other polyploids with an odd multiple of sets of chromosomes.

Artificially Produced Polyploids

Polyploid forms of many species of plants have been produced artificially by use of the drug *colchicine*, which is extracted from the autumn crocus (*Colchicum autumnale*). By exposing the growing points of shoots, buds or young seedlings to a very dilute solution of colchicine, or by soaking seeds in the solution, cell division can often be upset in such a way as to produce a polyploid condition in the cells. These polyploid cells may then develop normally to produce a polyploid shoot or plant.

If the solution of colchicine is too concentrated, or exposure to the solution too prolonged, the tissues may be killed. Preliminary experiment is therefore usually necessary before the precise conditions for treatment can be obtained.

The range of concentrations which has been used successfully with different plant species varies between 0·0006 per cent. and 1·0 per cent., and the time of exposure to treatment from merely wetting to soaking for 24 hours.

When seeds are treated some seeds which have received the correct dosage for the correct length of time produce polyploid plants, but often many seeds are killed in the process of treatment.

Although many new polyploid forms have been produced artificially by plant-breeders, the number which have been of immediate value have been small. In the case of flowering plants grown for decoration, polyploid forms, in which the flowers are larger and more showy, have proved of value, but in the case of many crop plants the polyploid forms have been of less value than existing types.

Useful polyploid forms seem to be obtainable more readily from species with low chromosome numbers. Those species which already possess high chromosome numbers, and are probably already natural polyploids, usually give less useful results following colchicine treatment. For example, red clover, *Trifolium pratense*, in which the somatic (*2n*) number of chromosomes is 14, has given useful tetraploid forms, whilst white clover, *Trifolium repens*, *2n*, 32, produced tetraploids which were inferior to the parent material. Tetraploid forms of wheat, *Triticum aestivum* (*2n*, 42), potato, *Solanum tuberosum* (*2n*, 48) and soya bean, *Glycine max* (*2n*, 40) were inferior to the parent material. Rye, *Secale cereale* (*2n*, 14), black mustard, *Brassica nigra* (*2n*, 16), buckwheat, *Fagopyrum esculentum* (*2n*, 16), mangels and sugar beet, *Beta vulgaris* (*2n*, 18) and alsike clover, *Trifolium hybridum* (*2n*, 16) produced tetraploids which were, in some respects, better than the parent material. In the latter group, however, some characteristics may appear which detract from their value. For example, tetraploid forms of rye have been produced in Sweden, Holland and U.S.A. which have larger grain with a higher protein content and producing better bread, but many of the lower spikelets shed their grain readily and consequently there is no significant increase in yield. Similarly, barley tetraploids have been produced in which the grains were 40 to 50 per cent. heavier, but the fertility was reduced and therefore the yield was poor. In addition, in this crop, there was a tendency, in some plants, for the ear to fail to emerge from the sheath completely and no grain was produced.

By crossing tetraploid lines of barley some improvement has been obtained. In other crops, although tetraploid forms may not be of immediate value for cultivation by the farmer, they may form valuable material for further breeding work.

Optimum Chromosome Content

The fact that some improvements may be obtained when dealing with species of low chromosome numbers, but little good results from polyploidy in species with high chromosome numbers, suggests that there may be an optimum chromosome content which has already been achieved by the high chromosome group. Some support is provided for this idea by the results obtained with sugar-beet. In this species tetraploids can be produced by the colchicine method and then, by cross-pollinating tetraploid plants with pollen from diploid plants, triploid seed may be obtained. Plants grown from triploid seed have, in some cases, given rise to roots superior both to the diploid and to the tetraploid. In this case the triploid may be the optimum form.

Species Hybrids and Genera Hybrids

Hybrids between different varieties of the same plant species are usually highly fertile. When, however, related species are crossed, if the cross is successful and seed is formed, the F.1 plants produced from this seed are often highly or completely sterile. Attempts to cross species belonging to different genera usually result in failure, but in a few cases when closely related genera are crossed some seed is obtained, but the F.1 plants grown from this seed are normally sterile.

For example, crosses between bread wheat, *Triticum aestivum*, and rye, *Secale cereale*, will produce some seed, but this seed normally produces sterile plants.

Some light is thrown on these results when the chromosomes involved in the wheat-rye cross are considered. The wheat plant carrying 42 chromosomes will give rise to gametes carrying 21 chromosomes, whereas the rye with 14 chromosomes produces gametes with 7 chromosomes. On cross-fertilization between the two a zygote is formed with 28 chromosomes, of which 21 are from the wheat parent and 7 from the rye parent, thus:

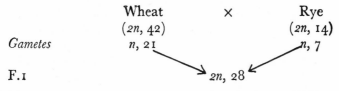

	Wheat	×	Rye
	(2n, 42)		(2n, 14)
Gametes	n, 21		n, 7
F.1		2n, 28	

Now, in the F.1 plants regular pairing of the 21 wheat chromosomes and the 7 rye chromosomes cannot take place during meiosis, i.e. there is an odd set of wheat chromosomes and an odd set of rye chromosomes. As a result, gametes are not produced and therefore, normally, no seed is formed.

On very rare occasions odd seeds have been produced naturally by such hybrid plants. Such seeds have been recorded in Sweden, Germany and Russia. These seeds germinated and gave rise to reasonably fertile plants which have been named *Triticale* (*Triticum-Secale* hybrid). Examination of the chromosome content of natural *Triticale* specimens revealed that the fertile hybrid plants had 56 chromosomes in their somatic cells, i.e. double the number found in a normal F.1 plant produced by fertilization between a haploid wheat gamete and a haploid rye gamete. The explanation of the odd seeds produced by the F.1 plants appears to be that some gametes were produced in the absence of meiosis, i.e. some unreduced pollen grains, and ovules were formed each carrying 28 (21+7) chromosomes. On fertilization of the 28-chromosome ovules by the 28-chromosome pollen grains zygotes with 56 (2×21+2×7) chromosomes were produced. In other words, an amphidiploid (or allotetraploid) was formed carrying two sets of wheat chromosomes and two sets of rye chromosomes. In such a plant regular pairing of chromosomes can occur during meiosis and fertile pollen and ovules may be produced.

In nature the occurrence of these tetraploid *Triticale* types is rare, but the use of colchicine has made possible the production of similar fertile hybrids between wheat and rye. The F.1 seed obtained from the wheat-rye cross is germinated and the coleoptiles treated with colchicine. Some of the seedlings which survive the treatment give rise to ears producing fertile pollen and ovules each with 28 chromosomes. Fertilization results in the formation of seed with 56 chromosomes from which fertile *Triticale* plants can be grown.

The first *Triticale* forms produced by the colchicine method were disappointing from an economic point of view. Yields were only about 50 per cent. of those of control wheat varieties in trials. More recently, however, as a result of experiment in the choice of the parent wheat and rye varieties for the production of *Triticale* varieties, and then, by crossing various varieties produced, more useful types have been obtained. The grain of these plants is of the wheat type, but is superior to control wheat varieties in protein content and baking quality. Yields approaching those of control wheat varieties have been obtained. The crop has the advantage of doing well, like rye, on poorer, lighter soils than are required for good yields of wheat.

Production of amphidiploids by means of colchicine has been used in America to obtain fertile and useful crosses between different species of tobacco.

A slightly modified method has been utilized in producing fertile crosses between some species of *Solanum*. For example, the cultivated potato, *Solanum tuberosum* (*2n*, 48) and the species *Solanum polyadenum* (*2n*, 24), which is resistant to Blight and to Colorado Beetle, will not cross. By first doubling the chromosome content of *S. polyadenum* by means of colchicine, successful hybridization can be achieved. Similar work has been carried out on coffee species.

Fertile species hybrids occur occasionally as a result of the natural production of amphidiploids. For example, the common hemp nettle, *Galeopsis tetrahit*, found on arable land in Britain, is thought to be a hybrid produced by the natural crossing of the two species *Galeopsis pubescens* and *Galeopsis speciosa*, the chromosomes of each having doubled, thus producing a fertile amphidiploid.

CUMULATIVE INFLUENCE OF GENES

Mention should here be made of the so-called *transgressive segregation*, which sometimes occurs in the F.2 and subsequent generations and results in one or more characters in individual offspring being expressed in excess of those characters in either original parent. An example of such a 'transgression' is the appearance of individual plants with shorter straw after crossing two long-strawed barley varieties. Characters such as straw-length and many other morphological and physiological characters are influenced by several pairs of genes, even in diploid species such as barley, and segregation after crossing may therefore result in combinations of genes which produce these apparent transgressions.

When the gene complex is produced by more than one set of paired chromosomes, as in polyploids, somewhat complicated results may often be obtained in breeding. These results may appear to transgress the laws of inheritance. For example, when red-grained varieties of bread wheat are crossed with a white-grained variety all the progeny in the F.1 are red-grained. In the F.2 red-grained and white-grained plants are produced, but the ratio of red-grained to white-grained varies with different original red-grained parent plants (P.1).

Some original red-grained parent varieties produce, in the F.2, a ratio of 3 red-grained plants to 1 white-grained; others produce a ratio of 15 red to 1 white and others a ratio of 63 red to 1 white.

These results show that red is dominant and white recessive, and the various proportions produced in the F.2 are the result of the action of three pairs of genes located on different chromosome pairs. Thus the genetic constitution of the red parent producing the 3 : 1 ratio must be R_1R_1, r_2r_2, r_3r_3 or r_1r_1, R_2R_2, r_3r_3 or r_1r_1, r_2r_2, R_3R_3 (where 'R' represents a dominant red-producing gene and 'r' a recessive white-producing gene). The constitution of the red variety giving the 15 : 1 ratio in F.2 will be R_1R_1, R_2R_2, r_3r_3, or R_1R_1, r_2r_2, R_3R_3, or r_1r_1, R_2R_2, R_3R_3, and that of the red variety giving the 63 : 1 ratio in the F.2 will be R_1R_1, R_2R_2, R_3R_3. The white-grained parent will, of course, be r_1r_1, r_2r_2, r_3r_3.

In the F.2 derived from the R_1R_1, R_2R_2, R_3R_3 parent crossed with a white-grained variety red-grained individuals may have anything from one to six 'doses' of red. These doses are cumulative; grains with a single red-producing gene being palest, those with six being deepest red.

Other characters, both morphological and physiological, are likely to be inherited in a similar manner. Thus, where more than one pair of genes affecting a particular characteristic is present they may supplement one another, producing increased effects. Such effects are particularly to be expected in polyploids, where more than two sets of chromosomes are involved.

THE GENE COMPLEX

In an elementary discussion of the effects produced by genes it is usual to consider a simple dominant and recessive pair, such as the genes regulating tallness and dwarfness respectively in peas. We have attempted to show that the effects of particular genes are not always so clear-cut as in this example. The influence of a particular gene may be modified by the presence of other genes in the same zygote. Also, a particular gene, when introduced, by breeding, into a different gene complex may produce different, and sometimes unexpected, effects.

An individual plant is not a representation of the separate effects of all the gene pairs in its nuclei, but of the whole gene complex. It is therefore of importance for a plant-breeder to know something of the behaviour of particular genes in different gene complexes in order to assess the value of plant material for breeding purposes. Such knowledge accumulates as a result of trial and recording of results.

CYTOPLASMIC INFLUENCE ON INHERITANCE

We have shown that inheritance is controlled by genes which make up the chromosomes. Normally the rest of the cell contents appear to have no influence on heredity. In a few cases, however, it has been demonstrated that the cytoplasm, which in most plants appears to be transmitted by the female side, may transmit certain characters or modify the expression of a particular gene combination. The cytoplasmic particles which influence heredity are known as *plasmagenes*.

PURE LINES

The progeny of a single homozygous self-fertilized plant is known as a *pure line*. A pure line shows constant genotypic uniformity. Variations will occur between individuals of a pure line, but these variations are not inherited; they are due to environmental conditions, and are therefore *fluctuating variations* or *phenotypic variations*.

Johannsen, a Danish botanist, demonstrated these facts in his experiments (1903) with the kidney bean, *Phaseolus vulgaris*, which is self-pollinated. He selected several single plants from a crop and saved seeds from them separately. The progeny of each single plant selection were grown separately, in a reasonably uniform environment, for a number of generations. In each generation the average seed weight varied between different pure lines. The heaviest and lightest seeds were next selected within a pure line, and these were grown on for a number of generations, selecting each time the heaviest and the lightest seeds. This time Johannsen found in each year that there was no significant difference in the average weight of seeds produced from the lightest as compared with those produced from the heaviest seeds within a pure line.

These experiments demonstrate the fact that by selecting single plants from a self-pollinated variety it is possible to build up pure lines, some of which may be superior to others in some respects, *but further selection within a pure line does not bring about any further improvement.* The pure line is homozygous, and because the plants are self-fertilizing no new genes are being introduced, and therefore it continues to breed constantly to type. The only possibility of genetic variation in a pure line is for mutation to occur. This happens only on rare occasions, and the pure line can normally be kept constant for many generations. When mutations do occur, the mutant plants, if observed, may be selected and may form useful breeding material. Many mutations, however, are of little value for this purpose.

INBREEDING

Many species of plants are normally self-pollinated, the pollen and the ovules being produced by the same plant and therefore having the same genetic make-up. Such species are therefore of necessity inbred. The crop plants barley, wheat, oats and peas, are examples of this normally self-pollinated, and therefore inbred, group. In these crops, in which inbreeding is normal, no adverse effect appears to result from this process, and vigour is maintained generation after generation.

Many plant species are normally cross-pollinated, and frequently they are specially adapted by various structural or functional means to achieve this and to prevent self-pollination. Some plants—for example, varieties of cherry—are completely self-sterile and cannot produce fruit and seed unless cross-pollinated. Other species, such as cabbage, will produce little fertile seed when allowed to be pollinated only by their own pollen. In many species when seed can be produced by compulsory self-pollination the offspring are less vigorous than those resulting from cross-pollination. Thus inbreeding in normally cross-fertilized plants may lead to deterioration.

Most detailed study of the effects of inbreeding has been made, in America, on maize which is normally cross-pollinated but which can readily be self-pollinated. The first generation resulting from self-pollination was usually inferior, to the parent, in vigour and yield of seed, and when self-pollination was continued for a number of generations the plants continued to deteriorate by progressively smaller amounts. In the lines which did not die out in the process a stage was reached, after a number of generations, at which further inbreeding had no further adverse effect. Various characters had become fixed in a homozygous condition, and no further deleterious recessives could be brought out by further inbreeding. In addition, the inbred lines had become pure for major characteristics such as colour, size and texture of the grain.

HYBRID VIGOUR OR HETEROSIS

In some plant species when different varieties are crossed the heterozygous plants resulting in the F.1 show markedly increased vigour above that of either parent. This is known as *hybrid vigour* or, because it is associated with the heterozygous condition, *heterosis*. The increased vigour is manifested in greater size, with more luxuriant growth of leaf and stem, and often in such characteristics as larger seed with more efficient germination, earlier flowering, higher yield of seed and greater resistance to disease. The hybrid vigour cannot be preserved and fixed, as it rapidly disappears in subsequent generations when the hybrid plants are inbred.

Hybrid vigour has been demonstrated, and utilized most widely for economic purposes, in the maize crop. When selected lines which have been inbred for a number of generations are crossed, very marked hybrid vigour may be obtained. The plants are considerably larger than the inbred parents and yield of grain often shows a gain of up to 200 per cent. above that of the inbred parents and over 20 per cent. above that of the original cross-bred variety from which the parents were produced. These hybrid plants of the F.1 also show marked uniformity as they are all similar heterozygotes.

Because the hybrid vigour cannot be fixed by inbreeding and rapidly disappears in succeeding generations, fresh hybrid seed must be obtained each year by growers. As a result, a flourishing industry has arisen in the U.S.A. for the production of hybrid seed from which farmers grow their crop for food, but not for seed purposes.

In 1933 about 0·2 per cent. of the total acreage of maize grown in the Corn Belt of U.S.A. was hybrid. The demand grew rapidly, and now practically all farmers in U.S.A. use hybrid seed for their maize crop. There is thus a huge annual demand for fresh hybrid seed.

In producing hybrid seed a good deal of preliminary trial is necessary. Inbred pairs, when crossed, do not always produce hybrid vigour in the offspring, i.e. they do not '*nick*'. Preliminary experiment is necessary in order to find pairs of inbred lines which will combine well, or 'nick', i.e. produce an F.1 showing hybrid vigour of economic worth.

The explanation of the cause of hybrid vigour is still open to discussion. One possible explanation on a genetic basis is that of Jones, an American geneticist. Jones's hypothesis suggests that a large number of genes is concerned in the control of size and vigour and that each chromosome may carry several of these genes. As a result of inbreeding, many of these genes will be present in a homozygous condition, some pairs being useful dominants, others deleterious recessives. Now, when two inbred lines are crossed and produce hybrid vigour in their offspring, they do so because the useful dominants of each mask the deleterious recessives of the other. Fig. 11 shows how this may work. In the diagram

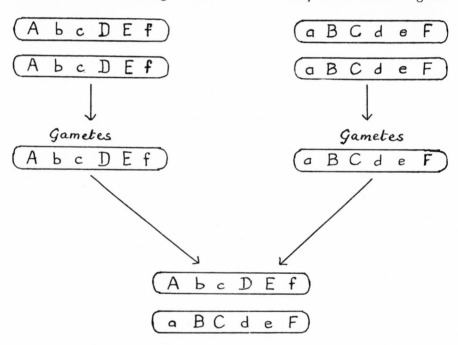

Fig. 11. Diagrammatic representation of a cross producing maximum heterosis in one pair of chromosomes in the offspring.

only one pair of chromosomes of each parent has been considered. It will be noted that crossing has produced the following pairing of genes, Aa, Bb, Cc, Dd, Ee and Ff, i.e. all the deleterious recessives are masked. In the F.2 and subsequent generations this condition would no longer be preserved.

It is not readily possible to breed out plants which would be homozygous for the dominants affecting vigour because the dominants are linked on the same chromosomes as recessives having adverse effects. All the chromosome pairs would have to undergo most complicated processes of crossing-over in order to produce a gamete containing all the dominants of all the allelomorphic pairs.

Reference to fig. 11 will suggest why it is necessary to select carefully the inbred parents for crossing. Each parent selected should have as many dominants as possible which will mask the deleterious recessives shown by the other.

In the actual production of hybrid maize seed for farmers in America it is usual to make a double cross like the following:

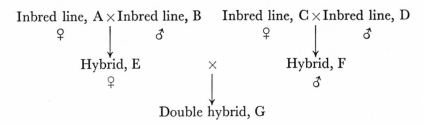

Or alternatively, a three-way cross, thus:

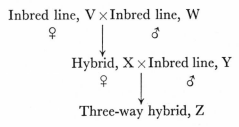

By these methods larger yields of hybrid seed are obtained. In a first cross between two inbred lines, although the seed produced by the female parent will give rise to plants showing hybrid vigour, the *amount* of seed is small because it is borne on a weak inbred plant. In the above methods strong hybrid plants (E and X) are first obtained to produce the ultimate seed crop, and therefore high yields of seed are produced. By careful selection of the inbred parents used, maximum masking of undesirable recessives and therefore maximum hybrid vigour is obtained.

Production of hybrid maize is relatively simple because of the structure of the maize plant (see Chapter XV). The male flowers are borne at the top of the plant in the so-called tassel, whilst the female flowers are in lateral shoots below. Prevention of self-pollination can be achieved simply by cutting off the tassels at an early stage. The inbred lines to be crossed are planted in separate rows, usually three or four rows of the female parent to one row of the pollen parent. The tassels are removed from the female parent plants and fertilization is therefore brought about by the selected male parent. The crop must, of course, be grown in isolation from other maize varieties which might pollinate it.

A further development in the production of hybrid maize is the utilization of male-sterile lines. Male sterility can be added to an inbred line;

this line, now male-sterile, can then be grown with a suitable pollinating inbred line, for the production of seed, without the necessity of removing the tassels of the seed parent.

In harvesting hybrid seed crops the seed produced on the pollen parent is harvested separately and, as it has been produced by pollen from similar plants, it can be used to produce further inbred plants.

In most other crops, in which the flowers are hermaphrodite and self-fertile, e.g. wheat, the phenomenon of hybrid vigour cannot be exploited so readily. In such crops emasculation (removal of the stamens) would have to be performed on each flower individually, and the amount of labour required to produce sufficient hybrid seed would be prohibitive. In crops in which a large amount of seed can be produced by each single pollination, as in the case of the tomato, artificial crossing is practicable, and quantities of seed for the commercial crop may be produced economically in this way.

Some progress has been made in the case of sugar-beet, which is normally cross-pollinated, but in which some degree of self-pollination may occur. Selected types are inbred by growing them in isolation with protective screens to prevent natural crossing. Inbred lines are then grown together and, although some 'selfed' seed is produced, a high proportion of the seed is hybrid. The hybrid seedlings grow more vigorously, and because they are more forward when the crop is chopped out, it is more likely that the weaker 'selfed' seedlings will be removed and an almost 100 per cent. hybrid crop will result.

As in maize, male sterile plants can be found in sugar-beet. By developing a male sterile line and then growing it alongside a male fertile inbred line to provide the pollen, 100 per cent. hybrid seed can be assured on the male sterile plants.

A useful amount of hybrid vigour often arises when different strains of beet, which have not previously been inbred, are grown together for seed. This is sufficiently valuable to be of use as a means of obtaining seed of superior quality. Again, the strains which will combine satisfactorily must be discovered by preliminary trial.

In species which are normally reproduced vegetatively, any hybrid vigour which arises on crossing two varieties is retained when further crops are produced by vegetative means. For example, any hybrid vigour which may appear when two potato varieties are crossed will persist, because later crops are produced from tubers, and there is no further reproduction by seed, which could reduce the heterosis.

INCOMPATIBILITY

Failure of self- or cross-pollination may be due to genetic factors. Many normally cross-pollinated plants will fail to set seed when forced to self-pollinate because incompatibility exists between the pollen and the style and the pollen grains fail to produce a pollen tube or produce one so slowly that the style withers and dies before the pollen tube reaches the ovules. Incompatibility may also exist between pairs of plants of the same species and cross-pollination between these plants will fail as a result.

Incompatibility exists in many species such as cabbage, beet and red clover. Growers of cherries are well aware of the importance of an understanding of the compatibility relationships of varieties of this crop. The sweet cherry, *Prunus avium*, is entirely self-sterile. All individual trees fail to set fruit when self-pollinated or when pollinated by pollen from other trees of the same variety (i.e. 'clone', see p. 48). When a particular

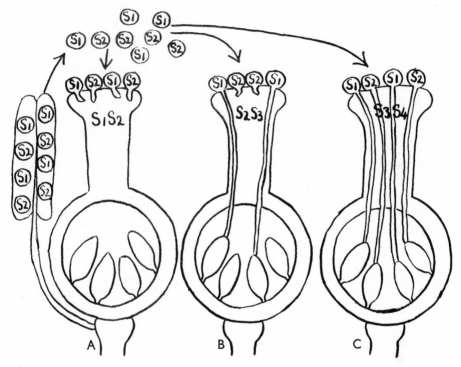

Fig. 12. Compatible and incompatible pollinations.

variety is pollinated by other varieties it is fertile with some varieties, but infertile or incompatible with others. For example, the variety Early Rivers is incompatible with Early Black, but compatible with Waterloo. Thus it is important, in planting cherry trees, to discover which varieties are compatible and to plant together suitable varieties to ensure successful fertilization and production of fruit.

A genetic theory which provides an explanation of incompatibility of this kind depends upon some physiological conditions of the pollen grains and of the style which are controlled by a series of allelomorphic genes S_1, S_2, S_3, S_4 . . . S_x. The influence of these genes is represented diagrammatically in fig. 12. The flower 'A' is heterozygous for S_1 and S_2; thus the pollen grains will carry either the gene S_1 or the gene S_2. The tissues of the style will carry S_1, S_2, and it is supposed that a physiological condition in the style is produced under the influence of these genes which prevents the effective growth of the pollen tube from either S_1 or S_2 pollen grains. The flower is thus self-sterile, and its pollen would also be ineffective in fertilizing any other flower carrying S_1, S_2 in its stylar tissues. Flower 'B' carries S_2, S_3 in its style. In this case S_2 pollen is prevented from growing, but as there is no S_1 in the style the S_1 pollen grains are effective. Thus half the pollen of flower 'A' would be effective when cross-pollinating flower 'B'. Flower 'C', which carries S_3, S_4, can be fertilized by both the S_1 and the S_2 pollen grains from flower 'A', because neither S_1 nor S_2 occurs in the tissues of the style 'C'.

Self-incompatibility or self-sterility may be overcome in some plants, such as cabbages and kales, by self-pollinating the flowers in the bud stage. In such plants the pollen tube grows slowly, and when self-pollination occurs after the flower has opened the style begins to wither before fertilization can take place. *Bud pollination* ensures that the maximum period of time is available for the growth of the pollen tubes, and therefore increases the probability of fertilization. This method is sometimes of use to the plant-breeder if he wishes to produce an inbred line of one of these crops.

CLONES

A clone is a group of plants descended from a single plant by vegetative reproduction. All members of a clone have the same genetic constitution as one another and as the original parent plant, because no sexual reproduction, and therefore no genetic segregation, has taken place in their production.

An example of a clone is provided by any variety of apple. For example, all the Cox's Orange Pippin apple trees in existence have descended, as a result of grafting, from one original tree which itself was grown from an apple pip or seed. Thus all the Cox's Orange Pippin trees in existence together form a clone. So long as these trees are propagated vegetatively their characteristics remain constant. Each tree will produce fruit readily recognizable as Cox's Orange Pippins. If the seeds from such trees were sown, and trees raised therefrom, it is highly improbable that such trees would be of the same type as the parent or that the fruit would be recognizable as the named variety. This is due to the fact that the parent plants are most probably heterozygous and, when reproduction by seed occurs, new characters are likely to appear as a result of segregation.

Similarly, any variety of potato has descended from a single seedling by vegetative propagation, by means of tubers, and all potato plants of any particular variety form a clone. Although the plants are most probably heterozygous, they remain true to type because masked recessives cannot appear during vegetative reproduction.

Clones are sometimes built up in order to increase the amount of breeding material available to the plant-breeder. Any plant which can be split up, in any way, and portions planted to produce new complete plants, may be used to build up a clone. For example, if it is desired to increase the number of plants of a grass or cereal of a particular genetic make-up, this may be done by splitting the original plant into tillers and planting-out the tillers. The tillers will produce fully developed plants all of the same genetic constitution as the parent plant. Clones of valuable plants of 'root' crops and clovers may be produced by means of cuttings.

APOMIXIS

Some plants are able to produce seed in the absence of fertilization. This process is known as *apomixis*. The embryo may be produced from the egg nucleus within the embryo sac or from somatic cells of the ovary. When the egg nucleus produces an embryo without fertilization the particular form of apomixis is known as *parthenogenesis*. In parthenogenesis in flowering plants meiosis has usually failed to occur during the formation of the egg nucleus; thus the egg, and the embryo it produces, will have the same chromosome content as the somatic cells of the parent plant. Embryos produced apomictically from somatic cells of the ovary will also have the same chromosome constitution as the parent. These forms of apomixis normally give rise to a group of plants genetically identical with the parent and with one another, and therefore comparable with a clone.

Common plants of agricultural interest which frequently produce seed apomictically are dandelion, *Taraxacum officinale*, and smooth-stalked meadow grass, *Poa pratensis*.

In some apomictic species numerous forms exist. For example, in *Poa pratensis* forms differing markedly from one another have been recorded. When the chromosome constitution of these different forms was examined it was found that the numbers varied between one form and another, and various even and odd numbers ranging from 28 to 124 ($2n$) are recorded.

Forms in which irregular chromosome constitution has developed are more likely to persist in apomictic species than in sexually reproduced species in which pairing of similar chromosomes and regular meiosis must occur.

PLANT CHIMAERAS

A *chimaera* is a plant in which there are two or more kinds of tissue differing in their genetic constitution. The term was originally used to describe a fabulous creature which had a goat's body with a lion's head and a dragon's tail.

Somatic mutations which affect only some of the somatic cells of a plant, giving rise to layers or zones of changed tissue, result in the production of chimaeras. It has been shown in some varieties of potatoes with coloured tubers that, by removing the eyes, new buds may be produced by division of cells of the internal tissue of the tuber, and that these buds will develop into shoots which produce uncoloured, white, tubers. It is therefore suggested that such coloured varieties are chimaeras, resulting from mutation of the surface layers of cells only, and derived from all-white varieties.

Many variegated forms of plants are chimaeras in which zones or layers of cells are genetically unable to produce chlorophyll. For example, the

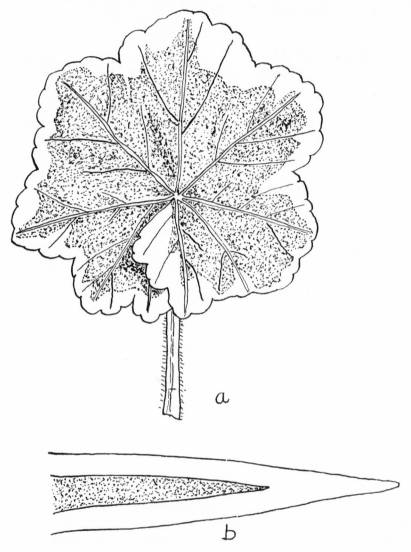

FIG. 13. *a*, Leaf of variegated Pelargonium. *b*, Diagram of a transverse section, showing inner green and outer white tissues.

variegated *Pelargonium* (commonly called *Geranium*) in fig. 13 possesses an outer layer of white tissue over an inner core of chlorophyll-producing tissue. In the leaves the white tissue extends beyond the inner green tissue at the margins, thus giving the variegated effect. It should be noted that variegation in plants is not always due to chimaera structure. It may result from disease, such as virus diseases, or it may, in some plants, be inherited in a Mendelian manner.

The term 'chimaera' is also applied to the so-called *graft-hybrids* produced from buds developed at the region of the union of stock and scion after grafting. After union of a graft has taken place, if the graft is broken or cut across at the point of union, any buds produced at the break may originate in any one of three different ways: (*a*) from cells of the stock only, (*b*) from cells of the scion only, and (*c*) from cells of both stock and scion. In the case of (*a*) the buds will produce shoots like the stock,

Fig. 14. *b*, A chimaera resulting from a graft between tomato *a* and black nightshade *c*. (After a photograph from Baur, *Vererbungslehre*, 5th and 6th Editions.)

and in the case of (*b*) shoots like the scion will be produced. The buds of mixed origin (*c*) may consist of an outer layer of cells of the scion and an inner core of cells of the stock, in which case the shoots which develop show characteristics intermediate between stock and scion. Alternatively, the buds of mixed origin may be derived from adjacent cells of stock and scion, in which case parts of the shoots developing from these show characteristics of the stock and other parts show characteristics of the scion.

A chimaera consisting of an outer layer of tissue 'A' surrounding a core of tissue 'B' is known as a *periclinal chimaera*. One consisting of distinct zones of the different tissues, one not enclosing the other, is called a *sectorial chimaera*.

Chimaeras of the graft-hybrid type have been produced experimentally. For example, by grafting together tomato (*Lycopersicum esculentum*) and black nightshade (*Solanum nigrum*) and cutting across the graft after union had occurred, both periclinal and sectorial chimaeras have been obtained. Periclinal chimaeras which have arisen spontaneously are also known—for example, the Adam's broom, which resulted from a graft of purple broom (*Cytisus purpurea*) on laburnum (*Laburnum anagyroides*). This tree has many characteristics of laburnum, but with purple flowers, although some branches may produce yellow flowers. Peach-almond and medlar-whitethorn graft-hybrids are also known.

Chimaeras are not usually of great importance to the breeder of agricultural crops, but they provide some attractive horticultural novelties.

VARIATION AND PLANT-BREEDING

The aim of the plant-breeder is to obtain variations which deviate from existing types within a variety or species in one characteristic or more of economic value.

It is important, therefore, to recognize the chief types of variation in plants and their causes. The types of variation which may occur may be summarized as follows:

1. *Non-hereditary Variations or Fluctuations*

Such variations, which are due to variations in environment and do not affect the genes of the plants, are of no value to the plant-breeder, but they may sometimes obscure hereditary differences between plants which are of some importance. For example, in sugar-beet, genetic differences between plants for yield of sugar may be slight, but valuable from a breeder's point of view. These differences may easily be obscured by differences in the fertility of the land on which the crops are grown. It is therefore important, in breeding work, to recognize variations of a fluctuating type and also to provide an environment for breeding material which will be as uniform as possible, in order to prevent genetic differences from being obscured by environmental effects.

2. *Heritable Variations*

Variations from the normal which can be passed on to the progeny are those sought by the plant-breeder. Such heritable variations may be quite small or they may be large and readily observed. The types of hereditary variation have been dealt with in the preceding pages, and may be summarized as follows:

(*a*) *Mutation* occurring naturally or as a result of artifice on the part of the plant-breeder. Some mutations are of value in crop improvement; many quite useless.

Somatic mutations may or may not be inherited through the seed produced on the mutant shoots (see p. 33). In vegetatively propagated plants somatic mutations may be useful even though they are not inherited through the seed. Clones of the mutant type may be built up and the new variation perpetuated—a method which is often of value more particularly with horticultural plants.

(*b*) *Polyploidy*—a special form of mutation involving complete sets of chromosomes rather than individual genes. Like gene mutations, polyploids are of varying value in plant-breeding.

(*c*) *New gene combinations* brought about by hybridization. This form of variation is of most value to the plant-breeder. The new gene combinations, over which the breeder has some control through his selection of breeding material and breeding methods, are the most important means of improvement of agricultural crops at the present day.

(*d*) *Continuous variation.* Although major genes may decide that a plant variety falls into a particular category, e.g., tall or dwarf in peas, often minor genes each having smaller effect may bring about differences in the particular character within the group. Thus within a dwarf variety of peas all plants would not be the same height under identical conditions. A continuous variation of height occurs within the group although the group as a whole can be designated 'dwarf'. Johannsen's work (p. 42) demonstrated that within a variety of self-pollinated plants selection of single plants and building up of pure lines from them results in groups of plants within which this type of variation is reduced in extent.

Chapter IV

PLANT-BREEDING: ORGANIZATION AND METHODS

CROP improvement by means of plant-breeding has been in progress for a considerable time. It was only, however, as a result of the work of Mendel, De Vries, Johannsen and others in comparatively recent times that a scientific basis was given to the methods of plant-breeding and further development of these methods became possible. Whilst plant-breeding, to some extent, remains an art depending upon the breeder's skill, it is now essentially a science depending for its success on the accumulated knowledge of the genetics of the breeding material.

For success the plant-breeder must be acquainted with the various sources of breeding material at his disposal and must know, or be able to discover by trial, the genetic characteristics of that material. Most plant-breeding stations maintain large quantities of plant material, consisting of different varieties and species of the crops in which they specialize. Some of this material may be of importance because it possesses so little as one valuable character—for example, resistance to a particular disease. Breeding material may be exchanged between breeding centres or individuals in various parts of the world. Organized expeditions may search for and find breeding material, often among wild plants, and sometimes in remote parts of the globe. Examples of the useful material found in such searches are the wild species of *Solanum*, collected in Mexico and South America, which have proved of value in potato-breeding, chiefly on account of their immunity or resistance to diseases, such as blight or virus diseases, or to pests such as potato root eelworm.

ORGANIZED PLANT-BREEDING

Contributions to crop improvement in the British Isles have been made by enthusiastic individuals, such as the late Donald McKelvie, who produced the Arran series of potato varieties on the Isle of Arran off the west coast of Scotland. With the introduction of *The Plant Breeders' Rights Regulations*, 1965, breeders in Britain now have legal rights regarding reproduction of their varieties comparable with rights which have existed for breeders in other countries for some years. Thus some financial gain may accrue and private plant breeders, in particular, are encouraged in their efforts.

Varieties of crop plants have been introduced from time to time as a result of breeding work carried out by some of the more enterprising

54

seeds firms in the British Isles. Some barley breeding has also been done on behalf of the brewing industry and rye improvement on behalf of rye biscuit manufacturers.

Plant-breeding centres, aided by finance from the Government and other sources, have been set up in various parts of the British Isles to deal with specific crops. Notable centres are:

The Cambridge Plant Breeding Institute, where breeding work is concentrated mainly on cereals, but work is done also on other crops, such as beans, field peas, potatoes, sugar-beet, kales, lucerne and sainfoin.

The Welsh Plant Breeding Station, near Aberystwyth, where herbage seeds and oats are the chief interests.

The Scottish Society for Research in Plant Breeding, which is centred at Pentlandfield, Roslin, Midlothian, where a variety of crops such as oats, potatoes, swedes, kales and herbage plants occupies attention.

The Ministry of Agriculture for Northern Ireland Plant Breeding Division at Stormont, where potatoes and flax are among the chief interests.

On the continent of Europe groups such as those of de Vilmorin-Andrieux in France and Weibull and Co. in Sweden have contributed valuable new crop varieties, as have individual breeders, such as Desprez and Blondeau in France, and Heine in Germany.

Of the Continental breeding centres the best-known is that at *Svalöf* in Sweden, where a wide range of new varieties of various crops has been produced since it commenced its activities in 1886. *The Abed Plant Breeding Station* at Abed in Denmark is also widely known; the *Plant Breeding Institute, Wageningen* in Holland and the *State Plant Breeding Station, Gembloux,* in Belgium, have also contributed cereal varieties which have proved of value in the British Isles as well as in the countries for which they were produced.

METHODS OF CROP IMPROVEMENT

The methods of crop improvement available to the plant breeder depend, to a large extent, upon the normal means of reproduction of the crop with which he is dealing. The systems of breeding vary as between self-pollinated, cross-pollinated, dioecious (male and female flowers on separate plants) and vegetatively reproduced crops. According to these distinctions common crops may be classified as follows:

Normally Self-pollinated. Wheat, barley, oats, rice, peas, kidney beans, flax or linseed and tomatoes. In these crops some small amount of cross-pollination may occur, but this amount is not usually of great importance. It is considered sufficient, however, in the case of the cereals, to make it essential to grow nucleus seed stocks of a variety in isolation from other varieties of the same species in order to maintain purity.

Normally Cross-pollinated. Rye, maize, field beans, sugar-beet, mangels, fodder-beet, Brassicas, carrots, parsnips, clovers and most perennial grasses. Self-fertilization is possible to varying degrees in most of these species, but under natural open pollination conditions cross-pollination is the rule. In the absence of sufficient suitable insect pollinators field beans produce a large proportion of their seeds by self-pollination.

Dioecious Crops. Hops and hemp. In this group breeding involves obtaining superior male and female plants, their superiority being proved by progeny tests.

Plants Normally Propagated Vegetatively. Potatoes and fruit trees. In these crops once a useful plant has been produced from seed a clone ('variety') is then built up by vegetative reproduction. The various individuals in a clone remain uniform in character.

Before considering the methods used in improving particular crops, let us first consider the general methods available.

MASS SELECTION

Mass selection involves the selection of a large number of plants within a variety. The best plants typical of the variety would normally be selected and the poorer types discarded. In the case of self-pollinated plants, such as the cereals wheat, oats and barley, little improvement can be expected by this method, but selection of this type, repeated at intervals, may be used to maintain the standard of a variety.

When practised with cross-pollinated plants, such as sugar-beet or rye, mass selection may be of more value. 'Varieties' of such crops consist of numerous cross-pollinating types, and by the rejection of the poorer types, those which are homozygous for inferior recessive characters, which can be identified in the phenotype, are eliminated. In this way improvement of the composite strain or variety can be effected. Because many of the plants will be heterozygous for inferior recessive characters, however, such characters will appear in subsequent generations, as a result of segregation giving rise to homozygosity for these characteristics. Any improved variety must therefore be reselected year after year to maintain its standard.

ROGUING

Roguing may be regarded as a form of mass selection, but in this case the undesirable plants are removed and the rest of the crop retained. Its value lies in maintaining the standard of a variety rather than in producing any improvement. Roguing is often practised in producing a uniform standard seed crop under one of the Seed Inspection or Certification schemes (see Chapter VI).

SINGLE-PLANT SELECTION

The work of Johannsen has shown that in a self-pollinating crop a mixture of numerous homozygous pure lines may exist. By selection of single plants and their subsequent propagation pure lines can be built up. Some varieties will show more variation than others; old varieties often show a considerable amount of variation, whilst new varieties are normally more uniform. Where single plants are observed which show promise, above the standard for the parent variety, these may be selected and from each a pure line produced. If the pure line differs markedly in some respects from the original variety it may be named as a new variety. For example, Victory oat was obtained at Svalöf in Sweden by single-plant selection from the variety Milton. When phenotypic differences are less obvious, the pure line may be introduced as a selected line of the original variety—for example, the wheat Squarehead's Master 13/4, which was derived by single-plant selection from a mixed population of the old variety, Squarehead's Master.

Many varieties of wheat and oats have been produced in the past by single-plant selection. This method, however, depends upon some considerable degree of variability within the existing variety. In most present-day commercial varieties which are subjected to selection to maintain their uniformity it is more difficult to discover single plants which may act as the parent of outstanding pure lines.

Often pure lines are built up in an attempt to obtain improvement in some character which is not readily discernible in the field, for example malting quality in barley, or resistance to specific diseases. It is then necessary to make selections and to carry out careful tests and trials in order to obtain desirable pure lines. When attempting to obtain new types by single plant selection usually a large number of selections are made, the progeny of each single plant being kept separately and grown on in a separate plot. Several parallel pure lines are thus produced and may be submitted to tests for the various qualities of commercial value. Many of the lines may be discarded early, others carried on for a number of generations and tested against the parent variety or other varieties of similar type. Eventually one pure line may finally be retained as the best of the selections if it shows promise of commercial value.

HYBRIDIZATION

Hybridization of varieties of different genetic make-up is performed with the object of increasing variability in the hope of obtaining new and valuable combinations of hereditary characters.

In the case of self-pollinated plants, such as wheat, oats, and barley, crossing is followed, in subsequent generations, by self-pollination, and plants can be selected in the F.2 and later generations which will be homozygous for the desired characteristics. It is difficult to select plants which are homozygous for all characters, but careful selection, over a number of years, can result eventually in the isolation of varieties combining most of the major characters in a homozygous condition, so that the variety breeds true for all but very unimportant characteristics. The variety thus produced will normally remain true to type generation after generation. Some variability may be produced in the new variety as a result of natural cross-pollination of a few plants with other varieties;

c

in most of the self-pollinated crops the amount of crossing is usually small. There is also the possibility of mutation occurring in some plants over a period of years, and in varieties which have been released into commerce some admixture of seeds of other varieties may occur. The bulk of the crop should, however, remain fairly uniform, and in the case of present-day varieties stocks of 'original' seed are maintained by plant-breeders or their agents for issue at intervals in order to maintain the standard of the variety.

In the production of new varieties by hybridization, if one or two characters of one parent 'A' are needed in combination with most of the characters of parent 'B' the *back-cross* method of breeding may be adopted. 'A' and 'B' are crossed first and the offspring are crossed again with parent 'B'. Back-crossing may continue for from two to five or six generations. Each back-cross will result in the concentration of the genes of 'B' and, by selection from the progeny, isolation of desirable homozygous forms, possessing most of the characteristics of 'B' in combination with the few desirable characters of 'A', may be achieved.

Good characters from three or more parents may be combined in a new variety by means of *multiple crossing*. This involves crossing two selected parents and at some stage (often at F.1) crossing the offspring with a third variety or with the progeny of another pair. By further crossing on similar lines the genes of any number of parents may be introduced. By this means combinations of genes from several parents are obtained and by subsequent selection new types combining good qualities from the various parents may result.

HYBRIDIZATION IN SELF-POLLINATED CROPS

The systems of breeding vary somewhat according to the particular crop which is being bred, and they may also vary from one breeder to another. There are two main systems in use: *the pedigree method* and *the bulk method*.

Pedigree Method

In this system careful records are made in each generation, and selection starts in the early generations. From the records each selected line can be traced from one generation to the next.

The F.1 generation resulting from a cross between two normally self-pollinated varieties will show uniformity of characters. If any seed has been produced by self-pollination—and this cannot always be avoided—the plants produced by such seed in the F.1 will be recognized by the correspondence of their characters with those of the seed parent, and they can be discarded. The true F.1 hybrid plants are allowed to produce seed by self-pollination.

The F.1 seed is sown so as to produce individually spaced plants. The number of F.2 plants grown from this seed may be anything from a few hundred to a few thousand.

Seed from each F.2 plant is harvested separately and threshed separately. The individual seed samples are kept separate and carefully labelled. Some F.2 plants showing undesirable characteristics may be discarded. Seed from the harvested plants may be examined for quality, and the produce of some F.2 plants may be discarded at this stage, but often such tests are postponed until later generations.

In the F.3 generation seed from individual F.2 plants is sown in *progeny rows* a separate row for the seed of each F.2 plant. A large number of rows, perhaps as many as 1,000 or more, may be grown in this generation. In the F.3 it is possible to discover which, if any, of the F.2 plants were homozygous for the major characters, by the uniformity of the plants in the rows. Promising homozygous rows are selected in the F.3 and subsequent generations. Plants from rows still segregating may be used to produce further progeny rows for further generations. From these, further homozygous rows may be selected.

Selections of rows are made, in F.3 and subsequent generations, on the basis of characters which are considered to be of importance in a new variety. For example, in cereals, characters such as frost resistance, length and strength of straw, earliness of ripening, grain colour and quality and resistance to certain diseases would be considered. Detailed quality tests may be postponed until later generations when a larger bulk of seed is available. In the F.3 and onward the most promising rows are selected first and then the best plants from these rows selected and harvested. Progeny rows are sown from the individual plant selections in the following generation. In each generation check rows of the parent varieties may be grown.

The seed of promising homozygous rows is finally multiplied for yield trials. This is usually done in the F.4 to F.6. Trials continue over a period of three years or more, during which selected varieties are tested alongside the best variety, or varieties, of comparable type. If early trials prove promising selected varieties may be tested over a wide range of soil and climatic conditions and, finally, after a variety has passed successfully through these trials, its seed may be further multiplied and released to the seed trade.

In this method of breeding many lines are discarded in each generation, but several lines may reach the stage of comparative yield trials.

Bulk Method

An alternative method, first practised at Svalöf, is followed by many breeders. This method consists of growing all the material together in a single plot until about the F.6 before any selection takes place. By the F.6 a large proportion of the plants will be homozygous and promising plants are selected for trial in progeny rows. Because of the elimination of selection, progeny row planting and recording in the early generations, a greater number of plants can be dealt with and a larger number of pure homozygous lines preserved. By F.6 a large number of plants will show undesirable characters; these will be plants which would have been eliminated in earlier generations in the previous system.

Natural selection will weed out many lines, such as those which ripen too late, those which are destroyed by any disease or pest attack which may occur during the period and, in the case of winter varieties, those which are not frost-resistant.

Seed of selected homozygous lines is finally multiplied for trials as in the previous system.

The bulk method is considerably less laborious than the pedigree method, and it has given very good results.

HYBRIDIZATION IN CROSS-POLLINATED CROPS

The production and maintenance of varieties of cross-pollinated crops presents greater difficulties. Hybridization cannot be used to produce types carrying the desirable characters of two parents in a homozygous condition. Such stability is prevented by cross-pollination in each generation.

Artificial crossing between two selected plants may be used to produce a family which, after selection for a number of generations, may be reasonably uniform, but which, because of its heterozygous condition, would require reselection of plants for seed production in each generation in order to maintain the uniformity of the family.

Hybridization in some species may be used to produce large quantities of F.1 seed which shows hybrid vigour. This has already been discussed in connection with maize and sugar-beet (Chapter III). This system depends on the possibility of large-scale hybridization in the field or of large quantities of seed being produced by each cross-pollination where this must be done artificially.

Hybridization may also be used in cross-pollinated crops to build up hybrid families which, after selection, are then grown with other selected hybrid families carrying desirable characters and allowed to cross-pollinate freely. Thus varieties composed of useful cross-pollinating families are built up. Such composite varieties deteriorate in later generations owing to the appearance of undesirable recessives in a homozygous state. It is therefore necessary for continuous mass selection to be followed each year to obtain parent plants for seed production. The breeder must annually produce nucleus stock seed in order to maintain the standard of the variety.

THE OBJECTS OF PLANT-BREEDING

The general object of the plant-breeder is to produce a new variety which will be superior to existing types. The detailed objects will vary with different crops. Yield is important, but in cereals it is yield of grain, in sugar-beet yield of refined sugar per acre, and in grasses yield of leaf. Quality is an important object—for example, malting quality in malting barleys, keeping and cooking qualities in potatoes. In wheat characteristics such as standing capacity of the straw, time of ripening, frost-resistance, resistance to shattering of the ear at harvest, resistance of the grain to sprouting in the stook and adaptation to particular soil and climatic conditions are some of the major considerations. In potatoes points of importance are time of maturity, shape, colour and cooking quality of the tubers, depth of the eyes and ease of lifting.

In addition, in all crops, resistance or immunity to diseases and pests is a desirable objective.

BREEDING FOR RESISTANCE OR IMMUNITY TO DISEASES AND PESTS

Farm crops are open to attack by many diseases and pests. Large numbers of a single plant species growing close together often provide ideal conditions for the rapid spread of disease or pest attack and such attacks may cause considerable financial loss to the farmer. In some cases the most valuable means of combating these troubles is the production of varieties which are immune or markedly resistant to them. Diseases and pests which cannot, easily and cheaply, be kept under control are those for which it is most important for the plant-breeder to provide immune or resistant varieties. Where a simple cheap method of control exists a costly programme of plant-breeding may not be justified. For example, in the wheat crop covered smut or bunt (*Tilletia caries*), which in former times was a serious cause of loss, can now be controlled cheaply by dressing the seed with an organo-mercurial fungicide (see Chapter XXV). This disease is therefore no longer a serious cause of loss to wheat-growers and production of resistant or immune varieties is of little importance.

When breeding is desirable, it is necessary as a preliminary to discover plants which show the necessary immunity or resistance. Having discovered such plants, which themselves may have little or no commercial value, the objective is to combine the genes controlling immunity or resistance with those producing the good qualities of the best commercial varieties.

One of the best examples of this type of work is the production of varieties of potato which are immune to wart disease. Wart disease, caused by the fungus *Synchytrium endobioticum* (see Chapter XXIII), threatened disaster to potato-growers at the beginning of the century. Fortunately, some immune varieties were discovered and immunity found to be inherited. Later, Salaman and Lesley (1921) showed that immunity was inherited in the Mendelian manner and was a dominant. By using immune varieties, for provision of the genes controlling immunity, modern immune commercial varieties were bred, and most present-day varieties are immune to the disease. Plant-breeders, with the assistance of legislation (see Chapter XXIII), have rendered wart disease relatively unimportant.

In some cases marked resistance, but not complete immunity, has been obtained as a result of plant-breeding. For example, varieties of wheat have been produced by plant breeders which show resistance to yellow rust disease (*Puccinia striiformis*). Resistance to potato blight (*Phytophthora infestans*) is being obtained by crossing the cultivated potato with wild species of *Solanum*, from Central and South America, which show resistance to this disease, e.g. *Solanum demissum*.

Breeding for immunity or resistance to diseases is complicated by the fact that various *physiological forms* or *races* of some disease-causing organisms exist, which exhibit various degrees of virulence and which may not all occur in any particular region. Thus a potato variety may be bred which exhibits resistance to two forms of the blight fungus, but develops the disease when it is exposed to a third form. The problem of the plant-breeder is to attempt to obtain immunity or resistance to all forms of a particular disease organism which are known to exist in the area for which the variety is being bred. A collection of races of the particular disease organism must be made and the breeding material submitted to infection trials. If complete knowledge of the reaction of the parent material to the various races is not available it will be necessary to perform preliminary trials with this material. New varieties are tested in the same way for a number of generations.

Varieties bred for a particular region may remain immune or resistant to attack whilst grown in that region, but when taken to another region where a different race of the disease organism is present they may succumb to the disease. For example, wheat varieties bred on the Continent may be highly resistant to yellow rust in the area for which they were bred, but may prove to be highly susceptible when grown in the British Isles.

A further complication in the problem of maintaining immunity or resistance lies in the fact that the fungi, bacteria and other disease-causing agents are organisms in which new genetic variations may arise at any time. Some of these new variations may prove to be more potent than those types already in existence, thus making further breeding of the crop necessary.

Breeding for resistance to pests presents similar problems. Some advance has been made in relation to certain crop pests. For example, varieties of oats markedly resistant to stem eelworm have been produced. Oat varieties with a high degree of resistance to frit fly have also been bred and, by use of some of the wild species of *Solanum*, resistance to Colorado beetle attack can be bred into potato varieties.

ARTIFICIAL CROSS-POLLINATION

Before attempting to cross two plants it is first of all important to understand the relationships of the two selected parents. Normally different varieties of the same species will cross successfully. Occasionally, however, incompatibility may exist between the two types and the pollen fail to bring about fertilization. In some plants, e.g. some sugar-beet and mangels, the flowers are male sterile and therefore cannot be used as the male parents in a cross. Male sterility also exists in some varieties of potato. In this crop also some varieties rarely produce flowers, and unless the plant can be forced to do so, by some cultural means, it is useless for breeding purposes. Other varieties of potato produce flowers which drop off early, and again unless this can be prevented they are useless as seed parents although they may be of value as pollen parents.

It is necessary to be familiar with the structure of the flowers; to know which flowers will produce strong seed; to know the time at which the pollen will be ripe on the male parent and the stigma receptive on the female parent. It may be necessary to force on the development of one parent in order to ensure that the stigmas are receptive at the same time as the pollen is available. Sowings at a number of dates may often achieve this object.

Crossing may be done in the field or in a glasshouse. The technique of crossing varies somewhat in different crop species; the fundamentals, however, are constant. The main consideration is to ensure that the pollen which fertilizes the selected ovaries is that which was chosen to be the male parent in the cross. To ensure this both the stamens of the male parent and the stigmas of the female parent must, usually, be protected from any possible contamination by extraneous pollen. In the case of the male parent the flowers may be covered whilst still in bud (this is most often done by placing them in a bag usually made of glassine or some similar material), to prevent air-carried or insect-carried pollen from becoming mixed with the selected pollen. The bag is placed over the flowers and tied at the mouth or plugged with cotton-wool. Self-pollination of the flowers of the seed parent is prevented by removal of their stamens before they have dehisced—known as *emasculation*. In many plants it is necessary to open the flower buds in order to do this in time. Usually the stamens are carefully lifted out with a pair of fine forceps or other fine instrument, care being taken not to burst the anthers and scatter pollen in the process. The flowers of the seed parent are then covered with a bag to protect the stigmas from extraneous pollen, which may be carried to them in the air or by insects. Inside the bags the flowers continue to develop and the stigmas become receptive. When the stigmas are receptive the flowers are uncovered and pollen is transferred to them from the flowers of the male parent. The technique of pollination varies in different species. In wheat mature stamens may be lifted out with forceps, the anthers split open, and one stamen inserted within each floret. In some species pollen, which may have shed within the bag, is collected and dusted on the stigmas with forceps or a camel-hair brush. After pollination the bags are replaced over the pollinated flowers to exclude contaminating pollen.

As an additional precaution against contamination by unknown pollen, any tools used for the transfer of pollen, such as forceps or brushes, may be decontaminated before use by dipping them in strong alcohol, which will kill adhering pollen grains. The alcohol is allowed to evaporate before the tools are used in pollination.

When dealing with plants which are self-sterile—for example, most red clovers—it is unnecessary to emasculate the seed parents. When the crop being bred is one in which a large number of flowers are produced close together in the inflorescence, some of the flowers may be removed in order to promote ease of handling of the rest and to ensure fewer, and therefore better-developed, seeds. For example, in hybridizing wheat the upper and lower spikelets may·be removed. The upper, less vigorous, florets within each spikelet may also be removed so as to retain two strong florets in each spikelet for crossing.

ARTIFICIAL SELF-POLLINATION

When seed produced by self-pollination is required from normally cross-pollinated plants it is necessary to protect the flowers before they open and until after pollination to prevent any cross-pollination. This is usually done by enclosing them in bags of glassine, or similar material, or by enclosing the complete plant in an insect-proof cage to prevent the entry of pollinating insects or, in the case of wind pollinated plants, a glass frame to keep out air-borne pollen. An alternative method is to grow single plants far enough away from other plants which might pollinate them. The distance will depend upon the species of plant, climatic conditions and the presence or absence of natural barriers to the spread of pollen. This method has been used by breeders of sugar beet and mangel in order to obtain 'selfed' seed for further breeding work.

THE TIME FACTOR IN PLANT-BREEDING

From what has been written in this chapter the reader will realize that the production of new varieties and strains of plants is normally a lengthy process involving several years' work before a new type is eventually available to the farmer.

The work of the plant-breeder can be speeded up a little, in some cases, by growing the breeding material in glasshouses with artificial illumination and control of temperature. Under these conditions two seed crops, and in some cases three, may be obtained from some annual species within twelve months, and the time required before seeding of biennial species can be considerably reduced. Thus, particularly in the early stages of a breeding programme, some time can be saved, but even so a number of years will be required after the commencement of breeding before new varieties can be made available to the farmer.

Chapter V

PLANT-BREEDING IN PRACTICE

LIMITATIONS of space prevent a detailed discussion of breeding problems and developments in all agricultural crops, but discussion of some of these, in connection with some of the more important crops, will serve to indicate how modern plant-breeders utilize the scientific discoveries and practices already discussed in an endeavour to produce new and improved varieties of crop plants.

BREEDING SELF-POLLINATED CROPS

Developments in the improvement of self-pollinated crops in modern times have involved, first of all, study and trials of existing varieties in order to determine the varieties most suitable for breeding work. Such varieties have, in some cases, then been improved by mass selection, but the first step leading to distinctive new types has usually been single-plant selection.

The advance possible by single-plant selection depends upon the variability of the existing varieties. This is limited in amount and a stage is eventually reached when single-plant selection from old varieties is unlikely to yield further valuable results. The next step in improvement of the crop involves crossing varieties in order to produce more variability in the breeding material from which new types may be selected.

Progressive improvement along these lines may be illustrated by reference to the breeding of certain malting barleys. The variety of most note in connection with the breeding of high-quality malting barleys in the British Isles is the old land variety Archer. (The term 'land variety' is used to denote a variety of unknown origin which has been in cultivation in a particular region for a very long time. Such varieties usually contain a considerable range of types.) Archer, which was formerly widely grown in the south-eastern counties and in Ireland, produced grain samples of high malting quality. It had a bent ear on a short, upright neck which did not break readily and cause the ears to fall off in the field, a fault common among the old varieties. It had a weak straw, however, and was late-ripening.

In Ireland, Archer was improved, first by mass selection and later by pure line selection. A pure line, Irish Archer, was then used by Dr. H. Hunter, in Ireland, for crossing with a variety called Spratt, which, although producing grain of poorer malting quality than Archer, had a stiffer, better-standing straw. From the progeny of this cross various types were selected and, after some years of trials and tests, a line named Spratt-Archer was first released for field cultivation in 1914. It is a variety capable of producing grain of high malting quality, but with a stronger straw than Archer; it also ripens a few days earlier. About the same time Beaven, who carried out breeding work at Warminster, introduced the hybrid Plumage-Archer, which combined good malting quality with a stronger straw than either Archer or Spratt-Archer.

Later, at the Cambridge Plant Breeding Institute, by crossing Spratt-Archer and Tschermak's two-row winter barley, the variety Pioneer (first recommended in 1945) was produced. This variety gives satisfactory malting samples and can be sown in the autumn; it ripens earlier than spring varieties, thereby helping to spread the harvest period.

More recently, at Cambridge, the popular spring variety Proctor (Kenia × Plumage-Archer) and the winter variety Maris Otter (Proctor × Pioneer, introduced 1965) have been bred. Both of these varieties produce grain of high malting quality.

In these examples it will be noted that the ability to produce good malting samples of grain is passed down from the old Archer, and new introductions show this character combined with other useful qualities obtained from other parents.

In a similar way, particular varieties of wheat and oats have played a prominent part in the origin of modern varieties of these cereals. For example, the varieties Squarehead's Master and Red Fife can be found in the ancestry of many wheat varieties, Grey Winter in that of winter oat varieties, and Victory in that of spring oats.

In the examples of barley-breeding quoted above, the major consideration was the production of varieties capable of yielding grain of high malting quality. Many other factors were taken into consideration in addition to this major one, and this must always be the case in breeding new varieties if they are to be of value. In wheat, for example, some of the important points to be considered in the production of new varieties are:

(1) Yield of grain.
(2) Quality of grain for milling and bread-baking; or for biscuit manufacture.
(3) Length and strength of straw.
(4) Time of ripening.
(5) Resistance to shattering of the ear and loss of grain when ripe.
(6) Resistance to sprouting of the grain in the ear at harvest time. With regard to this characteristic, red-grained varieties have been found to be more resistant than white-grained varieties, but within each group some varieties are more resistant than others.
(7) Resistance to diseases, such as loose smut (*Ustilago nuda*), yellow rust (*Puccinia glumarum*) and mildew (*Erysiphe graminis*).
(8) Suitability for autumn or for spring sowing.

A more detailed account of the origin and value of varieties of self-pollinated cereals is given in Chapter XV.

BREEDING CROSS-POLLINATED CROPS

In breeding cross-pollinated crops care is needed at all stages to prevent pollination by pollen from unknown parents, which may be carried in the air in some cases, such as rye; or by insects—for example, in the Brassicas. Protection of breeding material is achieved, in the case of controlled artificial crossing, by placing the flowers in bags before and after crossing (see p. 63). Where natural crossing between selected plants is desired, the plants may be grown in glasshouses, tightly sealed to prevent access of extraneous pollen, or in isolation, by distance, from other crops which might cross-pollinate them. In cases where cross-pollination between different species of the same genus is possible, as in the case of some of the Brassicas (see p. 124), isolation from such species may be necessary.

Breeding techniques with cross-pollinated crops show considerable variety. Usually the first steps toward improvement are those of *mass selection* of existing stocks. Any stock consists of numerous cross-pollinating forms, and usually heterozygosity exists in all plants of the stock. A stock which has been in cultivation for a long time will usually show considerable genetic variation. By repeated mass selection and trial, yields from such stocks can often be increased considerably and greater uniformity of type of plant achieved. Methods for further improvement depend to some extent on the type of crop and also upon the preferences of the particular breeding centre.

It is especially important for the work of the breeder and the seed-grower to go hand in hand in the case of cross-pollinated crops. The seed-grower should grow his crops in isolation to prevent deterioration due to free crossing with neighbouring crops. He cannot, however, prevent deterioration due to segregation of undesirable characters which must occur in cross-pollinated plants. It is therefore necessary for the plant-breeder to supply annually new stocks of seed of a particular variety (from which further seed is grown) in order to maintain a high standard for that particular variety.

In order to demonstrate some of the systems used in improving cross-pollinated crops, some of the methods for a few selected crops are discussed below:

Rye. In many Continental countries rye occupies a much more important position than it does in Britain, and it is in these countries, such as Sweden, Denmark and Germany, that most attention has been given to improving the crop.

The methods adopted in Sweden, at Svalöf, will serve to show the general procedure with this crop. In 1901, when work on this crop commenced, existing unimproved 'land varieties' were obtained and grown in yield trials. *Mass selection* was then commenced with the more promising. By this means superior varieties were obtained and put on the market. From one such variety known as *Steel* (introduced in 1921), single plants were selected. Each single plant would bear seed produced by cross-pollination. The progeny of each single plant selection were then grown in isolation from other rye crops and from one another. Thus stocks were built up each descended from a single original seed-parent and produced as a result of a mild degree of inbreeding between plants descended from that plant. After several years of mass selection of one of these stocks the variety *King II* was eventually introduced in 1939. It is a variety with a broad, dense ear and short, stiff straw which stands well on more fertile soils. On such soils it is widely grown in Sweden.

Further improved varieties, as yet without English names, have been obtained by crossing selected varieties followed by selection and testing of the progeny of the crosses.

Useful *tetraploid* varieties, produced with the aid of colchicine, have also been obtained. When tetraploid and diploid ryes are grown close together cross-pollination between the two results in some degree of sterility in each. This obviously must be avoided when a commercial crop is being grown. In yield trials, in which it is desired to compare the two types, it is necessary to grow them in isolation from one another and compare their yields against those of standard wheat varieties grown alongside each. In this way an indirect comparison is obtained between the yields of the two types of rye.

Root Crops. Somewhat similar methods of breeding may be adopted for all the cross-pollinated root crops, such as sugar-beet, mangels, fodder-beet, fodder sugar-beet, swedes, turnips, carrots. Crops such as cabbages and kales, although not grown for their 'roots' and therefore not strictly 'root' crops, might be included in the same general group.

Any variety in these crops consists of a population of large numbers of cross-pollinating forms which differ in some degree in external appearance, in their physiology and in important economic features, such as yield of roots per acre, yield of dry matter per acre (or of refined sugar in the case of sugar-beet), resistance to bolting and resistance to disease.

It should be mentioned here that there are often considerable differences between stocks of a particular named variety offered for sale by different seed firms. For example, in trials of mangels a stock of *Golden Tankard* supplied by firm 'A' may be near the top of the list for yield and/or dry matter content whilst the same named variety supplied by firm 'B' may be near the bottom. Even when two stocks have been derived from the same original stock, cross-pollination in the seed crop and different degrees of roguing may lead to very marked differences when stocks are reproduced for many generations.

In any variety repeated mass selection is necessary in order to maintain a satisfactory level of uniformity and productivity. By more rigorous mass selection the variety may often be improved considerably and sufficiently to be regarded as a type distinctive from the parent.

By selecting plants possessing superior economic qualities, in their first year of growth, and growing them on together so that interpollination occurs, then growing the progeny in the same way for a number of generations, repeatedly selecting desirable parents in each generation to produce seed for the next generation, new varieties exhibiting superiority to the old one can be built up. The number of roots selected from the parent stock is usually small, but the proportion of roots selected in later generations will increase as the stock becomes more uniform.

In mangels, swedes and turnips breeding may be based largely on dry matter yield of the roots, in sugar-beet on yield of refined sugar, but all other features of economic value must be taken into consideration in deciding the merits of the new varieties. For example, in mangels characteristics such as freedom from bolting, resistance to disease, keeping quality, ease of lifting and absence of fanginess in the root must be considered.

Selection within existing varieties, although it may result in new varieties markedly superior to the parent, has its limitations. Improvement is only possible within the limits of the genetic material available within the parent variety.

Further improvement can often be obtained by crossing varieties which are not too closely related. The progeny from such crosses between two heterozygous varieties will show considerable variability and must be tested and selected for a number of generations in order to obtain a more or less uniform type which can be released for growing a commercial crop.

Some degree of *hybrid vigour* can often be obtained by crossing similar, but not too closely related, varieties. Such varieties must be capable of producing, on crossing, F.1 seed which will produce a reasonably uniform crop and can therefore be used for production of the commercial crop. Much preliminary trial may be necessary in order to discover varieties which combine well in this way.

Another method, which ensures plants of fairly uniform type, involves a mild degree of inbreeding: this is the so-called *family breeding*. Single plants are selected within a variety and when they have produced seed (by free cross-pollination with other plants of the crop) the seed is saved separately and seed of each selected plant is sown in isolation. Thus in each isolation group the plants have descended from a single seed parent. These plants are allowed to cross-pollinate; thus brother-and-sister mating occurs. After trial and selection, the best families are grown together to produce seed by intercrossing. The seed is then multiplied for sale. This method is frequently used with Brassica crops, and is also utilized by some breeders for other 'root' crops.

A method utilizing a greater degree of inbreeding has been practised with sugar-beet and may be useful with other cross-pollinated plants. With beet, plants with high sugar content are made to self-pollinate and inbreeding is followed for several generations in an attempt to 'fix' lines. Inferior lines are eliminated by destroying *all* the offspring of any plant which produces a single plant not reaching the required standards. Selected lines, which have been found by preliminary trial to combine well, are then grown in pairs and allowed to cross-pollinate. This restores any vigour which may have been lost during inbreeding. Varieties produced by this means tend to show less variability in sugar content and to give higher yields than varieties produced, by other methods, from less inbred and selected parents.

In breeding root crops the breeder may be faced with *special problems*. For example, in Britain the problem of reduction of loss through virus yellows in sugar-beet is a very real one. By early sowing, plants are usually well established before the aphids which carry the disease are active. Thus early sowing helps in reducing loss through this disease. Early sowing, on the other hand, may increase the amount of bolting in the crop. It is therefore important to obtain varieties which can be sown early without loss through bolting. It is possible within a sugar-beet variety to select types which are resistant to bolting. By exposing seedlings to long daily periods of illumination and low temperatures for appropriate lengths of time (a treatment which encourages bolting) and then planting out the seedlings in the field, and later selecting the plants which do not bolt, *'non-bolting' varieties* can be built up. In connection with this problem, it may be significant that in Hungary a variety of sugar-beet has been produced which can be sown in the autumn for production of the root crop in the following summer. This variety withstands frost and is well advanced by the spring. It is reported to give high yields of roots and sugar and to show little tendency to bolt. There is thus the possibility of sugar-beet becoming an autumn-sown crop and, as a result, escaping serious reduction in yield due to virus yellows.

Developments in the artificial production of polyploid forms of sugar-beet, by means of colchicine, have already been mentioned (see Chapter III). Useful triploid sugar-beet have been produced which have more regular root shape with a more shallow vertical groove, and which therefore can be lifted with less soil adhering. Greater resistance to bolting is also characteristic of some of these forms. The triploids are produced by crossing tetraploids and diploids.

Tetraploid seedlings, produced by colchicine treatment, are grown on in glasshouses tightly sealed against the entry of diploid pollen. The air entering the houses may be filtered through silk-glass as an additional precaution. Selected tetraploid families are built up and then grown with selected diploids for cross-pollination. The seed produced is a mixture of triploid, tetraploid and diploid, since some self-pollination of tetraploid and diploid plants cannot be prevented. The production of 100 per cent. triploid seed is a possibility through the development of male-sterile tetraploid varieties for crossing with the diploid. The seed produced on such tetraploid plants would then all be triploid.

As triploid plants are sterile, they cannot be used for further seed production; fresh seed must be produced by the breeder each year by crossing tetraploid and diploid.

Herbage Plants. Towards the end of the eighteenth century in England Pacey produced an improved type of perennial rye-grass by selecting indigenous plants for seed production. During the following century various other 'improved' types of grasses, particularly perennial rye-grasses, were placed on the market, but interest in the improvement of herbage plants is largely a development of the present century. In Britain interest was more closely focused upon the differences to be found within species of herbage plants by the work of Professor A. D. Gilchrist at the Cockle Park Agricultural Experiment Station in Northumberland in the early years of this century. Gilchrist demonstrated, among other things, the superiority in persistence of native (*indigenous*) wild white clover as compared with the 'Dutch' white clover which was commonly used in seeds mixtures at the time. This demonstration of the importance of *variety* within species of herbage plants gave the lead to the development of a new and important line in plant-breeding in Britain.

In 1919 the Welsh Plant-breeding Station at Aberystwyth was in-augurated with Sir George (then Professor) Stapledon as its first Director. Here work was started on the breeding of improved herbage plants which has resulted in the introduction of valuable varieties, known as the 'S' strains, examples of which are the S.23 perennial rye-grass, S.143 cocks-foot and S.100 white clover (see Chapters XI and XVI). More recently breeding of herbage plants has also been carried out for the Scottish Society for Research in Plant-breeding at Corstorphine, resulting in useful varieties such as 'Scotia' timothy and cocksfoot.

Breeding of herbage plants has also progressed in other countries—for example, at Svalöf in Sweden, where work was started in 1904, and in New Zealand and U.S.A.

Productivity of herbage and, in the perennial species, persistence, are the chief points of concern in breeding varieties of herbage plants. Other points of importance are earliness of growth, length of growing season, time of maximum productivity, habit of growth, i.e. whether hay type, pasture type or pasture-hay type, winter greenness, and resistance to diseases.

It was obvious at the time when work commenced at Aberystwyth that commercial stocks of herbage seeds usually produced plants of a type which was undesirable from the farmer's point of view. These seeds were produced from stocks which had been grown for generations for seed harvested in the first or second years of a ley. As a result, early-flowering, short-lived stemmy types producing a large amount of seed had become concentrated in these stocks; any more-leafy, late-maturing types which may have been present in the original stocks having been eliminated automatically because, as a result of their delayed ripening, seed was not mature when the rest of the crop was harvested. On the other hand, examination of good old pastures, such as those to be found in Kent, Leicestershire, Northamptonshire and elsewhere showed that, as a result of the natural selection resulting from grazing management of the pastures for generations, more-leafy, more-persistent and later-flowering types flourished.

71

Methods of Breeding

(*a*) *Grasses*. Most grasses are normally cross-pollinated, and show a high degree of self-sterility. It is, however, possible, in most species, to discover occasional plants which show some degree of self-fertility, and in some cases a high degree of self-fertility exists. Self-pollination usually leads to a loss of vigour, but at Svalöf some useful varieties have been obtained by self-pollinating single plants and allowing the descendants of each selfed plant to pollinate one another in subsequent generations. This method depends upon the discovery of useful plants which will respond to this degree of inbreeding without loss of vigour.

Intercrossing of two or more inbred lines is another possible method of breeding. This method depends upon any depression in vigour resulting from some generations of inbreeding, being neutralized, on inter-crossing, and fertility and vigour being maintained in subsequent generations.

A method used at the Welsh Plant-breeding Station is not dependent upon the discovery of self-fertile plants, but depends rather upon the discovery of numbers of single plants which will combine well to produce a reasonably uniform composite variety on intercrossing.

The first step is to discover suitable breeding material. Single plants are obtained from various sources at home and abroad. These plants are grown on and their growth characteristics studied. From a large number of plants those which appear most suitable for the purpose in view are selected and their breeding qualities tested by crossing them with each other. Thus if three plants 'A', 'B' and 'C', were selected, these plants would be artificially crossed in all possible ways, i.e. A × B, A × C and B × C. Actually, more than three original plants would usually be selected. If twelve original plants are selected the number of possible crosses would be sixty-six. This system of crossing each plant with every other member of the group is known as *diallel crossing*.

The plants are grown in pots in a greenhouse, and crossing is usually done by hand. Seed parents are emasculated and covered with glassine bags before and after pollination. The flowers of the pollen parents are similarly protected from other pollen until the pollen has been collected.

Seeds from the crosses are grown on, and the plants produced are studied. F.2 seed is produced by growing the progeny of each cross in isolation. Some of the original parent plants may be discarded on the basis of the performance of their F.1 offspring, but more are likely to be discarded after the F.2 segregating generation has been studied. In this generation undesirable types are likely to be produced. By these progeny tests of the original plant selections those plants which combine well with the various other members of the group are discovered. These plants are then used as the parents for the new composite variety.

The selected plants are next broken up into *clone* plantlets which are grown on in pots, perhaps about ten plantlets from each original plant. The clones are grown all together in a glasshouse which is kept tightly sealed against extraneous pollen during the flowering period. The plants of the various clones intercross freely and the seed produced can then be used for building up a composite variety. After building up a nucleus stock of seed in pollen-proof glasshouses, the stock is next increased in isolation among arable crops; or in orchards; or on the Station's seed multiplication farm, where a section is devoted to one variety only of a particular species, in order to prevent cross-pollination between varieties.

Varieties are submitted to critical trials, and those which are of sufficient merit are passed out into commerce.

The grass varieties produced in this manner consist of a number of cross-pollinating types produced from original plants which were fairly similar to one another. The population within a variety is phenotypically fairly uniform, but, as the original plants were heterozygous and cross-pollination is the rule, there will always be less uniformity between individual plants than is the case with self-pollinating and largely homozygous varieties of wheat, oats and barley.

When stocks are passed out from the plant-breeding station to be grown on farms for seed there is liable to be deterioration in time as a result of cross-pollination with other types which may be growing near the seed crop, or of accidental admixture of seeds of other types—from threshing machines, storage sacks or seed drills, for example. Genetic variations may also occur when the seed is reproduced for a number of successive seasons. After leaving the plant-breeder, the seed will have been grown for multiplication for two or three generations before it reaches the farmer in his seeds mixtures. Therefore, if the plant types produced in the farmer's leys from this seed are to represent the types originally released by the plant-breeder careful technical supervision at the various stages of seed multiplication is important. Such supervision is provided by the herbage seed certification schemes described later (Chapter VI).

As stocks deteriorate when grown for a number of generations it is necessary for the breeder to be able to provide fresh basic seed each year from which to build up new seed stocks. For this purpose the original breeding plants are retained. They can be multiplied by breaking up into clones, in which the same genes will be present, for inter-pollination and production of new basic seed. Thus the standard of quality and uniformity of each variety may be maintained over the years.

(*b*) *Clovers.* The clovers, another group of cross-pollinating species, differ from the grasses in that they are insect pollinated. In the clovers there is a greater degree of self-sterility than in the chief grass species and, although a few highly self-fertile plants have been obtained, clovers are generally dealt with for breeding purposes as purely cross-pollinating species.

One of the chief methods for the production of improved varieties of clovers is similar to that described above for grasses. Large numbers of single-plant selections, from various sources, are made. These plants are grown as spaced single plants and their various features studied. From the collection a number of similar single plants is selected and their breeding potentialities determined by diallel crossing, as described above for grasses. In order to increase the amount of breeding material, clones may be developed from the original plants before these crossings are made. Emasculation is not necessary with clovers. Cross-pollination may be done by hand in glasshouses, or pairs of plants may be grown together enclosed within insect-proof cages into which one or two bees are inserted to carry out pollination. The bees are first washed by being shaken in a test-tube with a little distilled water. This removes pollen grains adhering to their bodies, or renders the grains harmless by causing them to swell up and burst. When dry, the bees are ready for use. In the case of most red clover plants, the corolla tube is too long and narrow to permit pollination by the hive bee, and pollination is normally performed by humble-bees (chiefly *Bombus agrorum* and *B. hortorum*).

The F.1 and F.2 generations of the various crosses are studied and a decision made as to which of the original plants are suitable for building up the new composite variety. The selected original plants are grown on, as clones, in glasshouses and inter-pollinated by washed bees to provide a nucleus stock of seed. The nucleus seed stock is further multiplied by growing on for further generations with precautions for isolation of the seed crops similar to those described for the grasses. Certified seed, of varieties proved by field trials to be valuable, is finally produced on farms in a similar manner (see Chapter VI).

BREEDING VEGETATIVELY-REPRODUCED CROPS

The possibility of building up clones (see Chapter III) from a single valuable plant simplifies the problem of maintaining the standard of a new variety of a vegetatively-reproduced crop. Having obtained a good plant from seed, the number of plants is multiplied vegetatively and all the plants so produced are genetically alike.

Potatoes. The cultivated potato appears to have originated in hilly districts of Chili and Peru, where it was grown thousands of years before Columbus discovered America. From these areas its cultivation spread to North America and Europe. Potatoes were first introduced into Europe toward the end of the sixteenth century. About this time two introductions were recorded, one a round white-skinned variety and the other a long reddish-purple-skinned type.

Potatoes are normally heterozygous, and when grown from true seed resulting from either self-pollination or cross-pollination, they produce a variety of offspring. It is probable that most of the varieties in cultivation in Europe up to about 1850 had descended from the two original introductions mentioned above. Records show that farmers realized that by sowing the true seed new varieties could be obtained, and it is probable that many stocks were somewhat mixed as a result of tubers from several seedlings being bulked together.

Interest in the production of improved varieties was stimulated by the potato famine of 1845-7. The famine was caused by a severe attack of blight (*Phytophthora infestans*) which spread across Europe, destroying at least half of the potato crop in 1845. The disease attacked again in Ireland in 1846, when about nine-tenths of the crop was destroyed and many deaths from starvation resulted among the population, which had become largely dependent upon the potato crop. Attention thus became focused upon the need for varieties showing resistance to blight. In an endeavour to produce blight-resistant varieties, new varieties were introduced into Britain from the American continent, from Australia and from India. Seedlings were raised from the increased range of varieties then available, and during the latter part of the nineteenth century some varieties were introduced which showed more resistance to blight than the older ones. The problem of breeding for greater resistance to blight is, however, still occupying the attention of plant-breeders.

At the beginning of the present century wart disease (*Synchytrium endobioticum*) became an additional problem for the plant-breeder. Fortunately, the spread of wart disease was successfully arrested after it was discovered that some varieties were immune to the disease, and most modern varieties have been bred for immunity to this trouble.

The realization, early in this century, that deterioration of potato stocks was due to virus diseases (see Chapter XXVIII) added a further problem for plant-breeders and one which is now only in the process of solution.

Resistance or immunity to diseases is an important aim, but these characteristics must be considered alongside commercial characteristics such as yield, shape and colour of tubers, thickness and texture of skin, cooking and keeping qualities and time of maturity. Interest is also being shown, in modern times, in the vitamin C content of varieties.

Breeding Methods. Varieties which produce normal flowers are usually self-fertile, but they are cross-pollinated freely. Choice of varieties for breeding work is occasionally restricted by the floral characteristics of the variety. Some varieties fail to produce flowers or produce them only rarely; this difficulty may often be overcome by grafting them on tomato plants. Male sterility and early dropping of the flowers provide further limitations (see p. 63).

As potatoes are normally reproduced vegetatively from tubers, and true seed is used only once, at the beginning of the production of a new variety, there is no need for the variety to be homozygous, indeed, varieties are normally heterozygous and do not breed true from seed on self-pollination. So long as tubers are used for reproduction, the variety (or clone) will remain constant in its characteristics unless somatic mutations arise, and these are of rare occurrence.

Because of the heterozygosity of varieties, seed produced by self-pollination will give rise to a diversity of seedlings. Thus new varieties may be obtained by sowing seed either from self-pollinated fruits or from fruits resulting from natural or artificial cross-pollination. Many notable varieties introduced in the latter half of the nineteenth century and the beginning of the present century were of unknown pollen parentage, and owed their origin to seeds produced either by self-pollination or by natural crossing between varieties growing close together. Frequently the raisers of new varieties collected any potato fruits available, and no record even of the female parent was kept.

In more recent times selection of two parent plants for artificial crossing has been more usual, the parents being selected on the basis of desirable qualities which it is hoped to combine in the new variety. The fact that the parents are heterozygous results in very varied material in the F.1, so that in selecting parents for characters desired in the offspring it is only possible to select for a few major characters, e.g. immunity to wart disease. Selection with the object of combining all the good characters of the two parents in one variety is unlikely to be successful unless a very large number of seedlings is raised.

For artificial cross-pollination the flowers of the seed-parent are emasculated before the flower buds open. The flowers are protected in glassine bags before and after pollination (some breeders regard this precaution as unnecessary in the case of potatoes). The pollen from the flowers to be used as male parents can be tapped out of the terminal pores of the anthers on to the thumbnail and then transferred to the stigmas of the female parent. More than one pollination, on successive days, may be necessary to ensure that the period at which the stigmas are receptive has been covered. About 100 to 200 seeds will be obtained from each successful pollination.

Having obtained true seed, it is of paramount importance that the seedlings raised from it should be grown under conditions where virus infection cannot take place. Once a stock is infected, it is of little further value. Thus precautions are particularly important in the first year, when a valuable seedling might be infected, and in the early years of multiplication of the tubers, when the stock of tubers is small and consequently the whole stock might become infected. Protection from aphids, which carry some virus diseases, may be obtained in the first year by growing the seedlings in pots in aphid-proof glasshouses. In later years when tubers are planted out in the open the crop may be planted at a distance from other potato crops, which may be a source of infection, and in the middle of a cereal crop, which provides further protection against aphids. Greatest safety from infection is ensured if the stocks are raised in districts where aphids are not abundant and which are noted for the production of virus-free seed potatoes (see Chapter VI).

The seedlings raised from the true seed will be very variable in type, and tubers from each seedling are harvested and kept in separate lots. Some seedlings may be discarded in the first year, but as tubers of adult form are not obtained until the third crop many seedlings must be propagated until the third crop before a preliminary appraisal is made. The first crop from a seedling will consist of a few small tubers varying in size, the largest being about the size of a broad bean. These tubers are planted out to produce the crop in the following year and so on. Large numbers of seedlings are usually raised, most of them being ultimately rejected for various reasons. Two or three thousand may be examined in order to discover a single useful variety.

Stocks from promising seedlings are submitted to yield trials, to laboratory tests for immunity to wart disease, resistance to blight and virus diseases, and to cooking tests. Data are also collected on time of maturity, type of top, shape of tuber, colour of tuber, depth of eyes, etc.

In modern potato-breeding use is being made of wild potato species from Central and South America, such as *Solanum demissum* and *S. lanciforme*, which resist blight, *S. andigenum*, which provides immunity to root eelworm, and *S. rybinii* and others, which promise to be of value in breeding for immunity to virus diseases.

The wild species is crossed with a cultivated variety of good commercial quality. Such a cross would be unlikely to produce seedlings of high quality in the F.1, owing to the large number of genes inherited from the wild parent. By back-crossing the hybrid to the good commercial variety (or by crossing it with another such variety) and repeating this process for a number of generations, it should be possible to obtain varieties of commercial value which also show resistance or immunity to specific diseases or pests. Such repeated back-crossing and the subsequent testing of new seedlings involves a breeding programme covering many years and the examination and testing of a considerable amount of material.

Somatic or Bud Mutations. Emphasis has been laid on the uniformity of characters in plants reproduced vegetatively. Occasionally, however, in potatoes, as in many other plant species, somatic or bud mutations occur. These may result in the formation of shoots, and sometimes of tubers, showing new characteristics. Mutation may result in changes in leaf shape, flower colour and other characters of no great economic importance. Occasionally mutations of some value may occur. Mutations may affect physiological characters as well as morphological ones—for example, increased or decreased resistance to specific diseases may occur in bud mutants. Whilst the search for useful somatic mutations, though laborious, might be of value, it cannot compete with hybridization as a certain means of crop improvement.

The best-known example of somatic mutation in potatoes is the variety Red King Edward, which has an all-red-skinned tuber and is said to have arisen by this means from the parti-coloured King Edward.

Chapter VI

VARIETY TRIALS AND QUALITY SEED PRODUCTION

WHEN the plant-breeder has completed his work of producing a new variety which appears to give promise of usefulness in commerce, it is then important to try it out over as wide a range of soil and climatic conditions as possible. Its performance is compared with that of existing commercial varieties at as large a number of centres as possible. Such trials are continued for at least three seasons, in order to reduce differences which may result from variations in seasonal climatic conditions. In this way the relative merits of varieties may be assessed, and new varieties may then be recommended for introduction into commerce.

It is then necessary to ensure that stocks of seed of the best varieties should be made available to the farmer and that these stocks should represent, as far as possible, the standard of the variety as released by the plant-breeder.

Extensive work along these lines is carried out by the National Institute of Agricultural Botany, Cambridge, and similar work, appropriate to their own particular interests, by the Scottish Society for Research in Plant-breeding and the Ministry of Agriculture for Northern Ireland.

The National Institute of Agricultural Botany

The organization in England responsible for testing both new and old varieties of agricultural crops is the National Institute of Agricultural Botany, briefly known as the N.I.A.B., which was founded in 1919 and has its headquarters at Huntingdon Road, Cambridge.

The work of the Institute is not confined, however, to the testing of crop varieties. It states its aims broadly as being 'To improve the yield and quality of farm crops by encouraging the use of better seeds'. The work in attempting to achieve this aim is divided into five main sections:

(1) *The Trials Branch* which deals with crops other than potatoes, and is concerned with trials of new and old varieties and the introduction of new varieties received from plant-breeding institutes and other sources.

(2) *The Potato Branch* performs similar work in connection with potatoes. Also, stocks of seed potatoes are tested for presence of virus, and virus-tested stocks are maintained and multiplied in seed-potato-growing areas in Northern Ireland and Scotland.

(3) *The Seed Production Branch* co-ordinates the production of seeds and encourages the production of high-quality seed.

(4) *The Multiplication Branch* multiplies seed for trials and basic seed from official plant breeding institutes.

(5) *The Official Seed Testing Station*, which carries out tests of seed

samples for germination and purity, on behalf of sellers of seed or individual users of seed.

Thus, between the plant-breeder and the farmer an organization exists to help to ensure that high-quality seed of the most meritorious varieties is available.

In connection with the work of the Institute a large number of plots is maintained at headquarters for identification and testing of varieties of crops. At the Institute's seed-multiplication farm, seed is raised for use in trials; old varieties of cereals which have been on the market for a number of years are reselected and fresh stocks of pure seed built up, and seed of useful new varieties received from breeders is multiplied from a few pounds to several tons for distribution chiefly to the seed trade.

Regional Trials. The variety trials of the N.I.A.B. are carried out mainly at Cambridge and at twelve regional centres, but a large number of secondary trials are performed, in co-operation with the National Agricultural Advisory Service, on farms all over the country. The regional trials are scattered as widely as possible over the country, so as to include a wide range of soil, climatic and management conditions, and they are usually located at institutions for agricultural education, universities, colleges and farm institutes. At each centre the trials are in the charge of a trained Trials Officer.

During the trials new varieties are grown alongside established varieties of comparable type, for comparison. Each variety is usually tested in eight separate plots suitably placed to enable any errors due to possible differences in soil fertility, etc., to be assessed. The relative yields of the varieties are obtained and observations made on the field characteristics of the crops and on the occurrence of diseases. The varieties under trial are also examined by specialists for characteristics of commercial importance, such as milling and baking qualities in wheat, malting quality in barley and cooking quality in potatoes. Quality testing is carried out in conjunction with appropriate consumer organizations, such as the Millers' Cereal Research Station in the case of wheat varieties.

After reasonably exhaustive trials, many new varieties show little or no material advantage over varieties already in cultivation, and are therefore never recommended for general cultivation. Such varieties may, however, be of some value for further breeding work.

Occasionally a new variety is found in the trials to be superior to some comparable commercial variety. It is then recommended that seed be multiplied, if necessary, and made available for sale to farmers.

Recommended Varieties. As a result of trials extending over a period of not less than three years for each variety, the N.I.A.B. is able to suggest that certain varieties are the most useful of their type and to issue lists of 'Recommended Varieties' which are available to farmers, seed merchants and others on application. As new varieties show their value in the trials, these may be introduced into the lists of recommended varieties and older varieties, which they may supersede, are withdrawn.

THE PRODUCTION OF HIGH-QUALITY SEEDS

After the plant-breeder has produced a new variety and the field trials have shown it to be worthy of introduction to commercial agriculture, it is important that seed of the type approved in the trials should become available to the farmer. Stocks may be bulked up by the breeder himself or nucleus stocks may be passed on to some agent, such as the N.I.A.B., for further seed production.

Before the seed reaches the farmer, for sowing for his crops, it will have passed through several years of multiplication since leaving the plant-breeder. Considerable care is necessary at all stages of seed multiplication, and most especially with cross-pollinated crops, if the farmer is to receive seed of high quality. Quality seed production may be regarded as a continuation of the work of the plant-breeder, and maintenance of a high standard necessitates technical supervision and organization.

After seed has left the plant-breeder it may deteriorate in value for a number of reasons. Seed from a variety of other sources may become mixed with the stock. Volunteer plants of other varieties of the same species, or of similar species, may appear in the seed crop from previous crops on the same field. Farmyard manure or straw left lying around from potato clamps or stacks may result in the introduction of seed of different cereal varieties into the seed crop. Seeds of other varieties may become mixed with the stock seed during drilling or during threshing and cleaning if machines are not cleaned out thoroughly before use. The growing of different varieties on headlands, or to finish off the field when the supply of stock seed is insufficient, may result in the mixing of varieties at harvest-time. Sacks in which seed is bagged after threshing may also introduce odd seeds of other types, if they have previously been used for seed.

Another cause of deterioration may be genetic variation due to cross-pollination with other varieties or to the occurrence of mutant types within the seed crop. In the case of normally self-pollinated crops, such as wheat, oats and barley, cross-pollination does not usually occur to any great extent, but some varieties, such as Little Joss wheat, are rather more liable to cross-pollinate with other varieties to a small extent.

Species which are normally cross-pollinated, such as rye, sugar-beet, mangels, Brassicas, grasses and clovers, must be grown for seed in isolation in order to prevent cross-pollination with other forms. As varieties of the cross-pollinated plants consist of a number of cross-pollinating types, in which there is a high degree of heterozygosity, variation in the standard of the seed must occur each time the stock is further propagated for seed purposes. It is therefore important for the breeder of such varieties to maintain nucleus stocks and to make available fresh *basic seed* each year for further propagation.

In order to maintain the standard of self-pollinated varieties new nucleus stocks may be produced at intervals by *re-selection*. This may be done by selecting single plants to produce a culture from which a new nucleus stock may be propagated. A number of single-plant selections is usually made, because even within a self-pollinated variety which appears to be uniform in character some slight genetic variations will exist between one plant and another. Absolute homozygosity of all plants for all characteristics is unlikely, and, although two plants, on inspection, may appear exactly alike, trials and tests may demonstrate differences in the pure lines built up from them. For example, small differences in nitrogen content of the grain of two plants of a bread wheat may result in differences of baking quality of the grain in the two pure lines built up from them. The stocks from a number of single plant selections will be submitted to trials and tests in order to discover which lines maintain the standard set by the breeder for the particular variety. When the desirable line has been obtained new nucleus stocks are built up and released for multiplication. In re-selected lines the standard for the variety must, at least, be maintained, but it is possible that lines may be obtained which show improvements in some respects over the old stock and, providing there is no reduction of standard in other respects, this is all to the good.

A method of maintaining pure stocks of cereals, adopted at the N.I.A.B., is the *ear-row* method. In this method a bundle of ears is selected at random from a large multiplication crop of a variety. The ears are then examined and 200 which are typical of the variety are selected. The grain from the individual ears is then sown in separate rows at least 50 yards from other cereals of the same species, and on land which has not been used for cereals for at least two years. The rows are examined throughout the growing season, and any rows showing undesirable characteristics are immediately destroyed. Each remaining row is harvested separately and threshed by hand and the grain characteristics examined. Further rows may be eliminated after this examination. The remaining grain is then bulked and multiplied for four seasons under careful supervision to ensure that the stock remains pure. At the end of this period the produce of some 70 to 80 acres will be available for sale for further seed production. This method has the advantage of being almost certain to maintain the standard of the variety, owing to the method of selecting the original ears, whereas with single plant selection it is possible accidentally to alter the agricultural characters of the variety. Seed produced in this way by the N.I.A.B. is also known as *basic seed*.

Organized Seed Production. A complete scheme for the further production of pure, healthy seed which could be 'certified' as being, as far as is humanly possible, of the standard set by the breeder; would involve supervision by some technical authority at all stages of production. It would involve (*a*) Approval of the stock of seed to be sown for seed production. (*b*) Inspection of the seed crop, in the field, for presence of other varieties, genetic variations, proximity to other crops which might cross-pollinate the seed crop in the case of cross-pollinated crops, presence of diseases and pests which could be carried by the seed, and presence of weeds whose seeds, or other reproductive parts, could not readily be separated from the seed crop when it is cleaned. (*c*) Supervision of threshing, cleaning and bagging to ensure that impurities could not gain access to the seed during these operations. (*d*) Supervision of sealing of the bags of seed with an official seal. (*e*) Testing of official samples for purity, germination and readily discovered seed-borne diseases. (*f*) Growing of check plots, from the 'certified' seed, in the following year, as a check on the efficiency of the administration of the scheme and for reference in the event of complaints from farmers who have used the seed.

In some countries—for example, Denmark and Sweden—certification schemes along these lines are in existence for certain types of agricultural seeds. In Britain there is a scheme of this type for herbage seeds, providing supervision at all stages, from choice of seed for sowing up to the official sealing of bags of threshed seed. Similar schemes are in operation for certain varieties of cereals. Complete supervision of all seed production along these lines would involve an organization employing a large number of inspectors and field and clerical staff and in the absence of such an organization modified schemes, involving approval of the seed sown and the inspection of the seed crop in the field, may be substituted.

The Cereal Field Approval Scheme. In order to assist in the maintenance of stocks of wheat, oats and barley seeds at a high standard of purity and health, the Seed Production Committee of the N.I.A.B. supervises a scheme for the inspection of growing crops of these cereals intended for seed. The varieties which may be entered in this scheme are those appearing in the lists of *Recommended Varieties* published by the N.I.A.B., and other varieties of special value which has been demonstrated by trials recognized by that body. This scheme does not involve technical supervision of production of the seed at all stages, and therefore the seed cannot logically be 'certified' as of undoubted authenticity. The scheme is purely one of *field inspection* of the growing crop which seeks to indicate those crops suitable for use for seed and those which should be rejected for seed purposes. The widespread use of such a scheme with the co-operation of seed merchants and seed-growers can do much to maintain a high standard of seed quality.

In order to qualify for inspection it is first important that the stock of seed from which the crop is grown should be of undoubted quality. Inspection is therefore restricted mainly to crops grown from seed, specially produced for the purpose of further multiplication and known as *multiplication seed. Field approved seed* produced under the scheme is for general use and not for further multiplication under the scheme.

Field inspection of seed crops is performed by qualified personnel who provide certain information on the basis of which the crop is approved or rejected by the Seed Production Committee. The inspectors satisfy themselves, so far as possible, that the crop is the stated variety. The presence and extent of impurities in the crop are determined. The impurities of greatest importance are: (*a*) weeds not readily removed during threshing and cleaning, (*b*) seed-borne diseases, (*c*) cereal impurities, and (*d*) genetic variations.

A. *Weeds.* The weed species which may cause rejection of the crop, if present in more than specified quantities, are: wild onion (*Allium vineale*), wild oats (*Avena fatua* and *A. ludoviciana*), wild radish, shepherd's needle, wild tares or vetches and cleavers.

B. *Seed-borne Diseases.* The presence of more than specified numbers per acre of ears showing the following diseases may lead to rejection: loose smut and bunt in wheat, loose and covered smuts in barley and smuts in oats.

C. *Cereal Impurities.* Identification of cereal impurities is restricted to those fairly readily observed. It is almost impossible to identify some varieties of cereals which may be present as impurities in a seed crop of a similar variety. Further, the grain colour of wheat, and to some extent of oats, is not readily seen in the standing crop. Field inspection, therefore, is limited in this respect. The following fairly readily distinguishable impurities, if present in more than specified amounts, may lead to rejection of the crop: any mixture of wheat, barley, oats and rye; very tall varieties in short varieties; black or grey oats in white varieties, or *vice versa*; tartarian panicles in open-panicled oats, or *vice versa*; bearded ears in beardless wheat, or *vice versa*; different chaff colour in wheat or clearly different ear shape; broad-eared barley in narrow-eared types, or *vice versa*; distinguishable rogues, but of similar varieties.

D. *Genetic Variations.* Common genetic variations, which cannot be prevented, are listed, some to be tolerated, others to be included among cereal impurities.

In order to achieve the required standards it may be necessary to *rogue* the crop before the date of the inspection. Careful growers may go through a crop methodically twice before inspection.

Dried Pea Seed Approval Scheme: Another scheme relating to a self-pollinated crop is the Dried Pea Seed Approval Scheme, which involves approval of the stock of seed used for producing the crop and field inspection and approval of the growing crop.

CERTIFICATION OF HERBAGE SEEDS

The first scheme for inspection and certification of herbage seed crops in the British Isles was introduced by the Montgomeryshire Late-flowering Red Clover Seed Growers' Association, which was formed in 1923. The success of this scheme stimulated interest in herbage seed 'certification', and schemes for other local varieties, such as Vale of Clwyd, Cotswold and Cornish Marl red clovers, were soon organized.

In 1930 a scheme for the 'certification' of wild white clover seed was introduced by the Ministry of Agriculture with the object of ensuring that true stocks of the persistent indigenous wild white clover should be available for further reproduction and for sowing in long ley seeds mixtures on farms.

In 1940 the Welsh Plant-breeding Station inaugurated a scheme for the inspection of crops and certification of seeds of the 'S' varieties of herbage plants bred at the station.

A national scheme for comprehensive certification of herbage seeds was introduced in 1956. Under this scheme bred varieties and certain local varieties of grasses, clovers and sainfoin are certified by an independent Certifying Authority which is representative of all interested bodies. Under the scheme certified seeds are provided with an official certification trade mark.

The scheme involves the inspection of the field to be used for seed production before the crop is sown. The seed used for multiplication must be approved and the crop produced from it is inspected in the field. The field inspection of the crop is concerned with the purity and isolation of the crop from any serious source of pollen contamination.

Rules are laid down with regard to the threshing, processing and labelling of the seeds. The processed seeds must achieve specified standards of total purity, freedom from weed seeds and from other crop seeds. There are also regulations with regard to particular weed seed impurities and to certain seed-borne diseases and also in connection with clover stem eelworm *Ditylenchus dipsaci* (*Anguillulina dipsaci*) (in relation to red clover seeds).

In growing crops of herbage seeds for certification, freedom of the crop from other strains which would cross with the strain being grown for seed is important, as is freedom from other species which might cross-pollinate with the crop (such as Italian rye-grass in perennial rye-grass). The crop must also be isolated from other varieties in neighbouring fields which may flower at the same time as the crop and bring about cross-pollination. The danger of contamination may be eliminated by hard grazing and repeated mowing of neighbouring fields so as to ensure that no flower heads appear. Cutting down herbage in neighbouring hedge-sides, roadways, headlands, etc., to prevent flowering, may also be necessary.

Seed Potato Certification. Certification schemes for seed potatoes were started in 1919 and were at first concerned only with varietal purity. Farmers, at that time, were finding difficulty in obtaining pure stocks of varieties immune to wart disease. Mixture of susceptible types with immune varieties has serious consequences in perpetuating the disease when stocks are grown on infected land. It was therefore of prime importance that pure stocks should be available. Later, in 1931, virus disease was also included as a factor in the certification of potato seed crops. The Agricultural Departments of Great Britain and Eire now adopt a uniform system of classification for certified seed stocks, in which there are three grades. 'SS' or Stock Seed is the highest grade, and is designed to be used for further seed production. 'A' is first quality commercial seed, which should be used for producing 'H' seed or for the ware crop. 'H' seed is intended exclusively for the production of ware crops; it is healthy seed of a slightly lower standard than 'A'.

On the certificate, the country of origin is indicated, by the addition, after the letter denoting the grade, of '(E)' for England, '(Scot)' for Scotland, '(W)' for Wales, '(Nor Ir)' for Northern Ireland, '(Eire)' for Eire and '(I.O.M.)' for Isle of Man. In addition, varieties which are not immune to wart disease are indicated by the addition of the letters 'NI'. Thus, a stock of Majestic (a variety which is immune to wart disease), grown in Scotland and of the highest grade, would be described on the certificate as 'SS.(Scot)'. An 'A' stock of King Edward (which is susceptible to wart disease) grown in England would be certified 'A.(E).NI'.

The standards adopted for the three grades by the various Agricultural Departments are in close agreement. The standards of health and varietal purity, at the time of inspection, laid down for crops grown in England and Wales, are as follows:

	Tolerance, not more than
'SS' Grade:	
Rogues, including undesirable variations, wildings and bolters	0·05 per cent.
Leaf roll or severe mosaic	4 plants per acre
Mild mosaic	0·25 per cent.
Blackleg	2·0 per cent.
'A' Grade:	
Rogues, including undesirable variations . .	0·5 per cent.
Wildings and bolters	1·0 per cent.
Severe virus diseases	0·5 per cent.
Mild mosaic visible under field inspection conditions	2·0 per cent.
'H' Grade:	
Rogues, including undesirable variations . .	0·5 per cent.
Wildings and bolters	5·0 per cent.
Severe virus diseases	2·0 per cent.
Mild mosaic visible under field inspection conditions	10·0 per cent.

'SS' and 'A' seed may be grown only in specified areas where virus diseases do not normally spread rapidly (see below) and on land which has been shown by laboratory examination to be free from potato root eelworm (*Heterodera rostochiensis*). All grades must be grown on land which has not grown a potato crop during the three previous years, and the type of seed to be used and the isolation distance from other potato crops are laid down for each grade. Crops may be rejected if they are rendered unsuitable for seed by reason of any disease or pest other than those mentioned above.

An explanation of the significance of leaf roll, severe mosaic and mild mosaic will be found in Chapter XXVIII, and of blackleg in Chapter XXVII. *Bolters* are tall plants with coarse upright branched stems; they usually flower freely and produce coarse tubers. *Wildings* are small bushy plants, often with a large number of stems; the stems are very thin, the leaf area is reduced, in comparison with normal plants, and usually there is a large, rounded, terminal leaflet and one or two pairs of small lateral leaflets. Underground, numerous very thin rhizomes are formed terminating in small tubers varying from the size of a pea to seed potato size, the former being more abundant.

Seed potato crops for certification are most easily grown in certain areas in Scotland, North and West England, Ireland and Wales where aphids, which carry certain virus diseases, are not prevalent. Such areas are usually exposed, often at high altitudes, and aphid movement is restricted by the frequent high wind velocity, low temperatures and heavy rainfall. For the higher certification grades it is essential to grow seed crops in such districts.

Certification is no absolute guarantee of freedom from virus diseases, as some forms of virus disease are impossible to detect by visual inspection of the crop, and also late infection with virus may produce little visible result until the following crop. Many stocks of potato varieties are infected with the mild form of virus known as virus X (see Chapter XXVIII). Scientists can build up nucleus stocks from single tubers which have been tested and found to be free from this virus. Such stocks are produced at the N.I.A.B., and nucleus stocks are then multiplied in virus-free areas to serve as a source of healthy seed for further propagation. (See also p. 591.)

A high standard of seed production has been achieved by many seed potato growers who *rogue* their crops for removal of 'off' types and those showing virus diseases. Professional roguers, who have received training in the recognition of varieties and virus disease symptoms, are often employed by growers. High varietal purity is thus obtained, but heavy roguing of virus-diseased plants may produce an apparently uniform healthy crop the seed from which may be disappointing in the following season, owing to virus already having spread from the rogued plants before they were removed, but infection having been sufficiently late to produce no visible symptoms in the inspected crop. Crops which have undergone an undue amount of roguing may be rejected for the highest grade of certificate.

Roguing involves digging (not pulling) the undesirable plants and removal of all tubers from the soil, so that tubers of the wrong varietal type or tubers carrying virus, are not harvested with the crop.

GROWING SEED OF 'ROOT' CROPS AND OTHER CROSS-POLLINATED CROPS

In the production of high-quality seed of all cross-pollinated crops it is important that the seed crop should be grown on fields where there is little danger of any material amount of cross-pollination with other types. *Isolation* distances of at least 1,000 yards are commonly recommended for Brassicas, but experiments have suggested that this distance could probably be reduced, in some cases, without undue risk of contamination. Further, in attempting to maintain the quality of seed, seed crops should be drastically *rogued*; plants which are visibly of the wrong type being removed before they flower. Finally, great care is necessary to prevent the deterioration of the seed stocks by preventing seed of other varieties from becoming mixed with them. All machinery through which the seeds pass at various times should be scrupulously cleaned, in order to eliminate other seeds, as should all containers used for the seed.

The 'root' crops are biennials and do not normally flower and seed until their second year. The usual practice for seed crops is to rear young plants on a small area of land in the first year. These are planted out in spaced rows in the autumn, or in the spring of the following year, for seed production in their second summer.

In the case of sugar-beet and mangel seed crops a complication arises owing to the incidence of the disease virus yellows, which is regularly to be found in crops of sugar-beet and mangels grown for their 'roots'. If young plants, or stecklings, as they are called, are grown for seed production in close proximity to infected root crops, they are liable to become infected with the virus by aphids which have fed on the infected crop (see Chapter XXVIII). Seed yield is considerably reduced in crops produced from infected stecklings. The virus does not infect the seed, however.

In order to overcome this difficulty, many stecklings are grown in areas, in the north and west of England and in Scotland and Wales, which are recognized to be suitable for the production of virus-free seed potatoes. The stecklings are lifted and clamped over winter and taken to the seed-growing areas of the eastern counties of England for planting out in the spring. In this way virus-free stecklings are planted out. In order to maintain their health they should, if possible, be planted at least 400 yards from root crops, or clamps, of mangels and beets which may act as a source of infection by virus yellows.

Zoning Schemes. In areas where much seed of cross-pollinated crops is grown, desirable isolation distances between crops which might cross-pollinate may be difficult to obtain. Isolation may be achieved, however, by devoting particular areas to the production of seed of only a single member of a cross-pollinating group. In such areas any seed crop which would cross with the selected type would be excluded.

On this basis zoning schemes have been devised for certain seed crops. An example of such an arrangement is the zoning scheme for sugar-beet, mangel and garden beet seed crops devised during the war. This scheme divided the area where seed of these crops is grown into zones. The area includes the counties of Norfolk, Suffolk, Cambridge, Essex, Lincoln, Nottingham, Leicester, Northampton, Bedford, Rutland, the Soke of

Peterborough and the Isle of Ely. In some areas sugar-beet could not be grown for seed; in other zones mangels were excluded as seed crops. In some small areas, set aside for production of garden beet seed, both sugar-beet and mangel were excluded. When the Order used to enforce the application of this scheme was revoked after the war the scheme was continued on a voluntary basis. In some of the mangel seed areas there are local arrangements for growing varieties of a particular colour in particular areas in order to prevent crossing between varieties of different colour. In Essex, where a large amount of Brassica seeds of various types is produced, there is a local zoning scheme for the isolation of the different types of Brassicas which would cross-pollinate freely.

Voluntary zoning schemes of this type, involving agreement among seed-growers, help to prevent crossing between different varieties or species grown for seed. Unfortunately, they cannot prevent pollination of seed crops by pollen from plants of other varieties which may be allowed to flower, in crops not being grown for seed, in neighbouring fields or gardens.

Chapter VII

SEED-TESTING

PLANT-BREEDING, crop-testing and seed crop inspection and certification each contribute much to crop improvement, but the crop ultimately produced by the farmer depends in addition upon certain characteristics of the seed he actually sows, in particular upon its germination capacity and purity.

In many countries legislation exists which requires the testing of seeds before they are offered for sale, so that the farmer is protected in some degree against the purchase of seed of inferior quality.

Before the introduction of such legislation the quality of seeds on the market was often very low. Seeds of poor germination and seed containing excessively large amounts of impurities, often consisting of serious weed seeds, were sold. Seeds deliberately adulterated with other similar seeds also came on to the market—for example, turnip seeds which had been adulterated with seeds of the weed charlock (often the weed seeds had been killed by heat so that they would not germinate, and would therefore pass undetected in the field).

Legislation has resulted in the improvement of the quality of seeds offered for sale in respect of germination and purity. It has also been a means of preventing detectable adulteration of seeds and in the farmer being provided with some degree of protection against the sowing of serious weed seeds along with his crop seeds.

In some countries the sale of seeds which do not conform to certain minimum standards is prohibited. In others the standards attained in official tests must be published so that the farmer may be able to judge the quality of the seeds he is offered, and although sales of seeds of low germination and purity may not be prohibited, the seed merchant is encouraged to ensure high quality in these respects.

The type of legislation concerned with the testing of seeds can best be illustrated by consideration of the *Seeds Regulations, 1961*. These regulations were issued under the *Seeds Act, 1920*. They replace the old Seeds Regulations, 1922, and will remain in force until such time as new Regulations may be introduced under the *Plant Varieties and Seeds Act, 1964*.

The Regulations are designed to protect growers from unwittingly buying seed of low quality. Sellers of seed are required to declare certain facts by means of which purchasers may assess the value of the seeds.

The Regulations apply to most farm seeds and most garden vegetable seeds together with seeds of certain forest trees (there are also regulations in respect of the sale of 'seed' potatoes).

The particulars which must be declared when seeds are sold or exposed for sale vary somewhat according to the type of seeds but the main requirements include (*a*) the seller's name and address, (*b*) a statement that the seeds have been tested in accordance with the provisions of the *Seeds Act, 1920*, (*c*) the kind of seeds, (*d*) if the seeds have been treated to control pests or diseases, or have been fumigated, pelleted or rubbed, (i) a statement whether the tests for germination and purity were made before or after these treatments, (ii) the nature or proprietary name of the liquid or powder used for pest or disease control, (iii) the nature or proprietary name of any fumigant used and the purpose of its use, (iv) the nature or proprietary name of any pelleting material used and its purpose. (*e*) In the case of hybrid seeds, whether F.1, double cross or of like character, a statement that the plants grown from them are unlikely to produce seeds which will produce plants true to the parent type. (*f*) In the case of mixtures of seeds the particulars must be given separately for each constituent of the mixture and the percentage by weight of each constituent in the mixture must be stated.

A statement of *variety and type* is required for certain specified seeds. The name of the *country of origin* is required for most seeds; this is important in that seed produced in widely different climatic conditions is often unsatisfactory for sowing under British conditions.

The actual percentage purity and percentage germination are required for herbage seeds and field seeds (vetches or tares, flax, linseed, buckwheat, lupin, sunflower) but in the case of cereals and root and vegetable seeds a statement that the seeds had a germination and purity not less than prescribed minimum percentages is acceptable. The prescribed minimum percentages include the following (germination in brackets):

Purity

99   Wheat and barley (90), oats (85), peas and rye (80), maize (75).
98   Field beans (90), rape (85), mustard, swede and turnip (80),
     kohl rabi and kale (75), cabbage, savoy, brussels sprout (70),
     cauliflower and broccoli (65).
97   Mangel, fodder beet, fodder sugar beet, sugar beet (70, of
     clusters), parsnip and celery (60).
93   Carrot (60).

The percentage of *hard seeds* must be declared in the case of clovers and other herbage legumes (see p. 96). The name and number of *injurious weed seeds* revealed by the purity test, if more than one seed was so revealed, must be stated in the case of herbage and field seeds (docks and sorrels being regarded as seed of the same kind for this purpose). For cereals the number of *injurious weed seeds* in a sample of 8 oz. For cereals, herbage and field seeds the percentage (by weight) of all weed seeds must be stated if it exceeds 0·5.

The *injurious weed seeds* mentioned above are wild oat (*Avena fatua* and *A. ludoviciana*), dodder (*Cuscuta* spp.), docks and sorrels (*Rumex* spp.), black grass or slender foxtail (*Alopecurus myosuroides*), and couch grass (*Agropyron repens*).

Wild oat, black grass and couch grass have been added to the list under the new Regulations as they are common impurities which are difficult to remove completely. Some species which were included in the 1922 Regulations have now been removed having become less important owing to changes in agricultural practice or being more easily removed by modern seed-cleaning methods. These species are cranesbills (*Geranium* spp.), soft brome grass and related species (*Bromus* spp.), wild carrot (*Daucus carota*) and Yorkshire fog (*Holcus lanatus*).

Seed-testing for England and Wales for the purposes of the Regulations is carried out at the Official Seed Testing Station at Cambridge (there is also an Official Seed Testing Station in Scotland and one in Northern Ireland). In addition, a number of private seed-testing stations, chiefly connected with seeds firms, are licensed by the Ministry of Agriculture and subject to inspection by appropriate officials of the Ministry. From these private stations check samples are collected officially at intervals and submitted to the official seed-testing stations for test.

The weight of seed submitted for an official test must be not less than the following amounts:

$\frac{1}{2}$ oz.	Cauliflower, celery.
1 oz.	Rough and smooth stalked meadow grasses.
2 oz.	Ryegrasses, meadow fescue, tall fescue, red fescue, timothy, cocksfoot, crested dogstail, meadow foxtail, most clovers and other small legumes, carrot.
4 oz.	Crimson clover, flax, linseed, kidney vetch, brassicas (other than cauliflower), parsnip, also herbage seeds mixtures.
8 oz.	Cereals, sainfoin, vetches or tares, buckwheat, sunflower, beet and mangel forms, lupin, also mixtures containing cereals, peas, beans or vetches.
16 oz.	Field bean.

Legislation requiring the testing of seeds and declaration of the results of such tests together with the improvement of machinery for cleaning seed stocks before they are submitted for test, has led to considerable improvement in the quality of seeds available to the farmer. This improvement has been further assisted by the development of selective weed killers and the certification and field approval schemes for seed crops.

SEED-TESTING TECHNIQUE AND INTERPRETATION OF RESULTS

The information required in connection with the Seeds Regulations may be summarized as follows:

(*a*) Percentage purity.
(*b*) Percentage germination.
(*c*) Percentage of hard seeds in the case of clovers and other small legumes.

(*d*) Percentage by weight of all weed seeds.

(*e*) Number of injurious weed seeds.

Other important information which may be obtained by a seed test includes *germination energy, presence of certain seed-borne diseases, moisture content, presence of other crop seeds, bushel weight* or *weight of 1,000 seeds.* This information is not however required for statutory declarations under the Seeds Regulations.

The details of methods of seed-testing show a certain amount of variety from one country to another, but the *International Seed Testing Association* seeks to obtain agreement between member countries upon problems connected with seed testing.

Sampling. It is important that a sample for testing should be representative of the bulk of seeds to be sold. Details of the method of sampling for official tests in Britain are laid down in the *Seeds Regulations 1961.* A single sample must not represent a bulk greater than 2 tons. Before sampling the bulk must be thoroughly mixed. If the bulk consists of not more than 5 sacks or other containers samples must be taken from each container; for larger bulks the proportion of containers to be sampled, at random, is laid down. In all cases a sample must consist of seed from the top, middle and bottom of the container. Special implements known as seed-triers or bag-samplers are used in drawing off seeds at various levels. The portions drawn off from the bulk must be thoroughly mixed and if the aggregate sample exceeds the required amount it is reduced by the halving method, i.e. dividing it into two equal parts, rejecting one half and again dividing the remainder into two, this process being repeated until a sample of the size required for submission for testing is obtained. Mechanical *seed dividers* may be used for this process.

Purity Test. The test for purity involves the examination of a representative sample particle by particle and for this purpose the regulation sample is normally too large and a smaller random sample is drawn from it, by the halving process, for actual examination. The final sample is weighed and may be brought to the prescribed weight by adding or removing small amounts of seed. As the purity test is done in duplicate, and the results averaged, two samples are drawn for testing.

The analytical sample is next spread out on a glass plate or a smooth table, examined particle by particle, and separated into the various grades, *pure seed, weed seeds* and *other impurities.* The other impurities include other crop seeds (which may be specified in the report), broken seeds consisting of one half or less of the original seed (in size), inert matter such as soil particles, stones, pieces of stem, pod or chaff and also ergot and other sclerotia. In the case of leguminous and cruciferous seeds any seed from which the seed coat has been removed must be included in these impurities; also, in the case of grass seeds any seed without an obvious caryopsis containing endosperm must similarly be included.

Under the Seeds Regulations pieces of seeds which are larger in size than half of the original seed are included in the pure seed. In some such pieces the embryo may have been damaged sufficiently to render the seed incapable of germination; thus this regulation, whilst increasing the purity, may reduce the germination capacity of some samples.

When grass seeds are examined it is somewhat difficult to determine whether a complete mature caryopsis is present within the husks. For some seeds this task is made easier by the use of an apparatus known as a *diaphanoscope*, which consists essentially of a glass plate on which the seed is examined and through which a beam of light shines from below. The seed is examined through a lens, and any seeds which by their diaphanous or semi-transparent nature are revealed as having no complete mature caryopsis are removed. In order to reduce the amount of seed to be examined in this way, the sample can first be separated into light, medium and heavy fractions by submitting it to a vertical blast of air in a specially designed *aspirator*. The lighter fractions are then examined as above.

When the various separations have been made the pure seed is weighed and the weight expressed as a percentage of the weight of the initial sample. The average of two samples is then recorded as the percentage purity (by weight). The impurities and weed seeds are similarly treated and expressed as percentages of the initial analytical sample. Any injurious weed seeds are counted and the *number* recorded.

The examination of a sample of small legumes or timothy seed for dodder (one of the injurious weed seeds) is a somewhat laborious process which can be eased by the use of a *dodder machine*; this feeds the seed slowly on to an endless belt of black velvet which passes under a lens through which the seeds are examined as they pass by.

The figures declared under the various headings mentioned in the Seeds Regulations are averages of a number of samples drawn from the sample submitted for test and the Regulations lay down limits of variation which may be permitted between the different samples contributing to these average figures.

It should be emphasized that the purity test has its limitations. In most cases the percentage purity can only represent the percentage of a particular species; the percentage of a particular variety or strain cannot usually be assessed. For example, tests of a sample of perennial rye-grass seed will reveal the percentage of perennial rye-grass, but they cannot discover what percentage of a particular variety (say Aberystwyth S.23) is present in the sample. In some cases varieties of cereals could be separated, particularly if grain colour varies within a sample, but there can be no certainty that a sample does not consist of a mixture of varieties of similar grain type. A reasonable degree of certainty as to the variety or strain of a sample can usually be provided only by seed crop certification, the more complete the system of certification the greater the degree of certainty.

The proportion of perennial rye-grass in Italian rye-grass seed and *vice versa* can be determined by special tests which are described later

(p. 309), and some idea of the type of white clover can be obtained by the *cyanophoric test* on germinated seeds (see p. 158).

Germination Tests. The percentage of seed which will germinate when sown under field conditions cannot be measured by laboratory tests, but normally a sample which gives satisfactory germination in a laboratory test will be satisfactory in the field if provided with suitable growth conditions. In order that results obtained from tests shall be comparable, and to eliminate the need for arbitrary decisions, tests are performed under conditions which have been proved to be the best possible for the particular species.

Tests are made on the pure seed separated during the purity test. Most usually 100 seeds are used for each test, and four or five such tests are made on each sample. The requisite number of hundreds must be drawn from the sample *at random*, selection of seeds being avoided. Mechanical aids can be used in drawing the hundreds. One such consists of a pad with 100 perforations which is connected by a tube to suction apparatus; by this means 100 seeds can be sucked on to the pad and then released, already spaced, on the seed-bed.

The seed-bed for the test may consist of filter or blotting paper or unglazed porcelain slabs, for smaller seeds, and sand or soil for larger seeds. The seed is germinated under optimum conditions. Moisture is provided in the requisite amounts, care being taken to avoid excess, which often has an adverse effect on germination. The most suitable temperature conditions for each particular species are provided. Most seeds germinate best at temperatures between 18° and 22° C., but for some seeds lower or higher temperatures are preferable. Certain seeds germinate more readily when the temperature alternates between about 22° and 30° C., e.g. mangel, sugar-beet, carrot and cocksfoot. Most seeds will germinate readily in diffused light or in the dark, but some, such as *Poas* and *Agrostis* species, germinate better in direct sunlight. Fresh air is required to remove the carbon dioxide and supply the oxygen involved in respiration; therefore provision is made for ventilation, without draughts, around the seeds.

Each test is continued for a period which has been agreed for each particular species, the time varying within a range from seven days for species which germinate evenly and rapidly up to twenty-eight days for those which germinate more slowly.

Seeds are considered to have germinated when they have produced a healthy root with root hairs.

The seeds which have germinated are counted at fixed intervals during the test; at each count those which have germinated are removed, and if necessary the remaining seeds may be transferred to a fresh seed bed. At the end of the test the total number of germinated seeds is obtained. The figures for the various test lots taken from the original sample are averaged and the figure obtained, expressed as a percentage, is known as the *germination capacity*, i.e. the percentage by number of the seeds capable of germination within the period of the test.

From counts made at the end of an agreed shorter period the *germination energy* may be calculated; this is the percentage by number which will germinate rapidly in a stated period.

If the figures for the various lots of seed from one sample show variations beyond fixed limits the germination test is repeated. Usually as a check on the reliability of a test a control sample, the figures for which are already known, is tested at the same time.

In testing seeds of *Beta* species clusters producing one or more seedlings are counted as one, a cluster of cocksfoot seeds is also germinated as a single seed.

Hard Seeds. When clovers and other small legumes are tested usually a proportion of the seeds will not absorb water, but remain small and hard and do not germinate during the period of the test. These seeds are not entirely useless, as some of them will germinate some time after being sown in the field (perhaps not until a year or two years or more later). The hard seeds are counted and reported separately; thus, for example, the germination capacity of a sample of red clover may be 85 per cent. plus six hard seeds. A high percentage of hard seeds is usually not desirable, especially if the seed is to be used for short duration leys.

Apparatus for Germination Tests. Various types of apparatus are utilized in testing seeds. Cabinets of the incubator type with the temperature thermostatically controlled may be used. In these the seeds may be placed, evenly spaced, on moist filter paper in Petri dishes or between filter papers kept moist by folds of moistened flannel, or large seeds may be sown in dishes of sand or soil. Water is applied when needed from a wash-bottle or spray. A small room with controlled temperature may be converted into a germinator of this sort.

Another type of germinator, the *Rodewald*, consists of a tray of wet sand on which unglazed porcelain dishes or blocks are bedded. The tray fits above a tray of water the temperature of which is controlled thermostatically. The seeds are arranged on the porous dishes or blocks which absorb water from the sand, which is watered by hand.

Other types of germinator in which the watering is automatic are also used. A type usually used for grass seeds, known as a *Copenhagen tank*, consists of a tank of water across the open top of which are placed glass strips. The seeds are arranged on filter papers along the glass strips and from beneath each filter paper a cotton wick or strip of filter paper dips into the water in the tank, the temperature of which is thermostatically controlled. Each filter paper with its seed sample is covered by a small ventilated bell-jar.

Rapid Tests. Normally a germination test covers a period of several days. On occasion it may be desirable to obtain the figures for germination within a shorter period. For this purpose a chemical method for discovering the germinability of seeds has been devised. The chemical used is 2, 3, 5-triphenyl tetrazolium bromide. The test depends upon the fact that when a solution of this substance is absorbed by healthy, active, embryonal tissues the tissues assume a red coloration. The test is more suitable for large seeds, such as cereals, peas and beans, as it involves bisecting the embryo, a difficult task with smaller seeds. Random samples of 100 seeds are soaked in tap-water overnight. The seeds are then bisected so that the embryo is halved longitudinally. One half of each seed is retained, and the hundred halves are placed in a dish and just covered with an aqueous solution (1 per cent.) of the chemical (the solution is almost colourless) and left in the dark at 20° C. for four hours. The seeds are then washed in water and examined. If the radicle and plumule stain red, they would have been capable of germination provided they have a healthy connection with the food store. Thus in wheat, for example, at least part of the scutellum, including its connection with the radicle and plumule, must stain in addition to the radicle and plumule; the endosperm does not stain, but in dicotyledons the cotyledons do so. By counting the number of properly stained half-seeds, the germination capacity can be determined.

This test has the advantage of being completed within twenty-four hours, but each test involves more laborious hand work than is necessary for an ordinary germination test and close scrutiny of each seed is required.

Plant Disease Organisms. During the examination of a seed sample for purity, certain disease organisms may be detected and reported upon. Sclerotia of ergot (p. 549) may be found in rye and grass seeds and occasionally in wheat. Among red clover seeds sclerotia of the clover rot fungus (p. 545) can be detected. Spores of certain smut fungi, such as bunt of wheat (p. 556), can be seen on the surface of the seeds under examination; these can be checked by microscopical examination. It is not possible to detect the presence of smut diseases which are present inside the tissues of the grain, such as loose smut of wheat (p. 557). Minute black dots (pycnidia) on the surface of celery seed indicate the presence of the leaf spot disease.

Some diseases may become evident during the germination test—for example, leaf spot of oats (p. 553), leaf stripe of barley (p. 554), blackleg of mangel and beet, and spot disease of peas (*Ascochyta pisi*).

Moisture Content. A knowledge of the moisture content of seed is particularly important for the merchant, who may require to store seed for some time before it is sold for sowing. A high moisture content may lead to rapid deterioration. For example, wheat with a moisture content of 15 per cent. can be stored safely, but if the moisture content is above 17 per cent. the sample will deteriorate much more rapidly; if it is 20 per cent. or more the seed may become valueless for sowing in a relatively short time.

Bushel Weight. The bushel weight, i.e. the weight of seed contained in an imperial bushel measure, was at one time thought to be a valuable figure, a high bushel weight being taken to indicate large well-developed seeds. This idea is not always correct, as the weight will depend upon how readily the seed packs down in the measure; in some cases—for example, oats—small seeds may pack well and weigh more per bushel than larger seeds.

The weight of 100 or 1,000 seeds is a much better guide in comparing seeds of the same kind.

The Evaluation of Germination and Purity Figures. The tests for germination and purity are of value not only in providing the information needed for statutory declarations with regard to the seeds, but also in providing information required by the merchant in evaluating his stocks and by the farmer who wishes to know what proportion of the pure seed is likely to grow and how much worthless or injurious impurity he is likely to be sowing.

The test figures for germination capacity are obtained under ideal conditions which rarely obtain in the field. Fewer seedlings are normally produced in the field per 100 seeds sown than are obtained in a laboratory test; the reduction, however, is normally less for samples with high figures for the germination test than for those with low figures.

The figure for *germination energy* is an important one. Of two samples of the same kind of seed with the same germination capacity, the sample with the higher germination energy will normally give better results in the field. A high germination energy usually indicates vigorous seed which will grow rapidly under field conditions with less risk of loss through attack by soil organisms, check by weather conditions or by competition with weed seedlings. A low figure may indicate old or badly conditioned seed; such seed is likely to give poor establishment when sown. Some seed may have a low speed of germination when tested if freshly harvested. For example, with cereals a period of after-ripening may be needed before satisfactory germination can occur. This type of dormancy of cereal seeds can be overcome by submitting them to temperatures about 5° C. before testing.

Purity as near to 100 per cent. as possible is desirable, but impurities which consist merely of inert matter are of little importance provided they will not interfere with mechanized sowing and that the price of the seed is adjusted in accordance with the amount of impurity present. Impurities of a weed nature are much more serious. Some seeds, such as wild oat, in very small amounts may introduce to arable land a source of trouble for many years. Other weeds, because of the lightness of their seeds, may be present in enormous numbers, although represented in the analyst's figures by a comparatively low percentage by weight. Thus a seed sample containing 1 per cent. or less by weight of certain weed seeds may result, when sown, in a large population of the particular weed appearing in the field (see p. 371).

In comparing two samples of seed of exactly the same kind, provided there are no serious impurities, it may be difficult from a study of the figures for germination and purity to decide which is the better sample.

For example, if two samples of the same strain of perennial rye-grass are under consideration and for sample 'A' the figures are percentage purity 90, germination capacity 90, and for sample 'B' percentage purity 95, germination capacity 85, one cannot distinguish the better sample at a glance.

In order to assist comparison, a single figure known as the *real value* may be obtained for each sample from the pairs of figures provided. The real value represents the percentage of pure germinating seeds and is arrived at by use of the following formula:

Real Value = Percentage Purity × Germination Capacity ÷ 100

Thus for sample 'A' the real value would be $90 \times 90 \div 100 = 81$, and for sample 'B' it would be $95 \times 85 \div 100 = 80 \cdot 75$. By comparing the two figures for real value, it is now seen that sample 'A' is slightly superior to sample 'B'.

In comparing two samples of seed, the nature of the impurities is of considerable importance. If, in the example quoted above, sample 'A' contained among its impurities 1 per cent. of serious weed seeds whilst sample 'B' contained only unimportant inert matter, the impurities in 'A' would far outweigh in importance any superiority in *real value*. Thus it is only occasionally that the real value figures have any significance.

In calculating the real value of small legumes it is permissible to add one-third of the percentage of hard seeds to the figure for germination capacity, except for red clover (half) and lucerne (total).

BOOKS FOR FURTHER READING

Akerman, A., *et al.* *Swedish Contributions to the Development of Plant Breeding*, 1938, New Sweden Tercentenary publications, Stockholm.

Allard, R. W. *Principles of Plant Breeding*, 1960, Wiley and Sons, N.Y.

Asimov, I. *The Genetic Code*, 1964, John Murray.

Babcock, E. B., and Clausen, R. E. *Genetics in Relation to Agriculture*, 1927, McGraw-Hill, N.Y. and London.

Crane, M. B., and Lawrence, W. J. C. *The Genetics of Garden Plants*, 1952, Macmillan.

Darlington, C. D. *Chromosome Botany and the Origins of Cultivated Plants*, 1963, Allen and Unwin.

Darlington, C. D. *Chromosomes and Plant Breeding*, 1932, Macmillan.

Darlington, C. D., and LaCour, L. F. *The Handling of Chromosomes*, 1960, Allen and Unwin.

Darlington, C. D., and Mather, K. *The Elements of Genetics*, 1949, Allen and Unwin.

Darlington, C. D., and Wylie, A. P. *Chromosome Atlas of Flowering Plants*, 1955, Allen and Unwin.

George, Wilma. *Elementary Genetics*, 1951, Macmillan.

Hagedoorn, A. L. *Plant Breeding*, 1950, Crosby Lockwood.

Hayes, H. K., and Garber, R. J. *Breeding Crop Plants*, 1927, McGraw-Hill.

Hayes, H. K., and Immer, F. R. *Methods of Plant Breeding*, 1942, McGraw-Hill.

Hunter, H. *Crop Varieties*, 1951, Spon.

Hunter, H., and Leake, H. M. *Recent Advances in Agricultural Plant Breeding*, 1933, J. and A. Churchill.

Lawrence, W. J. C. *Practical Plant Breeding*, 1951, Allen and Unwin.

Mercer, S. P. *Farm and Garden Seeds*, 1948, Crosby Lockwood.

Sansome, F. W., and Philp, J. *Recent Advances in Plant Genetics*, 1932, J. and A. Churchill.

Sinnott, E. W., Dunn, L. C., and Dobzhansky, Th. *Principles of Genetics*, 1950, McGraw-Hill.

Waddington, C. H. *An Introduction to Modern Genetics*, 1950, Macmillan.

Whyte, R. O., and others (editors), *Svalöf 1886-1946. History and Present Problems*, 1948, Lund.

White, M. J. D. *The Chromosomes*, 1961, Methuen.

Williams, W. *Genetical Principles and Plant Breeding*, 1964. Blackwell.

Also the following publications:

Journal of the National Institute of Agricultural Botany. Periodical publication.

Journal of the Royal Agricultural Society of England. Periodical publication.

Plant Breeding Abstracts. Published by the Commonwealth Bureau of Plant Breeding and Genetics.

O.E.E.C. publications:

1. *Development of Seed Production and the Seed Trade in Europe.* 1955.

2. *High-quality Seed, its Production, Control, and Distribution.* 1955.
3. *Seed Production, Testing and Distribution in European Countries.* 1954.

Other publications:
  Guide to Plant Breeders Rights.
  Plant Varieties and Seeds Act, 1964.
  Plant Breeders Rights Regulations, 1965.
  Seeds Regulations, 1961.

CROPS

Chapter VIII

THE BOTANY OF CROP PLANTS: GENERAL

THE TYPES OF PLANTS USED AS AGRICULTURAL CROPS

IN comparison with the number of different plants which can be grown in the climate of the British Isles, the number commonly grown as agricultural crops is extremely small. If we except a few uncommon crops grown only occasionally, and occupying a negligible fraction of the total area of farmland, we find that only eight families of flowering plants are represented. Of these eight, only two—the *Gramineae* (grasses and cereals) and the *Leguminosae* (pulse-crops, clovers, etc.)—show any wide range of crops; in the other six families the agricultural crop plants are confined to one or two genera, or even to a single species. It is evident, therefore, that there is a very rigid selection of plants for agricultural use, and that a plant must meet very special requirements if it is to become a common crop.

By far the greater part of the farmland of Britain is devoted to the production of food crops, either directly for human beings or for farm animals, and fibre-producing plants, such as flax, are of comparatively little importance. The primary requirement for a plant that is to be grown as a crop is thus that it shall contain a large proportion of edible material; in addition, it must produce as high a yield as possible and be conveniently and cheaply cultivated. It is desirable, therefore, to consider the effect of these requirements on the selection of plants for agricultural use.

Sources of Edible Material. Plants are made up of a number of different tissues, of which meristematic tissue, parenchyma and lignified tissue are the most extensive. Of these, only the first two are important food materials, and the food-crop plants are therefore those with a high proportion of meristematic or parenchymatous tissues. These tissues are found particularly in leaves and young stems, in special storage organs, and in seed reserves; food crops can thus be classified into three groups according to the part of the plant which is utilized.

1. *Leaves and Young Stems.* These provide mainly animal foods, since the proportion of cellulose is usually too high for them to form a staple human diet; some plants grown for leaf and young stem are, however, used as vegetables. Such 'greens' or leaf-vegetables are usually eaten in

comparatively small amount—mainly for their vitamin C and mineral content rather than as a source of energy—and are horticultural rather than agricultural crops. As crops used for animal feeding, the plants grown for their leaves and young stems provide non-concentrated foods; the water-content is usually high, and the food is available only for immediate consumption unless it is specially preserved by drying, or as silage.

The method of utilization of crops of this type depends largely on the growth-habit of the plant; plants with upright stems and aerial buds can usually only be cut or grazed off once (e.g. kales), while those with short or creeping stems and buds at or near ground-level will withstand repeated cutting or grazing (e.g. grasses and clovers). In both cases stock can be fed directly (i.e. the plants grazed), so that costs of immediate utilization are reduced to a minimum. The period over which such grazing can be carried out is dependent in Britain mainly on the ability of the plants to withstand frost and the treading of animals in wet soil conditions; in hot, dry climates it will be limited by drought conditions, although during drought periods animals may continue to feed on the dead, dry herbage.

Crops of this type, where leaves and young stems are eaten, thus normally form the main food of herbivorous animals, and it is only to carry them over the unfavourable periods, when such plants are not available, that the more costly storable crops of types 2 and 3 below are utilized.

2. *Special Storage Organs*. The storage organs found in food crops are mainly stems and roots with some form of non-lignified secondary thickening, giving moderately concentrated foods storable for some months and available for winter consumption. They are produced mostly by a few very specialized, long-cultivated plants, since species which form large volumes of edible parenchyma are rare. The majority are biennials, harvested at the end of the first season's growth, when the storage organ has reached its full size and while the plant is still in the vegetative stage. If conditions are such that flowering occurs in the first season, the value of the storage organ is much reduced. In potatoes, and the structurally similar Jerusalem artichoke, the plant is a perennial, dying down each year, and perennating only by means of underground stem-tubers; in these, production of the storage organ is largely independent of flowering.

Most of the crop plants of this type (2) have a storage organ which is mainly swollen tap-root, but the hypocotyl and the lower part of the true stem (epicotyl) may contribute to it. In kohlrabi the swollen part is, however, wholly stem, the root and hypocotyl being slender and woody; in potatoes the storage organ is a true tuber—that is, the enlarged apex of an underground axillary stem. Anatomically the storage organ of all these crops consists essentially of a mass of parenchyma, but the way in which this originates shows great variation. It may be primary tissue, as in potatoes; more commonly it is secondary tissue, derived either from a single cambium, as in turnips and carrots, or from a series of concentric cambia, as in mangels.

Crop plants of this type require to be grown at wide spacing to allow of full development of the storage organ, and they are therefore usually expensive crops to grow. If grown for animal consumption, only those with storage organs mainly above ground can be fed off *in situ*, and the remainder (including mangels, which, although mainly above ground, are chemically unfit for feeding before winter, and are not frost-hardy) must bear the cost of lifting, storing and feeding in addition. This cost of handling is necessarily high per unit of food owing to the comparatively high proportion of water present (dry matter ranges from about 9 per cent. in turnips to about 24 per cent. in potatoes). Originally garden crops for human consumption, plants of this type came into field use at a time when labour costs were comparatively low, and the need for winter feed for stock pressing. The introduction of turnips and swedes as winter feed for stock may indeed be said to have effected a revolution in British agriculture. With increased labour costs, however, and with the development of alternative winter foods, such as kale and grass silage (i.e. foods derived from the less expensive leaf and young stem crops of type 1), such root crops have become relatively less useful as animal foods. The development of efficient selective weed-killers has also reduced the necessity for their inclusion in the rotation as cleaning crops. There is therefore a tendency to reduce the acreage of these crops grown for stock, and where they are grown to utilize mainly those, such as fodder-beets, which give the highest dry-matter yield per acre. Potatoes and sugar-beet are normally grown only as direct cash crops for human consumption (in the latter it is the sugar only which is so utilized, the cellulose, etc., remaining as a by-product for stock food); carrots and parsnips, formerly grown to some extent for stock food, are now almost exclusively grown as vegetables for human consumption, and even swedes owe some of their popularity to the fact that they may be saleable for this purpose.

Storage of all these crops depends on the winter-dormancy of the plant, and cannot be continued after growth recommences in spring.

3. *Seed Reserves.* Seed reserves, present either in endosperm or cotyledons, have normally a very low percentage of water, and give highly concentrated foods which can be readily stored. The low cellulose content of many seeds makes them suitable as human food, and the fact that they remain dormant indefinitely if kept dry means that they can be stored for long periods.

Amongst the various large-seeded plants grown for their seed reserves the cereals are pre-eminent; these are grasses in which the bulk of the large seed consists of endosperm, parenchyma tissue densely filled with starch grains. Being upright annuals, with large seeds giving ready establishment, they can be comparatively cheaply grown in close stand, without interplant cultivation. The fruits, ripening all at the same time, and borne well above the ground, are readily and cheaply harvested.

Seed reserves are important sources of proteins and fats as well as of starch, but in this and other temperate climate countries with a comparatively high standard of living the tendency has been for proteins and fats for human consumption to be derived largely from animal sources. Where vegetable fats are required, oil seeds are imported from warmer climates, and the residues after oil extraction provide concentrated protein foods for stock. Oil and protein seeds are therefore of somewhat lesser importance among British crops, but such leguminous crops as peas and beans are grown to provide proteins for stock food.

Factors Affecting Yield. Whatever type of food-crop is being grown, it will normally be most profitable to grow the plant which gives the highest yield per acre of useful food. This will normally be the highest yield of edible dry matter, although it may be necessary to take quality into account, and for some purposes the farmer may prefer a lower total yield if the proportion of some valuable constituent, such as protein, is higher.

Yield of a plant is primarily a matter of the quantity of elaborated carbon-compounds produced; that is, it is dependent on the amount of photosynthesis carried out. The amount of photosynthesis is dependent on the intrinsic characters of the plant, and on the environmental conditions. The main plant characters concerned are:

(a) The net assimilation rate (i.e. the amount of dry matter produced per unit leaf-area per unit of time).
(b) The area of leaf or other green tissue.
(c) The length of growing period.

The chief environmental factors are:

(d) The amount of light.
(e) Temperature.
(f) The carbon-dioxide content of the air.
(g) Soil conditions, including water supply and availability of nutrients.

Some of these factors can be controlled by the farmer, while others cannot. The plant characters are genetically determined, and depend on the type of plant selected. The leaf area of any particular plant can be altered in a downward direction by grazing or cutting; normally a crop which can be treated in this way will give its highest total dry-matter yield when it is allowed to remain as long as possible without defoliation. Of the environmental factors, temperature and amount of light are usually controllable only to the extent that crops may be grown at the time of year when these are most favourable. Under field conditions, the carbon dioxide content of the air cannot be altered, although this may be possible in experimental glasshouses. Water supply can, to some extent, be altered by drainage or irrigation, but the factor which can be most readily changed is the supply of readily available soil nutrients.

The ideal high-yielding crop is thus one which has a high intrinsic photosynthetic rate, a high proportion of photosynthetic tissue, and a long growing season during the most favourable part of the year, and which responds well to heavy manuring. This ideal type of plant is in general the object aimed at in the choice of crop plants, although clearly all the requirements cannot always be met. Thus for some purposes a crop is required which comes to maturity early; here the growing period is shorter and the yield is thus reduced. Such a crop will only be desirable where the increased value of the early produce compensates for reduced yield, or where early maturity either allows the plant to be cultivated in an area where climatic conditions do not permit the growth of longer-growing, higher-yielding forms (e.g. spring wheats in northern Canada), or permits of a second crop from the same land being taken during the one year. Again, the requirement that the period of growth shall be during the most favourable part of the year cannot always be met; it may be necessary to grow a crop at a less favourable period in order to provide fresh food for stock at a particular time, or to use it as a catch-crop. Sometimes the physiological behaviour of a plant is such that the period during which it can be grown is limited. Thus, for example, sugar-beet and related crops, which are biennials grown for the food reserves in the storage organ, are normally sensitive to low temperature during the seedling and early-growth stages. Sowing early enough to give maximum growth during the most favourable part of the year is therefore impossible, as such plants respond to the low temperatures to which the seedling is subjected by bolting—that is, by behaving as annuals, so that little or no food reserve is built up.

The nutrient status of the soil is usually the factor most readily controlled, and with increased use of fertilizers there is an increasing tendency to use only crop plants adapted to conditions of high fertility. The great majority of newly-introduced crop varieties are ones which give high yields in response to heavy manuring, and crops and crop varieties which are suited only to conditions of low fertility are tending to become of less and less importance in British agriculture. This general tendency towards the use of high-fertility plants extends not only to arable crops, but also to grassland; even on poor hill grazings it will usually be considered better to build up the fertility to a level at which the higher-yielding grasses and clovers can be grown, rather than to try to find and grow the species which would give the maximum yield at the existing level of fertility.

Ease of Cultivation. The cost of growing a crop is largely controlled by the amount of labour which has to be expended on it; plants with a high labour-requirement will only be grown if they yield a high-priced product, usually for human consumption, and the growing of such crops (e.g. hops, celery, strawberries) tends to be a specialized horticultural operation rather than a matter for the general farmer. Where crops are grown for feeding to stock, or to provide low-priced human food, it is necessary that they should be grown cheaply. This means that as far as possible the plants must be readily established, that the cultivations required shall be simple and capable of being mechanized, and that the crop can be either fed off *in situ* if for stock, or harvested quickly and cheaply.

It might be thought that a perennial crop, in which the problem of establishment does not arise every year, would be an advantage; in fact, any advantages due to this fact are more than offset by the difficulties of maintaining high fertility and of keeping down weeds in perennial crops. Inter-row cultivations of standing crops are always more expensive and usually less effective than the thorough field cultivations which can take place during the interval between two annual crops; if hand-hoeing is involved, the expense may be prohibitive. As a result, long-lived spaced crops are found in this country only among specialized horticultural crops, such as hops and soft fruit. With close crops, where the plants are closely spaced with little or no bare ground between, the weed problem may not appear so serious, but it is still present. The problem of maintaining fertility is even greater, and it is only grass and grassland plants·which are grown as such a permanent crop. Even here the tendency for fertility and yield to deteriorate, and for weeds to come in, is very marked unless the crop is being grown under particularly favourable conditions. In many cases, therefore, one-year or short-term leys are preferred to permanent grass, the extra cost of re-establishing the crop at frequent intervals being more than offset by the increased yield obtained.

With the partial exception of grassland, then, perennial plants play little part in British agriculture, and the great majority of crops are annuals, or biennials and perennials grown as annuals. Such crops are usually grown from seed; crops which must be propagated vegetatively are normally more expensive to grow, and the potato is the only common agricultural crop in which this method is used.

It follows that for a plant to be satisfactory as an agricultural crop, it is necessary that it should produce seed readily, so that seed can be available at a low price, and that it can be easily established from this seed. The part sown need not be a true seed from the strict botanical standpoint, but may be an indehiscent fruit, sometimes enclosed, as in many of the grasses, within other parts of the inflorescence, but it is convenient to include all such bodies under the general name of 'seed'. (The terms *diaspore* or 'agricultural seed' may be used to distinguish such a structure from a true seed formed from the ovule only.) Occasionally, as in mangels and related plants, the 'agricultural seed' (cluster) is an indehiscent multiple fruit containing several true seeds, but this must be regarded as a disadvantage, as each cluster sown may give rise to several very closely-crowded plants, making hand-singling necessary.

The production of seed of plants normally grown for their seed reserves will, of course, present no difficulty, but plants which are usually grown only for their vegetative parts, such as fodder and herbage plants, may produce little seed, or the 'agricultural seed' may be a structure which is difficult or expensive to clean after harvesting. Meadow foxtail grass (*Alopecurus pratensis*) (see p. 339) illustrates both these difficulties; in the 'agricultural seed' the true fruit (caryopsis) is enclosed by a pair of relatively large, thin, hairy structures (glumes). This is not readily dealt with by seed-cleaning machinery, as the whole mass of 'seeds' tends to felt together, and does not flow freely over the sieves; spikelets in which the true seed has failed to develop differ only slightly in weight and not at all in size and shape from good 'seeds', and are therefore extremely difficult to separate out. Moreover, meadow foxtail, if grown for seed in Britain, is usually very seriously attacked by midges, with the result that the yield of 'seed' is often very low. In consequence, such 'seed' as comes on to the market tends to be expensive and of low purity and germination, with the result that meadow foxtail, in spite of its considerable merits as a herbage grass, is rarely regarded as worth sowing.

Ready establishment of a crop from seed means that the seed must be convenient to sow and must germinate uniformly and reasonably quickly under field conditions. Difficulty in sowing rarely occurs with true seeds, but may arise with some of the more complicated structures found in the grass family; for instance, bristle-pointed oat (*Avena strigosa*) (see p. 278) has the fruit surrounded by a husk (lemma) with two long points at the top and a still longer bristle-like awn on the back, and the whole 'seed' will therefore not pass through an ordinary corn-drill. Uniform germination implies more or less simultaneous development of all the seeds within a short time of sowing, that is that seeds do not remain dormant in the soil. This is often a striking difference between cultivated plants and related wild species, which often show very pronounced dormancy and irregular germination. Thus, while cultivated oats will normally all germinate within a few days of sowing if conditions are suitable, wild oats (*Avena fatua*) may show seedlings appearing at rather irregular intervals over several years. There is, of course, a natural tendency for this character of delayed germination to be automatically bred out when a species is brought into cultivation, as at harvest-time only those plants resulting from immediate germination will usually have matured seed. Thus in each generation the seed sown will have been derived only from the plants of the previous year which did not show delayed germination, and this character will therefore tend to be lost over the course of years.

In general, plants with large seeds, and hence with large food reserves, will establish more readily than those with small seeds. This will apply more particularly where conditions for establishment are unfavourable, and is perhaps rarely important in Britain. In Canada, however, some attempt has been made, by crossing herbage grasses with related cereals, to produce forage grasses with very large seeds, capable of establishing under very unfavourable conditions.

Plants which require special conditions for the germination of their seeds may be limited in their usefulness as crops. Thus, for example, maize, which has a rather high minimum temperature for germination, is limited in its value in Britain by the rather short growing season left after the soil has reached a sufficiently high temperature in spring for germination to take place. Some of the meadow-grasses (*Poa* spp., p. 319) have 'seeds' which are light-sensitive—that is, which germinate more readily in the light than in the dark. Hence 'seeds' drilled or harrowed in deeply may fail to germinate, and while those left on the soil surface can germinate satisfactorily if moisture is available, the seedlings are likely to be killed by drying-out unless weather conditions are very favourable. The proportion of the 'seeds' sown which actually produce a plant tends therefore to be very low.

The relations between plant type and the cultivation necessary after establishment have already been considered in discussing the sources of edible material. With plants which cannot be grazed off *in situ* it is desirable that the crop should be capable of being harvested quickly and cheaply; in plants grown for their seeds this necessitates good standing ability (since a lodged crop is more difficult to harvest), even ripening and a minimum of shedding. A comparison of buckwheat and the true cereals illustrates the first two points; buckwheat fruits are rather similar to cereal grains in composition and use, but buckwheat has weak stems, and the fruits ripen successively over a long period. It therefore compares unfavourably with the stiff-strawed cereals in which all fruits are ripe at about the same time. Ready shedding of seed as soon as it is ripe is a characteristic of most wild plants, but in the majority of plants successfully used as crops this character has been bred out by automatic selection. Thus the wild forms of wheat and barley have brittle spikes, which break up as soon as the fruit approaches ripeness, but cultivated forms have tough spikes, and the 'seeds' are not shed unless the crop is allowed to stand very late. Similarly, such crop plants as oil-poppy and linseed, the wild forms of which have dehiscent capsules, have fruits which either remain permanently closed or which open only at a very late stage. The use of the combine-harvester makes this character of late dehiscence even more important, since combined crops must necessarily be left standing until the fruits are completely ripe.

Chapter IX

PAPAVERACEAE AND CRUCIFERAE

PAPAVERACEAE

General Importance. Contains only one agricultural crop plant, oil poppy, grown in various temperate areas for its oil-containing seeds. Grown only experimentally in Britain. The plant is also the source of the drug opium.

Botanical Characters. A small family of mainly herbaceous plants. Leaves alternate, exstipulate, often pinnately divided. Flowers usually large, solitary, actinomorphic, insect pollinated. Sepals two, free; petals four, free, crumpled in bud. Stamens numerous, free; gynaecium superior, of two to many united carpels, unilocular, with numerous ovules on parietal placentas. Style very short or absent, stigma capitate or in the form of sessile rays on top of ovary. Fruit a capsule, often dehiscing by pores. Seed small, often reniform, with sculptured testa; endospermic, with very small embryo. The family includes a number of common weeds, for which see p. 410.

Papaver somniferum L.   Oil Poppy

An annual, 4 to 5 ft. high, glaucous with scattered stiff hairs. Leaves sessile, clasping, oblong, up to 30 × 10 cm., shallowly lobed, coarsely crenate-serrate. Stem stout, little branched. Flowers large, nodding in bud, erect in flower and fruit, on stout peduncles. Sepals caducous (falling when flower opens); petals large, 10 cm. broad by 7 cm. long, crumpled in bud, white with basal red-purple patch. Ovary globular, of nine to fourteen united carpels, top convex, marked by stigmatic rays; placentas forming incomplete vertical partitions not extending to centre, and bearing very numerous ovules. Fruit an ovoid or almost globular capsule, 5-6 cm. in diameter, glabrous and glaucous, dehiscence mechanism present in form of ring of pores below the flat, stellate, oblong-toothed stigmatic·cap, but not functional in cultivated varieties. Seed reniform, 1-1·5 mm., *c.* ¾ million per pound, testa pale grey-blue or almost white, marked with raised reticulations. Germination epigeal, expanded cotyledons linear, sessile, about 12 mm. × 2 mm.

The seeds contain a valuable edible drying oil; seed yields of 8 or 9 cwt. per acre are obtainable, giving an oil yield of some 300 lb. A fine seed-bed and very shallow drilling are necessary owing to the small size of the seed; a close stand with plants about 2 in. apart in 18-in. rows is necessary for high yields.

CRUCIFERAE

General Importance. The family includes a small number of species of outstanding importance as 'root' crops. These are plants producing

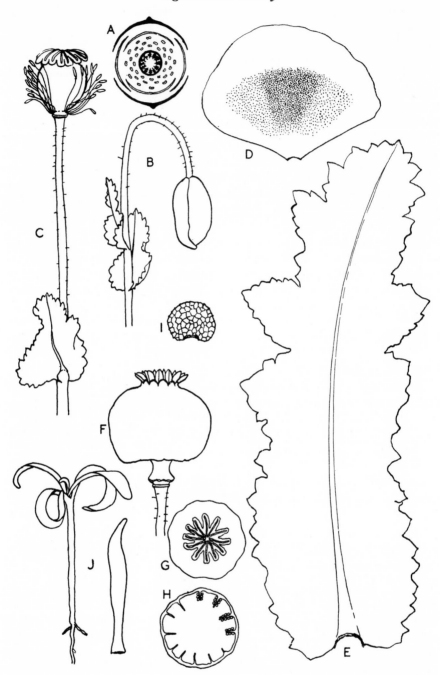

Fig. 15. Oil poppy, *Papaver somniferum*. A, floral diagram. B, bud. C, flower with petals fallen. D, detached petal. E, basal leaf. F, G, H, ripe capsule in side and top view and transverse section. All × ½. I, seed, × 10. J, seedling and detached cotyledon, × 3.

succulent leaves and young stems to provide bulk fodder for feeding green, or swollen storage organs suitable for folding-off or for temporary storage to provide winter fodder. Other forms of the same species are used for human consumption, and are important 'leaf' and 'root' vegetables. A few species are grown for their seeds, either as a source of edible oils (oil-rapes) or for use as condiments (mustards). The family includes also a number of purely horticultural crops, and some important farm weeds (p. 411).

Botanical Characters. A family of herbaceous plants of temperate regions, with alternate, exstipulate simple leaves, often pinnately lobed. Inflorescence racemose, with few bracts. Flowers conspicuous, insect-pollinated, actinomorphic, of very characteristic and remarkably uniform structure. Floral formula K2 +2, C4, A2 +4, G(2). Sepals erect or spreading, inner pair sometimes pouched; petals usually with narrow

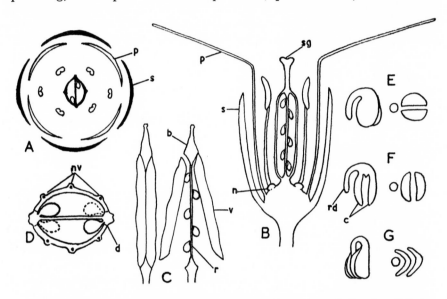

Fig. 16. Cruciferae. A, floral diagram. B, diagram of flower in vertical section. C, fruit (siliqua) entire and dehisced. D, fruit in transverse section. E, F, G, diagrams of side view and section of embryo to show arrangement in seed. E, accumbent. F, incumbent. G, conduplicate. *b*, beak. *c*, cotyledons. *d*, line of dehiscence. *n*, nectary. *nv*, nerve. *p*, petal. *r*, replum. *rd*, radicle. *s*, sepal. *sg*, stigma.

erect basal claw and broader erect or spreading limb, forming, as seen from above, the characteristic cross from which the family derives its name. Stamens six (occasionally reduced to four or two), the outer pair shorter than the four inner. Pollen-sacs two; nectaries present at base of filaments. Gynaecium superior, of two joined carpels, with a single short style and capitate or bilobed stigma. Ovules usually numerous, anatropous; placentation parietal, but the ovary divided into two chambers by the development of a false septum or *replum* as an outgrowth from the placentas. Pollination by insects, usually bees, sometimes by flies or small beetles, but self-pollination can occur. Fruit a specialized and characteristic form of capsule known as a *siliqua*, dehiscing by the carpel walls splitting longitudinally along the line of the placentas and becoming detached as separate *valves*, leaving the seeds temporarily attached to the replum. The siliqua is typically long and slender; the term *silicula* is used where the fruit is short and broad. Indehiscent or schizocarpic fruits occur in a few genera. Seeds are non-endospermic, with thick cotyledons with mainly oily food reserves. In some species glycosides are present which are broken down by enzyme action to give strong-tasting sulphur compounds; such seeds are used as condiments, but are distasteful to stock and may be poisonous.

The arrangement of the embryo in the seed varies and may be of value as a systematic character. The embryo is bent through 180° in the region of the cotyledonary node, so that the radicle lies parallel to the cotyledons. If it lies adjacent to the edges of the two cotyledons it is described as *accumbent*; if along the mid-rib of one of them it is *incumbent*; in the latter case the cotyledons may be either flat or longitudinally folded around the radicle—*conduplicate*.

The great uniformity of flower-structure in the *Cruciferae* means that members of the family are readily recognized as such, but it makes the subdivision of the family difficult, and the distinctions between the tribes and genera are necessarily based on small characters. The family contains some 220 genera and 1,900 species, but of these only a very small number are of economic importance.

BRASSICA

Brassica is by far the most important genus from the agricultural point of view. Plants of this genus are annual, biennial or perennial, with rather large pinnately-lobed or lyrate leaves, flowers with erect or somewhat spreading sepals and petals of some shade of yellow. Fruit a cylindrical or somewhat angular siliqua with globular seeds in one row in each loculus. Valves one-nerved, cotyledons conduplicate. Some forty species, of which the following are of agricultural importance:

Brassica oleracea L.   Cabbages and Related Plants

Leaves all glabrous and glaucous; racemes extended, not corymbose, so that the unopened buds stand out above the open flowers. Flowers large (2·5 cm.), sepals erect, petals pale yellow (very occasionally white). Outer stamens not much shorter than inner, filaments straight. Bracts sessile, narrowed to base, not clasping. Siliqua smooth with short conical beak. Seeds greyish-brown, 2 mm. Diploid chromosomes, 18.

Wild Form. The species occurs wild as the perennial *sea cabbage*, found on the sea-coasts of southern and western Europe, including southern Britain. It bears somewhat fleshy sub-evergreen pinnately-lobed leaves in irregular rosettes on much-branched, rather woody stems. Flowers, fruits and seeds are similar to those of the cultivated forms.

Cultivated Forms. No precise information is available on the place and time at which the species was brought into cultivation, but it may be assumed that the wild form was early used for human food, and probably favourable types selected for cultivation; certainly forms of the species

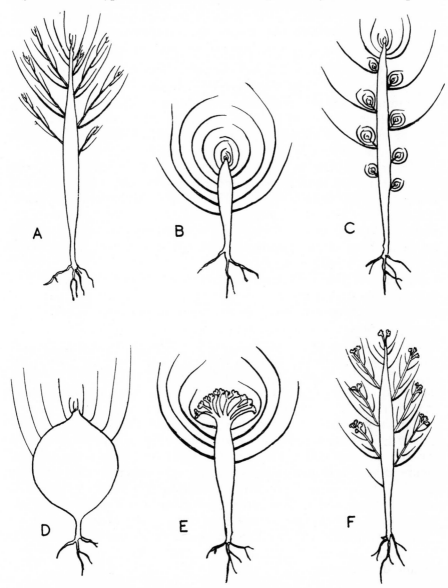

FIG. 17. *Brassica oleracea,* diagrams of cultivated forms. A, kale. B, cabbage. C, brussels sprouts. D, kohl-rabi. E, cauliflower. F, sprouting broccoli.

have been grown in the Mediterranean area for well over 2,000 years. Almost all the forms now in cultivation are biennial; they fall into a number of well-marked groups according to the particular part of the plant in which increased size and succulence have developed. The different groups represent enlargement of all parts of the plant other than root, fruit and seed. It should be emphasized that all forms are very similar in flower and fruit, and that they cannot be distinguished one from another in the seed stage.

GROUP I. KALES*

In the kales, which may be regarded as the nearest to the wild form, it is the young stems and loosely-arranged leaves which form the enlarged edible part. The larger-growing, higher-yielding type are the agricultural kales; the smaller forms of similar habit are garden vegetables. All forms are used in the vegetative stage, usually during the winter; if they are allowed to stand they produce inflorescences in the spring and die after ripening seed in the succeeding summer.

Thousand-head Kale. A tall plant (up to 1·5 m.) with rather slender woody main stem bearing on its upper part only leafy succulent branch shoots with plane or only slightly crinkled leaves. Moderately frost-hardy, and available, from a late spring sowing, for use during autumn and winter; development of inflorescences with consequent decrease in feeding value takes place in spring. *Canson kale* is a distinct selection with shorter, more branched stem.

Marrow-stem Kale (Chou Moellier). This closely resembles thousand-head kale, but the stem is much thickened throughout the greater part of its length. This thickened stem, up to 10 cm. in diameter, is edible, and shows in transverse section a very large succulent pith surrounded by a narrow ring of small vascular bundles. The stem-structure thus resembles that of kohlrabi (p. 116), from which marrow-stem kale is perhaps derived by crossing with thousand-head. The feeding value of the thickened stem (*c.* 12 per cent. protein) is less than that of the leaves (*c.* 20 per cent.).

Marrow-stem kale is rather less hardy than thousand-head, and is usually fed during autumn and early winter. Green and purple-skinned varieties exist, of which the former is much the more common. Both thousand-head and marrow-stem kale are very valuable crops providing large yields (*c.* 30 tons per acre) of high-protein fodder available for winter feeding, and as they can be grown without hand thinning, and fed off *in situ*, are cheaper to grow than the majority of 'root' crops.

Horticultural Kales. A very large range of *B. oleracea* kales are grown for human consumption. These are the garden kales, or *borecoles*. They include the following:

Cottager's kale .	.	Tall, hardy, plane-leaved.
Curly kale	.	Leaves closely crisped. Tall and dwarf forms.
Russian kale	.	Leaves thick, divided into rather narrow lobes.

* 'Kale' is a habit description, and plants referred to as kales are also found in the species *B. napus* (p. 119).

Hearting kale .	.	Upper leaves short and broad, forming a loose cabbage-like head.
Variegated kale.	.	Ornamental forms with white, purple or pink variegation of leaves.

GROUP 2. CABBAGES

In the cabbages, the main feature is the head of closely-packed leaves, which may be regarded as an immensely enlarged terminal bud in the vegetative stage. This stage is usually reached in autumn, winter or early spring, according to variety and time of sowing; if the plant is allowed to stand, the growing point enters the reproductive phase and the upper internodes lengthen, giving a long branched inflorescence in the succeeding summer. In the very dense-headed cabbage the closely-packed lower leaves may, however, interfere with the development of the flowering stems, and for seed production it is often necessary either to slash the leaves vertically to allow the inflorescence to emerge, or to cut the head and allow flowering branches to develop from the lower part of the stem.

Great variation exists in the size and shape of the head in different types of cabbage; the larger forms are used for fodder, the smaller for human consumption.

Cattle Cabbages. Large-headed cabbages, usually sown in special seed-beds and planted out at 3 ft. square; slow-maturing. The main form is the *drumhead* or *flatpoll* cabbage with broad, flattened heads, of which numerous varieties exist. Yields may be up to about 40 tons per acre, at about 11 per cent. dry matter, but the cost of growing is usually greater than for kales.

Horticultural Cabbages. Smaller forms, utilized as vegetables, include very many varieties, varying in size, in shape (mainly with round or pointed heads) and in time of maturity (from summer to late winter from spring sowings, and spring from late summer sowing). Other distinct forms are:

Red pickling cabbage .	Usually large, slow-maturing; anthocyanin pigments present in the leaves mask the chlorophyll.
Savoys . . .	Similar in habit to round-headed cabbage but with thick, puckered leaves; hardy.
Coleworts (collards) .	Hardy, loose- or non-hearting small cabbages.
Couve-tronchuda (Portugal cabbage)	Cabbage-like in habit, but leaves with much-enlarged white succulent petioles and midribs.

GROUP 3. KOHLRABI

Kohlrabi is a very distinct form in which the stem is enlarged to form a globular or fusiform 'bulb'. The mature plant at the end of the first year shows a short length of slender, woody stem surmounted by the 'bulb' which shows the widely-spaced leaf-scars on its lower part; leaves are present on the upper part of the 'bulb' and at the top is a very short leaf-bearing 'neck' which elongates only in the second year of growth.

The kohlrabi 'bulb' thus differs from that of the swede (see p. 120) in consisting of stem only. Its anatomical structure is also different, in that a transverse section shows a narrow ring of small vascular bundles with normal lignified xylem surrounding a much-enlarged pith, which forms

FIG. 18. Kohlrabi, young plant, × ¼.

the bulk of the 'bulb'. In the pith are slender branching strands of vascular tissue with some lignified cells.

Since the 'bulb', which stores well, forms the greater part of the yield, kohlrabi is comparable in its agricultural use to turnips and swedes; it may be used to replace these under conditions where its greater drought-resistance or its ability to withstand transplanting is an advantage. It is used also to some extent as a garden vegetable. Yields may be *c*. 20 tons per acre.

Little variation is shown in different stocks, but green-skinned and purple-skinned varieties exist.

The remaining groups contain comparatively low-yielding forms of horticultural value only.

GROUP 4. BRUSSELS SPROUTS

Comparable to cabbages, but here it is the axillary buds, not the terminal, which are eaten; the axillary buds forming in the vegetative stage a compact globular mass of tightly-packed leaves borne on a very short stem. The 'sprouts' are available for use in autumn and early winter only; numerous varieties exist, varying in length of stem and size of sprouts and, within the limited period, in date of maturity.

GROUP 5. CAULIFLOWER

Here the terminal bud is enlarged in the flowering stage, so that the head consists of short, much-swollen inflorescence branches bearing a compact mass of tightly appressed flower buds in an early stage of differentiation, the whole white or very pale yellow inflorescence (curd) being surrounded and protected by the upper leaves. The whole inflorescence, consisting mainly of meristematic cells, has a very high protein content.

Forms exist which come to the cutting stage at almost all periods of the year; the two main types are the *summer cauliflowers*, usually over-wintered under glass as young plants and planted out in spring for summer heading, and *winter cauliflowers* (*broccoli*) sown in spring and planted out in summer for autumn, winter or spring heading. The curd is readily damaged by frost, and winter-heading forms are therefore grown only in mild areas. *Nine-star perennial broccoli* is a distinct form occasionally grown in gardens, with a branching stem producing several heads and capable of persisting and heading for several years.

GROUP 6. SPROUTING BROCCOLI

In these the axillary buds form short, branching inflorescence-bearing shoots; it is these shoots, each terminating in a very small 'curd' comparable in stage to that of cauliflower, which are eaten. The majority of forms mature in late spring, but early forms exist. The small curd may be purple, white, or green (calabrese). Since the picked shoots do not travel well, sprouting broccoli is little grown on a commercial scale.

Brassica napus L. Swedes and Related Plants

The leaves of the mature plant of *Brassica napus* are glabrous and glaucous like those of *B. oleracea*, but the young plant shows leaves which are somewhat hairy. The flower is smaller than that of *B. oleracea*; sepals somewhat spreading, petals either bright yellow or buff; the filaments of outer stamens shorter and more curved. The inflorescence is more corymbose at the flowering stage, so that the unopened buds tend to be on the same level as the open flowers. Leaves on inflorescence with cordate partly clasping base. The siliqua is very similar to that of *B. oleracea*, but the seeds are purplish-black, without the brownish tinge seen in that species, and usually slightly larger (2·2 mm.). Diploid chromosomes, 38.

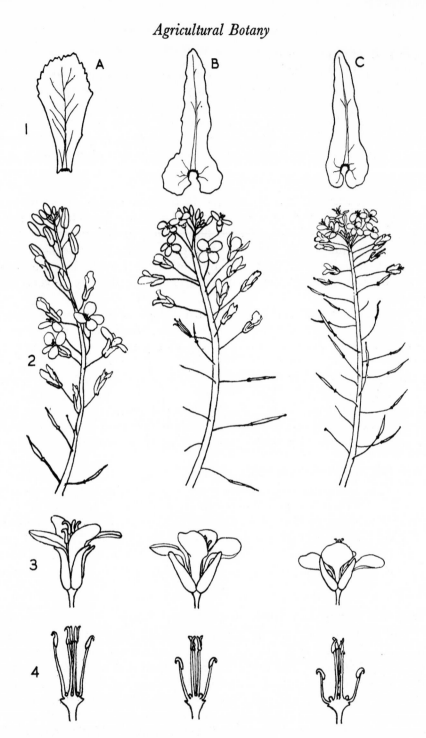

FIG. 19. 1, bract, × ⅔. 2, inflorescence, × ⅔. 3, flower, × 1¼. 4, diagram of arrangement of stamens, × 1½. A, *Brassica oleracea.* B, *B. napus.* C, *B. rapa.*

Brassica napus is not known as a wild plant, and can be regarded as a synthetic species derived from *B. oleracea* and *B. rapa* (see p. 124). The cultivated forms show considerable variation, and may be grouped as follows:

GROUP 1. RAPES (SWEDE-LIKE RAPES, COLESEED)

Rapes are forms with rather slender, usually branching stems, with rather small leaves and unthickened root. They are grown for two distinct purposes, (1) as an oil-seed crop, (2) as a leafy forage crop.

Oil Rapes. Swede-like oil rapes, rather extensively grown in various European countries for oil (rape oil, colza oil, formerly used for burning, and at the present day for lubrication and for margarine manufacture), exist in two forms, the biennial *winter oil-rape* and the very quick-growing *summer oil-rape*, sown in late spring or early summer and coming to harvest in about three to four months. Yields from the winter form are higher (*c.* 12 cwt./acre), but the spring form (*c.* 8 cwt./acre), owing to its suitability for catch-cropping, is perhaps more likely to be of value in Britain. Marketing of oil-rape seed is likely to be difficult unless a sufficient acreage is grown in Britain to justify the installation of the special processing equipment required for margarine manufacture. The seed residues after oil extraction form rape meal or rape cake, and are valuable stock food.

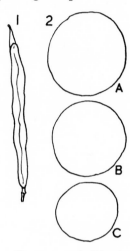

FIG. 20. 1, pod of *Brassica oleracea* × 1. 2, outlines of seeds of B, *B. oleracea*, A, *B. napus*, C, *B. rapa*, × 10.

Forage Rapes. Rape is commonly grown in Britain as a quick-growing forage crop for grazing off; the forms employed are similar to the winter oil-rapes in being biennial. Two distinct types are employed.

(1) *Early giant rape*, with a largely unbranched stem up to 2 ft. high.

(2) *Broad-leaved Essex rape*, with a shorter branching stem. The former gives a higher initial yield, but poor recovery from grazing; the latter, though a smaller and lower-yielding plant, may be grazed off two or three times before it is killed out. Forage rapes will not normally compare in yield with the *B. oleracea* kales, and are employed mainly where speed of growth is the main consideration, or where a 'nurse-crop' for grass and clover seeds is required.

GROUP 2. SWEDE-LIKE KALES

Forms of the species with rather stout stems and large leaves are referred to as kales, from their resemblance in habit to the *B. oleracea* kales. The yield per acre is much lower than from the latter, but they provide feed in late spring when few other forage crops are available. Two forms are grown for stock feed, *rape kale* (*sheep kale*), with stout, little-branched stems, and *hungry-gap kale*, with rather more slender, more branching stems, maturing later. *Asparagus kale* (*Buda kale*) is a horticultural form of which the young leafy axillary shoots are eaten in late spring.

GROUP 3. SWEDES (SWEDE TURNIPS, SWEDISH TURNIPS, RUTABAGAS (U.S.A.))

In swedes a swollen 'root' is produced in the first season, which can be fed off in autumn or lifted and stored for winter use. The swollen region forms a massive structure partly above ground; it consists of the upper

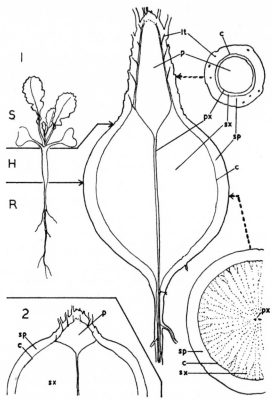

FIG. 21. 1, swede; diagram of seedling and of mature 'root' in longitudinal and transverse section. 2, turnip, longitudinal section of upper part of 'root' to show shorter 'neck'. S, stem region; H, hypocotyl; R, root. c, cambium. *lt*, leaf-trace. *p*, pith. *px*, primary xylem. *sp*, secondary phloem and cortex. *sx*, secondary xylem.

part of the true root (it must be emphasized that it is only a small part of the root system which is swollen, and that the lower part of the root forms an extensive branching system extending to a depth of 5 ft. and spreading laterally to a distance of 2-2½ ft. (Weaver)), the hypocotyl, and the lower part of the true stem. The greater part of the stem forms a conspicuous, leaf-bearing 'neck', which elongates in the second year to form a tall, branched inflorescence.

The swollen part of the plant consists mainly of parenchyma, arising not as pith (as in kohlrabi), but as unlignified secondary xylem. A transverse section through the lower part shows a slender diarch primary xylem, surrounded by a very broad ring of secondary xylem composed mainly of thin-walled parenchymatous cells, with only occasional scattered lignified cells. The secondary phloem, outside the cambium, also consists of thin-walled cells; it is surrounded on the outside by a thin layer of corky cells forming the 'skin' of the root. In the upper part of the root a small pith is present and the neck shows typical stem structure with a rather large pith surrounded by a narrow ring of xylem, here mainly lignified.

Cambial activity normally stops during the winter; in the following spring further and much more heavily lignified secondary xylem is produced, and food material stored in the parenchyma is withdrawn to provide for the rapid growth of the stem. The 'root' thus decreases greatly in palatability and feeding value if it is not used before growth recommences.

The mature 'root' of different forms of swedes varies in flesh colour, which may be yellow or white (flower colour is correlated with this, white swedes having yellow flowers, like those of rape, while the yellow-fleshed swedes have buff flowers), in 'skin' colour, and in shape. Yellow-fleshed forms are much more commonly grown than white; purple, green and bronze tops, due to the development of anthocyanin pigment or chlorophyll or both in the outer cells of that part of the 'root' which is exposed to light, are found associated with both types of flesh colour. Shapes are usually described as globe or tankard, but may be intermediate between these two. There appears to be no constant correlation between this colour and shape grouping and agricultural value, but green and dark-purple skinned forms are mainly frost-hardy, while the light-purple forms are readily damaged by frost. Within each of the more popular groups a number of named varieties exist; these differ from one another only in minor or in physiological characters. Swedes being normally cross-pollinated, variation will be found both from stock to stock of the same named variety, and from plant to plant within the same stock.

Swedes are normally grown only as a wide-drilled, thinned crop, and are therefore an expensive crop to grow. The yield, in the region of 15-20 tons, with a dry matter of 10-12 per cent., giving a dry matter yield of around 2 tons per acre, does not, at least in the south of England, compare favourably with that of mangels or fodder-beet. The main advantages of swedes are:

(1) Frost-hardiness, which enables them to be used for late autumn folding; for early folding the quicker-growing common turnips can be employed, and there appears to be little place for those swede varieties which show poor frost resistance.

(2) Their saleability, in some areas, for human consumption as a winter vegetable.

Brassica rapa L.*   Turnips and Turnip-rapes

B. rapa is distinguished from the two preceding species by its bright-green, not glaucous, densely rough-hairy lower leaves. The inflorescence forms a corymb at the flowering stage, with open flowers standing well above the unopened younger buds. Leaves on the inflorescence are usually glabrous and often somewhat glaucous, but with more deeply cordate and more markedly clasping bases than those of *B. napus*. Flowers smaller than in that species, the outer stamens with still shorter curved filaments. Siliqua closely resembling that of the two previous species; seed smaller and more variable in colour; some seeds are purple-black, but others are brighter red-purple, so that a bulk sample always has a paler and redder look than seed of *B. napus*.

Wild Form. A biennial form with a slender tap-root is found in Britain (possibly introduced) as a locally common riverside plant; an annual form is a charlock-like weed in some areas.

Cultivated Forms. The range of cultivated forms is less wide than in the swede species, and includes only oil-rapes and bulbous-rooted turnips; no forage-rape or kale forms are known.

Turnip-rapes. The two forms of turnip-like oil-rape, winter and summer, correspond to the two swede-like oil-rapes and are used in the same way; their yield is lower, but the plants are hardier and will tolerate poorer soils. They therefore replace the swede-rapes under these conditions; it does not appear likely that they would be of great value in Britain.

Turnips (Common Turnips). The turnips are biennial forms of this species, with the upper part of the root, the hypocotyl, and the lower part of the stem swollen by the development of extensive, little lignified secondary xylem. They thus correspond very closely in structure to swedes; the main difference is that the 'neck' in turnips is very short, the pith having the form of an obtuse cone, instead of a long cylinder, as in swedes. Turnips show a much greater range of 'root' shape than swedes, the length-breadth ratio varying from about 6 in extreme long forms to 0·5 in the flat forcing types; the agricultural turnips are, however, almost all globe or semi-tankard forms. Turnips are in general quicker maturing than swedes, and better adapted to poor conditions, but are of lower feeding value.

White-fleshed Turnips. Quick-maturing forms, with low dry-matter content (8 per cent.), normally sown in summer for folding off in autumn. They are not frost-hardy and do not store well, and must be used as soon as the 'root' has reached its maximum size; early-sown plants may produce elongated stems and inflorescence in the same year (bolt); when this occurs a rapid drying-out of the xylem-parenchyma takes place and the tissue becomes 'pithy' and inedible. White-fleshed turnips may be white, green, red, or bronze topped. Flowers bright yellow.

---

* The name *B. campestris* L. is also in use for this species; it appears to refer strictly to the wild form only, and has been so variously employed by different authors that its retention is likely to cause confusion.

Yellow-fleshed Turnips. (Scotch Yellows.) Yellow-fleshed turnips have a higher dry-matter content (9-10 per cent.), are slower-maturing and store better than white-fleshed turnips; they are normally sown earlier and used later, and are thus intermediate in agricultural use (but not in botanical characters) between white-fleshed turnips and swedes. The majority of varieties used are green or purple topped; the flowers are buff. The remarks made regarding named varieties in swedes (p. 121) will apply equally to turnip varieties.

Brassica nigra (L.) Koch. (**Sinapis nigra** L.). Black Mustard, Brown Mustard

An annual, with dark-green, sparsely-hairy lyrate leaves, base of inflorescence-leaves narrowed into a stalk; flowers small, bright yellow, with spreading sepals; siliquas smooth, more or less four-sided, short, with very short beak, erect on short pedicels. Seed small, brownish or reddish to black, conspicuously pitted.

Black mustard occurs as a wild plant in south England, occasionally as an arable weed. It is grown to a limited extent in east England as a crop plant for the seed, which is used in the production of table-mustard (cf. also *Sinapis alba*, p. 126). Its unpalatable nature and low vegetative yield, together with the ability of its seed to remain dormant in the soil (cf. charlock), and thus its tendency to persist as a weed in succeeding crops, limit its use and a form of *B. juncea* is preferred.

The seeds contain the glycoside sinagrin (potassium myronate), which is hydrolized by the enzyme myrosin on mixing with water to give a volatile, mustard-smelling allylthiocyanate. An oil, similar to colza oil, can be extracted from the seed, but the residues are unpalatable and may be injurious, and should not be used in oil-cake manufacture.

OTHER SPECIES

A form of *B. pekinensis* is a vegetable occasionally cultivated in gardens as 'Chinese cabbage', *pe-tsai*. It is an annual with thin, ovate, almost glabrous leaves. Flowers small, siliquas stout, spreading.

B. juncea (Chinese mustard, Indian mustard, Trowse mustard, etc.) is grown as a vegetable in climates too hot for the satisfactory employment of the other species. Annual, leaves swede-like, flowers small, bright yellow, siliquas cylindrical, spreading. Does not shed seed when ripe and can be combined. Replaces black mustard in table mustard.

Inter-relations of Brassica Species

Three primary groups of species exist with differing chromosome numbers:

$$n = 9 \quad B. \; oleracea$$
$$n = 10 \quad B. \; rapa$$
$$B. \; pekinensis$$
$$n = 8 \quad B. \; nigra$$

Crossing can take place between members of the same groups, and occasionally between members of different groups; in this last case the hybrids will be sterile. If, however, chromosome doubling takes place, then pairing of chromosomes derived from the same species can take place at meiosis, and these doubled hybrids (amphidiploids) are fully fertile and behave as a new synthetic species. In this way *B. napus* (rape and swedes) has arisen, by natural crossing (in itself very rare) between *B. oleracea* and *B. rapa*, followed by chromosome doubling. The cross apparently occurred in Central Europe some time during the seventeenth century: it has since been artificially repeated in Japan. Two other cultivated species, *B. juncea* (Indian mustard) and *B. carinata* (Abyssinian cabbage), have arisen in the same way.

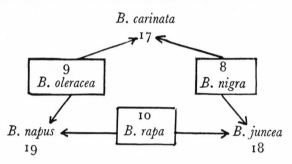

Crossing in Brassica Species

All *Brassica* species are normally cross-pollinated, and all forms belonging to one species cross readily. Thus all the different forms of *B. oleracea* will cross-pollinate one another, and the utmost care must therefore be taken when growing crops for seed, to ensure that crossing between different forms cannot take place. For instance, if a crop of cauliflower were being grown for seed, and, say, marrow-stem kale plants were allowed to flower in the same or an adjoining field; then, if flowers of both forms were open at the same time, cross-pollination would be likely, and the seed saved from the cauliflower crop would contain a proportion of worthless cauliflower-kale hybrids. Similarly, in the species *B. napus*, the different forms of swede, rape and swede-kale will all cross together.

In addition to this very ready crossing between different forms of the same species, crosses may occur between different species with sufficient frequency to make isolation desirable. *B. oleracea* can be assumed, for all practical purposes, not to cross with any other species, but the group of species with ten chromosomes in the haploid state, *B. rapa*, *B. pekinensis* and the amphidiploid 'synthetic species' *B. napus* and *B. juncea*, derived from them, will all cross together and should therefore be isolated from one another when grown for seed. Two only of these species—namely, turnip and swede (including swede-rapes and kales)—are common enough in Britain to be considered; here, crossing is more likely to be found where the swede is the seed parent than where the reverse is true.*

Isolation

For practical purposes a distance of over 1,000 yards is regarded as providing satisfactory isolation between two cross-pollinating crops, and it is normally considered necessary, therefore, that seed crops of different

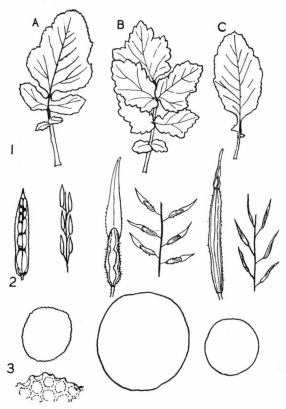

Fig. 22. 1, leaf, ×¼. 2, siliqua, ×1, and diagram of fruiting branch. 3, outline of seed, ×10, of A, black mustard; B, white mustard; C, charlock. A small part of the surface of black mustard seed is also figured, ×50.

forms of one species, or of different varieties within one form, should be separated by at least this distance. This figure of 1,000 yards is, however, a purely arbitrary one; the likelihood of cross-pollination falls off very rapidly in the first 100 yards, but the further decrease with distance is very slow, and while 1,000 yards is well beyond the distance at which any bulk crossing will take place, it is still not sufficient to exclude entirely

* The swede-turnip hybrids are normally sterile, but again doubling of chromosomes can give fertility, and a fertile hybrid behaving as a new synthetic species and named *B. napo-campestris* with a haploid chromosome number of 29 (i.e. 2 rapa sets+1 oleracea set) has been obtained artificially. The sterile swede-turnip hybrids sometimes show swellings on the roots which have been described as 'hybridization nodules'.

occasional cross-pollination by chance far-flying insects or even by the small but appreciable amount of wind-borne pollen. Such chance cross-pollination will, however, result in only a negligible proportion of hybrids in the seed, and from a practical point of view can be disregarded.

NOMENCLATURE OF GROUPS WITHIN BRASSICA SPECIES

Within the species of *Brassica*, many of the groups distinguished on growth-habit and agricultural or horticultural use have been given Latin names as botanical varieties, forms (formae) or sub-species, or even named as separate species. For practical purposes there appears to be little advantage in using such names for forms or groups of forms of agricultural origin; the following table is given for reference:

Species	Variety, forma or sub-species	Equivalent agricultural group
B. oleracea	sylvestris	(Wild cabbage)
	acephala (sabellica)	Kales
	capitata	Cabbages
	bullata (subauda)	Savoys
	gemmifera	Brussels sprouts
	botrytis	Cauliflowers
	italica	Sprouting broccolis
	caulorapa (gongylodes)	Kohlrabi
B. napus.	annua	Summer swede-rapes
	oleifera	Winter swede-rapes
	rapifera	Swedes
	including napobrassica	White-fleshed swedes
	and rutabaga	Yellow-fleshed swedes
B. rapa .	sylvestris (campestris)	(Wild turnip)
	annua	Summer turnip-rape
	oleifera	Winter turnip-rape
	rapifera (rapa)	Common turnips

SINAPIS

The genus *Sinapis* differs from *Brassica* in having the sepals always spreading and the valves of the fruit 3-5-nerved, not 1-nerved; the distinction is a small one and the species are often included in *Brassica*; they do not, however, cross with any of the true *Brassica* species.

Sinapis alba L. (Brassica alba (L.) Rabenhorst). White Mustard

White mustard is an erect annual, with pinnately-divided, stalked, hairy leaves. The flowers are similar in size to those of the swede; the fruit is a stiffly hairy siliqua with strongly 3-nerved valves and a stout, flattened, sword-like beak as long as the valves. The fruits are carried on long, spreading pedicels and stand out almost horizontally. Seed pale yellow, large (2·5 mm.). $n=12$. Not native; introduced probably from Mediterranean region.

White mustard (so called from the colour of the seed) is grown for its seed, used in the production of table-mustard in the same way as *B. nigra*, black mustard. The flavouring compound is, however, different, being pungent-tasting but not volatile, and produced by the action of myrosin on a different glycoside sinalbin.

White mustard makes a greater amount of vegetative growth than black mustard, and is more palatable; the seeds do not remain dormant in the soil. It can therefore be used, not only for seed production, but also as a very rapidly-growing catch-crop, either for grazing off in the same way as rape (it must be grazed early, as it rapidly becomes unpalatable when allowed to fruit) or for ploughing in as green manure. The young seedlings are also used in the expanded-cotyledon stage as salad (mustard and cress).*

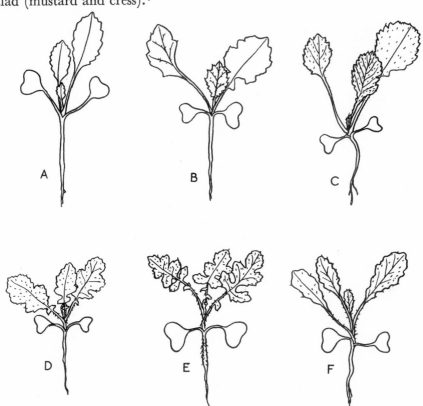

Fig. 23. Diagrams of seedlings of Cruciferae, × ½. A, *Brassica oleracea.* B, *B. napus.* C, *B. rapa.* D, *B. nigra.* E, *Sinapis alba.* F, *S. arvensis.*

Sinapis arvensis L. (Brassica sinapis Vis.; B. sinapistrum Boiss.). Charlock

Charlock is a weed, differing from white mustard in its rounded, shallowly-lyrate lobed or sinuate leaves, the upper ones sessile; the

* Cress is the white-flowered annual, *Lepidium sativum.* Rape seed is sometimes substituted for mustard seed.

siliquas with a shorter conical not flattened beak, usually hairy, and less stiffly spreading when mature. Seed small, dark red-brown, closely resembling turnip seed, but with more pungent taste. For the importance of charlock as a weed, see Chapter XIX.

KEYS FOR IDENTIFICATION OF BRASSICA AND SINAPIS SPECIES

LEAVES: Leaves glaucous 1
Leaves bright or dark green, hairy 2

1 { Leaves all glabrous . . . . . *B. oleracea*
{ Leaves with few hairs on nerves . . . *B. napus*

2 { Upper leaves stalked 3
{ Upper leaves sessile 4

3 { Lower leaves lyrate . . . . . *B. nigra*
{ Lower leaves pinnate, terminal lobe not large . *S. alba*

4 { Lower leaves deeply lobed, upper clasping . *B. rapa*
{ Lower leaves shallowly lobed, upper not clasping *S. arvensis*

FRUIT: Siliquas smooth, valves 1-nerved 1
Siliquas rough, valves 3-nerved 2

1 { Siliquas long, cylindrical, spreading *B. oleracea, napus, rapa*
{ Siliquas short, four-sided, erect . . . *B. nigra*

2 { Beak long, flattened . . . . . *S. alba*
{ Beak short, conical . . . . . *S. arvensis*

SEED: Testa pale, yellowish . . . . . . *S. alba*
Testa dark 1

1 { Testa brownish-grey . . . . . *B. oleracea*
{ Testa purple-black . . . . . *B. napus*
{ Testa red-brown 2

2 { Testa pitted . . . . . . *B. nigra*
{ Testa not pitted 3

3 { Taste acrid, biting . . . . . *S. arvensis*
{ Taste mild . . . . . . *B. rapa*

OTHER CRUCIFEROUS CROP-PLANTS

Raphanus sativus L., fodder radish, has been tried as a quick growing forage crop comparable to rape or white mustard. Horticulturally, radishes are grown for their swollen turnip-like 'roots'. Flowers white or lilac, fruits long, inflated, breaking up irregularly. Seeds large, cotyledons conduplicate. (**R. raphanistrum** L., wild radish, has the fruit a lomentum; see p. 411.)

Crambe maritima L., seakale, is a perennial, the blanched shoots of which are used as a vegetable. Fruit indehiscent, one-seeded, cotyledons conduplicate.

Lepidium sativum L., cress, is a white-flowered annual, with fruit a two-seeded silicula; cotyledons three-lobed, radicle incumbent. Used mainly in seedling stage as 'mustard and cress'. **Isatis tinctoria** L., woad, a biennial with large panicles of small yellow flowers; was formerly much cultivated for dye-production. Fruits one-seeded, winged, indehiscent; radicle incumbent.

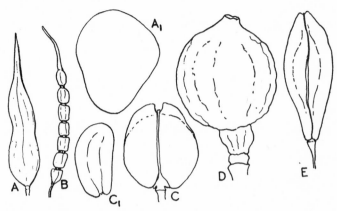

Fig. 24. Seeds and fruits of various Cruciferae. A, pod, × 1, and A₁, seed, × 7, of cultivated radish. B, wild radish pod, × 1. C, silicula, × 4, and C₁, seed, × 7, of cress. D, indehiscent fruit of seakale, × 4. E, indehiscent fruit of woad, × 2.

Armoracia rusticana Gaertn., horse-radish, is a perennial grown for its strongly-flavoured tap-roots. Flowers white, fruit a few-seeded silicula, radicle accumbent; seed not ripened in Britain. **Nasturtium officinale** R. Br., water-cress, is an aquatic perennial with white flowers and a slender siliqua with seeds in two rows in each cell; diploid. The brown winter variety is a sterile triploid derived from a cross between this and the tetraploid **N. microphyllum** (Boenn.) Rchb., with seeds in a single row.

Chapter X

CHENOPODIACEAE AND LINACEAE

CHENOPODIACEAE

General Importance. The *Chenopodiaceae* is a small family containing only one species of agricultural importance; this is *Beta vulgaris,* which includes sugar- and fodder-beets and mangels. Spinach and a few other plants are grown as garden vegetables. Several members of the family are common arable weeds (p. 419); these include species of *Chenopodium,* from which the family name is derived.

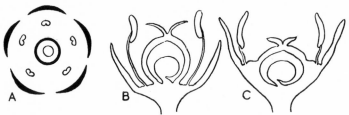

FIG. 25. Chenopodiaceae. A, floral diagram. B, diagram of vertical section of typical flower. C, of *Beta.*

Botanical Characters. Herbs and small shrubs, often halophytic. Leaves simple, often with 'mealy' covering of short, swollen hairs, alternate, exstipulate. Flowers small, inconspicuous, wind-pollinated, often in dense clusters. Perianth usually of five segments, stamens equal in number or fewer, placed opposite the perianth segments. Ovary of two or three united carpels, superior except in *Beta,* unilocular with a single basal curved ovule. Seed with embryo curved around the starchy food reserve tissue, which is mainly perisperm (the remains of the nucellus), not true endosperm.

Beta vulgaris L.   Beet

The wild forms of beet are sea-coast plants of Europe and Asia, very variable in habit and duration and perhaps referable to a number of different species. The cultivated forms, probably derived from eastern Mediterranean types, are biennials, grown either for their fleshy leaves, or more commonly for the swollen 'root'.

Life-history

Seedling. Germination is epigeal; the two cotyledons are almost sessile and lanceolate, with blunt tips. The hypocotyl is elongated and distinctly stouter than the root; the epicotyl remains short and a rosette of glabrous dark-green leaves develops. These leaves are ovate, tapering to a long, rather broad petiole.

First-year Plant. The primary root is diarch, and two vertical lines of lateral roots are produced. Secondary thickening commences in the usual way, by the development of a cambium between the primary xylem and primary phloem, but after this it proceeds in an unusual manner. Instead of the one cambium continuing to grow and produce more and more secondary tissue, a second cambium arises in the pericycle. The xylem produced by this cambium forms a ring outside the phloem from the

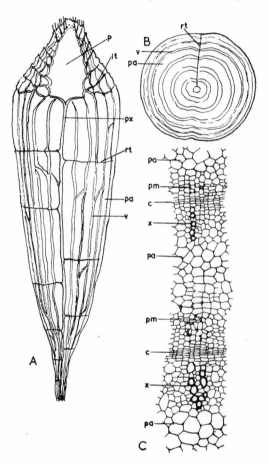

Fig. 26. A, diagram of longitudinal section of 'root' of a beet (long shape). B, transverse section. C, part of transverse section at higher magnification, to show arrangement of cells. *c*, cambium. *lt*, leaf-trace. *p*, pith. *pa*, parenchma. *pm*, phloem. *px*, primary xylem, closely surrounded by secondary xylem formed by first cambium. *rt*, root-trace. *v*, vascular ring. *x*, xylem.

first cambium, and separated from it by a ring of parenchyma. A third cambium arises outside the second, and then a fourth, until some eight or nine cambial rings have developed, each producing xylem internally and phloem externally. The mature root thus shows in transverse section a series of concentric rings of vascular tissue, separated by parenchyma.

In the wild beets, and in the forms cultivated for their leaves, the concentric zones are comparatively narrow, and the xylem is heavily lignified, so that a rather woody root is produced, 2 or 3 cm. in diameter. In mangels and other cultivated forms grown for their 'roots', the zones are very broad, and the xylem consists mainly of parenchymatous cells, so that a massive succulent 'root' is produced. The thickening involves not only the true root, but also the hypocotyl (distinguishable by the absence of lateral roots), and the base of the true stem, where the concentric rings of vascular tissue link up with each other and with the leaf-traces to form a complicated network. The stem in the cultivated forms remains very short during the first year (unless bolting occurs) and forms the 'crown' of the plant; from it arise the numerous closely-crowded large leaves.

Second Year Plant. The plants become dormant in late autumn, and the 'root' forms are usually lifted then. They are not resistant to hard frost, and mangels in particular may be severely damaged if left in the ground over winter. If the 'roots' survive, or if they are lifted and replanted, growth starts again in spring; this new growth is largely elongation of the stem at the expense of the food material stored in the previous year. A stout, ridged stem grows to a height of five or six feet, and bears numerous leaves, the lower ones large and stalked, the upper smaller and sessile. Branches in the axils of the leaves also grow out, and the upper parts of these and of the main stem form long, lax, spike-like inflorescences.

FIG. 27. Second-year mangel plant, in fruiting stage, $\times \frac{1}{4}$. Leaves omitted; fruit-clusters shown on some branches only.

Flowers. The flowers are borne in small sessile clusters (glomerules) in the axils of bracts. Each flower has a perianth of five greenish-yellow segments, and five stamens arranged opposite the perianth segments. The ovary is almost completely inferior and bears usually three short styles. Pollination is largely by wind, and cross-pollination is usual. The perianth does not wither and drop off as the single seed develops in the ovary, but persists and becomes almost woody in texture. Not only is the seed not set free, but all the enlarged and hardened flowers of each cluster remain fused together.

'*Seed.*' The 'seeds' obtained on threshing are thus complex structures, each containing from one to four or more true seeds (according to the number of flowers in the cluster) embedded in a mass of hardened receptacle and perianth tissue. When these 'seeds' or clusters (glomerules) are sown the true seeds germinate *in situ*, so that each cluster may give rise to several seedlings. Germination may be slow, as water penetrates rather slowly through the hard tissue of the cluster. It should be noted that,

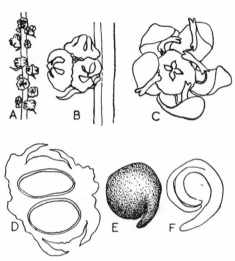

FIG. 28. Beet. A, part of fruiting branch, × ¼. B, single cluster, × 2½. C, individual flower, × 7. D, diagram of section through mature cluster, × 5. E, true seed, entire, and F, embryo dissected out, × 7.

in spite of the comparatively large size of the cluster (3-8 mm.), the true seed inside is small (1·5-2·5 mm.), and shallow drilling is therefore necessary. The fact that each cluster may give rise to several seedlings is a disadvantage when growing a crop, since however precisely the clusters are placed by the drill, the seedlings will be irregularly spaced. Two or more seedlings derived from the same cluster will be closely crowded together, and hand-singling is therefore essential. Various methods of overcoming this difficulty have been tried. One of these is to breed plants giving '*monogerm seed*'—that is, plants which have their flowers borne singly and not in clusters. Beet of this type have been selected, but the seed-yield is low, and it has so far not been found possible to combine the monogerm habit with all the other characters required; the method is therefore not at present in common use. The alternative is some form of mechanical treatment of the usual multi-germ clusters. No method of releasing the true seeds from the clusters has been devised, and the treatments adopted have been segmenting and rubbing. '*Segmented seed*' is produced by chopping the clusters into smaller pieces, '*rubbed seed*' by rubbing them against an abrasive wheel. In both cases the treated 'seed' is then graded by sieving so as to retain only those fragments likely to contain a single true seed. The rubbing method is the more popular in Britain, and the rubbed seed is usually graded from $\frac{7}{64}$ to $\frac{11}{64}$ in. (2·8-4·4 mm.).

Germination of beet clusters is expressed as a percentage of the clusters (or piece of cluster, in the case of rubbed seed) which produce at least one seedling. Additional seedlings from the same cluster are of no value, and for this purpose can be ignored. Germination of clusters is rarely

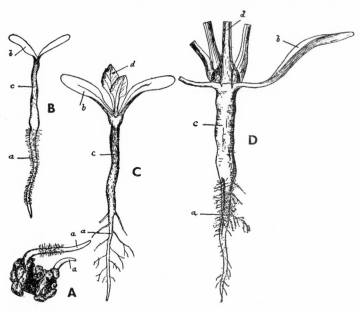

Fig. 29. Mangel. A, germinating cluster; B, C, D, stages in the development of a single seedling. *a*, root; *b*, cotyledon; *c*, hypocotyl; *d*, first foliage leaves. From Percival, *Agricultural Botany*.

above 85 per cent. Untreated 'seed' is extremely variable in weight, but has usually 15-20,000 clusters per pound; rubbed and graded 'seed' about 30,000 'seeds'.

Range of Types. The forms within the species can be divided into the wild sea beet (sub-sp. *maritima* (L.) Thell, originally described as a separate species, *B. maritima* L.), and the cultivated forms (sub-sp. *vulgaris*), which are again divisible into the forms grown for their leaves and those grown for their roots.

Wild Sea Beet. Usually perennial, low-growing, with branching prostrate stems arising from a woody root, and rather small angular leaves. Inflorescences like those of cultivated forms, but usually shorter, more or less prostrate, and with smaller flower clusters. A common seashore plant in Britain, extending in various forms to the shores of most of Europe and West Asia.

*Leaf Beets.** Biennials, grown for their large, succulent leaves; roots only slightly swollen, woody. Probably the first forms to be cultivated,

* Originally described as a separate species, *B. cicla* L., and sometimes referred to as *B. vulgaris* var. *cicla*.

but now relatively unimportant garden vegetables, not grown on a field scale. Two types are used: *Spinach Beet,* sometimes called *Perpetual Spinach,* in which the lamina only is used, as a substitute for the true spinach (*Spinacia,* see below, p. 140), and *Seakale Beet* or *Swiss Chard,* in which the petiole and midrib, which are white, thick and fleshy and up to 8 or 9 cm. wide, are used in the same way as the true seakale (*Crambe,* in *Cruciferae,* see p. 128). Forms with variously-shaped, brightly-coloured leaves also exist, which are used purely as orna-mental plants for bedding-out.

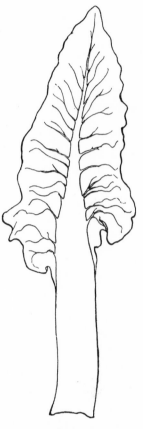

*Beets Grown for Their Swollen 'Roots'.** A large and variable group of biennials of considerable importance, in which specialized forms have been selected for use for three distinct purposes: (1) for human consumption—beetroot; (2) for the extraction of sugar—sugar-beet; (3) for stock-feeding—mangels and fodder-beet.

(1) *Beetroot* is the name used for the forms grown as root-vegetables for human consump-tion. They produce succulent 'roots' with very little hard, lignified tissue. In the past, various different colour forms have been used, but at present only deep red forms are grown. In these, the cell sap contains anthocyanin pigments, and selection is aimed at producing 'roots' of even, very dark red colour, with as little difference as possible between the rings of vascular tissue and the intervening parenchyma, both in colour and texture. In many varieties the red coloration extends to the leaves and also to the second-year stem. Half or more of the swollen 'root' usually stands above ground-level; long and intermediate varieties are grown for main crops for winter use, globe and flat varieties for earlier production and forcing.

FIG. 30. Seakale beet, single leaf, × ¼.

(2) *Sugar-beet* is a specialized type grown for processing in factories for the extraction of sugar. It was developed at the end of the eighteenth century in Europe from the white Silesian beet, which was then grown for fodder, and which was found to be the most suitable source of sugar as an alternative to the tropical sugar-cane (*Saccharum,* in the *Gramineae,* see p. 292). The strategic blockade of the Continental ports during the Napoleonic Wars cut off the supply of cane sugar from the West Indies, and thus favoured the development of an alternative source of sugar. The original forms contained only about 4 per cent. of sugar; careful selection, followed more recently by intensive breeding work (for methods,

* The name *B. vulgaris* var. *rapacea* has been used to include some or all members of this group.

see Chapter V), has resulted in the raising of this figure to a maximum of approximately 20 per cent. This, combined with a steady improvement in methods of sugar extraction, has resulted in sugar-beet becoming one of the outstanding arable crops of most temperate regions. In Britain, where it is primarily suited mainly to the warmer areas of the south and east, its cultivation dates from 1912.

Sugar-beet plants have white 'roots' of conical shape, growing deep in the soil with only the crown exposed. They usually show two shallow, vertical grooves (the so-called 'sugar-grooves') in which the two lines of lateral roots emerge. They tend often to be somewhat irregular in shape. Any pronounced irregularity or branching of the root is undesirable, as it results in greater adherence of soil to the root when lifted, and may make processing less efficient. The 'roots' are small compared with mangels, usually weighing from 1 to 2 lb. Larger roots tend to have a lower sugar content. The highest sugar concentration is associated with the phloem of the vascular rings and, other things being equal, 'roots' with numerous narrow rings show the highest sugar content.

The lower percentage sugar content of large roots means that the number of plants per acre has an important effect on the total yield of sugar. Plants spaced at 18 in. by 9 in., giving over 38,000 per acre, have been found to give the highest yield of sugar, but such close spacing makes cultivation expensive and difficult, and the usual recommendation is that a figure of from 25,000 to 30,000 should be aimed at. If the number of plants per acre is allowed to fall much below this, the increase in size of individual roots fails to compensate for the reduced number, and the root yield per acre also falls. Sugar-beet is usually drilled in rows from 18 to 22 in. apart, using about 15 lb. of whole clusters per acre, or about 9 lb. of 'rubbed seed'. It is essential that a good seed-bed should be provided, as otherwise germination and establishment may be low and irregular.

The time of sowing also has a marked effect on yield. In general, the earlier the 'seed' is sown the higher is the yield, providing that 'bolting' does not take place. The flowering of beet is influenced both by temperature and day length (cf. vernalization of cereals, p. 248). Plants change from the vegetative to the flowering condition when the day becomes sufficiently long (the necessary length varies in different strains), providing that the plant has passed through a preliminary period of exposure to low temperatures. With normal sowings this cold period is not experienced until the following winter, and the plant flowers during the second year. If, however, seed is sown very early, and cold weather follows sowing, the plant behaves as an annual, flowering during the first year—that is, 'bolting'. The useful yield of plants which bolt early in the season may be only half that of normal plants, and a high percentage of bolters therefore materially reduces the sugar yield per acre. Sowing before mid-March is likely to give, in most years, a high proportion of bolters, while late-sown crops are usually equally unsatisfactory since, although no bolting takes place, the yield is reduced by the shorter growing season.

Sugar-beet Varieties

A considerable number of varieties (often referred to as strains) of sugar-beet exist, all rather similar in appearance and differing mainly in physiological characters. The comparatively recent introduction of sugar-beet-growing into Britain has meant that Continental varieties, largely of German origin, have been commonly grown; more recently varieties bred in this country have come into use. It is not possible to combine the highest sugar percentage with the highest yield of roots per acre, and varieties may be grouped into three types on the basis of these two characters, yield and sugar percentage. These are *Type E* (from German *Ertrag*, yield) with high yield at rather low sugar percentage (say, 13 tons per acre at 16 per cent.); *Type N* (*Normal*), intermediate in both characters (say, 12 tons at 17 per cent.); and *Type Z* (*Zucker*, sugar), with a lower yield of higher sugar percentage (say, 11 tons at 18 per cent.). Developments in the breeding and cultivation of beet have tended to blur these distinctions, and varieties listed as E and N may be very similar. Almost all varieties now used are capable of producing yields of about 16 tons at between 17 per cent. and 18 per cent. sugar. Varieties show marked differences in resistance to bolting; thus Camkilt has about 1 per cent. bolters when sown at the normal time, the worst varieties about 7 per cent. Very early sowing would double these figures.

Varieties also differ in size of tops, i.e. of the crown and attached leaves which are cut off at harvest. Yield of tops varies from about 12 to 15 tons per acre. These tops, which have a nutrient value approaching that of kale, may be fed to stock after wilting, or as silage, and are a valuable by-product of the sugar-beet crop.

The yield of dry matter per plant is not so much greater in the large-topped forms as might be expected, since the small-topped forms have a higher net assimilation rate (amount of dry matter produced per unit leaf area); this partially compensates for the difference in leaf area.

Numerous triploid varieties have been developed; in sugar beet triploids tend to outyield both diploids and tetraploids. The available triploids give high yields, but do not necessarily surpass the best diploid varieties such as Klein E. They are largely sterile, so that seed must be produced by the interplanting of diploid and tetraploid parent stocks.

(3) *Mangels and fodder-beet.* These are the various forms of beet with swollen 'root' grown for stock-feeding. They might thus logically all be described as fodder-beet, but the very distinct large-rooted forms known as mangels have a much longer history in Britain than the others. They have thus retained their name, while 'fodder-beet' is used only for the more recently developed smaller-rooted types intermediate in character between mangels and sugar-beet.

*Mangels.** The typical mangel is a beet with a very large 'root', of which a high proportion is derived from the hypocotyl, and which stands high out of the ground, with only about one-third of the 'root' below ground level. It is therefore easily lifted, but is more readily damaged by frost than sugar-beet, and must be lifted and clamped early.

In Britain the breeding of mangels has in the past been directed mainly towards the production of large 'roots' (averaging perhaps 4 to 7 lb. each), easily lifted and of regular shape, with small tops. The 'root' shape is usually globe or tankard, less commonly long or intermediate; the skin colour is red, orange or yellow, while the 'flesh' often shows concentric rings of colour, the vascular rings being white and the intervening parenchyma of the same colour as the skin. Agricultural varieties

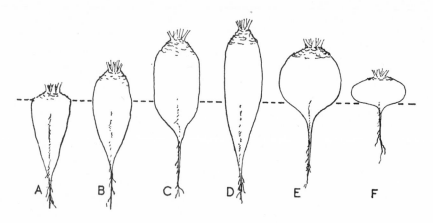

FIG. 31. Diagrams of shapes of mature 'root' in various beet forms. A, conical (sugar-beet). B, intermediate (most fodder-beets). C, tankard. D, long. E, globe (mangels and some red beet). F, flat (red beet only).

are usually named according to their shape and colour, e.g. Long Red, Golden Tankard, etc.

In Denmark and some other Continental countries mangels have been developed along rather different lines; selection has been based largely on dry-matter content of the 'roots', rather than on size and ease of lifting. The resulting high-dry-matter mangels are mainly of intermediate shape, with about half the 'root' above ground. The size of 'root' and the root yield per acre is smaller than with English mangels, but this is more than compensated for by the lower percentage of water in the 'roots'; the yield of dry matter per acre is therefore greater. The tops, which in Denmark are used for fodder, are larger than those of the English mangels, in which the leaves have usually been discarded.

* Also written 'mangolds'. *Mangold* is a German name of uncertain derivation for leaf-beet or chard; the forms with swollen 'root' appear to have been named from this *Mangold-wurzel* (i.e. chard root), and this later misinterpreted as *Mangel-wurzel* (i.e. scarcity root). The spelling 'mangel' is to be preferred, in spite of its derivation, since it avoids the possibility of confusion with the German name for leaf-beet.

Both types of mangel are grown primarily for storing and feeding to cattle in late winter and spring; they cannot be folded off, as the 'roots' are likely to cause digestive disturbances in autumn, and they can only be safely fed after a period of 'ripening' in store.

Fodder-beet. A considerable number of types of beet exist intermediate in characters between mangels and sugar-beet. These were developed particularly in Denmark and Holland and have been used in those countries since about 1930; they were not introduced into Britain until after 1940. They show a continuous range of variation from forms which are essentially special selections of sugar-beet grown for stock-feeding to ones which differ little in appearance from high-dry-matter mangels. All have large tops, and the 'roots' are suitable for feeding from autumn onwards, without the period of after-ripening necessary for mangels.

Since they present a continuous range of types, classification of fodder-beet varieties is difficult. Dry-matter content is not always closely correlated with appearance and depth in the ground, but for practical purposes the fodder-beets may be rather arbitrarily divided into two groups:

Fodder sugar-beet with dry-matter contents from 18 to 23 per cent. and 'roots' usually resembling sugar-beet, and *sugar-mangels* with 15 to 19 per cent. dry matter and 'roots' usually half to one-third exposed, often coloured like those of mangels. In general, the fodder-sugar-beet forms give a lower total yield per acre, but this is more than offset by their higher percentage of dry matter, so that the yield of dry matter per acre exceeds that of the other forms. The various types of fodder-beets and mangels may be compared as follows:

	Per cent. dry matter	Expected 'root' yield under good conditions, tons per acre	Proportion of 'root' exposed	Examples
Fodder-beet—				
Fodder-sugar-beet . .	18–23	20	$\frac{1}{4}$–$\frac{1}{3}$	Hunsballe, Pajbjerg Rex
Sugar-mangels. . .	15–18	25	$\frac{1}{3}$–$\frac{1}{2}$	Red Otofte, Yellow Danoe
Mangels—				
Danish type . . .	13–15	30	$\frac{1}{2}$	Barres Otofte, Stryno
English type . . .	8–13	40	$\frac{2}{3}$	Golden Tankard, Orange Globe

The highest yields of dry matter per acre (4 tons or more) are given by varieties of the fodder-sugar-beet type, and where maximum production per acre is required, this type of 'root' has great advantages. Its low water content means that it is sufficiently concentrated to be fed in quantity to pigs, which are not able to utilize more bulky 'roots'; and also means that the cost of handling is lower per unit of dry matter. On the other hand, the hard texture of the 'roots' makes this type of beet less suitable for feeding to cattle, and the deep-seated 'roots' make harvesting expensive.

Fodder beets are mainly important as alternatives to cereals; they were popular in the post-war years, but quickly went out of common use as grain became freely available.

For the feeding of cattle, the choice is likely to lie largely between the sugar-mangel and the high-dry-matter Danish-type mangels, depending on the extent to which the higher dry-matter production per acre of the former is offset by the greater cost of lifting.

Seed Production in Beets

All forms of the species *Beta vulgaris* are mainly cross-pollinated, and will all inter-cross freely. It is therefore essential that crops of different forms being grown for seed should be well separated. In order to ensure this, a system of zoning (see Chapter VI) has been developed in the seed-growing areas.

The cultivated forms, being biennials, usually flower in the second year, but in most cases plants grown in the normal way cannot be safely over-wintered in the field. Special methods of growing beet for seed production are therefore necessary. In areas where the winter is mild enough to allow over-wintering (but cold enough to provide the necessary stimulus for inflorescence production) seed is sown thickly in autumn and the small plants allowed to remain in position over winter, flowering in the following summer. In Britain seed is usually sown in summer and the resulting small 'roots' (stecklings) lifted in autumn, clamped, and replanted in the following spring, when they produce inflorescences and flower in summer. This method has the advantage that stecklings can be grown in areas free from other beet crops, and later transferred to the seed-growing areas for replanting. In this way the danger of infection with the disease Virus Yellows (see Chapter XXVIII) is reduced.

Spinacia oleracea L.   Spinach

An annual, grown as a vegetable for its thick, succulent leaves. The broad, dark-green, often crinkled leaves form a rosette in the young

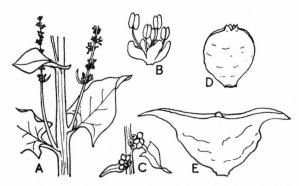

Fig. 32. Spinach. A, part of male plant in flowering stage, × ¼. B, single male flower, × 4. C, clusters of female flowers, × ½. D, E, mature 'seed' of round and prickly seeded forms, both × 4.

plant; later an erect leafy stem is produced, up to 2 ft. high. The flowers are borne in clusters in the axils of the upper leaves; they differ from

beet in being unisexual, the male flowers with four to five perianth segments, and four to five stamens, the female with a two- to four-toothed
perianth surrounding a single, one-seeded ovary with four to five short
styles. Spinach is usually dioecious, but occasional monoecious plants
occur. The perianth of the female flower hardens and persists around
the indehiscent fruit, and the 'seed' thus has approximately the same
structure as a monogerm beet 'seed'. The 'seed' is smooth in *round* or
summer spinach, or rough owing to the projecting calyx-teeth in *prickly* or
winter spinach. The latter is more hardy and can be used for autumn
sowings to stand over winter, but is more liable to 'bolt' in hot weather.
Even in summer spinach the period during which the plant remains in
the usable vegetative condition is short, and frequent successional sowings are necessary.

Chenopodium bonus-henricus L., Mercury or Good King Henry,
a low-growing perennial, and **Atriplex hortensis** L., Garden Orache,
a tall annual with pale green (or in one variety, deep-red) leaves, are
two other members of the family occasionally grown, and used in the
same way as spinach. **Chenopodium quinoa** Willd. is an annual
grown in S. America for its abundant seeds, used in the same way as
cereals.

Tetragonia expansa Murr., New Zealand Spinach, belongs to a
distinct but related family, the *Aizoaceae*. It is an annual with thick,

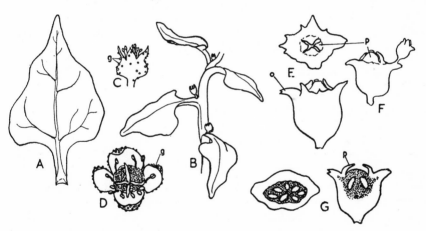

FIG. 33. New Zealand spinach, *Tetragonia expansa* A, leaf, × ½. B, flowering shoot, × ½.
C, immature flower, × 1½. D, open flower, × 3½. E, top and side views of mature indehiscent fruit. F, young fruit with flower borne on outgrowth of receptacle. G, transverse
and longitudinal sections of immature fruit, × 1½. *g*, glandular hairs. *o*, outgrowth of
receptacle. *p*, perianth.

fleshy, triangular, alternate leaves, and small greenish-yellow axillary
flowers, with four-partite perianth, numerous stamens and semi-inferior
ovary. Several ovules are present; the receptacle develops pointed, horn-
like projections and hardens around the mature ovary to give a large
(1 cm.) almost woody, irregularly-shaped 'seed', which absorbs water

very slowly. Discovered in New Zealand in 1770, coming into use in Britain about 1820, and thus one of the very few comparatively recently introduced species used as a vegetable. More tolerant of heat and drought than spinach, and occasionally replacing it for summer use.

LINACEAE

General Importance. The *Linaceae* includes only one species of agricultural importance. This is *Linum usitatissimum*, grown in two forms: one, linseed, for the oily seed; the other, flax, for its stem fibres, from which linen is manufactured. Neither form is now commonly grown in Britain.

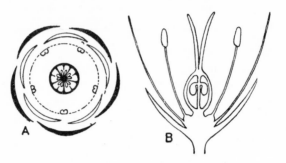

FIG. 34. Linaceae. A, floral diagram. B, vertical section of flower.

Botanical Characters. A small family, mainly herbaceous, with alternate simple leaves. Inflorescence usually cymose, flowers conspicuous, insect-pollinated. Sepals and petals five, free. Stamens five, sometimes with five staminodes. Gynaecium of five carpels, joined but with free styles; fruit usually a septicidal capsule. Placentation axile, ovules anatropous. Seeds with scanty endosperm, cotyledons with oil and protein food-reserves.

Linum usitatissimum L.   Linseed and Flax

Description. An annual, with erect, wiry stems, bearing numerous lanceolate entire leaves, glabrous and greyish-green, 3-4 cm. long. Stems (under closely spaced conditions of field crop) little branched, except near apex, where a series of short branches bear terminal flowers 2-2·5 cm. in diameter. The sepals are small and lanceolate, the petals wedge-shaped, crumpled in bud, bright blue, or in some forms white. Stamens five, with filaments broadened at base. Ovary ovoid, with five erect styles, and originally five-chambered, with two ovules in each loculus, but becoming almost completely divided into ten chambers by *false septa* growing in from the mid-rib of each carpel, and almost meeting the placenta between the ovules. Nectar is secreted by the disc at the base of the filaments, but under temperate conditions the plant is almost entirely self-pollinated. The ovary enlarges after fertilization to form a spherical or somewhat flattened capsule. In the majority of cultivated varieties the capsule is almost completely indehiscent, and the seeds are set free only on threshing, or by irregular shattering.

The seeds are oval, flattened, 4-6 mm. (40,000-90,000 per pound), pale to dark brown, distinctly shiny. The outer epidermis of the testa consists of large cells, which readily absorb water and swell up to form a structureless mucilage. The seeds contain 35-40 per cent. oil and about 20 per cent. protein, and form a very valuable animal food. They can be fed complete, or as linseed cake after extraction of the bulk of the oil. The extracted linseed oil is a valuable drying oil, used in the manufacture of paints, linoleum, etc., and also as human food. Care must be taken in the feeding of unextracted linseed owing to the presence of a cyanogenetic glycoside. If the seed is allowed to soak in cold water, enzyme action may result in the breakdown of this glycoside, with the production of the poisonous compound hydrogen cyanide (prussic acid); boiling water should therefore be used in the preparation of linseed gruel for calves, etc.

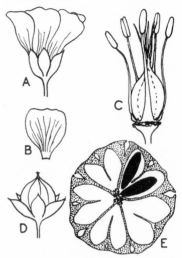

Germination is epigeal; the cotyledons elongate and become blunt-lanceolate in shape. The stem elongates rapidly and bears alternately-arranged leaves, the lowest very close to the cotyledons.

Fig. 35. Linseed. A, flower. B, petal, $\times 1\frac{1}{2}$. C, flower, with petals and sepals removed, $\times 4$. D, young fruit surrounded by calyx, $\times 1\frac{1}{2}$. E, diagram of transverse section of ripe capsule, $\times 4$ (two seeds only shown).

Stem Anatomy: Fibres

The stem shows a typical dicotyledonous structure, with a ring of vascular bundles surrounding the central pith. Immediately outside the

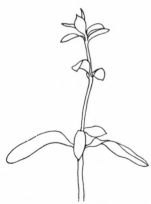

phloem of each bundle is a group of fibres; the individual fibres are very long, slender, thick-walled cells, 25-50 mm. long by about 20 μ thick. They differ from many fibre cells in being only very slightly lignified; the primary wall shows some lignification as the plant ages, but the bulk of the thickening consists of cellulose. The extracted fibres are therefore soft and flexible, but extremely strong, and it is to these characters of the fibre cells that flax owes its importance as a textile fibre. The fibres are extracted by *retting*, which is a process of controlled rotting, formerly carried out by immersing the pulled plants in ponds, or exposing them to damp air (dew-retting), but now completed more quickly and precisely at controlled temperatures in flax factories. The retting results in the breakdown of the middle lamella of the cell walls, so that

Fig. 36. Linseed seedling, $\times 1\frac{1}{2}$.

143

the cells can be readily separated. Mechanical treatment (scutching and hackling) of the retted stems removes the xylem and other tissues, leaving the linen fibre.

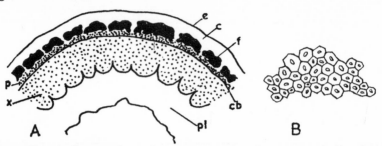

FIG. 37. Flax. A, diagram of part of a transverse section of a mature stem. B, a single small fibre-group more highly magnified. *e*, epidermis. *c*, cortex. *f*, fibres. *p*, phloem. *cb*, cambium. *x*, xylem. *pi*, pith.

Origin and Range of Types

Linum usitatissimum appears to have originated in South-west Asia, and has been in cultivation for some 5,000 years. Archaeological evidence suggests that the closely related *L. bienne* Mill. (*L. angustifolium* Huds.) native in the Mediterranean area and western Europe, including England, was also used. This species may therefore have played some part in the development of the cultivated forms. As the crop spread, specialization took place, with the Mediterranean and European forms developing as fibre plants—that is, flax—and the quicker-maturing forms grown in the warmer climates of S. Asia and particularly India, giving rise to typical linseeds, grown purely for seed.

There have thus developed two distinct cultivated forms within the species; both are largely self-pollinated and have therefore remained distinct, although crosses between the two are possible.

Flax. Grown for fibre-production, and typically a plant of cool, moist climates. Stems tall, little branched except in the upper part, number of flowers and yields of seed low, seed small. Flax is usually drilled at about 1½ cwt. of seed per acre, so as to give a dense stand which favours the production of slender, unbranched stems. A good seed-bed and fertile land is necessary, and, as flax is not frost-hardy, sowing should not normally take place before mid-April. Clean land is essential, as the yield is considerably reduced by weed competition, and the value of the produce reduced by an admixture of weeds; flax is rather readily damaged by selective weed-killers. Harvesting is by pulling, not cutting, so that the full length of stem is secured; it takes place soon after the petals have fallen. The immature capsules are combed off before the straw is retted; the seed yield under these conditions is, of course, low—perhaps 3 cwt. per acre.

Prior to 1927 the flax grown in the British Isles (mainly in N. Ireland) was largely derived from seed of N. European origin, but since that date a considerable number of improved varieties have been bred in N. Ireland.

Increased yield and higher quality was first obtained by the development of taller-growing forms, but progress along these lines cannot be continued very far, since very tall plants are likely to lodge. The quality of a lodged crop may be impaired, and harvesting costs are greatly increased if mechanical pulling becomes impossible. Further progress therefore depended on the production of varieties with a higher percentage of fibre in the stem, giving a higher yield of scutched flax from the same weight of crop; for quality to be maintained this increase must be due to an increase in number of fibres, and not to a greater diameter of individual fibre cells. This object was largely achieved, and the introduction of the Stormont varieties, produced by the plant-breeding station of the N. Ireland Ministry of Agriculture at Stormont, and the Liral series developed by the Linen Industry Research Association at Lambeg resulted in the raising of the yield of scutched flax from about 4 cwt. per acre to between 6 and 7 cwt. Examples are the early *Stormont Gossamer* and *Liral Crown*, and the later, higher-yielding *Liral Prince*. Since flax is almost entirely self-pollinated, varieties, once produced, remain relatively stable and uniform.

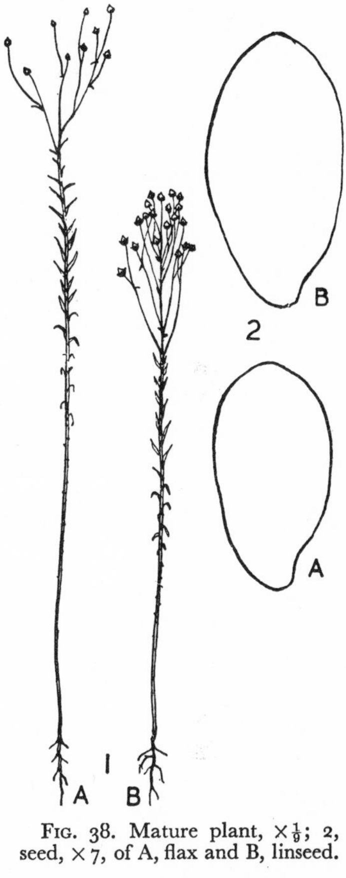

Linseed. Grown for the valuable oil and protein reserves of the seed; typically a crop for warm summer conditions. Plants are usually shorter, quicker-maturing and considerably more branched than flax varieties, the capsules more numerous and the seed usually (but not always) larger. High seed yields cannot be combined with good-quality fibre, and the 'straw' of linseed

FIG. 38. Mature plant, $\times \frac{1}{9}$; 2, seed, $\times 7$, of A, flax and B, linseed.

is a by-product of little value, occasionally used for the extraction of coarse fibre for packing, etc.

The acreage of linseed in Britain has never been large, but the high nutritional value of the seed sometimes made it a worthwhile crop, and small areas were often grown for consumption on the farm, rather than as a cash crop. Cultivation is somewhat similar to that of flax, but the seed-rate is usually lower (about $\frac{3}{4}$ cwt. per acre), giving a more open stand and hence more branching of individual plants. Harvesting by binder or combine takes place when the seed is fully ripe.

The small area devoted to linseed in Britain hardly justified the development of special varieties, and varieties of foreign origin were used.

Plate linseed, a rather variable series of forms from S. America, has been largely replaced by a series of N. American varieties, which ripen more uniformly and give usually higher yields. They include the early, rather small-seeded *Redwing* and *Sheyenne* and the larger-seeded, later *Royal* and *Dakota*. *Valuta* is a large-seeded, Swedish variety. It is derived from a Roumanian race, and like the later *Svalöf Oil Flax II*, often outyields the varieties of N. American origin. Although these varieties are more satisfactory than the older forms such as Plate, their yield, under British conditions, is not usually more than 9 cwt. per acre, and this is not high enough to justify anything but very occasional cultivation.

Chapter XI

LEGUMINOSAE

The *Leguminosae* is a very large family, divided into three sub-families, of which only one, the *Papilionatae*, is of importance in temperate regions. It is to this sub-family (sometimes treated as a separate family, the *Papilionaceae*) that the following particulars apply:

Habit. Very variable, trees, shrubs and herbs. The latter include annuals and perennials, and may be erect or climbing, tufted or creeping.

Leaves. Alternate, stipulate, usually compound, often with tendrils.

Flowers. Conspicuous, usually insect-pollinated, in racemose inflorescences. The flowers are of a characteristic and highly-specialized zygomorphic type, called papilionate from its fancied resemblance to a butterfly in the larger-flowered species. The calyx is composed of five joined sepals; the five petals vary in shape. The posterior one is often large and erect, forming the *standard* (vexillum) and partially overlapping the smaller lateral petals or *wings* (alae) which lie one on each side of the *keel* (carina) formed by the fusion of the two anterior petals. Within the keel lie the ten stamens; all ten may be joined by their filaments to form a tube surrounding the ovary (*monadelphous*), or the posterior one may be free, the other nine forming an incomplete tube (*diadelphous*). The gynaecium is of one carpel, usually with numerous anatropous ovules, the style emerging from the open end of the stamen-tube and curving upwards between the anthers.

Pollination is usually by bees. Nectar is secreted in diadelphous forms within the base of the stamen-tube, and can be reached only by long-'tongued' insects through the slits between the free stamen and those adjacent to it. In some *Leguminosae*, e.g. *Vicia*, projections of wing and keel petals interlock so that an insect alighting on the wings depresses the keel and exposes the stigma and anthers. In others, e.g. lucerne, the ovary and staminal tube tend to curve upwards and are held down by the rigid keel; dehiscence of the anthers takes place in the bud stage, and the stigma is thus covered with pollen. The stigma is not, however, receptive unless the flower is 'tripped'—that is, the ovary is released from the keel so that it springs sharply upwards and the stigmatic surface is ruptured. Tripping by bees usually results in cross-pollination; in some plants self-tripping may occur and give rise to selfing. In the majority of *Leguminosae* cross-pollination is usual, and many species are almost completely self-sterile. In such plants seed production is largely dependent on an adequate number of bees to effect pollination, and individual plants are usually highly heterozygous and the agricultural stocks are variable strains, rather than distinct uniform varieties (it is preferable to use the terms *variety* or *cultivar* rather than strain). In the few species, such as peas, which are usually entirely self-pollinated, well-defined uniform varieties exist.

Fruit. The fruit is usually a *legume*, with seeds forming a single row, splitting, sometimes explosively, along the full length of both sutures. Modifications of the type occur in some species; for example, the fruit

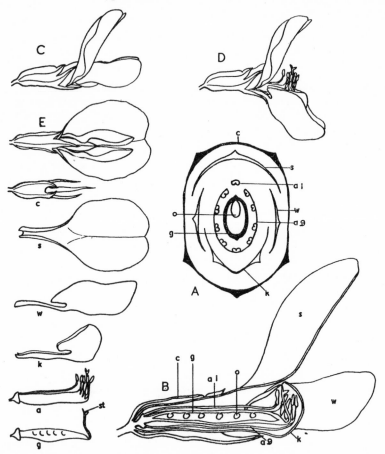

Fig. 39. Floral structure of Leguminosae. A, floral diagram. B, vertical section of broad bean flower, ×2. C, flower in normal position. D, with wings and keel depressed, both in side view. E, ventral view and separate parts of flower, all ×1. *a*, androecium. *a1*, separate stamen. *ag*, joined stamens. *c*, calyx. *g*, carpel. *k*, keel. *o*, ovule. *s*, standard. *sg*, stigma. *w*, wing.

may be one-seeded, either indehiscent (sainfoin) or opening as a pyxidium (red clover) or along one side (melilot), or the fruit may be constricted between the seeds to form a lomentum which breaks into single-seeded indehiscent mericarps (*Ornithopus*).

Seed. The seed is non-endospermic; the embryo consists of two oval cotyledons with starch and protein food reserves (oil in some species), a large radicle and small plumule. It is covered by a thick testa (seed-coat) with a conspicuous hilum. In some species the testa may become impermeable to water, giving what are known as *hard seeds*. (See seed-testing, p. 96.) These are unable to absorb water and swell, so that even when placed in water they will not germinate. The embryo is, how-ever, living, and if the testa is cracked by abrasion or frost, and water is able to enter, germination will take place. A large percentage of hard seeds is usually a disadvantage in an agricultural crop, as it results in poor initial germination, but may be a useful feature in some special cases. Thus, an autumn-sown ley in which the young clover seedlings are winter-killed may improve owing to the germination of hard seeds in the following spring. In the U.S.A. it has been found worthwhile to develop special strains of the annual crimson clover with a high percent-age of hard seed, which can persist in the soil and give a cover of clover after an intervening cereal crop, without any further sowing.

Root-nodules. The root system of leguminous plants is typically a branch-ing tap-root. It differs from that of the majority of families of flowering plants in bearing root-nodules. These are lateral outgrowths of the roots, mainly parenchymatous, but with a vascular supply connecting up with the vascular system of the roots. They are caused by the presence of par-ticular bacteria, *Rhizobium radicicola*, which enter through the root-hairs. They multiply in the root-hair and form an *infection-thread*, a slender filament of bacterial cells which becomes surrounded by a tube-like sheath secreted by the root cells. This infection-thread penetrates through the cortical cells, and in the inner cortex the sheath breaks down, setting free the bacteria in the host cells. Here they multiply and stimulate the host cells to divide, thus causing proliferation of the inner cortex and the development of a nodule.

Rhizobium radicicola is capable of utilizing the free nitrogen of the air, and if conditions are favourable a state of *symbiosis* is set up in which the bacteria supply nitrogenous compounds to the plant while the legu-minous plant provides the bacteria with carbohydrates. If satisfactory symbiosis occurs, the leguminous host plant becomes independent of combined nitrogen in the soil. This depends on soil conditions; for example, nitrogen fixation does not take place in waterlogged soils or in the absence of boron. It is also dependent on the strain of bacterium.

Rhizobium radicicola is a variable species, consisting of a number of distinct forms, sometimes treated as separate species, capable of form-ing nodules on certain leguminous genera, but not on others. Thus one form (*R. leguminosarum*, if it is treated as a species) produces nodules on species of *Pisum* and *Vicia*, another (*R. trifolii*) on clovers, and so on. Within each of these groups numerous strains exist, some effective nitro-gen fixers, others ineffective; ineffective strains may behave as parasites, and harm rather than assist the host plant. The bacteria set free by the decay of the nodules remain viable in the soil for some years, and a field which has carried a satisfactorily nodulated crop of a particular legu-minous species will give satisfactory results with the same species in later years. If, however, a new leguminous species is sown, which had not previously grown on that particular land, results may be poor, owing to the absence of the appropriate strain of *Rhizobium*. Inoculation with a suitable strain is then necessary. This may be done either by scattering over the land soil taken from a field where the legume is known to make good growth, or more conveniently by the use of a pure culture of the bacterium. Cultures can be kept growing on agar media, and transferred to a skim-milk medium, which is then mixed with the seed, which is dried, away from sunlight, and sown as soon as possible. If this is done, bacteria of the correct strain are present on the seed-coat at the time of germination, and infection of the young roots readily takes place. In Britain lucerne is the only crop which is commonly inoculated in this way; it can usually be assumed that the appropriate strains for clovers and the other common legumes are already present in all agricultural land.

Agricultural Value. The *Leguminosae* are of outstanding agricultural value because of their specialized form of nutrition. The nitrogen fixed by the *Rhizobium* cells in the root nodules is utilized by the leguminous plants, which are thus not dependent, as are almost all other plants, on nitrogen compounds present in the soil. They are valuable in themselves, therefore, as high-protein food plants, and also for their effect on other plants, since some of the nitrogen becomes available to nearby non-leguminous plants by decay of the nodules or, under some conditions, by excretion of nitrogenous compounds from the nodules.

Members of the family are used mainly in two ways (cf. cereals and herbage grasses), the large-seeded forms such as peas and beans are grown as arable crops for their high-protein seed reserves (pulse crops), while the smaller-seeded forms, such as the clovers and lucerne, are grown as forage crops, either alone or in mixture with grasses.

TRIFOLIUM. TRUE CLOVERS

Herbaceous plants, annual or perennial, leaves trifoliate, leaflets at least slightly toothed, with obtuse or emarginate tips. Flowers small in short, crowded racemes, standard only slightly diverging from other petals, stamens diadelphous. Pods one- to several-seeded, short, straight, dehiscent. First leaf of seedling simple.

A rather large genus including several species of outstanding importance as herbage plants in temperate regions.

Trifolium pratense L. Red Clover

Distinguishing Characters. Hairy perennial, with stout tap-root, not creeping. Leaves large, leaflets almost entire, usually with horseshoe-shaped leaf mark. Stipules large, often red-veined, broad and narrowing abruptly to a short, slender point. Flowers densely crowded in ovoid racemes subtended by leaf-like bract. Calyx hairy with narrow teeth. Petals purplish-red (occasionally white), forming a long tube at base, pollinated mainly by humble bees. Mainly self-sterile. Pod very short, single-seeded, opening transversely as a pyxidium. Seed 2 mm., $\frac{1}{4}$ million per pound, oval, but with radicle forming a conspicuous lobe $\frac{1}{3}$-$\frac{1}{2}$ length of cotyledons. Testa shiny, pale yellow with variable purple shading. Seed harvested under wet conditions may lose most of its purple pigment by weathering. Old seed darkens and becomes brown. Proportion of hard seeds usually low. Seedling with short-stalked, oval cotyledons, *c.* 5 mm. long. First leaf simple, rounded, sub-cordate, 4 mm. long by 6 mm. broad, hairy.

Growth Habit. The seedling develops a tap-root, and during the first

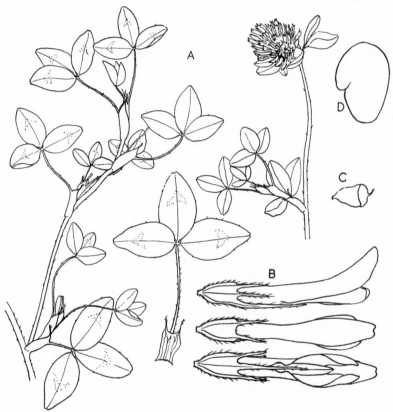

Fig. 40. Red clover. A, vegetative and flowering shoots and detached leaf, × $\frac{1}{2}$. B, side, dorsal and ventral views of single flower, × 3$\frac{1}{2}$. C, fruit, × 3$\frac{1}{2}$. D, seed, × 10.

year's growth the stem remains short so that a rosette of leaves is produced, with the axillary and terminal buds at or near ground-level. At this stage, therefore, red clover will tolerate hard grazing (contrast with lucerne, p. 164). In the following spring the buds grow out to produce more or less erect, leafy stems, on the upper part of which the flower heads arise. These elongated stems are annual and die off after setting seed, if not cut or grazed, and the plant overwinters in a rosette stage. This alternation of rosette and erect stages means that the plant is adapted to both grazing and hay; it is commonly used where hay is the primary purpose, and where grazing only is required will usually be replaced by the creeping white clover.

Range of Types. Red clover is a variable species, and is found in Britain in four rather distinct types; these are wild red (var. *sylvestre*) and three cultivated types (var. *sativum*), broad red, single-cut red, and late-flowering red.

Wild Red Clover. A long-lived perennial, earlier-flowering than the other types. The stems are semi-prostrate, with few rather small leaves; it is thus not suited for hay and gives a low yield under grazing. It is not in cultivation, but occurs fairly frequently in old pastures and may be of some value in maintaining soil fertility.

Broad Red Clover. Not derived from the indigenous wild red, but intro-duced from Holland as a cultivated plant in the seventeenth century. It is a short-lived, high-yielding, erect form suited to conditions of high fertility, starting growth early in spring and flowering early. The leaves are large and the leaflets always longer than broad (the name broad red refers to the width of the whole leaf, not the individual leaflet). In summer it produces a comparatively small number of erect, usually hollow, leafy stems with rather few nodes (*c.* 5-7), bearing at the top the flower heads, usually light reddish-purple in colour. The buds do not all develop at the same time, so that young, actively-growing shoots are present at the time when the older stems are producing flowers. This results in a rapid recovery if the plant is cut for hay, the young shoots growing rapidly to produce an abundant aftermath or a second hay crop; broad red is therefore often known as *double-cut* clover. The growing-out of a succession of buds during the first harvest year means that few dormant buds are left to continue growth in the following year, and broad red clover is typically a short-lived form, rarely persisting in quantity be-yond the second harvest year. (This is actually the third year of growth of a ley sown under corn.) Its main value is thus for short leys, and it is used, either alone or with rye-grasses, as the basis of most one-year leys where two hay-cuts are taken, or one hay-cut is followed by grazing, and as a constituent of longer leys which are to be cut for hay in their first year. It will not grow satisfactorily under conditions of low fertility, or on waterlogged or acid soils. It is very susceptible to clover rot (p. 545) and to attack by clover eelworm (*Ditylenchus dipsaci*, an important nema-tode pest causing a form of clover sickness, and sometimes spread by infected red clover seed); it cannot be satisfactorily grown on soils where these are present.

Varieties. It is usual practice to save broad red clover seed from the second growth, after cutting once for hay, as seed-setting in the first growth may be poor, and the very strong leafy growth makes harvesting difficult. It thus commonly happens that fields laid down primarily as hay leys are harvested for seed, and much of the broad red clover seed which comes on to the market as 'English' is of this origin and cannot be referred to any special variety. English broad red of this type will, however, usually be more satisfactory than imported seed.

Several special local varieties of broad red are produced in Britain, grown from authentic mother seed and field-inspected under certification schemes. Such are *Dorset Marl, West Sussex, Cotswold, Vale of Clwyd* and similar county varieties, differing slightly in time of flowering,

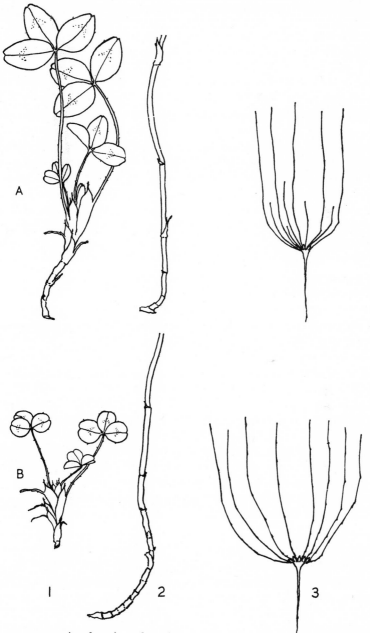

FIG. 41. 1, vegetative shoot in early spring. 2, base of flowering shoot. 3, diagram of habit of flowering plant of A, broad red clover, B, late-flowering red clover.

vigour and persistency, but generally more uniform and more reliable than uncertified stocks. The Aberystwyth variety *S.151* is not a typical broad red, but shows some approach to the characters of the single-cut type. *American Medium* is a distinct form of broad red, with more conspicuous and more spreading hairs; it is better adapted to hot, dry conditions than the British varieties. Numerous foreign varieties exist, but they are usually less satisfactory under British conditions.

Late-flowering Red Clover. (Often called extra-late flowering, to distinguish it from the single-cut clovers.) A continental form, long cultivated in S.W. England and in Wales. The true late-flowering reds are longer-lived plants than the broad reds, starting growth later (May) and flowering approximately four weeks later. The leaves are smaller and the leaflets of the leaves produced in spring are almost circular, although those produced later in the year show less difference from broad red. A very dense tuft is formed in spring, and at the flowering period late-flowering red shows many more elongated stems than broad red, each longer, with more nodes (*c.* 7-14,) less erect and more nearly solid. Flowers usually a rather deeper red-purple. All stems tend to elongate at the same time, so that there are few or no short shoots in active growth at the flowering period. The plant is thus slow to recover from cutting and produces little aftermath. Numerous dormant buds remain to continue growth the following year, and late-flowering red is a longer-lived type than broad red, often persisting well into the third harvest year and sometimes longer.

Late-flowering red is thus mainly used in leys of two or more years' duration which are to be cut for hay; it gives a rather late but heavy hay-cut, which may exceed that from broad red, but can only be cut once in the year. It is hardy and slightly more tolerant of poor conditions and hard grazing than broad red. Management for seed-production must, of course, be different from that for broad red; no hay-cut can be taken, but the crop may be grazed (or cut early for silage) up to mid-May. This treatment gives a seed harvest (usually in September) at about the same time as that from the second cut of broad red.

Varieties. Two rather similar British varieties are produced, *Montgomery* and *Cornish Marl.* The Aberystwyth variety *S.123* is derived from these two. *New Zealand Montgomery*, originally merely the Montgomery strain grown in New Zealand, has been developed into a bred variety of rather less extreme late-flowering types.

Single-cut Red Clover. (Also known as late-flowering red, in which case the type described above must be called extra-late.) A type intermediate between broad-red and the true late-flowering type; denser, more prostrate and some two weeks later than broad red, giving a very heavy hay yield with some aftermath growth, but not sufficient for a second hay-cut. Used for the same purpose as the true late-flowering red, but less persistent.

Varieties. Essex and *Cotswold* are certified English local varieties; *American*

Mammoth (with spreading hairs) and *Altaswede* belong also to this group.

Trifolium hybridum L.   Alsike Clover

This is a true species, in spite of its specific name, which may be taken to refer to the fact that it is in some ways intermediate in appearance between red and white clovers. It is not native in Britain, although now fairly well naturalized; its common name is derived from a village in Sweden, from where it was introduced in the early nineteenth century.

Distinguishing Characters. A short-lived, non-creeping perennial with a growth-habit somewhat similar to that of broad red clover. Leaves glabrous, without leaf-mark, more conspicuously toothed; stipules with long, tapering point, never red-veined. Stems more or less erect, with very short, almost spherical, axillary racemes of white or, more commonly, pale pink flowers. Individual flowers shorter than those of red clover, becoming reflexed after pollination. Pod 1 cm., with usually four to five small seeds (1 mm.; $\frac{3}{4}$ million to pound) which are mainly heart-shaped (i.e. with radicle and cotyledon lobes of almost equal size), light or dark green to almost black. Seedling with stalked oval cotyledons *c.* 4 mm. long. First leaf *c.* 4 mm. long by 5 mm. broad, sharply truncate at base, toothed, glabrous.

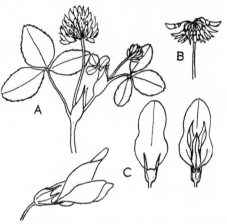

FIG. 42. Alsike. A, flowering shoot. B, flower-head, after pollination. Both × ½. C, side, dorsal and ventral views of single flower, × 2½.

Uses. Alsike is suitable for the same purpose as red clover but, being smaller and lower-yielding, it is of less value. It is, however, rather more resistant to acidity, to waterlogged conditions and to clover rot than red clover and is therefore used as a substitute for the latter where these are likely to cause difficulty. It is a common practice to include, say, 1 lb. per acre in a seeds-mixture including red clover as an 'insurance policy', so that there may be some clover present if the red fails to become established.

Range of Type. Alsike shows comparatively little variation within the species, and its minor importance in Britain would hardly justify the development and maintenance of distinct varieties; several Swedish varieties exist. The greater part of the seed employed is imported from Canada. Alsike and white clover are sometimes harvested together, and since the seeds are of very similar size and shape, they cannot readily be separated, and are sold as a mixture.

Trifolium incarnatum L.   Crimson Clover, Trifolium

An annual, introduced from S. Europe, rarely becoming naturalized.

Distinguishing Characters. Annual, with rather small tap-root. Leaves densely soft-hairy, leaflets very broad, stipules broad, truncate or rounded, often red- or purple-edged. Young plant growing rapidly to form a dense, rosette-like tuft of short shoots, elongating early to form erect stems. Flowers in long, dense terminal racemes; calyx with subulate teeth

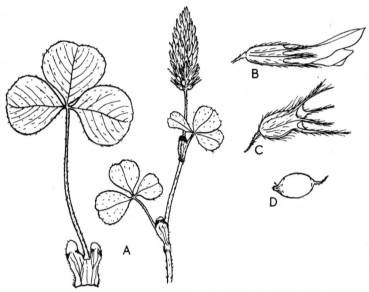

Fig. 43. Crimson clover, *Trifolium incarnatum*. A, single leaf and flowering shoot, × ½. B, C and D, single flower, fruiting calyx, and fruit, × 2.

and stiff hairs, persistent, becoming almost woody in fruit. Corolla bright crimson or white; pod one-seeded, fragile, enclosed in somewhat swollen calyx. Seed large (3 mm., ⅛ million to pound), yellow to pale orange (white in white-flowered forms), oval, radicle inconspicuous. Seedling large, cotyledons long-stalked, oval, up to 10 mm. long. First leaf rounded, *c*. 8 mm., sub-cordate, hairy.

Use and Range of Types. Crimson clover is mainly grown as a winter annual to provide spring keep; its rapid early growth gives plants from an August sowing after corn which are large enough to over-winter successfully. It is not, however, very hardy, and its use is therefore confined to southern England, where it is sown at about 20 lb. per acre, alone or with Italian rye-grass. The stiff, hairy calyx in the fruiting stage is unpalatable and may be dangerous to stock, and crimson clover must therefore be fed off or cut for hay not later than the early flowering stage (May-early June). It was formerly an important crop for arable sheep, for which it was desirable to provide a succession of keep for as long a period as possible. This cannot be done by successive sowings, since early-sown plants produce elongated stems in autumn and do not over-winter well, while later sowing will give very small plants which again do not survive the winter satisfactorily. A succession of keep could thus only be obtained by the selection of forms with varying dates of maturity, and some half-dozen different types were developed. Of these, only *Early Crimson* is commonly employed to-day; *Late White* (with white flowers and seeds) is occasionally used.

Trifolium repens L.   White Clover

Distinguishing Characters. A glabrous native perennial, forming small tufts with a tap-root in the early stages; buds in the axils of the rosette leaves soon grow out as horizontal, creeping, leafy stolons, rooting at

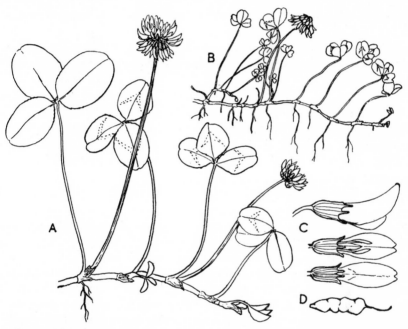

Fig. 44. White clover. A, part of stolon of a large white form (ladino) with leaves and flower-heads. B, of wild white (Kent); both × ½. C, single flower in side, ventral and dorsal views, × 3. D, fruit, × 3.

the nodes. Leaves glabrous; leaflets ovate to nearly circular, conspicuously toothed, usually with pale leaf-mark; stipules small, lanceolate, pointed, connate to form tube around stolon. Flowers in globular umbel-like heads, without bracts, borne singly on long peduncles in the axils of the stolon leaves. Individual flowers on short stalks, erect at first, becoming reflexed after pollination. Corolla white (very rarely pink) forming a short tube; cross-pollinated by hive bees. Pod five- to six-seeded; seeds heart-shaped, bright yellow, darkening to reddish-brown with age, not shiny, small (1 mm., ¾ million to the pound, with some variation in different forms). Hard seeds frequent, often about 10 per cent. Seedling small, cotyledons stalked, oval, up to 4 mm. long.

First leaf ovate, slightly toothed, glabrous, lateral veins inconspicuous.

Uses. White clover, typically a long-lived perennial, is essentially a grazing plant; its stems and buds, being all at or near ground level, are not readily eaten off by stock, and grazing therefore removes only leaves unless it is very severe, and hence causes comparatively little damage to the plant. The creeping habit of white clover allows wide vegetative spread, and it can therefore increase rapidly if conditions are favourable. The conditions needed are adequate lime and phosphate and absence of shade; thus if soil conditions are satisfactory, white clover will spread under hard grazing, which prevents its being overshadowed by taller-growing grasses. Such hard grazing is particularly effective in spring, since white clover normally starts active growth later than the better herbage grasses. Under good grassland management, which preserves a satisfactory balance between grasses and white clover, a dense network of stolons is formed between and around the grass shoots, so that nitrogen compounds produced by the clover are readily accessible to the grasses.

White clover is relatively shallow-rooted, and, although not readily killed by drought, makes little growth under dry conditions.

Range of Types. White clover shows very considerable variation in plant size, persistence and amount of adventitious root production. It also varies in the extent to which it is *cyanophoric*, that is, capable of producing hydrogen cyanide (prussic acid).

Cyanophoric plants contain the glycosides *lotaustralin* and *linamarin*, together with the enzyme *linamarase*, which hydrolizes these substances, with the production of hydrogen cyanide. Only plants with both enzyme and glycoside give cyanide; those with one only, or neither, are acyanophoric. The amount of cyanide produced is usually small, and it does not appear that stock suffer any direct harm from feeding on cyanophoric white clovers. The character is of interest mainly in distinguishing between different white clover forms; for this purpose the *picrate test* is employed. Leaves of the plant to be tested are incubated in closed tubes with strips of filter-paper previously soaked in sodium picrate solution; toluene or chloroform must be added, as no breakdown of the glycosides takes place in uninjured tissue. If the plant is cyanophoric the picrate paper changes from yellow to orange-red.

Wild White Clover. This is the wild form, native in Europe, including Britain, and widely naturalized elsewhere. It is a characteristic form of closely-grazed pasture, with small, dark-green leaves, numerous slender branching stolons with short internodes, producing copious adventitious roots at the majority of the nodes, so that stolons are very firmly attached to the ground. Commences growth late, flowering late (end of June), flower-heads small on rather short peduncles. Seed slightly smaller than other forms, but not readily distinguishable. Usually cyanophoric (this character has been shown to be related to winter temperatures; populations from S. and W. Europe consist mainly of cyanophoric plants, while those from areas in central and N. Europe with colder winters are mainly acyanophoric).

Wild white clover has been recognized since the pioneer work of Gilchrist at Cockle Park in the early years of the century as a plant of outstanding importance in pasture. Its value lies not so much in its own yield as in its effect on the grasses with which it is growing, although the high protein and mineral content of its foliage make it a valuable food. The nitrogen which becomes available to the grasses via the clover greatly increases their growth, so that although wild white clover grown alone tends to be late-growing and low-yielding, the combination of clover and grass provides one of the best possible swards for long grazing-leys and permanent pasture. Under such conditions the hardiness, permanence and ability to withstand hard grazing which are shown by wild white make it superior to any other leguminous plant.

Varieties. More importance is usually attached to trueness to wild type than to strain within the type. The Aberystwyth variety *S.184* is a very uniform, dense, dark-green, rather late-flowering form. *Kent* wild white was one of the earliest local forms to be introduced and has achieved a considerable reputation. Wild white clover from other parts of the country is not marketed as special local varieties, but produced under a national certification scheme (p. 83).

Large White Clovers. A number of large forms of white clover may be arbitrarily grouped together, as being distinguished from wild white by the greater size, particularly of leaves and stolons, and by their earlier flowering. The greater height and size means that their yield is considerably higher than that of wild white; they are also sufficiently tall to be of some value for hay.

The forms most used in Britain are those most nearly resembling an enlarged wild white. These are the Aberystwyth variety *S.100*, *Kersey White*, a strain derived from plants selected in Suffolk in 1924, and *New Zealand White*, primarily a local variety, but including some bred material. All are larger plants than wild white, with rather fewer, stouter stolons. These stolons are prostrate, but with longer internodes and fewer adventitious roots than those of wild white, and are thus less tightly rooted down to the ground; mainly cyanophoric. Flowering is usually a week to a fortnight earlier. All are high-yielding clovers, tolerant of grazing, perennial and usually persisting for at least six years. They are quicker-growing than wild white, and only slightly less hardy; one or other of them is usually included in all grazing leys of two years' duration or more, either alone in the shorter leys or mixed with wild white in the longer ones. S.100 and Kersey White are both very uniform varieties; Kersey White is rather earlier and more erect in growth. *S.100 No-mark* is a bred type similar to the ordinary S.100, but readily distinguished by the absence of the genetically dominant leaf-mark; out-crossing is thus very readily detected. New Zealand White is usually less uniform, containing some short-lived plants and some approaching the wild type.

Ladino is a distinct type of Italian origin, developed mainly under irrigated conditions. It is usually slightly larger than S.100, with less prostrate stolons not closely rooted down; it is high-yielding, but not tolerant of very hard grazing or of intense competition. Under British conditions it tends to be short-lived, and is little used, although very widely grown in the U.S.A. Acyanophoric. *Dutch White* (sometimes called ordinary white or English white) is a short-lived form lasting from one to two years only, developed under arable conditions, and originally introduced from Holland. It is more erect than S.100, with few stolons, producing very abundant large flower-heads about a week earlier. Now largely superseded by the much longer-lived and equally high-yielding S.100 and Kersey White. Acyanophoric.

Trifolium dubium Sibth.   Yellow Suckling Clover

An annual with prostrate stems and small greyish-green leaves. Leaflets narrow, terminal leaflet stalked. Flowers pale yellow, in globular axillary heads of from twelve to twenty-five individual flowers, which are at first erect, but become reflexed after pollination, withered corolla persisting. Pod usually one-seeded; seeds ovoid, 1 mm., pinkish-yellow to pale brown, slightly shiny, radicle inconspicuous. Seedling small, cotyledons stalked, oval, 3·5 mm. long. First leaf 3 mm. long by 4 mm. broad, not toothed, glabrous.

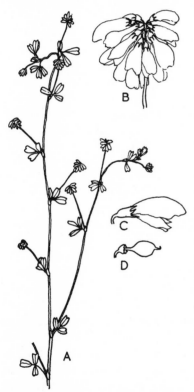

FIG. 45. Yellow suckling clover. A, flowering shoot, × ½. B, flower-head, × 2½. C, single flower, × 3. D, fruit, × 3.

A palatable but rather low-yielding annual, common as a wild plant and sometimes sown in short leys, where it may persist by self-seeding. Its main advantage is its ability to establish under dry conditions; it is used therefore mainly in the drier areas of eastern England. *Giant Suckling Clover* (sometimes called Giant Red Suckling) is a distinct agricultural form of the species, differing only in its larger size and more vigorous growth.

On account of its ability to establish readily from seed, yellow suckling clover is a common constituent of leys harvested for white clover seed. Since the seed of the two species is very similar in size and cannot be readily separated during cleaning, yellow suckling is a common impurity of white clover seed. Although it cannot be considered a weed, and a small proportion of it would not be objectionable, it is clearly less valuable for many purposes than white clover; the old Seeds Regulations of 1922 required that the presence of yellow suckling clover was disclosed if it formed more than 2 per cent. by weight of a sample of white clover seed.

Trifolium campestre Schreb. **(T. procumbens** auct.), Hop Clover, is an annual species resembling yellow suckling, but differing in its larger flower heads with from thirty-five to sixty flowers. It is a common, very stemmy, sprawling plant of dry banks, walls, etc., of no agricultural value. **T. micranthum** Viv. **(T. filiforme** auct). Small Yellow Clover, is also similar to yellow suckling, but much smaller, with short-stalked leaves of which the terminal leaflet is sessile, and very small flower-heads of from three to five flowers. A rather common weed of dry lawns.

Trifolium subterraneum L.   Subterranean Clover (Sub-clover)

An annual with long, prostrate stems; leaves large, hairy, leaflets very broad, rounded, often with irregular red splashes. Stipules broad, shortly

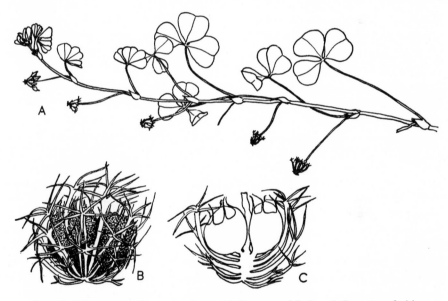

FIG. 46. Subterranean clover. A, shoot with flowers and fruit, × ⅓. B, mature fruiting head from soil, × 3. C, the same with some sterile calyces removed to show position of fruit.

pointed. Flowers in small axillary racemes, the lower flowers of the raceme rather large with white or very pale yellow corollas, the upper flowers sterile and consisting only of a small stiffly-toothed calyx. After pollination the peduncles turn downwards and the whole developing fruiting head is buried in the surface soil; the sterile flowers become reflexed and act as barbs retaining the burr-like mature head in this position. The plant dies off, leaving the naturally-buried seeds to germinate *in situ* in the pod. For seed-production purposes the burr-like fruiting heads are raked or swept up and threshed to free the seeds from the one-seeded pods enclosed within the calyx of the fertile flowers; the seed is almost twice the size of red clover seed (3 mm., *c.* 75,000 per pound), dark purple to almost black. Seedling large, very similar to that of *T. incarnatum*, but cotyledons usually more erect.

Subterranean clover behaves as a winter annual, germinating in autumn, producing its maximum growth in spring and dying off in summer. Its main value is in areas where summer drought is sufficient to kill the majority of perennial plants; its buried seeds germinate as soon as rain comes, and it therefore behaves as a self-seeding plant and gives what is in effect a permanent pasture on land only capable of supporting annuals. It is very extensively grown in Australia under such conditions, and a large number of strains have been developed there, differing mainly in the length of growing season required.

A small form of subterranean clover is indigenous in Britain, occurring in thin, dry pasture in the south, but it is of negligible importance. The much larger Australian varieties grow satisfactorily in southern England, but there appears normally to be little advantage in using them, as the yield does not compare favourably with crimson clover if they are grown purely as winter annuals, or with the larger white clovers if in a longer ley.

Trouble has sometimes been reported with ewes grazed on subterranean clover pastures; the production by the clover of an oestrogen-like substance may cause infertility.

Trifolium fragiferum L.   Strawberry Clover

A stoloniferous perennial resembling white clover, but distinguished in the vegetative stage by its less closely-prostrate habit and its long-pointed stipules, and in the flowering stage by bracts at the base of the individual flower-stalks and by the pale-pink flowers with hairy calyces. In the fruiting stage the plant is very readily recognized; the flowers become reflexed and the calyces much swollen and pink in colour, so that the whole fruiting head has some resemblance to a strawberry. The pods within the swollen calyces are one- to two-seeded; seeds heart-shaped, pale brown with darker flecks, 2 mm., about ½ million per pound. Seedling very similar to that of white clover, but cotyledons longer, first leaf narrower, more conspicuously toothed.

Strawberry clover occurs occasionally as an indigenous plant in wet pastures in Britain, and is exceptionally tolerant of waterlogging and of high salt concentrations. It has been used in the U.S.A., Australia and New Zealand under such conditions where other clovers will not grow, and a number of strains, including the large *Palestine* form, have been developed. It would perhaps repay more extended trial in Britain.

Several other species of clover occur in Britain. Among these may be mentioned **T. medium** Huds., Zigzag Clover, a perennial closely

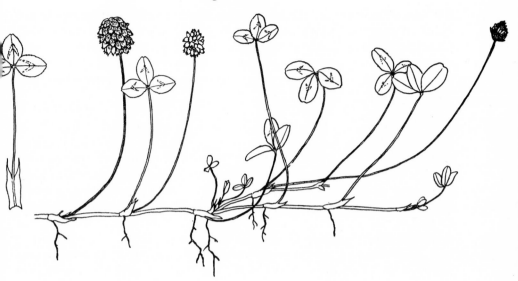

FIG. 47. Strawberry clover. Stolon and detached leaf, × ½.

resembling red clover in general appearance, but creeping by underground stems and with long, tapering-pointed stipules, and dying to ground level in winter; and **T. arvense** L., Hare's-foot Clover, a small, erect annual of sandy soils, with oblong pink hairy racemes. Clover species of some agricultural importance in sub-tropical areas are **T. alexandrinum** L., Berseem or Egyptian Clover, tall growing with white flowers in round heads; and **T. resupinatum** L., Persian Clover, a winter annual with pink twisted flowers and inflated calyx.

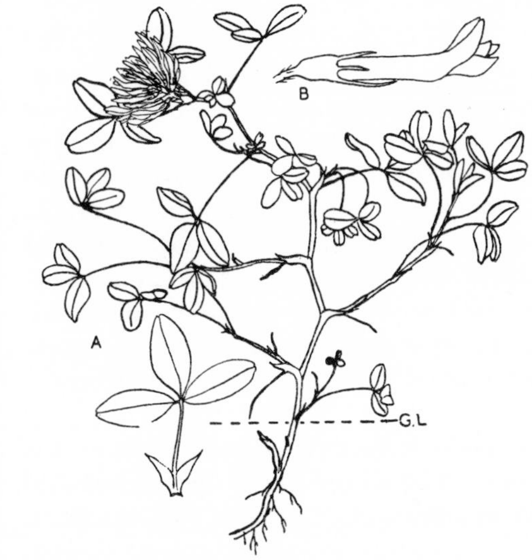

FIG. 48. Zigzag clover. A, flowering shoot and detached leaf, × ⅓. B, single flower, × 1½. G.L, ground-level.

FIG. 49. Haresfoot clover. A, flowering shoot, × ½. B, detached leaf, × ½. C, single flower after pollination, × 3½.

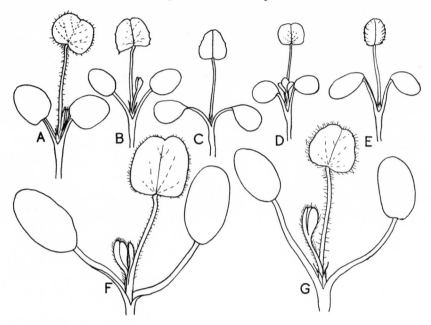

Fig. 50. Clover seedlings, × 2. A, red. B, alsike. C, white. D, suckling. E, strawberry. F, crimson. G, subterranean.

MEDICAGO

Distinguished from Trifolium by the pointed or mucronate leaflets, and by the curved or coiled pod. Includes the important perennial lucerne, the annual black medick sometimes included in short leys, and a few other annual species of little importance.

Medicago sativa L.   Lucerne, Alfalfa

Distinguishing Characters. A long-lived perennial, with long, stout tap-root, producing usually erect annual stems up to 1 m. (3 ft.). Leaves trifoliate, with pointed narrow-ovate toothed leaflets and toothed sti-pules. Flowers usually blue, in oblong axillary racemes; usually cross-pollinated by bees; 'tripping' necessary; pods smooth, loosely coiled in a spiral. Seeds numerous, *c.* 2 mm., *c.* 200,000 per pound, dull greenish-brown, angular, with conspicuous radicle, variable and often distorted and twisted owing to coiling of pod. Seedling with short-stalked, long-oval cotyledons up to 10 mm. long. First leaf 6 mm. long by 8 mm. broad, apex mucronate, base cuneate.

Growth-habit and Use. The young plant of lucerne is more slender and erect than that of the clovers, and does not form a rosette of leaves at ground-level. It is therefore much less tolerant of grazing at this stage, and can be readily damaged by the removal of buds if grazed during the first year. In the second year buds at the base of the stem grow out to form erect leafy stems, and these in turn produce further basal shoots so that a branched crown of short perennial stems is formed just above

164

ground-level. When this stage is reached the plant is much more resistant to grazing, but the fact that the bulk of the leaves are borne on the upright stems, well above ground-level, means that photosynthesis, and hence yield and vigour of plant, is very much reduced by continuous grazing. Lucerne can therefore only be used for grazing to a rather limited extent; it is primarily a plant for cutting for feeding green or as hay or silage, or for drying. Used in this way, it is capable of giving three or more cuts per year, and of producing a high total yield. Its deep tap-root makes it very resistant to drought, and it remains productive during a dry summer period when clovers and similar legumes are showing very little growth.

Lucerne is very intolerant of competition, particularly as a young plant, and must either be grown alone or in a specially-designed mixture. When

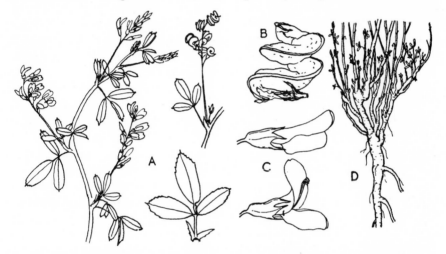

Fig. 51. Lucerne. A, flowering and fruiting shoots and detached leaf, × ⅓. B, fruit, × 3. C, flowers in early opening and tripped stages, × 2. D, crown and upper part of root of old plant, × ⅓.

grown alone, it is usually drilled in wide-spaced (10-12 in.) rows at 15-25 lb. per acre, and kept free from weeds by inter-row hoeing, and by harrowing during the winter dormant period. If it is sown in a mixture, the companion species should be sufficiently vigorous to keep down weeds, but not so strongly-growing that they compete seriously with the lucerne. The rye-grasses are too aggressive for the purpose; cocksfoot is satisfactory under dry conditions, but in wetter areas may become dominant, and in such areas timothy or meadow fescue is preferable. A typical mixture would be 14 lb. lucerne with 4 lb. of the grass and ½ lb. white clover per acre. Management must be such as to favour the lucerne, and grazing must be controlled, with long rest periods.

The high yield and high nutritive value of lucerne make it perhaps the most valuable of all legumes for stock-feeding, if the agriculture of the world is considered. In Britain, however, where the climate is particularly favourable for the growth of clovers, lucerne is mainly valued for its drought-resistance, and is more commonly used on the lighter and drier soils of S. and E. England. Good drainage is in fact always necessary for lucerne, as well as adequate lime and phosphate. Since lucerne is not a frequent crop in Britain, and is not widely naturalized, suitable strains of nodule bacteria are absent from many soils, and seed-inoculation is desirable.

Origin and Range of Type. Lucerne occurs wild in the Caspian Sea area, and was introduced from Persia into Greece in the fifth century B.C. Its use spread slowly through Europe, reaching England in the seventeenth century. It was introduced into Spain by the Moors, and thence to S. America and California, with the Arabic name *alfalfa*; it is now cultivated in almost all temperate and sub-tropical areas. A very large range of types has developed, extending from the wild-type Turkestan forms, which are very hardy but have a short growing season, to the non-hardy types, such as Arabian and Peruvian, which have a very long growing season, but are suited only to warm climates. It is the central part of the range of types which is of interest in temperate climates, and here the adaptability has been increased by crossing with another species. This is *Medicago falcata* L., a yellow-flowered hardy species, with small leaves, prostrate stems and sickle-shaped pods, which occurs in Asia and Central Europe, extending into a few areas in E. England. The hybrids, *M.* × *varia* Martyn (*M.* × *media* Pers.), are very variable and will back-cross with either parent. A whole series of hybrid types is therefore possible, and it is indeed probable that nearly all temperate-climate forms of lucerne now contain some *falcata* 'blood'. The most important hybrid types are the *variegated lucernes*, such as *Grimm*; the name variegated refers to the flowers, which vary from yellow to blue-purple. Grimm derives its name from that of a Bavarian farmer who introduced a local form of the hybrid lucerne, known as *Old Franconian*, into the U.S.A. in 1857. The forms previously available in N. America had been S. European types, and the introduction of the hardier Grimm enabled lucerne-growing to be extended much further north. Variegated lucernes derived from Grimm are now the main types of the northern U.S.A. and Canada, and they have been reintroduced into Europe.

Varieties Used in U.K. Seed-setting of lucerne tends to be rather poor under British conditions, and seed production is therefore very limited, the greater part of the seed being imported. The forms used are mainly rather variable local varieties, although some bred varieties of French origin are available. Source of origin is therefore important, and different forms of, for example, Grimm, may vary considerably if produced in widely different areas.

The main types useful in England may be grouped as follows:

EARLY . . Early spring growth and early flowering; long growing season, extending well into autumn. Stems erect, leaflets large. Mainly blue-flowered *sativa* forms of the *Flamande* type from N. France. Varieties include Ile de France, Ormelong (of which Du Puits is a selected bred variety), Chartainvilliers. Some English seed of the type is produced.

MID-SEASON — Later in spring, later flowering, shorter growing season, stems less erect, leaflets smaller. Blue-flowered *sativa* forms of the *Provence* type from S. France. Similar types are Hungarian and New Zealand Marlborough.

LATE — Later in spring, later flowering and still shorter growing season; more prostrate, leaflets smaller and narrower, yield lower, hardier. Mainly variegated *varia* forms of N. American origin, including Grimm and the still later, somewhat creeping Rhizoma, derived from a Grimm ×*falcata* back-cross.

It should be emphasized that this classification can be applied only with reference to a particular climate; thus Argentine forms (with short, broad leaflets), while agreeing with the early types in other respects, are late in spring and very late-flowering in England, although they show a very long growing season in the Argentine.

Medicago lupulina L. Trefoil, Black Medick, Yellow Trefoil

Distinguishing Characters. Annual, or sometimes biennial, with weak, trailing, much-branched stems, leaves trifoliate, leaflets small, ovate, mucronate. Flowers small, yellow, in oval, long-stalked axillary racemes. Pods single-seeded, short, curved, ridged, black when ripe. Seed symmetrical, not twisted, kidney-shaped with conspicuous projecting point near hilum, dull greenish-yellow, 2 mm., about ¼ million per pound. Seedling with almost sessile oval cotyledons, 7 mm. long. First leaf transversely oval, 4 mm. long by 7 mm. broad, mucronate, slightly toothed, veins conspicuous, occasional short hairs present. The plant somewhat resembles suckling clover (*Trifolium dubium*), but is readily distinguished by the broader, less grey, mucronate leaflets, the larger, brighter yellow racemes and the very different pods.

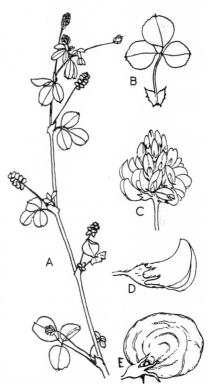

FIG. 52. Black medick. A, flowering shoot, ×½. B, detached leaf, ×½. C, flower-head, ×3½. D, single flower, ×7. E, fruit, ×7.

Uses. Trefoil is not conspicuously high-yielding, and can only be regarded as a rather poor substitute for red clover. It may sometimes be worth sowing alone at about 10 lb. per acre, or in mixture with Italian rye-grass, for a one-year ley if clover-rot (p. 545) prevents the growing of red clover, as it is somewhat resistant to this disease. The low price of the seed makes it suitable for ultra-short leys for stubble-grazing, where low cost of seeds-mixture is a primary consideration. Trefoil seed may also be included in small quantity (1 lb. per acre) in mixtures for longer leys as a precautionary measure, in case of red clover failure. It establishes readily providing that ample lime is present, but is very intolerant of acidity. It is a common wild plant on non-acid soils, and some variation exists, but its importance has not justified the development of distinct strains.

M. arabica (L.) All. (**M. maculata** Sibth.), Spotted Medick, a hairy, sprawling annual with very broad black-spotted leaflets and large

toothed stipules, orange-yellow flowers in short racemes and closely-coiled, almost globular spiny burr fruits, occurs as an unpalatable weed in S.W. England, germinating in autumn and dying out in summer, leaving bare patches in a ley.

FIG. 53. Fruits of A, *Medicago arabica* and B, *M. hispida*, × 3.

M. hispida Gaertn., Hairy Medick, with smaller unspotted leaves and flatter burr fruits, occurs occasionally in S. England, but rarely on farmland. Both are cultivated to a small extent as winter cover crops on cotton and maize fields in southern U.S.A. under the name of bur clover. These and other burr-fruited *Medicago* species may become serious weeds of sheep-pasture, as the fruits become entangled in wool and seriously reduce its value. (*M. hispida* Gaertn.=*M. polymorpha* L.).

MELILOTUS. MELILOTS, SWEET CLOVERS

Annuals or biennials, with rather woody erect stems, trifoliate pointed leaves and lanceolate entire stipules. Flowers white or yellow, diadelphous, in long axillary racemes, pods one-seeded, straight. Seed yellowish-brown, resembling red clover in size, but with longer radicle. Seedling with almost sessile long-oval cotyledons 9 mm. long. First leaf ovate, mucronate, with truncate base, toothed. Epicotyl elongating early.

Melilots are drought-resistant and tolerant of poor conditions, but are not of high agricultural value. If allowed to grow tall, they produce high yields, but the produce is very woody; if cut earlier, before the stems become woody, the yield is low. Growth is erect, with few basal buds, and the plants are therefore not tolerant of hard cutting or grazing. They contain *coumarin* (whence the name sweet clover; cf. sweet vernal grass, p. 333), which, although sweet-scented, is bitter in taste, and are therefore unpalatable. Spoiled melilot hay or silage may be toxic owing to the conversion of coumarin into compounds closely related to warfarin, used as a rat poison, and which, like warfarin, prevent normal clotting of blood. Melilots are extensively grown in N. America under conditions where clovers are unsatisfactory, and where

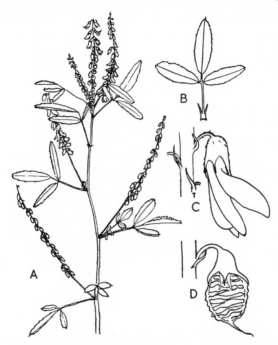

FIG. 54. Yellow melilot (*Melilotus officinalis*). A, upper part of flowering shoot, ×½. B, detached leaf, ×½. C, flower, ×4. D, unripe fruit, ×4.

the shortness of the ley prevents the use of lucerne; in Britain they are likely to be of value only for green-manuring, and are rarely sown.

The main species are: **M. alba** Medic., White Melilot, Bokhara clover, biennial with stout stems up to 5 ft., flowers white, 4-5 mm. long, wings and keel equal. *Hubam clover* is an annual selection.

M. officinalis (L.) Pall., Yellow Melilot, Common Melilot, is very similar, but with yellow flowers, with wing petals longer than keel. **M. indica** (L.) All., Small-flowered Melilot, is a smaller annual with small yellow flowers, occurring occasionally in waste places.

LOTUS. BIRD'S FOOT TREFOILS

Rather small herbaceous plants with pinnate leaves composed of five leaflets, the lower pair basal and resembling stipules (whence the name trefoil), true stipules minute.

Lotus corniculatus L.   Common Bird's-foot Trefoil

A deep-rooted herbaceous perennial, with stems prostrate or semi-erect. Leaves small; inflorescences axillary long-stalked umbels of from three to six yellow or yellow and orange-red flowers. Calyx teeth erect in bud. Cross-pollination by bees. Fruit a slender cylindrical straight pod, 1-2 in. long, with numerous seeds. Ripe pods spreading horizontally so that whole umbel resembles a bird's foot. Seeds shining brown with

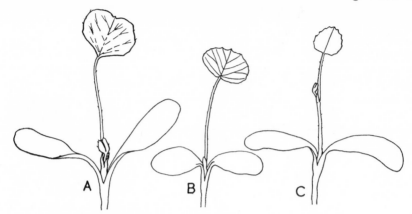

Fig. 55. Seedlings of A, lucerne; B, black medick; C, white melilot, × 2.

darker mottling, intermediate in size between red and white clover, *c.* 1·7 mm., 400,000 to lb. First leaf of seedling trifoliate.

Bird's-foot trefoil is common in dry pastures on poor land; it is a useful plant on such soils, but is not usually considered worth sowing in

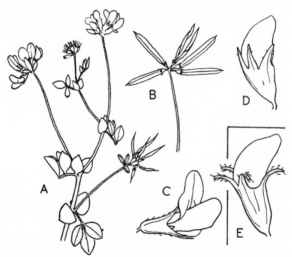

Fig. 56. Birdsfoot trefoil, *Lotus corniculatus*. A, flowering shoot, × ½. B, fruiting head, × ½. C, flower, × 2. D, bud, × 3. E, bud of *L. uligonosus*, × 3.

Britain. It does not compete well with clovers on the better soils; establishment is slow, and the proportion of hard seeds high (up to 50 per cent.). Cultivated in France and the U.S.A. alone or with grasses, sown at 5-15 lb. per acre.

The indigenous British form is a small prostrate plant with broad leaflets. The cultivated forms are larger and more erect; some of these are referred to *L. tenuis* Waldst. & Kit., a diploid with narrower leaflets and smaller flowers, less drought-resistant.

Lotus uliginosus Schkuhr. (**L. pedunculatus** Cav., **L. major** Scop.). Greater or Marsh Bird's-foot Trefoil

A larger plant, with larger leaves, wide-spreading stems and short rhizomes. Umbels with eight to twelve smaller flowers, calyx teeth spreading not erect, pods more slender, seeds smaller, 1·2 mm., about 800,000 per lb.

Occurs in Britain on marshy soils, and is almost the only legume tolerant of such conditions. Rarely sown here, but has been employed in New Zealand for the improvement of marsh land.

Anthyllis vulneraria L. Kidney Vetch.

A perennial with stout tap-root and branching crown. Leaves pinnate with from three to five pairs of lanceolate leaflets, terminal leaflet larger; leaves forming a rosette-like tuft in winter. Erect leafy stems in summer up to 18 in., softly hairy. Inflorescence terminal or sub-terminal, consisting of several short crowded racemes subtended by bracts, each with about thirty almost sessile yellow flowers. Calyx inflated, hairy, with short teeth. Stamens monadelphous. Fruit a one-seeded pod enclosed in persistent calyx. Seed oval, radicle-lobe inconspicuous, 2·5 mm., about 200,000 to lb., upper half green, lower half yellow. First leaf of seedlings simple, obovate.

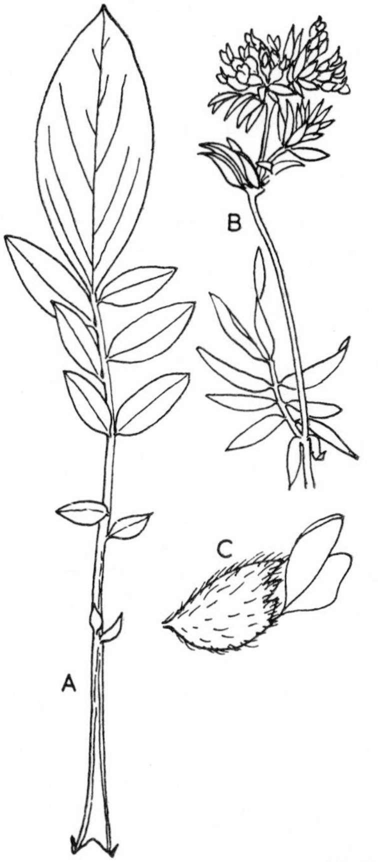

FIG. 57. Kidney vetch. A, basal leaf, × ½. B, flowering shoot, × ½. C, single flower, × 2.

Kidney vetch occurs occasionally in dry, calcareous pastures. It is rarely sown, but is sometimes employed in E. England to replace red clover under dry conditions. It gives only a single hay cut, does not compare favourably in yield with red clover, and under ley conditions tends to be short-lived.

Onobrychis viciifolia Scop. (**O. sativa** Lam.). Sainfoin

Distinguishing Characters. A perennial, with stout tap-root, producing numerous erect leafy stems. Leaves pinnate, with numerous pairs of lanceolate lateral leaflets, terminal leaflet small. Stipules broad, pointed, membranous, red in colour, fused to form tube around stem. Long axillary racemes of large flowers. Calyx teeth long narrow, petals pink with red veins; standard semi-erect, wings very small. Stamens diadelphous. Fruit a one-seeded indehiscent pod, with straight ventral suture and semicircular, usually strongly-toothed dorsal suture. Pericarp pale

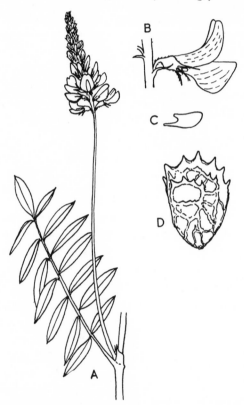

brown when ripe, surface marked with reticulate ridges, about 7 × 5 mm., about 20,000 fruits to lb. True seed, obtained by milling fruits after threshing, large, dark olive-brown, kidney-shaped, about 4×3 mm., 30,000 to pound. First leaf of seedlings simple, second trifoliate.

Use. Sainfoin is almost confined in Britain to the southern half of the country and to chalk and limestone soils, where it provides valuable sheep-feed and hay. Hay is difficult to make, as the leaflets tend to become brittle before the midribs and stems are dry, but when well-made is regarded as the most valuable of all hays for racehorses. Sainfoin is usually sown under corn, at about 100 lb. per acre unmilled 'seed' ('in husk') or 50 lb. of the milled seed; 1 lb. of unmilled sainfoin contains about two-thirds the number

FIG. 58. Sainfoin. A, leaf and axillary raceme, × ½. B, single flower, × 1¾. C, wing petal, × 3. D, ripe fruit ('unmilled seed'), × 3.

of seeds present in 1 lb. of true seed, but the sowing rate is doubled to allow for the greater proportion of hard seeds. Unmilled sainfoin is very likely to be contaminated with the somewhat similar woody fruits of burnet (p. 186); milling of the seed enables this to be cleaned out.

Types. Sainfoin is cross-pollinated, and a number of local varieties exist; these can be divided into two fairly distinct groups:

Giant Sainfoin, giving two cuts per year, but persisting only for about two years. Flowers in first year if spring sown, and has long flowering period and comparatively few long stems. Introduced from France about 1830.

Common Sainfoin, a long-lived perennial persisting for five years or more, but giving only a single hay cut each year. Does not flower in first year;

in second and later years has a shorter flowering period than giant, with more numerous but rather shorter stems. Possibly indigenous, but probably introduced into cultivation from France in seventeenth century. More commonly grown than giant.

The distinctions between the two types correspond roughly to those between broad red and late-flowering red clovers, but giant sainfoin does not commence flowering earlier than common, and the correlation between the single-cut character and long life is not always close. The two forms cannot be distinguished on characters of seed or seedling; the mean number of leaflets per leaf is slightly greater (about twenty-five) in giant than in common (about twenty-three), but this distinction is only evident if large samples are counted under comparable conditions. The purchase of certified (field-inspected) seed is therefore the only guarantee of trueness to type.

Ornithopus sativus Brot., Serradella, is a Portuguese annual with pinnate leaves, pink flowers and curved, indehiscent pods which break up into one-seeded pieces. It grows to a height of 18 in., has been used as a fodder and green-manuring crop on poor dry soils in Europe. It is not cultivated in Britain; the much smaller **O. perpusillus** L., Bird's-foot (from the arrangement of the pods; cf. *Lotus*, p. 170), occurs on dry, sandy soils in S. England, but is of no agricultural importance.

LUPINUS. LUPINS

Lupinus is a large genus of perennials (including the common garden ornamental *L. polyphyllus* Lindl.) and annuals, of which a number of species are used as fodder and green-manuring plants.

The annual lupins used in agriculture are stout, erect plants up to 5 ft. high, with palmately compound leaves, narrow stipules, and racemes of large flowers with two-lipped calyx and monadelphous stamens; the pods are straight, hairy and contain several large seeds. They are not frost-hardy, but have the advantage that they will grow on light acid soils, where almost all other legumes fail. It is only on soils of this type that they merit consideration; in Britain they have been used to some extent on the lighter soils of E. England for sheep-folding, silage and green-manuring. Utilization for fodder is complicated by the fact that lupins are often poisonous, owing to the presence of lupinine and other toxic alkaloids. The concentration of the toxic substances is variable, and tends to be higher in the pods and seeds; they are not destroyed by drying, but may be removed by leaching or steaming. Feeding of large amounts of lupins may result in *lupinosis*, the sheep showing jaundice, staggering and loss of appetite; death may result from asphyxia.

Strains of lupins have been developed in Germany, New Zealand and elsewhere which have a low alkaloid content; these are known as *sweet lupins,* and sweet strains of both yellow and blue lupins are available, with alkaloid contents of 0·01-0·03 per cent. in the seed, as against 0·8-0·9 per cent. in the 'bitter' forms. The sweet lupins are to be preferred for stock-feeding, and can be fed to sheep with greater safety, although care is still necessary.

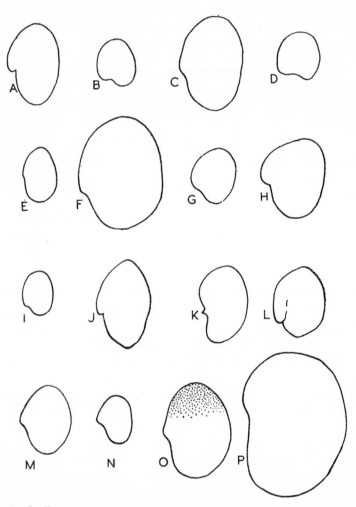

Fig. 59. Outlines of seeds of clovers and other forage legumes, × 10. A, red clover. B, alsike. C, crimson clover. D, white clover. E, suckling clover. F, subterranean clover. G, strawberry clover. H, zigzag clover. I, haresfoot clover. J, lucerne. K, black medick. L, white melilot. M, common birdsfoot trefoil. N, greater birdsfoot trefoil. O, kidney vetch (stippling indicates position of green coloration). P, sainfoin (milled).

Lupins are usually drilled at 50-100 lb. per acre, either alone or in mixture with rape, oats or sometimes buckwheat. Seed production is difficult, and yellow and white lupins are usually too late in ripening for seed to be produced in Britain. Blue lupins are usually earlier, but loss of seed by shattering (early dehiscence of pods) is a serious problem, and yields are rarely more than 10 cwt. per acre.

The three species occasionally employed in Britain are:

Fig. 60. Upper part of flowering plant of A, white lupin; B, yellow lupin; C, blue lupin; all × ⅓.

Lupinus angustifolius L.   Blue Lupin

Up to 3 ft. high, branching, with rather woody stems. Leaves small with usually from seven to eleven narrow, rather obtuse leaflets, flowers small, pale blue (white forms exist) in short racemes, pods about 5 cm. long, with from four to six ovoid seeds. Seeds buff with darker markings, 9 mm., about 2,000 per lb. Quick-growing, early ripening.

L. luteus L.   Yellow Lupin

Up to 3½ ft. high, less branched, leaves larger with from seven to nine broader leaflets; flowers larger, bright yellow, whorled in longer racemes. Pods similar; seeds smaller, 7·5 mm., about 3,000 per lb., white with black markings. Establishment slow under cool conditions, late-ripening.

L. albus L.   White Lupin

Up to 5 ft., stout, little branched, leaves larger with from five to nine ovate-lanceolate leaflets with ciliate margins. Flowers white in continuous racemes,

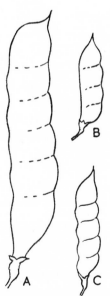

Fig. 61. Pods of A, white; B, yellow; and C, blue lupins, × ½.

175

calyx with upper lip entire. Pods large, up to 13 cm., seeds white, flat, large, varying in size up to 15 mm., 750 per lb. Large-seeded forms have been used as a pulse crop in S. Europe, the seed being apparently safe after steeping and cooking. Used in Britain only as a green-manuring crop.

Fig. 62. Seedlings of A, white; B, yellow; and C, blue lupins, × ½.

VICIA. VETCHES AND FIELD BEANS

Vicia species have weak climbing or straggling stems (stout, erect in *V. faba*), pinnate leaves with small stipules and the terminal leaflet replaced by a tendril or point, flowers in axillary racemes, stamens diadelphous with staminal tube obliquely truncate, pods long, straight, dehiscent. Several weak-stemmed species are common in Britain as wild vetches (see weeds, p. 423), the only one commonly cultivated is:

Vicia sativa L.   Common Vetch, Tare

An annual with long straggling four-sided stems and large pinnate leaves ending in a branched tendril, leaflets numerous obovate or oblong, 10-20 mm. long, mucronate; stipules lanceolate, pointed, often toothed, with dark mark in centre. Flowers short-stalked, axillary, solitary or in pairs, red-purple or very occasionally white. Pods 50-70 mm., four- to ten-seeded, seeds round, somewhat flattened, varying from pale brown with darker mottling to dark brown, hilum elongated, pale, 4-6 mm., 6,000-8,000 per lb. Germination hypogeal, first leaf with two leaflets and short central point.

Grown alone, or more commonly in mixture with cereals, as a forage crop to be folded off or used for silage or occasionally for hay. Valuable for its rapid growth and high yield of green fodder; may be used as a 'smother-crop' to control weeds by its heavy shading effect.

Two main types are used: *winter vetch*, hardy and used for autumn sowings; and *spring vetch*, less hardy, but quicker-growing. The difference is mainly a physiological one; the winter type tends to have smaller seeds

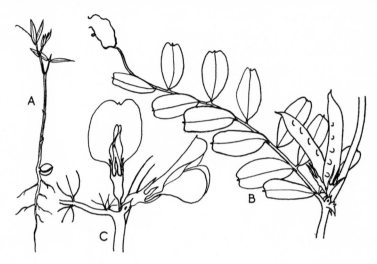

FIG. 63. Common vetch *Vicia sativa*. A, seedling, × ½. B, part of stem with leaf and young pods, × ½. C, pair of flowers in axil of leaf, × 1¼.

and smoother, more cylindrical pods, but these morphological differences are variable and not well-defined.

(*V. villosa*, with flowers in long axillary racemes, is hardier than *V. sativa*, and is known as winter vetch in the U.S.A., where winter forms of common vetch do not survive; it is also commonly cultivated in central Europe.)

Vicia faba L. (Faba vulgaris Moench.). Field Bean, Broad Bean

Cultivated in Europe since prehistoric times, and not known wild; perhaps derived from the somewhat similar but smaller *V. narbonensis* L., an erect Mediterranean annual.

An erect annual with stout, square, slightly winged stems, large leaves with toothed stipules and usually two pairs of large ovate leaflets; no tendrils are present, but the mid-rib ends in a short, fine point. Short axillary racemes of from two to six large flowers. Corolla white, or occasionally lilac or purple, with black blotch on wing petals. Pods large, straight, fleshy when young and with inner surface downy; seeds varying in size and number in different types. Partially self-pollinated.

Two main types are used within the species: broad beans grown as a vegetable for human consumption, and field beans grown for stock-feeding.

Broad Beans. Seeds large (usually 15-25 mm.), flat and with pale testa, either white or green. Grown for picking in the unripe seed stage, as a market garden crop. A number of fairly distinct varieties exist, falling into two groups: (*a*) *Longpods.* Sufficiently hardy to allow of autumn or very early spring sowing under favourable conditions; pods long, several together, with from four to nine seeds; (*b*) *Windsors.* Less hardy, suited to spring sowing only; pods usually borne singly, shorter, broader, with from two to five larger seeds.

Field Beans. Seeds smaller (usually 10-17 mm.), short-cylindrical or somewhat flattened, testa pale brown darkening with age; grown on field scale for harvesting ripe and threshing for stock feed, or as a constituent of arable silage or forage crops for cutting green.

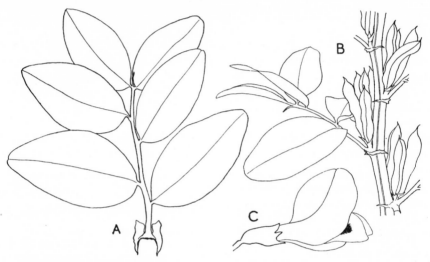

Fig. 64. Field bean (Tick). A, leaf, × ¼. B, part of stem with leaves and young pods, × ¼. C, flower, × 1⅓.

Cross-pollination occurs to the extent of about 50 per cent., and stocks of field beans tend therefore to be rather variable, and are usually somewhat mixed. The majority fall into one or other of the following groups:

Winter Beans. Hardy, slow-growing, stems branching at base. Seed short cylindrical, about 6–700 per lb. E.g. Throws MS, SQ, Maris Beaver.

Tick Beans. Suited spring sowing, less hardy, less branched, quicker growing. Seeds smaller, about 8–1100 per lb., used for pigeon food. E.g. Albyn, Maris Bead.

Horse Beans. Plants similar to ticks, seed as winters but flatter. E.g. Suffolk Red, Strubes. (*Mazagan*, old N. African type, seeds very large.)

Field bean seeds (protein about 25 per cent., carbohydrate about 50 per cent.) are valuable stock food, but the crop is often unreliable. Beans could provide a convenient break in a largely cereal rotation, and the use of residual pre-emergence herbicides, together with effective aphis control, may result in their greater use. Winter beans are not completely hardy, and may suffer severely from chocolate spot disease (p. 548); spring beans require early sowing, and if late may be badly damaged by black aphis. Bean 'straw' has a higher protein content than cereal straw, and is of potentially high feeding value, but can rarely be harvested in good condition if seed is allowed to ripen fully.

Pisum sativum L.   Pea

A climbing annual, glabrous and glaucous, with slender cylindrical stems from 1 to 6 ft.; leaves with from two to three pairs ovate leaflets and ending in branched tendril, stipules very large, leaf-like. Flowers from two to four in long-stalked axillary racemes; calyx with broad teeth, corolla white or red-purple, standard broad, erect, stamens diadelphous, stamen tube short transversely truncate. Self-pollinated. Pods smooth, almost cylindrical, with numerous seeds, varying in size and colour in different types. Germination hypo-geal, first two leaves represented by trifid scales of which the shape varies in different varieties.*

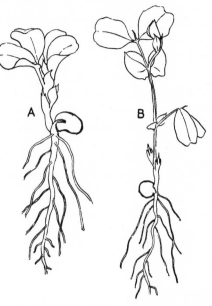

FIG. 65. Seedlings of A, field bean and B, field pea, × ½.

Cultivated since prehistoric times; probably originating in S.W. Asia. No truly hardy winter varieties.

The fact that peas are normally self-pollinated, and natural crossing very rare, means that a large number of distinct true-breeding varieties have been developed. These fall into two distinct groups, sometimes treated as separate species, but completely interfertile if artificially crossed:

(a) *Garden Peas* (*P. sativum* in the narrow sense). White-flowered with blue-green or white seeds, testa colourless, plants tender, stipules un-marked. Cultivated for seeds for human consumption. Varieties of this type may be arbitrarily divided into two groups according to use:

(i) *Green Peas* (*Vining Peas*). Grown as a crop for picking green, for use fresh, frozen or canned; very variable in height (dependent on internode length), from 1 to 5 ft.; taller varieties as garden crop only, usually supported on pea-sticks. Length of growing period varies from about ten to fifteen weeks (dependent on num-ber of non-flowering nodes at base of stem). Mainly with green, wrinkled seeds; but a few hardier early varieties have round seeds. Round seeds have a lower water content and harden earlier;

* See Morris, G. P. *J. nat. Inst. agric. Bot.* **6,** 489, 1953.

179

they have simple starch grains, while those of wrinkled peas are compound.

(*Sugar Peas* (Mangetout) are a distinct form in which the inner fibrous layer of the pod is not developed; the immature pod is cooked whole; not grown on field scale.)

(2) *Dry Peas*. Varieties grown on a field scale without supports for harvesting ripe and threshing for human consumption as packeted, processed or split peas. The main groups of varieties are:

Marrowfats, with wrinkled seeds, cotyledons green. Fair yield of high quality. Harrison's Glory is main variety.

Blue Peas, with round seeds and green cotyledons. The Small Blue, with small seeds and long straw, is hardier and suited to poorer soils than the short-strawed Large or Dutch Blue. Less popular than marrowfats.

White Peas, with round seeds and yellow cotyledons, mainly varieties of Dutch or Swedish origin, are grown only for use as split peas.

(*b*) *Field Peas* (*P. sativum* var. *arvense* (L.), Poir, or sometimes separated as *P. arvense* L.). Flowers bicoloured, purple and red, with seeds brownish or mottled owing to coloration of testa, plants hardier,

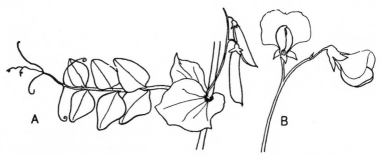

Fig. 66. Field pea (Dun). A, part of stem, with leaf and young pods, × ⅓. B, flowers, × ½.

stipules with purple coloration at base. Grown only for stock-feed, for ripe seed or cut green for forage or silage, either alone or in mixture with cereals. (It may be remarked that, while these are commonly known as field peas, the field acreage devoted to them in Britain is considerably exceeded by that of the garden peas.)

Field peas may be grouped into:

Dun peas, with large seeds, testa dull brown, cotyledons yellow, early ripening, medium length 'straw'.

Maple peas (also called Partridge), with smaller seeds, testa brown, speckled, cotyledons yellow, usually later than duns, and with longer straw. Used, like duns, for stock-feeding, but also has special sale for pigeon-feeding, for which purpose small peas with light hilum are preferred. Named bred varieties are *Marathon*, small-seeded, storing well, hilum black, and the earlier, even-ripening *Minerva* with light hilum, higher-yielding and shorter-strawed than Marathon.

Grey peas, seeds smaller, spherical, testa pale grey speckled violet, cotyledons yellow. Late ripening. Little grown in Britain, used in southern U.S.A. as winter cover crop (Austrian winter peas).

Peas provide useful stock food of approximately the same composition as beans, but, as with beans, the yields are very variable. Drilled at about 40-180 lb. per acre according to size and use, in 7-14-in. rows; suited to medium or light soils. Harvesting difficult except under dry conditions; in wetter areas usually grown in mixture with cereals to provide support. They may also, like field beans, be included in arable silage and forage mixtures.

Glycine max. (L.) Merr.   Soya Bean

(The original description has been variously interpreted, and the names *G. soja*, *G. hispida* and *Soja max* have also been used.)

Annual, erect, 2-3 ft.; leaves trifoliate with large, ovate, mucronate, hairy leaflets, narrow, pointed stipules present at base of leaflets as well as of leaves. Flowers small, yellowish-white, in short axillary racemes. Pods straight, hairy, with from three to five seeds. Seeds varying in colour and size in different varieties. Eastern Asiatic in origin, cultivated at least 4,000 years. Very numerous varieties.

Soya bean seeds are of exceptionally high feeding value, with some 20 per cent. oil, 35 per cent. protein and 30 per cent. carbohydrates; no starch is present. Very widely cultivated, giving, under favourable conditions in N. America, yields of a ton or more per acre of ripe seed, or from 2-4 tons of hay if cut green. Numerous attempts have been made to grow the soya bean in Britain, but it behaves as a short-day plant requiring high temperatures, and only the earliest and therefore lowest-yielding varieties will ripen seed, and that very late in the year. In these varieties pods are borne at nodes very near the ground, and harvesting is therefore difficult. Requires a distinct form of *Rhizobium radicicola* (sometimes separated as *R. japonicum*) for nodulation, but in fertile soil will make apparently healthy growth without inoculation.

PHASEOLUS

A considerable number of species of *Phaseolus*, with pinnate, usually trifoliate leaves and twining stems, are grown in various parts of the world as beans. Two only are grown in Britain as market garden crops:

P. coccineus L. **(P. multiflorus** Willd.**).**   Runner Bean

Tall perennial with fleshy root, grown as an annual. Inflorescences axillary, longer than leaves, with from twenty to thirty flowers, scarlet, white or bicolour, pods broad, rough, green, seeds large, pink with black mottling, or white in white-flowered varieties. Self-pollinated. Germination hypogeal. Grown only for immature pods as a vegetable.

P. vulgaris L. French or Kidney Bean (or Field Bean in U.S.A.)

Annual, climbing or dwarf. Inflorescence fewer-flowered, shorter than leaf. Flowers white or scarlet, pods smooth, narrower, various colours.

FIG. 67. Soya bean. A, whole plant in fruiting stage, ×⅕. B, leaf, ×⅕. C, pods, ×½. D, seedling, ×¼.

Self-pollinated. Seeds smaller, but varying much in size and colour in different varieties. Germination epigeal. Grown for immature pods, or ripe threshed seed known as *haricot beans*. (For varieties, see North and Squibbs, *J. Nat. Inst. Agric. Bot.*, **6,** 196, and Sneddon and Squibbs, *ibid.*, **7,** 121.)

Other members of the *Leguminosae* not grown in Britain, but sometimes imported and used in stock-feeding, include:

Arachis hypogea L., ground-nut; a low-growing, tufted annual with pinnate leaves and yellowish flowers turning down after pollination, gynophore (base of ovary) elongating to bury developing fruit in ground. Ripe pods fibrous, containing from two to three pea-like seeds of high oil and protein content. Widely cultivated in tropics and sub-tropics.

Ceratonia siliqua L., carob bean, locust bean, a large tree of Mediterranean area, belonging to sub-family *Caesalpinioideae*. Pods broad,

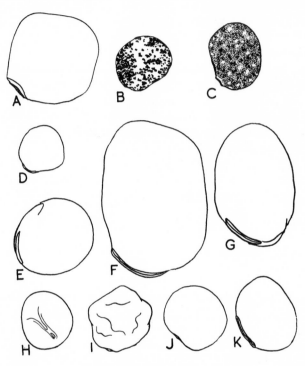

FIG. 68. Seeds of various large-seeded Leguminosae, × 2. A, white lupin. B, yellow lupin. C, blue lupin. D, common vetch. E, tick bean. F, broad bean. G, Scotch horse bean. H, blue pea. I, marrowfat pea. J, maple pea. K, soya bean.

flattened, fleshy, with high sugar content; used whole or ground for stock-feed.

Trigonella foenum-graecum L., fenugreek. Erect Mediterranean annual with long, pointed, narrow pods containing yellow, flattened, very angular, strongly-scented seeds, sometimes ground and the meal included in cattle feeds as spice.

KEY TO GENERA. VEGETATIVE CHARACTERS

Leaves trifoliate.
    Leaflets large, 1½ in. (4 cm.) wide or more.
        Leaves glabrous, stem twining   .   .   .   .   *Phaseolus*
        Leaves hairy, stem not twining   .   .   .   .   *Glycine*

Leaflets small.
    Leaflets emarginate or obtuse   .   .   .   .   *Trifolium*
    Leaflets mucronate.
        Stipules lanceolate or broad, toothed .   .   .   *Medicago*
        Stipules linear, not toothed   .   .   .   .   *Melilotus*
Leaves with five or more leaflets.
    Leaflets palmately arranged   .   .   .   .   .   *Lupinus*
    Leaflets pinnately arranged.
        Terminal leaflet present.
            Leaflets 5, lower pair stipule-like .   .   .   .   *Lotus*
            Leaflets numerous.
                Terminal leaflet largest .   .   .   .   *Anthyllis*
                All leaflets similar.
                    Stipules membranous, broad.   .   .   .   *Onobrychis*
                    Stipules green, minute   .   .   .   .   *Ornithopus*
        Terminal leaflet replaced by tendril or point.
            Stipules smaller than leaflets   .   .   .   .   *Vicia*
            Stipules larger than leaflets   .   .   .   .   *Pisum*

Chapter XII

ROSACEAE, UMBELLIFERAE, POLYGONACEAE AND CANNABINACEAE

ROSACEAE

General Importance. A family of outstanding horticultural importance, containing many of the main cultivated fruits, but with very few members of agricultural value. Forage burnet is an agricultural crop of very minor importance; hawthorn, and to a lesser extent blackthorn, are farm hedging plants.

Botanical Characters. A very large family, including numerous shrubs and small trees. Leaves alternate, usually stipulate, often compound. Inflorescence racemose; flowers actinomorphic, insect-pollinated, very variable in structure. Calyx of five free sepals, sometimes with an epicalyx; petals five, free; stamens usually ten or more; gynaecium of from one to many carpels, sometimes united, with one or more ovules, the style of free carpels often lateral or basal. The flower is usually perigynous, but in some forms the carpels are so deeply sunk in the receptacle that the flower becomes epigynous, while in others the central part of the receptacle is strongly convex, bearing the carpels on its outer surface. The fruiting receptacle may be either dry or succulent, as may also the pericarp, so that a very wide range of fruit types is found.

The family is divided into a number of tribes, the classification being based on these differences of flower and fruit structure. The only strictly agricultural crop-plant, forage burnet, belongs to the *Sanguisorbeae*, and this and the tribes which contain important fruit crops are discussed below.

Sanguisorbeae, the Burnet tribe. A small and relatively unimportant tribe with a very deeply concave persistent receptacle becoming hard and enclosing the one or two achenes.

Poterium polygamum W. & K. (**P. muricatum** Spach.), forage burnet, is a tufted perennial growing to a height of about 2 ft. The radical leaves are pinnate, with numerous toothed ovate leaflets; the rather wiry, erect, flowering stems bear numerous leaves of similar structure, but with rather narrower leaflets. Ovate toothed stipules are present at the base of the leaves. The plants are monoecious, or sometimes polygamous, with the usually unisexual flowers crowded together in short, ovoid racemes. The lower flowers of the raceme are male, and the upper ones female; hermaphrodite flowers may be present in the middle. Four green or purplish sepals are borne on the rim of the tubular receptacle; petals are absent. The male flowers have numerous stamens, the female flowers usually two one-seeded carpels sunk in the receptacle and each bearing a long style with red, brush-like stigma; pollination is by wind. The receptacle persists in the female and hermaphrodite flowers, and tightly encloses the mature achenes. The 'seed' thus consists of achenes and hardened receptacle; it is pale brown, about 6 mm. long, oval in side-view, roughly rectangular in cross-section, with four toothed, longitudinal wings and with the surface between the wings coarsely toothed and reticulated.

Forage burnet is an introduced plant, of Mediterranean origin, sometimes grown as a grassland 'herb'. It is deep-rooted, drought-resistant and relatively high-yielding, but may become somewhat unpalatable if allowed to develop its rather hard flowering stems. It does not persist well in herb mixtures on non-calcareous soils. It has become widely naturalized on calcareous soils, and is probably more important as a weed of sainfoin crops than as an intentionally-sown crop. The 'seed' is a common impurity of unmilled sainfoin seed (see p. 172), which it somewhat resembles was a common impurity of unmilled sainfoin portion of burnet plants in a sainfoin ley would be unobjectionable, it would clearly be undesirable that a large percentage of a sample purchased as sainfoin should consist of burnet, and the old Seeds Regulations therefore made the declaration of burnet 'seed' compulsory if present to the extent of 5 per cent. or more.

Poterium sanguisorba L., salad burnet, is a similar but smaller plant, usually only 1 ft. high, with rather rounder leaflets and few cauline leaves and globular racemes; the 'seed' is about two-thirds the size of forage burnet, with entire wings and finer reticulations. Salad burnet is a native plant, common on dry limestone soils, but rarely if ever sown, and considerably less frequent as a weed of sainfoin and similar crops.

Sanguisorba officinalis L., greater burnet, is a larger plant up to 3 ft. tall, sometimes found in damp grassland. It somewhat resembles forage burnet in general appearance, but has all flowers hermaphrodite, insect-pollinated, with four stamens only, and a single carpel. The 'seed' is smooth between the wings. It is not sown, and the 'seed' does not occur as a common impurity.

FIG. 69. Forage burnet, upper part of flowering shoot, × ½.

The members of the *Rosaceae* grown as fruit crops are almost all vegetatively propagated, and the horticultural varieties are clones. Methods of propagation vary; in strawberries a natural means of vegetative spread is present in the runners, while in raspberries and similar plants the shoots which arise from below ground-level, and which naturally produce adventitious roots, can be separated and replanted. In the tree fruits, however, no natural means of vegetative propagation are present, and cuttings rarely produce adventitious roots. For these plants it is therefore necessary to resort to budding or grafting, the clone which it

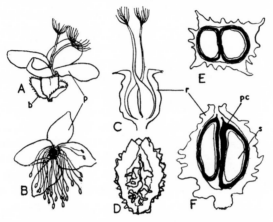

FIG. 70. Forage burnet. A, female flower, × 4. B, male flower, × 2. C, vertical section of female flower to show position of carpels. D, ripe fruit, × 4. E, transverse and longitudinal sections of fruit, × 6. *b*, bract. *p*, perianth. *pc*, pericarp. *r*, receptacle. *s*, seed.

is desired to propagate being used as the *scion*. The *root-stock* is a form of the same or a closely-related species which can either be readily grown from seed, or of which rooted cuttings can be obtained, usually by means of the *stool-bed* method. This involves the cutting-back and earthing-up of stock plants in such a way as to encourage the development of rooted shoots from below ground-level; these can be later separated and re-planted as stocks. The type of root-stock used has no genetic effect on the scion, but does markedly affect the size, vigour and longevity of the resultant tree; it is therefore an advantage to use root-stocks vegetatively propagated by the stool-bed method, since these are clones of uniform type, whereas 'free' stocks grown from seed will usually show considerable variability. The East Malling series of root-stocks for apples, e.g. Malling IX, are examples of such clonal stocks.

Although seeds are not used in propagating fruit crops (except in the production of new varieties), it is essential that seed should be set in order that full development of the fruit may take place. Many clones either produce little or no viable pollen, or are partially or entirely self-incompatible, that is to say, will only set seed when cross-pollinated. Plantings of one single variety are useless in such cases, and interplanting

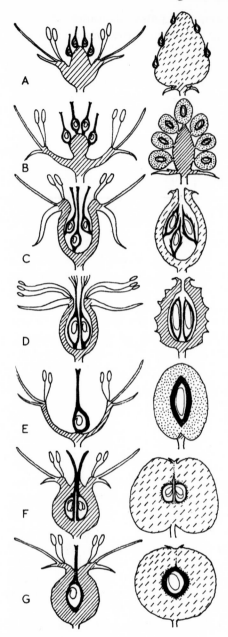

with a suitable pollinator is necessary. This must be another variety which is compatible with the first (cross-incompatibility is common, e.g. in cherries), which produces sufficient viable pollen, and which flowers at the same time. An adequate number of pollinating insects, usually bees, is also necessary.

Tribes of *Rosaceae* which include important fruit-crops are: *Potentilleae*, the Potentilla tribe. Receptacle convex, bearing numerous separate carpels, which may develop into achenes, either on a dry receptacle as in *Potentilla* (p. 425) or on an enlarged succulent edible receptacle as in *Fragaria*, the strawberry. The modern cultivated strawberry varieties are clonal forms of the octoploid *F.* × *ananassa* Duch., a series of hybrids between the two wild octoploid species *F. virginiana* Duch. from N. America and *F. chiloensis* Duch. from S. America. They are large-fruited, with glabrous leaves. Usually self-compatible, but some varieties, e.g. Tardive de Leopold, are male-sterile and must be interplanted. Other species are the diploid *F. vesca* L. (wild strawberry, cultivated forms of which are known as Alpine strawberries) with hairy leaves and small fruits, and the tetraploid *F. moschata* Duch. (hautbois, of European origin, now almost obsolete as a crop), also with hairy leaves, and with larger purplish fruit with achenes on the upper part of the receptacle only.

Rubus has the receptacle dry, but the carpels develop as small drupes (drupels or drupelets), the mesocarp forming the succulent edible part, while the endocarp, the inner layer of the ovary wall, forms the hard

FIG. 71. Rosaceae. Diagrammatic vertical sections of different types of flower and fruit. A, strawberry. B, blackberry. C, rose. D, burnet. E, plum. F, apple. G, hawthorn. The receptacle is marked by diagonal shading; broken diagonal lines in the fruiting stage indicate that the receptacle is succulent. Carpels solid black; parts of carpel-wall which are succulent in fruit stippled. Not to scale.

'pip' containing the single seed. The genus includes a considerable number of species and hybrids forming a polyploid series. *Rubus idaeus* L. (raspberry) is a diploid with pinnate leaves and succulent drupelets separating from the receptacle when picked; *R. fruticosus* L. (blackberry) is mainly tetraploid but very variable and usually split into a large number of separate species, some forms cultivated, others wild and common weeds of neglected grassland (see p. 426); it has palmate leaves and drupelets which remain attached to the receptacle. The hybrid *R. × loganobaccus* Bailey (loganberry) is a hexaploid of American origin derived from parents belonging to the two previous species; the leaves are pinnate, and the elongated aggregate fruit resembles the blackberry in the drupelets not separating readily from the receptacle. Numerous other forms of hybrid origin exist; the odd-number polyploids are usually of lower fertility and therefore lower yield than the even-number.

Pruneae, the plum tribe. Trees and shrubs with simple leaves; receptacle concave, not persistent; one carpel, fruit a single drupe. *Prunus* is a large genus, divisible into several sections or subgenera. In the plum section (leaves deciduous, rolled in bud) *Prunus spinosa* L., blackthorn or sloe, is a spiny shrub, with white flowers produced in spring before the small lanceolate leaves. The fruit is a small drupe with purple skin and green flesh. Blackthorn is a common shrub in farm hedges, but less satisfactory than hawthorn or quick (see *Crataegus*, below) and rarely planted. The cultivated plums, *P. domestica* L., are allo-hexaploids derived from a crossing of the tetraploid sloe with the diploid cherry-plum (*P. cerasifera* Ehrl.) followed by chromosome doubling. In the cherry section (leaves deciduous, folded in bud) the diploid *P. avium* L. includes the cultivated sweet cherries, all self-incompatible and showing marked cross-incompatibility. *P. cerasus*, sour and Morello cherries, is a tetraploid, usually self-compatible.

In the almond section (leaves as cherry, axillary buds in threes, endocarp rough) *P. persica* L., probably of Chinese origin, includes the peach and nectarine. In *P. amygdalus* Batsch., the almond, from W. Asia, the mesocarp is inedible, and it is the seed which is eaten after removal of the endocarp which forms the shell. In the laurel section (leaves evergreen) *P. laurocerasus* L., cherry-laurel, is a shrub or spreading tree with oval, leathery leaves, small white flowers in erect leafless racemes and black, cherry-like fruits. It is commonly planted in garden hedges and is often naturalized; it is an undesirable shrub on farms, as it is markedly *poisonous* owing to the presence of a cyanogenetic glycoside in the leaves (see p. 384).

Pomarieae, the apple tribe. Flowers epigynous, with from one to five carpels sunk into the receptacle and fused with it. Fruit a pome. Haploid chromosomes 17.

Pyrus communis L., common pear, has five carpels with styles free throughout their length. Each carpel contains two ovules, and the endocarp becomes horny, forming the core. Stone-cells are present in the 'flesh' of the enlarged receptacle. Cultivated varieties often self-incompatible; diploid, triploid and tetraploid varieties exist. Fruits mainly on short spur-shoots.

Malus sylvestris (L.) Mill. (*Pyrus malus* L.), the apple, is similar, but with the styles joined at the base, and stone-cells absent. Cultivated varieties mainly diploid, some triploid; self-incompatibility frequent.

Cydonia oblonga Mill., the quince, has a fruit similar in structure to that of the apple, but with several ovules in each carpel; grown occasionally for fruit and some forms also used as a root-stock for pears.

Crataegus has the fruit a pome, but the endocarp of the carpel wall becomes hard, so that the seed is enclosed in a 'stone'.

C. monogyna Jacq., hawthorn, whitethorn or quickthorn, is a spiny shrub or small tree, with deeply-lobed leaves and conspicuous stipules. The small white flowers, produced in corymbs in May and June, have only one carpel, single-seeded; the pome is red, about 10 mm. in diameter. Hawthorn is the best and commonest plant for farm-hedges; non-poisonous, spiny, hardy and withstands laying. Propagated by seed, which requires a period of after-ripening and germinates slowly. *C. oxyacanthoides* Thuill., is a very similar shrub, with more shallowly-lobed leaves and two carpels; less commonly used.

UMBELLIFERAE

General Importance. The *Umbelliferae* are not of great agricultural importance, but include a number of plants grown as vegetables for human consumption and occasionally as root-crops for stock-feeding. Many members of the family contain strongly-scented resin-like substances, and are used as flavouring herbs. A few contain alkaloids and are important poisonous weeds (see p. 428).

Botanical Characters. A large family with between 2,000 and 3,000 species, almost all very uniform in structure, so that the family (like the Cruciferae) is usually easy to recognize, but distinction within the family is often difficult. Nearly all are herbaceous plants with erect, hollow stems and alternate exstipulate leaves, often much divided and with broad sheathing bases to the petioles. The flowers are small, but massed together in conspicuous umbels. The umbels (from which the family takes its name) are usually compound; a whorl of bracts (*involucre*) is sometimes present at the base of the primary umbel, and whorls of bracteoles (*involucels*, or partial involucres) at the base of the secondary umbels. The individual flowers consist of five sepals, which are often reduced to minute points or may even be completely suppressed, five free petals, five stamens and two joined inferior carpels. A single pendulous anatropous ovule is present in each of the two chambers of the ovary. The ovary is surmounted by a fleshy disk (*stylopodium*), around which nectar is secreted; the two short styles are borne on the disk. Pollination is usually by small flies; selfing is largely prevented by marked protandry. The fruit is a schizocarp, splitting when ripe into two single-seeded mericarps which may remain for a time attached to a slender branched 'stalk' (*carpophore*). It is these mericarps or half-fruits which form the 'agricultural seed' in the *Umbelliferae*. They vary considerably in shape, and classification of genera and species within the family is

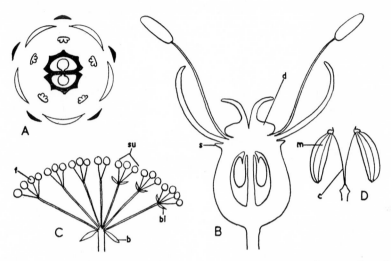

FIG. 72. Floral characters of Umbelliferae. A, floral diagram. B, diagram of vertical section of flower. C, diagram of compound umbel. D, fruit separating into two mericarps. *b*, bract of involucre. *bl*, bracteole of involucel. *c*, carpophore. *d*, disk (stylopodium). *f*, individual flower. *m*, mericarp. *s*, sepal (often much reduced or absent). *su*, single secondary umbel.

very largely based on them. The inner (*commisural*) surface by which the two mericarps were attached is usually somewhat flattened, the outer surface usually convex with five longitudinal ridges, between which lie oil-canals (*vittae*). Within the rather thick, leathery wall of the mericarp is the single seed, with abundant endosperm in which is embedded the small, straight embryo.

Daucus carota L.   Carrot

A biennial with tap-root which is woody in the wild form, thick and succulent in the cultivated forms. Leaves thrice-pinnate with small lanceolate pointed lobes, forming a rosette in the first year. Stem lengthening in the second year, ridged, solid, leafy, up to 3 ft. high, bearing numerous compound umbels which are flat or slightly convex in flower, and deeply concave in fruit, giving a 'bird's nest' appearance. Bracts usually from three to six, divided into several narrow, pointed lobes. Individual flowers small, petals notched, white (petals of central flower of umbel sometimes reddish). Fruit ovoid, primary ridges small, bearing short, stiff hairs. Secondary ridges are present between the primary ridges, and are much more conspicuous, forming on each mericarp four lines of stiff, hooked spines.

Life-history. 'Seed.' The spiny mericarps which are the structures obtained on threshing a carrot-seed crop are difficult to deal with, as they mat together and cannot be drilled readily. They are therefore 'rubbed' during the cleaning process; this does not set free the true seed, but rubs off the spines and part of the ridges, and the 'seed' normally sown consists of the rubbed and more or less smoothed, roughly hemispherical mericarps, about 3·5 mm. long, about 300,000 per pound. Germination is usually low, and 70 per cent. is accepted as satisfactory.

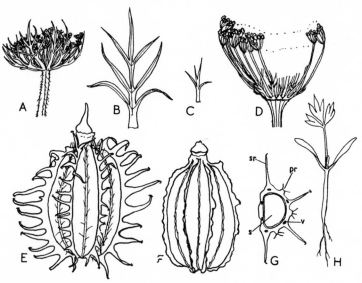

Fig. 73. Carrot. A, small compound umbel in flowering stage, ×½. B, bract, ×1. C, bracteole, ×1. D, umbel in fruiting stage (part omitted), ×½. E, mericarp in unrubbed state, ×10. F, after rubbing. G, diagrammatic transverse section of E. H, seedling, ×1. *pr*, primary ridge. *sr*, secondary ridge. *s*, seed. *v*, vitta.

Seedling. Seed is usually drilled in wide rows, at about 5 lb. per acre; germination is slow. The cotyledons are elongated, strap-shaped, the first foliage leaf deeply divided and about as long as broad. The succeeding leaves are much longer. The hypocotyl and the upper part of the root become swollen; the epicotyl remains very short.

Structure of Swollen Root. The primary root is diarch; four vertical rows of lateral roots are produced. These are not confined to the true root, but adventitious roots are produced on the hypocotyl, which in most varieties remains rather short and is pulled down into the ground. Normal secondary thickening takes place, but the secondary xylem is largely unlignified, and the secondary phloem forms a wide zone around it. The structure is thus similar to that of a turnip, but the proportion of phloem to xylem is very much greater, and only root and hypocotyl are involved.

Second-year Growth. Occasional plants may 'bolt', producing inflorescences in the first year and then dying, but the majority of plants behave as biennials. They are usually lifted and stored at the beginning of the winter dormant period, as they are easily damaged by frost. Growth re-commences in the spring, new leaves are produced, and further secondary thickening takes place. The secondary xylem produced in this second year is heavily lignified, and the feeding value of the root therefore de-creases when new growth starts. If the root has been left in the ground the stem (epicotyl) elongates, and the reserve food stored in the root is used in the production of the inflorescence and fruit. The whole plant dies when the fruit is ripe.

Range of Types. The wild form (Wild Carrot) has a rather slender, woody tap-root, and occurs as an occasional weed in Britain (p. 427). The cultivated carrots, with swollen, succulent root, have been in culti-vation for over 2,000 years, and are perhaps derived from western Asiatic forms of the species. They vary in colour, size and shape of root. The *White Belgian* has large, tapering roots with white flesh, standing out of the ground to a height of about 3 in. The skin of the exposed part is often greenish. This form gives the highest total yield per acre (20 tons or more) but is of rather lower feeding value; it was formerly used as a field crop for stock food, but has now largely gone out of use. *Yellow Belgian* was

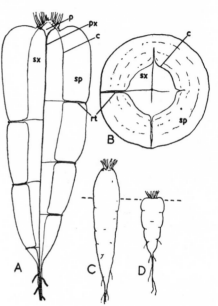

Fig. 74. Carrot. A, diagrammatic longi-tudinal section of root at end of first year's growth. B, transverse section. C and D, com-parison of habit of cattle carrot (White Belgian) and garden carrot (Intermediate). *c*, cambium. *p*, pith. *px*, primary xylem. *rt*, root-trace. *sp*, secondary phloem. *sx*, sec-ondary xylem.

similar, but with yellow flesh and somewhat higher feeding value. Carrots are now rarely grown in Britain for stock food, although surplus or un-saleable roots may be used in this way. The varieties grown for human consumption are all red carrots, which have about 13 per cent. dry matter, of which some 40 per cent. consists of sugars. Carotene, which is largely responsible for the colour and is nutritionally valuable as a precursor of vitamin A, is present to the extent of about 0·25 per cent. of the dry weight. Selection in carrots for human consumption is directed towards the production of roots with as little 'core' as possible—that is, with the secondary xylem as similar as possible to the phloem both in texture and colour. Fungal diseases are not important; the main pest is the carrot-fly, *Psila rosae*, but no varieties are known which show resist-ance to the attacks of this insect. Maincrop varieties are grown often on a field scale for lifting mature for winter consumption; these may be either of long (e.g. Altringham and St. Valery) or intermediate (Scarlet

Intermediate) root shape. For production of 'bunched carrots' for summer use, shorter-rooted varieties are employed, such as Short-horn (stump-rooted), Chantenay (short conical) and French Forcing (round).

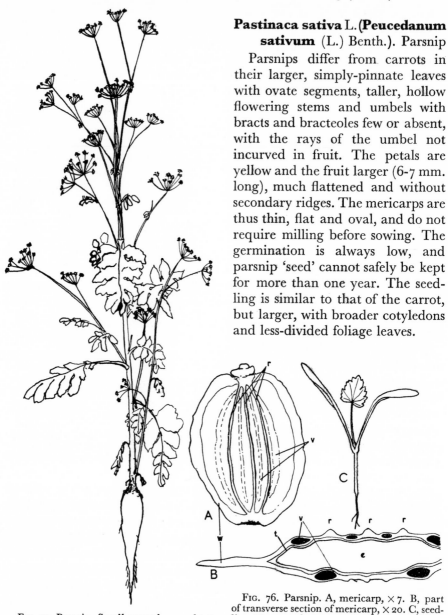

Pastinaca sativa L. **(Peucedanum sativum** (L.) Benth.). Parsnip

Parsnips differ from carrots in their larger, simply-pinnate leaves with ovate segments, taller, hollow flowering stems and umbels with bracts and bracteoles few or absent, with the rays of the umbel not incurved in fruit. The petals are yellow and the fruit larger (6-7 mm. long), much flattened and without secondary ridges. The mericarps are thus thin, flat and oval, and do not require milling before sowing. The germination is always low, and parsnip 'seed' cannot safely be kept for more than one year. The seedling is similar to that of the carrot, but larger, with broader cotyledons and less-divided foliage leaves.

FIG. 75. Parsnip. Small second-year plant in unripe fruit stage, $\times \frac{1}{11}$.

FIG. 76. Parsnip. A, mericarp, $\times 7$. B, part of transverse section of mericarp, $\times 20$. C, seedling, $\times 1$. *e*, endosperm. *r*, three primary ridges of outer surface. *t*, testa. *v*, vittae. *w*, wing.

Wild parsnip is an unimportant biennial grassland plant of some limestone soils in Britain; it has a slender, rather woody tap-root. The cultivated forms have swollen roots similar in structure to those of carrots, but with an even larger proportion of secondary phloem. Only white (really pale yellow) forms exist. Parsnips were formerly grown to some extent for stock food on soils heavier than those suited to carrots, and gave yields of about 20 tons. The dry matter is about 15 per cent., so that prior to the development of fodder-beets parsnips had the highest nutritive value of all true root-crops. Their use is now confined to growing mainly on a market-garden scale as a winter vegetable for human consumption. Only long (e.g. Hollow Crown) and half-long (e.g. Offenham) maincrop types are used, although shorter 'turnip-rooted' forms exist, and a very long growing season is required. Parsnips are rarely attacked by diseases, and usually only slightly damaged by carrot-fly.

Apium graveolens L. Celery

Celery is a biennial with coarsely bi-pinnate leaves, and greenish-white flowers with small entire petals in small, short-stalked umbels. The fruits are small (1·5 mm. long), broadly ovoid, with entire slender primary ridges; they have the characteristic celery odour, and are sometimes used for flavouring. Leaf-spot disease of celery is seed-borne, and black pycnidia of the causal fungus *Septoria apii-graveolentis* are often present on the mericarps.

Wild celery occurs in Britain as a waterside plant. Cultivated celery (sometimes treated as a separate species, *A. dulce* Mill.), which came into use in the seventeenth century, is grown only as a vegetable for human consumption, both in gardens and, particularly on fen soils, as a field crop. The 'seed' is sown in special beds and the seedlings transplanted into

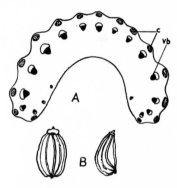

Fig. 77. Celery. A, diagrammatic transverse section of petiole, × 1½. B, dorsal and side views of mericarp, × 10. *c*, collenchyma strands. *vb*, vascular bundle (xylem black, phloem white).

rows. The plants are 'blanched' by earthing up towards the end of the first year of growth, and the short stem and very thick, succulent petioles are used. 'Self-blanching' varieties also exist in which the petioles do not become green on exposure to light. The petioles are broad and consist largely of parenchyma, with a series of vascular bundles of varying size extending through it. A strand of collenchyma occurs immediately inside the lower (abaxial) epidermis in association with each bundle; 'stringy' celery is the result of excessive development of these collenchyma strands under unfavourable growing conditions. *Celeriac* (var. *rapaceum* (Mill.) DC.) is a form of celery occasionally grown in gardens, in which the short stem and upper part of the root are much swollen to form a rather irregular globular structure mainly above soil level; it is used as a 'root' vegetable.

Petroselinum crispum (Mill.) Airy-Shaw. Parsley

(The nomenclature of parsley is somewhat confused, and the names *Petroselinum sativum* Hoffm., *P. hortense* Hoffm. and *Carum petroselinum* Benth. have also been used.)

Parsley is a perennial of Mediterranean origin with tri-pinnate leaves with wedge-shaped segments, and greenish-yellow flowers in flat umbels, bracts and bracteoles both present. Fruit, 2-3 mm., ovoid, with entire primary ridges. *Sheep's parsley* is a form with large leaves with broad, wedge-shaped segments and a woody, usually branched tap-root. It is grown occasionally as a grassland herb, but although very palatable is not usually persistent under grazing conditions.

Curled parsley has smaller leaves with the segments much curled and crisped; it is commonly grown as a garden herb for flavouring and garnishing, and is usually treated as a biennial. The root resembles that of sheep's parsley. *Hamburg parsley* or turnip-rooted parsley is a form very occasionally grown as a garden root vegetable; the tap-root is swollen and succulent, resembling a small parsnip.

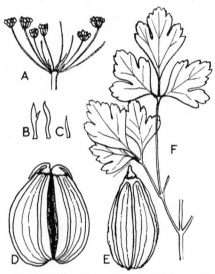

Fig. 78. Sheep's parsley. A, fruiting umbel (part omitted), × ½. B, bracts. C, bracteole, × 1. D, whole fruit, side view, × 10. E, single mericarp, dorsal view, × 10. F, part of leaf, × ½.

Other members of the Umbelliferae grown as garden herbs or vegetables are Chervil (**Anthriscus cerefolium** (L.) Hoffm.) used in a curled-leaved form in the same way as parsley, and Fennel (**Foeniculum vulgare** Mill.), of which the very large, succulent sheathing leaf-bases are used. A considerable number of species are grown for their strongly-scented 'seeds', used for flavouring; these include the biennial Caraway (**Carum carvi** L.), which has also been used as a grassland herb in the same way as sheep's parsley, and the annuals Aniseed (**Pimpinella anisum** L.) and Coriander (**Coriandrum sativum** L.).

POLYGONACEAE

General Importance. The *Polygonaceae* is a family in which the weed species are of much greater importance than the crop-plants. The only agricultural crop is buckwheat; rhubarb is the most important of the very few horticultural crops. Family name derived from the genus *Polygonum, q.v.* under weeds.

Botanical Characters. A small family of mainly herbaceous plants, with alternate simple leaves. Stipules united to form a membranous tube surrounding the stem, known as the *ochrea*. Inflorescences racemes or axillary clusters or whorls; flowers small, actinomorphic, hermaphrodite or unisexual. Perianth variable, either of six segments, in two often dissimilar whorls of three; or five segments, spirally arranged; petalloid (and then usually pink or white) or sepal-like. Stamens variable in number,

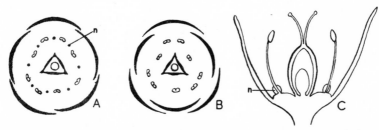

FIG. 79. Polygonaceae. A, floral diagram of *Fagopyrum*. B, of *Rheum*. C, vertical section of flower of *Fagopyrum*. n, nectary.

often six or nine. Gynaecium superior, of three (rarely two) united carpels, with a single basal orthotropous ovule. Pollination by wind or insects. Fruit a three-cornered achene or nut; seed with a curved embryo embedded in copious mealy endosperm.

Fagopyrum esculentum Moench. (Polygonum fagopyrum L.)
Buckwheat, Brank

Buckwheat is an annual with rather weak erect stems, swollen at the nodes. The leaves are alternately arranged, cordate or triangular in shape with sagittate base. The lower ones are large on long petioles, the upper smaller and almost sessile. The inflorescences are stalked axillary clusters; the individual flowers are cymosely arranged and each cluster contains flowers of very varying age. Flowers consist of (usually) five white or pink petaloid perianth segments, eight stamens, and three united carpels forming the triangular superior ovary, bearing three short styles. Small spherical nectaries are present between the bases of the stamens, and pollination is by insects, mainly bees. The flowers are dimorphic—that is, two types of plant are found, one with long filaments and short styles, the other with flowers in which the anthers are on short filaments and the styles longer. Crossing normally takes place from a long-styled to a short-styled plant, and vice versa. The perianth segments do not increase in size after pollination, but the ovary enlarges to form a three-cornered achene, which is the agricultural 'seed'. The ripe achene is (in the form usually grown) greyish-brown in colour, slightly shiny, acute-angled, about 6 mm. long, about 18,000 per pound. The pericarp and testa (husk) form about 40 per cent. by weight of the whole achene, the remainder being white, floury endosperm (starch-parenchyma) with the slender, curved embryo embedded in it.

Buckwheat is usually grown for the achenes, which are milled into flour for human consumption, or used for stock-feeding. It is generally a less satisfactory flour-crop than the true cereals, and is normally only used when these cannot be grown. Its advantages are its quick growth and its tolerance of low fertility and of soil acidity. Its disadvantages (in addition to the very high husk content) are its very weak stem, which is likely to lodge on even moderately fertile soils, and its uneven ripening.

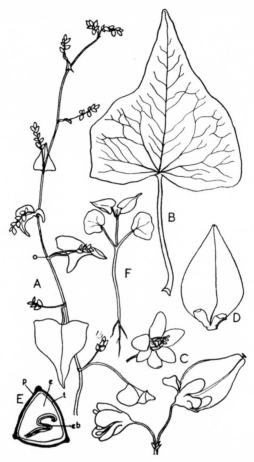

Fig. 80. Buckwheat. A, upper part of stem with leaves and flowers, $\times \frac{1}{5}$. B, leaf, $\times \frac{1}{2}$. C, flowers in various stages, $\times 3$. D, fruit, $\times 4$. E, diagrammatic transverse section of fruit. *e*, endosperm. *eb*, embryo. *o*, ochrea. *p*, pericarp. *t*, testa.

In the true cereals flowering is confined to a week or two at most, and all fruits ripen at about the same time, but in buckwheat flowering is continuous over a long period. In consequence of this, some flowers are still in bud at the time when the earliest-formed fruits are mature. Moreover, the plant is still actively growing at the time when it is necessary to harvest it in order to avoid undue loss of this early seed, and drying of the cut crop is therefore difficult.

Buckwheat is therefore comparatively rarely grown in Britain for seed; it is occasionally used as a green-manuring crop for ploughing in, or sown in small patches to provide food for game. Some danger of stock-poisoning attaches to its use as green fodder. When grown for seed it is drilled at about 50 lb. per acre, or at up to 150 lb. for green manuring. Drilling must be in late spring, as buckwheat is not frost-hardy and does not germinate well at low temperatures. Yields of 12-15 cwt. of 'seed' may be expected.

Buckwheat probably originated in Central Asia, and was introduced into Europe during the Middle Ages. A number of distinct forms exist, including *Japanese*, with rather larger 'seeds', and *Silver Grey*, with pale grey pericarp, but *Common Grey*, the type already described, is the only one used in Britain. *Tartarian Buckwheat*, hardier, and with smaller, rounded achenes, is a distinct species, *Fagopyrum tartaricum* Gaertn., cultivated in Asia. The name buckwheat means 'beech-wheat', from its use for flour and the resemblance of the achene to a miniature beech-nut.

Rheum rhaponticum L.   Rhubarb

A perennial with short rhizomes forming a thick, irregular root-stock, from which arise very large radical leaves, of which the petiole is eaten. Inflorescence a massive panicle 6 ft. tall, with very numerous small white hermaphrodite flowers. Perianth segments six, stamens from six to nine, ovary with three styles, maturing to form an oblong, slightly winged achene. Usually propagated vegetatively by splitting of root-stock, and named varieties are thus clones, but can be grown from achenes. Grown on large scale either in open ground, or lifted roots 'forced' in darkness, after preliminary freezing, to give earlier, more tender, brighter-red etiolated petioles. Of Central Asian origin; other species such as *R. palmatum* L. (with deeply-lobed leaves) possibly involved in development of modern cultivated varieties. Not commonly grown until early nineteenth century. Leaf blades not eaten, often poisonous owing to high oxalic acid content.

Two species of *Rumex* (for characters, see p. 434) are very occasionally grown in gardens: **Rumex patienta** L., spinach dock, as a spinach-like plant for early spring use, and **R. acetosa** L. (of which the wild form is the weed common sorrel) in a special cultivated broad-leaved form known as garden sorrel.

CANNABINACEAE

General Importance. Only one species, *Humulus lupulus*, the hop, is of importance in British agriculture, and that as a localized crop in the hands of specialist growers. Hemp is of some importance as a fibre and drug plant in warmer countries, but its cultivation is now obsolete in Britain.

Botanical Characters. A very small family of two genera only, with inconspicuous unisexual flowers, formerly united with either Urticaceae or

Moraceae, but sufficiently distinct to merit treatment as a separate family. Plants herbaceous, with stipulate, palmately-lobed or divided leaves. Dioecious, the male plants with axillary panicles, the female with sessile flowers in dense, spike-like clusters. Male flowers with five perianth segments and five stamens. Female flowers with small, entire cup-like perianth, and a single, one-seeded ovary with two large stigmas. Bracts

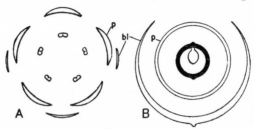

Fig. 81. Cannabinaceae. Floral diagrams of A, male flower; B, female flower. *bl*, bracteole. *p*, perianth.

and bracteoles conspicuous, surrounding female flowers. Fruit an achene, seed endospermic, embryo coiled.

Humulus lupulus L.   The Hop

A perennial climbing plant grown for the female inflorescences which are used in brewing. Annual stems arise in spring from an underground

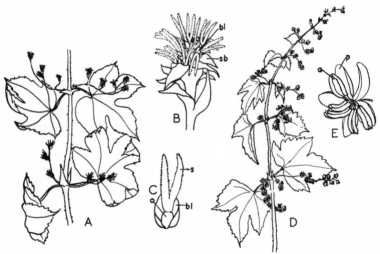

Fig. 82. Hops. A, part of female plant with leaves and young strobili, × ½. B, strobilus at 'burr' stage, × 2. C, single female flower at same stage, × 4. D, upper part of a stem of male plant in flower, × ½. E, single male flower, × 4. *a*, anther. *bl*, bracteole. *p*, perianth segment. *s*, stigma. *sb*, stipular bract. *o*, ovary.

root-stock, and may climb by twining (clockwise) around a string or other support to a height of some twenty feet. The stems are angular, hollow, and hairy with stiff reflexed hairs; they bear opposite palmately-lobed leaves of rather variable shape, with pointed scarious stipules at the base of the petiole. Male plants produce in summer branched axillary and terminal panicles of loosely-arranged flowers 4-5 mm. in diameter, consisting of five blunt, lanceolate perianth segments and five anthers on short filaments. The female plants produce smaller axillary panicles of hop-cones, or *strobili*. Each strobilus consists of a short axis (the 'strig') on which are borne a number of spirally-arranged bracts, or strictly of

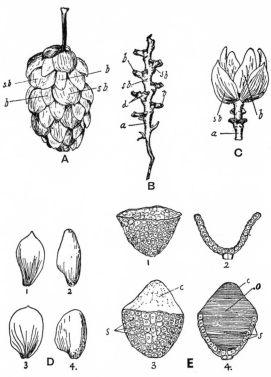

Fig. 83. Female inflorescence of the hop. A, whole strobilus. B, strig, with bracts and bracteoles removed. C, part of strobilus, showing one pair of stipular bracts and the associated bracteoles. *a*, strig, the main axis of the strobilus. *d*, the short branch-system in the axil of the undeveloped bract. *sb*, stipular bract. *b*, bracteole. (In B, *sb* and *b* indicate the scars left by the removal of these structures.) D, 1, stipular bract and 2, bracteole of the variety Fuggles; 3 and 4, of the variety Bramling. E, lupulin glands, × about 150; 1, side view and 2, vertical section of young gland; 3 and 4, of mature gland. *s*, secretory cells of gland. *c*, cuticle. *o*, resinous secretion. (From Percival, *Agricultural Botany*.)

paired structures representing the stipules of the bracts. The bract lamina is only very occasionally developed in abnormal inflorescences. In the axil of each pair of stipular bracts is a very short, branched axis bearing four flowers each subtended by a bracteole. Each flower consists of a single ovary surrounded by the cup-like perianth. Two large papillose stigmas are present which reach a length of about 4 mm. when receptive and stand out well beyond the bracts and bracteoles, giving a characteristic brush-like appearance to the strobilus at this ('burr') stage.

The stigmas receive wind-borne pollen from male plants; shortly after pollination the stigmas are shed and rapid growth of the bracts and bracteoles takes place, so that the appearance of the strobilus changes and becomes fir-cone-like. When mature, the strobilus is some 4 cm. long, the individual stipular bracts and bracteoles having a length of about 15 mm., varying in size and shape according to variety. The stipular bracts are only slightly concave, but the base of the bracteole curves round to envelop the achene and its surrounding perianth.

The perianth and the lower parts of the bracts and bracteoles bear numerous epidermal glands, the *lupulin glands*. These arise as shortly-stalked, cup-like structures one cell in thickness. At about the time of pollination the cells of the cup start secreting a yellow resinous fluid, which accumulates under the cuticle covering the inside of the cup. The secretion of resin continues during the growth of the strobilus, until the

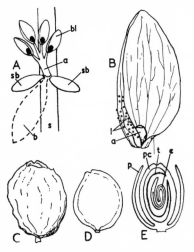

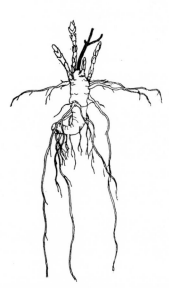

FIG. 84. Hops. A, diagram to show relation of stipular bracts to flowers in female strobilus. *a*, short axis in axil of bract, *b*, of which only the stipules, *sb* (stipular bracts), are developed. *bl*, bracteole subtending flowers. *s*, 'strig', or main axis of strobilus. B, bracteole with mature fruit, × 2½. C, achene surrounded by cup-like perianth, × 7. D, with perianth removed. E, diagrammatic vertical section of C. *a*, achene. *l*, lupulin glands. *p*, perianth. *pc*, pericarp. *t*, testa. *e*, embryo.

FIG. 85. Young hop plant grown from seed; beginning of second year, × ½.

cuticle becomes strongly convex, and the gland with its enclosed resin almost spherical. The resin solidifies and becomes somewhat opaque, so that the glands appear like a dusting of fine sulphur over the surfaces of the mature strobilus.

It is for these lupulin glands that the hop plant is grown. Their secretion, lupulin, is a complex mixture of resin and resin-like substances which not only impart to beer its bitter taste, but also act as an efficient preservative, by preventing rapid bacterial growth.

Fruit an achene, dark brown, 2·5 mm., partially covered by persistent cupule. Sown only for the production of new varieties. Germination epigeal, cotyledons blunt-lanceolate, first foliage leaves ovate, coarsely-toothed, not lobed. A short, thickened tuberous root-stock is produced during the first year of growth and from the crown of this the aerial stems arise.

Cultivation. Since the strobili are the parts of the plant which are of value, only female plants are grown, except for a small proportion (normally about 1 in 200) of males, which are necessary to provide pollen. The mature achenes are of no value and a heavy set of seed is undesirable, but if no pollination takes place the growth of the strobili is greatly reduced, and the yield therefore low. In this connection *triploid* plants, in which pollination induces the necessary growth of the strobilus, without any actual set of seed, may be a desirable development.

Hops are propagated vegetatively; the aerial twining stems die at the end of the year, but the base of the stems below ground remains alive, and these stem bases are used as cuttings. Each cutting (sett) consists of a 4-in. length of stem-base removed from the parent plant; it bears buds and readily produces adventitious roots. Cuttings are placed in a nursery bed and planted out the following year in their permanent positions. The usual spacing is about seven feet square, depending on variety, and plants remain productive for many years. Hops require good soil, heavy manuring, and shelter from winds and a large expenditure is involved in the provision of a wire framework to support the strings up which they grow, and in the stringing, training and removal of excess stems and spreading rhizomes, as well as cultivations to destroy weeds and spraying to control insect pests and fungus diseases. Harvesting, formerly by hand-picking of the mature strobili and therefore requiring a very large amount of seasonal labour, has become increasingly mechanized. Mechanical picking differs from hand-picking in that the stems ('bines') must be cut and fed to the machine, so preventing the translocation of remaining food material from the leaves and stems to the rhizomes.

The picked hops must be artificially dried in kilns (oast-houses) and exposed to sulphur dioxide as a bleaching and preservative agent. During drying and subsequent packing careful handling is necessary to avoid loss of the dry lupulin glands.

Origin and Range of Types

Hops are probably native in Britain, although many of the hop plants found wild are escapes from cultivation, but the use of this species in brewing was introduced in the sixteenth century from continental Europe. It is probable, therefore, that the cultivated forms are derived from Continental rather than British plants. Since the hop is normally propagated vegetatively, the varieties are strictly speaking clones. New varieties are produced from seed—that is, by sowing the achenes; about half the resultant plants are males which must, of course, be discarded. Breeding work is necessarily unusually difficult in a dioecious plant such as hops. Certain characters, such as vigour of growth and disease resistance, are visible in the male parent, but there is no method except some form of progeny testing, of assessing its genetical make-up as far as yield and quality are concerned. Nevertheless, considerable progress has been made, notably at Wye College, Kent, in the development of new and improved varieties.

Varieties. Some 75 per cent. of the hop acreage is occupied by the variety *Fuggles*, a mid-season hop which is of rather low quality, but adapted to a wide range of soil conditions. It has narrow bracts and bracteoles. Seriously damaged by *Verticillium* wilt. *Golding* and similar varieties occupy the greater part of the remaining acreage, mainly on the better hop soils. Golding is an early variety, of high quality, with broad bracts and bracteoles. Numerous new varieties, mainly bred at Wye, occupy comparatively small areas. Among the more important are *Bullion* and *Brewer's Gold*, varieties of special 'American' type intended to replace the hops formerly imported; *Keyworth's Midseason*, a wilt-tolerant replacement for Fuggles; and *Northern Brewer*, of Golding type.

Cannabis sativa L.   Hemp

Hemp is a tall-growing, slender, rather tender annual, with large alternate leaves palmately divided into lanceolate, coarsely-toothed, pointed leaflets. Like hops, it is dioecious, the male plants bearing small axillary panicles of yellowish-green flowers, the female axillary leafy clusters not forming a compact strobilus. The male flowers are similar to those of hops; the female flowers have more slender stigmas and are closely surrounded by the inrolled tube-like bracteole. The fruit is a greyish-brown achene, about 4 mm. long (about 35,000 per pound) used to some extent as bird-seed.

Hemp was formerly widely cultivated in Britain for its fibre; this, like that of flax (p. 143), is derived from the groups of fibre cells which occur on the outer side of the vascular bundles of the stem. The fibre cells differ from those of flax in being stouter and more lignified, and the extracted fibre, obtained by retting and scutching in the same way as with flax, is used for coarse fabrics and ropes. The cultivation of hemp somewhat resembles that of flax, 'seed' (achenes) being drilled or broad-cast at about 100 lb. per acre in April or May. The resultant crop consists of about equal numbers of male and female plants, and since the male plants mature earlier than the female, the best quality fibre is only obtained by hand-pulling the male plants first and then harvesting the female plants separately a month or more later. Yields of about 5 cwt. of fibre might be expected, together with a similar weight of seed. Hemp is thus an expensive crop to grow, and is not now economic in Britain owing to the competition of imported fibres, including not only true hemp but also the technically similar monocotyledonous leaf-fibres,

Manila hemp (from the banana-like *Musa textilis*), sisal (from *Agave sisalana*) and New Zealand hemp (from *Phormium tenax*, which has also been experimentally grown in S.W. England).

In hot climates the glandular hairs of the hemp plant secrete resins

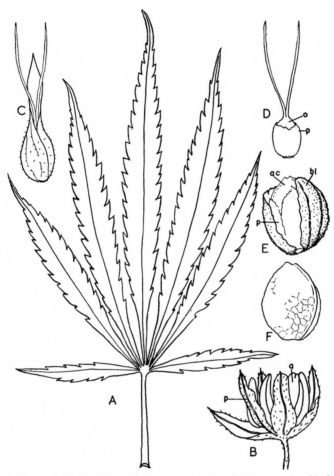

FIG. 86. Hemp. A, leaf, × ⅓. B, male flower, × 4. C, female flower enclosed in bracteole; D, with bracteole removed. E, ripe achene surrounded by remains of perianth and bracteole. F, achene alone, × 4. *a*, anther, *ac*, achene. *bl*, bracteole. *o*, ovary. *p*, perianth.

containing narcotic alkaloids, and it is thus an important and dangerous drug plant (hashish, marijuana).

Chapter XIII

BORAGINACEAE, SOLANACEAE, DIPSACACEAE AND COMPOSITAE

BORAGINACEAE

General Importance. Contains only one agricultural crop, Russian Comfrey, which has been recommended as a forage crop, but is not in general cultivation. Named from genus *Borago*, borage.

Botanical Characters. Plants herbaceous, usually rough-hairy; leaves simple, alternate, exstipulate. Inflorescence a monochasial cyme. Flowers actinomorphic, insect-pollinated. Calyx of five joined sepals; corolla tubular or with rotate limb, five-lobed, mouth of corolla-tube partly closed by scales. Stamens five, epipetalous. Gynaecium superior, of two united carpels each divided into two lobes, giving four single-seeded nutlets around the central style.

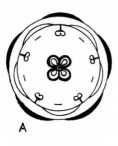

Fig. 87. Floral characters of Boraginaceae. A, floral diagram. B, vertical section of flower.

Symphytum × peregrinum Ledeb. Russian Comfrey

A hybrid, or more strictly a hybrid swarm (i.e. a series of hybrids together with their back-crosses with both parents), between *S. officinale* L., common comfrey, and *S. asperum* Lepech. (*S. asperrimum* Donn.), prickly comfrey. (May be included under name *S.* × *uplandicum* Nyman.)

A perennial, with stout, somewhat tuberous roots, forming a series of branching crowns. Radical leaves hispid, broadly-lanceolate, stalked. Stems erect, 4-5 ft. high, branched, bearing similar but smaller sessile leaves, variably decurrent. Flowers pendulous in branched cymes at top of stems; calyx with pointed teeth, corolla broadly tubular, usually dull pinkish-purple. Mature nutlets rarely produced, 4-5 mm., rugose, black.

S. asperum has smaller leaves, not decurrent, and bright blue flowers with blunt calyx-teeth; *S. officinale* is usually a lower-growing plant, with leaves strongly decurrent, dull purple or white flowers, and smooth black nutlets. The form of Russian comfrey now grown is nearer to *S. officinale* in appearance than to *S. asperum*; it is reported to have been introduced from Russia about 1870, but crosses between the wild British *S. officinale* and the earlier-introduced *S. asperum* (formerly used as crop-plant, now sometimes grown as garden ornamental, and occasionally naturalized) may have contributed to the present range of forms.

A quick-growing plant producing a large bulk of foliage; not palatable in the fresh state and not tolerant of hard grazing. The treatment recommended is cutting and feeding wilted or as silage; with 5-8 cuts per year, annual yields of 50-100 tons green weight per acre have been reported from established stands under good conditions. With a dry-matter content of about 12 per cent., of which 20-25 per cent. is crude protein,

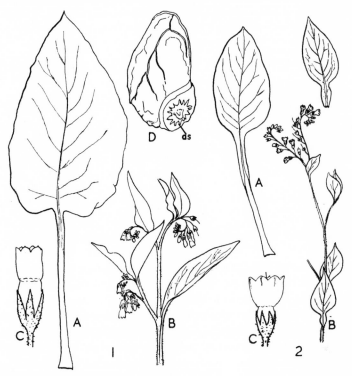

FIG. 88. 1, Russian comfrey (*Symphytum peregrinum*). 2, Prickly comfrey (*S. asperum*). A, basal leaf, × ¼. B, upper part of flowering shoot, × ¼. C, flower, × 1. D (one only), nutlet (rarely formed), × 7. *as*, attachment surface.

this yield compares favourably with that of other, more commonly grown crops. That comfrey has not become established as a common crop may be attributed partly, perhaps, to the very considerable confusion which has surrounded the plant, and the fact that many of the trials carried out have been with *S. asperum* or other lower-yielding forms, but still more to the inherent disadvantages of the plant as a general farm crop. It can only be propagated vegetatively; this involves the planting-out of root-cuttings or divided crowns in autumn or spring (the plant dies down to ground level in winter) at about 5,000 per acre and a consequent very high cost of establishment. Row-crop cultivation is necessary to control weeds, and a high level of fertility must be maintained; maximum yields are not attained in the first year or two, and the plant must be treated as a long-duration crop. Costs of utilization involving frequent cutting are likely to be high; further, the plant, once established, is often difficult to eradicate completely when this is required, and may persist as a weed.

SOLANACEAE

General Importance. The *Solanaceae* includes only one species of outstanding agricultural importance, the potato. Tomatoes and a few other plants are horticultural crops, but many members of the family are poisonous, including a few species found wild in Britain (see Chapter XIX).

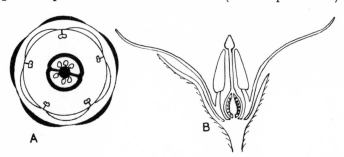

Fig. 89. Floral characters of Solanaceae. A, floral diagram. B, vertical section of flower of *Solanum*.

Botanical Characters. Herbs and shrubs, including a few climbers. Leaves exstipulate, simple or pinnately compound, alternate but often partially adnate to the stem so that they diverge from the stem some distance above the node. Inflorescence usually cymose; flowers conspicuous, usually insect-pollinated. Calyx and corolla both of five joined segments, actinomorphic. Stamens five, epipetalous and alternating with corolla segments. Ovary superior, of two joined carpels, surmounted by a single style. Placentation axile, ovules numerous; fruit a capsule or berry, seeds small, endospermic.

SOLANUM

A large genus, very variable in habit. Flowers with rotate corolla, anthers forming a cone around the style and dehiscing by apical pores. Fruit a berry.

Solanum tuberosum L.   Potato

The potato is of S. American origin and had been long cultivated there before the discovery of that continent by Europeans. It is not known with certainty in a wild state, but forms one of a large polyploid series of tuber-bearing species, some wild and some locally-cultivated in South and Central America. The poisonous alkaloid solanine is widely distributed in the green parts of the plant, which are therefore not usable for fodder. It is absent from the tubers, except where these are greened by exposure to light.

Tubers. The potato is cultivated for its tubers; these are stem structures formed by the enlargement of the tip of an underground stem. They bear 'eyes'—that is, buds or groups of buds originally formed in the axils of scale-leaves. These scale-leaves are short-lived, and their position is marked in the mature tuber by slight ridges, the enlarged leaf-scars, which form the 'eyebrows'. It is desirable that the tuber should be of regular shape, with shallow eyes, in order to avoid waste in peeling. In most present-day varieties the shape is more or less spherical (*round*) or preferably ovoid (*oval*) or flattened-ovoid (*kidney*); varieties with cylindrical tubers are occasionally grown as salad-potatoes. The eyes are not uniformly distributed but tend to be more closely-spaced towards the apical (rose) end than towards the point (heel) where the tuber was attached to the unthickened part of the rhizome.

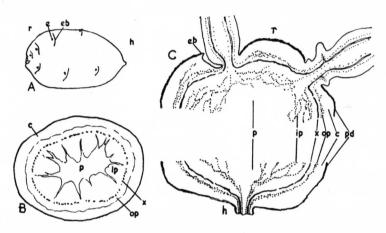

FIG. 90. Potato. A, small tuber, × ½. B, diagrammatic cross section of young tuber, × 1. C, parts of longitudinal section of sprouted tuber, × 2, xylem strands shown in solid line, phloem dotted. *r*, 'rose end'. *h*, 'heel end'. *e*, eye. *eb*, 'eyebrow'. *p*, pith. *ip*, internal phloem. *x*, xylem. *op*, outer phloem. *c*, cortex. *pd*, periderm.

Anatomically, the tuber shows stem structure. There is little secondary tissue present; the great increase in diameter is mainly due to the proliferation of the primary tissue, and not to secondary thickening as a result of cambial activity. In transverse section a ring of vascular bundles, which are not clearly separated from one another, surrounds a large irregularly-circular or stellate pith. The amount of xylem is small, and very few lignified cells are present, and the main bulk of the vascular tissue consists of phloem, mainly parenchymatous but with sieve-tubes and companion cells running through it. This phloem is present not only outside the xylem and cambium, but also, and in greater amount, within the xylem, between it and the pith. The internal phloem (also known as medullary, or intra-xylary phloem) occupies a considerable proportion of the cross-sectional area of the tuber. Outside the outer phloem is a rather narrow cortex, surrounded by a well-developed periderm, the thick cork layer forming the skin of the tuber. The original epidermis is only visible in very young tubers. The continuous cork layer of the skin is interrupted at intervals by lenticels, small circular areas in which the cork-cells are loosely arranged, so allowing the exchange of oxygen and carbon-dioxide through the otherwise relatively impermeable skin. These lenticels are usually rather inconspicuous, but may increase in size to form raised white dots in tubers grown in partially-waterlogged soil. The main food reserve of the mature tuber consists of starch in the form of large oval starch grains; these are present in all the parenchyma cells, but are more densely packed in the phloem tissue, which therefore appears more opaque than the pith or cortex.

In addition to the normal cork-cambium which produces the tuber skin, further cork cambia may arise in response to wounding. The consequent healing of cut surfaces is made use of in the cutting of large tubers into smaller pieces for planting; this practice is not common in Britain on a field scale, but is sometimes used in gardens. The first result of cutting is the deposit of a layer of suberin on the surface; this is followed by division of the underlying cells to form a new cork cambium parallel to the cut surface, and if conditions are favourable a continuous layer of cork is formed. This depends on the rate of drying out, since if the underlying cells are killed by desiccation before they have produced a cork layer, no healing is possible. If freshly-cut tubers are planted in moist soil, healing is usually satisfactory, but if the soil is dry many pieces may fail to heal, and a 'gappy' plant results. Under such conditions it is better to store the cut pieces in a moist atmosphere for a week or more before planting. Tubers may be cut almost through at the time of boxing, so that the two halves are joined by a narrow strip of tissue. The two cut surfaces thus remain in contact and heal satisfactorily, owing to the fact that they protect each other from drying out. A slight twist is sufficient to separate the two halves at planting time, leaving only a very small area of unhealed surface on each. Dressing the cut surfaces with lime, which was at one time recommended, appears to hinder rather than help the progress of cork-formation. Varieties differ in their behaviour; some (e.g. Great Scot) produce cork very readily, while others (e.g. Majestic) heal only slowly.

Dormancy. The buds which form the eyes of the tuber are initially dormant, and remain in this condition for a varying period, depending on the variety. In early varieties (see below, p. 217) dormancy is comparatively short, and sprouting (i.e. the growing-out of the buds into shoots) may commence in early autumn in tubers produced during the early summer. In late varieties, dormancy may last until the winter or the following spring; the actual time of sprouting is affected by temperature, and tubers intended for consumption in late spring should be stored under cool (but frost-free) conditions. It has been shown that the period of dormancy can be artificially shortened or lengthened by exposure of the tubers to various chemical substances.

Treatment of dormant tubers with the vapour of ethylene chlorhydrin, for example, results in the breaking of dormancy at an early stage. This is rarely of direct economic value, but has been used in southern U.S.A. to provide a second crop during the year, tubers of the normal early summer crop being replanted after treatment to produce 'new' potatoes in autumn. A more generally important use of dormancy-breaking treatments is in testing for the presence of virus diseases. Samples of tubers intended for replanting in the following year are treated soon after lifting, and grown under glass, thus enabling the presence of disease to be detected before the main bulk of tubers is planted.

Treatments which lengthen the period of dormancy are of more direct economic value in that they enable tubers to be kept in good condition for a longer period. Sprouting results in loss both of dry matter and of water from the tubers, and it is often difficult to keep naturally-stored tubers in such a way that they remain in good condition until the following year's crop is available. A nitro-benzene compound (2-3-5-6-tetra-chloro-nitrobenzene) originally introduced to control the spread of dry rot in stored tubers (see Chapter XXVI), was found to prolong dormancy, as does also the hormone-like substance α-naphthyl acetic acid. Addition of either of these substances at the rate of a few ounces per ton of tubers when the clamp is being made, and the consequent exposure of the tubers to their vapours, results in a marked delay in sprouting. The treatment should not be used with tubers intended for replanting as 'seed', except under the conditions described for the control of dry rot, as sprouting may be so much delayed that a normal crop is not produced. Where tubers are stored indoors, with controlled ventilation, the alcohol *nonanol* can be introduced into the air blown through the stored bulk, and gives effective control of sprouting. This treatment is repeated at intervals, as may be necessary.

Sprouting. At the end of the period of dormancy, the buds forming the eyes of the tuber grow out if the temperature is high enough. If sprouting starts early, apical dominance is shown, and only a few shoots, near the 'rose' end, develop. If sprouting is delayed by low temperatures all the buds tend to grow at the same time, giving numerous sprouts. Shoots produced in the light are short with crowded green leaves; in the dark, shoots are etiolated, long and slender. Etiolated shoots are very liable to damage in handling and planting, and it is therefore desirable to plant as 'seed' either unsprouted tubers or ones which have sprouted in the light. The sprouting or 'chitting' of tubers before planting results not only in an earlier crop, but also often in a higher yield. The number of underground nodes on a stem produced from a tuber previously sprouted in the light will be greater than that on a stem from a tuber planted unsprouted, since in the latter the shoot will develop entirely in the dark. New tubers are produced from stems arising at these underground nodes and, other things being equal, an increase in the number of nodes will tend to result in an increase in number of tubers.

Development of the Planted Tuber. The sprouts develop at the expense of the starch and other materials present in the tuber, and form stems which bear alternately-arranged leaves. Below ground, these leaves are small and scale-like, and the stems round and colourless, with numerous adventitious roots arising at their nodes. Above ground the stems are square or triangular in section, with conspicuous, sometimes wavy wings at the corners, formed by the decurrent bases of the petioles. The leaves

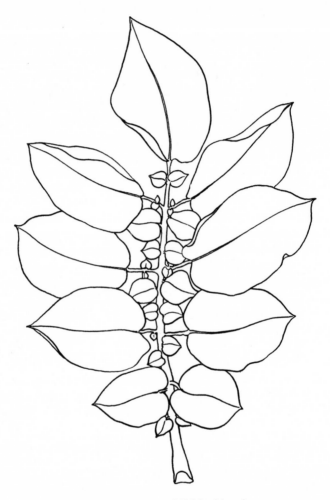

FIG. 91 Potato leaf (Majestic), × ½.

are large and pinnately compound, with a single terminal leaflet and a number of pairs of large, stalked, lateral leaflets. Between these large primary leaflets are a number of almost sessile small secondary leaflets or folioles, and still smaller tertiary leaflets are usually present on the stalks of the primary leaflets. The leaflets are entire, usually ovate with cordate base, but the size and shape varies considerably in different varieties, as does the length and degree of erectness of the stems.

Buds in the axils of underground scale-leaves grow out to form hori-
zontally-directed rhizomes, which bear scale-leaves and adventitious roots,
but do not usually branch. The tip only of each of these slender rhizomes
acts as a food-storing organ, and swells to form a tuber, which is thus
connected to the upright stem by the unswollen part of the rhizome.
This is short in the majority of potato varieties, but may reach a length
of several feet in the related wild species; long rhizomes are usually
associated with low tuber yields.

Meanwhile, the food material stored in the planted 'seed' tuber has
been used up by the developing stems, and is not replaced. The 'seed'

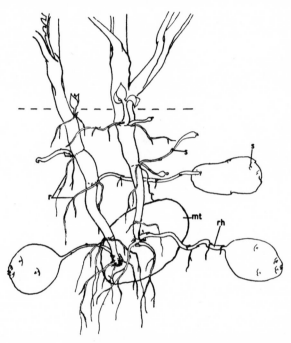

FIG. 92. Lower part of potato plant, shortly before stage for lifting
as first early, × ⅓. Simplified, some shoots and numerous roots omitted.
mt, mother tuber. *r*, adventitious root. *rh*, rhizome. *s*, scale leaf.

tuber thus dies, and the stems which arose from different eyes and which
were previously only connected by the tissue of the 'seed' tuber become
entirely separated from one another. The apparent potato plant, derived
from a single 'seed' tuber, is therefore no longer strictly one plant, but
a colony of independent unconnected plants growing close together. This
lack of organic connection between the different stems in the later stages
of growth is of importance in limiting the spread of virus diseases (see
Chapter XXVIII) in cases where infection takes place late in the year.

As the aerial stems approach their full size they produce flowers, which
are borne in rather lax cymes in the axils of the upper leaves. Each
flower has usually a green calyx with five spreading blunt teeth, and a

rather flat corolla, 2-3 cm. in diameter. The corolla is not deeply divided, and varies in different varieties from stellate to almost circular in outline; the colour varies from white to mauve or blue-purple. The five stamens arise from the base of the corolla; they have short, stiff filaments, and the anthers form a cone around the style. Since potatoes are propagated vegetatively (except for plant-breeding purposes) the flower is of no distinct economic importance, and many varieties, selected for their desirable vegetative characters, rarely flower or have distorted and partially or wholly sterile flowers. In such varieties the anthers are often malformed or partially aborted and form an irregular, twisted, pale yellow cone, producing little or no viable pollen. In fertile varieties the anthers are usually broader and deep orange in colour. The ovary is globular,

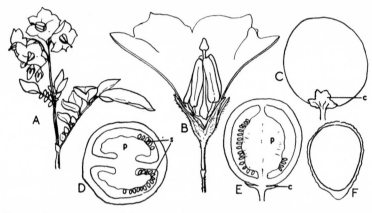

Fig. 93. Potato flower and fruit. A, inflorescence, × ⅓. B, flower, with part of corolla removed to show style and stamens, × 2. C, mature fruit, × 1. D, transverse, and E, longitudinal sections of fruit, × 1. F, seed, × 10. *c*, calyx. *p*, placenta. *s*, seeds (a few only shown).

with a slender style of variable length, bearing a capitate or slightly-notched stigma.

In many varieties the flowers are shed at an early stage, but in those in which they are retained, and in which pollination takes place, the ovary develops to form a globular berry, two-chambered and with large, fleshy placentae on which numerous seeds are borne. The ripe seeds are pointed-oval in shape, about 2 mm. long, flattened and slightly winged, pale brown in colour and rough or slightly hairy in appearance, owing to the partial breakdown of the epidermal cells. The embryo is curved and embedded in the endosperm.

These true seeds are used only when it is desired to produce a new variety and not (in Britain) for the production of a crop. Germination is epigeal and the cotyledons become green, ovate and leaf-like. The epicotyl elongates quickly and bears a succession of alternately-arranged simple ovate leaves. While the plant is still small, buds in the axils of the cotyledons and lower leaves grow out as slender stems which turn downwards and enter the soil; there their tips enlarge to form tubers. These first-year tubers usually reach a diameter of only 1-3 cm.; in the breeding of new varieties they are lifted, stored, and replanted the following year, when they give rise to plants bearing rather larger tubers. These are treated in the same way and full-sized tubers are produced in the third or fourth year.

Yield. Potatoes require a high level of soil fertility, and heavy manuring is necessary for high yields. For satisfactory growth of the tubers it is also necessary that cultivations shall be such as to give as little consolidation of the soil as possible, and to prevent weed competition in the early stages. Given these conditions, yield will depend largely on the amount of photo-synthesis which the plants are able to carry out. In the early stages the plants are not self-supporting, but are dependent on the food reserves in the planted tuber; this food reserve is, of course, much greater in amount than in a crop grown from the true seed. Weight of tubers planted per acre has therefore an important effect on final yield, and the yield per acre increases with increase of 'seed' rate up to at least 2 tons of 'seed' per acre. The increased yield resulting from increased 'seed' rate is, however, very small at rates over 1 ton per acre, and does not normally pay for the extra seed. The most profitable 'seed' rate can only be decided by comparing the costs of 'seed' and ware potatoes;

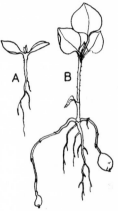

FIG. 94. Potato. A, seedling. B, young plant from seed, showing origin of tuber-bearing stems from cotyledonary node, × 1.

rates of 17-18 cwt. per acre are common. Providing that spacing is adjusted according to size of 'seed', so that the total weight of tubers planted per acre reaches this figure, the size of 'seed' is within limits comparatively unimportant. Tubers of about 2 oz. weight are usually preferred for planting; very large seed tubers may give a crop of the same total weight per acre, but consisting of a larger number of smaller tubers. Crops can be grown from small chips, including an eye, or even from detached eyes, but the yield is normally low.

The foliage produced at the expense of the planted food reserves carries out photosynthesis; the products of photosynthesis are used partly in the production of further leaves, partly in the development of tubers. Varieties which produce tubers early are thus not able to develop as large a leaf area as varieties in which tuber-production is delayed; the total amount of photosynthesis, and consequently the total yield, is thus lower in early varieties. Any factors which tend to decrease the area or duration of the leaves will, of course, tend to decrease yield; thus blight (see Chapter XXIII) is of outstanding importance, not only because of the direct tuber damage it may cause, but also owing to the premature defoliation it produces, which markedly lowers the yield even when the tubers escape infection. Flowering has a much less marked effect on yield than it has in biennial crops, but does make some demands on the available food materials. It has been shown experimentally* that in varieties which flower and fruit abundantly, tuber yield is increased by up to about 20 per cent. if fruiting is artificially prevented, and by up to about 40 per cent. if both flowering and fruiting are stopped.

Quality. Since potatoes are grown primarily for human consumption, quality is of very great importance. A large number of factors contribute to quality and requirements differ in different countries and in different areas. Even-shaped tubers of even size, with shallow eyes, are always preferred; cracked, hollow tubers are undesirable. Second growth, or 'super-tuberation', in which partially mature tubers grow out to form attached daughter-tubers, is a serious defect. Skin colour is of no direct importance, but purple-skinned varieties are not popular in England; there is a demand for tubers with red coloration around the eyes, since this is associated in the consumer's mind, but not necessarily in fact, with the good quality of the variety King Edward. 'Flesh' colour is regarded as important, with a marked preference in Britain for white flesh; Duke of York is almost the only accepted yellow-fleshed variety. Dry-matter content is not in itself important; the usual percentage is about 23 for the whole tuber, but it is not uniformly distributed, and the pith may contain less than 10 per cent. Cooking quality may, however, be better in tubers with a high dry-matter content, although this character is difficult to assess precisely. For most purposes British taste calls for tubers which are floury when cooked, but firmer flesh is desirable in tubers for frying, and also in early varieties to be eaten as 'new' potatoes. Blackening of tubers after cooking is a serious defect, of uncertain origin, but associated partly with variety and partly with soil conditions.

A number of other tuber characters also have an important effect on the value of a variety; among these are resistance to mechanical damage and resistance to various storage diseases. Varieties which bruise easily during lifting and grading may show various types of internal discoloration in apparently sound tubers. Susceptibility to diseases which spread during storage (such as dry rot, see Chapter XXVI) is particularly important in the tubers kept for 'seed', which may appear healthy but may, if infected, fail to produce shoots.

Origin and Range of Types

A large range of tuber-bearing *Solanum* species occurs in South and Central America, extending as far north as Mexico. They form a polyploid series, including diploids (e.g. *S. rybinii*, cultivated), triploids (e.g. *S. commersonii*, wild), tetraploids (e.g. *S. tuberosum* and *S. andigenum*, both cultivated), pentaploids (e.g. *S. edinense*, wild) and hexaploids (e.g. *S. demissum*, wild). The interrelations of the different species have not been fully worked out, but some of the polyploids may well be amphidiploids derived from the crossing of other species. A large number of the species

---

* W. L. Bartholdi, *Univ. of Minnesota Agr. Expt. Station Tech. Bulletin*, 150, 1942.

have been used in recent years in endeavours to introduce the disease-resistance, which many of them show, into cultivated potatoes (see Chapter V), but only two have been concerned in the main development of potatoes in Europe. These are *S. tuberosum* L., cultivated in Chiloe and the adjacent mainland area of Chile, and the morphologically very similar *S. andigenum* Jug. et Buk. from Peru and Ecuador. The recent cultivated potatoes of Europe more closely resemble the forms from Chile, particularly in their ability to produce tubers under the long day-length of temperate summers. Historical evidence suggests, however, that the potatoes introduced into Europe towards the end of the sixteenth century were probably of the Peruvian type, forms adapted to the short days of the equatorial region and producing tubers in Europe only in the short days of late autumn. If this was so, the modern European potatoes must have been derived either from these *S. andigenum* forms by selection (in which case the distinction between the two species cannot be maintained) or from a later unrecorded introduction of the *S. tuberosum* type from Chile.

Whatever their origin, the cultivated potatoes of Europe and other temperate regions now comprise a series of long-day forms. The short-day forms maturing tubers only in very late autumn have been discarded, but those now grown show a continuous range of maturity dates from early summer to early autumn. They can be arbitrarily divided into first earlies, second earlies, early maincrops and maincrops; but it should be emphasized that this classification is based on agricultural rather than botanical characters. Thus first earlies include not only such varieties as May Queen, which produces its full tuber-yield early, but also the much more commonly grown Arran Pilot, the full yield of which is not reached until the second early period. This latter variety shows, however, early 'bulking-up', and a sufficient proportion of the yield is produced early in the season to make it economic to lift it as a first early. All varieties other than maincrops are normally consumed soon after harvesting, and keeping quality is not important except in relation to 'seed'. Maincrops, which commonly produce the highest yield per acre, may need, however, to be kept until the following June, and long dormancy and good keeping quality is therefore required.

Varieties. Since potatoes are vegetatively propagated by means of their tubers, the varieties are strictly clones, and each variety is derived from one single true seed. Occasionally somatic mutation takes place, and the mutated forms may be selected and multiplied up so that a second variety is produced, derived from the same original seedling. Thus King Edward, with tubers coloured red around the eyes only, has given rise to the all-red but otherwise similar Red King. Usually such mutation affects only certain tissues, and the resultant plant is a chimaera (see Chapter III); thus if the eyes are removed from a tuber of the russet-skinned Golden Wonder, and adventitious shoots arise from the deeper layers of the tuber, the tubers which these shoots produce are smooth-skinned, and indistinguishable from those of Langworthy, from which variety Golden Wonder presumably arose.

The requirements of a good potato variety are so many and varied that no very clear picture of the development and interrelations of varieties can be presented. Out of the very large number of new varieties produced, very few prove to be of sufficient all-round excellence to displace the existing older varieties. Although much progress has been made in the development of disease-resistant varieties by crosses with other *Solanum* species, the majority of such varieties have so far suffered from defects in their field characters or quality which have prevented their extensive use. Thus the most widely grown in Britain of all varieties in 1954 was Majestic, introduced in 1911, followed in popularity by King Edward, introduced in 1902.

Some 50 per cent. of the acreage devoted to *first earlies* in 1954 was occupied by the variety *Arran Pilot* (introduced 1930), early-bulking and high-yielding, although not of the highest cooking-quality. *Home Guard* (1943), usually of rather better quality, occupied a further 25 per cent. *Ulster Chieftain* (1938), early, but very susceptible to blight (p. 534), and to cracking of tubers, was the next most popular variety. All these have oval or kidney-shaped tubers with shallow eyes and white skin and flesh.

Among *second earlies* the older, round, rather deep-eyed *Great Scot* (1909) has been to some extent replaced by newer oval or kidney varieties with shallow eyes, including *Craigs Alliance* (1948) and *Craigs Royal* (1948).

The variety *Majestic* (1911) occupied 50 per cent. of the *maincrop* acreage; although not outstanding in any one direction, it maintains a high general level of yield and quality which makes it difficult to displace. *King Edward* (1902), which is of very high cooking-quality, but is lower in yield, requires high fertility, and is very susceptible to blight, was responsible for about 25 per cent. Among newer varieties may be mentioned *Pentland Crown* (1958), resistant to common scab and severe mosaic, and *Pentland Dell* (1964), resistant to blight; both these varieties are capable of outyielding Majestic. *Record* (1932) is a yellow-fleshed variety of high dry-matter content, suitable for processing.

Solanum melongena L., aubergine, is a non-tuberous species cultivated for its edible fruit. It is a perennial, cultivated as an annual, with large simple ovate lobed leaves, purple flowers, and usually elongated deep purple fruits (ovoid white in one non-edible form, whence the alternative name, egg-plant). Of Indian origin, occasionally cultivated under glass in Britain.

Lycopersicum esculentum Mill. Tomato

An annual, closely related to *Solanum*, leaves potato-like, but with leaflets pinnately cut or divided, glandular-hairy; stem weak, sprawling, flowers in apparently leaf-opposed cymes, corolla deeply-lobed, yellow, anthers with longitudinal not porose dehiscence. Grown for the edible, succulent fruit which is almost solid owing to pulpy outgrowths from placentae around seeds. Seeds similar in form to those of potato.

Native in north-western S. America, in small-fruited (cherry-like) form with short calyx teeth, flowers pentamerous with two carpels. Introduced to Europe early in sixteenth century, now widely grown in great variety of cultivated self-pollinated varieties, with large or small, globular, elongated or pear-shaped red or yellow fruits. Important commercial varieties hexamerous with red globular fruits formed from two (or in some, up to six) carpels. Not important in Britain until end of nineteenth century, now extensively grown, mainly under glass, but some outdoor varieties (not frost-hardy) exist, including some dwarfs.

The close-related **L. pimpinellifolium** Dun. (**L. racemigerum** Lange), with glabrous leaves and red-currant-like fruits, crosses readily with tomato and has been used in the production of disease-resistant forms.

Capsicum annuum L., the red and sweet peppers, is an annual or biennial grown for its hot-flavoured fruits. **Nicotiana tabacum** L., tobacco, is a tall annual, with pink-tinged short tubular flowers and the fruit a capsule with numerous very small seeds, grown for its large ovate-spatulate leaves, which contain nicotine and are used after curing and fermenting.

DIPSACACEAE

General Importance. Includes only one crop-plant, teasel, of which a small acreage is grown, the dry inflorescences being used in the finishing of woollen cloth.

Botanical Characters. A small family of herbaceous plants, with opposite leaves and rather small flowers usually massed together in a compact head, often somewhat resembling that of the Compositae (see below, p. 220), but readily distinguished by the free, not joined, anthers.

Dipsacus fullonum L.   Teasel

A prickly biennial with long tap-root, producing in the first year a rosette of large broadly-lanceolate leaves, and in the second year an erect, much-branched stem to 5 ft. high. Stem leaves connate, so that the bases of the two opposite leaves at each node join to form a cup. Branches terminated by dense, erect, capitulum-like flower heads, about 8 cm. long by 4 cm. in diameter. At the base of each head is a whorl of long, spiny bracts forming the *involucre,* and above this the swollen axis (*receptacle*) bears numerous shorter *receptacular bracts.* In the axil of each of these latter bracts is a single flower surrounded at its base by a cup-like *involucel* formed from fused bracteoles. Each flower consists of an inferior ovary enclosed in the involucel and surmounted by a short, four-toothed calyx and a tubular, four-lobed mauve corolla, on which are borne the four free stamens. The inferior ovary, which is composed of two united carpels, contains a single pendulous anatropous ovule, and bears a single style with undivided stigmatic tip. Cross-pollinated by bees and flies. Fruit an achene, about 5 mm. long, with persistent involucel and calyx.

In the cultivated form, fuller's teasel (subsp. *fullonum*), the bracts of the involucre are comparatively short and spread horizontally, and the

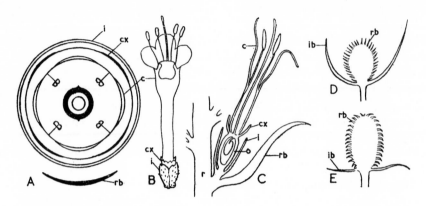

FIG. 95. Teasel. A, floral diagram. B, single flower in ventral view. C, in diagrammatic vertical section. D, diagram to show general shape of flower-head of wild teasel; E, of cultivated teasel. *i*, involucel. *cx*, calyx. *c*, corolla. *o*, inferior ovary. *r*, receptacle (main axis of flower-head). *rb*, receptacular bract. *ib*, involucral bract.

receptacular bracts are stiff and recurved. It is these receptacular bracts which are the effective part of the inflorescence when it is dried and mounted on roller frames and used to raise the knap of woollen cloth. In the wild teasel (subsp. *sylvestris*, often treated as a distinct species *D. sylvestris* Huds.), the involucral bracts are longer and curved upward around the head, and the receptacular bracts are softer and straight, and therefore useless for cloth-finishing.

Teasels are cultivated in small areas in various parts of the temperate regions, in England almost entirely in Somerset. They are a crop which requires a large amount of hand labour. 'Seed' (achenes) sown in April, often in special seed-beds, and young plants transplanted after shortening of the tap-root and spaced at about 13,000 per acre. They bloom in July of the following year, and individual heads are cut by hand as they become ready. Yields of some 200,000 heads per acre may be obtained; very careful drying and packing of the heads is necessary to avoid damage to the bracts. 'Seed' is obtained from a proportion of heads left to become fully ripe.

COMPOSITAE

General Importance. The *Compositae* provides no crops of outstanding importance in British Agriculture; chicory and yarrow are herbs sometimes included in leys, and sunflowers are sometimes grown as an arable crop. Among horticultural crops, lettuce is of greatest importance.

Botanical Characters. The largest of all families of flowering plants, including about one-tenth of all known species. Members of the family are world-wide in their distribution, and occur in almost every possible type of habitat.

The habit is very varied, including trees, shrubs and herbaceous plants of many types. Leaves are exstipulate, usually alternate, very variable in shape, but often pinnately cut or divided. The most characteristic feature of the family is the inflorescence, which is always a *capitulum*. Each capitulum consists of an enlarged stem-structure, the *receptacle*, which is surrounded by one or more whorls of bracts and bears on its upper surface a number of sessile individual flowers. The bracts around the receptacle form the *involucre*; the individual flowers, which may be subtended by

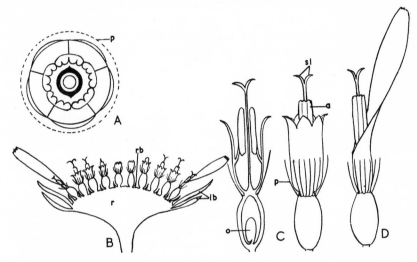

FIG. 96. Floral characters of Compositae. A, floral diagram (of single floret). B, diagrammatic vertical section of capitulum. C, vertical section and side view of tubular floret. D, side view of ligulate floret. *a*, anther tube. *o*, ovule. *p*, pappus. *r*, receptacle. *rb*, receptacular bract. *ib*, involucral bracts. *sl*, stigmatic lobes.

scales arising from the surface of the receptacle, are usually known as *florets** on account of their small size compared with that of the whole capitulum. The receptacle may be flat, convex or cylindrical, and may bear from a few (in certain genera, one only) to many hundred florets.

Each individual floret has an inferior ovary from which the other floral parts arise. The calyx is either absent or replaced by a ring of hairs (or, in some genera, scales) known as the pappus. The corolla is formed of five united petals, and on it are borne five stamens which are united by their anthers to form a tube surrounding the single style. The inferior ovary is formed from two united carpels, and contains a single basal anatropous ovule. The appearance of the floret largely depends on the shape of the corolla, and two distinct types are recognizable: (1) *tubular*

* It should be noted that *floret* is used in a different sense in describing the *Gramineae*, where it refers to an individual flower together with its associated lemma and palea. See p. 230.

florets, with an actinomorphic cylindrical or bell-shaped corolla, divided at the top into five broad lobes; and (2) *ligulate florets*, in which only the base of the corolla is tubular, and the remainder forms a flat, strap-like or lanceolate structure, often with five minute teeth at the apex. The capitulum may consist entirely of tubular florets (as in thistles) or entirely of ligulate florets (as in dandelion), or may have a central *disk* of tubular florets surrounded by a single ring of ligulate florets forming the *ray* (as in daisies).

Cross-pollination is by insects, and the whole capitulum forms a conspicuous attractive structure, in spite of the small size of the individual florets. If insect-pollination does not take place, it is still possible for selfing to occur, and in some forms self-pollination is the general rule. The style is terminated by two stigmatic lobes, of which only the inner surface is receptive. Dehiscence of the anthers is introrse, and pollen is shed into the tube formed by the united anthers. The two stigmatic lobes are not separated when the style grows up through the anther tube, and pollen is therefore deposited only on their outer non-receptive surface. Later they separate so that the inner surface of the stigmas are in a position to receive pollen from visiting insects. Still later they curve downwards, so that the receptive surfaces make contact with the pollen earlier deposited on the outer surface of the style, and self-pollination takes place if crossing has failed.

The inferior ovary develops into a single-seeded, dry, indehiscent fruit usually called an achene (since it is derived from two carpels, and is inferior, the special term *cypsela* is sometimes used). The pappus, if present, usually remains attached to the achene, and forms a very efficient means of wind dispersal. The seed is almost non-endospermic, with a large, straight embryo, usually containing oil as a food-reserve.

The large size of the family, and the very uniform structure of the inflorescence and flower, make classification difficult, and the *Compositae* is usually divided into numerous tribes, separated by very small differences. It is sufficient here to note the two main divisions or sub-families, *Tubiflorae* and *Liguliflorae*.

Tubiflorae. Some or all of the florets tubular; oil canals often present, but no latex.

Helianthus annuus L.   Sunflower

A tall annual, with large, rough-hairy, cordate leaves, alternately arranged on the stout, little-branched stem, and very large terminal capitula. The receptacle is flat or slightly convex, with several rows of large, pointed, involucral bracts. Florets subtended by broad scale, corolla yellow; disk florets very numerous, tubular, fertile; ray florets ligulate, large, sterile. Achenes broad, angular, large (*c.* 10 mm.); pappus scaly, not persistent. Seedling with long-oval, short-stalked cotyledons; first two leaves opposite, lanceolate, almost sessile, hairy.

Of N. American origin, widely cultivated in very varying forms, mainly as an oil seed, but occasionally for green fodder (and frequently as ornamental flowers).

Although a very important oil-producing crop in E. Europe and else-

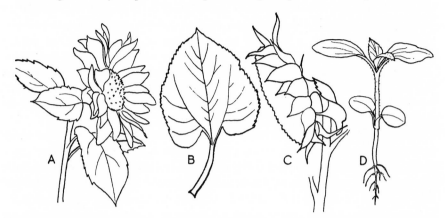

FIG. 97. Sunflower (Mars). A, small lateral capitulum, in flowering stage, × ¼. B, leaf, × ⅙. C, capitulum at ripe achene stage, × ⅙. D, seedling, × ¼.

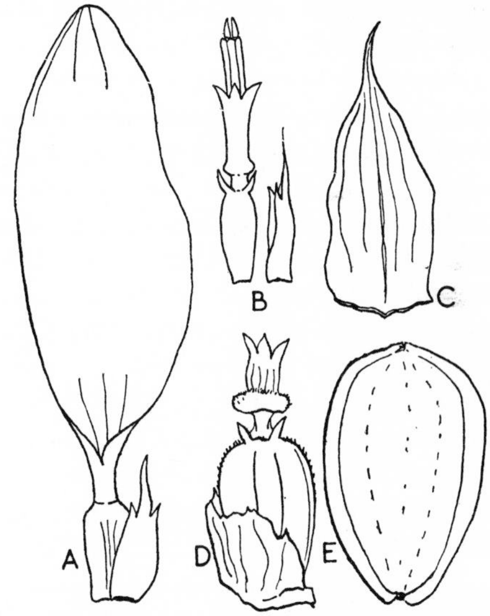

where, sunflowers are grown only to a limited extent in Britain; dry conditions are essential for satisfactory ripening and harvesting, and only the southern and eastern parts of England are suitable. 'Seed' (achenes) is drilled at 6-10 lb. per acre and seedlings thinned to give a spacing of about 15 × 10 in. or rather more. Crops may be combined if sufficiently dry when mature, but cutting and stooking of individual plants is often necessary; the thick, fleshy receptacle dries very slowly and mould growth may take place. Yields of from 10 to 20 cwt. of achenes may be obtained; bird damage is often very severe on small areas. About 40 per cent. of the achene consists of 'husk'; the oil content of the whole achene including husk is approximately 20 per cent., with 12 per cent. protein.

Forms of sunflower exist varying in size from the giant Russian types,

FIG. 98. Sunflower (Mars). A, ligulate floret and receptacular bract, × 1½. B, tubular floret and bract, × 1½. C, involucral bract, × ½. D, tubular floret with nearly mature achene, × 1½. E, mature achene, × 3.

7 ft. high with capitula 20 in. across, to dwarf forms 3-4 ft. high. Intermediate forms have been found most satisfactory in Britain, giving

223

capitula about 10 in. in diameter on 5-ft. plants. Varieties used include *Pole Star*, early, with white-striped black achenes, and *Mars*, rather later, achenes all black. A considerable amount of cross-pollination may take place.

Helianthus tuberosus L.   Jerusalem Artichoke

Similar to sunflower, but perennating by tubers; leaves mainly opposite, with broad, winged petiole; stems more branched; capitula small, rarely produced in Britain. Named artichoke from the resemblance in flavour of tubers to the globe-artichoke (*Cynara*, see below); Jerusalem is a corruption of Girasole, the Italian name for sunflower, and the plant is of N. American origin, having no connection with Palestine.

Grown primarily for its tubers, which are more irregular in shape than those of the potato, borne on shorter, stouter rhizomes, and with larger persistent scale-leaves subtending the buds. Internally the tubers consist mainly of parenchyma, partly primary tissue produced by proliferation of the pith cells, partly secondary tissue produced by the cambium. The well-marked cork layer found in potatoes is absent, and tubers wilt rapidly during storage. Since they are frost-hardy, they are usually left in the ground over winter and lifted as required. The food reserve in the tubers is mainly inulin, not starch. Artichokes are mainly grown as a vegetable for human consumption but, being fairly tolerant of low fertility and poor cultivations, they are sometimes recommended as a farm crop on difficult land.

Although artichokes are vegetatively propagated, few distinct varieties exist, and varietal names are not commonly used; the form commonly used in Britain has white-skinned tubers, but purple-skinned forms exist.

Topine is a German form grown as a double-purpose crop, the stems and leaves being cut for silage in early autumn and the tubers later lifted and either processed for inulin extraction or used directly for stock-feeding. Yields of up to 18 tons of green fodder (at 18-20 per cent. dry matter) per acre, together with 8 tons of tubers (about 16 per cent. dry matter), have been recorded. Topine (like some French clones of artichoke) is reported to be derived from a cross between *Helianthus tuberosus* and the related N. American *H. strumosus* L., which has smaller, more oval tubers on longer rhizomes. The name appears to be a contraction of *Topinambur*, the usual German name for artichokes, derived (via the French name, *topinambour*) from that of a Brazilian tribe with whom the artichoke was mistakenly associated at the time of its introduction to Europe at the beginning of the seventeenth century.

Achillea millefolium L., yarrow (for description, see p. 458), is sometimes used as a constituent of leys, or of special herb-strip mixtures for grazing, on account of its high mineral content. The 'seed', consisting of the very small, flat, silvery-white achenes (1·8 mm., 5 million per pound), is expensive, and is usually sown at the rate of ½ lb. or less per acre.

Chrysanthemum cinerariifolium (Trev.) Vis., pyrethrum, is grown for its flowering capitula, from which the insecticide pyrethrum is extracted. **Cynara cardunculus** L., globe artichoke, is a tall, thistle-like plant, with all florets tubular, grown occasionally as a garden vegetable, the fleshy receptacle and involucral bracts being eaten. *Cardoon* is a form of the same species in which the young etiolated shoot is used.

Liguliflorae. All florets ligulate; latex vessels present throughout the plant, associated with phloem.

Cichorium intybus L.   Chicory

A perennial with stout tap-root and a rosette of large, somewhat hairy leaves with pointed, shallow lobes. Erect annual stems are produced, growing to about 5 ft. high, and bearing similar but smaller leaves, and axillary clusters of almost sessile, few-flowered, blue capitula, 3-4 cm. in diameter. Achenes angular, pale brown, rather irregular in shape, about 3 mm. long, *c.* 300,000 per pound, with a pappus of short, finely-divided scales.

A common wild plant of chalk and limestone soils in England. Cultivated forms used in three distinct ways:

(1) As a grassland herb in the same way as yarrow. High-yielding and usually palatable, but rather difficult to manage; not persistent under hard grazing, and may become coarse and unpalatable under lenient grazing or hay. Sown at rates up to 2 lb. per acre.

(2) As a root-crop, in the same sort of way as sugar-beet, the roots being processed for the manufacture of a coffee substitute. The form used is the large-rooted *Magdeburg* chicory (which is also the form usually supplied for use (1) above), drilled at about 5 lb. per acre. Yields of 10 tons per acre of washed

FIG. 99. Chicory. A, leaf, × ⅛. B, capitula, × ½. C, single floret, × 2. D, mature achene, × 10.

roots are obtained, but lifting of the long roots is difficult, and roots incompletely removed may develop adventitious shoots, and the plant persist as a weed.

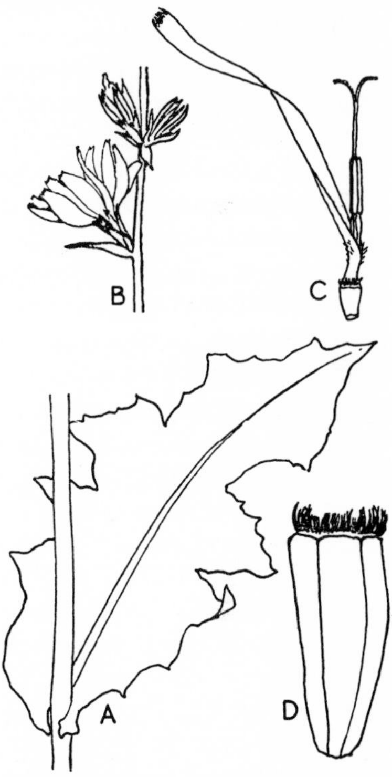

(3) As a vegetable, the young etiolated leafy shoot being eaten. The form usually used is *Witloof*, resembling Magdeburg, but with broader leaves.

Cichorium endivia L., endive, is a very similar species with the leaves glabrous, less lobed, the stems shorter, and the achenes slightly larger, with longer scales. Grown as a leaf vegetable, often blanched, in either plain or curled-leaved forms. Usually annual or biennial.

Lactuca sativa L., lettuce, is an annual grown for its very tender, compactly-arranged entire leaves, the whole plant being cut in the vegetative condition. In plants which have reached the 'bolting' stage, the stem elongates, producing a much-branched system of leafy shoots up to 2 ft. high, with very small cylindrical capitula. Corolla pale yellow; upper part of ovary elongating rapidly after pollination to form slender beak on which is borne the pappus of simple hairs. Beak and pappus removed in threshing; achene as sown about 4 mm. long, flattened, ribbed, black or white according to variety. Lettuce is almost entirely self-pollinated, and very numerous varieties exist. The main division on form is into the short-leaved flat or round-headed *cabbage lettuce* (var. *capitata*) and the larger-leaved upright *cos lettuce* (var. *romana*). Physiological differences are important, since they control the time of year at which varieties can be used. Many varieties can be satisfactorily grown only within a limited range of day-lengths; below this range they fail to heart, and above it they show rapid bolting.

Tragopogon porrifolius L., salsify, is a biennial occasionally grown as a garden vegetable for its thickened tap-root. It has long, narrow entire leaves and, in the second year, large capitula on leafless, swollen peduncles. Corolla purple, achenes large (12 mm.), with large pappus of compound hairs on long beak. **Scorzonera hispanica** L., black salsify, with shorter lanceolate leaves and somewhat smaller capitula of yellow flowers on leafy stems, achenes not beaked, is used in the same way.

Chapter XIV

LILIACEAE AND GRAMINEAE: GENERAL

LILIACEAE

General Importance. Contains numerous ornamental plants, but only one genus important as food-crops, the onions and related plants.

Botanical Characters. Mainly herbaceous plants, often bulbous. Leaves alternate, often sheathing at the base. Inflorescence usually a raceme; an umbel only in Allium and related plants.* Flowers actinomorphic, usually insect-pollinated, with a perianth of six usually petaloid seg-- ments, six stamens, and a superior gynaecium of three united carpels. Placentation axile; fruit a capsule or berry; seeds usually numerous, endospermic.

Allium cepa L.   Onion

A bulbous plant, behaving usually as a biennial. Stem in vegetative condition very short, conical, bearing numerous distichously-arranged leaves. Leaves consisting of two parts, leaf-sheath and leaf-blade (cf. *Gramineae*, p. 235). The leaf-sheath forms a tube open only at its junction with the leaf-blade; its lower part is much thickened and in the older (outer) leaves expanded to form a hollow sphere. It is these swollen, concentrically-arranged leaf-sheath bases which form the greater part of the bulb. The upper part of each leaf-sheath is a thinner tube, and these form the neck of the bulb. The leaf-blade is initially solid, approximately hemispherical in cross-section, but becomes hollow and tubular as it matures. The central cavity of the leaf-blade is not continuous with that of the leaf-sheath. The roots are adventitious, arising from the short basal stem. Buds in the axils of some of the lower leaves may develop to form structures similar to the main shoot, still enclosed within the outer leaf-sheaths.

Bulbs are usually harvested when they become dormant at the end of the first year's growth. If they are left in the ground, or replanted in spring, the main stem and those of the axillary buds elongate to produce hollow, swollen, flowering stems, about 4 ft. high. These bear no leaves above the bulb, and terminate in a large simple umbel of up to several hundred flowers. The umbel is subtended by a spathe formed of two membranous bracts. The individual flowers are borne on long pedicels; they consist of six free white or lilac perianth segments, about 4 mm. long, six stamens of which the three inner have filaments which are very

---

* The tribe *Allieae* is transferred to the family *Amaryllidaceae* in the classification proposed by Hutchinson, on account of its umbellate inflorescence initially enclosed in a spathe. It differs, however, from the typical members of that family in having the ovary superior, in which it agrees with other Liliaceae.

broad and shortly-lobed at the base, and a somewhat triangular ovary with a single slender style.

Cross-pollination is by insects, mainly flies, and the fruit, which usually ripens late in the year, is a loculicidal capsule, with only one or two seeds in each of the three chambers. The seed is black, angular, about 3 mm.; the embryo is sharply curved, with a single cylindrical cotyledon and very short radicle. On germination, the radicle emerges and is followed by the greater part of the cotyledon; it is the central part of the coty-ledon, bent to form an inverted V, which first comes above ground, while the tip remains in contact with the endosperm in the seed, and acts as a haustorium. Later, the cotyledon straightens, and the first foliage leaf emerges through a slit in the side.

Grown, sometimes on a field scale, for human consumption, either direct from seed, or from 'onion setts'. These are very small dormant bulbs, obtained by very late close sowing of seed in the previous year. Very many varieties exist, varying in size, shape, colour of skin (outer leaf-sheaths) and keeping quality. Cultivated from very early times, not known wild, perhaps derived from related species in Central Asia. The *shallot* is a perennial form (var. *ascallonicum* (L.) DC.) producing offset bulbs.

Other cultivated species are **Allium porrum** L., leek, with broad, flat leaf-blades and cylindrical, not bulbous, thickened leaf-bases, fila-ments of inner stamens very broad with long lateral teeth exceeding the anthers; **Allium sativum** L., garlic, similar but with numerous offset bulbs and small bulbils in inflorescence; and **A. schoenoprasum** L., chives, perennial, non-bulbous, slender cylindrical leaf-blades edible, flowers purple, filaments of all stamens simple.

Asparagus officinalis L., asparagus, belongs to a distinct tribe, with flowers in racemes. It is a rhizomatous perennial, with erect annual stems; it is the tips of these stems which are eaten in the young stage. Fully-developed stems bear only small scale-leaves; photosynthesis car-ried out by needle-like *cladodes*, stem structures borne in clusters in the axils of the scale-leaves. Dioecious, flowers greenish-white axillary, single or in pairs; female plants bear red globular berries. Grown as perennial, but propagated by seed, not vegetatively. Male plants outyield female.

GRAMINEAE: GENERAL

The **Gramineae**, the grass family, is a large family of world-wide distribution, with some 500 genera and well over 5,000 species. Both floral and vegetative structure are highly specialized, and members of the family are readily recognized; with the exception of the bamboos, which are mainly tropical or sub-tropical and have woody stems, all are herbaceous plants. The majority show the special growth-habit of grasses, making vegetative growth with very little elongation of the stems, so that at this stage most of the aerial part of the plant consists of leaf, the stem and buds being at or near ground-level. It is this habit which makes them ideal grazing plants, since animals feeding on them eat off only the leaves, and the stem and buds remain undamaged. Grasses form the main food of all grazing animals, and hence are of outstanding importance in any agriculture involving livestock. In addition, the cereals, which are large-seeded annual grasses grown for the food-reserves in the endosperm, are amongst the most important of arable crops. The Gramineae is thus unquestionably the most important family of flowering plants from the agricultural point of view.

THE GRASS FLOWER

The grass flower may be regarded as an extremely reduced form, of the basic monocotyledonous type, adapted to wind-pollination. In this basic type, as exemplified by the Liliaceae, there is a perianth of six

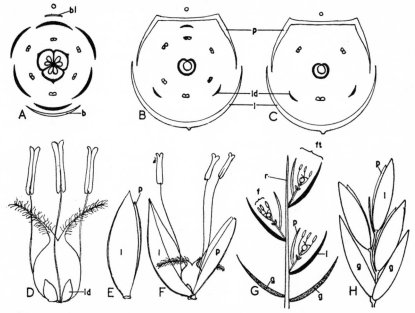

Fig. 100. Gramineae, flower and inflorescence. A, floral diagram of Liliaceae; B, of bamboo; C, of typical grass. D, grass flower. E, single floret, closed; F, open. G, diagram of structure of typical spikelet. H, spikelet in side view. *b*, bract. *bl*, bracteole. *f*, flower. *ft*, floret. *g*, glume. *l*, lemma. *ld*, lodicule. *p*, palea. *r*, rachilla.

segments in two whorls, six stamens also in two whorls, and three united carpels. In the Gramineae the perianth is reduced either to a single whorl of three, as in some bamboos, or more commonly to two segments only; these are small scale-like structures known as *lodicules*. Six stamens are found in some grasses, as, for example, in rice, but in the majority only one whorl of three is present. The gynaecium is reduced always to a single-chambered, one-seeded ovary, which bears usually two feathery styles. Such styles with their feathery, stigmatic branches may be considered as an adaptation to wind-pollination, as providing a large receptive area to catch wind-blown pollen. The stamens also, with their long filaments and large versatile anthers, are adapted to this method of pollination.

The perianth segments, being reduced to small, scale-like lodicules, provide no protection for the developing flower, and the protective function is carried out by bracts. Each flower is subtended by a bract, the *lemma*, and bears on its axis a bracteole, the *palea*. Both lemma and palea are strongly concave on their inner face, and the margins of the lemma usually enclose the edges of the two-keeled palea, so that the true flower is completely surrounded by them. This association of lemma and palea with the true flower (lodicules, stamens and carpel) is so constant that it is usual to speak of the whole structure as a grass *floret*.

Inflorescence

The florets are arranged to form short spikes known as *spikelets*. The axis of the spikelet, on which the sessile florets are borne, is known as the *rachilla*. At its base is a pair of bracts not subtending flowers; these are known as *glumes*. The spikelet then consists of a pair of glumes, and a rachilla bearing a number of florets; the number varies from one to about twenty. This spikelet is the basic unit of the whole inflorescence, which consists always of a series of spikelets. These are arranged to form either a *spike* (strictly a spike of spikelets) where they are sessile on the axis or *rachis*; a compound raceme or *panicle* (strictly a panicle of spikelets) where the spikelets are arranged on a repeatedly branched axis; or occasionally as a simple raceme (raceme of spikelets), where the structure is similar to that of a spike, but the spikelets are stalked, not sessile.

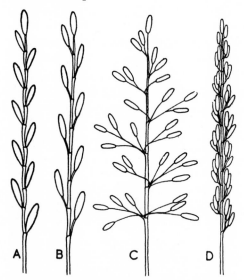

Fig. 101. Diagrams of types of grass inflorescence. A, spike. B, raceme. C, spreading panicle. D, spike-like panicle. Each ellipse represents a complete spikelet.

Spikes are usually simple, but branched or clustered spikes are found in some grasses (e.g. *Cynodon, Spartina*). The number of spikelets at each node of the spike also varies; there is, for instance, one spikelet per node in wheat, three in barley. Panicles also show considerable variation, particularly in the length of the branches on which the spikelets are borne, and the distance apart of the nodes at which the branches arise. Thus in oats, where the nodes are distant and the branches long, an open or *spreading panicle* is formed; in timothy, where the nodes are closely spaced and the branches short, the spikelets are tightly packed to form a dense cylindrical ear, known as a contracted or *spike-like panicle*.

Pollination. The developing stamens and carpel are completely enclosed within the lemma and palea, and cross-pollination can only take place if these structures separate. In the majority of grasses this takes place when the anthers are mature; the lodicules become fully turgid, swelling up to force apart the lemma and palea. The filaments of the stamens increase rapidly in length and the anthers come to hang freely outside the lemma and palea, and dehisce, setting free the loose, powdery pollen, which is carried by the wind to other plants. The stigmas are usually exposed later—that is, the flowers are *protandrous*. After pollination has taken place the lodicules shrivel, and the lemma and palea resume their original closed position and remain covering the carpel during the whole development of the fruit. This account of the actual flowering or *anthesis* applies to the majority of grasses, but some exceptions occur. A small number of grasses are *protogynous* (e.g. *Anthoxanthum*); in these there are no lodicules, and the stigma emerges first between the apex of the palea and the lemma, and is followed by the anthers. Occasionally, as in wheat, the anthers dehisce and deposit pollen on the stigma before the floret opens so that self-pollination is the general rule. The subsequent opening of the floret is usually too late to be effective, although it may allow a very small and, for most purposes, negligible percentage of cross-pollination to occur.

Caryopsis. If pollination is effective, the single ovule in the carpel is fertilized, and develops to form an endospermic seed. This remains always enclosed within the *pericarp* formed from the carpel wall. The mature pericarp is very thin (except in some bamboos, in which it becomes succulent), and it adheres to the still thinner testa and the special type of indehiscent fruit so formed is known as a *caryopsis*. In the great majority of grasses the caryopsis remains enclosed within the lemma and palea even when mature, and the inflorescence breaks up (*disarticulates*) so that the caryopsis is not set free, but is shed as part of a more or less complicated structure, which may include not only lemma and palea but also glumes. The whole structure, although not a true seed in the botanical sense, is usually referred to as the 'seed'. (See note on 'Agricultural Seed', p. 106.) Only in a rather small number of naturally-occurring grasses, not found in Britain (e.g. *Sporobolus*, the drop-seed grasses), is the caryopsis shed without coverings; in a number of cereals mainly used for human food (e.g. wheat, rye, maize) forms have been selected in which the naked caryopsis threshes out.

A wheat grain may be taken as an example of a caryopsis. It is an ovoid structure, pointed at the lower end, where it was attached to the floret, and blunt at the upper end, where the style branches were originally present. It is rounded on the dorsal surface (the surface facing the lemma when the caryopsis was enclosed in the lemma and palea) and marked by a deep groove on the other, ventral side. The whole surface is covered by the fused pericarp and testa, which consist of a few layers only of dead, crushed cells. At the lower end of the dorsal surface the embryo shows up as a small oval area, over which the pericarp and testa are somewhat wrinkled. The remainder of the interior of the caryopsis consists of the endosperm, a mass of polygonal thin-walled cells containing starch grains and some protein. Its outer layer is specialized as the *aleurone layer*, in which the cells are approximately cubical, and contain protein grains. A very thin residue of nucellar tissue (perisperm) may sometimes be seen between the testa and aleurone layer.

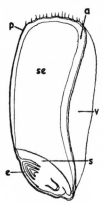

FIG. 102. Diagrammatic vertical section of wheat caryopsis, × 7. *a*, aleurone layer. *e*, embryo. *p*, pericarp and testa. *s*, scutellum. *se*, starch parenchyma of endosperm. *v*, ventral groove.

The embryo consists of a flattened oval structure, the scutellum, in contact with the endosperm, and the cylindrical shoot and root region attached to the scutellum on its outer surface. The shoot region consists of the hollow tubular *coleoptile*, within which is the small conical stem apex, surrounded by two or three rudimentary leaves. The root region consists also of a hollow tubular structure, the *coleorhiza*, which is fused with the scutellum for the greater part of its length, and encloses the short primary root, which shows a well-marked root-cap. Rudimentary lateral roots are present as small projections at the sides of the lower part of the stem region where this joins the scutellum; each of these is covered by a sheath continuous with the coleorhiza.

The morphological interpretation of these structures is not easy, and cannot be fully discussed here. The view most generally accepted, and based on the comparison of wheat with various other grass embryos, and on the course of the procambial strands which represent the rudimentary vascular system of the embryo, is that scutellum and coleoptile together represent the single cotyledon of the embryo. On this interpretation, the scutellum is regarded as a part of the cotyledon which has become modified as a food-absorbing organ; it may be noted that on germination it secretes enzymes and is responsible for transfer of food material from the endosperm to the other parts of the embryo, but does not itself show any further growth.

Variations in Spikelet Structure

It has already been mentioned that the spikelet may contain from one to many florets; the various parts of the spikelet may also show very considerable variation.

Glumes. The two glumes present may be equal or unequal in size; they are usually separate, but may be joined as in slender foxtail. They vary in size from the large, thin, multi-nerved glumes of oats, which completely surround and exceed in length the two or three florets, to minute, almost negligible, scales or facets in mat-grass and rice. They may be stiff and firm as in wheat, or thin and translucent as in tall oat-grass. The apex is often pointed; only rarely, as in timothy and barley, is the

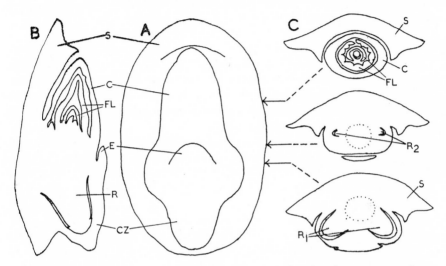

Fig. 103. Wheat embryo. A, in surface view. B, in vertical section. C, transverse sections at three levels, × 20. S, scutellum. C, coleoptile. FL, foliage leaves. E, epiblast. R, radicle. R1, R2, first and second pairs of lateral root initials. CZ, coleorhiza. Adapted from Percival, *The Wheat Plant.*

point prolonged into an awn-like structure; in *Aegilops* numerous long points are present.

Lemma. The lemma, like the glumes, shows considerable variation in size and texture; it may be round-backed or keeled, awned or awnless. The *awn*, usually a slender, bristle-like outgrowth, may be *terminal* when it arises as a prolongation of the tip of the lemma, *dorsal* when it arises on the back of the lemma, below the tip, or *basal* when its origin is even further down the lemma. It has been shown that large awns such as those of the common varieties of barley, may be responsible for a considerable part of the transpiration of the inflorescence. In addition they may play an effective part in distribution and burying of the seed. This is particularly true of *geniculate awns*, in which the lower part of the awn is spirally twisted and makes a marked angle with the usually finer, straight upper part. The spiral coils and uncoils according to water-content, causing the upper part of the awn to rotate. The shed lemma, enclosing the caryopsis, can be moved about on the surface of the ground by this action, and its sharp lower end tends to enter any cracks present, giving a self-burying effect.

Palea. The palea usually shows little variation; it is typically thin and two-keeled, and is never awned.

Rachilla. The rachilla may be either hairy or glabrous. In a spikelet which breaks up at maturity the rachilla usually disarticulates immediately below the individual florets, so that each separate floret bears a single internode of the rachilla. In one-flowered spikelets the floret may be terminal, as in timothy, in which case no rachilla is present on the floret after separation; or it may be lateral, as in barley, in which case the rachilla is visible standing up from the base of the floret.

'AGRICULTURAL SEED' OF GRASSES

The 'agricultural seed', or diaspore, that is the structure actually sown, either by natural shedding or after harvesting and threshing, varies according to the structure of the inflorescence and the way in which this breaks up. The true seed of a grass is never seen, since the caryopsis itself is an indehiscent fruit in which the single seed always remains covered by the pericarp. The main types of structure found are:

(1) Caryopsis only; this is rare and can only occur where the lemma and palea do not wrap closely around the caryopsis. Examples: wheat, rye.

(2) Caryopsis with lemma and palea; the commonest type of 'seed' in grasses. It is found where the rachilla separates above the glumes and, if the spikelet has more than one flower, also between the florets. Examples: rye-grass, cocksfoot, derived from many-flowered spikelets; timothy, bent, from single-flowered spikelets.

In such cases the rachilla (in many-flowered spikelets it is, strictly speaking, only a single internode of the rachilla) forms part of the 'seed' and is visible at the base of the palea. Exceptions to this are those one-flowered spikelets, such as timothy, in which the rachilla is not prolonged beyond the base of the floret. 'Seeds' in which lemma and palea are present will also include the lodicules, but these are not visible without dissection.

(3) Caryopsis with lemma and palea plus one or more male or sterile florets. This is derived usually from a spikelet with only one complete floret. Examples: tall oat-grass (one fertile floret containing caryopsis and one male floret), sweet vernal (one fertile floret containing caryopsis and lemmas only of two sterile florets).

(4) Complete spikelet; this is found where the spikelet separates below the glumes. Examples: slender foxtail (one-flowered spikelet), Yorkshire fog (two-flowered spikelet, of which one floret male only).

(5) Two or more complete spikelets; this is found where the rachis breaks into single-noded sections, each carrying more than one spikelet. Example: wall barley-grass, with three single-flowered spikelets at one node, only the centre one being fertile.

It will be observed that the more valuable species are included in the first two groups, and that the species in the later groups are largely weeds.

Increasing complexity of 'seed', while it may make for effective natural distribution and therefore favour the spread of a weed species, makes the cleaning and drilling (and in cereals, grinding) more difficult, and therefore tends to reduce agricultural value.

VEGETATIVE STRUCTURE

The shoot of grasses, like that of other plants, consists of a stem bearing leaves at the nodes. Its appearance, however, may be very different from that of a typical leafy stem, owing to the fact that the lower part of a grass leaf forms a tubular structure, the *leaf-sheath*, which surrounds and may completely hide the stem. In the majority of common grasses the stem, in the vegetative stage, is extremely short, and the arrangement of the leaves is not readily seen. It is simpler, therefore, to consider first a grass such as bamboo, in which the stem internodes are elongated. A single leaf arises at each node; the leaf arrangement (*phyllotaxy*) is *distichous*—that is, the leaves lie in two opposite ranks. Each leaf arises at a node and its sheath encircles the internode above. The base of the leaf-sheath is attached to the node around the whole circumference of the stem, but the tube so formed is split down one side, and the axillary bud will be found between the sheath and stem on the side opposite to this split. If the leaf-sheath is shorter than the internode above its point of origin, a length of uncovered stem will be visible between the top of the leaf-sheath and the node above. If, however, the leaf-sheath is longer than the next internode, then no stem will be visible, and only by stripping away the next lower leaf will it be possible to see the node at which a leaf originates.

The elongated stem of non-flowering bamboo shoots is exceptional, and the typical vegetative shoot of herbage grasses is one in which the internodes remain very short, so that the apparent axis of the shoot is merely a series of concentric tubular sheaths, with the true stem confined to the base of this. Such a shoot is seen in fig. 105; a vertical section of the basal part shows that the stem is roughly conical in form, with leaves arising at the closely-crowded nodes. Young leaves originate as collar-like projections around the apex of the cone and, as they increase in size, grow up through the tube formed by the older leaves.

Axillary buds are formed in the axils of these leaves,

Fig. 104. Diagram of bamboo shoot to show relation of nodes and leaves. The lowest node shown is labelled N1, and the sheath and blade of the leaf arising at this node LS1 and LB1. N2 is the next node above, and so on.

235

and these buds develop to form axillary shoots, each similar in structure to the shoot from which it arises. Usually the axillary shoot so formed grows up between the leaf-sheath of its subtending leaf and that of the next younger leaf, and is first seen when the tips of its leaves emerge above the subtending leaf-sheath. Such a shoot with developing axillary shoots is

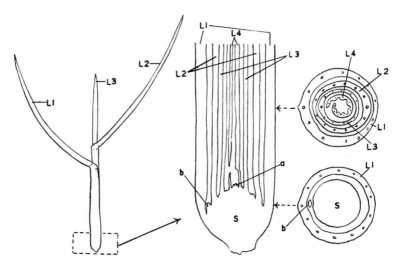

FIG. 105. Single vegetative grass shoot, and diagrammatic longitudinal and transverse sections of its base. L1-4, leaves numbered in succession from oldest to youngest. *a*, stem-apex. *b*, axillary bud. S, stem.

shown in fig. 106. Buds in the axils of the leaves of these axillary shoots may in their turn develop to form similar shoots, so that a dense rosette-like tuft of leafy shoots, all with extremely short stems, is gradually built up. This process is particularly conspicuous in cereals, where it is known as *tillering*, and this term is conveniently used as a general name for this type of branching from unelongated stems, the shoots themselves being known as *tillers*.

Structure of Leaf

Each leaf arises as a crescentic projection around the stem-apex; this projection increases rapidly in size and becomes differentiated as an upper part, the leaf-blade, and a lower part the leaf-sheath; in typical leaves little growth of the sheath takes place until the blade has reached a considerable length, and then the growth of both continues together, the growing zones being at the base of the blade and the base of the sheath. The developing leaf-blade is carried up through the tube formed by the leaf-sheath of the next older leaf, and at this stage is either folded in two or rolled longitudinally. If folded, its outline as seen in transverse section will be a more or less flattened oval; if rolled the section will be round. The shape of the tube formed by the leaf-sheaths conforms to the shape of the young leaf-blades, so that grasses with leaves folded in

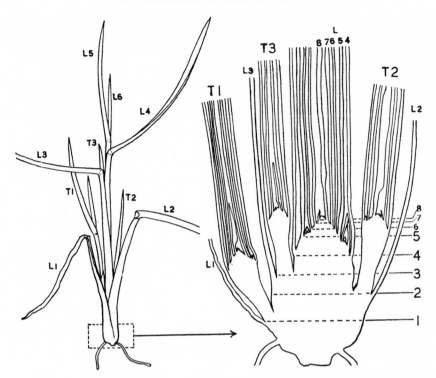

FIG. 106. Shoot after commencement of tillering, and diagrammatic longitudinal section of basal part. L1-8, leaves of main shoot. T1-3, tillers in axils of leaves 1-3. Numbers at right indicate nodes of main shoot.

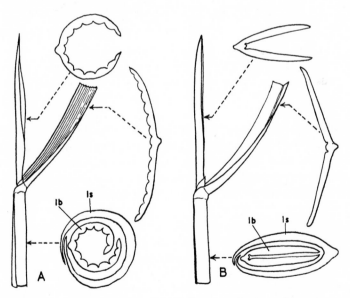

FIG. 107. Diagrams of upper part of vegetative grass shoots, and transverse sections at various levels. A, round shoot, leaf rolled in bud. B, flat shoot, leaf folded in bud. *lb*, leaf-blade. *ls*, leaf-sheath.

the young stage have flattened vegetative shoots, while those with rolled leaves have cylindrical shoots. *It should be noted that this distinction applies only to vegetative shoots, flowering shoots in which the stem has elongated are circular in outline whether the leaf-blade is folded or rolled.*

The leaf-sheath may be either *closed* or *open,* that is, may form a complete tube or may be split; this split may extend almost or quite to the base. Frequently the edges of a split sheath overlap. A keel may be present as a projecting ridge down the centre of the sheath.

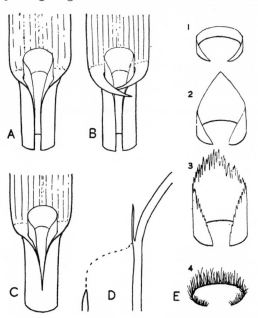

FIG. 108. Junction of leaf sheath and blade. A, auricles absent, sheath open. B, auricles present, sheath open. C, auricles absent, sheath closed. All shown with medium-length blunt ligule. D, diagrammatic vertical section of C. E, ligule types: 1, short, blunt; 2, medium length, acute; 3, long, toothed; 4, represented by ring of hairs.

When the leaf first emerges from the older sheaths surrounding it, the young leaf-blade is erect. As it matures, it gradually approaches the horizontal, making a right angle with the sheath. The junction of blade and sheath is always well-marked, and there is usually a projecting flap, the *ligule,* at this point. This is a thin, erect sheet of non-vascular tissue; it varies in length and shape and is often of value in the identification of grass species in the vegetative stage. The leaf-blade in the majority of grasses flattens out as it matures, and is usually wider than the sheath. At its lower end it may narrow abruptly to the sheath, or its lower corners may be extended as a pair of claw-like projections, the *auricles.*

The mature blade of a typical leaf is always long in proportion to its width, and usually considerably longer than the sheath. It may be *tapering,* with the margins straight and the width greatest at the base, *parallel,* with the margins straight except at the tip, where the blade narrows abruptly to a blunt point, or *broadest near the middle* and tapering to the tip and base. In some grasses the leaves are *bristle-like* (needle-like, acicular), remaining permanently folded so that the blade forms a more or less solid 'bristle', usually narrower than the sheath.

The upper surface of the leaf-blade may be flat or ribbed; the lower surface is usually flat, but may show a central keel. Both sheath and blade may be glabrous or hairy. The leaf-blade is usually a darker green than the sheath; the lower part of the sheath, not exposed to light, is often white, but may show other colours, e.g. red in the rye-grasses and fescues, yellow in dog's-tail. Such differences are frequently of value in the identification of grasses when not in flower.

The first leaf of a tiller is usually distinctly different from the later leaves; it consists of a two-keeled sheath without blade, and is known as a *prophyll*. Short, bladeless scale-leaves occur on underground stems, and transitional leaves, intermediate between those and typical foliage leaves, may also be found.

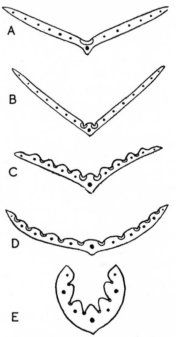

Leaf Anatomy

The venation of grass leaves is parallel; that is, a number of vascular bundles enter the leaf at the node and extend throughout its length without branching. These veins are surrounded by loosely-arranged chlorophyll-containing parenchyma, the mesophyll, which in turn is covered by the epidermis. This forms a continuous 'skin' over the leaf, the only apertures in it being the stomata, the apertures between the specialized guard-cells. The stomata, through which the bulk of the exchange of gases and water-vapour between the intercellular spaces and the external atmosphere takes place, are present on both surfaces of the leaf-blade of many grasses. In the more xerophytic species, however, they are found only on the upper (adaxial) surface, so that if the leaf-blade is rolled up, either permanently as in the bristle-leaved grasses, or temporarily in response to dry conditions, they all open in to the more or less enclosed space within the tube formed by the rolled blade.

FIG. 109. Diagrammatic transverse sections of leaf-blades of different types. A, folded, upper surface plane, one line of motor-tissue (cocksfoot). B, as A, but two lines motor-tissue (meadow-grass). C, folded, upper surface ribbed (dogstail). D, rolled (timothy). E, bristle-like (small fescue). Motor-tissue outlined, vascular bundles solid black.

Folding and rolling of the leaf-blade is facilitated by the presence of lines of *motor-tissue* consisting of greatly-enlarged, thin-walled cells of the upper epidermis. In folded leaves, a single line of motor-tissue in the centre of the blade (e.g. cocksfoot) or two closely-spaced lines, one on each side of the centre vein (e.g. meadow grasses), act as a hinge, allowing the two halves of the blade to close together. In leaves which roll up, a number of lines of motor-tissue are present. When, as is frequently the case, the upper surface of the blade is ribbed, these lines of motor-tissue lie in the grooves between the ribs, and contraction of the cells results in the upper surface becoming strongly concave. Motor-tissue is absent or poorly developed in permanently-folded, bristle-like leaves.

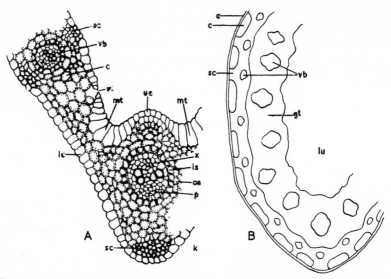

Fig. 110. A, transverse section of part of leaf-blade of smooth-stalked meadow-grass to show arrangement of cells. B, diagram of part of a transverse section of almost mature flowering stem of cocksfoot, to show arrangement of tissues. *vb*, vascular bundle. *x*, xylem. *p*, phloem. *is*, *os*, inner and outer bundle sheaths. *sc*, sclerenchyma. *le*, *ue*, lower and upper epidermis of leaf. *mt*, motor-tissue. *st*, stoma. *c*, chlorenchyma. *e*, epidermis. *gt*, parenchymatous ground-tissue. *lu*, lumen, space formed by breakdown of central ground-tissue of stem. *k*, keel.

Each vein consists of a single vascular bundle with xylem and phloem surrounded by a bundle-sheath of two layers of cells. In the majority of temperate-region grasses the outer layer is poorly-developed, the inner conspicuous with lignified walls; in the *Paniceae* and related tribes (p. 245) the outer layer is more conspicuous. Additional mechanical strength is provided by sclerenchyma associated with the veins. The amount of sclerenchyma present has a marked effect on the palatability of the leaf, and is discussed further on p. 301. Special siliceous cells, with a high silica content, and varying in shape in the different tribes, are present in the epidermis.

Stem Anatomy

In the relatively small number of grasses with a solid stem, of which maize may be taken as an example, the stem structure is that of a typical monocotyledon, with scattered bundles embedded in a ground tissue of parenchyma. Each vascular bundle consists of relatively small strands of xylem and phloem, surrounded by a bundle sheath; no cambium is present. In the majority of grasses, however, the vascular bundles are confined to the outer part of the stem, and the central part of the ground tissue breaks down, so that the mature stem is hollow (except at the somewhat swollen nodes, where a solid septum separates the cavities of adjacent internodes). The bundles, being thus confined to the relatively narrow region left, appear less scattered than in maize, and tend to be arranged in two rings as seen in transverse section. The bundles of the inner ring are usually larger; the ground tissue surrounding the bundles of the outer ring becomes thick-walled and lignified, so that these bundles are embedded, in the mature stem, in a ring of sclerenchyma. This sclerenchyma ring has, spaced at intervals around it, projections which extend out to the epidermis, and divide the chlorenchyma, which forms the outer ground tissue, into a series of narrow, vertical strips. The stomata open into the intercellular spaces of these strips, which remain green and carry on photosynthesis until the final ripening of the fruit and death of the stem. Creeping stems show a somewhat similar structure, but are more often solid. In rhizomes, which grow underground, no chlorophyll is present.

LIFE HISTORY

Germination. Germination is essentially the growth of the root and shoot regions of the embryo at the expense of the food reserves contained in the endosperm. Wheat may be taken as an example in which the grain is large and consists of the caryopsis without any other parts of the spikelet, and in which the progress of germination is therefore readily followed. The grain absorbs water, and the cells of the embryo, living but up to this time dormant, become active. Enzymes present in the aleurone layer and scutellum break down the starch and protein contained in the endosperm cells, and the soluble products are absorbed by the enlarged outer epithelial cells of the scutellum, and pass to the other parts of the embryo. Cell division recommences, and the first slight increase in size of the coleoptile and coleorhiza results in the rupture of the combined pericarp and testa covering them. The coleorhiza increases only slightly in length, and the primary root breaks through it and elongates; the lower pair of lateral roots also break through their sheaths, followed usually by the upper pair. Rather later a fifth lateral root may appear. Meanwhile, the coleoptile elongates and its upper part comes above ground as a tubular structure which surrounds and encloses the remainder of the shoot. Increase in length of the first foliage leaf (the next leaf after the coleoptile) results in this growing up through the tubular coleoptile and emerging through the slit at the top. Successive leaves develop from the short, conical stem-apex to give a shoot-structure similar to that described (p. 235) for a typical vegetative tiller. This may occur without any marked elongation of the stem, but if the grain has been rather deeply drilled, the lower one or two internodes above the coleoptile node may elongate to form the so-called rhizome. This has the effect of bringing the remaining unelongated part of the stem, from the nodes of which tillering will take place, into position just below the soil surface.

Meanwhile the primary and lateral roots have increased further in length and become branched, forming the *seminal root system*, which may persist throughout the life of the plant, but is soon supplemented by adventitious roots developed from the nodes above, and it is these which form the main bulk of the root system of the mature plant.

Tillering. As the main shoot increases in size and number of leaves, tillering begins. This, as has been explained (p. 236), is the development of the buds in the axils of the leaves to form shoots, the internodes of which, like those of the stem from which they arise, remain very short. Secondary tillers arise in the axils of the leaves of these primary tillers, so that a cluster of leafy shoots is developed. As each tiller enlarges, adventitious roots arise from its lower nodes, so that the size of the root system keeps pace with that of the aerial parts. The actual amount of tillering which takes place is very much dependent on conditions, and is discussed further in Chapter XV.

Flower Initiation. Each tiller during the period of vegetative growth has a conical stem-apex, from which new leaves continually develop. At a certain stage, however, the stem-apex changes from this vegetative condition and produces instead a rudimentary inflorescence. After this change no more leaves are produced by that tiller, and the last one formed is the 'flag' leaf. The change from the vegetative to the flowering condition is primarily a response to day-length, but previous exposure to low temperatures is necessary in some cases.

Stem Elongation. Once the change from the vegetative to the flowering condition has taken place in a particular tiller, its further development consists in the increase in size of the structures already present. The remaining immature leaves develop successively to their full size, and at the same time the internodes elongate, carrying the nodes bearing the younger leaves up through the tube formed by the older leaf-sheaths. Elongation of the lower internodes takes place first (the actual growing region being at the base of each internode); each internode starts its growth before that of the one below has ceased, so that normally two or three internodes are elongating at the same time. The final length reached by each internode usually increases progressively up the stem; it is always less than that of the corresponding leaf-sheath, except for the final and longest internode immediately below the inflorescence. This carries the inflorescence, which meanwhile has been increasing in size and complexity, and by now is almost mature, up through the leaf-sheath of the final or flag leaf, a process sometimes known as the 'shooting of the ear'. It usually continues growth until there is a considerable length of bare stem (neck) between the top of the flag leaf sheath and the base of the ear.

FIG. 111. Life cycle of wheat. A-D, germination. E, young plant before tillering. F, beginning of tillering; elongation of internode above coleoptile to form rhizome has brought tillering nodes near to ground-level, and development of adventitious roots from those nodes has begun. G, further tillering has taken place, and the stem-apex of the larger tillers has changed from the vegetative to the flowering state and elongation of their stems has started. H, tillering has ceased, lower internodes of fertile tillers have elongated, inflorescence well developed, but not yet emerged. I, ear of few fertile tillers emerged, later-formed tillers dying; after this stage pollination and fertilization lead to the development of the mature grain, followed by the death of the plant. (H and I one fertile tiller shown in full; roots largely omitted.) *c*, coleoptile. *cz*, coleorhiza. *p*, primary root r_1, r_2, first and second pairs of seminal roots; *ar*, adventitious roots from lower nodes of shoots *rz*, rhizome. *s*, position of spike.

243

Fruiting and Death of the Tiller. Pollination and fertilization take place, and the caryopsis matures; during the latter process food materials are absorbed from the fertile tiller, and the whole of this tiller is dead by the time the grains are fully mature. In wheat and other annual grasses all tillers die in this way; in perennial grasses (see p. 300) vegetative tillers are also present, and these remain alive, only the fertile tillers dying.

TRIBES OF GRAMINEAE

The *Gramineae* is a very large family showing a wide range of structure, and since a large number of different members of the family are of agricultural importance, and need to be considered here, either as cereals or as herbage plants, it is convenient to split it into a number of groups. These large groups within the family are known as *tribes*; members of one tribe have a good many characters in common, and a knowledge of the characters of the different tribes provides therefore a useful framework for the knowledge of the individual grasses.

The older classification of the family was based purely on the structure of the inflorescence and spikelet. More recently a number of anatomical characters, the type of starch-grains in the endosperm, and the size of the chromosomes, have been taken into consideration as well, in order to produce a less artificial classification. There have therefore been recently considerable changes in the grouping of grasses into tribes; the following somewhat simplified arrangement is based on that of Hubbard:*

Mainly temperate climate tribes; first foliage leaf narrow:

Festuceae. Panicle (except *Lolium*), spikelets many-flowered, glumes short. Starch grains compound, ovary glabrous, chromosomes large. (The *Glycerieae* are similar but differ in a number of anatomical characters and in having chromosomes small.)

Brachypodieae. Inflorescence as in *Festuceae*, or reduced to simple raceme. Starch grains simple, ovary hairy.

Hordeae. Spike, spikelets one- to many-flowered. Starch grains simple, ovary hairy, chromosomes large.

Aveneae. Panicle, spikelets few-flowered, glumes large. Awns often geniculate. Starch grains compound, chromosomes large. (*Phalarideae* similar, but one floret only complete.)

Agrostideae. Panicle, spikelets one-flowered, glumes larger than floret. Starch grains compound, chromosomes large.

Danthonieae. Panicle, spikelets few-flowered, glumes variable, starch grains compound, chromosomes small, ligule replaced by fringe of hairs.

Nardeae. Spike, spikelets one-flowered, glumes minute, starch grains compound, chromosomes large.

* C. E. Hubbard, *Grasses*, 1954. See also Hubbard's chapter on grasses in Hutchinson, *British Flowering Plants*, 1948, and Clapham Tutin and Warburg, *Flora of the British Isles*, 1952.

Mainly tropical, first foliage leaf broad (except in *Oryzeae*):

Oryzeae. Panicle, spikelets one-flowered, glumes minute, starch grains compound, chromosomes small.

Paniceae. Panicle, spikelets two-flowered, one fertile. Lemma hardened. Mesophyll radiating round vascular bundles. Starch grains simple, chromosomes small.

Andropogoneae. As *Paniceae*, but spikelets in pairs, lemma soft, glumes hardened.

Maydeae. As *Andropogoneae*, but separate male and female inflorescences.

Certain members of several of these tribes are large-fruited grasses grown for their seed-reserves, that is, are cereals; for convenience of treatment these are considered separately here. Wheat, rye and barley belong to the *Hordeae*, oats to the *Aveneae*; these cereals are considered in some detail, and a brief description is given of the mainly tropical or sub-tropical cereals rice (*Oryzeae*), millet (*Paniceae*), sorghum (*Andropogoneae*) and maize (*Maydeae*). The last four tribes contain no plants of importance as herbage- or weed-grasses in Britain, and are therefore not considered further, although members of the *Paniceae* and *Andropogoneae* are of great importance as grassland plants in other areas.

Chapter XV

GRAMINEAE: CEREALS

CEREALS: GENERAL

THE cereals are annual grasses grown primarily for their large 'grains'. In general, they provide the main concentrated carbohydrate food for man and for livestock and are to a considerable extent interchangeable for this purpose, the particular cereal grown in a given area depending largely on the climatic conditions. Thus wheat is the cereal mainly grown for human food in temperate climates; it is replaced for this purpose by rye under conditions of low temperature and low fertility. Barley, grown for stock-feed and for malting in areas where wheat can be grown, becomes the main human food-grain in parts of Asia; oats are the main cereals of cool temperate regions with high rainfall. In warmer regions these are replaced by maize, and in still hotter climates by rice (usually where irrigation by controlled flooding can be practised) or, where conditions are unsuitable for rice, by millet or sorghum.

Life-history and Behaviour under Field Conditions

The life-history of annual grasses has been discussed (p. 241), but it must be emphasized that the behaviour of plants grown under the close-spaced conditions of a cornfield is different from that of plants grown without competition.

The behaviour of winter wheat under field conditions may be taken as an example.* If sowing takes place in early November, germination may be complete in early December; leaves of the main shoot appear in succession through January and February, the first side tiller being visible towards the end of February at about the same time as the fourth leaf. Further leaves and side tillers appear during March, April and May; early in April the apex of the main shoot shows the first rudiments of the inflorescence. Further tillers usually become visible after this date, but rarely develop, under field conditions, to the ear stage, and dying off of the youngest tillers may be observed in May. Meanwhile, development of the inflorescence of the earlier-formed tillers continues, with florets forming successively from the base of each spikelet during May; in wheat up to nine florets per spikelet may be formed, of which the ninth develops for only one day, the eighth for rather longer, and so on, so that usually only four or five florets per spikelet reach maturity, the others remaining rudimentary. Growth of the stem internodes takes place in the fertile tillers, so that eventually the inflorescence becomes visible

---

* See Engledow and Ramiah, 'Investigations on Yield in Cereals', VII, *J. Agric. Sci.* **20,** 1930, and other papers in this series.

above the uppermost leaf-sheath. This emergence of the ear usually takes place during the middle of June; the ear of the main tiller emerges first, but there is a relatively quicker growth of the side tillers, so that, although the latest-formed tiller to produce an ear may not have become visible until nearly three months after the appearance of the main shoot at germination, its inflorescence emerges within at most from two to three weeks of that of the main shoot. This tendency for all ears to emerge at about the same time under field conditions is of great importance, in that it results in an evenly-ripening crop; if cereal plants are grown at wide spacing, so that there is less competition, and a large number of tillers are able to develop an ear, it will often be noticed that the ears of younger tillers are still green when those of older ones are ripe. The same effect can be seen under field conditions if ears develop on younger tillers, as, for instance, in an oat crop attacked by frit-fly in which the earlier-formed tillers are killed.

Flowering occurs some ten days after emergence of the ear in wheat, and although individual florets remain open for less than an hour, the whole process may be spread over a week or more for all the florets of any one ear. In wheat, barley and oats, self-pollination is the rule, with pollen shed on to the stigma before the floret opens; in rye a considerable amount of crossing takes place. Fertilization takes place within a few hours of pollination, and embryo and endosperm develop; starch begins to appear in the endosperm some ten days after fertilization and increases in quantity partly owing to the photosynthesis of the ear itself, partly by translocation from the leaves. By about a month after fertilization, the water content of the grain ceases to increase, and a few days later the grain reaches its maximum size. The embryo is mature and becomes dormant, and desiccation of the grain begins, and the endosperm becomes harder, passing through 'milk-ripe' to the fully ripe, hard stage. Meanwhile, gradual death of the whole plant, from the roots upwards, has taken place. In most cereals, breaking-up of the inflorescence to set free the grain takes place readily when the dead-ripe stage is reached, or the straw becomes brittle so that whole ears are lost. Although such shedding is very much less rapid and less complete than in wild forms, it is still necessary to take precautions against it, and to select varieties which do not shed readily when ripe; this is particularly important with crops which are to be combined and which must therefore be left standing until fully ripe.

Dormancy of Grain. The embryo, which has shown rapid development during the early stages of caryopsis formation, ceases growth and shows no further changes during the later stages of ripening. Germination involves the restarting of active growth of the embryo; this is dependent on a supply of water, and germination normally starts when the mature grain is soaked. In the cereals, however, the freshly-ripened grain may show a period of dormancy, during which germination will not take place, even when ample water is supplied. This dormancy is not due to any immaturity of the embryo, nor (as in 'hard' seeds of Leguminosae) to failure to absorb water, but is dependent on the character of the outer layers of the grain, which at this stage may prevent an adequate oxygen supply to the embryo. Where the caryopsis is closely invested by lemma and palea, as in barley and oats, these may have some effect, and their removal may reduce dormancy, but it is primarily the pericarp and testa which are important and dormancy can be broken by removing or puncturing them. This effect of the pericarp and testa is a transient one, and dormancy of the freshly-ripened grain is therefore only temporary. Its duration varies in different species and in different varieties, and its length is of considerable agricultural importance. If it is very short, grain in the ear may germinate if it is wetted, so that in a wet harvest much of the yield may be lost by sprouting of standing or sheaved corn; while if it is very long, the value of the grain for sowing or malting will be reduced.

Factors Affecting Yield under Field Conditions

(1) *Time of Sowing.* Inflorescence production in the grasses is largely controlled by day-length; the temperate cereals are long-day plants which change from the vegetative to the flowering stage when a certain length of day is reaching in spring. Alteration of time of sowing, therefore, does not greatly alter time of flowering and harvest for any particular variety, and late sowing will tend to give a low yield at about the normal harvest time, owing to reduction in the total photosynthesis, rather than a normal yield at a later date. In winter varieties of wheat, rye and barley the position is complicated by the fact that a cold period is necessary before the plants can respond to increased length of day; if such varieties are sown in spring they do not flower in the year of sowing, but make vegetative growth only and flower the following year. The stage of growth at which the low temperature occurs is not important, and Russian work has shown that it can be effective before the corn is sown. Storage of the dry, dormant grain at low temperature has no effect, but if just sufficient water is added for the embryo to become active, and the moist grain then stored for several weeks at a temperature a little above freezing-point, the treatment is effective. The treated grain, if then sown, will develop and flower without any further cold period. This conversion of a winter variety into a spring form is known as *vernalization*; while it is of considerable theoretical interest, it is of no economic importance in this country.

In general, the winter varieties, with their longer growing period, are higher-yielding than the spring forms, but the difference is usually not great. It is, of course, essential that winter varieties shall be sufficiently hardy to withstand the winter climate; thus, for example, winter oats, which do not show a very great resistance to hard winters, are rarely grown in northern England or in Scotland. Winter wheats can be grown throughout the British Isles, but only certain varieties are hardy enough for use in Sweden, while in the greater part of the Canadian wheat area only spring varieties can be used. While true winter varieties, which have a definite low-temperature requirement, cannot be sown in spring, the reverse process, the sowing of spring varieties in winter, is satisfactory providing they are sufficiently hardy, and spring barleys, for example, are sometimes winter-sown in southern England.

The optimum date of sowing varies not only according to district, but also with the variety. Thus, within the winter wheats, some, such as Rivet, require very early sowing, say October, whereas others can be sown up to February; among the spring wheats, while the majority must be sown by March, others such as Fylgia and April Bearded can be sown up to the end of April.

The tropical cereals are mainly short-day plants, and their season of growth in the tropics, with uniform short day-length throughout the year, is largely controlled by temperature and distribution of rainfall. They are, of course, not frost-hardy, and have a high minimum temperature for germination, so that the effective growing season in Britain would be extremely short. Millet can be grown in southern England, but is not economic; maize can be used only in the form of quick-maturing, and therefore low-yielding, varieties.

(2) *Spacing.* Cereals are grown at spacings which will give the greatest yield of grain per acre; this is quite distinct from spacing for maximum yield per plant. A winter wheat plant grown alone, with ample nutrients and no competition, may produce 100 or more tillers, of which a large proportion form ears; in a field crop the average number of ears per plant is usually between one and two. Close spacing is adopted because the increased yield per plant obtained by wider spacing does not fully make up for the smaller number of plants per acre. As the seed-rate is raised there is, in wheat, a reduction in percentage establishment (that is, in the proportion of 'seeds' sown which actually produce a plant), in the number of tillers per plant, in the number of these tillers which produce an ear, and in the size of ears. All these factors tend to offset the effect of increased seed-rate, but at rates below about 1¼ cwt. per acre (equivalent to about eighteen 'seeds' per foot-run of drill) the compensation is not complete. The yield per acre therefore increases with increase of seed-rate up to about 1¼ cwt. Increases in seed-rate above this figure are usually fully offset by reduction in percentage establishment and in yield per plant, so that further raising of the seed-rate has little or no effect on yield.

At all seed-rates there is a considerable excess production of tillers which are not normally able to produce an ear. High tillering ability is of value primarily only under adverse conditions, where the survival of tillers is low, or in giving partial compensation in areas of the field where the plant-density is abnormally low owing to irregular sowing or to dying-out of whole plants.

In barley and oats compensation for varying plant density takes place

I   249

mainly by variation in the weight of the inflorescence, with little variation in the average number of inflorescences per plant. Here again, there is a considerable excess production of tillers, and although the total number of tillers produced by a high-tillering variety such as 'Potato' may be double that of a low-tillering variety such as 'Marvellous' sown at the same rate (2 cwt. per acre), the average number of panicles per plant is about one in both varieties.*

Maize is very different in growth-habit from the other cereals; little tillering takes place, but the individual shoots are massive, with a very large leaf-area. The female inflorescences, in which the grain is produced, are lateral, not terminal, and one shoot may bear several inflorescences (cobs), each of far greater weight than a wheat ear. Maize therefore gives its greatest yield per acre under wide-spacing conditions.

(3) *Soil Fertility.* Cereals vary considerably in their soil-fertility requirements, with rye most tolerant of low fertility, and wheat and maize needing the most fertile conditions. In general there has been a continuous progress towards forms suited to high fertility levels; the modern cereal species are mainly less suited to poor conditions than the more primitive species, and within the species, modern varieties have a higher fertility requirement than the older ones. Rye and oats are tolerant of somewhat acid soils, but wheat and barley need adequate lime. Application of phosphate and potash may be necessary, but the most conspicuous response is usually to nitrogen. The addition of 1 cwt. sulphate of ammonia per acre usually gives an increased yield of some $2\frac{1}{2}$ cwt. grain per acre from wheat, barley and oats, and this order of increase may continue up to a total application of some 4 cwt. Increases of yield by increased applications of nitrogen are in practice, however, strictly limited by the standing ability of the plant.

(4) *Standing Ability.* It has been seen that increased yield per acre in cereals is due mainly to increased weight of the individual inflorescence; this inflorescence is borne on a comparatively long, slender culm, and the full potential yield can only be obtained if this culm is strong enough to carry it. In addition to the weight of the ear, the culm also has to withstand the additional weight of water standing on the ear in wet weather, and the beating effect of heavy rain and wind. There may be some recovery from bending-down of the culm (*lodging*) if this occurs at an early stage; the nodes of the stem retain their meristematic activity after growth of the internodes has ceased and respond to the geotropic stimulus of laying by one-sided growth, so that the upper internodes resume a more or less vertical position. If, however, lodging takes place later, or if breaking of the culms is involved, no recovery can be expected. Lodging may cause very serious reduction in yield; grains may fail to 'fill' completely and will ripen slowly and incompletely and, if badly

* S. G. Stevens, 'Yield Characters of Selected Oat Varieties', *Journal of Agricultural Science,* *32*, 1942.

laid, may sprout or rot under wet conditions. Harvesting is more difficult and expensive, and rarely as efficient as with standing corn.

Standing of a crop is partly a function of the individual cereal variety,
and partly of the cultivation conditions. The standing ability of the plant
depends on its shape and on the character of the straw. Winter varieties
of the common cereals tend to be prostrate in the early stages, so the
lower internodes of the culms are almost horizontal; this gives a broad-
based plant somewhat less readily laid than the narrow-based erect spring
type. Much the same effect is produced in maize, where the rigid upright stem is supported by *prop-roots*, which grow outwards and downwards from the nodes immediately above ground level. The characters
of the straw which affect standing ability are its length and its strength.
Long straw provides more leverage for the beating action of wind and
rain, and short-strawed varieties are therefore much more resistant to
lodging. Strength of straw varies considerably; it is mainly controlled by
the amount of thickening and lignification of the cells of the ground tissue.
Straw diameter and size of the internal cavity (*lumen*) also affect strength.

The main factors affecting the ability of any given variety to stand
in the field are the supply of soil nutrients and the density of the crop;
the actual amount of lodging which occurs will depend largely on weather
conditions. Severe storms may, of course, beat down any crop, and standing ability must be assessed in relation to normal weather conditions to
be expected at harvest and during the preceding few months. The presence
of weeds and of disease may also have an important influence on standing.

The main soil nutrient influencing standing is nitrogen; high nitrogen
not only increases the weight of inflorescence to be supported, but also
decreases the strength of the straw. With a high nitrogen supply the
straw tends to be longer, and is also more succulent; this may be particularly marked if the manuring is unbalanced, with an excess of nitrogen. The level of nitrogen supply is thus the preponderating influence,
and from a practical point of view the cereal varieties can be classified
into those suitable for low, medium and high nitrogen levels, and in
general the highest yield will be obtained by growing a cereal at the
highest level of fertility at which it can be relied on to remain standing.

Density of crop influences lodging mainly by its effect on the light
reaching the developing culm. A high seed-rate will give a larger number
of tillers in a given area, even after allowing for the compensating effect
of reduced percentage establishment and reduced number of tillers per
plant. The light reaching the base of tillers will thus be reduced, and
partial etiolation occur, giving more elongated, thinner and less lignified
stems. The presence of weeds may have the same effect, and external
shade from trees or tall hedges may also result in weaker straw and consequent lodging.

Any disease which weakens the straw is likely to result in increased
lodging; the most important in Britain is Eyespot, caused by the fungus
Cercosporella herpotrichoides, of which an account is given in Chapter XXVI.

251

CEREALS: SPECIAL

WHEAT

Wheat belongs to the genus *Triticum*; this is a member of the tribe *Hordeae*, and is closely related to *Agropyron*. The inflorescence is a typical spike, with a single spikelet at each node. Each spikelet consists of a pair of rather stiff glumes, and from two to nine florets borne on a very short rachilla; the upper one or more florets being sterile. The glumes are of about the same size as the lemmas, keeled and asymmetrical, with the side away from the rachis larger. The lemmas are of thinner texture, awned or awnless; the large caryopsis is hairy at the apex, and in some species threshes out from between the lemma and palea. All members of the genus are annuals.

A whole series of wheat species exists, of which some are found wild, while others are known only in cultivation. They can be divided into three groups on chromosome numbers; the basic haploid number is 7, and diploid species thus have fourteen chromosomes, tetraploids twenty-eight, and hexaploids forty-two.

DIPLOID SPECIES

Triticum aegilopoides Bal. (*T. boeoticum* Boiss.) Wild Small Spelt

Stem slender, hairy at nodes. Rachis very fragile, whole spike breaking up at maturity. Spikelets two-flowered, lower floret only maturing grain. Glumes tough, long, lemmas awned, caryopsis long narrow. Wild in eastern Mediterranean region.

Triticum monococcum L.   Small Spelt or Einkorn

Very similar to wild small spelt, and derived from it. Rachis fragile, but not breaking up except on threshing. Spikelets three-flowered, but maturing only one grain, which is rather shorter than in the wild form. The ear of both these species is very much narrower in face view than in side view, so that the ear at first glance looks more like a two-rowed barley. Small spelt was formerly cultivated in Asia Minor and western Europe, now rare. (Spelt is a general term for wheats in which the caryopsis does not thresh out.)

TETRAPLOID SPECIES

Triticum dicoccoides Körn.   Wild Emmer

Stem slender, hairy at nodes. Rachis very fragile, breaking up above spikelets when ripe. Spikelets three-flowered, one- to two-grained, lemmas awned. Wild in S.E. Asia.

Triticum dicoccum Schülb.   Emmer

Closely resembling wild emmer, and derived from it. Rachis fragile, spikelets three- to four-flowered, two-grained. Less hairy. Formerly widely cultivated, now rather rare. (*T. carthlicum*, Nevski. (*T. persicum* Vav.) is a similar form with tough rachis.)

Triticum durum Desf. Macaroni Wheat

Rachis tough, spikelets five- to seven-flowered, two- to four-grained. Lemmas awned. The caryopsis is large, very flinty, and tends to be triangular in cross-section; it threshes out from the lemma and palea, which remain attached to the tough rachis. Macaroni wheat is a much higher-yielding form than emmer, and is an important wheat of hot, dry countries; the grain is not suited for bread-making, but is used for the manufacture of macaroni and similar products. (*T. orientale*, Perc., Khorasan wheat, with pubescent leaves and glumes, spikelets three- to four-flowered, two- to three-grained, cultivated in Persia; and *T. pyramidale*, Perc., Egyptian cone wheat, with short, dense, tapering ears, cultivated in Egypt, are local forms related to *T. durum*.)

T. polonicum L. Polish Wheat

A species related to *T. durum*, although very different in appearance owing to the very long lanceolate, almost leaf-like, glumes. A form of little importance, having no advantages over *T. durum*, from which it probably originated. Occasionally cultivated for macaroni in the Mediterranean area; not Polish in origin, nor grown there.

T. turgidum L. Rivet Wheat

Rachis tough, caryopsis threshing out. Spikelets five- to seven-flowered, three- to five-grained. Glumes short, broad, lemmas awned, caryopsis short, plump, very floury, not suited to bread-making. High yielding. Cultivated to a small extent in the Mediterranean region and a hardier form in southern England.

Rivet wheat is the only species other than bread wheat (*Triticum aestivum*) which has been recently cultivated in Britain. The form grown (usually the variety Rampton Rivet) was a tall-growing wheat, with very large ears, square in section, strongly *bearded*, that is, with the lemmas bearing long awns and with the chaff (glumes and lemmas) markedly hairy, and bluish-grey in colour. The straw, although very long, is strong and wiry and the crop stands sufficiently well to be grown on soils of low fertility. The upper part of the straw is semi-solid and bends freely so that the mature ear is pendulous.

The caryopsis, which is very firmly held by the lemmas, may not thresh out easily unless fully ripe, and Rivet usually suffers less from bird-damage when grown in small plots than bread wheats. The caryopsis is distinct in shape, with a marked dorsal 'hump'; it is red in colour, owing to pigment present in the testa. The endosperm is of a type which makes the grain of fair milling quality, but which is very 'weak' (see p. 260); it can be used for biscuit-making, but not for bread.

Rivet long retained its place in cultivation as a winter wheat for poor, heavy soils, and under these conditions outyielded available bread wheat varieties. It has a long growing period, and must be sown early (preferably not after mid-October) and even then is late-maturing. The young plant is markedly prostrate, but is not very winter-hardy, and can only be grown in areas of comparatively mild winters.

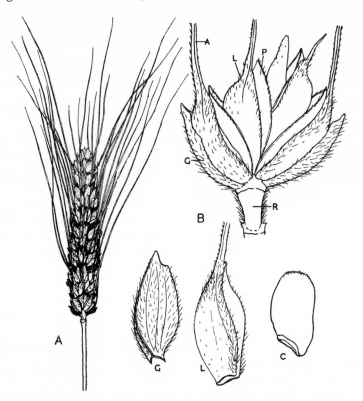

FIG. 112. Rivet wheat (*Triticum turgidum*). A, spike in face view, × ½. B, single spikelet and separate parts, × 3. A, awn. C, caryopsis. G, glume. L, lemma. P, palea. R, rachis.

T. timopheevi Zhuk.

A distinct wild species found in Georgia (U.S.S.R.); rachis brittle, ear short and broad, grains small. Probably not closely related to the other tetraploid wheats.

HEXAPLOID SPECIES

Triticum spelta L.   Large Spelt

Rachis fragile, breaking below spikelets, caryopsis not threshing out. A very distinct-looking wheat with narrow spikelets and square-topped glumes. Spikelets three- to four-flowered, two- to three-grained. Lemmas awned or awnless. Cultivated to some extent in S.W. Germany and Spain, never very widespread. Requires special milling treatment.

(*T. macha* Dek. & Men. is a Georgian form resembling *T. spelta*, but with rachis breaking above spikelets; *T. vavilovi* (Tum.) Jakub. has large, lax, broad ears.)

Triticum aestivum L.* (T. vulgare Host.)   Bread Wheat

Rachis tough, caryopsis threshing out. Spikelets five- to nine-flowered, with up to five grains. Glumes loose, rather short, keel not usually distinct to base. Lemmas awned or awnless. Caryopsis large, plump but not 'humped', variable in appearance, but less flinty than *T. durum*, less floury than *T. turgidum*, and many varieties suitable for bread. By far the most important and generally the highest-yielding of the wheat

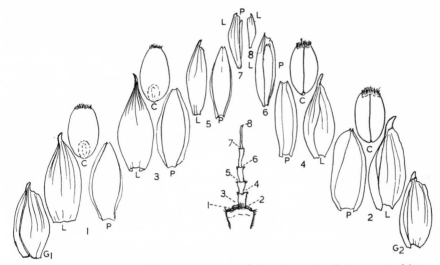

Fig. 113. Bread wheat, *Triticum aestivum* (var. Juliana); single spikelet separated into its constituent parts. The rachilla is shown in the centre, with the points of attachment of the eight florets numbered; the separated florets are numbered to correspond. Parts on left are shown in dorsal view, parts on right in ventral view; lodicules are omitted. G_1, G_2, glumes. L, lemma. P, palea. C, caryopsis (matured only in florets 1-4). × 2.

species. All wheats grown in Britain, with the single exception of Rivet, belong to this species, which will therefore be discussed in more detail later.

T. compactum Host. Club Wheat, with short, dense ears and small grains, spikelets six- to seven-flowered; and **T. sphaerococcum** Perc., Indian Dwarf Wheat, with spikelets six- to seven-flowered and very short, round, flinty grains, are locally-cultivated forms similar to *T. aestivum*.

INTERRELATIONS OF SPECIES, AND THE ORIGIN OF CULTIVATED WHEATS

The polyploid series shown by the wheat species is not due to simple replication of chromosomes (autopolyploidy); the chromosome groups (genoms) are different, and may be represented as follows:

Diploid species.   Chromosome number, 14.   Genom AA
Tetraploid species. Chromosome number, 28.   Genom AABB
Hexaploid species. Chromosome number, 42.   Genom AABBDD

* Used originally for bearded spring wheat only, but now regarded as synonymous with and having priority over *T. vulgare*.

Here A represents the haploid group of seven chromosomes found in *T. aegilopoides* and *T. monococcum*. These two species are clearly very similar, and *T. monococcum*, Small Spelt, may be regarded as derived by cultivation from the wild species. It appears to have been one of the earliest-cultivated of all crop plants, and archaeological evidence shows that it was widespread in southern Europe during the Neolithic period.

Emmer, *T. dicoccum*, is again very similar to the wild *T. dicoccoides*, and can be regarded as the cultivated form of the latter. Both these have the AABB genom—that is, are allopolyploids, resulting from a cross of a Small Spelt type with another plant. There is evidence that this other parent may have been *Aegilops speltoides*, an annual also occurring in the eastern Mediterranean area, and it may be assumed that *T. dicoccoides* arose from a natural cross between these two grasses, followed by chromosome doubling to give a fertile allotetraploid. Emmer, with two grains per spikelet and a larger ear, is a higher-yielding plant than Small Spelt, and became a most important cereal of the ancient world. It has, however, the disadvantage of a fragile rachis with the caryopsis not threshing out, and was largely replaced, during the classical period, by other tetraploid species, particularly *T. durum* with a tough rachis and naked caryopsis. These have the same genom as emmer, and it is assumed that they were derived from it, by mutation and selection in cultivation.

The hexaploid wheats, which are unknown as wild species and occur only as cultivated crop-plants, have the AABBDD genom, and thus involve a third parent. This has been shown to be another member of the related genus, *Aegilops*, probably the diploid annual *Aegilops squarrosa*. McFadden and Sears in America obtained in 1946 hexaploid amphidiploids from crosses between this species and *Triticum dicoccoides*, which closely resembled *T. spelta*; more recently Kihara in Japan, using the nearly-related *T. carthlicum* instead of *T. dicoccoides*, has obtained forms of the *T. aestivum* type. The original crossing and doubling to produce hexaploids must have taken place somewhere in S.W. Asia, where these species occurred together, but there is not sufficient evidence to say when. The resulting hexaploids combined (in *T. aestivum*, but not in *T. spelta*, in which the caryopsis does not thresh out, and which has never been of more than rather local importance) the naked caryopsis of the better tetraploids with a greater number of grains per spikelet, and thus a higher yield. They had, as well, great variability, and an enormous range of forms has developed in cultivation, including many types of particular value for bread and also many hardy types, which are not found in the other species. The result has been that they, and in particular bread wheat, *T. aestivum*, have not only very largely replaced the other species in the areas where these were formerly grown, but have spread over almost the whole world to become by far the most important cereals of the present day.

Triticum aestivum. Bread Wheat

RANGE OF TYPES

Winter and Spring Forms. Both winter and spring forms are found in the one species. Different varieties vary in the time at which they can be safely sown, and may be grouped into true winter forms, as, for instance, the majority of winter wheats of Scandinavian origin, which must be sown in autumn; the intermediate winter forms, including most of the English and French winter wheats; and the spring wheats, which may be sown during March or even April. A few dual-purpose wheats, such as Bersée (now obsolete), are satisfactory for either winter or spring sowing.

In general, the winter wheats are more prostrate in the early stages, and have a higher tillering capacity. Winter wheats, with their longer growing period, are usually higher-yielding, but with the improved spring wheats, such as Kloka and Opal, this difference is not as marked as it formerly was.

Straw Characters. Straw length varies in commonly-grown varieties from, say, 3 ft. (90 cm.) in the very short varieties such as Hybrid 46 to about 4 ft. 6 in. (140 cm.) in the obsolete April Bearded. Short-strawed varieties are normally much more resistant to lodging, and there has therefore been a progressive tendency away from the taller-growing varieties. The upper internode of the culm is almost solid in varieties of French origin, hollow with thin walls and large lumen in most others. Some colour variation occurs; a few varieties, such as Steadfast, showing distinct purple coloration.

Ear Characters. Many wheats have bearded ears—that is, the lemmas have well-developed awns. This character is, however, regarded as a disadvantage, and the only bearded wheat of the *T. aestivum* group recently grown in Britain was April Bearded. Many varieties commonly grown show, however, some 'tip-bearding'—that is, some of the upper lemmas of

Fig. 114. Spikes of Bread wheat, *Triticum aestivum*. A, face view, and B, side view of dense beardless variety (Juliana). C, D, lax bearded variety (April Bearded). × ½.

the spike bear short awns. Hairy chaff is also a disadvantage, in that there is some tendency for hairy forms to hold water more readily, and all Bread Wheat varieties now grown in Britain are smooth chaff forms. (Rivet and the *turgidum × aestivum* hybrid Alpha have hairy chaff.)

Density of ear varies considerably, from lax-eared varieties with long rachis internodes, such as April Bearded and Little Joss, averaging twenty

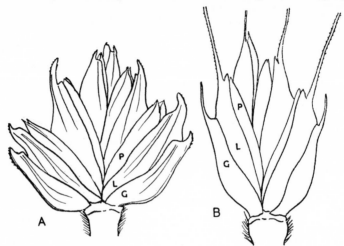

FIG. 115. Wheat. Single spikelet of A, a beardless variety (Juliana); B, a bearded variety (April Bearded); × 3. G, glume. L, lemma. P, palea.

spikelets or less per 10 cm. length of ear, to very dense varieties like Victor, with up to thirty-five. The dense ears are, however, usually shorter than the lax, so that the total number of spikelets shows little variation, and is usually approximately from twenty-two to twenty-four. Some of the lower and upper spikelets may be less well developed than those in the centre of the ear, giving a tapering outline. Colour of the ear, i.e. colour of the glumes and lemmas, may be red (usually dull reddish-brown) or white (pale yellow or 'straw'); this difference is only visible shortly before harvest, when the ear has 'turned colour'.

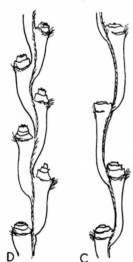

FIG. 116. Wheat. Part of rachis (in side view, with spikelets removed) of D, a dense-eared variety (Juliana); C, a lax variety (April Bearded); × 3.

Grain Characters. Size of grain varies, with the French wheats having large caryopses weighing about 60 g. per thousand, and most spring wheats smaller caryopses, of which 1,000 weigh about 40 g. Colour of the caryopsis is either red, of varying shades, or white; this colour is due to pigmentation of the testa, and though not in itself of great importance (the testa is so completely removed by modern milling methods that its colour has little or no effect on that of the resulting flour), is closely linked with seed-dormancy. The red-grained wheats are dormant at harvest-time and show little or no sprouting under wet conditions; the white wheats, however, do not show dormancy at this period and are all liable, therefore, to very severe damage in wet harvest years. The character of the endosperm has a very marked effect on the suitability of the grain for bread-making and other purposes, and is discussed below in the section on quality.

MINOR CHARACTERS USED IN IDENTIFICATION OF VARIETIES

The identification of individual wheat varieties presents considerable problems; at the time of a field inspection the colour of chaff and grain may not be developed, and even if it is, will only serve to separate the varieties into a number of groups (see 'botanical varieties', below). It is therefore necessary to take into account a number of minor characters, which although of no economic importance, have the advantage of being very little affected by cultural or weather conditions. Such characters are the size and shape of the glumes, which are, for example, long and rather narrow in Yeoman, short and broad in Juliana; the type of 'beak' (apex of keel) on the glume, which may, for example, be long and sharp, as in Koga II, or small and blunt as in Svenno, and the shape of the 'shoulder', broad and square in Svenno, narrow in Cappelle-Desprez. Short hairs present on the upper part of the inner face of the glume are also a useful guide; these vary from a few, confined to the inside of the keel, as in Svenno (Type 1) through an intermediate condition (Type 2) with hairs few but not confined to the keel (e.g. Professeur Marchal) to forms (e.g. Champlein) in which the whole upper third of the inner surface is hairy (Type 3). The 'imprint', a semi-translucent area at the base of the glume, visible from the inner side, may also be of value for identification; this is, for example, large and broad in Professeur Marchal, but small in the variety Atle.

The phenol reaction of the grain may also be of assistance, although this test is not suitable for use in the field. Grains are wetted with 1 per cent. aqueous phenol and allowed to stand in the presence of air for eight hours and the degree of coloration observed. This test may be used, for example, to distinguish between the morphologically very similar varieties Wilhelmina and Victor, as the former blackens whereas the latter remains unchanged in colour.

'Botanical Varieties'

A classification into 'botanical varieties', based on the presence or absence of awn on the lemmas, and hairs on the glumes and lemmas, and on the colour of the chaff and grain, may be mentioned. It serves to divide up the agricultural varieties (cultivars) into a series of groups, each of which has been given a Latin varietal name. The only groups which need be included here are those into which varieties now or recently cultivated in Britain fall. They are:

Bearded, smooth chaff, red chaff, red grain; *T. aestivum*, var. *ferrugineum*. Only example: April Bearded.

259

Beardless, smooth chaff, white chaff, white grain; *T. aestivum*, var. *albidum*. Examples: Holdfast, Victor, Flamingo, etc.

Beardless, smooth chaff, white chaff, red grain; *T. aestivum*, var. *lutescens*. Examples: Cappelle-Desprez and majority of current varieties.

Beardless, smooth chaff, red chaff, white grain; *T. aestivum*, var. *albo-rubrum*. Only example: Steadfast.

Beardless, smooth chaff, red chaff, red grain; *T. aestivum*, var. *milturum*. Examples: Squarehead's Master, Little Joss, Jufy I, etc.

(For the full classification, under the specific name *T. vulgare*, reference may be made to Percival, *The Wheat Plant*.)

QUALITY IN WHEAT

Although one may speak of a sample of wheat as being of good or bad quality according to whether it is well or badly harvested, plump or shrivelled, clean or mouldy, the term 'quality' denotes particularly the suitability of a given variety, at its best, for the purpose for which it is to be used. Since the main use of wheat is for milling and baking, quality normally means suitability for these two purposes.

Milling Quality. In the traditional method of milling wheat between stones, the whole of the grain was ground up, giving a flour from which the larger flakes of bran might be sifted out, but which otherwise contained all the constituents of the caryopsis; pericarp and testa (=bran) and embryo (germ) as well as endosperm. Modern methods of large-scale milling between rollers give almost complete separation of the different parts of the caryopsis, enabling a flour to be produced which is derived from the endosperm only; such a flour is whiter and, owing to the absence of the oily embryo, longer-keeping, although of lower feeding value than stone-ground flour. It is, then, the endosperm which is of importance to the present-day miller, and the character of the endosperm which determines whether a variety is of good or bad milling quality. Some wheats are *hard*, and the endosperm breaks down to give a 'gritty' product passing readily through the sieves of the mill without clogging; others are *soft* and give a light, 'fluffy' flour, clogging sieves and reducing considerably both the rate of production and the extraction rate. Maris Widgeon is a hard wheat, of high milling quality, and Elite Lepeuple and Svenno are also hard, while Hybrid 46 and many French wheats are soft and of low quality from a milling point of view.

Baking Quality. In the production of bread, flour is moistened with water and yeast added. The yeast ferments sugars present to produce carbon dioxide, which forms numerous small bubbles which increase the volume of the dough. If these bubbles are retained during the handling and baking of the dough, a large, light-textured loaf will result; if not, then the volume of the loaf will be smaller and its texture closer. The ability of the dough to retain the carbon dioxide is spoken of as *strength*; it depends on the quantity and quality of the mixture of proteins known as *gluten*. Strong wheats have a high proportion of gluten of good quality, which is deficient in weak wheats. Accurate assessment of strength is difficult without actual baking tests; nitrogen content may give some information, a strong wheat having perhaps 1·9 per cent. nitrogen, and a weak one 1·6 per cent., but the figures tend to be very variable and can only be used for comparison under similar conditions. A strong wheat has usually a translucent, flinty endosperm, and that of a weak one tends to be more floury and opaque in appearance.

It was at one time claimed that strength was largely dependent on climatic conditions, but, although it can be influenced by these, and there are certain European wheats which are strong when grown in a continental climate, but weak when grown in Britain, it was proved early in this century that strong wheats can be grown in Britain. This was shown by Biffen at Cambridge, who found that Red Fife, the source of the very strong imported Canadian wheat, retained its strength when grown here, and, further, that this strength could be maintained in new varieties derived from it. Thus, while the older English varieties, such as Squarehead's Master, are weak; newer varieties, such as Yeoman, and more recently Maris Widgeon, are of high quality for bread-making.

Strong wheats are usually hard wheats, and it is of course true that to be a satisfactory wheat for bread a variety must be of good milling quality, as it has first to be made into flour. Not all varieties of good milling quality are strong, however, and many of those which are of good or fair milling quality, but weak, are the most satisfactory wheats for biscuit-making, where the dough is not required to rise in the same way as for bread. Squarehead's Master and Victor are examples of such biscuit wheats; a more recent variety is Flamingo.

VARIETIES OF BREAD WHEAT IN CULTIVATION

The combined requirements of the farmer for high-yielding, strong-standing, disease-resistant varieties and of the miller and baker for high quality present a very difficult problem for the plant-breeder. It has been met by the successive crossing of varieties, each with their particular merits, derived from almost all over the world, in an endeavour to produce new varieties combining as many as possible of the qualities required. Outstanding work has been done in Britain at Cambridge, and by individual firms, and at the same time there has been a constant introduction of varieties developed in other countries with sufficiently similar climatic conditions. Field experience, and the systematic trials undertaken by the N.I.A.B., have acted as a sieve, sorting out and retaining the best varieties and rejecting the inferior ones, whether old and formerly valuable varieties now superseded, or new introductions of insufficient merit. Few of the older varieties remain in cultivation, and the 'life' of the majority of varieties is short. Thus, of the twenty wheats in the 1955 revision of the N.I.A.B. lists of recommended wheat varieties, only six were included in the recommended list for 1960, and of these six, two only remain into 1965. It is therefore only possible to give here an account of the trends observable in wheat varieties; for detailed recommendations, the current N.I.A.B. lists should be consulted.

The English wheats at the end of the nineteenth century were mainly weak winter wheats, giving satisfactory yields and standing reasonably well under conditions of moderate fertility; outstanding amongst them were the squarehead types, then amongst the best standing wheats available. Crosses between wheats of this type, or between them and a Dutch high-yielding variety, Zeeuwsche, gave first Victor and Wilhelmina, and later Juliana and Wilma, a series of closely-similar, white, weak winter wheats of high-yielding and standing ability on moderate soils, which have proved very useful biscuit wheats, although with the disadvantage, common to all white wheats, of growing out in wet harvests. They were in turn replaced by the Dutch hybrid, Staring, in which the high biscuit quality of one parent, Juliana, was combined with the higher-yielding and better standing ability of the French wheat Vilmorin 23, and by the Belgian variety Minister, and later by Flamingo.

Meanwhile, the problem of increasing bread-making quality was dealt with at Cambridge. A genetically strong variety was found in Red Fife, a Canadian spring wheat of Galician origin, very low-yielding under British conditions. A cross of this with a squarehead type (Browick) now obsolete gave Yeoman (1916), of good quality and good standing ability. This crossed with White Fife (closely related to, and probably a derivation of, Red Fife) gave Holdfast (1935), even better both in quality and yield, but a white wheat with the attendant disadvantage of growing out in the ear. Holdfast crossed with Squarehead's Master, the latest surviving old English variety, gave Masterpiece, which was free from this defect. A later cross of Holdfast and the French Cappelle-Desprez gave Maris Widgeon, combining high bread quality with high yield. All these good bread wheats, it will be observed, owe their strength to Red Fife, which has also been of outstanding importance as a parent variety in N. America. There, by crossing with various Indian and Russian wheats, it has given rise to the very important Marquis, and the still earlier Ruby and Garnet, which greatly increased the Canadian wheat acreage by allowing cultivation to spread northward into areas of very short growing season.

The old English squarehead types, introduced into Scandinavia towards the end of the nineteenth century, gave rise by crossing with local wheats to the Scandinavian white chaff, red grain, winter wheats, such as Iron, Steel, Scandia, etc. Many of these were introduced into Britain during the 1930s and 1940s, and proved useful farmers' wheats, but were unsatisfactory on account of their low milling quality. More recently, the better-standing and higher-yielding variety, King II, has been used, but suffers from the same defect. The Scandinavian spring wheats have, however, proved extremely useful in Britain. Many of them are derived from crosses of Extra Kolben, itself a derivative of Galician Kolben,

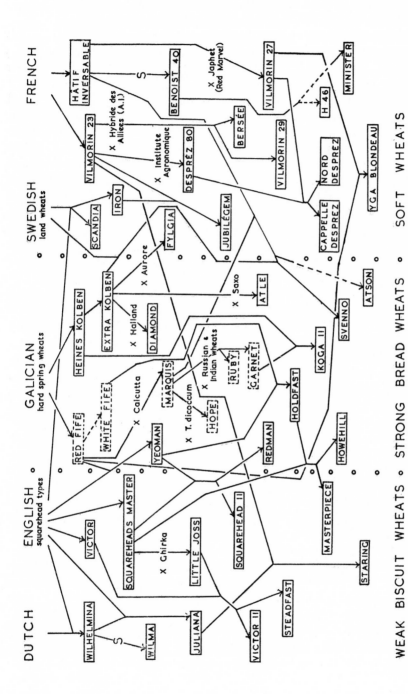

WEAK BISCUIT WHEATS ○ STRONG BREAD WHEATS ○ SOFT WHEATS

Fig. 117. Origin and interrelation of wheat varieties. Broken connecting lines indicate that pedigree has been simplified; S, that variety was obtained by selection without crossing. Names in dotted frames are American varieties.

coming from the same area as Red Fife, and probably related to it. Atle, derived from Red Fife. Svenno, with the same high quality and slightly and strength equal or even superior to the best winter bread wheats derived from Red Fife. Atson, with the same high quality and slightly greater yield and earliness, is of rather more complicated parentage, including, in addition, the Canadian Marquis and the French Hâtive Inversable. Fylgia, also a derivative of Extra Kolben, was suited to very late sowing, and so replaced the old April Bearded. Koga II was derived from Kolben, Garnet, and a German variety; Kloka and Opal are high-yielding varieties of German origin.

The earlier French wheats introduced into Britain were mainly spring varieties, such as A1 (Hybrid des Alliés) and Red Marvel (Japhet), and these, although valuable at the time, have been superseded by the Scandinavian varieties. More recently, very high-yielding French wheats, mainly winter, with short, semi-solid straw, and large red grain of low milling and baking quality, have been developed. From Hâtive Inversable (already mentioned as one of the parent forms of Atson) have been derived Vilmorin 27 and Benoist 40; from the latter Hybrid 46 has been produced in England, and Minister in Belgium. From Vilmorin 23 (previously noted as one of the parents of Staring) have come, by crosses with other French wheats, Vilmorin 29, Bersée and Desprez 80, and, by a cross with the Swedish variety Iron, Jubilégem. Desprez 80 crossed with Vilmorin 27 has given Nord Desprez and Cappelle-Desprez. Many of these varieties have had to be eliminated under British conditions on account of their susceptibility to disease, as, for example, Desprez 80 and Nord Desprez to yellow rust (see p. 564) and Vilmorin 27 to loose smut (p. 557). The best of them, however, are outstanding as very high-yielding, short, stiff-strawed varieties for high fertility, and their superiority in these respects outweighs, for the farmer, their low quality.

For the immediate future it may be expected that interest will continue to centre on yield, and that very high-yielding varieties of the type of Rothwell Perdix and Champlein will be grown more than higher quality varieties such as Elite Lepeuple and Maris Widgeon. Disease resistance is likely to be increasingly important; most currently recommended varieties show good resistance to one or more important diseases, but not to all. Thus Capelle-Desprez and Maris Widgeon are resistant to eye-spot, but susceptible to loose smut; whereas the position is reversed in Rothwell Perdix and Champlein. The two former are also rather susceptible to yellow rust, while Hybrid 46, which is very resistant to yellow rust, is highly susceptible to both eye-spot and loose smut.

For the distant future, it may be guessed that the wheat genus is capable of still further development, and that *Triticum aestivum*, the hexaploid product of the crossing of three different species, which has so largely superseded the earlier wheat species, may perhaps in its turn be replaced by some new and even more valuable synthetic species.

RYE

Rye belongs to the genus *Secale*; this is closely related to *Triticum*, and has a very similar spike, but with much smaller, narrow glumes.

Secale cereale L. is the only species cultivated. This is an annual with rather lax spikes of usually three-flowered spikelets; the third flower is nearly always abortive and minute. The glumes are narrow and acute, the lemmas longer than the glumes, tapering gradually into long, rather stout awns, and bearing stiff hairs on the keel. The lemma and palea of each floret tend to diverge, so that the tip of the mature caryopsis is

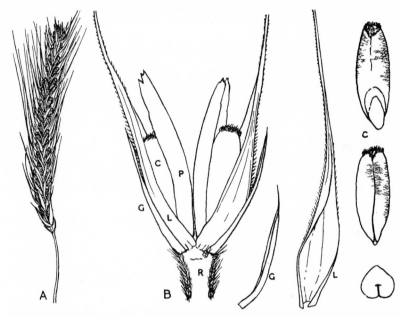

FIG. 118. Rye. A, spike in side view, × ½. B, single spikelet and separate parts, × 3. G, glume. L, lemma. P, palea. C, caryopsis (shown in dorsal and ventral views and cross-section). R, rachis.

clearly visible. The caryopsis, which threshes out in all cultivated forms of rye, is similar in structure to that of wheat, but considerably longer and more slender.

Germination is similar to that of wheat, but usually only three lateral seminal roots are produced. The young plant closely resembles wheat, but the coleoptile and leaves tend to show a purplish tint, and the auricles are small, very narrow and hairless. The straw is long, slender, solid and wiry.

Origin. Cultivated rye appears to have been derived from *S. montanum* or a related species. This is a wild plant of E. Europe and W. Asia, similar to cultivated rye and, like it, a diploid with fourteen chromosomes. It differs in being perennial, in having smaller grains and a brittle rachis. Annual and biennial forms with brittle rachis, which have been described as *S. ancestrale*, occur as weeds of other cereals in S.W. Asia, and these

appear to be the primitive forms of *S. cereale.* Rye has never been cultivated in the area in which these wild forms occur, and it appears probable, therefore, that they were carried westwards and northwards into
central Europe quite unintentionally as weeds of wheat. As the mixed
crop was taken north, conditions became less and less favourable for the
wheat, so that the crops harvested contained ever-increasing proportions
of rye, which in primitive agricultural conditions could not, of course,
be cleaned out. Ultimately, in central and northern Europe, the non-
hardy Mediterranean wheat would disappear entirely, and the rye remain
as a secondary or replacing crop.

Uses and Distribution

Rye is used for bread-making, but the bread is inferior to that made
from wheat, and rye is used only because of its greater hardiness and
ability to grow on somewhat acid soils of low fertility. The cultivation
of rye for bread is thus only practised where wheat cannot be grown
satisfactorily, and there is always a tendency, with greater efficiency of
farming and rising standards of living, for rye to be replaced by wheat.
It was formerly an important bread-corn in Britain, but its cultivation
for this purpose is now largely confined to E. Germany, Poland and
Russia. Rye is grown as a cereal in Britain only for the production of
rye biscuits, and in N. America for whisky manufacture.

The thin, hard straw of rye is of little or no value for animal feeding
and is used for litter, thatching, packing, etc. Rye is, however, often
included in arable forage and silage mixtures for use in the green condition; its hardiness, high tillering capacity and ready establishment
make it a useful plant for this purpose, and for early spring grazing.

Varieties

Rye differs very conspicuously from wheat in being largely cross-
pollinated; individual plants therefore tend to be mainly heterozygous,
and varieties are much less constant and well-marked than in wheat.
This fact, together with its very minor importance in Britain, means that
little attention is paid here to variety in rye, and it is often sold and
grown merely as 'winter rye'. A considerable number of Continental
varieties are available, however, and King II, a comparatively short-
strawed, rather dense-eared, winter variety is grown to some extent.
Spring varieties differ from winter varieties in the same way as in wheat;
they are not grown in Britain. Forage rye is sown in September and
grazed in early spring and is usually ready well before Italian ryegrass.
Varieties include the German Bernburg and the Hungarian Lovaszpa-
tonai. These may be grown for grazing only, but with extra nitrogen, an
early forage cut will allow grain to be harvested.

Polyploids and Hybrids

Autotetraploid forms of rye, with twenty-eight chromosomes, have
been produced, and show promise of increased grain size and yield.

Their use is, however, complicated by the necessity for isolation from normal diploid rye, since cross-pollination with pollen of different chromosome number will result in sterility and loss of yield.

Crosses with *Aegilops* and *Triticum* species have also been made; some varieties of bread wheat will cross rather readily with rye and fertile amphidiploids (*Triticale*; see p. 39) and some aneuploid forms with one or more rye chromosomes added to the wheat nucleus, have been produced, and may be of value in combining the grain-quality of wheat with the hardiness and tolerance of poor conditions of rye.

BARLEY

Barley belongs to the genus *Hordeum*. The inflorescence, like that of wheat, which is placed in the same tribe of the *Gramineae*, is a spike. The arrangement of the spikelets is, however, quite different from that seen in wheat; in barley each node of the rachis bears three single-flowered spikelets.

Cultivated barley, **Hordeum sativum** Jess., is an annual with large spikes; each node of the rachis bears three spikelets, each consisting of a pair of small linear glumes, and a single floret with a lemma larger than the glumes, partly enclosing the palea. The rachilla is prolonged above the base of the floret. The rachis is tough in the cultivated barleys and the caryopsis either threshes out (naked or hull-less barleys, not grown in Britain) (fig. 124) or threshes off the rachis enclosed within the lemma and palea which not only tightly enwrap it, but are stuck to it by a secretion produced by the pericarp.

The caryopsis differs from that of wheat in minor details only; it is more pointed at the apex, and the aleurone layer consists of several layers of cells instead of one. In the 'hulled' barleys grown in Britain, the caryopsis is completely hidden by the lemma and palea; the five-nerved lemma extends some two-thirds of the way round, its margins overlapping those of the palea. The palea shows a ventral groove corresponding to that of the caryopsis; in the lower part of the groove lies the slender rachilla. Within the base of the lemma, and between it and the embryo region of the caryopsis, is the pair of lodicules, which may be large or small.

Germination is similar to that of wheat, but the coleoptile, in the hulled barleys, grows up inside the lemma and therefore appears to emerge from the apex of the grain. Seminal roots may be up to eight in number. The young plant is distinguished from wheat by its much larger auricles and usually by its glabrous leaf-sheaths; in some winter barleys hairs are present, but not on the auricles themselves. The leaf blades show usually some fifteen to twenty nerves as against eleven to thirteen in wheat; as in wheat, the leaf blades tend to be twisted in a clockwise spiral. The life-history of barley also resembles that of wheat, and the same distinction into winter and spring forms exists. Like wheat again, cultivated barley is self-pollinated, the florets of the large-lodiculed forms usually opening for a short period after anther dehiscence, those of the small-lodiculed forms remaining closed throughout.

Range of Types

If all three spikelets of each node produce a grain, six vertical lines of grains will be visible on the ear. If the internodes of the rachis are short —that is, if the ear is dense, these vertical lines will be spaced equidistantly around the rachis, giving a typical *six-rowed barley*. If, however, the ear is lax, the lateral two spikelets at each node have room to stand more nearly opposite to each other, and hence come almost in a vertical line with

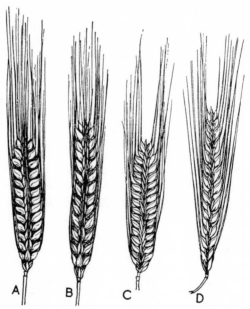

Fig. 119. Barley spikes. A, dense six-row. B, lax six-row (i.e. four-row). C, dense two-row. D, lax two-row. (A and B in face view, C and D in side view.) × ½.

those of the node above, giving the so-called *four-rowed barleys*, in which there are two single vertical rows, formed by the grains of the central spikelets, and two double rows formed by those of the lateral spikelets. In many barleys, however, the lateral spikelets are much smaller than the central one at each node, and do not produce a grain, so that a *two-rowed barley* is produced.

Four- and six-rowed are distinguished only by difference of density, and grade one into the other. The distinction from two-rowed forms is, however, quite clear-cut (intermediate types, in which the lateral spikelets are fertile but smaller than the central ones do occur, but are of no economic importance) and the appearance of the ear is very distinct. Samples of threshed grain can also be distinguished; in two-rowed barleys all the grains are symmetrical but in four- or six-rowed forms the lateral grains are asymmetrical and slightly twisted, and the sample thus consists of one-third straight grains and two-thirds twisted grains.

Differences of ear density are also shown in the two-rowed barleys; where the ear is lax and the internodes of the rachis long, the grains make only a small angle with the rachis, giving a *narrow-eared barley*. Where

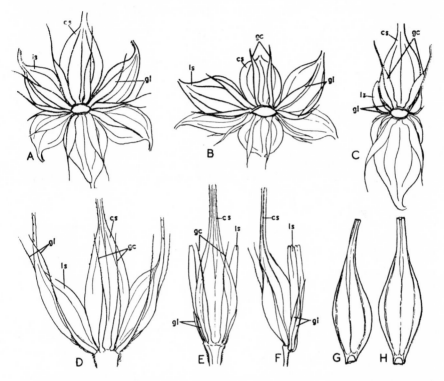

Fig. 120. Barley. A, B, C, part of spike seen from below, to show arrangement of fertile spikelets at two successive nodes to form A, six rows; B, four rows; C, two rows. D, E, F, group of three spikelets at one node; D, of a four-row barley in face view; E, of a two-row barley in face view; F, in side view. G, H, dorsal view of threshed grains of a four-row barley; G, a lateral grain, H, a central grain. All × 3. *cs*, single floret of central spikelet. *ls*, of a lateral spikelet. *gc*, glumes of central spikelet. *gl*, of lateral spikelet.

the ear is dense, the grains stand out more nearly horizontally, making a larger angle with the rachis and giving a *broad-eared barley*. Within each of these groups various degrees of density occur.

The base of the mature grain varies in shape. It may be square as seen in side view, often with a shallow, transverse 'nick' across the base of the lemma about 1 mm. from the point of attachment (*verum type*); or it may be bevelled off to a blunt, chisel-like edge (*falsum type*). The lodicule characters are correlated with those of the grain-base; varieties with *verum*-type base have small lodicules lying wholly on top of the caryopsis, as seen when the lower part of the lemma is dissected off. Varieties with *falsum*-type bevelled grain-base have larger lodicules, partially hidden in the dissected grain by the base of the caryopsis, and with their tips curving round it in a collar-like fashion. Hairs are present on the lodicules and also on the rachilla, and the type of hair found is the same on both; these may be either long and fairly straight (Archer type, conveniently called 'hairy') or short and curved (Chevallier type, 'woolly').

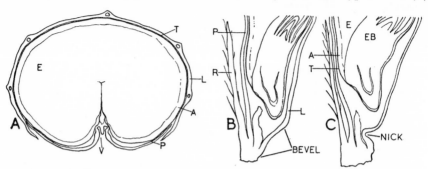

FIG. 121. A, diagrammatic transverse section of mature barley grain. B, diagrammatic median vertical section through lower part of grain with *falsum* type base. C, with *verum* type. All × 12. R, rachilla. L, lemma. P, palea. T, pericarp and testa. A, aleurone layer. E, endosperm. EB, embryo. V, ventral groove.

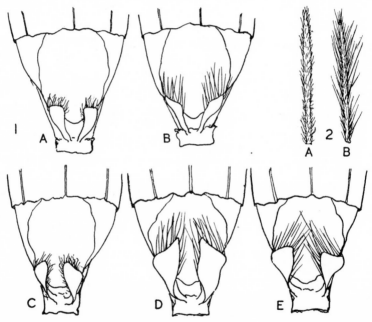

FIG. 122. 1, barley grains with basal part of lemma dissected off to expose lodicules and embryo region of caryopsis; A, lodicules small (bib-type) hairs woolly (Maltster); B, lodicules small, hairs straight (Plumage Archer); C, lodicules large (collar-type) hairs woolly (Chevallier); D, lodicules large, pointed, hairs straight (Spratt-Archer); E, as D, but lodicules blunt (Kenia). 2, detached rachilla: A, with woolly hairs (Chevallier type); B, with straight hairs (Archer type). All × 9.

Type of hair is not correlated with grain-base, and each of the two rachilla and lodicule hair types may be found associated with either *verum* or *falsum* grain-base.

Type of grain-base is not necessarily correlated with density, but in fact all the narrow-eared two-rowed barley varieties grown in Britain show the bevelled *falsum* base, while all the broad-eared forms, with the exception of Spratt, have *verum* base.

Nomenclature. All the forms of cultivated barley will cross with one another, and many of the distinctions between them are single-factor differences. It seems desirable, therefore, to regard them as belonging to

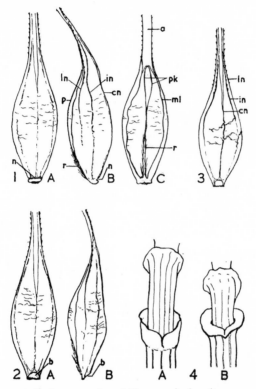

FIG. 123. Barley. 1, grains of Plumage-Archer (two-rowed, dense, *verum* base): in A, dorsal; B, side view; C, ventral view. 2, Spratt-Archer (two-rowed, lax, *falsum* base, English type); A, dorsal view; B, side view. 3, Freja (as 2, but Scandinavian type), dorsal view. All ×3. 4, collar at base of lowest internode of spike: A, Spratt-Archer (cup type); B, Freja (plate or platform type); ×7. *a*, awn. *b*, bevel. *n*, nick. *p*, palea. *pk*, the two keels of palea. *r*, rachilla. *cn, in, ln*, central, intermediate and lateral nerves of lemma. *ml*, margin of lemma.

a single species, and *Hordeum sativum* Jess., which is used here, is the earliest name used in this sense. The different forms had, however, previously been named as separate species:

H. hexastichon L. . Six-rowed forms.

H. vulgare L. . . Four-rowed forms (*H. polystichon* covers six- and four-rowed).

H. distichon L. . . Two-rowed forms, divided sometimes into three varieties:

zeocriton (originally as a distinct species)—Fan
 barleys, e.g. Spratt.

erectum—broad-eared, two-row forms, e.g. Plumage.

nutans—narrow-eared, two-row forms, e.g. Chevallier.

(The intermediate narrow-eared forms such as
 Spratt-Archer have been variously placed
 under either *erectum* or *nutans*.)

H. deficiens . . Extreme two-rowed forms with lateral spikelets
 minute.

H. trifurcatum Jacq. . Hooded forms, known as Himalayan or Nepaul
 barley.

Origin and History of Cultivated Barley

Barley has been in cultivation for a very long period, and remains of
grains of both two- and six-rowed forms have been recorded associated
with archaeological finds at least 5,000 years old. Cultivated barleys are
diploid with fourteen chromosomes, and appear to have been derived
from the very similar wild species, *Hordeum spontaneum* Koch, with the

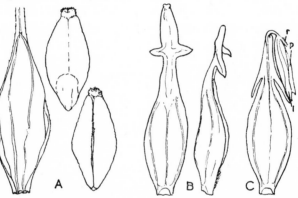

Fig. 124. A, naked barley; ventral view of spikelet to show loosely fitting palea and
lemma, threshed caryopsis in dorsal and ventral views. B, hooded (Himalayan) barley
grain in dorsal and side views. C, hooded grain in which an extra spikelet has developed
on hood. *r, p,* and *l,* rachilla, palea and lemma of extra spikelet. All × 3.

same chromosome number. This is wild in S.W. Asia, and resembles a
two-rowed barley, but has smaller grains and a fragile rachis which
breaks up at maturity into single internodes, each bearing a central
fertile spikelet, and two lateral infertile spikelets, in the same way as the
wild English wall barley, *Hordeum murinum*. *Hordeum agriocrithon* Aberg,
a similar but six-rowed barley, found wild in Tibet, may have been
concerned in the origin of the six-rowed cultivated forms.

Uses

Barley was formerly used largely as a cereal for human food, and many
of the forms cultivated were naked barleys, in which the caryopsis alone

threshes out. Such naked barleys (mainly six-rowed, but two-rowed forms exist) are still cultivated in areas in Asia, unsuited to wheat-growing; in regions such as Britain, where barley is now used either for stock-feeding or for malting, only hulled forms, in which the caryopsis remains firmly enclosed within the lemma and palea, are used. These may be either two- or six-rowed forms; in Britain six-rowed forms are of little importance, but in the United States, for example, they are the main malting barleys. For stock-feeding the character of the grain is not critical, although a high protein content may be an advantage, but for malting purposes grain characters are of very great importance, and quite small differences may have a marked effect on quality and value. In neither case is the character of the awn important, since it is removed in threshing, but where barley is cut green for fodder or hay the rough awn of the common malting and feeding varieties is a distinct disadvantage, and either smooth awned or awnless (hooded) forms are used.

Malting Quality. The malting process consists essentially in soaking the barley grain and allowing it to germinate for a period of usually rather over a week. During this time enzymes are produced by the scutellum and aleurone layer, and the cellular structure of the endosperm is largely broken down. Considerable root growth takes place, and the coleoptile grows part way up under the lemma; this growth is at the expense of part of the starch originally present. Germination is then stopped by kiln-drying, and the shrivelled roots are sieved out. The resulting malt can then be incubated with water and the diastase present breaks down the remainder of the starch to maltose; in brewing, the extract so obtained is fermented by yeast to give alcohol.

For the barley to malt satisfactorily it is essential that germination shall be very high, very rapid and very uniform. Dead grains will not merely not malt, but are likely to give rise to undesirable fungal growth; dormant grains will delay the process, and if some grains germinate more rapidly than others, it will be impossible to stop germination at the optimum stage for all grains. The physical state of the endosperm must also be satisfactory; 'steely' grains, which show a semi-translucent surface on cutting, are undesirable, as the endosperm structure breaks down incompletely or more slowly than in a grain showing an opaque, floury cut surface. This necessitates a longer germination period with increased growth of the embryo, and therefore greater loss of carbohydrate from the endosperm. High nitrogen content is undesirable, since it means a lower carbohydrate content; in addition, it gives a higher percentage of nitrogen compounds in the final extract, which is for most brewing purposes a disadvantage.

These characters of the grain, on which the malting value of a sample depends, are determined partly by the variety and partly by the way in which it is grown. Slow ripening and complete maturity are essential for high malting value; quality is decreased by drought or excessive rain, by late sowing, and by late or excessive nitrogenous manuring; it is also very much influenced by soil conditions. Quality can ultimately only be judged by malting and brewing tests, but nitrogen percentage may be a good guide. It varies from about 1·3 per cent. in good malting samples to nearly 2 per cent. in poor ones, and it has been shown that for any given variety the yield of extract from the malt is decreased by an amount proportionate to any increase in the nitrogen content of the grain. Size of grain, as expressed by weight per 1,000 grains, also affects yield of extract, as smaller grains tend to have a higher proportion of lemma and palea, and therefore a lower starch content. On appearance, a sample is judged by the type of endosperm as seen on cutting, on the absence of threshing damage or moulding, on the size, uniformity and well-filled condition of the grain, and on the clear, pale yellow colour and finely-wrinkled appearance of the lemma and palea. This latter character is due to the thin lemma and palea adhering to the caryopsis during its final slight shrinkage resulting from loss of water after it has reached its full size.

BARLEY VARIETIES CULTIVATED IN BRITAIN

Six-rowed barleys have, in recent times, been of little importance except in the upland areas of Wales and Scotland, where the hardy land race Bere has been cultivated as a winter feeding barley. More recently, a lax six-rowed winter variety, Prefect, was unsuccessfully tried as a malting barley. For feeding, the early, high-yielding but thick-husked German variety Dea is sometimes used. Dea shows good resistance to leaf-blotch, *Rhynchosporium secalis*.

With these exceptions, all barleys grown in Britain are of the two-rowed type. In the early nineteenth century the main malting barleys were land races with very slender arching ears and hairy rachilla. They were weak-strawed and low-yielding; some of them at least had useful malting qualities, as, for instance, Scotch Common, with very low seed-dormancy and very rapid germination. About the middle of the century these were largely replaced by the similar but higher-yielding, woolly-rachilla variety, Chevallier, and this in turn at the end of the century by the denser, narrow-eared form Archer and by the broad-eared Gold-thorpe. These, however, still had the disadvantages of weak straw, and of a tendency to a slightly brittle rachis, which made clean threshing difficult. Goldthorpe had also the further drawback of a long and fragile 'neck' between the uppermost leaf-sheath and the base of the ear, which resulted in loss of grain by ears falling off before harvest.

These disadvantages were to a large extent overcome by crosses using Archer as a parent. In one of these, Spratt-Archer, the other parent was Spratt, an old, very broad-eared variety long grown on fen soils in E. England on account of its very stiff straw. In the other, Plumage-Archer, the cross was made with Plumage, a variety of Scandinavian origin somewhat similar to Goldthorpe. These two varieties, although different in type, Plumage-Archer being a broad-eared, and Spratt-Archer a narrow-eared barley, are very similar in yield, in their exceptionally high malting quality, and in their field characters, although Plumage-Archer is suited to rather heavier soils on higher rainfall than Spratt-Archer. Their malting quality soon made them the most widely-grown varieties, and by 1940 they were together responsible for 80 per cent. of the malting barley acreage.

Although almost ideal from the maltster's point of view, neither of these barleys is very easy to grow satisfactorily; both are rather weak-strawed by modern standards, and both are late-maturing. The latter difficulty was, however, largely overcome by the development of Earl as an early selection from Spratt-Archer, ripening some ten days earlier. The two varieties Spratt-Archer and Plumage-Archer were also crossed together; one such cross was Golden Archer, of the same general type as Spratt-Archer and not sufficiently good to supersede it; another was of the Plumage-Archer type, and indeed so similar to it that it retained the same name, and Plumage-Archer of 1935 and later years was, in fact, the progeny of this cross. Other crosses of Spratt-Archer gave two winter barleys, Prefect, already mentioned as a six-rowed form, and Pioneer, similar to Spratt-Archer in appearance and malting quality, but with real winter hardiness; Pioneer and its derivative Maris Otter are satisfactory winter malting varieties.

Meanwhile, considerable development had taken place in the Scandinavian countries. Gold, derived from a Swedish land race, was one of the first improved forms to be produced and, when introduced into Britain, achieved some popularity as a stiff-strawed, early-ripening variety, although, by British standards, of low malting quality. It was soon superseded by other varieties. From Hanna, an old variety of Czechoslovakian origin, were derived Binder and Hannchen; and from crosses between these and Gold came Opal, Kenia and Maja, and Victory, of which Kenia and Maja soon became popular in Britain in spite of their low malting quality. They, in turn, have been superseded by the still earlier Freja (Victory × Opal), ripening even before Earl, and by the even stiffer-standing varieties Herta and Rika (both Kenia × Isaria, a Bavarian variety). These varieties thus have very great advantages from the grower's point of view (although more susceptible than the English varieties to loose smut), and for feeding purposes are superior even to Camton (Spratt × Archer-Goldthorpe), a late, very dense, broad-eared barley bred at Cambridge expressly as a high-yielding, stiff-strawed feeding barley.

As might be expected, the next step was to try to combine the high malting quality of the English varieties with the very desirable field qualities of the Scandinavian barley. Numerous crosses between the two groups have been made. Carlsberg, a Danish cross between Maja and Archer, has a malting value which for British maltsters is only moderate; the British crosses Maythorpe, Proctor and Provost have, however, a malting quality comparable to that of Spratt-Archer, and are also resistant to loose smut (see p. 558). Maythorpe (Maja × Goldthorpe) is almost as early-ripening as Freja, but, like that variety, not exceptionally stiff-standing; Proctor (Kenia × Plumage-Archer) is a better-standing variety, although somewhat later; Provost (Kenia × Spratt-Archer) is similar in standing ability, but not greatly earlier than Spratt-Archer.

Of these varieties, Proctor was outstanding, as combining high malting quality with a yield equal to the best of the Scandinavian varieties then available. It came to occupy the same commanding position that Spratt-Archer and Plumage Archer had previously held; its lead was later challenged by the very similar but mildew-resistant Maris Badger and by Maris Baldric (Spratt-Archer × Freja) of only slightly lower malting quality and distinctly earlier.

As the premium for malting barley has become less and barley is increasingly grown for stock food, yield has become more important than malting quality. A further series of varieties of purely continental origin, giving higher yields than Proctor, have thus become popular; these include Cambrinus, Impala and Europa, all derived from crosses between Balder (Gold × Maja) and other, mainly German, varieties. These all show some resistance to mildew and loose-smut, but are all susceptible to leaf-blotch (see p. 578).

All these varieties are rather similar morphologically; the tow-rowed broad-eared barleys with small lodicules and *verum* base have gone out of use in Britain, as have varieties with woolly hairs of the Chevallier type. All two-row varieties used are thus narrow-eared barleys with large straight-haired lodicules, and *falsum* base. Within these the English group with pointed lodicules, cupped collar at base of spike, and no teeth on the intermediate nerves of the lemma, could be distinguished from the Scandinavian with rounded lodicules, flat collar and at least occasional lateral nerve teeth. Crossing between these two groups has to some extent obscured these differences.

see p. 578

OATS

Oats belong to the genus *Avena*, characterized by the inflorescence being a panicle, few-flowered spikelets, with large, thin glumes enclosing the florets. They are distinguished from the oat grasses and other members of the tribe *Aveneae* by their annual habit and large, pendulous spikelets.

The panicle is always of the spreading type, with comparatively long internodes and branches, but considerable variation occurs in its shape. The spikelets are usually three-flowered, and the glumes thin, multi-nerved and enclosing the florets. In the wild species and most cultivated forms, the caryopsis remains enclosed within the stiff, tapering lemma and the palea. The structure of the grain base and of the rachilla varies considerably in the different species and will be discussed separately. The awn if present is dorsal and often strongly geniculate.

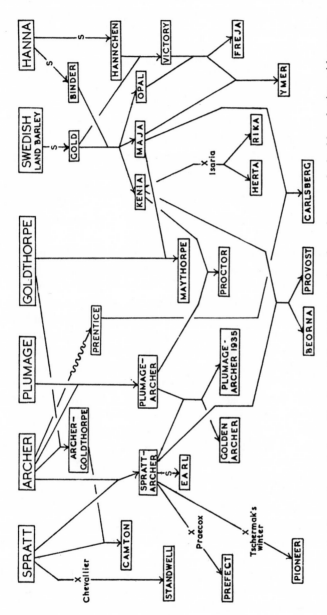

Fig. 125. Origin and interrelations of barley varieties. S indicates that the variety was obtained by selection, without crossing. A wavy connecting line indicates close similarity, but not necessarily a direct derivation.

277

The caryopsis resembles that of wheat in general structure, but is longer and pointed at both ends; the pericarp is hairy over the whole surface, and not merely at the tip as in wheat. On germination three seminal roots only are usually produced; the seedling also differs from that of wheat in that the region below the origin of the coleoptile elongates to form the so-called 'mesocotyl'. The complete absence of auricles distinguishes oats in the vegetative stage from the other cereals; the leaves are usually twisted in an anti-clockwise spiral, and have from eleven to thirteen nerves.

OAT SPECIES

A polyploid series exists in the genus *Avena*; the basic chromosome number is seven, and diploid species with fourteen, tetraploids with twenty-eight, and hexaploid species with forty-two chromosomes occur. Size of spikelet increases with increased chromosome number, but wild and cultivated forms are found in each group.

DIPLOID SPECIES. **Avena strigosa** Schreb. Bristle-pointed Oat

Spikelets small, lemma narrow, tapering into two long awn-like points, dorsal awn also present. Wild forms occur in the Mediterranean region; this oat was formerly important as a cultivated cereal in W. Europe, and its occurrence in Britain (particularly in Scotland and Wales) as a weed is due to its persistence from earlier cultivation. It is, in fact, still in cultivation on the extreme limits of arable cropping, in mountainous areas of Wales and on calcareous sands in the Hebrides and Shetland; under these conditions only it is preferred to the commonly-cultivated hexaploid *Avena sativa*, which elsewhere in Britain has completely replaced it. Most of the old land forms of bristle-pointed oat are very susceptible to smut (see p. 559); S.75 is an improved smut-resistant variety bred at Aberystwyth. Bristle-pointed oat with its narrow grain and long awn-points is only suitable for broadcasting; an Aberystwyth variety S.171, produced by crossing it with *Avena brevis*, is free from this disadvantage. *Avena brevis* Roth., the short oat, is an oat closely related to *A. strigosa*, but with a shorter, broader grain and much shorter awn-points; it occurs wild, and is occasionally cultivated, in S.W. Europe.

Pilcorn was a naked form of bristle-pointed oat formerly cultivated in England for human food.

TETRAPLOID SPECIES

These are of little importance, and none occurs either wild or cultivated in Britain. *Avena abyssinica* Hochst. is cultivated in Ethiopia; *A. barbata* Brot., slender oat, resembling *A. strigosa*, but with shorter awn-points and articulated grains (see below) is wild in the Mediterranean area and naturalized in California, where it is utilized as a forage-grass, not as a cereal.

HEXAPLOID SPECIES

Three wild hexaploid oat species may be distinguished; these are *Avena fatua*, the common wild oat, important as a widespread weed in Britain; *A. ludoviciana*, winter wild oat, of recent introduction but now important as a weed in central England; and *A. sterilis*, the wild red oat, a Mediterranean weed.

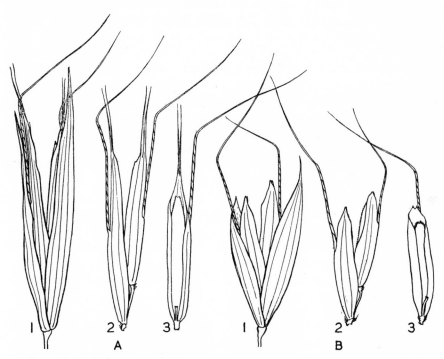

FIG. 126. Diploid oats. 1, whole spikelet. 2, spikelet without glumes. 3, lower grain (ventral view) of A, bristle-pointed oat (*Avena strigosa*). B, short oat (*A. brevis*). All × 3.

Avena fatua L.   Common (Spring) Wild Oat

Panicles large, closely resembling those of the common cultivated oat, spikelets usually of two grains, with special *articulation surfaces* at the base of each. These form joints which readily separate, so that the grains are shed as soon as the caryopsis is mature and the two grains fall separately. Each grain has a tapering lemma with the lower half covered with stiff brown hairs, which are particularly conspicuous around the rachilla and the oval scar of the articulation. Each grain bears a strong dorsal awn; the tip of the lemma shows two minute blunt teeth.

The common wild oat is an important weed of cereal crops, widespread in Britain and particularly in the eastern half. Vegetatively it cannot be distinguished from cultivated oats, and in an oat crop usually only becomes conspicuous when its tall panicles stand above those of the crop. It cannot be controlled by any form of selective weed-killer in a cereal crop, and control must be by cultivation in either a fallow or a root-crop, or alternatively by using the herbicide T.C.A. (see p. 403) at 5-10 lb. per acre at least three weeks before sowing a crop. Some of the grains are shed before harvest; these germinate erratically and may show prolonged dormancy. They are capable of persisting in the soil for several years, some germinating each year, mainly in the spring, and thus contaminating future crops. Grains which have not been shed will be harvested with the crop; such grains are difficult to remove from any cereal and particularly from oats. Wild oats are therefore very readily spread as impurities of seed corn, and it is most important that grain contaminated with wild oats should not be used for seed (see p. 83, cereal seed inspection). Scheduled as an injurious weed seed (Chap. VII).

Avena ludoviciana Dur.   Winter Wild Oat

This species closely resembles *A. fatua*, but can be distinguished by the two or three grains of the spikelet falling together; there is an articulation surface at the base of the lower grain only. If the grains separate, they do so by fracture of the rachilla above the base of the lower grain, and

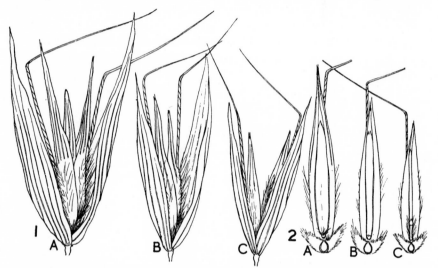

Fig. 127. Wild oat species. 1, whole spikelet. 2, lower grain in ventral view. A, *Avena sterilis*. B, *A. ludoviciana*. C, *A. fatua*. All × 2.

not by disarticulation. Germination is delayed and erratic as in *A. fatua*, but tends to take place mainly in winter rather than in spring. This wild oat species has only been comparatively recently recorded in Britain; it is a weed species of S. Europe and appears to have been introduced, probably with imported seed-corn, at some time prior to 1920. It is now widespread in southern central England. Injurious weed seed.

Avena sterilis L.   Mediterranean Wild Oat; Wild Red Oat

This species is similar in structure to *A. ludoviciana*, but has a much larger spikelet and grains; it is a weed of the Mediterranean area, and does not occur in Britain. Its strongly-geniculate awns show very conspicuous movements with changes of moisture content, giving it the name of 'animated oat'.

CULTIVATED HEXAPLOID OATS AND THEIR ORIGIN

Two series of cultivated hexaploid oats exist, **A. sativa** L., the **Common Oats** of cool climates, and **A. byzantina** Koch, **Red Oats,** the main cultivated oats of warmer climates. In both, the articulation has been lost, so that the grain is not readily shed. In *A. sativa* fracture of the rachilla occurs (on threshing, or when over-ripe) at the top of the internode, i.e. just below each grain; in *A. byzantina* the fracture between the

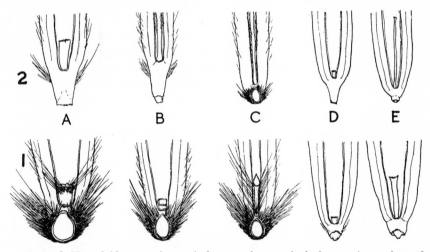

FIG. 128. Hexaploid oat species; grain bases to show method of separation. 1, base of lower grain in ventral view; 2, of second grain. A, *Avena sterilis.* B, *A. ludoviciana.* C, *A. fatua.* D, *A. byzantina.* E, *A. sativa.* All × 5.

grains tends to be close above the lower grain, so that part of the rachilla forms a 'stalk' on the second grain. Remains of an articulation may sometimes be made out on the lower grain. *A. sativa* is usually regarded as representing the cultivated derivations of *A. fatua*, and *A. byzantina* those of *A. sterilis*; the species will, however, cross together, and fatuoid oats (i.e. forms resembling *A. fatua*) arise not infrequently by mutation from cultivated varieties, and all four species have probably had a common origin. There is no evidence for the cultivation of oats at a very early date, and it appears probable that, like rye, oats originated as a secondary crop, first appearing as weeds of wheat and barley crops in S.W. Asia, perhaps 2,000 years ago, and being carried westwards and northwards. The process of harvesting and sowing seed would eliminate by gradual automatic selection the long-dormant forms and those shedding readily. Under the cooler and more humid conditions of N. Europe the *A. sativa* forms became the predominant cultivated oats, while further south the heat-resistant *A. byzantina* forms were more important. This latter group, the red oats, are still important in the warmer oat-growing areas, and show some disease-resistant characters not found in the common oat *A. sativa.* In Britain they are never grown as such, and are of interest only as parent material for the production of crosses with the common oat.

CHARACTERS OF AVENA SATIVA, COMMON OAT, AND RANGE OF TYPES

Vegetative Habit. Winter and spring varieties of oats are not distinguished by variation in cold-requirement for flowering, as in wheat. The winter varieties are slower-maturing, hardy forms, although none of them shows extreme winter hardiness, and winter oats are mainly confined to the southern half of Britain and to other areas with comparatively mild winters. Grey Winter, from which all the commonly grown winter varieties are derived, is very distinct in its vegetative habit as a young plant, being free-tillering and almost prostrate. The spring varieties are all more upright; the typical 'grain-producing' varieties of the Swedish type such as Victory being erect, with comparatively few tillers even under wide-spacing conditions, while the older 'straw-producers', of which Potato is an important but not extreme form, are intermediate, with a larger number of semi-erect tillers. This distinction into straw- and grain-producers reflects the greater importance that attaches to the straw of oats than to that of other cereals, but is in fact of little importance at the present day; under high-fertility conditions many of the more modern varieties will outyield the 'straw-producers' in grain and give at least as great a yield of straw. Grey Winter and some related

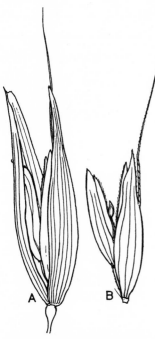

FIG. 129. Cultivated oats, *Avena sativa* (Grey Winter). A, whole spikelets. B, spikelet without glumes, showing awned lower grain and abortive third floret. × 3.

varieties have the leaves fringed with hairs, while those of most spring oats are glabrous.

Panicle Characters. The panicle-branches, although they arise on one side of the main axis at any one node, spread out around the axis; the branches at the lower nodes are longer than those at the upper nodes, so that the general form of the panicle is conical. The most noticeable departure from this form is in the Tartarian oats, where the panicle branches are more erect and tend to stand to one side. These are sometimes distinguished as a separate sub-species or variety *A. sativa orientalis,* but numerous intermediates exist between the extreme form as seen in Black Tartar, and the usual equilateral panicle. Equilateral panicles vary in size, number and size of spikelets, and also in the angle of the branches, from, for example, the large, open panicle of Grey Winter with numerous small spikelets, to the small, closed one of the Swedish type with fewer, larger spikelets.

Variation also occurs in the number of grains per spikelet. There are usually three florets present, but in some varieties, such as Potato, only

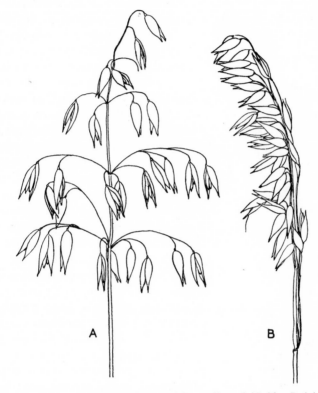

A   B

FIG. 130. *Avena sativa*. A, spreading panicle, equilateral (Golden Rain). B, dense, one-sided panicle (Black Tartar). × ½.

the lowest one usually produces a caryopsis, while in many varieties two grains develop and the third remains abortive. In a few varieties, such as Orion III, three grains are often produced, but these vary very considerably in size. Only in the naked oats does the number of florets normally exceed three; these are rather distinct forms with thin lemmas, similar in texture to the glumes, which allow the naked caryopsis to thresh out. Seven or eight florets are borne on a long, lax rachilla, so that the upper ones stand out well beyond the glumes. Naked oats are not grown in Britain; they are used in China for human food, and to some extent in Canada for poultry, but must be harvested with great care to avoid shattering.

In all varieties other than the naked oats, the threshed grain consists of the caryopsis enclosed by the palea and the rather stiff lemma. This is glabrous, or almost glabrous, in the cultivated varieties, with at most a few hairs at the base and on the rachilla. The colour varies in different varieties and may be white, yellow, grey or black; for stock-feeding the colour is of no importance, but for milling for oatmeal white oats are preferred. This is because removal of the lemma in the first stage of milling may not be quite complete, and any fragments of a darker-coloured lemma would be conspicuous in the oatmeal. The extent to which awns are developed varies; cultivated oats rarely have more than the lowest floret of the spikelet awned, and often awns are almost completely absent.

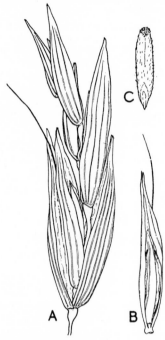

FIG. 131. Naked oats. A, single spikelet. B, single floret, ventral view. C, threshed caryopsis. All × 2.

Grain Quality. The oat caryopsis is of high feeding-value, with some 13-14 per cent. protein and 7-8 per cent. oil in addition to starch. The feeding value of the lemma and palea is, of course, much lower, and the value of the whole grain therefore depends on the proportion of lemma and palea (husk) to caryopsis (kernel), and a high-quality oat is thus one with a thin husk. The husk percentage varies from rather over 20 per cent. to about 35 per cent.; it is affected by climatic conditions, and may be lower in Scottish-grown oats than in the same variety grown in S. England.

VARIETIES OF OATS IN CULTIVATION

As with wheat, there is a constant flow of oat varieties in and out of cultivation. New varieties are always replacing older ones, and the current N.I.A.B. lists of recommended varieties should be consulted.

The main groups of oat varieties, considered from the point of view of their suitability for various conditions, are (1) winter oats, (2) spring oats; but these latter show much more localization geographically than do the wheat varieties, and they can to a larger extent be divided into two groups, those used primarily in S. England and those adapted to the cooler and generally more humid conditions of N. England, Scotland and Ireland. There are in addition a number of special-purpose varieties, such as the very early-ripening spring oats.

Winter oats are all only moderately hardy, and their use is mainly confined to the southern half of Britain; they have the advantage of ripening early, and are particularly valuable in areas where spring droughts are a problem. All the winter oats commonly grown are derived from the very old variety Grey Winter, a tall, slender-strawed oat with rather small grain of high quality; this is so weak-strawed that it can only be relied on to stand on soils of quite low fertility, and cannot therefore be expected to give high yields. The winter varieties which have replaced it are crosses in which an endeavour has been made to combine the winter-hardiness of Grey Winter with the stronger straw of other oats; thus Picton, a tall but stiff-standing and high-yielding variety, was produced at Cambridge by crossing it with an Argentine oat, while at Aberystwyth a series of improved winter varieties has been developed. S.147, a tall oat with large grain of high quality, was produced from a cross with Marvellous, an old variety of rather complicated parentage, including Grey Winter itself and forms of *A. fatua*. S.147 does not, however, show the resistance to stem eelworm (*Ditylenchus dipsaci*) possessed by Grey Winter and by the other Grey Winter hybrids. S.81, from a cross with the Cyprus oat, Kyko, has shorter straw; S.172, from a similar cross also including Bountiful (another old variety, partly related to Marvellous) has extremely short, stiff straw, adapted to conditions of the very highest fertility, but a small grain of lower quality. S.226 (Powys) is an intermediate derived from a cross between S.147 and S.172, and combines the quality of S.147 with a rather shorter straw. The association between stiff, stout straw and thick husk is a very close one and makes the breeding of varieties combining high standing ability with high quality an extremely difficult problem.

The main spring oats used in S. England are of the Swedish type. Abundance (Gartons, England) was one of the first of these to be produced; since then a large number of varieties derived from the old Probsteier land oats have been selected and intercrossed. Of these Victory (Svalöf, Sweden) has been of outstanding importance, both as a high-yielding variety and as a parent of still better forms which have now superseded it. Crossed in Sweden with Crown, another Probsteier selection, it gave Star, and with the old German frit-fly-resistant oat Von Lockow's Yellow, Eagle. These two were again crossed in Sweden to give Sun II and Blenda, both outstanding as high grain-yielders for fertile conditions. At Aberystwyth, Victory was crossed with the old Welsh oat Radnorshire Sprig to give S.221 (Maldwyn), and with the extremely short-strawed winter oat S.172 to give the closely comparable S.225 (Milford), suited to very high fertility only.

In Scotland and N. England, and also in Ireland, varieties based largely on the old variety Potato, producing large amounts of straw of high quality, have been of more importance. Ayr Bounty and Craigs Afterlea are Potato-Tartarian derivatives; Early Miller, Stormont Arrow and Glasnevin Triumph are essentially crosses of Potato with oats of the Swedish type. In southern England such varieties tend to be thick-husked and unsatisfactory, but under northern conditions give good yield of good-quality grain and straw.

Derivatives of the very early-maturing Kherson, or sixty-day oat, have

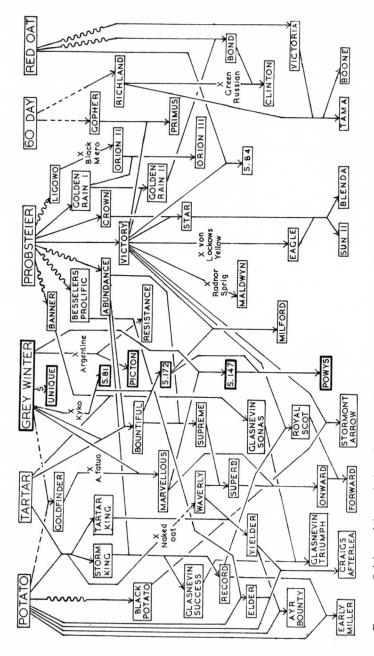

Fig. 132. Origin and interrelation of oat varieties. S indicates that the variety was obtained by selection, without crossing; broken connecting lines that the pedigree has been simplified. Wavy lines indicate similarity of type, but not necessarily direct derivation. Names in heavy frames are of winter oats.

been largely used in the U.S.A., and Primus and Clinton are varieties of this origin which have been recommended for use in Britain, where particularly early-ripening forms are required.

Disease-resistance is becoming of increasing importance in oat-breeding. The main oat diseases in Britain are crown rust (p. 566) and mildew (p. 543); resistance to both these is shown by different forms of the red oat, *A. byzantina*, and crosses between such forms and varieties of *A. sativa* have to some extent replaced the older varieties. Blenda has been to a large degree superseded by the higher yielding but otherwise rather similar Condor and Astor, but for Wales and south western England Manod is recommended. This had Tama, derived from a cross between an American sixty-day and a red oat, as one of its parents; it shows resistance to crown-rust and stem eelworm, and fair resistance to mildew. Among newer winter oats, Peniarth and Padarn, both derived from S.172, S.147, and a red oat, outyield Powys and are resistant to mildew. Peniarth, which stands better than Powys, but has rather smaller grain, is also resistant to stem eelworm.

Resistance to insect and nematode pests has already been mentioned in discussing varieties; Eagle, for example, may show resistance to frit-fly, while the majority of the Grey Winter derivatives show resistance to stem eelworm. Cereal root eelworm (*Heterodera major*) remains, however, as an outstanding problem.

RICE

Rice, **Oryza sativa** L., is not closely related to any of the other cereals, and is a member of the tribe *Oryzeae*, of which the only British representative is a rare plant of wet places, cut-grass, *Leersia oryzoides* (L.) Swartz. The inflorescence of rice is a panicle, with numerous one-flowered spikelets. The glumes are almost absent, being reduced to small facets, but a pair of extra empty lemmas (cf. Phalaris, p. 333) are present outside the lemma and palea, which are both large, keeled and rough. The lemma bears a terminal awn in many varieties. The flower is unusual in having six stamens. Lodicules are present and the floret opens for about half an hour at anthesis; self-pollination is usual, but up to about 0·5 per cent. crossing may occur.

The caryopsis does not thresh out, and the threshed grain (paddy) must be hulled to remove the lemma and palea. It is then usually 'polished' before being used for human consumption—that is, the pericarp and testa, together with the embryo, are removed by abrasion, although this considerably reduces the nutritive value of the grain.

Vegetatively rice resembles the temperate cereals in having narrow leaf-blades; the sheaths are split, and a short ligule and very narrow toothed auricles are present. It is usually grown on land which is kept flooded for the greater part of the growing period, and both roots and leaves show the very large intercellular air-spaces characteristic of water plants.

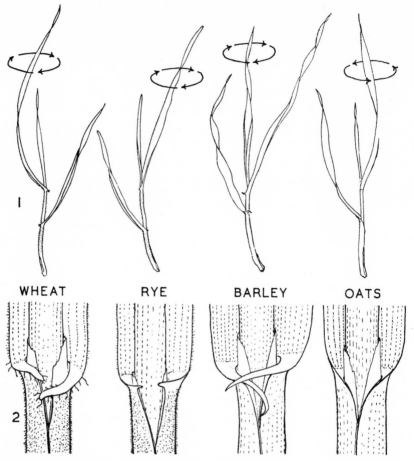

WHEAT RYE BARLEY OATS

WHEAT: auricles blunt, hairy; leaf-sheath and blade always hairy. Ligule medium
length. Blades with about 12 veins, twisted clockwise.

RYE: auricles very short, not hairy; leaf-sheath and blade variably hairy, greyish. Ligule
short. Blades with about 12 veins, twisted clockwise.

BARLEY: auricles long, slender, glabrous; leaf-sheath and blade usually glabrous (scattered
long hairs in a few varieties). Ligule medium length. Blades with about 20 veins,
twisted clockwise.

OATS: auricles absent; leaf-sheath and blade usually glabrous, scattered long hairs in
some varieties, especially of winter oats. Ligule medium length. Blades with about
12 veins, usually twisted anti-clockwise.

FIG. 133. Characters for recognition of common cereals in vegetative stage. 1, single
tiller of young plant, × ⅔. 2, junction of leaf-sheath and blade, ×6.

Rice is a short-day plant needing high temperatures (germination
minimum about 13° C., optimum 30-35° C.), and its cultivation is therefore confined to the tropical area between 40° N. and 40° S. latitude.
Varieties differ considerably in their water requirement; 'dry rice' includes those which can be grown on moist but not flooded soils, and
usually gives lower yields than those grown in water. The usual method
of cultivation involves sowing in special seed-beds and later planting out

the young tillering plants in flooded fields; where, as in the southern U.S.A., the cultivation is mechanized, the seed is drilled and the ground later flooded, and finally drained again for harvesting. Yields vary up to about 25 cwt. per acre, but the average world yield is perhaps half this.

Varieties also differ in size and shape of grain, in rapidity of growth and in texture of endosperm. No gluten is present, and the 'hard' rice which is the usual commercial form, with translucent endosperm, has a high starch content, while the less important 'soft' or 'glutinous' varieties, with opaque white endosperm, have the starch partially replaced by dextrin.

MILLET

Millet is a name used for a number of different small-grained cereals of warm climates; they belong to various genera of the tribe *Paniceae*, with broad leaves, and panicles of two flowered spikelets, of which only the upper is fertile, with hardened lemma and palea enclosing the short, broad caryopsis.

Panicum miliaceum L. Common or Proso Millet

This is an annual, growing some 2 to 4 ft. high, with often unilateral panicles varying in compactness. The leaf-sheaths are split, ligule short, auricles absent, leaf-blades hairy, from 1 to 3 cm. broad. Branches are frequently produced from nodes well above ground-level.

The panicle bears numerous spikelets, each with a pair of thin, membranous glumes, the inner larger than the outer. Within these are a lower sterile floret,

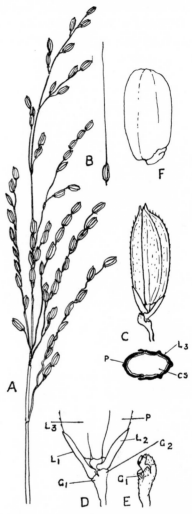

Fig. 134. Rice. A, panicle of awnless variety, × ½. B, single spikelet of awned variety, × ½. C, single spikelet, × 3, in side view and diagrammatic cross-section. D, base of spikelet, × 7. E, base of rachilla, and vestigial glumes, × 10. F, caryopsis after hulling (soaked), × 4. G_1, G_2, glumes. L_1, L_2, sterile lemmas. L_3, fertile lemma. P, palea. CS, caryopsis.

with lemma similar in size and texture to the inner glume, and palea minute, and an upper fertile flower. This has, when mature, a short, rounded caryopsis some 3 mm. long, with no ventral furrow and enclosed in the thick, shiny lemma and palea. The colour of the lemma and palea varies according to variety; white, yellow, grey and black forms occur.

Common millet is of considerable antiquity in the Mediterranean region, although now largely replaced by maize. It is still used in E. Asia for human consumption, but elsewhere tends to be replaced by higher-yielding, larger-grained cereals. It will ripen in S. England, but is not an economic crop; in N. America it is used mainly as a forage plant.

Fig. 135. Millet, *Panicum miliaceum*. A, part of plant with unripe grain (spikelets shown only on some panicle branches) × $\frac{3}{16}$. B, part of panicle, × 3. C, single spikelet and separate parts, × 7. G_1, G_2, glumes. SL, SP, lemma and palea of sterile floret. FL, FP, lemma and palea of fertile floret (the caryopsis remains enclosed between these).

Setaria italica (L.) Beauv. **(Chaetochloa italica).** Italian or Foxtail
Millet

This millet differs from *Panicum miliaceum* in having a more compact
panicle, often cylindrical and spikelike. The structure of the spikelet is
similar, but in addition a number of bristles, usually
from one to three, are present below each; these
represent reduced sterile spikelets (cf. Cynosurus,
p. 315). The grain is rather smaller than that of
common millet, and flattened on one side. Italian
millet is grown as a grain crop in warm areas,
especially in E. Asia. A form with narrow, cylindrical
panicle is used as a forage grass in the U.S.A. under
the name of Hungarian Grass; it resembles the wild
species, green millet (*Setaria viridis* (L.) Beauv.), of
southern Europe, which is an occasional casual in
England.

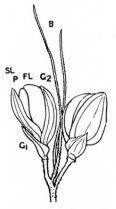

Fig. 136. Italian millet, *Setaria italica*; part of panicle showing bristles and two spikelets, × 7. B, bristles; G_1, G_2, glumes. SL, lemma of sterile floret. FL, P, lemma and palea of fertile floret.

SORGHUM

The sorghums, forms of **Sorghum vulgare** Pers.
(=**Andropogon sorghum** (L.) Brot.), are warm-
country cereals, which somewhat resemble millet,
but are usually taller plants with broader leaves.
The structure of the inflorescence is more complex,
and the sorghums are placed in a distinct tribe,
the *Andropogoneae*, to which the sugar-cane also belongs. The spikelets
are paired, with one pedicellate and male, the other sessile and
hermaphrodite. The structure of the hermaphrodite spikelet somewhat
resembles that of millet and the other members of the *Paniceae*, but
the outer glume is as large as the inner, and both are hardened.
The lower sterile floret is represented by the lemma only; the upper
fertile floret has a narrow, bicleft, shortly-awned lemma, two lodicules,
three stamens, and ovary with two long styles; the palea is absent or
very small. Up to about 50 per cent. cross-pollination may take place;
the threshed grain, which consists either of the whole fertile spikelet with
the caryopsis enclosed, or of the naked caryopsis, is usually broadly oval
and larger than the millets.

The sorghums, which are of African origin, are extremely variable in
form and use; the main groups are:

(1) The grain sorghums, extensively grown for stock food.
(2) The broom corns, with stiff, open panicles used (after deseeding)
     for the manufacture of sweeping brooms.
(3) The sweet sorghums, or sorghos, grown for the high sugar content
     of the immature stem, used for forage.

Sudan grass, sometimes called grass sorghum, is a related and intercrossing species, *Sorghum sudanense* Stapf., grown as an annual forage grass.

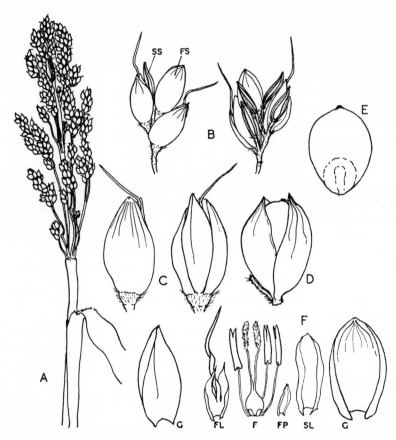

FIG. 137. Sorghum. A, panicle, × ½. B, group of spikelets seen from outer and inner sides, × 3: FS, fertile spikelet; SS, sterile spikelet. C, single fertile spikelet of awned variety in pre-flowering stage, dorsal and ventral views, × 7. D, single fertile spikelet of awnless variety, with apex of mature caryopsis exposed, × 7. E, threshed caryopsis, × 7. F, as C, but dissected to show separate parts. G, G, glumes. SL, lemma of sterile floret. FL, FP, lemma and palea of fertile floret. F, flower.

Saccharum officinarum L., and other species.   Sugar-cane

Perennial grasses up to 15 ft. high, widely grown in the tropics for sugar, which is extracted from the stout, solid stems. Inflorescence resembling that of sorghum, but spikelets all hermaphrodite. 'Seed' very small (1-2 mm.); normally vegetatively propagated.

MAIZE

Maize, **Zea mays** L., belongs to a small, highly-specialized tribe, the *Maydeae*, closely related to the *Andropogoneae*. It is an annual, usually producing only a single shoot, with stout, solid stem and very large leaves with broad blades. The terminal panicle bears only male flowers, and is known as the tassel. The panicle branches are long and bear closely-spaced, short-stalked pairs of spikelets. Each spikelet consists of a pair

of glumes enclosing two male florets, each with lemma and palea, lodicules and three stamens. The male florets open widely and pollen is shed
to be carried by wind to the female flowers. These are borne on special

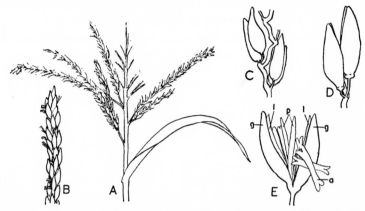

FIG. 138. Maize; male inflorescence. A, tassel (a few branches only shown in full), × ⅙.
B, part of single branch of tassel, × ½. C, part of branch, × 1¼, to show arrangement of
spikelet-pairs on rachis. D, spikelet-pair, × 1¾. E, single spikelet in flower, × 2: *g*, glumes;
l, lemmas; *p*, paleae; *a*, anther.

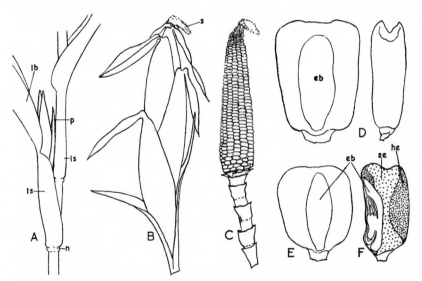

FIG. 139. Maize, female inflorescence. A, part of plant to show young cob in axil of
leaf. B, almost mature cob (Goudster) surrounded by husk leaves. C, the same with husk
leaves removed. All × ⅛: *n*, node at which cob is borne; *p*, prophyll of cob shoot; *ls*, leaf-
sheath; *lb*, leaf-blade; *s*, withered silks (styles). D, grain of White Horse Tooth in face
and side view; E, of Goudster. F, diagrammatic vertical section of dent-corn grain: *eb*,
embryo; *he*, horny endosperm; *se*, starchy endosperm.

female inflorescences, the cobs, in the axils of some of the middle leaves
of the main stem. Each cob consists of a short, stout axis, bearing on its
lower part a series of closely-packed, imbricating, almost bladeless leaves,
forming the husk, and completely enclosing the upper fertile part. This

is a dense spike with a number of vertical double rows of very much reduced spikelets; it may be regarded as representing the coalescence of a branched structure like the male infloresence, each double row corresponding to the series of pairs of spikelets borne on one branch. Reduction of the spikelet has progressed so far that, in the mature infloresence, all that is visible is a series of tightly-packed, naked caryopses. Only in the immature stage can it be made out that each grain has around it a series of scales, the two glumes and the two lemmas and two paleas of the two-flowered spikelet. These structures do not normally develop further, and their protective function is taken over by the husk leaves, which form a continuous and persistent cover to the whole cob. Pollination is made possible by the very great development of the single style of each ovary, which forms a long thread extending up from each flower to the apex of the husk, where the numerous threads emerge as a conspicuous tuft, known as the silks. The upper part of each style is receptive, and wind-borne pollen germinates on its surface, the pollen-tube growing down through the whole length of the thread to reach the ovule. Growth of the style continues until pollination is effected, so that the styles may reach a length of 1 ft. or more. After pollination the silks wither, and enlargement of the grain takes place. The husk leaves become dry and papery, but remain in position around the mature cob.

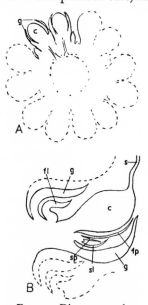

FIG. 140. Diagrams to show, structure of maize cob. A, transverse section of young cob; one pair of spikelets only shown in solid line. B, vertical section through single spikelet before pollination: *g*, glumes; *fl*, *fp*, lemma and palea of fertile floret; *sl*, *sp*, of sterile floret; *c*, ovary; *s*, style.

There is thus no normal means of seed-dispersal, and maize is not known as a wild plant. It was already an old-established cultivated plant in America in Columbus' time, and it can only be assumed that it arose from *Euchlaena*, an American member of the same tribe, or from some similar form now extinct.

Maize now exists in a wide variety of forms, varying in height, growth-period and grain characters. The main variation found in the grain is in the character of the endosperm, and the following groups may be distinguished.

FIG. 141.
Maize leaf, × ⅓.

*Flint corn;** the whole of the outer part of the endosperm is hard and horny in consistency, and the grain remains round-topped when ripe.

Dent corn; the inner soft endosperm extends to the apex of the grain and in ripening shrinks more than the surrounding hard endosperm, so that the apex of the mature grain is indented. Flint and dent maize store well, and are by far the most important forms grown for grain.

Flour corn; the whole of the endosperm is soft and floury. Flour corn was formerly preferred by the American Indians on account of the ease with which it could be ground, but it stores badly and is now of little economic importance.

Waxy corn; a recently-developed form in which the endosperm is waxy in texture; it can be milled to give a product closely resembling tapioca. (True tapioca is prepared from the root of cassava, *Manihot utilissima* Pohl., a tropical member of the Euphorbiaceae.)

Pop corn; the endosperm of the rather small, pointed, grain expands explosively on heating, turning the grain inside out to give a product which is eaten fresh, without milling.

Sweet corn; the endosperm remains sugary to a late stage. Used only as a vegetable, the immature cobs being cooked.

Pod corns are forms of little economic importance, in which the glumes and lemmas are well-developed and surround the mature grain. This character may be associated with any of the endosperm types.

Maize has now spread from America to almost all the warmer areas of the world and, among cereals, is second only to wheat in total acreage. The most important types are the high-yielding, relatively slow-maturing dent corns, grown at wide spacing (10,000 to 20,000 plants per acre) and giving yields of some 45 cwt. on good soils. The separate male and female inflorescences makes the production of F.1 hybrids (see p. 43) comparatively simple, and such 'hybrid corn', with its greater uniformity and hybrid vigour, has largely replaced the older open-pollinated varieties in America.

Britain and N.W. Europe lie outside the main area of maize cultivation owing to climatic conditions. The majority of maize varieties will not germinate satisfactorily in soil temperatures below 50° F., and the period required for the production of ripe grain under British conditions is about double that for the same variety in the U.S.A. 'corn belt'. This means that the choice of varieties is confined to those that will mature in about ten weeks in the U.S.A., or twenty weeks here—namely, the early flint and dent varieties, and crosses between these.† A number of these, such as the early Wisconsin hybrids, and the open-pollinated Dutch variety Goudster, will ripen grain satisfactorily in S. England in

---

* 'Corn', used as a general synonym for cereal in England, refers exclusively to maize in N. America.

† J. L. Harper, 'Problems Involved in the Extension of Maize Cultivation into Northern Temperate Regions, *World Crops*, 7, 3, p. 93, March, 1955.

favourable years. Spacing for these smaller, quicker-growing varieties needs to be closer, say 30,000 plants per acre.

For silage or forage, ripening of grain is not necessary, and in the past the southern U.S.A. variety White Horse Tooth has been largely used; under long-day conditions in England this makes profuse vegetative

FIG. 142. Maize; appearance of whole plants at end of August. A, tall late variety (White Horse Tooth). B, dwarf early variety (Wisconsin 240). $\times \frac{1}{30}$.

growth with little cob production. A greater yield of more easily handled material can be obtained by the use of the early varieties, harvested when the grain is unripe; under these conditions the cobs may contribute about half the total weight of the crop. It is questionable, however, whether maize for fodder can compete here in total dry-matter production with such crops as kale, and the protein production is certainly lower.

Chapter XVI

GRAMINEAE: HERBAGE GRASSES

Tiller Production and Growth-Habit

IN the annual grasses all tillers are of the type described on p. 236—that is, they grow up within the sheath of the subtending leaf; their internodes remain short while they are in the vegetative condition, and do not elongate until an inflorescence is produced. Such tillers are described as *intravaginal* (within the sheath). In some perennial grasses, however, another type of tiller is produced; this grows horizontally, bursting out through the base of the leaf-sheath subtending it, and forms a spreading stem which is described as a *rhizome* if underground and as a *stolon* if above-ground. In both these types of stem the internodes are more or less elongated. Such a tiller is described as *extravaginal* (outside the sheath).

The presence or absence of such extravaginal shoots, and the length to which they grow, has a marked effect on the general appearance or *growth-habit* of the plant. Grasses with all shoots intravaginal (e.g. cocksfoot, perennial rye-grass) will form dense tufts with the tillers tightly packed together and not show any great ability to spread. Those with short rhizomes (e.g. meadow foxtail) will form looser tufts and spread more rapidly to form a continuous turf, while those with long rhizomes (e.g. red fescue) or stolons (e.g. creeping bent) will form creeping plants which may spread to occupy large areas. On rhizomes, growing underground in the absence of light, the leaves are represented by scales, which usually cover only a small part of the internode; if the buds in their axils develop they grow out to form branch rhizomes. Eventually the tip of the rhizomes turns upwards and produces transitional leaves, intermediate between scale-leaves and normal foliage leaves; when it comes above ground normal foliage leaves are produced, and the newly-formed internodes remain short, so that the apex of the rhizome takes on the structure of a typical vegetative tiller. If only extravaginal shoots are produced, then such tillers will appear singly as scattered shoots separated by greater or less lengths of rhizome (e.g. the creeping fescue of sand dunes, *Festuca juncifolia*). Many grasses, however, produce both kinds of shoot, and in them the apex of the rhizome, coming above ground, may produce intravaginal shoots, giving small tufts of shoots, each tuft being separated from the next by a length of rhizome (e.g. couch).

Short stolons may be formed by the slightly-elongated internodes at the base of a tuft of intravaginal tillers; these stolons gradually increase in length as the plant grows older and further internodes are added to

297

them. Such short stolons are formed in the gradual spread of old plants of tufted grasses; if no treading takes place there may be few roots produced, so that the outer tillers of the clump merely lie on the surface of the ground, but on plants which are grazed and trampled so that the base of the tillers is pressed into the ground, numerous roots may arise, so that these gradually-lengthening stems behave as true stolons.

Longer stolons of typical creeping grasses usually arise as extravaginal shoots, with uniformly-elongated internodes. The leaves produced on such stolons are usually similar to normal foliage leaves, but are often small and with very short sheaths. Buds in their axils may grow out either intra- or extravaginally (the distinction where sheaths are short may not be very clear-cut) to form either more or less erect, leafy tillers, or branch stolons.

The majority of grasses of first-class agricultural value in this country are either tufted or with very short rhizomes or stolons. In them the bulk of the tissue produced during the vegetative period is leaf, which is not only the most valuable part of the plant for animal feeding, but is also capable of photosynthesis. Thus a large proportion of the material produced by photosynthesis is devoted to increasing the leaf area, and hence to increasing still further the amount of photosynthesis; yield, both total and useful, is therefore at a maximum in these grasses. The production of long, horizontal stems implies the diversion of food material to tissue, which is not merely not photosynthetic, but which is also either inaccessible to stock or is of low feeding value. Hence in such creeping grasses both the total yield, and the proportion of it which is useful to stock, are reduced.

Many grasses with far-spreading rhizomes will grow satisfactorily only in loose soil or in sand or mud; they tend therefore to be arable weeds (e.g. couch) or at best useful sand-binding plants for preventing erosion by wind or water (e.g. marram grass). The tufted grasses are, however, often less resistant to drought than rhizomatous ones and, being much less able to spread, often compete poorly with grasses with either stolons or rhizomes. It is thus essentially only in cultivated grassland, under good conditions, and in short leys, where strong, early growth is more important than later competitive spread, that these tufted grasses show to full advantage.

General Physiology and Agricultural Requirements

The method of growth of grasses makes them, in general, ideal plants for grazing or repeated cutting, in that their stems, during the vegetative period, either remain very short or creep horizontally. All stems and buds are thus at or near ground-level, and grazing or cutting removes only leaves, since these are the only parts of the plant standing above this level. The growing points of the stems, and the axillary buds, remain intact, and the production of further leaves and shoots is not interfered with.

The value of a particular grass for herbage use will depend on its total annual yield (and, for long leys, on its persistence) and on the palatability and nutritive value of this yield. The yield will depend on the rate of growth of the plant and on the length of time for which this growth continues. Each individual tiller is constantly producing new leaves during the period of vegetative growth, but there is also a constant dying-off of older leaves, so that the number of living leaves per tiller remains approximately the same. Increase in size of the plant takes place by the production of new tillers, and during the vegetative phase, the rate of growth in total size mainly depends on the rate at which new tillers are produced. Thus, in a vigorously-growing young plant of perennial rye-grass, every axillary bud produces a tiller, and the development of the bud takes place while the subtending leaf is still growing, so that the new tiller is visible above the leaf-sheath of one leaf by the time the next leaf but one on the main shoot has emerged. These axillary tillers similarly commence tillering at once, so that the total number of tillers increases geometrically.

In slower-growing species, only a small proportion of the axillary buds develop, so that the rate of tiller production is very much lower; this is particularly marked where rhizomes or stolons are produced and food material thus diverted to the production of non-photosynthetic structures. Even in the very rapidly-growing grasses like perennial rye-grass, the rate of increase in tiller number tends to fall off as conditions become less favourable. Reduction in light owing to the shading effect of the crowded tillers is an important factor in this; tillering rate being lower at lower light intensity. Tillering rate falls off rapidly with the onset of winter; this falling-off of tillering is, in perennial rye-grass, greater than the falling-off in leaf production, so that leaves are formed with no axillary tillers. When new tillers begin to arise again in spring, they are formed in the axils of newly-produced spring leaves, and not by development of dormant buds in the axils of over-wintered leaves. The date of the beginning of vigorous growth in spring is partly a character of the particular grass; thus in general perennial rye-grass and cocksfoot are species which start growth early, while timothy and bent are late, but there is considerable difference between different plants of the same species (see below, p. 306). It is also partly controlled by previous treatment; thus, in cocksfoot entering the winter grazed down hard, and hence with little stored food reserves, growth starts later in spring than when the plant has been allowed to grow and build up reserves in the previous autumn.

Behaviour of the grass plant during late spring and summer is largely a matter of the change from the vegetative to the flowering condition. When an individual tiller changes to the flowering state, not only does production of further leaves stop, but development of buds in the axils of leaves already initiated also stops. In the great majority of grasses of temperate regions, the change to the flowering condition is a response to increasing length of day, but tillers must have reached a certain minimum age and size before they can respond in this way; a tiller which has reached this stage can be described as 'ripe to flower'. If a grass requires a very short period to become ripe to flower, then, once the day-length is sufficient for that particular plant, all tillers formed will reach this stage before the day-length decreases again. In this case, the plant will behave as an annual, all tillers flowering and dying off after producing seed, or, if they become ripe to flower while still very small,

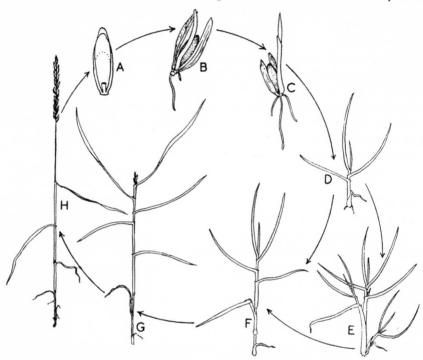

Fig. 143. Life-cycle of a perennial grass (perennial rye-grass). A, 'seed'. B, C, stages in germination. Tillering then takes place; a single tiller is shown at D. An individual tiller may either become fertile, developing as in F, or may remain in the vegetative condition, producing further tillers, as in E, and not reach stage F until later in the year, or the following year. Plants in which a large proportion of the tillers follow the direct path from D to F will be stemmy and short-lived, while those in which the majority of tillers go through stage E will be leafy and long-lived. Further development of the fertile tiller is shown in G, emergence of inflorescence, and H, mature inflorescence, which produces 'seed', A, and dies. Not to scale.

dying without being able to produce seed. If, however, the period required is longer, then only the larger and older tillers will flower, and some will remain as 'barren' tillers, which will produce more new tillers before they themselves flower. If the period is sufficiently long, or if a period of exposure to cold is needed to cause flower initiation, then only tillers produced in the previous year will flower, and there will be only one flowering period per year, as in the extreme pasture forms of perennial rye-grass. If rather shorter, tillers not ripe to flower at the normal first flowering period in early summer may reach this stage in the late summer, giving a second, 'aftermath' flowering. In general, the longer the period of active vegetative growth before the flowering stage is reached, the greater will be the proportion of barren to flowering tillers, and, since perennation depends on overwintering barren tillers, the longer will be the total life of the plant.

Total growth during the year will depend on the number of tillers produced and on their size, and total yield may not be much influenced by the proportion of barren to flowering tillers, although yield will fall

off considerably from year to year in plants with relatively few barren tillers. Usually plants with tillers having a long vegetative period will produce a greater total number of tillers, and therefore a greater total yield per plant, but this may not be important, except in widely-spaced plants; under the usual crowded conditions of grassland competition between plants may be too great to allow of increased yield being produced in this way. The proportion of flowering tillers will, however, have a considerable effect on the nutritive value and palatability of the herbage, since the feeding value (and usually the palatability) of stem is considerably less than that of leaf. Plants with few barren tillers will tend to be more stemmy and therefore less valuable than otherwise comparable ones which have a large proportion of leafy vegetative shoots.

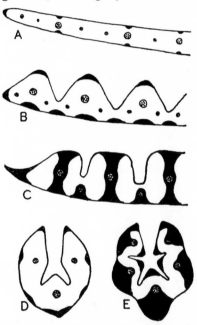

Fig. 144. Diagrams of transverse sections of grass leaf-blades to show varying amounts of sclerenchyma. A, rough-stalked meadow-grass. B, tussock grass. C, marram. D, sheep's fescue. E, *Nardus*. Sclerenchyma black; vascular bundles stippled.

The feeding value of a grass will be influenced not only by the proportion of leaf to stem, but also very much by the structure of the leaf. The leaf-blade is normally of higher value than the sheath, but very marked differences exist between the leaf-blades of different grass species. The general structure of the leaf-blade has already been described (p. 239); while the structure of the vascular bundles is rather similar in all species, and the amount of xylem always small, the extent to which sclerenchyma develops as strengthening tissue above and below the bundles varies very much, and has a profound effect both on the nutritive value and the palatability. Thus in a palatable grass of relatively high value, like rough-stalked meadow-grass, sclerenchyma is present only as very slender strands adjoining the epidermis above and below the main vascular bundles, and along the margins. In an unpalatable grass, such as tussock grass, which is usually avoided by stock, stout and closely-spaced sclerenchyma strands develop on the lower side, together with other strands capping the ridges and edging the margins. In a completely inedible grass, such as sea lyme-grass, which is of value only as a sand-binder, the main vascular bundles are embedded in a stout 'girder' of sclerenchyma, extending the whole way from the lower to the upper epidermis. The same trend can be seen in the grasses with permanently-folded, bristle-like leaves; thus in the relatively palatable sheep's fescue forms there is a comparatively small sclerenchyma strand outside each main bundle, whereas in the similarly-shaped but very unpalatable leaf of mat-grass (*Nardus*) at least a third of the whole cross-sectional area is occupied by sclerenchyma.

Palatability is reduced by hairiness and by bitter-tasting substances as well as by high fibre content. Fibre content has also a marked effect on the nutritive value of the leaf; lignin is not only largely indigestible in itself, but increased lignification is accompanied by decreased digestibility of the cellulose. The effect is more marked if the whole shoot is considered; in most grasses digestibility falls off sharply after the emergence of the inflorescence. Even among 'good' grasses differences exist, thus cocksfoot has a lower percentage digestibility than ryegrass at the same stage.

Varieties (Herbage grass varieties are often referred to as *strains*)

Plants belonging to the same grass species will all have the same general structure of inflorescence and vegetative parts, but may show considerable variation in physiological and quantitative characters. Thus we may find plants which, while they are all clearly recognizable as belonging to one species, differ in size, rate of tillering, length of vegetative period, proportion of fertile tillers, time of flowering, winter-greenness, disease-resistance and other characters which considerably affect their agricultural value. The great majority of grasses used for herbage are grown from seed produced as a result of cross-pollination, and variation from plant to plant always occurs. It is not practicable to build up a stock of identical or nearly identical plants, as it is with a vegetatively-propagated plant such as potato, or with a self-pollinated plant such as wheat (refer to plant-breeding, Chapter V). The most that can be done on an economic scale is to develop a series of plants, which, although not identical, are all somewhat similar, and show much less than the total range of variation found in the species as a whole. Such a group of plants, varying within more or less narrow limits, is described as a *variety* or *strain* of the particular species (see also Leguminosae, p. 147).

Any naturally-occurring population of grass plants of a single species will have been subjected to a natural selection, so that it will consist only of types suited to the particular local conditions prevailing. (Such types selected by natural ecological conditions are known as *ecotypes*.) Thus in Britain, where most grassland is only maintained as such by the influence of grazing animals preventing the establishment of trees and shrubs, the types found in any area of old grassland will be those which withstand grazing best, as well as being suited to the prevailing climate and soil. In addition, since establishment by natural re-seeding is not usually easy under hard grazing, they will be mainly long-lived perennial forms if the grazing has been close, any short-lived plants which may have been present originally having died out.

The old practice of establishing grassland by allowing arable land to 'tumble-down' to grass, which was prevalent until the eighteenth century, meant that the land was seeded down by seeds carried in from neighbouring wild grass plants. When the pasture was eventually established it contained, therefore, plants essentially of the same type as the surrounding old grass. Some of the earliest of the artificially-sown pastures were seeded down with 'seed' hand-collected from existing grassland, and this again involved no great change of type. It was soon found, however, that grass 'seeds' could be more cheaply obtained by harvesting fields specially laid up for this purpose, and that the seed so produced (or, in some cases, seed imported from other countries) could be used to sow other fields as leys, which in turn would provide further seed, and so on. Harvesting for seed was most conveniently done in the first years of the ley, before other species had crept in, and consequently seed came to be harvested, generation after generation, from one-year-old leys. This entirely altered the selective influences acting on the plants present; instead of selecting the hardy, long-lived, grazing types, the new method tended to select the plants which grew most quickly in the first year, and particularly those which produced the most seed. The fact that such plants were the more stemmy forms, and likely to be short-lived, meant that such commercially-produced seed consisted of types different from, and mainly inferior to, the plants present in old grassland.

The effect of this entirely unintentional but none the less effective selection of the worst types from the grazing point of view was aggravated by the development of an international trade in grass seeds, which often resulted in the sowing of seed harvested from plants which had been subject not only to the adverse selective action of this method of seed-growing, but also to that of climatic conditions which might differ widely from those of the area in which it was sown. The importance of this selection was for long unrecognized, and dissatisfaction with its effects resulted, as with perennial rye-grass during the nineteenth century, in criticism of the species as a whole, rather than of the particular types being used. Even although occasional better stocks did appear, such as Pacey's rye-grass, their importance was not appreciated, and they were allowed to die out—in fact, if not in name. It was not until the pioneer work of Stapledon and his colleagues at Aberystwyth that the importance of selection within the species came to be appreciated, and steps taken to ensure that the types employed were the best available within each particular species.

The present position is that it is generally recognized that varieties of grass (and the same also applies to other herbage plants) produced under climatic conditions differing widely from those of Britain are unlikely to be satisfactory here. Seeds imported from north-western Europe, and from New Zealand, usually give good results, as these areas have climate not very widely different from our own; grasses from, for example, parts of N. America, with a more continental climate, are less satisfactory. The converse is, of course, also true; British varieties are unlikely to be useful if exported to areas with a very different climate.

Within the range of type suited to the climate, varieties are available which are suited to the particular agricultural conditions under which they are to be used. A number of these are *local varieties*, where seed is obtained from old pastures of good type in a particular locality; the plants present have been subjected for many years to the selective effect of grazing and will include, therefore, only types which are suited to this. The seed yield from old pastures is usually low, and the mother-seed so harvested must be multiplied up under ley conditions before it can be placed on the market in sufficient quantity, but care is taken that the period of multiplication is confined to very few generations, so that adverse selective effect of growing generation after generation from short leys does not occur.

Bred varieties, which form the majority of the improved varieties available, are similar, but the basic plants which provide the mother-seed are selected, not by the gradual effects of pasture conditions on a particular local population, but by the conscious choice of the plant-breeder. It is thus possible for a greater range of bred strains to be produced, each designed to suit a particular set of agricultural conditions. It is also possible for the breeder to combine in one variety material from a number of different areas, so that the adaptability of a bred variety to different districts may be greater than that of a local variety.

It is impossible to determine the variety of a grass by examination of a sample of seed; certification schemes have therefore been developed (see Chapter VI) to safeguard the purchaser, and it is advisable to use only 'certified' stocks of the local and bred varieties.

HERBAGE GRASSES: SPECIAL

FESTUCEAE

LOLIUM. THE RYE-GRASSES

The genus *Lolium* has the typical spikelet of the tribe *Festuceae*—that is, a many-flowered spikelet not completely enclosed by glumes; but it differs from other members of the tribe in that the spikelets are borne on a spike instead of a panicle. The spike, however, is differently arranged from that of wheat and other similar plants of the tribe *Hordeae*. In them the spikelet has its flat side towards the rachis, but in *Lolium* it is placed edgewise-on to the rachis. If two glumes were present in this type of spike, one of them would lie against the rachis; in fact, in *Lolium* only one glume (the upper) is present on the majority of spikelets, and the internodes of the rachis are slightly hollowed out and may be considered to take over the protective function of the other glume. The terminal spikelet, at the apex of the spike, has the usual two glumes.

The inflorescence thus consists of a spike, with a variable number (usually from twelve to twenty) of spikelets placed singly at the nodes of the rachis, and edgewise-on to it. Each spikelet consists of one rather narrow boat-shaped glume, and some six to twenty florets, each with a usually five-nerved lemma, rounded on the back, and with or without a terminal awn.

The common name 'rye-grass' is not particularly appropriate, as there is no very close resemblance or relationship to rye (p. 265); it is, in fact, a corruption of the earlier name 'ray grass', itself derived from the old French name, *ivrai* (*ivré*=intoxicated), applied to the poisonous species, *Lolium temulentum*, darnel, on account of the symptoms it produces. The name then came to be extended to cover all the species; 'eaver', a local name in S.W. England, is derived from the same source.

The genus contains some six species, of which two, perennial and Italian rye-grasses, are of outstanding importance in British agriculture.

Lolium perenne L. Perennial Rye-grass

A native perennial, extremely common and of great agricultural value.

Inflorescence. In *L. perenne* the glumes are short, usually not more than half the length of the whole spikelet, and the lemmas end in a rather blunt point, with no awn. The spikelets usually have some six to twelve florets.

'*Seed.*' On threshing, the rachilla breaks up, and the 'agricultural seed' consists of the caryopsis, which may be purple in colour, enclosed within the pale brown lemma and somewhat transparent palea. The rachilla is flattened and widens gradually from below upwards (cf. meadow fescue, p. 311). The length is usually 4-6 mm., and about ¼ million go to the pound.

Vegetative Characters. The whole plant is perennial, tufted in growth and with intravaginal tillers only. All parts are glabrous. The leaves are folded in the bud, giving distinctly flattened vegetative shoots. The expanded leaf-blade is tapering, rather narrow; it is ribbed, dark-green and dull on the upper surface; keeled, lighter green and very shiny on the lower surface. Auricles are present, but these are small and often reduced on the leaves of vegetative tillers to mere ledge-like projections. The ligule is blunt and very short. The leaf-sheaths are split (not quite to the base), shiny, with a bright, cherry-red coloration at the base (a form without red colour exists, and was at one time available under the name of 'golden rye-grass'. It is, however, uncommon; it is a double recessive for the two genes controlling anthocyanin production). The leaves develop little sclerenchyma, and the old leaf-sheaths are not persistent, but rot away comparatively quickly.

Agricultural Importance. Perennial rye-grass is very common, and perhaps the most important of all grasses in British agriculture. It is palatable, stands up to hard grazing well, and under conditions of high fertility gives high yields of leafy herbage. It is winter-green, commencing growth early in spring and continuing well into autumn. It is not, however, a grass for poor conditions or low fertility, and is not drought-resistant. While the total growing season is long, the main 'flush' of growth occurs around May, and this period of maximum growth is not readily altered by management methods. It may be possible by selection of different strains within the species, and by top-dressing, to shift this flush of growth perhaps a month, but it is not usually possible to arrange for it to be produced at other times, or to avoid a depression of yield in the middle of the season. For good, fertile lowland conditions, however, perennial rye-grass is usually the most generally useful species, and forms the basis of most leys and pastures under such conditions. Its comparatively cheap seed and ready establishment make it suitable for short leys, and as a result a greater tonnage of perennial rye-grass seed is used annually than of any other grass.

Owing to its large seed and the rapid growth of the seedling, perennial rye-grass establishes well, under good conditions the field establishment may be 60 per cent. or more (see p. 354). Its rapid early growth may cause difficulty when it is sown with other grasses, the rye-grass being very *aggressive* and tending to compete so strongly with other slower-growing grasses that they are at least partially suppressed.

Varieties. Perennial rye-grass is a very variable species, and crossing may take place not only between the different forms of the species, but also with Italian rye-grass and some other species, and also with some species of fescue, although in the latter case the resultant hybrid is usually sterile.

Perennial rye-grass plants can thus be found varying from extremely long-lived forms with very numerous barren tillers to short-lived, almost annual plants which are stemmy and produce few non-flowering shoots. This wide range of types is reflected in the large number of strains, commercial, local and bred, of which seed is available in Britain.

The most conspicuous difference between varieties is the date of flowering, and the strains used can be conveniently divided into early- and late-flowering groups. Crosses between early and late plants give intermediate progeny, but such plants have not been selected in the development of British varieties, and the two groups remain fairly distinct. In general, early flowering is associated with early spring growth, and although late-flowering plants are not necessarily late in starting growth, they do usually show this character.

EARLY-FLOWERING VARIETIES

Irish Commercial. Produced in very large quantity in N. Ireland; usually in first harvest year of three- to four-year mixed ley. No special selection of mother seed. Seed low-priced, but plants give small proportion of barren tillers, and tend, particularly under rather poor conditions, to be stemmy and short-lived. *Scottish Commercial* (*Ayrshire*) is similar.

Devon Eaver is a local variety derived from old pastures in Devon, early flowering and more persistent.

S.24. An Aberystwyth-bred variety, designed to replace Commercial. Flowers a day or two later, has a larger proportion of barren tillers and is hence more leafy and relatively persistent.

Grasslands Ruanui is a New Zealand variety similar to S.24.

LATE-FLOWERING VARIETIES

S.321. An Aberystwyth-bred intermediate variety, similar to S.101 but giving higher hay yields and remaining green in autumn.

Taptoe. A Dutch variety, of the same type as S.101 but an *autotetraploid*, and showing the special characters of tetraploid ryegrasses. Tetraploids differ from diploids in having larger 'seeds' and larger tillers with lower dry-matter but higher soluble carbohydrates. They are markedly more palatable, and this may result in a higher dry-matter intake by grazing animals. This advantage is however offset by the high cost of seed, which, since it is larger, must be sown at at least one and a half times the normal rate.

Kent Indigenous. A local variety, produced originally from old pastures in the Romney Marsh area, multiplied under ley conditions. Flowers about three weeks later than Commercial, and distinctly later in starting growth in spring. Persistent, with a fairly high proportion of barren tillers; plant rather small.

S.101. An Aberystwyth-bred variety, described as a pasture-hay type, flowering slightly later than Kent, some three to four weeks after Commercial. Leaves long, plant large, with high proportion of barren tillers. Late starting in spring, very few flowering heads in aftermath.

S.23. The pasture variety bred at Aberystwyth. Very late-flowering, some four to five weeks after Commercial, with very high proportion of barren tillers, producing extremely large spreading plant. Very persistent. Late starting in spring, very few flowering heads in aftermath.

(Numerous continental European varieties exist, some of which may be available in Britain. Among these may be mentioned the Swedish Otofte Early, comparable to S.24; Hunsballe, somewhat similar to Kent; and the Belgian Melle, which closely resembles S.23.)

Lolium multiflorum Lam. (**L. italicum** A. Br.).   Italian Rye-grass

An important introduced species, behaving as an annual or short-lived perennial. The name *L. italicum*, or *L. multiflorum* var. *italicum* Beck., is often used for the commonly grown two- or three-year plant, the type

---

* Caused by the fungus *Phialea temulenta*. Causes no visible damage to plants, but infected 'seeds' fail to germinate.

of the species *L. multiflorum* being the strictly annual form (see Wester-wolds rye-grass).

Inflorescence. The inflorescence closely resembles that of perennial rye-grass, but there are normally more (sixteen to eighteen) florets per spike-let, and the lemmas bear a long, fine terminal awn.

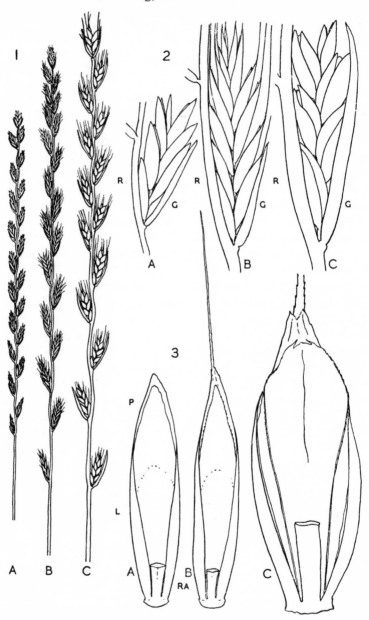

FIG. 145. Rye-grasses. 1, inflorescence, × ½. 2, single spikelet, × 3. 3, 'seed', × 10, of A, perennial rye-grass; B, Italian rye-grass; C, darnel (awned form of darnel shown in 1 and 3, awnless in 2); R, rachis; G, glume; L, lemma; P, palea; RA, rachilla.

'*Seed.*' The threshed 'seed' is very similar to that of perennial rye-grass, but easily distinguished by the awn. This awn is not usually lost in the threshing or cleaning processes; if it is, then seeds can only be distinguished by the *Hellbo test*, the examination of the intermediate nerves of the lemma for minute teeth, present in Italian but absent from most forms of perennial, or by the *Gentner test*, which depends on the fact that roots of Italian rye-grass germinated on filter paper fluoresce under ultraviolet light, while seedlings of perennial (except for a small proportion in the early strains) show no fluorescence. The 'seed' is often slightly larger than that of perennial, with some 200,000 per pound, but this difference is by no means constant.

Vegetative Characters. Italian resembles perennial rye-grass, but has usually larger tillers, with broader leaves. The plant is usually more erect, with a tendency to produce tillers at nodes well above ground-level. Young leaves are rolled, not folded as in perennial, so that shoots are round, not flat. Auricles are large, well-developed, long and clasping around the sheath.

Italian rye-grass can usually be distinguished from meadow fescue (p. 311) by its more succulent, quickly-grown appearance and by its less-persistent old leaf-sheaths, but plants may be encountered in which these characters are not clearly visible; it is then necessary to depend on very small details. The shape of unexpanded tiller buds (really the outline of the young prophyll) exposed by stripping down the older leaf-sheaths provides a clear distinction; in Italian rye-grass the bud is narrow, pointed and with ciliate margin, while in meadow fescue it is broad, rounded and glabrous.

Agricultural Importance. Italian rye-grass is probably the quickest-growing and highest-yielding of all temperate-climate grasses under high-fertility conditions. It is therefore of outstanding importance in short leys, where its lack of permanence is not a disadvantage. It establishes readily and grows very rapidly, so that it may be fit to graze within a few weeks of sowing, and is amongst the most palatable of all grasses. Flowering normally takes place about the same time as that of the late strains of perennial, and a considerable amount of aftermath flowering occurs. It lends itself more readily, however, than perennial to treatments designed to prolong the grazing period, and by selecting suitable times of sowing and methods of management, keep can be obtained at almost any desired time of year. It is thus not only used as the basis of most one-year hay and grazing leys, but for out-of-season grazing leys, catch crops and green-manuring. May die out in severe winters.

It has in the past been used in considerable quantities as a constituent of three-year and longer leys; its exceedingly vigorous and aggressive early growth makes this a dangerous practice, as, unless very carefully managed, it competes too strongly with other slower-growing grasses. If this happens the ley may appear very satisfactory in its first and perhaps second year, but degenerate rapidly after this as the Italian dies out, leaving behind it only few and weakened plants of the less aggressive and more permanent species.

Italian rye-grass is not known in a wild state, and appears to have originated in cultivation in N. Italy. It was introduced into Britain in the early nineteenth century.

Varieties. The usual forms of Italian rye-grass are biennials or short-lived perennials, giving a very high yield in the first harvest year, and tending to die out during the second harvest year, with only occasional plants surviving longer. *Commercial* Italian ryegrass is produced in Northern Ireland; the Aberystwyth-bred *S.22* is somewhat higher yielding, later flowering and longer lived. Of the continental varieties, *Tetila*, from Holland, is a tetraploid and shows the same special characters as the tetraploid perennial ryegrasses. A number of Danish diploid varieties are outstanding in their early spring growth.

The variety *Combi*, from Holland, appears to be somewhat more winter-hardy than other varieties, but it must be emphasized that winter-hardiness is very much influenced by time of sowing and by management.

Westerwolds Ryegrass (Western wolths). This is a strictly annual form of *L. multiflorum*, originating in Holland. It is similar to ordinary Italian, but even quicker growing, and flowering in the same year if sown in spring or summer. Used only for very short leys or catch crops, where the total period of growth is six months or less.

Hybrid Ryegrasses. Some varieties resulting from crosses between Italian and perennial are in use. New Zealand Short Rotation, or H.1, now renamed *Grasslands Manawa*, achieved considerable popularity as combining longer life with the desirable characters of Italian, but proved, in a severe winter, rather less hardy. Very similar to Italian in appearance, but with rather frequent branched spikes.

Different hybrid varieties show a range from those essentially Italian to *long rotation* types which are very near perennial ryegrass.

Lolium temulentum L.   Darnel

Darnel is a strictly annual, southern European species, very similar in the vegetative stage to a sparsely-tillered plant of Italian rye-grass, with rather rougher leaves. It is readily distinguished when in flower by the greater length of the glumes, which extend beyond the top of the uppermost floret of the spikelet. The florets are considerably broader than those of Italian; the lemma may be awnless (var. *arvense* Lilj.) or bear a fine terminal awn.

Darnel is valueless as a herbage grass, but was formerly important as a weed of cereal crops. The 'seed' (caryopsis enclosed in lemma and palea) is much larger than that of the other rye-grasses; and sufficiently near to a wheat grain in size and shape for it not to be separated by primitive cleaning methods. The seed may be poisonous, owing to the presence of a sterile fungus mycelium, and wheat contaminated with darnel was therefore dangerous to use for food. Improved methods of seed-cleaning have reduced the importance of darnel to negligible importance, and it is now a rare plant in Britain.

L. rigidum Gaud., Wimmera rye-grass, is a small, very quick-growing annual species used in Australia as a herbage grass in areas of extremely short growing season.

FESTUCA. THE FESCUES

The genus *Festuca* is closely related to *Lolium*, and crosses are possible between many species of the two genera. It is distinguished by the inflorescence being a panicle, not a spike; all spikelets have two glumes. The members of the genus are all perennials, annual species being placed in the genus *Vulpia*. (The bromes, genus *Bromus*, have panicles resembling fescues in general appearance, but are distinguished by the hairy ovary with enlarged tip, and by the dorsal, not terminal, awns on the lemmas.)

The species of *Festuca* of agricultural importance fall into two groups: (1) the large fescues, with all leaves broad and flat—meadow and tall fescue; and (2) the small fescues, with permanently-folded, bristle-like leaves—sheep's fescue and related species.

Festuca pratensis Huds. (**F. elatior var. pratensis** (Huds.) Hack).
Meadow Fescue

A tufted perennial, palatable and of considerable value in leys.

Inflorescence. A spreading panicle 2-3 ft. high; panicle branches usually in pairs, unequal, some with only one to two spikelets. Spikelets cylindrical, six- to twelve-flowered.

'*Seed.*' Caryopsis enclosed in palea and blunt, awnless, round-backed lemma. Very similar in size and shape to perennial rye-grass, but distinguished by cylindrical (not flattened) rachilla, widening abruptly at top.

Vegetative Characters. Tufted perennial, tillers intravaginal. Leaves rolled in bud, shoot round, glabrous. Leaf blades broad, tapering ribbed, dull above, shiny below. Upper surface of blade slightly rough. Auricles conspicuous, glabrous, ligule short. Sheaths split, shining, bright cherry-red at base. Very similar to Italian rye-grass, distinguishable usually by harder, less succulent, slower-grown appearance, and persistent pale-brown old sheaths. (For distinction by bud-shape, see Italian rye-grass, p. 309.)

Agricultural Importance. Meadow fescue is a useful herbage grass for longer leys, palatable, high-yielding and winter-green. Growth in the seedling and young plant stages is rather slow, and meadow fescue suffers very badly in competition with the rye-grasses. Its inclusion in general-purpose leys based on rye-grass is therefore not to be recommended. It has, however, advantages over perennial rye-grass for some purposes as being more flexible in its reactions to varied management, and capable of providing keep during the winter and midsummer periods, when rye-grass yield is low. For these purposes it is best grown in separate non-rye-grass leys, usually combined with timothy, which is also non-aggressive in the young stage, and such timothy-meadow fescue leys (sometimes with the addition of cocksfoot) have become popular as alternatives to the rye-grass ley.

Varieties. Meadow fescue shows the same sort of division into early hay and late pasture types as perennial ryegrass. *Canadian Commercial* is fairy early, somewhat, stemmy; Aberystwyth *S.215*, and the continental hay varieties such as *Combi Hay* and *Trifolium* give good spring growth. Later-flowering varieties such as Aberystwyth *S.53*, *Mommersteegs Pasture* and *Garton's Own Leafy* tend to be more persistent. They flower some ten or twelve days later, but do not usually give better autumn growth than the early varieties.

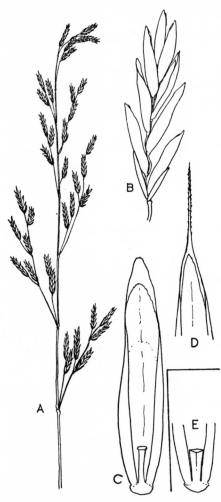

F. arundinacea Schreb. **(F. elatior var. arundinacea** (Schreb.) Celak.). Tall Fescue

A very variable species, similar to meadow fescue, but always larger and coarser. It is only the finer forms (i.e. those nearest to meadow fescue) which are of any agricultural importance, the larger forms being stiff, harsh-leaved plants of roadsides and sea-coast of little or no grazing value. It can be distinguished from meadow fescue by the larger panicles, with all branches bearing three or more spikelets, by the pointed or shortly-awned lemmas and by the ciliate auricles. Most forms are very early, with heavy spring yields.

Fig. 146. Meadow fescue. A, panicle, × ½. B, spikelet, × 3. C, 'seed', × 10. D, apex only of 'seed' of tall fescue for comparison with C. E, base only of 'seed' of perennial rye-grass for comparison of rachilla.

Commercial tall fescue, of German or American origin, is one of the intermediate forms of the species, but none the less a rather large, coarse plant of doubtful palatability. An Aberystwyth variety *S.170*, somewhat nearer to meadow fescue is intended for winter or early spring grazing, comparable in yield to

Italian rye-grass, but unpalatable in summer. North African forms, softer and capable of winter growth, may be of value.

F. rubra L. Red Fescue

Small, needle-leaved grasses, agriculturally important only on hill-grazings, but useful for lawns and sports turf. Very variable.

Inflorescence. A rather narrow, open panicle, up to 2 ft. high. Spikelets small, about 10 mm., four- to eight-flowered.

'*Seed.*' Caryopsis enclosed in palea and round-backed lemma, tapering into fine terminal awn; hairy in some forms; ¾ million per pound.

Vegetative Characters. Perennial, with both intra- and extra-vaginal shoots, usually creeping (except Chewing's fescue) by slender, brownish rhizomes. Leaves permanently folded, bristle-like (except on flowering shoots), auricles and ligule small, sheaths closed, often reddish.

Agricultural Importance. Red fescue varies considerably, but in its better forms it is, in spite of its needle-leaves, a palatable grass of fair nutritive value. Yields are rather higher than might be expected from its appearance, and although it cannot compare with the better lowland grasses, it is, under the more difficult conditions, and lower fertility, of hill and mountain grazing, a very valuable species. It is commonly found in semi-natural hill pastures; it is rarely considered worth sowing as a herbage grass, as the percentage establishment is low, and the seed (partly owing to the demand for it for sports turf) is somewhat expensive, particularly for use on the poor land to which it is suited.

Forms

F. rubra sub-sp. rubra (F. rubra genuina). Creeping Red Fescue

This is the typical red fescue; it is very variable, but the bulk of the seed available is the Aberystwyth-bred strain *S.59*, which has rather softer, lighter-green leaves and is more winter-green than many of the wild forms. It was designed as a grass for hill-reclamation, but appears in fact to be mainly used for sports turf.

F. rubra sub-sp. commutata Gaud. (F. rubra var. fallax (Thuill.) Hack.). Chewing's Fescue

A non-creeping form of red fescue occurring in New Zealand, and named after the original producer of seed there, where it is used as a constituent of hill pastures. Seed is imported into Britain mainly for lawn and sports turf.

Festuca ovina L. Sheep's Fescue

A needle-leaved perennial very similar to red fescue, but with all tillers intravaginal, not creeping, and with split leaf-sheaths. Panicle and seed available is the Aberystwyth-bred variety *S.59*, which has rather what smaller, with shorter awns. Occurs in similar situations, and may be the main species of hill pasture, probably less valuable as grazing than red fescue. Seed rarely available for agricultural purposes.

Related forms are **F. tenuifolia** Sibth. **(F. capillata** Lam., **F. ovina var. tenuifolia),** fine-leaved fescue, with shorter, narrower leaves and smaller, awnless 'seeds', sometimes recommended for lawns; **F. longifolia** Thuill. **(F. ovina var. longifolia),** hard fescue, a rather larger plant of which seed was formerly imported from Germany; and **F. vivipara** (L.) Sm. **(F. ovina var. vivipara** L.), viviparous fescue, resembling fine-leaved fescue, but always viviparous, i.e. spikelets becoming

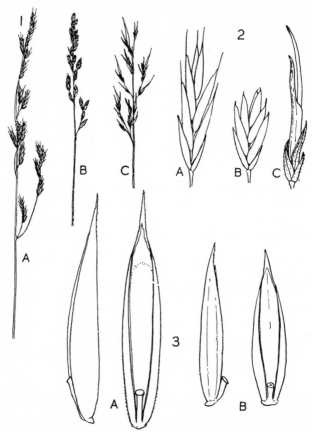

Fig. 147. Small fescues. 1, panicle, × ½. 2, spikelet, × 3. 3, 'seed', × 10 of A, red fescue; B, sheep's fescue. C, viviparous fescue (no 'seed' produced).

leafy and developing as young plants. No seed is therefore formed. Common in wet mountain pasture and retaining viviparous habit if transplanted to lowland.

VULPIA

A genus of small annual grasses, sometimes included in *Festuca*, with similar panicles, but very slender long-awned 'seeds'; flower with one stamen only.

Vulpia bromoides (L.) S. F. Gray, rat's-tail fescue (squirrel-tail fescue, 'hair'), is an annual with panicle up to 2 ft. high, occurring in poor, under-grazed dry grassland, important only as a weed of grass seed crops, especially perennial rye-grass. The panicle is able to develop during the period the field is laid up for seed, and some rat's-tail is shed before harvest, so that if a seed crop is taken several years in succession, a very serious infestation of this weed may build up. Although the seed is much more slender than rye-grass, it is a difficult impurity to clean out, and may cause some clogging of screens. Under normal grazing conditions rat's-tail is not a serious weed, soon dying out if not allowed to seed.

Vulpia myuros (L.) C. C. Gmel., or **Festuca myuros** L., is a name which is often used to include this species; it refers strictly to a closely-related but much less common grass of waste places, distinguished by the panicle not being completely exserted from the upper leaf-sheath.

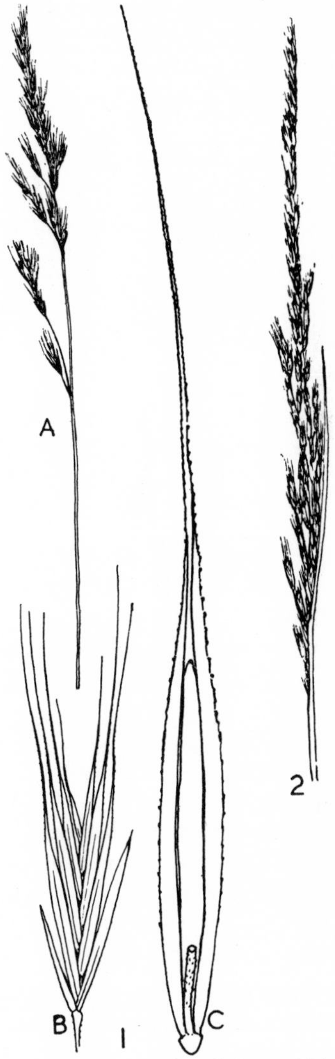

CYNOSURUS. DOG'S-TAILS

Panicles with very short branches, spike-like in appearance. Fertile spikelets similar to those of *Festuca*, but sterile reduced spikelets also present.

Cynosurus cristatus L. Crested Dog's-tail

A common perennial of rather poor pastures, occasionally sown but not of great agricultural value.

Inflorescence. A one-sided spike-like panicle 18 in. to 2 ft. high. The very short panicle branches bear both fertile and sterile spikelets, the latter towards the outside, so that the fertile ones are largely hidden. Fertile spikelets some 5 mm. long, with two nearly equal pointed glumes and from

FIG. 148. 1, Rat's-tail fescue, *Vulpia bromoides*: A, panicle, × ½; B, single spikelet, × 3; C, 'seed', × 10. 2, panicle of the closely-related *V. myuros*, × ½.

three to five florets. Sterile spikelets of about the same size, but with glumes and lemmas represented only by narrow, bristle-like structures.

'*Seed.*' Caryopsis enclosed in lemma and palea, *c.* 4 mm. long, ¾ million to pound. Lemma narrow, rounded on back, sharply-pointed or very shortly-awned, rough on upper part. The yellowish-brown colour is very characteristic; 'seeds' all bright yellow may be an indication of under-ripeness, but there are nearly always sufficient yellow 'seeds' in a sample to make recognition easy.

Vegetative Characters. A tufted, rather small, glabrous perennial, with leaves folded in bud, shoots oval in section. Leaf-blades short, stiff, tapering, deeply-ribbed above, shiny below; ligule very short, blunt; no auricles. Sheaths split, yellow at base.

Agricultural Importance. A fairly palatable grass, but its small size and short leaves result in a low yield. It is hardy, winter-green and persistent under low-fertility conditions, and therefore often found in quantity in rather poor upland pastures. It may be sometimes worth sowing under such conditions, but requires careful management, as the inflorescence is very wiry and unless kept grazed down early, quickly becomes unpalatable, and is therefore able to produce and shed seed even under grazing conditions. Such self-seeding may result in the dog's-tail becoming dominant, with a resultant low pasture yield.

Dog's-tail is sometimes recommended for lawns and playing-fields, but although its stiff, short foliage is very suitable, the wiry inflorescence stalks often prove impossible to mow cleanly.

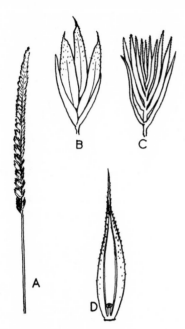
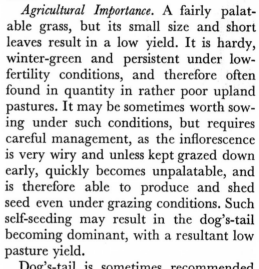

Fig. 149. Crested dogstail. A, panicle, × ⅔. B, fertile spikelet, × 6. C, sterile spikelet, × 6. D, 'seed', × 10.

Cynosurus echinatus L., rough dog's-tail, is an introduced annual of no agricultural value, distinguished by its irregular, much broader panicles and long-awned lemmas.

BRIZA. QUAKING GRASSES

Briza has a spreading panicle, with pendulous, very broad spikelets; glumes and lemmas rounded, almost as broad as long.

B. media L., common quaking grass, is a low-yielding perennial of poor grassland, fairly common, but rarely present in great quantity, and of little agricultural importance. Panicles are spreading, up to 18 in. high, branches flexuous, very slender so that the pendulous spikelets 'quake' in the wind. Spikelets small, roughly triangular in shape, some 5 mm. long with *c.* eight florets. Glumes and lemmas very broad, blunt, awnless, cordate at base.

B. minor L., lesser quaking grass, is an annual with similar but smaller spikelets found occasionally in S. England; **B. maxima** L. is a Mediterranean annual with very large, ovate spikelets, sometimes cultivated in gardens for its ornamental panicles.

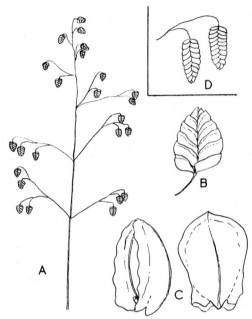

FIG. 150. Quaking grass, *Briza media*. A, panicle, × ½. B, spikelet, × 3. C, 'seed', side and dorsal views, × 10. D, two spikelets of *Briza maxima*, × ½.

DACTYLIS

Panicle spreading but ultimate branches short, lemmas sharply keeled.

Dactylis glomerata L.   Cocksfoot, Orchard Grass (U.S.A.)

A high-yielding perennial of major importance, frequently sown in leys.

Inflorescence. Panicle large, up to 3-4 ft., primary branches long, so that the general outline is that of a spreading panicle, but ultimate branches short, so that the spikelets are crowded together in dense clumps (glomerata=clumped). Spikelets flat, 6-9 mm. long, three- to five-flowered, glumes and lemmas strongly keeled.

'Seed.' Caryopsis enclosed by lemma and palea, 5 mm., ½ million to the pound. Lemma very sharply keeled, so that 'seed' is compressed laterally and tends to lie on its side. Lemma very shortly-awned, rough, pale brown, hairy on keel, curved or twisted. The upper florets of the spikelet do not separate readily on threshing, and double or treble 'seeds' are frequent in some samples.

Vegetative Characters. A stout, tufted, glabrous perennial, tillers all intravaginal, large. Leaves folded in bud, tillers very flat. Leaf-blades broad, long, tapering, dull grey- or blue-green on both surfaces, upper flat with single median line of motor-tissue, lower deeply-keeled. Auricles absent, ligules large, white, conspicuous. Leaf-sheaths broad, thick, fleshy, white at base, strongly-keeled, rather persistent, dying off pale brown.

Agricultural Importance. A valuable, high-yielding perennial, coarser, less digestible and less palatable than rye-grass, but growing well at slightly lower fertility levels, and showing marked drought resistance. Establishment from seed is fairly good (40 per cent.), but the seedling growth is rather slow, and cocksfoot does not compete well with the rye-grasses in the first year. Aggressiveness in later years is very dependent on management. The thick, fleshy leaf-sheath bases act as a food reserve, and cocksfoot is very markedly benefited by long rest periods, which enable such reserves to be built up. Under lenient grazing it may become dominant in an originally mixed sward, individual plants building up into large and often rather unpalatable clumps. This difficulty of managing cocksfoot in a mixed sward has tended to make cocksfoot unpopular in some areas; the danger of clump formation is, however, much less with the grazing strains, and with the ready availability of S.143 cocksfoot has increased in popularity, and is now commonly included in most general-purpose leys where drought-resistance is required. It is also used in cocksfoot-white clover leys managed so as to take advantage of its food-storing ability.

Fig. 151. Cocksfoot. A, panicle, × ½. B, part of panicle to show clustered spikelets, × 3. C, single spikelet, × 3. D, 'seed', side and ventral views, × 10.

Varieties. Commercial cocksfoot was often stemmy and is now little used; various English and continental bred varieties exist. Aberystwyth *S.345* flowers very early, with good spring and autumn growth, but moderate hay yield. Other bred varieties are *S.37*, hay type; *S.26*, intermediate, and *S.143*, pasture type. All are somewhat similar leafy forms, later-flowering than Danish and varying in growth-habit, S.143 being the least erect, and also the least likely to form unpalatable coarse clumps. As large-scale seed-production from wide-drilled rows has enabled seed of this strain to be sold at a price comparable to that of commercial cocksfoot, it has become the most popular of the cocksfoot varieties in England.

Panicle spreading, spikelets small, flattened. Lemmas keeled, awnless. Leaves folded, with two lines of motor tissue.

Poa trivialis L.   Rough-stalked Meadow-grass

A common and fairly useful grass of damp soils, rarely sown.

Inflorescence. Panicle spreading, open and feathery in appearance, with numerous small spikelets, 3-4 mm. long, usually three- to four-flowered. Culm immediately below lowest node of panicle sometimes slightly rough with minute, downward-pointing spines (it is to this that the not very helpful common name refers).

'*Seed.*' Caryopsis, with lemma and palea, with at the base a *web* of fine, cottony hairs (removed during cleaning). 'Seed' small, *c.* 3 mm., 2 million per pound, triangular in cross-section owing to sharply-keeled lemma; tapering narrow-oval in side view. Lemma five-nerved, awnless, hairy on lower half of keel only.

Vegetative Characters. A stoloniferous creeping perennial (loosely-tufted under dry conditions). Leaves folded in bud, tillers flat. Leaf blades bright green, soft, tapering, rather short, shiny below, rather dull above, but not ribbed, with a double line of motor tissue. Auricles absent, ligule pointed, short on barren tillers but long on upper leaves of flowering tillers. Sheaths split, flattened, pale.

Agricultural Importance. Rough-stalked meadow-grass is a palatable but rather low-yielding grass very common in most damp, lowland grassland; under these conditions it may make an important contribution to the spring growth, as, for instance, in irrigated 'meadows', but the later yield, particularly during dry periods, is low. The 'seed' is light-sensitive (requires light for good germination) and establishment from seed is often very low (5 per cent.), so that it is rarely considered worth sowing.

Rough-stalked meadow-grass may under some conditions appear as a minor arable weed; it is then a loosely-tufted plant with leaves much broader and rougher than under grassland conditions.

Poa pratensis L.   Smooth-stalked Meadow-grass

A common grass of rather low value, never normally sown.

Inflorescence. A spreading panicle, more compact and with spikelets larger than rough-stalked, 5-6 mm. long with from four to five florets.

'*Seed.*' Very similar to rough-stalked, but rather broader, with blunter lemma, about 1½ million per pound. It can be distinguished in the fresh state by the presence of hairs on the intermediate nerves of the lemma as well as on keel (keel only in rough-stalked), but these are usually removed together with the web during the seed-cleaning. The slightly coarser teeth on the keels of the palea of smooth-stalked may also be used as a distinction, but it is necessary to dissect out the palea to observe these.

Vegetative Characters. A rhizomatous creeping perennial, with rather stout, white, underground stems bearing scale and transitional leaves. Foliage leaves similar to those of rough-stalked, but blade longer, stiffer,

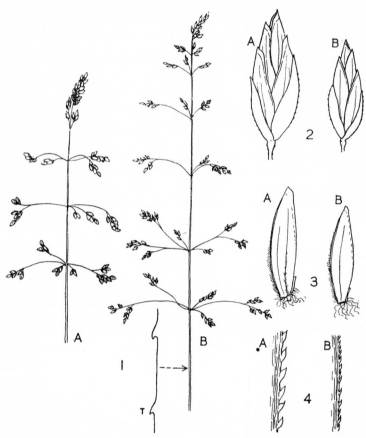

Fig. 152. Meadow-grasses. 1, panicle, × ¼. 2, spikelet, × 7. 3, 'seed' (unmachined, web and hairs still present), × 10. 4, teeth on nerves of palea, × 60, of A, smooth-stalked, and B, rough-stalked meadow-grass. T, margin of culm of rough-stalk × 60, to show teeth sometimes present.

darker green, parallel-sided narrowing abruptly to a boat-like tip, ligule always blunt, sheaths smooth.

Agricultural Importance. The stiff leaves of smooth-stalked are rather unpalatable, and it has little to recommend it, other than its drought-resistance and ability to withstand treading. It is a very common grass, being found in small amount in most old pastures, but is rarely a dominant species. Establishment from seed is usually poor, and in Britain it is even less commonly sown than rough-stalk, although under the rather more difficult conditions of the eastern U.S.A. it is highly valued as a pasture grass, under the name of Kentucky bluegrass.

Varieties. *Poa pratensis*, as usually defined, is a variable species, and includes plants with chromosome numbers varying from 28 (tetraploid) to 124. Many of the higher polyploid forms are apomictic, i.e. produce seeds without fertilization, and therefore do not show normal segregation. Numerous American and Scandinavian varieties have been developed, but the importance of the species in Britain is not sufficient to warrant much attention to varieties here.

Poa annua L.   Annual Meadow-grass

An annual or ephemeral, producing at almost all times of year its small panicle of few, relatively large webless spikelets. Vegetatively it somewhat resembles rough-stalked, but has blunter leaves, broader in proportion, light green, often crinkled and with more conspicuous ligule. A very common arable weed, readily controlled by cultivation, and frequently found in grass land, where its presence is often an indication of earlier bare patches. Not unpalatable, but yield very low, and drying up completely in hot, dry weather. Tetraploid; perhaps an amphidiploid from two similar but much less widespread diploid species, *P. infirma* H.B.K. and *P. supina* Schrad. Common impurity of grass seeds.

Poa compressa L., flat-stemmed meadow-grass, a rhizomatous perennial with rather rough, greyish leaves and small panicles with distinctly flattened stem occurs in dry lowland grassland, but rarely in quantity. Cultivated in N. America as Canadian bluegrass. **Poa nemoralis** L., wood meadow-grass, a tufted perennial, with slender, dark-green leaves and large spreading panicles, and with nodes of flowering tillers black, is found in woods and is sometimes recommended for lawns in shade.

Puccinellia maritima (Huds.) Parl., sea meadow-grass (distinguished from *Poa* by rounded, not keeled, lemmas) and related species provide useful salt-marsh grazing.

GLYCERIEAE

Glyceria is a genus with an inflorescence of the festucoid type, with lax, cylindrical spikelets and very blunt, round-backed lemmas; it differs, however, in its small chromosomes and connate lodicules and has therefore been referred to a separate tribe. **Glyceria fluitans** (L.) R.Br., floating sweet-grass, has slender panicles and vegetative characters resembling those of a much-enlarged, very succulent, rough-stalked meadow-grass. **G. maxima** (Hartm.) Holmb., reed meadow-grass, has large, spreading panicles, stout rhizomes and upright shoots forming large clumps. These, and some related species and hybrids, are common and palatable grasses of water-meadows, riversides and very wet lowland grassland, where they may provide useful herbage.

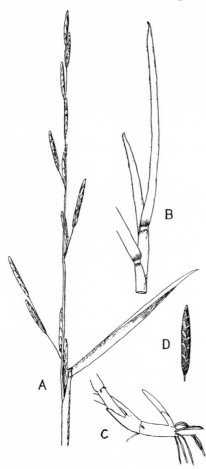

A

B

C

D

BROMUS. THE BROME GRASSES

Inflorescence festucoid, with lemmas either keeled or rounded on back and with dorsal awn. Ovary with hairy process above lateral styles, and starch grains simple, not compound, and therefore referred to separate tribe. A large genus, divisible into a number of sections, sometimes treated as separate genera. British species mainly hairy, unpalatable weeds.

Bromus mollis L.   Soft Brome

Usually annual, common in overhayed grassland, and as an impurity of grass seed.

Inflorescence. Spreading panicle with large, oval spikelets, 15-20 mm. long, eight- to ten-flowered, with lemmas of adjoining florets overlapping, lemmas hairy, awned.

'*Seed.*' Lemma shortly hairy, very much broader than caryopsis and palea and tending to stand out at sides, variable, *c.* 10 mm. long, with fine, rough dorsal awn of about the same length. Typical large 'seeds' considerably bigger than those of rye-grass, but the smaller 'seeds', and those in which the lemma is

Fig. 153. Floating sweet-grass, *Glyceria fluitans.* A, panicle, ×½. B, leaves, ×½. C, base of stem, ×½. D, spikelet, ×¾.

more closely rolled about the palea, are difficult to remove from rye-grass and similar-sized seed.

Vegetative Characters. Tufted annual or sometimes biennial, leaves rolled, shoots round. Leaf blades broad, dull grey-green, hairy, soft, no auricles, ligule blunt. Sheaths closed, hairy, keeled, pale.

Agricultural Importance. An unpalatable grass spreading rapidly by self-sown seed if not prevented by hard grazing or early cutting; it is therefore most common in grass fields cut for hay each year, particularly where hay is cut late enough for the bulk of the brome seed to have ripened. Control by hard grazing; soft brome is not completely unpalatable and will usually be eaten down in spring and again in autumn; not persistent if not allowed to seed. It is, of course, much favoured by seed-production conditions, where the late cutting allows complete ripening; in a broadcast rye-grass crop cutting for seed may not be possible for more than two successive years owing to the rapid build-up of soft brome. The seed, together with related species, was scheduled under the Seeds Regulations, 1922, as an *injurious weed seed* owing to the difficulty of ensuring its complete removal from rye-grass and similar-sized seeds; now less important; omitted from 1961 list.

Numerous closely-related species and forms occur. The most distinct forms from an agricultural standpoint are **B. arvensis** L., field

FIG. 154. Brome grasses. 1, Soft brome, *Bromus mollis*: A, panicle, × ½; B, spikelet, × 3; C, 'seed', × 10. 2, spikelet of *B. arvensis*, × 3. 3, spikelet of *B. secalinus*, × 3.

brome, with rather lighter-green leaves and narrower spikelets, a rather uncommon grassland weed in Britain, sometimes sown for hay in northern Europe, and **B. secalinus** L., rye brome, with very broad spikelets, the mature florets spreading so that the lemmas of adjoining florets do not overlap, and almost glabrous leaf-sheaths. This occurs mainly as an arable weed in winter cereals, and may be distributed as an impurity of poorly-cleaned seed corn.

Bromus sterilis L. (**Anisantha sterilis** (L.) Nev.), barren brome, is a very common annual with large, drooping panicles of very large wedge-shaped spikelets, up to 5 cm. long, consisting of from six to ten florets. The 'seed' is up to 20 mm. long, with an even longer dorsal awn. Although often abundant in field hedges and occasionally spreading by seed into cultivated land, it is rarely a serious weed, as it does not persist in a grazed sward, and the 'seed' is too large for it to be a common impurity even of seed corn.

Bromus erectus Huds. (**Zerna erecta** (Huds.) Panz.), upright brome, is a tufted, slightly hairy perennial with erect panicles and parallel-sided spikelets. It is coarse and unpalatable and may become dominant in under-grazed grassland on limestone soils.

Bromus ramosus Huds. (**Zerna ramosa** (Huds.) Lindm., **Bromus asper** Murr.), wood brome, is a common hairy perennial distinguished by its very large, drooping panicle, almost confined to woodland, and rarely appearing on farmland. **Bromus inermis** Leyss. (**Zerna inermis** (Leyss.) Lindm.), awnless brome, is an almost hairless, strongly rhizomatous perennial, with cylindrical spikelets, awns very short or absent. Not native, and although extensively grown (as 'brome', or 'smooth brome') in N. America, is not generally considered worth cultivation in Britain. **Bromus unioloides** Willd. (**Ceratochloa unioloides** (Willd.) Beauv.), Schräder's brome or rescue grass, is another species cultivated in America and in Europe, but only occasionally introduced in Britain. It is a large-growing perennial with broad leaves and extremely large, flat spikelets.

BRACHYPODIUM. FALSE BROMES

Perennials of no agricultural value, resembling the bromes, but with spikelets in a simple raceme, not panicle, and awns terminal, not dorsal.

Brachypodium pinnatum (L.) Beauv., tor grass or heath false-brome, is a stout, coarse, rhizomatous perennial of chalk and limestone soils, with harsh, yellowish-green, slightly hairy leaves. Inflorescence a simple raceme of short-stalked, erect, cylindrical, often curved, many-flowered spikelets. Lemmas glabrous, rounded on back, shortly-awned. Tor grass rapidly becomes unpalatable and may spread to become dominant in undergrazed chalk downland and similar areas.

Brachypodium sylvaticum (Huds.) Beauv., wood false-brome, differs in having no rhizomes, thinner, papery, more hairy leaves and less smoothly-cylindrical, straight spikelets, with more tapering, longer-awned, hairy lemmas. It is confined to shady conditions, and although often abundant in hedges, is not found in agricultural grassland except occasionally as a relic of cleared woodland.

HORDEAE

AGROPYRON. COUCH GRASSES

Inflorescence a spike, with a single, many-flowered spikelet at each node. Each spikelet has much the same structure as that of the *Festuceae*, with a pair of rather short glumes, and four or more florets. In Britain, one species only is important, and that as an arable weed; some foreign species are cultivated as forage grasses.

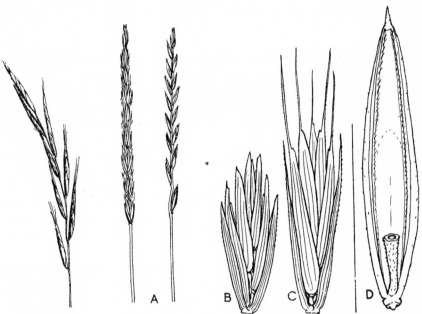

FIG. 155. Wood false-brome. Raceme,×½.Spikelets on short stalks.

FIG. 156. Couch, *Agropyron repens*. A, spike in face and side views, ×½. B, spikelet of awnless form, ×3. C, of awned form. D, 'seed', ×10.

Agropyron repens (L.) Beauv.   Couch, Twitch

A common and serious perennial weed of arable land.

Inflorescence. A rather stiff spike with a single three- to eight-flowered spikelet some 15 mm. long at each node. Two glumes present per spikelet; spikelets flat side on to rachis (not edgewise, with one glume only, as in rye-grass). Lemma pointed or awned. 'Seed'. 7 mm. or more, rough, keeled towards top, rachilla rough with terminal pit. Often empty, and then florets not separating. *Injurious weed seed* under 1961 Regulations.

Vegetative Characters. Perennial, with very extensive, stout, white, sharply-pointed rhizomes, spreading to form loose tufts of tillers above ground. Leaves rolled in bud, shoots round. Leaf blades large, broadest in middle, dull green, variably hairy. Auricles present, usually small, ligule short. Sheaths open, not keeled, pale, variably hairy.

Agricultural Importance. Couch rarely occurs in any quantity in grassland; its habit of growth makes it essentially a grass of disturbed soil and open vegetation, and it is as an arable weed that it is important. Spread by seed may take place, but it is mainly due to its very great capacity for vegetative spread that it is so common. Control by cultivation usually involves the killing of the rhizomes by working them to the surface to dry out; repeated rotary cultivation, or the use of TCA or dalapon (p. 402), may also control. Found on all types of soils, but perhaps more serious on the heavier ones, owing to the greater difficulty of carrying out the necessary cultivations, particularly under wet conditions.

Agropyron pungens (Pers.) Roem. & Schult., with tough rachis, and **A. junceiforme** Löve, with very broad spike readily breaking at nodes, are sea coast plants of similar habit to couch; **A. caninum** (L.) Beauv., tufted couch or bearded wheat-grass, is a tufted non-creeping perennial with slender spikes and long-awned lemmas, found in woods.

Triticum, the wheat genus, is closely related to *Agropyron*, and hybrids are possible between the two genera. It differs in its broader glumes, larger caryopses and in the fact that only the lower flowers on the spikelet are fertile. *Secale*, the rye genus, with two florets only per spikelet and very narrow glumes, is also closely related. No wild species of these two genera occur in Britain. For wheat and rye as cultivated cereals, see Chapter XV.

Elymus has spikelets somewhat similar to those of *Agropyron*, but two spikelets are borne side by side, at each node of the rachis, instead of only one. **E. arenarius** L., sea lyme grass, is a seacoast perennial, with broad, very hard, harsh grey-blue leaves, stout rhizomes and large spike, sometimes planted on sand-dunes to control wind erosion.

HORDEUM. BARLEYS

Spikes with three spikelets at each node; spikelets one-flowered only. **H. sativum** Pers., the cultivated barleys, with large caryopsis and tough rachis, is dealt with in Chapter XV; the smaller wild species are known as barley-grasses.

Hordeum secalinum Schreb. (**H. pratense** Huds.), meadow barley-grass, is a tufted, short-lived perennial of moist grassland, rather local in distribution. It is neither palatable nor high-yielding, and is to be regarded as a weed. It has hairy, rolled leaves and small auricles; the spike is small, with the centre spikelet at each node fertile, the lateral ones male only, and shortly-stalked. The two glumes of each of the three spikelets are very narrow, bristle-like. The rachis is fragile—that is, the spike breaks up at maturity into single internodes to which the three spikelets remain attached. The 'seed' is thus a very complex structure consisting of a short length of rachis plus three complete, single-flowered spikelets, with the single caryopsis enclosed within the lemma of the central one. Its sharp-pointed and strongly-barbed character give it great powers of penetration, and it may cause irritation to grazing stock.

Hordeum murinum L., wall barley-grass, is a very common annual of disturbed waste ground, suburban roadsides, etc., very rarely becoming a farm weed. It is an annual, distinguished by its lighter-green leaves with larger auricles and its larger, broader spike, with the glumes of the central spikelet broad at the base, not bristle-like throughout. The spike breaks up in the same way as that of meadow barley-grass.

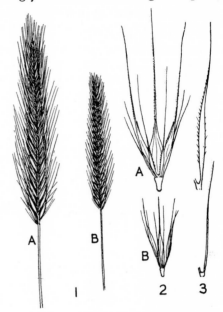

FIG. 157. Barley-grasses. 1, spike, ×½. 2, 'seed' (three spikelets attached to single internode of rachis), ×1. 3, glume of central fertile spikelet, ×3, of A, wall barley (*Hordeum murinum*), and B, meadow barley (*H. secalinum*).

AVENEAE

Avena, the oat genus, as now defined, includes only the cultivated and related wild oats, annuals with panicles of large, pendulous spikelets, with the florets surrounded by the many-nerved glumes. These are dealt with in Chapter XV. The following three genera of perennial oat-grasses were formerly included in *Avena*, but are clearly not very closely related to the cultivated oats, and are now kept separate.

ARRHENATHERUM

Spikelets erect, two-flowered, with few-nerved glumes. The generic name means 'male-awned'; the lower floret of the spikelet is male only, and is more conspicuously awned than the upper.

Arrhenatherum elatius (L.) J. & C. Presl.* Tall Oat-grass

A very common large grass, of little importance in present-day British agriculture. A tuberous variety is a serious arable weed of light soils.

Inflorescence. Erect panicles, up to 4 ft. high, usually rather dense. Spikelets 8-10 mm. long, with two unequal translucent glumes and two florets. Lower floret male only, lemma blunt rounded, with very strong geniculate awn arising almost at its base. Upper floret smaller,

* The name *Arrhenatherum avenaceum* Beauv., sometimes used, is not valid, since the species had already been named *Avena elatior* by Linnaeus, and the specific name (with the necessary change of gender) must be retained in the new genus.

hermaphrodite, and hence producing a caryopsis, lemma awnless or with short, fine, straight dorsal awn.

'*Seed.*' This consists of the whole spikelet apart from the glumes—that is, the empty lemma and palea of the lower floret are present as well as those of the upper floret, which contains the caryopsis. The 'seed' is thus unusually large, *c.* 10 mm. long, 150,000 to the pound, and bears two awns. It is difficult to clean and also to drill; in the U.S.A., where tall oat-grass is of greater importance than in Britain, some work has been carried out on the 'hulling' of the 'seed', so that the much smaller and more readily-drilled caryopsis only is sown.

Vegetative Characters. Perennial, tufted; tillers large, leaves rolled in bud, shoots round. Leaf-blades long, broadest in middle, dull green, variably hairy. No auricles, ligule long. Sheaths split, hairy, pale. Roots chrome yellow.

Agricultural Importance. Tall-oat is an early, high-yielding grass, but it is rather coarse and unpalatable, with somewhat bitter taste. It is very intolerant of hard grazing and treading. Although formerly included in some permanent pasture mixtures, it is unsuited to pasture conditions, and it is only in un-grazed turf, roadsides, etc., that it is common. If used agriculturally its proper place is in short leys for hay, on land too poor or too subject to drought and heat to support the better grasses; its high yield and rapid recovery from cutting are utilized in this way in France, and in parts of the U.S.A. too dry for timothy. Its use in Britain is now negligible.

FIG. 158. Tall oat-grass. A, panicle, ×¼. B, spikelet, ×3. C, 'seed' (whole spikelet without glumes), ×10.

In the tuberous form, var. *bulbosum*, onion couch, the lower internodes of the shoots are swollen to form short chains of bead-like corms

5-10 mm. in diameter. These corms readily break apart, and each is capable of producing a new plant. This onion-couch form of tall-oat may therefore become a serious weed if it is present in arable land, owing to the practical impossibility of removing such round, bead-like structures by any form of mechanical cultivation.

TRISETUM has all florets fertile; the lemmas are split at the top to form two slender, awn-like points which, together with the dorsal awn, give the 'three bristles' which is the meaning of the name.

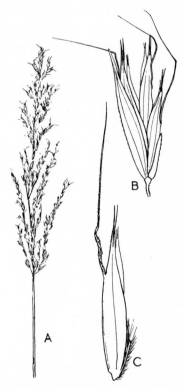

Trisetum flavescens (L.) Beauv., golden oat-grass, also called yellow oat-grass, is a palatable but low-yielding perennial of dry, especially calcareous, pastures. It has a panicle similar to that of tall-oat, but much smaller, and with smaller three- to four-flowered spikelets, becoming distinctly yellow as it ripens. Vegetatively it is most easily recognized by its slightly hairy, rolled leaves, without auricles, with downward-pointing hairs on the split, pale sheaths. It provides useful sheep-keep on upland pastures, and may make an important contribution to the yield of downland swards, but is not considered worth including in seeds-mixtures, and 'seed' is rarely available in Britain.

HELICTOTRICHON has larger spikelets, with all florets fertile, lemmas not two-pointed. **H. pratense** (L.) Pilger, meadow oat-grass, and **H. pubescens** (Huds.) Pilger, downy oat-grass, are two rather similar tufted perennials of minor importance, occurring in the same sort of semi-natural pasture as golden oat-grass,

FIG. 159. Golden oat-grass. A, panicle, × ½. B, spikelet, × 5. C, 'seed', × 10.

but less generally common. Downy oat-grass has more hairy leaves and is less strictly confined to dry conditions.

KOELERIA has small spikelets on a compact, almost spike-like, panicle. The glumes are rather short and the lemmas awnless. **Koeleria gracilis** Pers. (**K. cristata** (L.) Pers.), crested hair-grass, is another perennial of dry, calcareous pastures, of very minor agricultural importance.

DESCHAMPSIA has spikelets with two florets only, both fertile; plants perennial.

Deschampsia caespitosa (L.) Beauv., tussock grass or tufted hair-grass, is a very large, unpalatable, tufted perennial forming dense clumps. The panicles are very large, silvery, spreading, with very numerous small spikelets. The spikelets have two flowers, each with a blunt lemma, short basal awn and hairy rachilla. Leaf blades broad, hard, dark green, deeply ribbed on upper surface.

Tussock grass is a serious weed of rather poor pastures on heavy or badly-drained soils; it establishes readily from seed and is extremely unpalatable, so that, unless prevented by hard grazing or cutting at an early stage, the seedlings quickly develop into large tufts and ultimately into the characteristic tussocks or 'hassocks'. If plants are allowed to reach this stage they are far too tough to be grazed off by any stock, and may even be impossible to mow closely; ploughing and reseeding is then the only method of improving the pasture, and even that may be impeded by the difficulty of ploughing large tussocks under.

D. flexuosa (L.) Trin., wavy hair-grass, is a smaller grass with panicles only half the size of those of tussock grass. The panicle branches are flexuous (whence the common name); the comparatively few spikelets are slightly larger than those of tussock-grass, and the awns longer and stouter. Vegetatively, wavy hair-grass is very different; it is a low-growing, loosely-tufted or slightly-creeping perennial with permanently-folded, bristle-like, short leaves. It, also, is very unpalatable and of no value for grazing, but is confined to acid hill and heath land, and does not invade sown pastures.

The genus *Aira*, in which the *Deschampsia* species were formerly included, is now regarded as covering only annual grasses with rather similar spikelets; of these, *Aira praecox* L. (*c.* 6 in. high, panicle compact, very early) and *A. caryophylla* L. (*c.* 1 ft., panicle spreading) are common but unimportant heath grasses.

HOLCUS has spikelets of two florets, the upper male only, the lower hermaphrodite (the reverse of the position in *Arrhenatherum*).

Holcus lanatus L.   Yorkshire Fog

A common and important perennial weed of grassland, and a common impurity of grass seeds.

Inflorescence. A spreading panicle, usually rather dense, but very variable in general appearance and in colour, which varies from green through almost white to pink. Spikelets *c.* 5 mm., with two florets almost completely hidden by the broad, keeled, hairy glumes. Florets small, lemmas half length of glumes, lower floret awnless, hermaphrodite and producing caryopsis, upper male only, with dorsal hooked awn, usually hardly extending beyond glumes.

'*Seed.*' Occurs in two states: (1) the whole spikelet including glumes giving a fairly large but proportionately very light 'seed' found as an impurity of rye-grass and similar seeds; (2) rubbed-out, as the caryopsis enclosed only in the short, ovate, shiny brown lemma and palea, with,

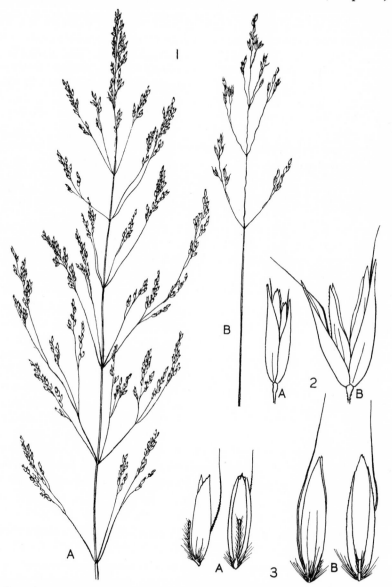

FIG. 160. Hair-grasses. 1, panicle, × ⅓. 2, spikelet, × 3. 3, 'seed' in side and ventral views, × 10, of A, tufted hair-grass (tussock grass), and B, wavy hair-grass.

or more commonly, without, the narrower, awned, empty lemma of the upper male floret; this stage is more commonly found as an impurity in samples of smaller grass seeds, such as timothy. Scheduled as injurious weed seed under the Seed Regulations, 1922, but not in current list.

Vegetative Characters. A loosely-tufted perennial, densely soft-hairy. Leaves rolled in bud, shoot round. Leaf-blades dull grey-green; auricles absent, ligule long; sheaths open, keeled, pale with conspicuous red veins.

Agricultural Importance. A common but unpalatable grass, usually only grazed when very young, and thus often left to form conspicuous tufts, which, however, tend to die away in winter, and rarely reach very large size. Tolerant of acidity and of rather low fertility, and may spread rapidly if allowed to seed owing to under-grazing or to late hay-cuts; it is one of the commonest grass weeds of poorly-managed long leys, and is present in small quantity in all but the very best of old pastures.

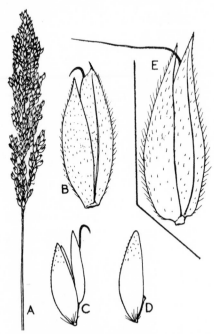

Although Yorkshire fog is to be regarded as a weed under lowland conditions, it has been used in temporary pioneer mixtures for mountain reclamation under extreme conditions, as giving rapid establishment to provide a sward somewhat better than the original vegetation, at low cost.

Fig. 161. Yorkshire fog. A, panicle, × ½. B, spikelet, × 10. C, spikelet without glumes, × 10. D, fertile floret only, × 10 ('seed' may be B, C, or D). E, spikelet of creeping soft-grass, × 10.

Holcus mollis L., creeping soft-grass, is primarily a woodland plant, but may occasionally become an arable weed. It is distinguished in the flowering stage by its larger, more acute glumes and by the long, nearly straight awn on the lemma of the upper male flower standing conspicuously out beyond them. Vegetatively it is distinguished by its creeping habit, with stout rhizomes and long, sprawling surface stems; the leaf-sheaths are less conspicuously red-veined, and less hairy than Yorkshire fog, but with a conspicuous ring of long hairs at the nodes. A common plant in rather dry woodland and in hedges, rare and usually unimportant in grassland, but may become a difficult arable weed of light land, behaving in the same way as couch. 'Seed' is not usually found as an impurity.

ANTHOXANTHUM has spikelets which can be regarded as basically three-flowered, but only the uppermost is fertile, the two lower being represented only by their lemmas.

Anthoxanthum odoratum L. Sweet Vernal Grass

A common but unpalatable, low-yielding grass, frequent in rather poor pastures.

Inflorescence. A rather lax spike-like panicle; spikelets *c*. 8 mm. long with unequal, pointed, thin, translucent, yellowish glumes, enclosing a pair of short, blunt, empty lemmas (representing the reduced, sterile lower florets) which are densely covered with dark brown hairs, and bear dark brown awns, that on the upper one geniculate and basal, and the other straight and dorsal. Between these two extra lemmas, and hidden by them, is the fertile floret, with short, shiny, awnless lemma and small palea. Two stamens only are present, and no lodicules; the flower is protogynous and the stigmas emerge at the apex of the spikelet.

'Seed.' The whole spikelet above the glumes is set free as the 'seed', which thus consists of the caryopsis enclosed not only by its lemma and palea, but also by the two awned, hairy, extra lemmas. It is thus very distinct and easily recognized, but is not now normally in commerce in Britain, and rarely occurs as an impurity.

Vegetative Characters. A loosely-tufted perennial, with rather dark-green, somewhat hairy foliage. Leaves rolled in bud, shoot round. Leaf-blades soft; auricles absent, ligule long; sheaths split, pale, hairy, with a conspicuous tuft of rather long white hairs at juncture of sheath and blade.

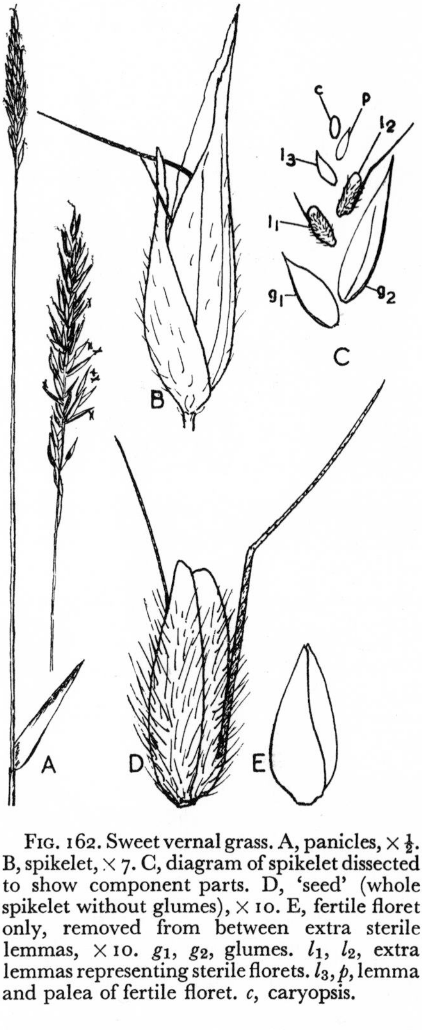

Agricultural Importance. Sweet vernal is a very common perennial occurring under a wide range of conditions, and tolerating drought and low fertility. It derives its common name from its early flowering and its sweet scent when dry; this

FIG. 162. Sweet vernal grass. A, panicles, × ½. B, spikelet, × 7. C, diagram of spikelet dissected to show component parts. D, 'seed' (whole spikelet without glumes), × 10. E, fertile floret only, removed from between extra sterile lemmas, × 10. g_1, g_2, glumes. l_1, l_2, extra lemmas representing sterile florets. l_3, p, lemma and palea of fertile floret. c, caryopsis.

scent is, however, due to the presence of coumarin (cf. melilot, p. 168) which is bitter in taste and makes the grass unpalatable. This, combined with its low yield, has resulted in sweet vernal losing its former reputation as a useful grass; it is never now sown in Britain.

PHALARIS resembles *Anthoxanthum* in structure of spikelet, but the two empty lemmas, representing the basal sterile florets, are reduced to small scales, and the usual three stamens and two lodicules are present in the fertile floret. The two genera are usually placed in a distinct tribe, the PHALARIDEAE, but *Anthoxanthum* shows close resemblances to the typical members of the *Aveneae*.

Phalaris canariensis L., canary grass, is a Mediterranean annual sometimes grown in England as an arable, cereal-like crop for bird-seed. It has broad, oval, spike-like panicles up to 5 cm. long, with large, very

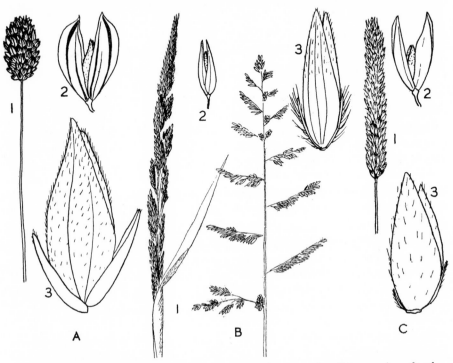

FIG. 163. *Phalaris* species. 1, panicle, × ½. 2, spikelet, × 3. 3, 'seed' (caryopsis enclosed in lemma and palea, plus two narrow sterile lemmas), × 10, of A, canary grass, *P. canariensis*; B, reed canary grass, *P. arundinacea* (panicle shown in closed and open states); C, *P. tuberosa*.

deeply-keeled green and white-striped glumes, completely enclosing the three florets of each spikelet. The threshed 'seed', as used for bird-seed, consists of the caryopsis enclosed in the hardened lemma and palea, pointed oval, *c.* 5 mm. long, shiny but shortly-hairy, with the small, glabrous, empty lemmas at the base.

P. arundinacea L., reed canary grass, is a coarse perennial of wet places, creeping by rhizomes. It has a much larger, irregular, slightly-spreading panicle, with smaller spikelets and seed, and hairy empty lemmas. Common in wet lowland conditions in Britain, dying down to ground-level in winter, and not considered of agricultural value here, but sown on wet land in the U.S.A., where a number of strains have been developed.

P. tuberosa L. is a species of Mediterranean origin, but developed and much cultivated in Australia, where several strains have been selected. It is a large, glabrous perennial with broad, succulent leaves, somewhat resembling timothy in appearance, making considerable growth in winter and perhaps meriting consideration in the milder parts of England. Readily identified by the anthocyanin in the sap of the leaf-sheaths— young shoots 'bleed' when crushed; and by the stout cylindrical panicle, intermediate in appearance between *P. canariensis* and *P. arundinacea*. Hybrids with the latter species have been developed at Aberystwyth, and may be of value in British agriculture (*S.230*).

AGROSTIDEAE

AGROSTIS. BENT GRASSES

Inflorescence a spreading panicle, spikelets one-flowered, small; glumes narrow, pointed; 'seed' very small, consisting of caryopsis enclosed in small palea and round-backed awnless or dorsally-awned lemma; rachilla not usually continued above lemma base.

Several similar species, each showing considerable variation, are commonly found in Britain. All are grasses of low agricultural value, some useful under hill-grazing conditions, but all, under lowland conditions, are important primarily as weeds, mainly in grassland, but sometimes in arable. They are therefore conveniently considered together.

Inflorescence. A delicate, more or less spreading panicle, with slender branches. Spikelets one-flowered, very small, *c.* 3 mm.

'Seed.' The smallest of all British grass 'seeds', usually recognizable on size alone; *c.* 2 mm. long, 5-6 million to pound. Round-backed, narrow oval, usually hairless, awned only in *A. canina*. Not sown, except for lawns and sports turf.

Vegetative Characters. Perennials, widely-creeping by rhizomes or stolons; low-growing. Leaves rolled in bud, shoots round. Leaf-blades linear, acute, ribbed above, thin, dull. Auricles absent, ligule variable, sheaths split, slender, glabrous, green or sometimes reddish.

Agricultural Importance. The bents are all low-yielding grasses, with a large proportion of creeping stem, starting growth very late in spring. They are very tolerant of low fertility and, being creeping, are very aggressive when once established. Invasion by bent grasses is thus one of the commonest causes of degeneration of leys (see Chapter XVII). Bent is also extremely common in permanent pasture; in the poorer types it is the dominant grass, and only in the very best old pastures is the proportion of bent negligible. Under extreme hill and mountain pasture conditions the bent grasses are of value; their hardiness and winter-greenness and relatively high palatability make them preferable to such grasses as Nardus and Molinia. The larger and coarser forms of bent, particularly those with well-developed rhizomes, may become arable weeds. Although they are not usually as serious a problem in arable crops as couch, it must be remembered that they, unlike couch, are also capable of persisting and spreading in grassland. It is very important,

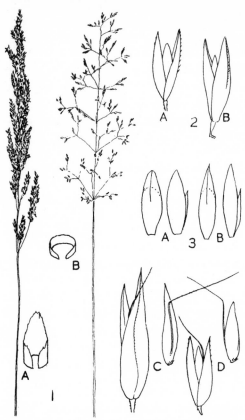

Fig. 164. Bent grasses. 1, panicle, ×½, and diagram of shape of ligule. 2, spikelet, × 10. 3, 'seed', dorsal view, and side view partially separated to show palea, × 10 of A, creeping bent (*Agrostis stolonifera*), and B, fine bent (*A. tenuis*). C, spikelet and 'seed' of bristle bent (*A. setacea*), × 10; D, of velvet bent (*A. canina*).

therefore, that arable land overrun with bent should be thoroughly cleaned before sowing down to a ley.

DISTINCTION BETWEEN DIFFERENT AGROSTIS SPECIES

A. stolonifera L.   Creeping Bent, Fiorin

Stoloniferous, with panicle contracted in fruit, awnless; ligule long, rounded. Common in grassland, occasionally as an arable weed. Rarely, if ever, sown.

A. gigantea Roth. (**A. nigra** With.), Black Bent, Red-top

Rhizomatous, panicle always spreading, awnless, leaves broad, coarse, ligule long blunt. Mainly an arable weed; occasionally in grassland.

Sown in the U.S.A. on wet acid soils; not used in Britain. (These two species have sometimes been grouped under the name of **A. alba.**)

A. tenuis Sibth., Brown Top, Fine Bent

Short rhizomes or stolons, panicle always spreading, awnless, ligule short. Common in poor grassland, especially on hills and mountains. Seed produced in New Zealand, sown in Britain for lawns.

A. canina L. Velvet Bent

Leaves narrow, ligule pointed. Lemma awned, palea minute. Subsp. *canina* stoloniferous, in wet lowland grass; subsp. *montana* rhizomatous, in dry hill pasture, sometimes used in lawns.

A. setacea Curt., bristle bent, is a very distinct plant of acid heath and moorland in S.W. England; closely-tufted, not creeping, leaves resembling sheep's fescue, panicle slender, lemma awned, palea minute. Negligible agricultural value.

Gastridium ventricosum (Gouan) Schinz & Thell., nitgrass, is an annual somewhat resembling *Agrostis*, but with dense panicle and glumes longer and swollen at base. Occasionally found as arable weed in S. England.

Ammophila arenaria (L.) Link., marram grass, is a much larger grass with large, dense panicle, very stout rhizomes and large, stiff, inrolled leaves. A valuable sand-binding grass, often planted (not sown) to prevent movement of sea-coast dunes.

PHLEUM. TIMOTHY OR CAT'S-TAIL

Panicles dense, spike-like, cylindrical; spikelets one-flowered; glumes equal, stiff, keeled; lemma short, blunt, awnless.

Phleum pratense L. Timothy

A high-yielding, palatable perennial for moist conditions, important and frequently sown in leys.

Inflorescence. Dense, cylindrical, spike-like panicle, up to 15 cm. long; spikelets *c.* 3 mm., with glumes square-topped, but keel extended as long, stiff, awn-like point; keel fringed with stiff hairs. The single floret is only about half the length of the glumes and completely hidden by them.

'*Seed.*' The single floret threshes out of the glumes, and the 'seed' thus consists of the caryopsis enclosed in the thin, blunt, oval, silvery lemma and palea. No rachilla is present. The 'seed' is shorter and rounder (*c.* 2 mm.) than most grass 'seeds', running freely and readily cleaned; 1 million to pound. The lemma and palea are rather readily rubbed off, exposing the brown pericarp, and most seed samples contain a proportion of such 'brown seed'; germination is not affected by this shelling-out, and the presence of 'brown seed' is no disadvantage, except for seed that is to be stored for some years, although a very large percentage in a sample may be an indication of old or badly-machined seed.

Vegetative Characters. A large, tufted, glabrous, rather succulent perennial. Leaves rolled in bud, shoots round. Leaf-blades broadest near middle, thick in texture, ribbed above, light grey-green. Auricles absent, ligule short obtusely-pointed; sheaths split, not keeled, usually pale. Base of tillers often bulbous, due to formation of haplocorm, i.e. swollen lowest internode.

Agricultural Importance. Timothy is a high-yielding, palatable grass for moist soils of medium or high fertility. It is sometimes sown alone, as in the Scottish timothy meadows, primarily for hay. It is not aggressive as a young plant and, although establishment alone is fairly good, it establishes poorly in competition with the rye-grasses, and particularly under grazing conditions the proportion of timothy in the sward resulting from the sowing of a timothy-rye-grass mixture may be very low (see Chapter XVII). For this reason, timothy-meadow fescue mixtures are to be preferred, as these two species do not compete seriously with each other. Timothy is a late-flowering species, and usually late to start growth in spring, but summer and autumn production is high.

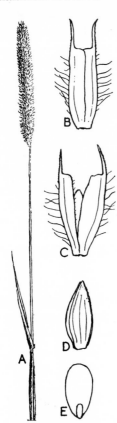

FIG. 165. Timothy, *Phleum pratense.* A, panicle, × ¼. B, spikelet, × 7. C, the same with glumes separated to expose 'seed'. D, 'seed', usual state with caryopsis enclosed in lemma and palea, × 10. E, 'brown seed' state, caryopsis only, × 10.

Origin. Timothy as usually grown is a hexaploid plant with forty-two chromosomes in the somatic cells. Gregor and Sansom (*J. Genetics*, 1930) found that a plant indistinguishable from the hexaploid timothy could be obtained if chromosome doubling took place in a sterile triploid hybrid produced by crossing two smaller species *P. nodosum* L. and *P. commutatum* Gand. *P. nodosum* is a common lowland pasture species (see below, p. 339) with fourteen chromosomes, i.e. diploid; *P. commutatum* a form of alpine timothy occurring in Britain only in the mountains of N. England and Scotland, with twenty-eight chromosomes, i.e. tetraploid. There is thus good reason to believe that *P. pratense*, the cultivated timothy, is a synthetic species, an allopolyploid comparable to *Brassica napus* (p. 124). The time and place of its origin is not known, but it appears possible that it may have been in the seventeenth century in N. America, where *P. commutatum* is widespread, *P. nodosum* being introduced from England. It was first recorded in the seventeenth century in New Hampshire, and later introduced into Maryland by Timothy Hansen about

1720. Introduced to England with the name 'timothy' in 1760, and shortly after into continental Europe, it quickly came into general cultivation.

Varieties. Commercial forms of timothy are upright, relatively early types, suited to short-ley conditions only. Commercial *American* is, under British conditions, stemmy and susceptible to rust; *Scotch* is generally superior and more persistent. Aberystwyth *S.352* is an early high-yielding hay type, less competitive than *S.51* and best suited to simple mixtures. The Aberystwyth *S.51* is a very distinct hay type, with long, yellowish-green leaves, later than Commercial, but producing better aftermath. *S.48* is the Aberystwyth intermediate pasture type, shorter and later-flowering than the hay varieties, denser and more leafy. (For *S.50* see *P. nodosum*, below.) Numerous other British and European varieties also exist.

Phleum bertolonii DC. (**P. nodosum** auct). Small Timothy, Cat's-tail

This diploid species is similar to the hexaploid timothy, but much lower-growing, with smaller panicle and narrower leaves, and slightly smaller 'seed'. It is strongly-creeping, with spreading stems below and above ground, and distinctly more drought-resistant than large timothy. It is found commonly in well-grazed pastures on rather thin soils, such as the lower hill pastures of fairly high fertility. Very persistent under grazing, but not high-yielding.

The Aberystwyth variety *S.50* is the main form of this species of which seed is available; it is recommended for long grazing leys and permanent pasture mixtures only, as its comparatively low yield and rhizomatous habit make it unsuitable for short leys. The seed yield is low, and threshing sometimes difficult, so that the seed price tends to be high, usually nearly double that of ordinary hexaploid timothy.

The diploid and hexaploid timothy species do not usually cross with each other.

ALOPECURUS. FOXTAIL GRASSES

Alopecurus differs from *Phleum* in its softer glumes usually joined at the base and shed as part of the 'seed', and in the lemma being awned, and palea and lodicules absent, flowers protogynous.

Alopecurus pratensis L.   Meadow Foxtail

A palatable early grass of moist, old grassland, rarely sown in leys.

Inflorescence. A dense, spike-like panicle 5-10 cm. long, more tapering than that of timothy. Spikelets ovate, flat, hairy, *c.* 5 mm., consisting of a pair of equal keeled glumes, joined at base, and enclosing a single floret. Lemma with long, almost basal, awn extending well beyond tip of glumes.

'*Seed.*' The whole spikelet drops entire; the seed is thus large, *c.* 5 mm., but light, *c.* $\frac{3}{4}$ million to pound, hairy and awned, and thus of a type difficult to clean satisfactorily, not flowing readily over sieves, and with empty spikelets, in which the caryopsis has failed to develop, difficult to separate from full ones.

Vegetative Characters. A loosely-tufted, rather large perennial spreading slightly by very short rhizomes. Leaves rolled in bud, shoot round, glabrous. Leaf-blades long, dark green, ribbed above, dull below. Auricles absent, ligule medium length, square-topped; sheaths split, somewhat ribbed, base of old sheaths becoming dull purplish-brown.

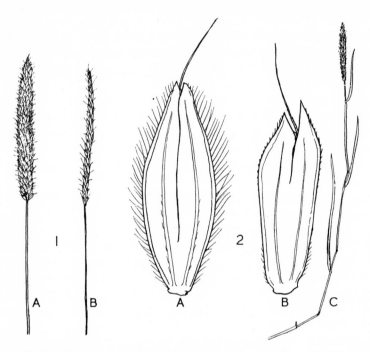

Fig. 166. Foxtail grasses. 1, panicle, × ½. 2, 'seed' (whole spikelet), × 10, of A, meadow foxtail (*Alopecurus pratensis*), and B, slender foxtail (*A. myosuroides*). C, fertile tiller and panicle of floating foxtail (*A. geniculatus*), × ½.

Agricultural Importance. A palatable, moderately high-yielding, very early perennial of moist grassland of medium to high fertility; not very tolerant of hard spring grazing and found more commonly in fields used mainly for hay. For this purpose and type of land it is a valuable grass, and to be welcomed when it volunteers in old grassland, but the difficulties involved in establishing it largely preclude its use in leys. Not only is the seed difficult to clean, and therefore usually of low germination and purity, but the percentage establishment is low, *c.* 20 per cent., and seedlings grow slowly and suffer severely in competition with other more aggressive plants. Meadow foxtail rarely makes much contribution to the sward if included in a mixed ley; in the U.S.A., where it is of rather greater importance, it is usually sown alone. A further disadvantage is that seed production in Britain presents considerable difficulties, mainly owing to attack by gall midges. A leafy variety *S.55* has been bred at Aberystwyth, but on this account it has not been found possible to distribute it generally. The limited amount of commercial seed coming on the market is imported, mainly from Finland.

Alopecurus geniculatus L., floating foxtail, is a small, shortly-creeping perennial of very wet lowland grassland, with culms conspicuously angled at the nodes (geniculate=kneed) and small greyish cylindrical panicles *c.* 3 cm. long in May. Palatable, but too low in yield to be of any real value. Hybrids with *A. pratensis* exist.

Alopecurus myosuroides Huds. (**A. agrestis** L.), slender foxtail, black grass, is an annual arable weed, usually germinating in autumn, and forming a compact tuft of narrow leaves with panicles up to about 18 in. high in May and June. The panicles are considerably more slender than those of meadow foxtail, with relatively few large, oblong spikelets, and setting abundant seed. The 'seed' is the whole spikelet, similar to that of meadow foxtail in structure, but narrower, heavier and almost hairless.

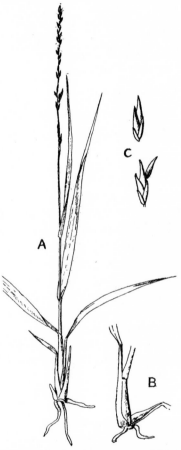

Slender foxtail is rather local in its distribution, but in those areas where it is prevalent it is, on heavy soils, one of the most serious weed grasses, its abundant early seeding before cereals are fit to harvest resulting in very heavy contamination of the soil. Control is by continued cultivations, either in root crops or fallow; seed does not normally remain dormant in the soil more than two years.

It is not an important weed of grassland, but may persist in seed crops and be an impurity of rye-grass and fescue. Scheduled *injurious weed seed* under 1961 Regulations.

DANTHONIEAE

Molinia caerulea (L.) Moench, called purple moor grass, but usually known by its generic name, is a large tufted perennial of wet peat. The inflorescence is a rather narrow panicle *c.* 3 ft. high, with few-flowered spikelets *c.* 6 mm. long,

FIG. 167. Purple moor-grass, *Molinia caerulea*. A, flowering shoot, × ¼. B, swollen base of stem, × ½. C, spikelets, × 2.

often purplish in colour; anthers and stigmas purple. Culms with very long upper internode, and lower part swollen. Leaves broad, thin, dry, dying off

341

FIG. 168. Heath grass, *Sieglingia decumbens*. A, panicle, × ½. B, spikelet, × 3. C, 'seed', ventral view, × 10.

brown in winter and blades deciduous. Ligule replaced by fringe of hairs.

A very common plant of wetter peaty areas, often dominant on mountain grassland; palatable only in extremely young stage and thus of very low grazing value.

Sieglingia decumbens (L.) Bernh. (**Triodia decumbens** (L.) Beauv.), heath grass, more commonly known as *Triodia*, has a smaller panicle than Molinia, with longer glumes and three-cleft, blunt tip to lemmas; flowers cleistogamous. A tufted perennial, smaller than Molinia, common in mountain grassland but rarely in any great quantity. Fairly palatable and usually kept well grazed down.

NARDEAE

Nardus stricta L., mat grass, is a common perennial of mountain and moorland, not closely related to other British grasses. It has a one-sided spike (*c.* 1 ft. high) with one single-flowered spikelet at each node; the glumes are reduced to minute scales at the base of the sharply-pointed lemma. Style single, no lodicules, protogynous.

Nardus forms densely-packed tufts, with tough, persistent sheaths, making tillers stiff, comb-like; leaf-blades bristle-like, very wiry. Plant rather pale grey-green, leaves dying off almost white. Often abundant in almost pure stand on damp, thin peat; very unpalatable and of very low grazing value, but provides some winter keep by sheep eating the 'heart' of plant.

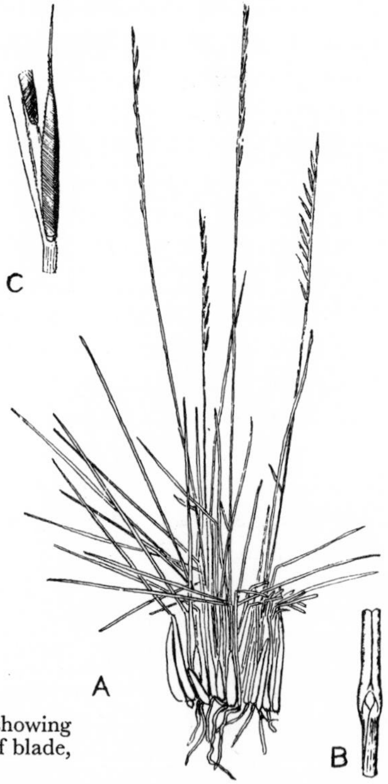

C

A

B

FIG. 169. Mat-grass, *Nardus stricta*. A, plant showing tufted habit, × ½. B, ligule and base of rolled leaf blade, × 3. C, spikelet, × 4.

Illustrated Key for Identification of Common Grasses in Vegetative Stage

The key includes only the species most commonly found as constituents of lowland grassland swards. The illustrations for each species include a single vegetative tiller, or a group of tillers; a single leaf; an enlarged view of the junction of leaf-sheath and blade; and diagrammatic transverse sections of leaf-blade and shoot.

LEAVES BRISTLE-LIKE

LEAVES EXPANDED, FOLDED IN BUD

UPPER SURFACE RIBBED

AURICLES PRESENT, BASE RED

AURICLES ABSENT, BASE YELLOW

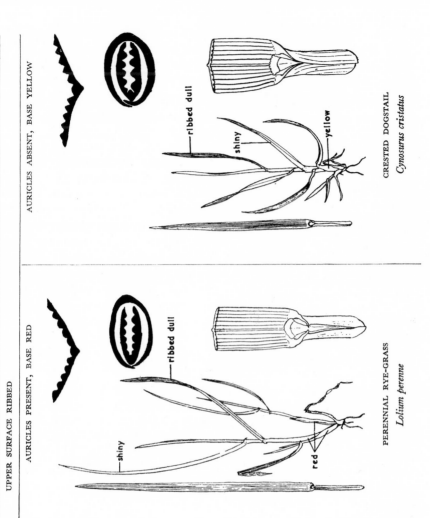

RED FESCUE
Festuca rubra

PERENNIAL RYE-GRASS
Lolium perenne

CRESTED DOGSTAIL
Cynosurus cristatus

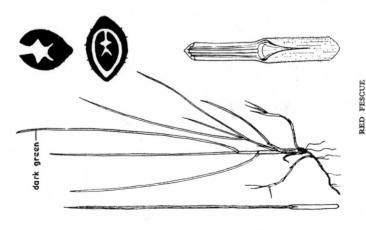

LEAVES EXPANDED, FOLDED IN BUD

UPPER SURFACE NOT RIBBED

ONE LINE MOTOR TISSUE

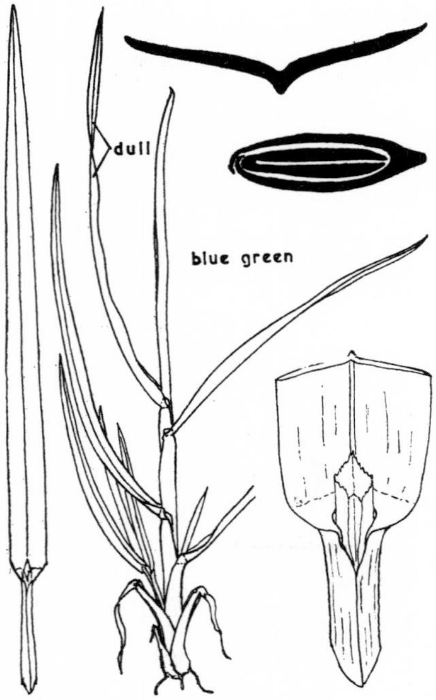

TWO LINES MOTOR TISSUE

PERENNIAL, RHIZOMES PRESENT

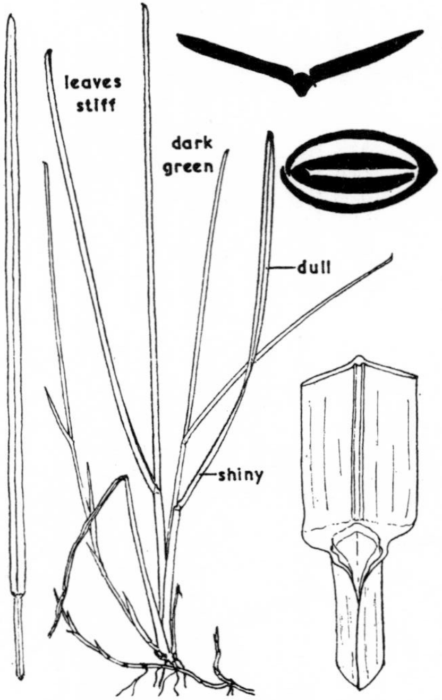

PERENNIAL, STOLONS OFTEN PRESENT

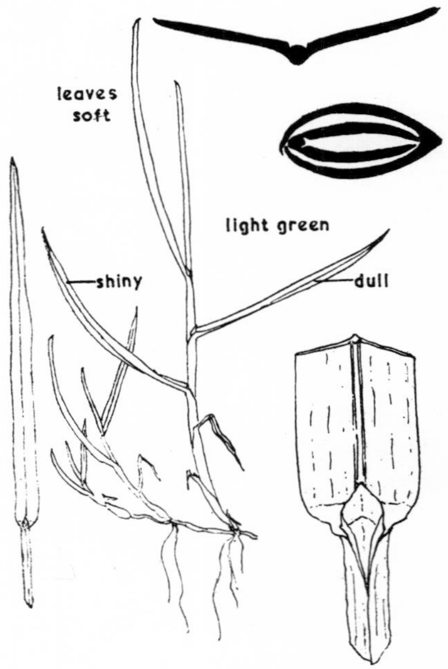

leaves soft

light green

dull

shiny

ROUGH-STALKED MEADOW-GRASS
Poa trivialis

dark green

leaves stiff

dull

shiny

SMOOTH-STALKED MEADOW-GRASS
Poa pratensis

blue green

dull

COCKSFOOT
Dactylis glomerata

344

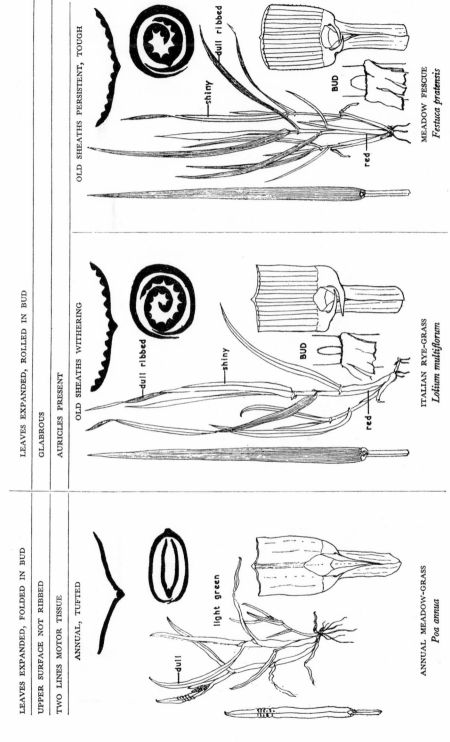

LEAVES EXPANDED, ROLLED IN BUD

GLABROUS

AURICLES PRESENT

OLD SHEATHS PERSISTENT, TOUGH

dull ribbed

shiny

BUD

red

MEADOW FESCUE
Festuca pratensis

OLD SHEATHS WITHERING

dull ribbed

shiny

BUD

red

ITALIAN RYE-GRASS
Lolium multiflorum

LEAVES EXPANDED, FOLDED IN BUD

UPPER SURFACE NOT RIBBED

TWO LINES MOTOR TISSUE

ANNUAL, TUFTED

light green

dull

ANNUAL MEADOW-GRASS
Poa annua

M

345

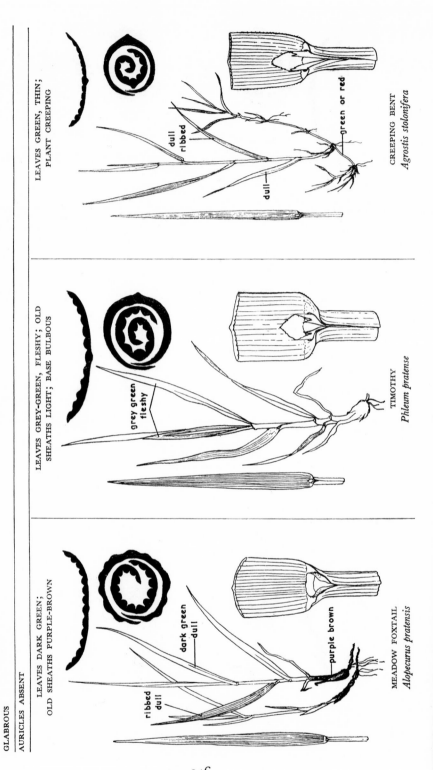

LEAVES DARK GREEN;
OLD SHEATHS PURPLE-BROWN

ribbed
dull

dark green
dull

purple brown

MEADOW FOXTAIL
Alopecurus pratensis

LEAVES GREY-GREEN, FLESHY; OLD
SHEATHS LIGHT; BASE BULBOUS

grey green
fleshy

TIMOTHY
Phleum pratense

LEAVES GREEN, THIN;
PLANT CREEPING

dull
ribbed

dull

green or red

CREEPING BENT
Agrostis stolonifera

HAIRY

AURICLES PRESENT

AURICLES ABSENT

SHEATH OPEN

SHEATH RED-VEINED

TUFT OF LONG HAIRS AT BASE OF LEAF-BLADE

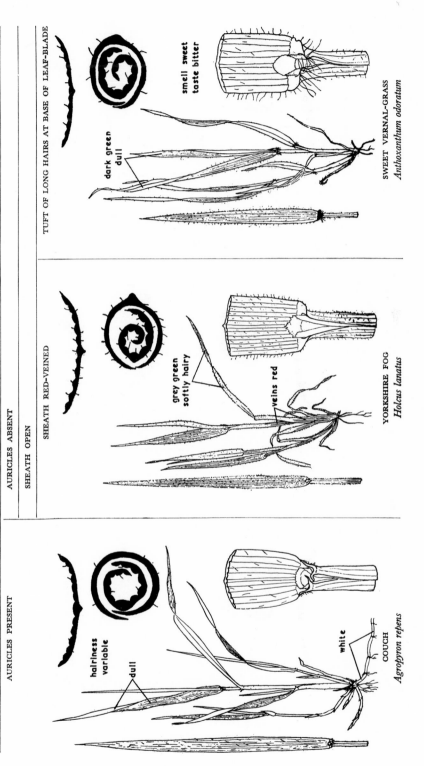

hairiness
variable

dull

white

COUCH
Agropyron repens

grey green
softly hairy

veins red

YORKSHIRE FOG
Holcus lanatus

smell sweet
taste bitter

dark green
dull

SWEET VERNAL-GRASS
Anthoxanthum odoratum

LEAVES EXPANDED, ROLLED IN BUD

HAIRY

AURICLES ABSENT

SHEATH OPEN	LONG REFLEXED HAIRS ON SHEATH	SHEATH CLOSED
HAIRS FEW, LEAVES LARGE		

hairiness
variable

dull

Base of
bulbous
form

roots
yellow

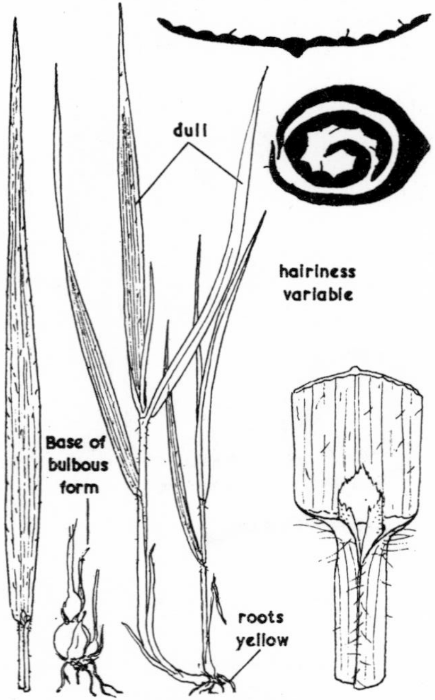

TALL OAT-GRASS
Arrhenatherum elatius

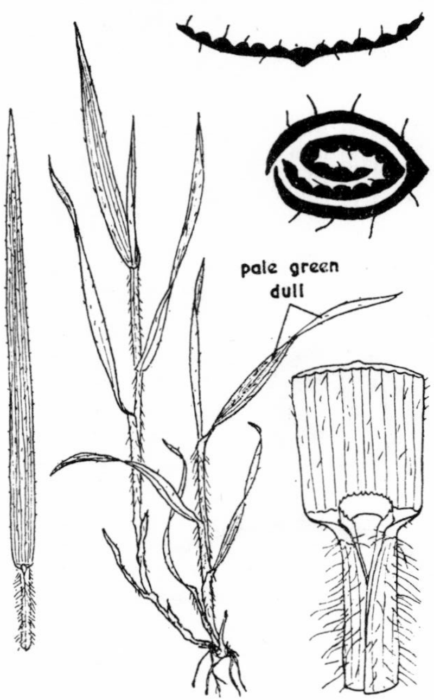

pale green
dull

GOLDEN OAT-GRASS
Trisetum flavescens

grey green
dull

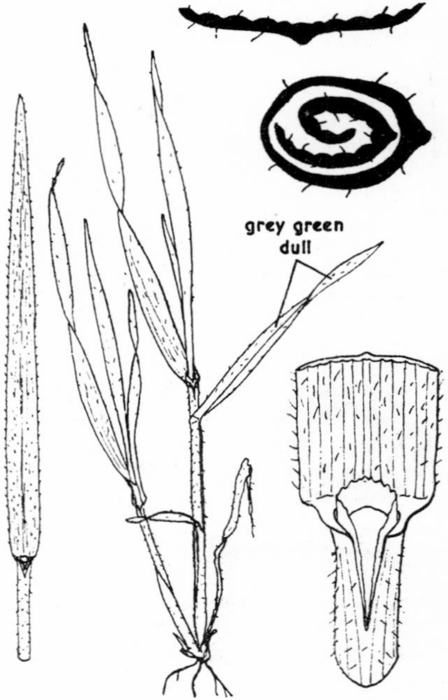

SOFT BROME
Bromus mollis

348

Chapter XVII

GRASSLAND

TYPES OF VEGETATION

THE type of natural vegetation found in any area depends partly on climatic conditions, partly on soil conditions and partly on biotic conditions. Biotic conditions are those produced by other organisms, and here the effects of grazing animals are particularly important. Grasses show a very wide range of adaptability to different climatic and soil conditions, and, as has been pointed out in discussing their mode of growth, are usually very tolerant of grazing. Their usually low growth, with vegetative stems and buds at or near ground-level, while making them resistant to damage by grazing, at the same time makes them susceptible to shading-out by taller-growing plants. Grassland is consequently only found where conditions do not allow of the establishment of a dense cover of shrubs or trees. The main natural grassland areas of prairie and steppe occur where conditions are too dry for tree growth, but all gradations exist from semi-desert through grassland with scattered trees to open woodland. Mountain grassland also occurs above the level of tree growth. In these cases, grassland is the ecological climax, and does not tend to be replaced by other types of vegetation. In other areas, however, grassland is not the climax, and is only found because the woodland climax vegetation is prevented from establishing itself. This is true of almost all grasslands in Britain except the mountain areas; in Britain the natural climax is forest, and grassland is only maintained as such by grazing, preventing the normal succession through bushes and scrub to woodland.

TYPES OF GRASSLAND

Grassland can thus be divided into three types: natural, semi-natural and cultivated. True natural grassland is, as has been said, of limited occurrence in Britain, and even those areas where it is a true climax are considerably influenced by grazing. Semi-natural grasslands in Britain include rough grazing and hill land, where the vegetation reflects largely the climatic and soil conditions modified only by the effect of the grazing animal, and in some areas by periodic burning. Cultivated grassland is more directly controlled by the farmer; not only is grazing more precisely managed, but soil conditions can be altered by manuring and drainage, and at least in temporary leys the main species present can be decided by choice of seeds mixture. Clearly no hard and fast line can be drawn between these types, and old pasture, even although originally sown, may be regarded as semi-natural if it receives little attention. The plants present in such old pastures reflect the climatic and soil conditions and the effect of grazing, and may bear little relation to the species originally sown.

The greater part of the grassland of Britain, other than short leys, can thus be regarded as semi-natural, in that, although maintained as grassland mainly by grazing, the composition of the sward is determined largely by climate (here mainly a function of height above sea-level) and soil. Three main types can be distinguished: mountain and hill grassland, downs, and lowland grassland.

Mountain and hill grassland occurs mainly above 1,000 ft. on acid soils with high rainfall. Leguminous plants are usually absent, and only grasses tolerant of acid conditions and low soil fertility are present. Bents (*Agrostis* spp.) and small fescues are the most general species, partially or wholly replaced by Molinia on deep peats and by Nardus on thin peat or damp mineral soil. Plants other than grasses may be common; on the thin peats the heathers *Erica* and *Calluna*, and deer-grass (*Trichophorum caespitosum*) with gorse (*Ulex* spp.) on lower slopes, and bracken on deeper soils.

Downs occupy a comparatively small area, and are chalk or limestone uplands with fairly low rainfall. The porous subsoil results in relatively rapid leaching, and the soils are thin, but the general level of fertility is higher than that of the typical hill soils. Bents and small fescues are present together with such grasses as golden, meadow, and downy oat grass, crested dog's-tail and others. Small legumes such as birdsfoot trefoil are usually common. In less well-grazed areas the less palatable heath false brome and upright brome may become dominant.

Lowland grassland varies considerably in type, but in general may be regarded as a series extending from *Agrostis*—dominant on the poorer soils, through varying proportions of bent and perennial rye-grass to a rye-grass-dominant sward with abundant white clover on the better soils. Cocksfoot, timothy, the larger fescues and the meadow-grasses may be associated with the bent and rye-grass of the better swards; Yorkshire fog, dog's-tail and sweet vernal with the poorer ones. In wet areas of high fertility, meadow foxtail and *Glyceria* may be important. A wide range of plants other than grasses may be present as weeds.

TEMPORARY GRASSLAND, LEYS

The initial composition of a ley can be controlled by the choice of seeds mixture sown, and it is thus possible to produce leys containing the grasses and clovers most suited to the particular purposes for which the leys are designed. Usually the higher-yielding, more palatable species only are included. These require high fertility and appropriate management, and if these conditions are not provided, tend to be replaced by other species of which seeds are already present in the soil, or which spread in from outside. These replacing species will be ones better adapted to the existing soil and other conditions, and there is always a tendency therefore for a ley, whatever its original composition, to approximate as it becomes older to the local type of semi-natural grassland. This change of composition can be delayed by careful management and suitable manuring, and should not normally be of very great extent during the first three years of the life of the ley. Leys of up to three years' duration provide, therefore, a very valuable type of grassland, of which the composition can be comparatively readily controlled.

COMPOSITION OF LEYS

A discussion of the utilization and value of leys belongs rather to husbandry than to botany, but some consideration may be given here to the types of ley available. The characters and value of the individual grass and legume species have already been discussed, and it has been seen that the number of high-yielding species suitable for use in Britain is comparatively small. Among grasses, the rye-grasses, cocksfoot, timothy and meadow-fescue are by far the most important species. Important members of the *Leguminosae* include red and white clovers and lucerne; alsike, sainfoin and black medick are of more limited use. Almost all leys consist of one or more of these grasses with one or more of the legumes mentioned. The legumes have, in general, a higher protein and mineral content than the grasses, and therefore increase the value of the produce as food for animals; the combined nitrogen which they make available to the grasses increases the yield of these.

There is normally little difference in total yield between the grasses mentioned, and the choice of grasses for a ley will usually depend on its duration, on the method and time of utilization, and on soil conditions. For short duration leys, a grass making rapid growth in the young plant stage is essential; the rye-grasses are pre-eminent in this respect, and one-year leys are normally based on Italian rye-grass. Short-rotation and perennial rye-grass may replace it in leys to last more than one year. Longer leys may be based on any of the species mentioned, other than Italian rye-grass. Perennial rye-grass establishes readily and will withstand continued hard grazing, and is therefore the most commonly-used species; it is, however, not drought-resistant, and is not readily adapted to produce out-of-season herbage. Cocksfoot is more resistant to dry conditions when established, and, together with timothy and meadow fescue, which are more suited to damp conditions, more adaptable than rye-grass to utilization at different times of the year.

There is thus no one ideal grass, and it may be necessary to use more than one species to obtain the full range of advantages required. In very favourable climates it may be possible to utilize two species making their main growth at different times of year; thus in N. New Zealand leys of perennial rye-grass and *Paspalum dilatatum* (*Paniceae*, not hardy in Britain) with clovers can be managed so as to give heavy yields of *Paspalum* during the summer and of rye-grass in winter. In Britain, however, the most that can be done by the use of more than one species is to extend the grazing season into earlier spring or later autumn, and to level up the production at different times of the season. This can be done either by the inclusion of species with different times of maximum production (see fig. 170) in one ley (a general-purpose mixture) or by growing a number of different leys, each containing one grass species only (ultra-simple mixtures). The former method is often the most convenient and has been very widely used, but has some serious disadvantages. The chief of these are, that it is not easy to design a seeds mixture which gives any particular desired proportions of two or more species where these show differences in competitive ability, and that it is equally difficult to devise a system of management which will not favour one species to the exclusion of the others. This question of competition between

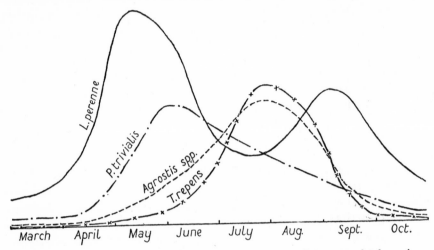

FIG. 170. Variation in the time of maximum growth in different grassland species; diagrammatic seasonal productivity curves for perennial rye-grass, rough-stalked meadow-grass, bent, and white clover. From Blackman, G. E., *Emp. J. Expt. Agric.*, **1**, 1933, by permission of the author and the Clarendon Press.

species will be discussed further in dealing with seeds mixtures and management.

The choice of legumes for inclusion in leys is more limited; of the species already mentioned, lucerne requires too specialized a system of management to be included in many mixtures, and is thus usually grown alone, or in special mixtures in which the grasses are of secondary importance only. Red clover is rapid in its early growth and therefore suitable for use in short leys; it is not very tolerant of hard grazing, and is therefore mainly confined to leys to be cut for hay. White clover, in one or more of its different forms, is an almost ideal legume for grazing conditions, and is normally included in mixtures for all but the shortest leys. Alsike may replace or supplement red clover where the latter may suffer from disease; the annual black medick is normally included only for short leys where low cost is important.

Plants other than grasses and clovers are usually regarded as weeds when they occur in grassland, but many of them are palatable to stock, and some may be worth cultivation. Such useful broad-leaved plants are usually known as *grassland herbs* (the term 'herb' is also used in two other senses: as a general name for herbaceous, i.e. non-woody plants; and as a special term for horticultural aromatic and flavouring plants). Those commonly employed are ribwort plantain (p. 451), chicory (p. 255), yarrow (p. 224), burnet (p. 185) and sheep's parsley (p. 196). Many of these were originally introduced as palatable, deep-rooted plants included in the Clifton Park mixtures advocated by Elliot at the end of the nineteenth century. Their main advantage is their high mineral content— as high as, or slightly higher than, that of the legumes, and very markedly superior to that of the grasses. The yield and protein-content may also be as good as that of the other herbage species, but in general their management is not easy. Chicory and sheep's parsley are rather easily killed-out by hard grazing, while yarrow (also capable of persisting as an arable weed after ploughing), plaintain and, on calcareous soils, burnet, may become over-abundant. Chicory tends to become coarse and unpalatable if allowed to produce flowering shoots. The desirability, therefore, of including such herbs in leys, either in mixture throughout the field, or in special herb-strips, remains a controversial question.

DESIGN OF SEEDS MIXTURE

Once the desired type of ley and its composition has been decided on, it is necessary to consider the seeds mixture which will give this type of sward. A number of factors need to be taken into consideration; these include the size of seed, the number of plants required per acre, the proportion of seeds sown which actually produce a plant, and the effects of competition between plants of the same, and of different, species.

Seed size and weight show considerable variation between the species commonly sown in leys; using approximate figures, the rye-grasses, meadow fescue and red clover have $\frac{1}{4}$ million seeds per pound, cocksfoot $\frac{1}{2}$ million, white clover and alsike $\frac{3}{4}$ million, and timothy 1 million. Thus a given weight of timothy would contain four times as many seeds as the same weight of rye-grass seed. The proportion of seeds sown which produce a plant capable of surviving depends on the seed-bed conditions, on the species, and on the rate of sowing. Clearly, if the seed-bed is very poorly prepared, or the weather conditions very unfavourable, very few are likely to become established, but even under good field conditions the number of plants produced is always considerably less than the number of seeds sown. The proportion varies with different species, and may be expressed as the *percentage establishment*; the following figures, quoted from Aberystwyth trials, illustrate the way in which different species vary when sown alone under the same (good) conditions:

	Percentage establishment (averages of numerous field and garden trials at various seed rates)
Perennial rye-grass	56
Italian rye-grass	48
Meadow fescue	38
Cocksfoot	37
Timothy	30
Dog's-tail	22
Meadow foxtail	15
Rough-stalked meadow-grass . . .	14
Smooth-stalked meadow-grass . . .	9
Red clover	39
Alsike	27
White clover	33

(From Stapledon and Davies, 'Seeds Mixture Problems, III', *Welsh Plant Breeding Station Bulletin*, Series H, No. 6, 1927.)

The actual figure will, of course, vary with conditions, but the same relative differences remain. If the seed-rate is increased, the percentage establishment decreases; again quoting Aberystwyth results,* the percentage establishment of timothy and perennial rye-grass, each sown as a single grass in mixture with red clover, at different seed rates, was as follows:

Timothy:				
Pounds per acre . . .	3	6	12	18
Percentage establishment . .	18	15	10	8
Perennial rye-grass:				
Pounds per acre . . .	$5\frac{1}{2}$	11	22	33
Percentage establishment . .	65	50	36	25

The effect of increased competition between seedlings was thus to reduce the percentage establishment at the highest seeding rate to less than half that at the lowest rate; that is, increasing the number of seeds sown six times only increased the number of plants which became established by less than three times.

One pound of rye-grass evenly sown over an acre would give seeds spaced about 5 in. apart, or, assuming a 50 per cent. establishment, one plant every 7 in. Vigorously-growing rye-grass plants could produce clumps of 7-in. diameter within a year, so that a continuous cover from a seed-rate as low as 1 lb. per acre is theoretically possible. In fact, seed-rates as low as this are never used, but rates as low as 4 or 5 lb. have

* Wm. Davies, 'The Factor of Competition between One Species and Another in Seeds Mixtures', *Welsh Plant Breeding Station Bulletin*, Series H, No. 8, 1928.

been found satisfactory in some areas, while in others 30 lb. or even more is commonly sown. There is no evidence that high seed-rates increase the yield of the resulting sward and, as we have seen, the number of plants persisting does not increase proportionately with increased seed rate. An increased seed-rate does, however, reduce the time during which bare ground is present, and therefore reduce the chance of weeds establishing; this appears to be the main factor in deciding what seed-rate is necessary. In general, the lower seed-rates are more satisfactory in the drier eastern half of England, where conditions for germination of weed seeds on the soil surface are less favourable, while the higher rates are normally used in the wetter areas where rapid weed establishment is a more serious problem.

If more than one species is included in the seeds mixture, competition between the different species must also be taken into account. In the establishment of leys, it is the competitive ability, or *aggressiveness*, in the young plant stage which is important. This may be markedly different from the aggressiveness of the mature plant; thus, for example, creeping bent has a small seedling and does not compete strongly in the early stages of growth, but the mature plant, with its strongly-creeping habit, can be highly aggressive and spread at the expense of other species.

Of the grasses commonly sown in leys, Italian rye-grass is the most aggressive in the early stages, closely followed by perennial rye-grass. Cocksfoot, timothy and meadow fescue are much weaker competitors at this stage; the following figures* illustrate the effect on the percentage establishment of timothy of varying quantities of other species:

Mixture (per acre)	6 lb. timothy+5 lb. PRG	6T+11PRG	6T+33PRG
Per cent. establishment of timothy	22	13	7
Mixture	6 lb. timothy+5 lb. cocksfoot	6T+11C	6T+33C
Per cent. establishment of timothy	22	17	14
Mixture	6 lb. timothy+10 lb. meadow fescue	6T+20MF	6T+40MF
Per cent. establishment of timothy	17	22	21

The establishment of timothy is thus markedly reduced by the competition of perennial rye-grass unless the latter species is present in very small quantity (it should be remembered that 33 lb. rye-grass contains less than one and a half times the number of seeds present in 6 lb. timothy). The competition from cocksfoot is much less severe, and that from meadow fescue negligible. Thus a mixed timothy-meadow fescue sward (with cocksfoot also, if required) is comparatively easily produced, whereas mixtures of perennial rye-grass (or still more, Italian rye-grass) with the other species normally give a sward dominated by rye-grass, unless the management is such as to hold the rye-grass severely in check.

Competition between different varieties of the same species is not so readily observed as that between different species, and there is little information available, therefore, on the comparative establishment and

* Wm. Davies, *loc. cit.*

mutual competition when more than one variety of a species is included in a seeds mixture. In general, it may be said, however, that different varieties are not mutually exclusive, and that their reactions to different types of management show less difference than that between those of different species. It is therefore possible to establish and maintain, at least for some time, swards containing two or more varieties; thus, by using varieties of different growing period, the production of a simple mixture can be extended or levelled out, without the attendant management difficulties consequent on including other species. It is therefore a very common, and usually desirable practice, to include, for example, an early and a late perennial rye-grass, or a large white and a wild-white clover, both in ultra-simple and in general-purpose leys.

MANAGEMENT OF GRASSLAND

The primary object of the management of grassland is the production of the maximum possible food for animals. It is necessary, therefore, to consider the methods of management and utilization which will give this maximum yield of food; and, in addition, since grass is a crop that is expected to continue to yield throughout the season, and in many cases for several or even many years, to consider the effects of such management on the plants themselves, and hence on their future yield.

Although grasses are tolerant of frequent cutting or grazing, they, like other green plants, depend on their leaves for photosynthesis. Cutting or grazing will reduce the area of leaf, and hence the amount of photosynthesis, and consequently the yield. The maximum total yield of dry matter is therefore obtained by the most lenient cutting or grazing. On the other hand, the longer the grass is allowed to grow, the lower will be the quality of the produce, since protein content is at a maximum and fibre content at a minimum in the youngest grass. The art of management for the production of maximum useful food lies largely in balancing these two opposing tendencies. In general, the higher yields are obtained by on-and-off (*rotational*) grazing in which growth is allowed to proceed unchecked for several weeks, and the produce then grazed off, followed by a further rest-period, and so on. Continuous grazing for long periods, if it is sufficiently hard to keep the grass always short, will result in low total yields, although the yield which is produced will be of high nutritional ·value. Lighter continuous stocking may give higher yields, but is normally less satisfactory. It necessarily involves the use of a comparatively large area per head of stock, and there is then a considerable danger of unequal and selective grazing, with overgrazed patches giving low yields, and undergrazed parts being allowed to grow so long that they become unpalatable.

The frequency of defoliation will affect not only the yield; it will also affect the root system and other non-photosynthetic parts of the plant. A plant which has been grazed hard will have a smaller root system and smaller reserves than one which has been allowed to retain a larger leaf

356

area. This is illustrated by the following figures* for weight of roots and plant bases in a block of turf 4 in. in diameter and 6 in. deep taken from swards which had previously received different treatments:

Sward	Lightly grazed gr.	Hard grazed gr.
Three-year mixed ley . .	29	19
Old pasture	58	40
Perennial rye-grass only . .	33	27
Cocksfoot only . . .	41	19

It will be seen that in all cases the weights were lower in the samples from areas which had previously been hard grazed. The higher weight in the old pasture samples shows the tendency towards the formation of a 'mat', a dense accumulation of roots and plant bases which may be deleterious if it proceeds too far, but even here the difference is still apparent. It will also be seen that different grasses are differently affected; perennial rye-grass is comparatively little reduced by hard grazing, whereas cocksfoot shows a very marked difference. This is due largely to its ability to store food reserves in its succulent white leaf-sheath bases if photosynthesis is allowed to proceed. A grass plant with large root system and food reserves is naturally able to make stronger growth, and to compete more strongly with other species, than one in which these are reduced. Cocksfoot is thus favoured by lenient grazing or long rest periods, and may become dominant in undergrazed swards on soils of fairly high fertility. Perennial rye-grass is very tolerant of hard grazing, and is favoured, compared with cocksfoot (and to a lesser extent with timothy and meadow fescue) by the resulting absence of shading.

Not only do different species react differently to varying intensities of grazing, they are also differently affected by the actual time of grazing. Different species grow at different times during the season; hard grazing during the growing period will cause a check because young leaves are eaten off as fast as they grow, while grazing during a dormant period will have comparatively little effect. Perennial rye-grass (particularly the early types) is amongst the first grasses to commence growth in spring, followed by cocksfoot (this may be earlier if it has large reserves resulting from autumn resting) and then usually by meadow fescue and timothy. White clover is also late in starting spring growth, as also are bent and Yorkshire fog. The proportion of the different species in a sward can be greatly altered by the timing of the grazing. Thus Martin Jones found that a young ley grazed hard throughout the spring (and rotationally grazed during the rest of the year) for three successive years, had a final composition of 41 per cent. rye-grass, 16 per cent. cocksfoot and 34 per cent. clover. Another part of the same ley, treated in exactly the same way

* Martin Jones, 'Grassland Management and Its Influence on the Sward', *Empire Journal of Experimental Agriculture*, I, 1933.

except that hard grazing was confined to early spring, showed only 11 per cent. rye-grass and 4 per cent. clover, but 82 per cent. cocksfoot. In the first case both grasses were kept in check until late spring, allowing strong growth of the clover, but not seriously harming the rye-grass. In the second case the hard grazing stopped at the time cocksfoot was beginning to grow, and the ensuing rest-period strongly favoured this species and enabled it to become dominant and to shade out much of the rye-grass and white clover.

He obtained even more striking results on old pasture by varying the intensity of stocking only, all other conditions being kept the same. One section was very well grazed, the number of sheep being carefully adjusted to suit the amount of keep available, so that both overgrazing and undergrazing were avoided. The composition of the sward at the end of two years was 33 per cent. useful grasses (mainly rye-grass), 54 per cent. white clover and 13 per cent. weed grasses. On another section of the same sward a constant number of sheep were grazed throughout the whole time, so that there was excessive overgrazing in winter and early spring and very marked understocking in summer. The composition of this section at the end of the two years was 7 per cent. useful grasses, 3 per cent. clover and 89 per cent. weed grasses, mainly bent and Yorkshire fog. While the large differences obtained in this trial were the result of very carefully managed grazing on the one hand, and of intentionally very bad management on the other, the same tendencies operate under normal farm conditions. There is almost always greater pressure on the available keep when this is short in spring, and difficulty in keeping abundant growth in summer adequately grazed. The tendency towards overgrazing at one period, and undergrazing at the other, is thus difficult to avoid, and is one of the main causes of the deterioration of grassland swards.

The maintenance of a balance between grasses and legumes is, as the trials quoted illustrate, largely a matter of grazing management. Providing adequate lime and phosphate (and to a lesser extent, potash) are available, the white clover content of a sward can be readily increased by hard grazing, particularly in late spring. Conversely, an excessively clovery sward can be improved by favouring the growth of grasses by increasing the length of rest-period. Nitrogenous manuring will also favour the grasses; heavy nitrogen dressings plus long rest-periods will give high yields, but will result in an almost pure grass sward.

Cutting of grass for silage or dried grass has approximately the same effect as grazing if the period of growth is the same, except that the treading action of stock, which may be beneficial in causing increased rooting from nodes near ground-level, is absent, and that there is no return of manurial ingredients in dung and urine. The period between cuts is often long, and if this is so, shading effects come in. These are still more important in the case of cutting for hay, which markedly favours the taller-growing plants and those capable of benefiting, by storage of food reserves, from an unusually long period of undisturbed growth. Cocksfoot and timothy, for example, are both favoured by haying in comparison with the higher light-demanding perennial rye-grass and white clover. Red clover is also favoured at the expense of white clover. The effects of haying are most marked if the field is laid up for a long period and the hay cut at a late stage. If this stage is so late that some of the plants present are able to produce ripe seeds an opportunity is offered for very marked change of sward type by self-seeding. Such a change is, under British conditions, almost always a change for the worse, since the early-ripening seeds are mainly those of weedy annuals or short-lived perennials. Among grasses, the most important of these are soft brome and Yorkshire fog, the former in particular being a characteristic weed of over-hayed grassland. Among non-gramineous plants, yellow rattle and hog-weed are also characteristic of such swards.

The higher-yielding herbage plants all require a high level of soil fertility, and cannot be grown satisfactorily unless this is maintained. Establishment of the sown species is poor under conditions of low fertility, and complete manuring is usually desirable when sowing down to grass. This should include nitrogen, since at this stage combined nitrogen from legumes is not yet available. None of the high-yielding herbage plants will tolerate high acidity or continuous waterlogging, and liming and drainage may therefore also be necessary.

In an established grazing ley under good conditions there is a constant and rapid circulation of nutrient elements; nitrogen, phosphorus, potassium and calcium are absorbed from the soil by the grazing plants; these are grazed by the stock and the dung and urine of the grazing animal returned to the soil, where it rapidly decomposes and its elements are again taken up by the plants. The circulation is, however, incomplete; only part of the nutrient elements is returned to the sward, the remainder, varying in proportion with the class and age of stock, goes to provide milk or meat. Losses by leaching from the soil also occur, and although an ample nitrogen supply may be maintained if clover is abundant, the available supply of other elements will be gradually reduced if additional fertilizers are not supplied. The first effect of this reduction in fertility will be that the yield of the plants present will fall off; as their yield falls so their competitive ability falls also, and other plants, better adapted to the lower fertility conditions now prevailing, will tend to replace them. Under these conditions decay of dead plant residues tends to be slower, with a resultant increase of mat formation, so that further manurial elements remain locked up and unavailable. If available lime and phosphorus are so reduced that the clovers become less abundant, the nitrogen supply will also be reduced, and a further lowering of the level of fertility will result.

The rye-grasses are the plants least adapted to low fertility, and reduction in the proportion of rye-grass in the sward is usually one of the first effects of such a lowering of fertility. Cocksfoot, timothy and meadow fescue are somewhat more tolerant, but still need at least a moderately high level; at lower fertility levels, bent, with its vigorously competitive creeping habit, Yorkshire fog, and perhaps crested dog's-tail, sweet vernal, and the small fescues as well as many non-gramineous weeds, will come in. The change from a sward dominated by perennial rye-grass to one in which bent is dominant is perhaps the commonest of all forms of deterioration of leys. Bent is favoured not only by a reduction in fertility, but also, as has been seen, by the natural tendency towards overstocking in spring and understocking in summer. Invasion by bent so commonly accompanies the ageing of leys, and is so commonly the main reason why they are eventually broken up, that it is often regarded as an almost inevitable stage; certainly the preservation of a productive rye-grass sward, free from bent, is a good test of grassland management.

The change of sward-composition with change of fertility level is a reversible one, and adequate manuring of a sward composed of low-yielding, low fertility-demanding plants can result in a very marked improvement. Even an extremely low-yielding mountain sward, dominated by Molinia and Nardus, can be changed, by heavy manuring and liming only, to a reasonably good white clover-grass sward of lowland type, the seeds of the new species being brought in by wind and stock. Lowland swards of low fertility often respond well to lime and phosphorus only, the increased white clover content resulting from the addition of these elements having the effect of increasing the nitrogen supply, and this in turn favouring the growth of better grasses. Bent, however, once established, is not easy to eradicate by manuring and management alone, and it may often be more profitable to destroy the existing vegetation by ploughing, or the use of paraquat, and to start again with a new ley, with a higher fertility level produced by manuring.

Where it is undesirable to plough, improvement may be assisted by grassland cultivations. Severe harrowing and surface cultivation may tear out some of the surface-creeping species such as bent; they also, by increasing aeration, assist in the breakdown of mat and therefore in the setting free of locked-up fertility. Without adequate manuring, however, such cultivations can rarely be expected to produce very marked results.

EVALUATION OF GRASSLAND

Botanical Analysis. Since different grassland species vary in their yield and nutritive value, the botanical composition of a sward gives a measure of its agricultural value. For many purposes simple inspection and a visual estimate of the approximate abundance of different species is sufficient. Where, however, it is desired to compare different swards, as, for instance, in trials of the effect of different treatments, it is necessary to use some more precise numerical measure of the proportions of different species present. The figure assessed may be proportion by number, proportion of ground area covered, or proportion of total weight of herbage.

Proportion by Number. It is rarely possible to determine the extent of individual plants, particularly of creeping species, in dense herbage. The unit used is therefore the individual tiller, and the method is sometimes known as the *percentage tiller frequency* method. A grid of convenient size (often 6 × 6 in.) is thrown repeatedly at random within the area to be assessed, and the number of tillers of each species standing within the grid area reckoned. Figures from repeated throws are totalled and the average figure for each species expressed as a percentage. For very accurate work actual counts are made (with very short herbage it may be necessary to lift the square of turf enclosed by the grid); but often sufficiently close estimates of numbers can be made without actual counting. The main disadvantage of the method is that it cannot be strictly applied to non-gramineous herbage; various arbitrary conventions have to be adopted to deal with white clovers and weeds.

Proportion of Ground Area Covered. If the proportion of the area of each quadrat (the individual area sampled, i.e. the space enclosed by the grid at one throw) covered by the different species is recorded instead of tiller number, an average number for *percentage area* can be obtained. This method has the advantage that it can be readily applied to all types of herbage plants, including clovers and rosette plants, and also used to give the proportion of bare ground, which is necessarily ignored in the counting method. Its main disadvantage is that it depends on eye estimation; it can be made more accurate by subdividing the grid into small squares, but is never strictly objective.

A useful modification of the area method is the *point quadrat* method, which may be regarded as the use of a very large number of quadrats, each reduced to negligible size. A horizontal frame carries ten movable wires, each of which can be brought down vertically or diagonally until the point touches vegetation or bare ground. The number of times a given species is touched in, say, 200 'points' can be regarded as proportional to the percentage area occupied by that species. Since the method avoids estimation, and involves only recognition of the species touched, it is readily reproducible, and closely comparable results can be obtained by different observers. It is, however, not readily applied to tall herbage.

Proportion of Total Weight of Herbage. Herbage can be clipped at a standard height (usually as near ground-level as possible) from a number of quadrats, and the cut herbage sorted out into the constituent species, which are then weighed. This technique, known as the *percentage productivity* method, gives a figure for each species which represents the percentage of the whole yield at the time of sampling which is contributed by that species. It is thus a more directly useful method when considering the productivity of a sward, but is necessarily extremely slow and laborious. A similar method, but using estimated proportions of yield instead of actual weights, is quicker, but, like all estimation methods, is reliable only when used by an experienced observer, and results obtained by different observers are not always strictly comparable.

Grassland Yield Trials. Botanical analysis, by recording the proportions of high- and low-yielding species in the herbage, enables an approximate estimate of the potential yield of a sward to be made. Such an estimate depends, of course, on a previous knowledge of the yielding ability of the different species, and to obtain this knowledge, and to compare actual yields of different swards, yield trials are necessary. Yields may be recorded as total production per acre over a given period, expressed either as fresh weight, dry weight, or starch and protein equivalent; or, since animal feeding is the object of growing grass, directly as live-weight gain or in terms of milk production.

Herbage Yields. Figures for yield of herbage can be readily obtained by direct cutting and weighing, but they will vary very much according to the frequency of cutting. Except where an attempt is being made to estimate production of silage or hay, yield figures so obtained will bear little relation to yield under normal farm conditions. A closer approximation to yield under pasture conditions can be obtained by the *movable-cage* method, where areas of pasture are temporarily protected from grazing. Cuts are taken from similar areas of protected and of grazed sward, the difference in weight between the two giving an estimate of the weight of herbage grazed off. Various precautions are necessary, but, providing the individual grazing periods are short, the method gives results of considerable value, and it has been widely used.

Animal Production. In the movable-cage technique the animals are used only to provide grazing conditions, and are not themselves directly recorded. The most complete assessment of the value of a sward is, however, provided by figures for the animal production obtained from it; these can only be obtained by directly recording the animals themselves. Such methods are necessarily laborious and expensive and, while of great value in providing yield figures directly in terms of animal production, are clearly not suitable for small-plot trials where numerous different swards are being compared.

LAWNS AND SPORTS TURF

Lawns and sports turf may be briefly considered as a type of grass sward very distinct from those of agricultural grassland. The object desired is a dense, low-growing cover of evergreen herbage; yield is of no importance, and high yield is, in fact, a disadvantage as necessitating more frequent mowing. The main requirements in a lawn grass are that it shall tolerate close mowing and shall produce a dense, uniform stand; where the turf is used for games it must not be slippery when wet (ruling out white clover) and must be capable of withstanding hard wear. If used for games where the ball must run true, the individual tillers must be as small as possible.

It is thus the low-growing, low-yielding grass species, mainly of low agricultural value, which are the best lawn grasses. The smaller bents, *Agrostic tenuis* (brown-top) and *A. canina* (velvet bent) and forms of *Festuca rubra* (red fescue) are the best for first quality lawns and sports turf. For general lawns and playing-fields, perennial rye-grass (pasture strains only), diploid timothy (S. 50) and crested dog's-tail may be used; although less fine-growing they tend to withstand puddling in wet weather better, and are somewhat cheaper in cost of seed. Smooth-stalked meadow-grass is occasionally used where drought and wear resistance is important, but tends to produce a 'patchy' turf; for very shady conditions wood meadow-grass (*Poa nemoralis*) may be worth including.

Lawns and sports turf are established either by turfing or seeding. Turfing is expensive, but gives a usable sward quickly; turves can usually be readily established during the winter, but must not be allowed to dry out during the critical period before new roots have penetrated into the underlying soil. The composition of the sward produced will, of course, initially be that of the sward from which the turves were cut, but the changed conditions resulting from transplanting to a new environment may result in considerable alterations of composition. Thus, for example, Cumberland sea-washed turf, extensively used for the production of bowling greens, consists mainly of specialized ecotypes of red fescue, selected by the particular conditions of the salt-marsh environment; when this is transplanted to a different soil under very different environmental conditions very marked changes of composition may take place.

For the establishment of lawns from seed, very high seed-rates are usually employed in order to give quick cover and to prevent as far as possible the establishment of weeds. Rates of 2 oz. per square yard (equivalent to some 6 cwt. per acre) are often recommended, but for most purposes there is little advantage in exceeding $\frac{2}{3}$ oz., while for grass paths and similar areas $\frac{1}{3}$ oz. (say 100 lb. per acre) is usually satisfactory if very quick cover is not essential. Very high purity of seed is desirable, as a small proportion of weed grasses, too low to be of any significance in agricultural practice, may result in considerable disfigurement of a lawn; the effect is, of course, much enhanced by high seed-rates. A typical seeds mixture is 7 parts by weight of red fescue ($\frac{1}{2}$-$\frac{3}{4}$ million 'seeds' per pound) to 3 of brown top (about 4 million); a uniform sward is more likely to be obtained if the red fescue is the non-creeping form, Chewing's fescue, since a mixture of two creeping species may result in patchiness. The creeping red fescues, such as S.59, may be sown alone. Mixtures including perennial rye-grass will usually give swards which initially consist almost exclusively of this species; but since rye-grass is less tolerant of hard mowing than the bents and small fescues, it may be worth using these latter in the mixture in the hope that sufficient plants of them will establish to give partial replacement of the rye-grass in later years.

Management of lawns and sports turf differs markedly from that of agricultural grassland. Frequent mowing is normally essential, but, since constant close mowing has a weakening effect on all grasses, by keeping the leaf area very small, mowing height should be varied when conditions permit, to allow of some reserves being built up. Nitrogenous manuring is necessary; sulphate of ammonia is normally used, and the acidifying effect of repeated dressings encourages the acid-tolerant bents and fescues and discourages clovers. Ferrous sulphate is also used with this object. Phosphate and lime are used only in the minimum amount necessary for the growth of the required grasses; excess will tend to give a clovery turf. Constant machine-mowing, even without extra rolling, tends to produce an over-consolidated soil surface, and raking, aerating by means of hollow-tine forks or spiked rollers, and top dressings of screened humus. etc., are necessary to maintain satisfactory growth. Since clovers are not required, selective weed-killers (Chapter XVIII) may be freely used for the destruction of dicotyledonous weeds.

BOOKS FOR FURTHER READING

CROP PLANTS: GENERAL

J. M. Hector. *Introduction to the Botany of Field Crops*, Central News Agency, 1936, Johannesburg.

H. E. Hayward. *The Structure of Economic Plants*, 1948, Macmillan, New York.

G. D. H. Bell. *Cultivated Plants of the Farm*, 1948, Cambridge.

H. Hunter. *Crop Varieties*, 1951, Spon, London.

R. Good. *Plants and Human Economics*, 1933, Cambridge.

S. P. Mercer. *Farm and Garden Seeds*, 1958, Crosby Lockwood, London.

C. D. Darlington. *Chromosome Botany and the Origins of Cultivated Plants*, 1963, Allen and Unwin, London.

L. S. Cobley. *An Introduction to the Botany of Tropical Crops*, 1956, Longmans, Green, London.

P. M. Zukovsky (transl. P. S. Hudon). *Cultivated Plants and their Wild Relations*, 1962, Commonwealth Agricultural Bureaux.

Sir Joseph Hutchinson (ed.). *Essays on Crop Plant Evolution*, 1965, Cambridge.

DICOTYLEDONS

D. H. Robinson. *Leguminous Forage Plants*, 1947, Arnold, London.

A. G. Erith. *White Clover*, 1924, Duckworth, London.

C. H. Oldham. *Brassica Crops*, 1948, Crosby Lockwood, London (horticultural).

W. G. Burton. *The Potato*, 1948, Chapman and Hall, London.

E. F. Hurt. *Sunflower*, 1946, Faber, London.

L. D. Hill. *Russian Comfrey*, 1953, Faber, London.

J. L. Bolton. *Alfalfa*, 1962, Leonard Hill and Interscience.

J. D. Ivins and F. L. Milthorpe (Editors). *The Growth of the Potato*, 1963, Butterworth, London.

British Atlas of Potato Varieties, 1965, Potato Marketing Board.
A. H. Burgess. *Hops*, 1964, Leonard Hill, London.

GRAMINEAE

A. Arber. *The Gramineae*, 1934, Cambridge.
C. E. Hubbard. *Grasses*, 1954, Penguin, London.
S. F. Armstrong. *British Grasses and Their Employment in Agriculture*, 1950, Cambridge.
Burr and Turner. *British Economic Grasses*, 1933, Arnold, London (identification in vegetative stage).
C. Barnard (Editor). *Grasses and Grasslands*, 1964, Macmillan, London.

CEREALS

R. A. Peachey. *Cereal Varieties in Great Britain*, 1951, Crosby Lockwood, London.
J. Percival. *The Wheat Plant*, 1921, Duckworth, London.
E. S. Beaven. *Barley*, 1947, Duckworth, London.
H. Hunter. *The Barley Crop*, 1952, Crosby Lockwood, London.
H. Hunter. *Oats*, 1924, Benn, London.
W. M. Findlay. *Oats*, 1956, Oliver and Boyd.
Descriptions of Cereal Varieties, 1954 (Loose-leaf), National Institute of Agricultural Botany, Cambridge.
F. A. Coffman (Editor). *Oats and Oat Improvement*, 1961, American Society of Agronomy, Madison, Wisconsin.
G. Aufhammer, P. Bergal and F. R. Horne. *Barley Varieties*, EBC. Elsevier, Amsterdam, 1958, and supplements.
D. M. Barling. *An Introduction to Cereal Structure and Identification*, 1963, Institute of Corn and Agricultural Merchants, London.
R. F. Peterson. *Wheat*, 1965, Leonard Hill, London.

GRASSLAND

W. Davies. *The Grass Crop*, 1960, Spon, London.
S. J. Watson. *Grassland and Grassland Products*, 1951, Arnold, London.
E. Bruce Levy. *Grasslands of New Zealand*, 1951, N.Z. Education Dept., Wellington.
D. Brown. *Methods of Surveying and Measuring Vegetation*, 1954, Commonwealth Agricultural Bureaux.
R. B. Dawson. *Practical Lawn Craft*, 1954, Crosby Lockwood.
J. R. Harlan. *Theory and Dynamics of Grassland Agriculture*, 1956, Van Nostrand, Princeton, N.J.
Experiments in Progress (annual). The Grassland Research Institute, Hurley.
J. D. Ivins (Editor). *The Measurement of Grassland Productivity*, 1959, Butterworth, London.

JOURNALS

Papers dealing with agricultural crop plants appear in a large number of journals, including:

Journal of the National Institute of Agricultural Botany.
Journal of the British Grassland Society.
Journal of Agricultural Science.
Journal of Ecology.
Empire Journal of Experimental Agriculture.
Annals of Botany.
World Crops.

Papers in these and other journals, including foreign publications, are abstracted in:

Plant Breeding Abstracts.
Herbage Abstracts.
Field Crop Abstracts.

Section Three

FARM WEEDS

Chapter XVIII

WEEDS: GENERAL

THE general importance of weeds as hindrances to the growing of crops is immediately evident, but it is difficult to give a definition of a weed which covers all cases. A plant which may be useful under some conditions may be a weed under others, and the simple definition of a weed as 'a plant out of place' is perhaps the best that can be given. In an arable crop, grown for one particular product, any other plant, of whatever sort, may be regarded as a weed. In grassland, however, the usual object is the production of the maximum amount of food for cattle, and plants other than those sown would only be regarded as weeds if they were inferior in yield or value. In either case, however, the weed is a plant which comes in on its own, without being intentionally sown or planted.

TYPES OF PLANTS OCCURRING AS WEEDS

The fact that a weed is able to establish itself in cultivated land means that it must be a plant naturally adapted to the conditions provided. These conditions differ so markedly between arable and grassland that it is desirable to consider the two separately. Arable land, with the soil surface frequently disturbed, provides conditions which are very rarely found in natural habitats; only in areas of unstable soil, landslips, mud-banks and similar positions does such disturbance occur naturally. Plants adapted to such conditions are therefore usually rare under natural conditions, and we find that many of the most important arable weeds are, in fact, not native plants at all in the countries where they occur as weeds, but have been unintentionally introduced with foreign crop plants. Many of them occur naturally only in limited areas, often under semi-desert conditions which provide the same short growing period, and the same necessity for rapid establishment from seed or rapid regeneration from underground shoots, that are met with in arable fields. Such plants, accidentally transported by human agencies to other countries, are often much better adapted to the unnatural conditions of arable cultivation than are the majority of the native species. Consequently, we find that many of the more important arable weeds are now world-wide in their distribution; and that it is only comparatively rarely that plants which formed part of the original natural vegetation of an area persist as serious weeds when it is cleared and brought under arable cultivation.

The conditions in grassland are very different, and where, as in lowland Britain, grassland is only maintained as such by the action of the grazing animal, weeds may be normal members of the natural succession to forest, which forms the normal climax vegetation of the area. Shrubs and trees are, however, only able to establish themselves when the grassland is very inadequately grazed, and it is therefore only in long-neglected fields that such woody plants become important as weeds. A more common type of grassland weed consists of plants which are well adapted to grazing conditions and are regarded as weeds only because they are lower in yield or value than the species sown; the grasses Yorkshire fog and bent are examples of this type. Where serious overgrazing occurs, rosette plants, better adapted even than the grasses to very hard grazing, may come in as very low-yielding weeds. In extreme cases, where the sward is broken up by hard grazing and excessive trampling, highly-specialized 'gateway' weeds may come in, or arable weeds may establish themselves.

Means of Spreading. To be able to invade cultivated land, whether grassland or arable, a weed must possess an efficient means of spreading. This spread may be by vegetative means or by seed. Vegetative spread, which is confined to perennials, may take place by the production of long rhizomes or stolons, or offsets in the form of corms, bulbs or tubers. Such spreading perennials, particularly those with deeply-placed rhizomes, are often amongst the most difficult weeds to control. Single plants may spread to cover very large areas; in bracken vegetatively-spread patches may cover several acres, while in creeping thistle a single small cutting of creeping root has been recorded as producing in two years a patch 60 ft. across.

If spread is solely by vegetative means, with no production of seeds (or spores in non-flowering plants) the weed is unable to become widely distributed, although it may be extremely serious in limited areas. Examples of such plants are the terrestrial form of *Polygonum amphibium* (amphibious persicaria or lakeweed), which flowers only when growing in water, but spreads vegetatively by deep rhizomes to become a very difficult weed of adjacent damp arable land; and winter heliotrope (*Petasites fragrans*) introduced as a garden plant, and spreading in some south-western areas as a coltsfoot-like weed, but not normally setting seed in England and therefore found only where planted. Other garden plants with spreading rhizomes may behave in a similar way; goutweed (*Aegopodium podagraria*) is an old-established example, formerly grown as a medicinal plant and now a pernicious weed of some gardens, but not commonly spreading by seed, and therefore rarely found as a weed of farmland.

All annual and biennial plants, as well as those perennials which have no special means of vegetative propagation, are entirely dependent on the production of seed for their spread. Weeds are thus usually plants which produce abundant seed; many of them are able to do so even under very unfavourable conditions; thus many weeds, even if cut in the flowering stage, are still able to produce germinable seed.

Seed Dispersal. For a plant to become a widespread weed, it is necessary not only that abundant seed shall be set, but also that some efficient method of distributing seed shall exist. This distribution of seed may be due either to natural adaptation for fruit or seed dispersal, or to human activities.

Natural dispersal may be due to (*a*) explosive fruits, (*b*) wind, (*c*) water and (*d*) animals.

(*a*) *Explosive Fruits and Similar Mechanical Means.* Common examples are cranesbills (*Geranium* spp.), where the ovary breaks up at maturity, the outer part of each carpel curling suddenly upwards so that the seed is slung out; hairy bitter-cress (*Cardamine hirsuta* and *flexuosa*), in which the valves of the mature siliqua open explosively when touched, throwing the small seeds, and amongst garden weeds, the introduced small yellow oxalis (*O. corniculata*), in which the seeds are forcibly squeezed out by the sudden contraction of the aril. The censer mechanism, where movement of the stem results in the loose seeds being shaken out of the capsule, either through pores, as in poppies, or between teeth, as in campions and other members of the *Caryophyllaceae*, has a similar effect.

(*b*) *Wind.* Dispersal by wind is most conspicuous in plants with winged or plumed fruits or seeds; of these, the most important as weeds are the numerous species belonging to the family Compositae, which have a pappus present on the single-seeded, indehiscent fruit. Common examples of these are the thistles, ragwort, dandelion and groundsel; in all these, extensive wind transport may take place over considerable distances. In thistles, however, the extent of this wind-transport may appear greater than it really is; the achene very readily becomes detached from the pappus, and clouds of thistle-down seen blowing about often consist of the pappus only, and are therefore quite harmless, the seed having been left behind.

Although less conspicuous than with winged or hairy fruits or seeds, wind transport of very small seeds may be equally important, particularly where the testa is finely pitted or toothed so that the ratio of surface area to weight is large. Poppy seeds, and those of the chickweeds, are examples of such seeds with sculptured testa; in them the censer mechanism already mentioned shakes the seeds out forcibly, so that they may then be carried away by the wind. Many grasses, where the surface/weight ratio is high owing to the presence of glumes or other structures around the fruit, are readily distributed by wind.

(*c*) *Water.* The dispersal of weeds by water is necessarily limited to areas where surface water may occur; it is often responsible for the spread of weeds along ditches and stream banks; in times of flood floating seeds or fruits may be spread over adjacent fields. A large proportion of weed seeds or fruits are capable of floating for at least short periods; dock 'seeds', consisting of the fruit surrounded by perianth segments bearing a corky tubercle, are well adapted to dispersal by water.

(*d*) *Animals.* Transport of seeds by animals may be either internal or external. Plants with succulent fruits, the commonest type of adaptation to internal seed transport by animals, are rare as weeds, black nightshade being one of the few examples, although sloe (blackthorn) and bramble may occur as grassland weeds under some conditions. Fruits with no special attractions for animals are, however, often eaten by cattle along with other herbage, and seeds may pass undamaged through the alimentary canal and be distributed in the dung. External transport by animals may take place by casual carriage of seeds in mud adhering to feet, etc., but is most important with weeds having burr fruits—fruits with hooked hairs or spines which become attached to hair or wool and are later rubbed off. Cleavers, wild carrot and spotted medick are examples of plants distributed in this way.

The natural dispersal of weed seeds is clearly a very important method of introduction of weeds into agricultural land. It can only be prevented by ensuring that weeds readily spread in this way are not allowed to seed. While this is the responsibility of the farmer on his own land, some measure of protection against ingress of seeds from outside is given by the *Injurious Weeds Order*, made under the Corn Production (Repeal) Act of 1921, and continued as the responsibility of the County Agricultural Executive Committees under the Weeds Act of July 1959. This order permits the serving on the occupier of any land of a notice requiring him to cut or destroy any of a number of scheduled weeds; failure to comply with such notice renders the occupier liable to fines. The weeds scheduled as injurious weeds are: spear thistle, creeping thistle, curled dock, broad-leaved dock and ragwort.

Dispersal by human agency may be caused by (*a*) the sowing of imperfectly-cleaned seed, (*b*) the use of hay, farmyard manure, etc., containing weed seeds, and (*c*) the casual carriage of weed seeds by implements, vehicles, etc., and in packing material, ballast, etc.

(*a*) *Seed Impurities.* The sowing of seed containing weed seeds as impurities is unquestionably the most important way in which weeds are spread by human agency. It is responsible for both long-distance transport of weeds from country to country, and for their general dispersal over cultivated land. Any weed which ripens seed at the same time as a crop-plant may be carried in this way, providing that it is tall enough to be harvested with the crop, and that its 'seed' is sufficiently similar to that of the crop for it not to be separated out in the threshing or later operations. How close this similarity needs to be depends on the methods used. Under primitive conditions, with threshing by treading or flailing and cleaning of the threshed seed confined to winnowing by tossing it in the wind, weed 'seeds' would remain in the sample even if they were very different in size and weight from the crop seeds. Of the period of, say, 5,000 years during which crops have been harvested and sown for seed, only the last 100 years or so have witnessed any real alterations in the procedure. Consequently, the main spread of crop plants throughout the world has taken place under conditions in which seed samples would never be truly clean, but would always contain varying proportions of weeds. The spread of weeds, therefore, kept pace with the spread of crops, and many of the most serious and important weeds are now almost world-wide in their distribution.

The more similar the weed-seed was in size and weight to the crop-plant seed, the more likely it would be to be present in large amount. With very similar seeds (and with any weed showing variation in seed size there would be an automatic selection of the forms with seeds most nearly resembling the crop seed) it might readily happen that in successive generations the proportion of weed to crop steadily increased, if local conditions tended to favour the weed at the expense of the crop-plant. Ultimately the crop would have to be abandoned, if the weed were quite useless; or if the weed could be utilized it might itself become the object of cultivation, replacing the original crop (cf. origin of rye, p. 266).

With the development of higher standards of farming, and particularly of seed threshing and cleaning machinery, weed seed impurities have decreased, both in amount and in range of type likely to be found associated with any one crop. Nevertheless, the sowing of seed contaminated with weeds still remains the most important of all the methods, other than natural seed dispersal, by which weeds are spread. Under modern conditions, only weeds with seeds rather closely resembling those of the crop seed are likely to be found in any particular crop, but it still is very difficult to ensure complete purity. The resultant association of certain weeds with certain crops because of the resemblance of their seeds is discussed further on p. 374. When assessing the effect of seed impurities it must be remembered that even a small percentage of weeds in a seed sample can give rise to a large number of plants when sown, as the following table illustrates:

Table I

NUMBER OF WEED SEEDS

Name of weed	*Number of weed seeds in 1 lb. of herbage seed containing 1 per cent. by weight of the weed*	*Number of weed seeds per square yard if this seed is sown at 16 lb. per acre*
Curled dock	3,240	11
Dovesfoot cranesbill	2,950	10
Yorkshire fog	18,140	60
Slender foxtail	4,320	14
Creeping buttercup	1,890	6
Yellow suckling clover	9,070	30
Broad-leaved plantain	22,680	75
Mouse-eared chickweed	45,360	150

(*Data from Report of the Committee on Qualitative Control of Seeds, H.M.S.O.,* 1950.)

It is evident, therefore, that a high degree of purity is necessary if weed dispersal by this means is to be kept in check; this involves very thorough seed-cleaning and careful testing to ensure that this is effective. In most countries legislation makes this testing compulsory, and lays down standards for the amount of weed impurity permissible (p. 89).

It is sometimes possible to distinguish weeds derived from seed impurities by the fact that they tend to be uniformly distributed through the crop, whereas weeds derived from seeds previously present in the soil, or carried in by other methods, are more likely to vary in quantity in different parts of the field. In a drilled crop, weeds derived from seed impurities will, of course, be confined to the actual drill lines. Any such distinctions based on appearance should, however, be regarded as indications only, and need to be confirmed by weed-seed analysis of a sample of the seed sown.

(*b*) *Dispersal in Hay, etc.* Grassland weeds are readily dispersed by the carting of *hay* on to grass fields for feeding when fresh grass is scarce; trouble is most likely to occur where the hay has been cut late so that a large number of weeds were able to mature seed before cutting. The danger from *silage* is normally less; grass silage is usually cut at a stage when few mature seeds are present, and storage in silage has been shown to reduce very considerably the germination of the majority of weed seeds. A number of weeds, such as field bindweed, seeds of which might be present in a late-cut arable silage crop are, however, very resistant and may remain viable in silage.

The extent to which *farmyard manure* may be a source of weed seeds depends largely on the method of making. Fresh dung may contain large numbers of viable weed seeds; germination of these is, however, very much reduced by storage for two months, providing that the manure is managed in such a way that fermentation takes place and temperatures of 150° F. are reached in the heap. Field bindweed is again an example of a very resistant species. Storage in loose, dry manure has little effect in reducing the viability of weed seeds, and old, neglected manure heaps may, in fact, be a further source of more weed seeds if they are allowed to become overgrown with such weeds as fat hen. *Composts* of various types can also be responsible for the spread of weeds, particularly where such materials as wool waste (likely to contain burr-fruits) are used. Where it is particularly important that compost shall be free from weed seeds, as in the top-dressing of lawns and sports turf, sterilization by heat, steam or chlorpicrin is employed.

(*c*) *Implements and Miscellaneous Methods of Spread.* Almost any farm implement or vehicle may be responsible for the casual carriage of weed seeds from one field to another, but the implement most likely to cause large-scale spread of seed is the combine. The majority of combines discharge weed seeds over the harvest field, whereas the use of a binder and stationary thresher results in the majority of the weed seeds being discharged at one point, where they can be conveniently burnt.

Packing materials, ballast and similar materials are often contaminated with weed seeds. It is not often that these are brought directly on to farmland, but such materials are often the means of introducing foreign plants, as witness the common occurrence of exotic species near ports, on ballast heaps and rubbish dumps, from which the danger of their spread to agricultural land always exists.

Persistence of Weed Seeds in the Soil. The seeds of most crop plants either germinate quickly when sown, or die and rot; but many weed seeds are capable of remaining alive, but dormant, in the soil. This dormancy may be either natural or induced. A naturally dormant seed does not germinate even when conditions of moisture, aeration and temperature are favourable. This failure to germinate may be due to the necessity for a period of *after-ripening*, as in some *Polygonum* species, or more commonly to an impervious seed-coat preventing the entry of either oxygen, as in wild oats, or water, as in hard seeds of *Leguminosae*. The seed remains alive and, when after-ripening is complete, or the seed-coat is cracked by frost or other causes, it will germinate. Induced dormancy is caused by unfavourable conditions; a seed buried deeply cannot germinate owing to lack of aeration, but if under these conditions it becomes dormant, then, when it is later brought to the surface by cultivations, germination may take place.

This ability of many weed seeds to remain alive in the soil, often for many years, means that the introduction of weed seeds into a field, whether by natural means or as an impurity, will affect not only the current crop, but those of future years. The old saying, 'One year's seeding means seven years' weeding', illustrates this point; seeds ripened and distributed over farmland in one year may remain dormant for varying periods, so that weed seedlings appear each year for many years after. The length of time for which seeds can remain alive varies with the species; a few, like small-flowered buttercup, germinate only in the autumn of the year in which they were produced, others, such as slender foxtail, survive for about two years, while others again may remain alive for many years. Docks, charlock and poppy are common weeds in which at least a proportion of the seed may survive for forty years or more.

There is thus in most fields a large population of buried viable weed seeds in the soil. The effect of this is most noticeable when a ley is broken up; arable weed seeds, persisting from the period before the ley was sown, germinate and may give rise to numerous weeds which had not been seen at all during the period the field was in grass. The total population varies considerably; figures of up to 100 million viable buried seeds per acre have been recorded in rather poor, acid grassland. Under arable conditions where the greater rate of germination and also of dying and rotting of old seeds more than offsets the greater production of seed, figures are usually lower, varying from 2 to about 50 million, although under the exceptional conditions of the permanent wheat plots at Rothamstead a figure of over 150 million was reached.

ASSOCIATION OF WEEDS WITH PARTICULAR CROPS AND CONDITIONS

Of the many different types of plants which can become weeds of agricultural land, usually only a small proportion are found in any one crop. Many weeds are confined to, or at least are more common in, a particular type of crop, or a particular type of soil. This association between weeds and crops or conditions may be due (*a*) to the frequent introduction of particular weeds as impurities with the seed of particular crops, (*b*) to the method of management of the crop favouring certain weeds, or (*c*) to the special ecological, and particularly soil, requirements of the weeds. These three causes may, of course, operate together, and a weed introduced as a seed impurity will naturally only be of importance if management and ecological conditions in the crop are such as to favour it.

(*a*) *Weeds Associated with Particular Crops as Seed Impurities.* It has been pointed out, in discussing seed impurities as a factor in the dispersal of weeds, that, under modern conditions, only weeds with seeds fairly closely resembling those of the crop are likely to be found as impurities. Thus wild oats, wild radish, cleavers and black bindweed are commonly found in cereal crops because of the similarity of size of their 'seeds' to cereal grains; wild onion is another weed often associated with cereals, but here it is the vegetative bulbils formed on the inflorescence which are difficult to clean out of seed corn. Smaller-seeded weeds are commonly found in clovers; ribwort plantain and various *Geranium* species are frequent examples. The main weeds associated with grasses are other grasses; Yorkshire fog, soft brome, ratstail and slender foxtail are examples of weed grasses often found in leys owing to their presence as impurities in the seed sown.

(*b*) *Weeds Associated with Particular Management Conditions.* The most conspicuous example of the effect of agricultural management on the weed flora is the difference between the weeds of arable and grassland. In the first year of a ley, numerous arable weeds may be present, but most of these cannot survive grassland conditions and are soon replaced by other species, better adapted to the new conditions. The majority of arable weeds are either annuals or are perennials spreading rapidly through loose soil; in grassland there is, unless the sward is rather poor, comparatively little opportunity for establishment of seedlings. Perennials, which, once established from seed, are able to persist, are therefore most important as weeds under such conditions and many non-creeping perennials, such as plantains, knapweed and acrid and bulbous buttercups, are common as grassland weeds. Grassland weeds must, of course, be plants which will tolerate grazing or repeated cutting; they are therefore nearly all plants with their main stems and growing points at or near ground-level, and only under conditions of extreme undergrazing do erect, tall-growing weeds become important.

Not only are the weeds of grass usually different from those of arable crops, but different types of grassland management result in different associations of weeds. Grassland frequently cut for hay tends to have

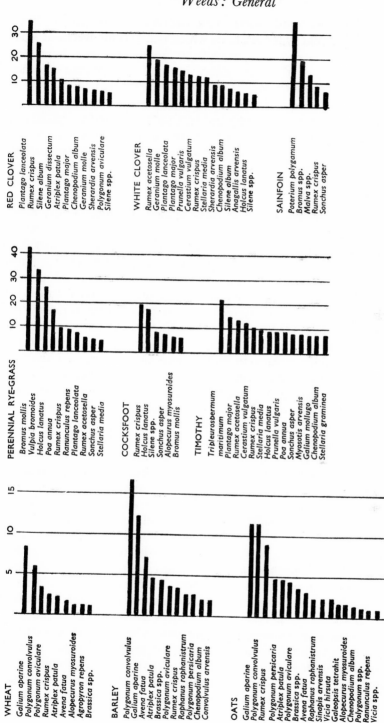

Fig. 171. Diagrams to show the weed seeds most commonly associated with certain crops, and the percentage of samples of the crop-plant seed in which they were found as impurities in 1951–2. Adapted, with alteration of proper names of some weeds, from Broad, P. D., *J. Nat. Inst. Agric. Bot.* **6**, 1952, by permission of the Director of the N.I.A.B.

375

a rather open sward, making establishment from seed easier than in pasture, and early-flowering weeds, which are able to mature and shed seed before the hay is cut, may become frequent. Soft brome is often abundant under these conditions; on poor land yellow rattle may spread, and on better soil hogweed and other *Umbelliferae* of upright habit, and common sorrel, are frequent. In pasture, serious undergrazing often results in the establishment of erect, woody plants; bramble, hawthorn and (on acid soils) gorse or broom are common in neglected grassland. Less serious undergrazing, unless soil fertility is high, may give swards including rather upright herbaceous or slightly woody plants, such as ragwort and lesser knapweed. Overgrazing tends, on the other hand, to encourage low-growing weeds, particularly plants of rosette habit, and may give swards containing daisy, self-heal, bulbous buttercup, dandelion and many other weeds, among which members of the *Compositae* are conspicuous. Under conditions of extreme overgrazing and trampling, annual plants may come in on bare patches, and such weeds as annual meadow-grass, rayless mayweed and swine-cress may be found. Broad-leaved plantain and knot-grass are common gateway weeds.

In arable crops, the type of weed found is perhaps more closely related to seed impurities sown and to soil conditions than to management. All arable weeds must, of course, be plants that are not readily destroyed by the usual arable cultivations; they are thus either perennials with some form of underground vegetative propagation or annuals. The former are able to make new aerial shoots from underground stems (or in some cases, e.g. docks, dandelion, creeping thistle, from roots), while the latter pass through their whole life cycle from seed to seed during the period between successive cultivations. Lucerne, which from this point of view may be regarded as intermediate between an arable crop and a ley, is almost the only crop in which cultivations are far enough separated to allow of the growth of biennial weeds; such biennials as viper's bugloss, wild mignonette (*Reseda lutea*) and wild carrot are common weeds of this crop. In most root crops cultivations are continued during the early growth of the plant and the time during which weeds can develop is very short; rapid-growing ephemerals such as chickweed may appear if shading by the crop is not too intense, as, for example, in a potato crop when the haulm has begun to die down. In cereal crops the period between pre-sowing and post-harvest cultivations is long enough to allow of full development of many annuals; weeds germinating in autumn, such as corn buttercup, hairy buttercup and shepherd's needle are, however, confined to autumn-sown corn crops. Spring-germinating weeds may be found in both winter and spring corn, but are more commonly associated with the latter, since winter corn, unless very thin, casts too deep a shade in late spring to allow of ready establishment then.

(*c*) *Weeds Associated with Particular Soil Conditions.* While many weeds are capable of growing under a very wide range of soil conditions, others are commonly met with only on particular types of soils. Such weeds are often referred to as *indicator plants,* and may be of value in assessing soil character. While the character of the weed flora as a whole is usually a useful guide to soil conditions, too much stress should not be laid on the presence or absence of any one particular species, since this may be very much influenced by other conditions, such as the previous history of the field. Thus, while spurrey may normally be regarded as a reliable indicator of light, strongly-acid soil, it may sometimes persist, owing to heavy seeding in previous years, on land which has been limed and is no longer markedly acid. Again, sheep's sorrel is also commonly an indicator of acid soil, but, in the absence of competition, makes stronger growth in neutral soil. Its frequency on acid soils is due to its ability to tolerate such conditions better than many other weeds, rather than inability to grow under other conditions.

A considerable number of plants, known as *calcicoles,* are confined to *calcareous soils.* Very few of these, however, are important weeds, and the arable weed flora of chalk and limestone soils is not usually markedly different from that of neutral or only slightly alkaline soils. The grassland weeds, stemless thistle, purging flax and tor-grass are, however, largely confined to chalk and limestone soils. A considerable number of weeds occur on *any soils that are not acid*; among these may be listed charlock, corn poppy, various annual speedwells (*Veronica persica* and related species), red dead nettle, corn buttercup, nipplewort and shepherd's needle.

Arable weeds common on *slightly acid soils* are wild radish, corn marigold, wild chamomile and, in some areas, field woundwort. On *strongly-acid soils* the most characteristic arable weeds are spurrey, sheep's sorrel and annual knawel. In grassland, the presence of bracken or foxgloves (usually only in shade) are indications of acidity; the heathers and ling (*Erica* spp. and *Calluna vulgaris*) occur only on strongly acid soils.

Weeds which are normally confined to *wet soils* include a number of creeping perennials occurring both as arable and grassland weeds, such as creeping buttercup, silverweed and corn mint. In grassland, ragged robin, together with such unsown grasses as the sweet grasses (*Glyceria* spp.), floating foxtail and reed canary grass can be found in wet areas. Rushes are usually also indications of wet conditions, but, once established, may persist in relatively dry soils. A number of weeds with very deep rhizomes are found in areas where wet conditions occur in the deeper layers of the soil, as, for instance, coltsfoot and lakeweed (*Polygonum amphibium,* terrestrial form).

Soils with a relatively *high nitrogen level* usually show a characteristic flora of annual weeds; these conditions occur most commonly in market-garden crops. Such weeds include common chickweed, fat hen, groundsel, annual spurges (*Euphorbia helioscopia, E. peplus* and *E. exigua*), annual nettle, black nightshade and common sow-thistle.

The common perennial stinging nettle is commonly an indicator of loose surface litter; its shallow rhizomes are readily destroyed by cultivations, and it is therefore rarely found as an arable weed, but they are unable to spread in consolidated soil in grassland. It usually occurs, therefore, where rubbish heaps, piles of hedge-trimmings or similar materials have allowed the accumulation of surface litter and prevented consolidation by stock. At the other end of the scale, such weeds as broad-leaved plantain and knotgrass, already mentioned as occurring in overtrodden grassland, and the comparatively recently introduced weed rayless mayweed, are characteristic plants of heavily-consolidated soil, and are frequent on headlands, rick-sites and path-sides.

THE DAMAGE DONE BY WEEDS

Reduction of yield of crops, due to competition, is, of course, the most important harmful effect of weeds, but damage may also be done in other ways. The value of the crop may be reduced, altogether apart from the reduction of yield; the presence of poisonous or tainting weeds for example, may make it impossible to use a crop for feeding even where they are not present in sufficient quantity to cause any serious reduction in total yield. The presence of weeds may also increase the difficulty, and therefore the cost, of harvesting a crop; and finally, weeds may have an indirect harmful effect by acting as hosts for insect pests or fungal diseases of crops.

Competition and Reduction of Yield. Competition may take place between weed and crop for light, for water and for soil nutrients, and may result in any degree of reduction of the yield of the crop from a negligible decrease to almost complete loss. It is most likely to be serious where very rapid weed growth takes place while the crop is still small; crops such as potatoes and lucerne, which are comparatively slow in making a complete ground cover of leaves, are particularly sensitive to weed competition at this time. Even the more rapidly-growing crops, such as the cereals, may show very large reductions in yield if weeds are present in abundance.

Competition takes place below ground as well as above; thus, measurements made on the total length of roots of mature wheat plants gave a figure of about 6,000 in. of root per plant where there was no competition from weeds, 4,000 where charlock was competing with the wheat (the charlock itself having some 2,700 in. of root per plant), and only 2,000 where the competing weed was wild oat, which had nearly 9,000 in.* Above ground the competitive ability of the weed largely depends on its height and leaf area, and hence on the extent to which it is able to shade the crop. Weeds which make use of the crop itself for their own support have an advantage in this respect, and such climbing weeds as field bindweed, black bindweed, cleavers and hairy vetch may very seriously reduce the yield of cereals.

The parasitic habit may be regarded as the ultimate extension of this type of competition. Parasitic plants may be *hemi-parasites*, attached to

* Pavlychenko and Harrington, 'Root Development of Weeds and Crops in Competition under Dry Farming', *Sci. Agr. 16*, **151**, 1935 (Canada).

the roots of crop plants, and dependent on them for their mineral nutrition, but with green leaves carrying out normal photosynthesis; or *total parasites*, devoid both of normal roots and of chlorophyll, and entirely dependent on the host plant. A number of hemi-parasitic weeds occur in poor grassland; they are attached to the roots of various grasses, but do not normally result in the death of the host plant. All are members of the *Scrophulariaceae*; they include yellow rattle, red rattle and eye-bright. Only two total parasites are commonly found as weeds of British farm crops; these are broom-rape and dodder. Broom-rapes parasitize various leguminous crops; they are most common on red clover, but appear occasionally on white clover and other species. The upright flowering stem is readily destroyed by the trampling of stock, and they are therefore most commonly seen in ungrazed aftermath or fields put up for a seed harvest. The host plant is not normally killed, although it may be somewhat stunted; broom-rape plants are rarely seen at a greater density than one in several square yards, and this level of attack, although very conspicuous, probably has little effect on the total yield of clover per acre. Dodder is a much more serious weed and may result in the killing-out of the host plant; again clovers are most commonly affected among the crop plants. Dodder seed is normally distributed as an impurity of clover and other similar-sized seeds; very stringent legislative control (Chapter VII) has effectively reduced its importance, and, although potentially serious, it is now a comparatively rare plant as a weed in Britain.

Reduction of Value of Produce. The extent to which weeds reduce the value of crop produce depends on the ease with which they can be separated out. In a seed crop, weeds will only seriously reduce the value of the crop if they produce seeds which cannot be cleaned out. The presence of any weed seeds may increase the cost of cleaning, but weeds which cannot be removed completely, such as soft brome in rye-grass, wild oats in oats or wild onion bulbils in wheat, may render the crop completely unfit for use as seed, and therefore reduce very considerably its monetary value. Where the crop is to be used for purposes other than sowing, seeds or other parts of weeds present in small quantity will cause little reduction in value unless they are poisonous or cause tainting. Thus a wheat sample contaminated with wild onion bulbils is not only unfit for seed, but also for milling, since the ground-up bulbils will give an onion taint to the flour. Similarly, darnel (*Lolium temulentum*) and corn-cockle, which have poisonous seeds, have in the past made wheat valueless because of the danger of poisoning; with modern methods they can be removed comparatively readily, and are now of very minor importance.

In root crops, where plants are lifted separately, the danger of contamination of the resulting produce with weeds is very slight, but in forage and grassland crops, where the herbage is either mown for hay or silage or is grazed *in situ*, there is no opportunity for selection. Thus in them any weeds which are present are available to the animal; if any of these weeds are harmful to the animal, the value of the whole crop is reduced. The harmful weeds may either be directly poisonous or mechanically injurious to the animal, or may bring about a reduction in value of the animal products, as in the tainting of milk by strong-smelling weeds or the spoiling of fleeces by burrs.

Poisonous Plants. A large number of different plants are capable of causing more or less severe poisoning of some animals under some conditions. Of these, those which grow in places accessible to stock are most likely to cause losses, so that it is primarily the poisonous grassland weeds which are important, although arable weeds and plants of gardens and woodland and waste places may give trouble if stock are allowed access to them. Grazing animals normally exercise considerable selection in feeding, and in many cases, but unfortunately not in all, will avoid poisonous plants. Much less selection can be exercised by the animal where the herbage is cut and fed as hay, but not all plants which are poisonous in the fresh state retain their injurious properties when made into hay.

The important poisonous plants are thus the grassland weeds which are not always avoided by stock in the fresh state or which remain poisonous in hay. Ragwort and bracken appear to be the most serious causes of loss of stock; the former because it is not always avoided by grazing cattle (it is readily grazed by sheep, which are usually, but not always, resistant to its effects) and remains poisonous in hay; the latter because, although usually avoided, it is abundant on such an immense acreage of hill land. Of the other poisonous plants found in Britain, yew and laurel, evergreen shrubs or trees which are commonly planted in places where stock may be able to reach them, are probably the most frequent offenders. They are usually not eaten, but during snow or at other times when herbage is scarce they may be attractive to animals; discarded hedge-trimmings or clippings of these shrubs are often dangerous.

Table II lists the plants found wild in Britain or commonly planted which are known to be poisonous and which would normally be looked for in investigating any case of suspected poisoning. Many are not weeds in any ordinary sense of the term, and many are plants that would only be accessible to stock under exceptional conditions. An attempt has been made to give some estimate of their toxicity, but it must be remembered that this can be, at best, only a very rough guide. The concentration of poisonous material will vary in different parts of the plant and between different individuals of the same species, as well as being affected by time of year, stage of growth and climatic and soil conditions. The susceptibility of stock will vary with the type of animal, and with age and weight and general health, and with the amount of other herbage consumed at the same time, as well as according to the idiosyncrasies of the individual beast. Some poisons may be taken in small amounts without any obvious effects, but when such small amounts are taken regularly over a period they accumulate in the body until finally the amount present is sufficient to produce symptoms. Such poisons are said to be *cumulative*.

Experimental evidence regarding poisonous plants is necessarily difficult and expensive to obtain, and cannot cover a very wide range of conditions; clinical evidence is bound to be scanty in the case of rare plants or plants rarely eaten. The details given are therefore often based on old and possibly unreliable reports, or on reports from other countries where conditions may be widely different.

The position may perhaps best be summarized by saying that, while the presence of poisonous plants in places where they are accessible to stock does not necessarily mean that any animals will ever be poisoned, it does mean that some danger exists. The extent of the danger is difficult to assess, but precautionary measures may be taken to reduce it to the lowest possible level. These include the destruction of poisonous plants in grassland, the fencing-off of woods or ornamental grounds where poisonous plants are known to exist, the avoidance of hay containing ragwort or other weeds which remain toxic when dried, and the exercise of great care in the disposal of garden trimmings, hedge-clippings, ditch-cleanings and similar materials.

Plants which are likely to cause mechanical injury to stock are rare in Britain, but grasses with sharp-pointed, barbed 'seeds', such as the barley grasses, may occasionally injure the mouths of grazing animals.

Milk-tainting Plants. The flavour and quality of milk is to some extent affected by the animal's food, and a large number of plants have been suspected of causing tainting or other abnormalities in milk. The evidence is, however, often unsatisfactory in so far as taints of bacterial origin have not always been excluded. There seems good evidence that the flavour of some strong-smelling weeds can pass directly into the milk secreted by animals feeding on them. Such weeds include the wild onions or garlics (particularly ramsons, *Allium ursinum*, which has also caused tainted meat in animals slaughtered shortly after grazing it) and probably also garlic mustard (*Alliaria officinalis*) and the strongly-scented mayweeds (*Anthemis* and *Matricaria* spp.).

Many of the species included in the list of poisonous plants have also been recorded as having a deleterious effect on milk; it is to be expected that among the symptoms of most forms of poisoning in a lactating animal would be a reduction in quantity and quality of the milk. The secretion of poisonous milk has been recorded in a number of cases, notably in poisoning by meadow saffron.

Honey may be noted as another product which may be reduced in value by weeds; tainting of honey by ragwort is recorded as frequent in New Zealand, and poisonous honeys may occur.

Increase of Cost of Growing Crops. Weeds may increase the cost of crops in various ways. In addition to the extra cost of operations such as cultivation and spraying for weed control, further costs may have to be met owing to the greater difficulty of harvesting weedy crops. Cereal

Table II

POISONOUS PLANTS

	Frequency	Toxicity	Probable serious or fatal dose (fresh weight)	Poisonous principle	Hay or dry state	Symptoms and time before death, if fatal	Notes
GRASSLAND WEEDS:							
Ranunculaceae:							
Ranunculus bulbosus, bulbous buttercup	v.c. (dry soils)	m	large	protoanemonin (a volatile yellow oil)	H	Inflammation and narcosis	Unpalatable; very rarely eaten
R. acris, acrid buttercup .	v.c.	s	,,	,,	,,	,,	Occasionally eaten; rarely serious
R. repens, creeping buttercup	v.c. (damp soils)	vs	v. large	,,	,,	,,	,,
R. sceleratus, celery-leaved buttercup	f. (wet)	m	large	,,	,,	,,	Very succulent; may be attractive when other herbage scarce
R. flammula, lesser spearwort	,,	,,	,,	,,	,,	,,	Rarely eaten
R. lingua, greater spearwort	r. (wet)	s	,,	,,	,,	,,	,,
Caltha palustris, marsh marigold	f. (wet)	,,	,,	,,	,,	,,	,,
Umbelliferae:							
Conium maculatum, hemlock	l.c.	vm	5-10 lb.	coniine and other alkaloids	H*	Narcosis and paralysis; few hours	Strong smell; very rarely eaten
Oenanthe crocata, hemlock water dropwort	c. (wet)	,,	1 lb. root	oenanthetoxin	T	Narcosis and paralysis; 1 hour .	Foliage usually avoided; exposed roots may be eaten

382

	Frequency	Toxicity	Probable serious or fatal dose (fresh weight)	Poisonous principle	Hay or dry state	Symptoms and time before death, if fatal	Notes
Cicuta virosa, cowbane	r. (wet)	vm	1 lb. root	cicutoxin	T	Delirium, convulsions; 1 hour	Foliage usually avoided; exposed roots may be eaten
Scrophulariaceae: *Digitalis purpurea*, foxglove	v.c. (acid, shade)	,,	¼ lb.	digitoxin and other glycosides	,,	Contracted pupils, laboured breathing, convulsions; few hours	Very rarely eaten fresh; dangerous in hay
Compositae: *Senecio jacobaea*, **ragwort**	v.c.	vm CUM	2-10 lb.	jacobine and other alkaloids	,,	Straining, staggering, liver degeneration; up to 1 month	Dangerous fresh and in hay; affects all stock; less common in sheep
S. aquaticus, marsh ragwort	l.c. (wet)	,,	,,	,,	,,	,,	,,
Liliaceae: *Colchicum autumnale*, meadow saffron	l.c.	,,	3-5 lb.	colchicine	,,	Vomiting, diarrhoea, stupefaction; 1-6 days	Leaves may be eaten in spring or flowers in autumn
Polypodiaceae: *Pteridium aquilinum*, bracken	v.c. (hill land)	m CUM	large	thiaminase and ? toxins	,,	Internal haemorrhages; some days or weeks	Horses and cattle affected; usually avoided, but so abundant that poisoning common
Equisetaceae: *Equisetum palustre*, horsetails	l.c. (wet)	m	,,	thiaminase and alkaloids	,,	Wasting, loss of muscular control	Rarely eaten fresh; very dangerous in hay; other spp. also dangerous

TREES AND SHRUBS:

	Frequency	Toxicity	Probable serious or fatal dose (fresh weight)	Poisonous principle	Hay or dry state	Symptoms and time before death, if fatal	Notes
Buxaceae: Buxus sempervirens, box	c. gardens, l.f. wild on chalk	m	2 lb.	? alkaloids	? T	Purging, congestion of lungs	—
Leguminosae: Laburnum anagyroides, laburnum	c. gardens	vm	1 lb.	cytisine (alkaloid)	T	Excitement, convulsions, coma; few hours	All parts toxic, seeds most dangerous; horses more susceptible than cattle
Rosaceae: Prunus laurocerasus, cherry laurel	c. gardens, often naturalized	s-vm	varies	cyanogenetic glycoside	H	Difficult breathing, convulsions; sudden	Effects v. variable, but poisoning not uncommon
Thymelaeaceae: Daphne laureola, spurge laurel	r. woods	vm	small	glycosides	? T	Purging, intestinal inflammation, narcosis	Rarely accessible to stock
D. mezereum, mezereon	r. woods, f. gardens	,,	,,	,,	,,	,,	,,
Fagaceae: Quercus spp., oak	v.c.	vs	very large	? tannins	—	Constipation, blood in urine	Leaves may cause trouble, but acorn poisoning more common, esp. young cattle; sheep and pigs immune
Ericaceae: Rhododendron spp., rhododendron	c. gardens, naturalized acid heath	vm	small	andromedotoxin and other glycosides	? T	Violent vomiting, vertigo; death from failure of respiration	Dangerous to all stock
Oleaceae: Ligustrum spp., privet	c. garden hedges	s	large	glycosides	—	Vomiting, diarrhoea	Rarely serious
Taxaceae: Taxus baccata, yew	c. garden hedges; wild in woods some areas	vm	1-10 lb.	taxine (alkaloid)	T	Irritation and narcosis; sudden	Probably most dangerous of all trees; cases of poisoning frequent

ARABLE WEEDS:

	Frequency	Toxi-city	Probable serious or fatal dose (fresh weight)	Poisonous principle	Hay or dry state	Symptoms and time before death, if fatal	Notes
Papaveraceae: *Papaver rhoeas*, poppy	v.c.	s	large	rhoeadine	T	Excitement followed by coma	Rarely important
Cruciferae: *Sinapis arvensis*, charlock	,,	m seed only	—	'mustard oils'	,,	Acute gastro-enteritis	Danger only if grazed when in fruit, or if seed fed in cake or meal
Caryophyllaceae: *Agrostemma githago*, corn cockle	o.	,,	½ lb. seed	saponin	,,	Diarrhœa, wasting	Danger from feeding cereal 'tailings' containing cockle seed
Euphorbiaceae: *Euphorbia* spp., spurge (annual)	c.	s	large	? euphorbio-steroid	,,	Irritation and inflammation of mouth	Danger to stock probably negligible
Umbelliferae: *Aethusa cynapium*, fool's parsley	f.	m	small	coniine	H	Purging and narcosis	,,
Primulaceae: *Anagallis arvensis*, pimpernel	c.	vs	large	glycosides	—	Irritation and narcosis	,,
Solanaceae: *Solanum nigrum*, black nightshade	,,	s to nil	,,	solanine (alkaloid)	—	Stupefaction, convulsions	,,
Gramineae: *Lolium temulentum*, darnel	v.r.	m seed only	1-2 lb. seed	temuline (alkaloid)	T	Giddiness, stupefaction	Formerly common; now of negligible importance

HERBACEOUS PLANTS OF WOODS, HEDGES, WASTE PLACES AND GARDENS:

Frequency	Toxicity	Probable serious or fatal dose (fresh weight)	Poisonous principle	Hay or dry state	Symptoms and time before death, if fatal	Notes
Ranunculaceae:						
Anemone nemorosa, wood anemone	c. woods	m	? large	protoanemonin	H	Narcosis and diarrhoea	Rarely eaten (*A. pulsatilla* rare on chalk, and other spp. in gardens similar)
Helleborus spp., hellebores	r. woods, f. gardens	vm	½-1 lb.	helleborin and other glycosides	T	Narcosis and diarrhoea; some weeks	Dangerous poisons, but rarely eaten by stock
Aconitum spp., monkshood	v.r. woods, f. gardens	,,	1 lb.	aconitine (alkaloid)	,,	Depression and convulsions, paralysis; few hours	,,
Delphinium spp., larkspur	v.r. arable, c. gardens	,,	,,	alkaloids	,,	,,	,,
Papaveraceae:						
Chelidonium majus, greater celandine	o. waste places	s	large	,,	—	Vomiting and purging	Probably rarely serious
Euphorbiaceae:						
Mercurialis perennis, dog's mercury	v.c. woods	m CUM	? small	,,	H	Irritation, narcosis	May be eaten in early spring
Solanaceae:						
Solanum dulcamara, woody nightshade	c. hedges	s	? large	solanine (alkaloid)	? T	Narcosis and diarrhoea	Rarely eaten
Atropa belladonna, deadly nightshade	l. waste places, chalk, shade	vm	varies with animal	hyoscyamine and other alkaloids	T	Narcosis, dilatation of pupils, convulsions	Very toxic to man; cattle and horses less susceptible; sheep and rabbits resistant
Hyoscyamus niger, henbane.	o. waste places	,,	small	,,	,,	,,	Strong unpleasant smell; unlikely to be eaten
Datura stramonium, thornapple	casual, rubbish heaps, etc.	,,	,,	,,	,,	,,	Probably rarely eaten

	Frequency	Toxicity	Probable serious or fatal dose (fresh weight)	Poisonous principle	Hay or dry state	Symptoms and time before death, if fatal	Notes
Cucurbitaceae:							
Bryonia dioica, white bryony	l.c. hedges	m	5 lb. root	bryonin and other glycosides	—	Inflammation and convulsions .	Foliage rarely eaten; dug roots very dangerous
Dioscoriaceae:							
Tamus communis, black bryony	,,	,,	—	glycosides	—	Vomiting and paralysis . .	Roots and fruit dangerous foliage harmless
Iridaceae:							
Iris spp., flags .	c. marshes, etc.	,,	—	iridin	T	Diarrhoea . . .	Rarely eaten fresh; hay and dug rhizomes dangerous
Araceae:							
Arum maculatum, wild arum	c. waste places, shade	? s	—	acrid juice	H	Acute irritation . . .	Rarely eaten

387

EXPLANATION OF SYMBOLS USED

Frequency: v.c., very common; c., common; l.c., locally common; f., frequent; o., occasional; r., rare; v.r., very rare.

Toxicity: vs, very slight; s, slight; m, marked; vm, very marked; cum, cumulative poison.

Hay or dry state: T, toxic; H, harmless; H*, poisons evaporate slowly, as hay matures, so that matured hay is usually safe.

crops may be partly laid owing to climbing weeds; or crops cut with a binder may require a longer period of drying in stook if weeds are present in the sheaf. Potatoes may be difficult to lift if the soil surface becomes overgrown with weeds after the haulm has died down. Weeds in hay may dry more slowly than grass and necessitate extra labour in haymaking. Any crops intended for seed will have to bear extra costs if weedy; not only will the cleaning process be more difficult and expensive, but there will also be some loss of crop, since it is normally impossible to clean out weed seeds without losing some crop seeds as well.

Encouragement of Pests and Diseases. Weeds may harm crops indirectly by harbouring insect and other pests and by acting as hosts for the organisms causing diseases of crop plants. Many pests and diseases rapidly build up if crops of the same type are grown year after year on the same ground, and rotation of crops is therefore necessary if they are to be kept in check. The object of the rotation is, however, defeated if susceptible weeds are allowed to develop. Thus, for instance, weeds such as charlock and shepherd's purse, which belong to the same family as the cruciferous root-crops, are susceptible to the disease club-root (p. 527), which attacks these crops. Attempts to control this disease by rotation of crops may therefore be quite ineffective if such weeds are present to carry the disease over the intervening years. Similarly, the control of insect and nematode pests of crops may be more difficult in the presence of weeds which are capable of acting as alternative host-plants.

THE CONTROL OF WEEDS

A very large range of methods can be used to combat weeds, and the choice of the method to be used in any particular case will depend both on the type of weed and on the type of crop in which it is growing.

Suitability of Control Methods According to Type of Weed. The most important characters of the weed which will affect the suitability of different control methods are its duration and the type of vegetative propagation, if any, which it shows. For this purpose, therefore, weeds can be classified into (a) annuals, (b) biennials, (c) perennials without special vegetative propagation, (d) perennials with special methods of vegetative propagation.

(a) *Annuals.* Annual weeds are usually readily killed by cultivations, and the main difficulties in controlling them arise from their rapid growth and copious production of seed. No economic method exists by which they can be killed in the dormant seed stage; soil-sterilization by steam or dry heat or by the volatile chemicals, such as chlorpicrin, are effective, but can only be used on a glass-house scale. All killing on a field scale must, therefore, take place after germination, and many of the most difficult annual weeds are those which remain dormant in the soil for a long period. Working the soil down to a seed-bed to encourage weed seed germination, and then cultivating to destroy the seedlings before sowing the crop seeds may be effective. Its success depends largely on whether or not the particular weed species present show marked periodicity of germination. Stubble-cleaning involves the production of a seed-bed shortly after the harvest of a cereal crop; it will assist in the destruction of autumn-germinating weeds, but will not be effective against such weeds as *Polygonum* species or fat hen, which will usually only germinate in spring. It is thus usually impossible to induce all seed present in the upper layers of the soil to germinate before sowing the crop, and some will germinate with the crop. Many of these are capable of flowering and shedding seed before the crop is removed, and trouble in future crops can only be prevented by control measures which can be used while the crop is still present.

(*b*) *Biennials.* Biennials present less of a problem than annuals, since they do not flower during the first year and in annual crops will be destroyed by after-harvest cultivations before they have produced seed. It is therefore only in semi-permanent crops, such as lucerne and leys, that biennials are important.

(*c*) *Perennials without Vegetative Propagation.* Like annuals and biennials, perennials which have no special adaptations for vegetative propagation are readily destroyed by cultivations. Like biennials, they do not flower in the first year, and are therefore found only in semi-permanent crops. In grassland, those which have their buds at or near ground-level—as, for instance, plantains—are difficult weeds, while those which have aerial buds—as, for instance, tree seedlings—are readily controlled by cutting or hard grazing.

(*d*) *Perennials with Special Adaptations for Vegetative Propagation.* Perennials with creeping or underground stems, or with roots which can give rise to adventitious shoots, are more difficult to control by cultivation. Since they spread vegetatively it is not sufficient to prevent their flowering and seeding, and destruction of the whole plant must be aimed at. The extent to which this can be achieved depends on the position and nature of the stems (or shoot-producing roots). If these are deep (e.g. field bindweed, horsetails), that is, below the level to which it is practicable to plough, then the weed cannot be directly destroyed by cultivations and can only be killed by indirect methods, or possibly by chemical weed-killers. If they are shallow, that is, within reach of the plough or cultivators, the difficulty of killing them will depend largely on their shape. Stolons or long, shallow rhizomes (e.g. couch) can be readily worked to the surface and removed or killed by drying out. Shorter structures, such as the shoot-producing tap-roots of docks and dandelions, are less readily removed or brought to the surface, while the greatest problem of all is provided by weeds with small bulbs or corms. Such structures, which are usually approximately spherical, cannot be brought to the surface by any of the usual implements. Weeds with vegetative structures of this type are fortunately rare; wild onion and onion couch (the tuberous form of tall oat-grass) are the only two commonly found in Britain, although some bulb-forming species of *Oxalis* have become established in the milder areas of the south-west. Control measures are confined either to very expensive hand-picking or to cultivations carefully timed to coincide with the period when the majority of old bulbs or corms have grown out, and new ones have not yet formed.

Bare ground allows of the greatest freedom of choice in weed-control operations and a permanent broadcast crop the least; wide-drilled crops are intermediate in position. These three cases may be considered separately.

(*a*) *Bare Ground.* Permanently bare ground permits of the use of any form of weed-control, but is unlikely to occur under agricultural conditions. Fire-breaks in forests are perhaps the only example of land kept permanently free from all growth by cultivations and long-lasting weed-killers. Roads, railway tracks, etc., are areas on which no growth is allowable, but where the surface must not be disturbed; here cultivations are impossible, but any type of chemical weed-killer may be used.

Agricultural land is normally bare for comparatively short periods. Such temporary bare ground is available for varying lengths of time, from a few weeks between crops to a whole year in the case of a full fallow. Any form of cultivation may be carried out, and the only limitation on weed-control methods is that chemical weed-killers must not be so persistent that they affect the succeeding crop.

(*b*) *Spaced Crops.* Spaced crops, in which the plants are grown sufficiently far apart to allow of cultivations between them, permit weed-control to be continued after the plants are in position. Cultivations are largely confined to relatively shallow hoeing, since deeper working might cause damage to spreading roots of the crop. Most agricultural spaced crops are temporary, as in the annual root crops, but grass seed crops grown in wide drills and a number of horticultural crops such as soft fruits provide examples of spaced crops kept down for several years. Spaced crops are often regarded as cleaning crops, in that they allow of some cultivations, but the very effective control of many weeds in cereal crops, now possible with selective herbicides, has greatly reduced their importance for this purpose.

(*c*) *Close Crops.* Broadcast or closely-drilled crops do not usually allow of any cultivations during the time the crop is in the ground. Weed-control in temporary close crops, such as cereals, depends on cultivations before sowing and after harvesting, and on the application of selective weed-killers during the intervening period. Permanent or semi-permanent close crops such as long leys prevent all cultivations other than surface treatment, and weed-control in them is primarily a matter of cutting and grazing management, supplemented by the use of selective weed-killers.

WEED-CONTROL METHODS

The methods available for the control of weeds may be divided into (*a*) cultivation and similar mechanical methods, including cutting, in which the plant is attacked directly, (*b*) ecological methods, in which the plant is attacked indirectly, by altering the environmental conditions so as to make them less favourable to the weed, (*c*) biological control, where insect pests are introduced which will attack the plant, and (*d*) herbicides or weed-killers, including a wide range of different chemical substances sprayed or dusted on to the plant to kill it.

(*a*) *Cultivation.* In weed-control by cultivation, direct *removal* of the living plant is rarely necessary and is usually employed only for docks (hand-pulling or forking, or hand-picking of ploughed-up roots), and occasionally for onion couch. The majority of cultivations aim at killing by *desiccation*, weeds being cut through at or a little below ground-level and left on the surface to dry out. Perennials with underground stems can be dealt with in the same way, providing that the rhizomes can be dragged to the surface to dry out. Killing by this method is dependent on dry weather; under wet conditions even annuals may be able to produce adventitious roots and re-establish themselves.

Burying, usually by ploughing under, is effective with annuals, and may be effective with stoloniferous or shallow-rhizomed perennials. In the latter case deep ploughing with complete inversion of the furrow slice is essential, as otherwise shoots will grow up between the furrows and no kill will result. A method comparable to burying is *mulching*, where a layer of straw or similar material is laid on the surface of the soil; sheets of paper have sometimes been used, laid between rows of crop plants. The method is usually only effective for the control of seedling weeds, and can normally only be used on a horticultural scale. *Flooding* has much the same effect on weeds as burying, but is effective against deep-rhizomed perennials. Controlled flooding (with fresh water) for three to eight weeks during summer has been used in the U.S.A. for the killing of weeds of this type, including hoary pepperwort. Casual natural flooding in winter, when weeds are largely dormant, is usually without effect.

Weeds with rhizomes too deep to be reached by implements can be controlled by repeated shallow cultivations. Here the effect is comparable to repeated mowing, and death results from *starvation* of the rhizome. Food material stored in the rhizomes is used up in producing vertical shoots, which are cut off, either below ground-level by hoeing or above-ground by mowing, before they reach the stage of growth at which surplus food, produced by photosynthesis, is available for storage in the underground parts. The food material used up is thus not replaced, and repeated production and cutting of such shoots will result in weakening of the rhizome and eventually, if the process is continued, in its death. The effect of repeated hoeing on the food reserves in the rhizome of field bindweed is illustrated in fig. 172; it will be seen that, while the percentage increases steeply during the growing season in undisturbed plants, it decreases slightly in plants kept regularly hoed. Field bindweed is a particularly difficult weed to control, and hoeing would need to be continued for at least two seasons to kill it.

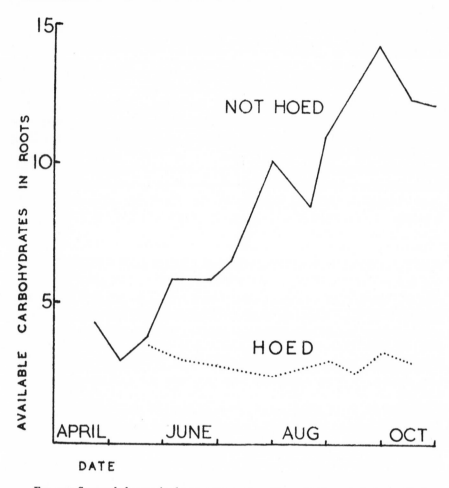

FIG. 172. Seasonal changes in the percentage of readily available carbohydrates (fresh weight) in the 'roots' of field bindweed. Solid line, plants undisturbed; broken line, plants hoed once a fortnight. Redrawn and adapted from Barr, C. G., *J. Agric. Res.*, **60**, 1940, by permission of the U.S. Department of Agriculture.

The control of bracken by cutting may be used as an illustration of the effect of timing of operations on the process of killing by starvation. Fig. 173 represents the relation between strength of bracken, expressed as weight of fronds per sq. yard, and the time of cutting during each of the four preceding years. Plots cut early showed only small decreases, owing to the fact that the fronds were small at the time of cutting, and the amount of food reserves used up and lost in their production was therefore also small. Cutting at the beginning of July gave the greatest weakening of the bracken, and almost complete control, since at this time the maximum amount of food material had been utilized in production of the fronds, but these had not yet produced a surplus of food which could be stored. Later cutting resulted in poorer control, since it allowed the new fronds to replace, by photosynthesis, the food reserves used up; cutting after the middle of August gave only slight reduction in strength. The actual dates given apply only to the particular area in Scotland where the trial was carried out, and would be somewhat different in other districts.

The *burning-off* of weeds by implements of the 'flame-thrower' type is comparable to mowing, but may be more effective owing to the formation of toxins in scorched plant tissues and their translocation to roots and other underground structures. Under some conditions the effect may

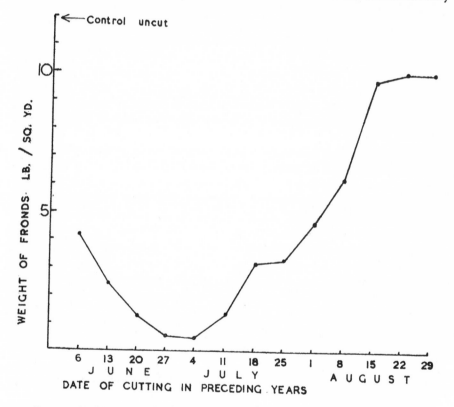

FIG. 173. Weight of bracken fronds in pounds per square yard fresh weight at end of July on plots cut once a year at various dates. Redrawn and adapted from Braid, K. W., *Scottish Jour. Agric.*, XXII, 1939, by permission of the Controller of H.M. Stationery Office.

be increased by the deposition on the plant surfaces of unburnt oil, which acts as a herbicide.

(*b*) *Ecological Methods.* Alteration of the environment, to make it less favourable for weed growth, provides an indirect method of controlling weeds. *Manuring*, by favouring the growth of crop-plants, which usually have a high fertility requirement, may enable them to compete more strongly with weeds. *Liming* may have the same effect and enable crops to compete successfully with acid-tolerant weeds. *Drainage* may be used where excess water favours the weeds associated with wet conditions. The use of *smother crops*, such as vetches, is an example of weed-control by very vigorous competition from the crop, the main effect here being of competition for light, with the weeds being shaded out by the crop. Similar alterations in the environment of grassland weeds may be obtained by varying management, as, for example, in the suppression of low-growing pasture weeds by haying or by long rest periods enabling the grasses to grow up and cast a dense shade.

(*c*) *Biological Control*. The term biological control might be used to cover all cases of weed-control by the action of other organisms, such as competition from other plants, or the influence of the grazing animal, but is commonly confined to the special case of control by insect pests. Spectacular results have been obtained in Australia in the biological control of prickly pear (*Opuntia* spp.) by a moth, *Cactoblastis cactorum*, but the method is not one which is generally applicable. Prickly pear is an American plant, not closely related to any indigenous Australian plants, and introduced without insect pests. It was thus able to multiply at a very great rate in those parts of Australia where the climate was favourable. Control was achieved by the large-scale introduction of the *Cactoblastis* moth from the Argentine; this was introduced free from predators, which in its natural habitat would keep its numbers in check. It thus multiplied rapidly, and has given virtually complete control of prickly pear in Australia.

The native or long-introduced weeds of Britain are attacked by numerous insects, which in turn are kept in check by numerous predators and parasites, so that a state of equilibrium has been reached which is not readily upset. Even if it were possible to discover some new and aggressive insect pest, its introduction would only be effective if it were not attacked by any of the native parasites or predators. Its introduction would only be safe if it were certain that it would not damage any crop plants; this requirement would only be met by an insect of very specialized feeding habits attacking a weed not closely related to any useful species. Biological control of weeds by fungal or virus diseases is a theoretical possibility which has sometimes been considered—as, for example, for bracken control. The limitations of this method are perhaps even stricter than for control by insects, and no successful use of it has been recorded.

Although the opportunities for planned biological control of weeds are thus limited, there is no doubt that biological control in the wider sense does play an important part in determining the relative abundance of different plants. The upsetting of an established equilibrium by the spread of myxomatosis among wild rabbits may well result in changes in the weed flora of rough grassland and waste places; tor grass (*Brachy-podium pinnatum*) and deadly nightshade (*Atropa belladonna*) have been suggested as species which are showing signs of increase in some areas as a result of the cessation of rabbit-grazing.

(*d*) *Herbicides.* Very many chemical substances are capable of killing plants; their usefulness as herbicides depends on the quantity required and its cost, on the length of time they remain toxic, and on their selectivity. For use on permanently bare ground, a herbicide is required which is not selective—that is, which will kill all plants and which will remain toxic for as long as possible. On temporary bare ground, such as a fallow between crops, a quick-acting, non-selective weed-killer is required which will no longer be toxic when the succeeding crop is sown. With herbicides to be used for killing weeds in a growing crop, selective action is the most important character. Here a chemical is required which, when applied at a rate which will not harm the crop, kills all, or as many as possible, of the weeds.

Permanence and selectivity are both variable characters, depending on the amount of the herbicide used. In nearly all cases, the greater the quantity applied, the longer will be the time for which it persists and the less will be its selectivity. It is none the less possible to distinguish three main groups of substances: the non-selective, long-lasting herbicides, used mainly on roads and railways, and of little agricultural importance; the short-period non-selective, sometimes useful on temporarily bare farmland, but employed mainly only for weeds resistant to selective herbicides; and the selective herbicides, which are by far the most important agriculturally.

Various methods of application are used; non-selective weed-killers are often applied as dry granules or as a coarse spray to the surface of the ground, the weed-killing action being due to absorption into the plant from the soil. Oil sprays, sometimes used as general non-selective weed-killers, require, however, to be sprayed so as to form a film over the plant surfaces, while volatile substances, such as carbon bisulphide, are injected into the soil, and the vapour spreads through the air-spaces in the soil. The majority of selective weed-killers are applied directly to the plant, either as dusts or more commonly as sprays, either high volume (usually about 100 gallons of spray fluid per acre) or low volume (often 6-10 gallons per acre) according to the type of herbicide (see p. 401). The latter method, if effective, has the advantage that smaller spray-tanks are adequate, and that less cartage of water is needed. The amount of chemical applied per acre is usually about the same in both cases. Low-volume spraying has, however, the disadvantage that the danger of spray drift on to neighbouring susceptible crops is greater; the very small droplets produced are readily carried long distances before they settle, and low-volume spraying is usually impracticable with winds of over twelve miles per hour. With contact herbicides such as the dinitro compounds and sulphuric acid, which act directly on the leaf surface, it may be necessary to include a wetting agent in the spray fluid to ensure complete wetting of weeds with hairy or waxy surfaces. Where no satisfactory selective herbicide exists for a particular combination of crop and weed, good results can sometimes be achieved by the use of *pre-emergence sprays*; a quick-acting spray is applied after the crop is sown, but before it emerges, and kills recently-germinated weeds which would otherwise compete with the crop.

Non-selective Herbicides. *Arsenic* compounds were formerly used as long-lasting general weed-killers; they are very effective, but so poisonous to man and animals that their use has been abandoned. *Borax* and other boron compounds are somewhat less effective but much safer, and may still be used. Organic *residual herbicides* such as the triazines *simazine* and *atrazine* can be employed. Simazine is extremely insoluble and very long-lasting in the soil; the killing of established weeds is slow, and it may be advisable to add other herbicides where rapid kill is required, but doses of as low as 5 lb. per acre can prevent re-establishment of many weeds for a year or more. Simazine shows very little movement in the soil, and can thus be used close to susceptible plants, or under deep-rooted trees. Atrazine is rather more soluble, and penetrates deeper. Other residual herbicides are the substituted ureas, such as *monuron*, and carbamates such as *propham*; in general these residual herbicides are very effective in preventing seed germination, but established plants of many weeds are resistant to them. Since some crop plants are also resistant, some selective weed-killing is possible. Thus *propham* can be used as a pre-emergence spray in sugar beet; *diuron* or *endothal* (toxic; special precautions necessary) is added to increase the range of weeds killed. Dosage of the mixture must be strictly related to soil type.

Chlorates are useful herbicides which have a wide range of effectiveness; they control a large number of species in the first few months, but will usually allow of a crop being grown after about six months, unless heavy applications are used. They have the great advantage of being non-poisonous, but some danger of fire exists; chlorates are powerful oxidizing agents, and any dry mixture of a chlorate with organic matter is explosive. Sodium chlorate is commonly used and is safe, providing that precautions are taken and that, for example, clothes saturated with chlorate solution are not allowed to dry without washing. The hygroscopic calcium and magnesium chlorides are sometimes added to reduce the danger of fire.

Chlorates may act by penetrating directly through the leaf surfaces, but are usually absorbed by the roots and translocated within the plant; like arsenites, they are relatively more effective on sandy soils than on clay. The amount required to give an adequate kill depends on the weed species, and varies from about 15 lb. per acre for chickweed (i.e. a 1·5 per cent. solution if sprayed at 100 gallons per acre) up to 50-100 lb. for other annuals and surface-rooting perennials, such as creeping buttercup and ragwort. Rhizomatous perennials, such as couch, nettles and coltsfoot, may require 150-200 lb., and especially resistant ones, such as docks, field bindweed and goutweed, 400-500 lb. Rates of application of this latter order are commonly used in the U.S.A., but are not usually regarded as economic in Britain. They are, moreover, semi-permanent in effect and will not permit of the land being cropped in the following year; rates up to 100 lb. acre are the only ones that are usually safe for use during a short fallow. Spot treatment of such weeds as docks is sometimes economic; here a pinch of dry sodium chlorate is applied to the individual plant, producing a local concentration sufficient to kill it.

Carbon bisulphide is a non-selective weed-killer which is effective against plants with deep rhizomes; it is injected 18 in. to 2 ft. deep in the soil, and its vapour, which is highly toxic to plant tissue, spreads through the soil spaces. *Tetrachlorethane* has been used in the same way.

Mineral oils, cresylic acids, and other substances can be used as contact herbicides to kill a wide range of plants. *PCP* (pentachlorphenol) can be added to the oil, or used alone as a pre-emergence spray.

The quaternary ammonium compounds *diquat* and *paraquat* are particularly useful; the latter is translocated to some small extent and may therefore give some kill of perennials, but both are inactivated on contact with the soil. They can thus be used for immediate pre-sowing spraying, as well as pre-emergence. Diquat kills a wide range of dicotyledonous annuals; paraquat is more effective against grasses. Where both are present, a mixture of the two is employed. They can also be used for purposes other than weed-killing; diquat for the desiccation of potato and other foliage, paraquat for the partial or complete killing of grassland swards. In the latter case the sward is left for two weeks to allow maximum kill, and then cultivated to produce a seed bed.

Selective Herbicides. Selective herbicides which can be used to kill the weeds in a growing crop are of outstanding importance, since they allow of weed-control at a time when cultivations may be impossible. No known substances are completely selective at all rates of application, but a considerable number exist which are sufficiently selective to be of value—that is, which can be applied at a rate high enough to kill many weeds without damaging certain crops. Selectivity depends, of course, on a difference of effect of the herbicide on the crop and on the weeds, and the more similar the two are the more difficult is selective control. In general, effective control of many dicotyledonous weeds is comparatively easy in a cereal or grass crop, and is possible in certain dicotyledonous crops—such as peas, lucerne, linseed and, to some extent, beet. Control of monocotyledonous weeds is more difficult, but some annual grass weeds can be selectively killed under some conditions.

Selective herbicides suitable for application as a spray may be divided into *contact herbicides* (groups (*a*)-(*c*), below) in which killing is mainly confined to tissue actually covered by the spray, and *growth-regulator herbicides* (group (*d*)), in which there may be in addition considerable transport of the herbicide within the plant.

The selective killing of dicotyledonous weeds in cereal crops depends largely, in the case of contact herbicides, on the fact that the weeds present a large surface of mainly horizontally placed leaves which retain a greater amount of spray or dust than the narrow, vertically-standing leaves of the cereal, and that their stems and growing points are relatively exposed, while those of cereals are protected by surrounding leaf-sheaths. Some differences in the actual susceptibility of the plant tissues may also exist. Resistance to most selective herbicides increases with age; cereals in the seedling stage are susceptible and cannot safely be treated. The weeds also in many cases become more resistant as they become older, so that spraying should usually be carried out as soon as the crop will bear it. While the susceptibility of different weed species to the various selective herbicides varies widely, it is in general true to say that the younger the weeds the better will be the control. Many species can be satisfactorily controlled in the seedling or young plant stage which are to a large extent resistant as mature plants. Control of established perennials is more difficult, and complete killing is often impossible in cereal crops; it may, however, be practicable in grassland which will usually tolerate higher concentrations of herbicide. Even in cereal crops the perennials may, however, be sufficiently checked to prevent their being serious competitors during the growing period of the crop.

Selective Herbicides for Control of Dicotyledonous Weeds. (*a*) *Salts.* Salts of heavy metals such as *copper sulphate* and *copper chloride* were amongst the first substances to be used for the selective control of weeds in cereal crops. *Ferrous sulphate*, at one time used as a spray, is still used as a constituent of lawn sand* for the control of lawn weeds. Large quantities of very soluble salts may be also applied to certain crops as a spray; advantage is taken of the high salt tolerance of the various beet and mangel forms by using *sodium nitrate* as a 25 per cent. solution at 100 gallons per acre. The majority of weeds are killed by this concentration, but those, such as fat hen, which belong to the same family as beet are unaffected.

(*b*) *Sulphuric Acid.* Sulphuric acid at about 5–10 per cent. is an effective contact herbicide for many broad-leaved weeds, and causes little damage to the common cereals. It has the advantages that it is rapid acting, is little affected by temperature, and has no residual effect. It therefore came into wide use, but has been now almost completely abandoned, except in certain special cases, on account of its highly corrosive nature, which necessitates the use of special spraying apparatus.

(*c*) *Dinitrophenols.* DNOC (dinitro orthocresol, also known as DNC) is a methyl-dinitrophenol. It is a yellow dye, originally used as an insecticide, and later shown to be an effective selective contact herbicide. It can be used on cereals at up to 8 lb. of the sodium salt (6 lb. of the ammonium salt) and kills a very wide range of seedling dicotyledonous weeds. It is however highly toxic to man and is therefore unpleasant and dangerous to use; pro-

---

* A typical lawn sand mixture is 3 parts sulphate of ammonia, 1 part ferrous sulphate (calcined) and 20 parts sand; applied at 4 oz. per square yard.

tective clothing must be worn. It remained in general use after the development of the earlier growth-regulating herbicides since it kills several important weeds which are resistant to MCPA and 2,4-D. With the development of special herbicides effective against many of these resistant weeds (see p. 403) DNOC has largely gone out of use.

Dinoseb (dinitro secondary butyl phenol, or DNBP) is a methylpropyl dinitrophenol. It is as toxic as DNOC, and the same special precautions are necessary, but it is still sometimes used since it is less harmful to the *Leguminosae*, and therefore capable of being used for weed control in leguminous crops. It is used in the form of the ammonium salt, usually at a rate of $1\frac{1}{2}$ lb. per acre at high volume, i.e. in about 100 gallons of water. At this rate it can be applied to field peas between 4 and 10 in. high (garden peas are more liable to injury), winter-sown field beans about 3 in. high, and to lucerne, sainfoin and clovers with at least two trifoliate leaves. In all cases the rate must be reduced to 1 lb. if the temperature is over 70° F.: spraying at below 55° F. is not usually effective. The control of weeds with $1\frac{1}{2}$ lb. dinoseb is closely comparable to that obtained with 8 lb. DNC, but a few weeds such as speedwells (*Veronica* spp.) are not so well controlled. Dinoseb is not suitable for general use in cereal crops, but may be used in cereal-legume mixtures if necessary; some scorching of oats is likely to be produced.

(*d*) *Growth-regulating Substances.* Physiological studies of the bending-over of oat seedlings exposed to light from one side resulted in the discovery that curvature was controlled by substances produced at the top of the coleoptile and diffusing down towards its base, where they affected the rate of elongation. These substances were referred to as auxins, or as plant hormones, since they resembled hormones in animals in being secreted in one region and affecting physiological processes in other parts of the organism. One such substance, hetero-auxin, was shown to be β-indolyl-acetic acid, and the physiological action of a large number of chemically-related substances was therefore investigated. It was found that a considerable number of them were able to affect plant growth, and some have proved valuable, particularly in horticulture, in inducing the formation of adventitious roots on cuttings, causing the swelling of unpollinated ovaries (e.g. in tomatoes) preventing fruit-abscission, and in various other ways. Such physiologically active compounds are often called hormones, although this term is not strictly applicable to those which have not been shown to exist naturally in plants; the terms 'growth-regulators' or 'plant-growth substances' are perhaps therefore preferable.

It was found that some of these hormone-like substances when applied to plants in larger quantities caused a breakdown of the normal growth pattern, producing irregular, distorted growth and eventually death of the plant. The effect was selective, many dicotyledonous weeds being readily killed, while the cereals were relatively unaffected. The most effective substances from this point of view were certain substituted phenoxyacetic acids and their compounds, and these have come into general use as the growth-regulator or hormone-type weed-killers. These are MCPA (2-methyl-4-chloro-phenoxyacetic acid) and 2,4-D, which is also known as DCPA (2:4-dichloro-phenoxyacetic acid). TCPA (2:4:5-trichloro-phenoxyacetic acid, known also as 2,4,5-T) is rather different in its effects, being particularly toxic to woody plants, and will be considered separately.

MCPA and 2,4-D are, in general, similar in their effects; applied at rates varying from ¼ lb. for very susceptible weeds under favourable conditions up to 2 lb. per acre (expressed in terms of the pure acid) they give good control of many annual weeds, although the total number of species controlled is not as great as with DNC. The plants must be actively growing for them to be effective, and control is therefore poor at low temperatures. Killing of weeds is much slower than with contact herbicides, and the full effect may not be evident for four weeks or even more. Since they are hormone-like substances capable of being transported to some extent within the plant, their action is not confined as with contact sprays like DNC to the plant organs actually covered with spray. They are therefore effective against a number of perennials, although plants with deep rhizomes are rarely killed completely. Spraying must not be done when the plants are dormant; control of perennials is usually more effective when the aerial shoots are well developed, so that a large leaf surface is presented to the spray. Distorted inflorescences and decreased fertility are common results of the growth disturbances produced, and even plants that are not killed may be prevented from setting seed. A further result of the mode of action of these growth-regulators is that they can be applied at low volume. With contact sprays it is usually necessary to apply sufficient fluid to cover a large proportion of the surface area of the weeds to be killed; with growth-regulators the spray may be in the form of very fine droplets which should be evenly distributed over the weed but need not actually cover a very large proportion of the total leaf surface. Low-volume spraying at rates from 20 down to 5 gallons per acre (or even down to 1 gallon when spraying from the air) is therefore commonly employed for these herbicides. They may also be prepared as dusts; the active compound is absorbed in a large quantity of a finely-powdered inert carrier, so that 1 cwt. or more per acre of the mixture can be applied with a fertilizer-distributor. This is a convenient method when no sprayer is available, but it is less efficient than spraying, and the figures quoted for amounts of active substance to be applied as a spray should be doubled if dusting is used. Great care must be taken, both with dusts and with low-volume sprays, that wind does not cause drift into neighbouring susceptible crops.

MCPA and 2,4-D are not used as free acids, but in the form of their sodium or amine salts, which are soluble in water. 2,4-D is also used as ethyl, propyl or other esters of the acid; these are dissolved in oil and sprayed as an emulsion in water. Different formulations may vary somewhat in their effects on different plants; in general the esters are usually most toxic and least selective. The compounds of the two acids are usually closely comparable in effect, but MCPA is in many cases slower-acting and more selective. MCPA salts can be applied as a spray to all cereals except oats at rates equivalent to 2 lb. per acre of the free acid, and to oats at 1 lb.; for 2,4-D salts the safe figure is about 1 lb., and for esters from $\frac{1}{4}$ to 1 lb., neither being safe for spring oats. MCPA (but not 2,4-D) may also be used in linseed, but not at low volume.

The figures given for safe rates of application refer to crops at their most resistant stage; for the cereals this is usually after six leaves are visible on the larger tillers. The factor which is important is not the size of the plant, but the stage reached by the stem apex; normally by the time six leaves are visible on a tiller the initiation of the inflorescence is complete, and the rudiments of all spikelets have been formed. Spraying, even at very low rates, before this stage, may result in very seriously deformed inflorescences which sometimes fail to emerge completely from the flag leaf; in wheat and barley whorled or supernumerary spikelets may be present, in oats bunched panicle branches and deformed spikelets. Very late spraying at the time when the ear is shooting may also cause damage if esters are used, and may result in shortened straws and reduced seed-set.

The use of these growth-regulators is not recommended in cereal crops undersown with grass and clover, as the seedlings, particularly those of clovers, are rather readily killed. If, however, weeds are present in quantities which make control essential, and they are ones which, like charlock, are very readily killed, then it may be worth applying not more than 1 lb. per acre of sodium MCPA (or smaller amounts of other compounds). Spraying should be done as late as safely possible, as both grass and clover seedlings increase in resistance with age. The use of butyric acid compounds (see below) is preferable in such undersown crops.

On established leys higher rates of application may be used, since mature clover plants are relatively resistant. Up to 2 lb. per acre of the salts, or 1 lb. esters, may be used, and will not usually result in more than a temporary check to the clovers. Established grasses will tolerate heavy applications, and on lawns and sports-turf, where clovers need not be considered, rates of up to 5 lb. per acre MCPA salts may be used.

2,4,5-T, the related trichloro compound, is used mainly in the form of esters, either alone or in mixture with 2,4-D esters, as a 'brush-killer', and gives good control of, for example, brambles; rather poorer control of gorse, and is ineffective against ling (*Calluna*). The effect is partly dependent on the extent to which translocation takes place within the plant, and effectiveness and selectivity vary according to the time of year. Hawthorn is relatively resistant, so that some selective control of brambles, etc., in hedges is possible, by using 2,4,5-T as a foliage spray.

Butyric Acid Compounds. It was shown by Professor Wain at Wye College in 1954 that, while the corresponding butyric acid compounds are ineffective as growth-regulators, they can be broken down in some plants to give the effective acetic acid compounds. Thus, MCPB (4-(2 methyl-4-chlorophenoxy) butyric acid) is inactive, but in certain plants which possess the appropriate β-oxidation enzymes, it is converted to MCPA. The result is that if two plants, both susceptible to MCPA, are sprayed with MCPB, if one has the appropriate enzyme system and the other has not, then the former will be killed and the latter unharmed. This opens up greatly increased possibilities of selective weed-killing; it does not increase the range of weed species which can be killed, but it does increase the range of crops in which control can be undertaken. Thus clovers and celery do not convert the butyric acids to acetic acids, or do so only very slowly, and are therefore unharmed by MCPB (or 2,4-DB), while many weeds are as well controlled by it as by MCPA. MCPB does not cause damage even to very young cereals; clover seedlings and young peas (some varieties only) will tolerate up to 2 lb. per acre, and established clovers up to 4 lb.

Herbicides for the control of weeds resistant to MCPA and 2,4-D. Some common annual weeds of cereals are resistant to MCPA and 2,4-D; these include chickweed and some other members of the *Caryophyllaceae*, *Polygonum* spp., hemp-nettle, cleavers, mayweeds and nipplewort. Against such weeds, the corresponding propionic acid compounds can be effective; *mecoprop*, also known as MCPP or CMPP, is 2-(4-chloro-2-methylphenoxy) propionic acid; *dichlorprop*, or 2,4-DP, is 2-(2,4 dichlorophenoxy) propionic acid. Mecoprop controls the chickweeds and cleavers, as well as many, but not all, of the species controlled by MCPA. Dichlorprop is effective against *Polygonum* spp. Other herbicides which can be used for the selective control of these resistant weeds are *2,3,6-TBA* (2,3,6 trichlorobenzoic acid) and *dicamba* (3,6-dichloro-2-methoxybenzoic acid). 2,3,6-TBA is effective against chickweeds and other members of the same family, and against mayweeds; dicamba against chickweeds, hempnettle, nipplewort and *Polygonum* spp. These two benzoic acid compounds are used in mixture with MCPA since they have a rather narrow range of effectiveness if used alone.

A more recent introduction is *ioxynil*, a benzo nitrile not related to these growth-regulating substances. It behaves as a contact herbicide, and kills chickweeds, mayweeds, and some species of *Polygonum*.

Herbicides for the Control of Monocotyledonous Weeds. Selective weed-killing in the reverse direction—that is, the killing of monocotyledonous weeds (especially grasses) in dicotyledonous crops is difficult. *TCA* (trichloracetic acid, used mainly in the form of its salts) and *dalapon* (2,2-dichlorpropionic acid) are good grass killers, but neither is very selective. TCA is absorbed mainly through the roots; it can be used at rates up to about 7 lb. per acre applied to the soil well before drilling peas or some root crops to kill annual grasses such as wild oats; at higher rates it is used non-selectively to kill perennial grasses, including couch. Couch is best controlled by not less than 40 lb. per acre preferably as two separate applications during cultivations, so that the spray may come in contact with exposed rhizomes. Dalapon is absorbed mainly through the leaves, as a translocated herbicide; couch is controlled by spraying at about 10 lb. per acre when in active growth. It is usually necessary to plough at least two weeks later to discourage regeneration, and normally there must be an interval of two months (longer for cereals) before a crop is sown. Paraquat can be used to kill annual or tufted grasses, but is not effective against couch, and cannot be used as a selective herbicide.

Some carbamates, particularly *barban* can be used for the selective killing of wild oats. Barban at about 5 oz. per acre kills young (2 leaf) plants of wild oats and of black grass, and is selective enough to be used in many varieties of wheat and barley (not oats) as well as in beans and peas.

Weed killing in susceptible crops. Crops which are susceptible to the growth-regulating herbicides must usually be kept weed-free by inter-row cultivations, but there are some cases in which herbicides may be used. In kale *SMA* (sodium monochloracetate) or *desmetryne* (a triazine) may be used as selective sprays at the young plant stage, and both control a fairly wide range of seedling weeds. Where fat hen is the main weed, desmetryne should be used. Carrots are resistant to certain mineral oils which are toxic to the great majority of plants, and these can therefore be used as selective foliage sprays for this crop.

Where there is no foliage spray to which the crop is resistant, a pre-emergence herbicide may be used. Residual pre-emergence herbicides will prevent weed seedlings from appearing for some time and are therefore used where the crop is not damaged by them. Thus *simazine* and *atrazine* can be used with maize, and *propham* with peas and sugar beet. Where, as with turnips and swedes, such residual herbicides would cause damage, a pre-emergence contact herbicide such as *diquat* or *pentachlorphenol* can be used, but this will kill only those weeds which germinate before the crop. In such a case, a stale seed-bed technique is likely to give the best results.

Chapter XIX

WEEDS: SPECIAL

In this chapter some of the more common weeds are described. In addition a few species are included on account of some special interest, rather than because of their abundance as weeds; for example, certain weeds which are poisonous to livestock (see Chapter XVIII); also parasitic weeds, such as dodder.

It is impossible in a book of this nature to describe all species which may be encountered as weeds on farms, but those considered to be of most interest are included. The student wishing to extend his knowledge of species beyond these limits is referred to one of the standard floras mentioned at the end of this section.

Descriptions of the seeds of a number of species have been included—chiefly those seeds which are likely to be encountered as impurities in agricultural seed samples or in waste from threshing or seed-cleaning machines and those which may assist in the identification of a plant. The measurements quoted for seeds normally represent the approximate length of the longest axis. The term 'seed' as used here is not strictly correct in the botanical sense, as it is taken to include the fruits, or parts of fruits, of some species, which are commonly referred to as seeds.

For the general characters of families already dealt with in Section II, students are referred to the appropriate chapter. Brief descriptions of general characters are included for the other important families.

In the case of a few species which are difficult to control by general methods, and where special techniques are involved, some notes on control have been included. For other species which may be troublesome an indication of the value of selective herbicide sprays is included. In some cases mention is made of the value of DNC (DNOC) and dinoseb. The use of the former for cereal crops has declined but dinoseb is often used as a post-emergence spray for peas and to some degree for undersown cereals and seedling lucerne. The herbicides should be used for appropriate crops only, as indicated in Chapter XVIII. Where 2,4-D is mentioned the recommendation includes the amine and ester forms unless otherwise indicated. Proprietary herbicides containing the active substance in diluted form will normally be used and, as different products containing a particular active substance differ somewhat in composition, application rates recommended by the manufacturer should normally be used.

It should be borne in mind that often specific weeds are normally controlled by methods of good husbandry, discussed in Chapter XVIII, and recourse to the use of herbicides may be necessary only when such methods are unsuccessful or uneconomic, or when weeds have become abundant as a result of neglect of these methods of control.

In connection with the choice of herbicides, it is important to be able to identify weeds in the early stages of growth. In practice weed seedlings will be found in crops before adult plants are available. It has therefore been thought desirable, for ease of reference and for comparison, to deal with seedlings in a separate chapter, after the descriptions of the weed plants.

Notes. 1. In the notes describing the weeds the following abbreviations have been used:

st—stem; *lvs*—leaves; *lf*—leaf; *lflt*—leaflet; *inf*—inflorescence; *fl*—flower; *frt*—fruit; *cots*—cotyledons.

2. The months quoted indicate, approximately, the period during which plants may be found in flower.

3. The families of flowering plants are arranged in the systematic order indicated in Chapter I. Pteridophyta are placed after the flowering plants for convenience, although logically they should precede them.

DICOTYLEDONS

I. ARCHICHLAMYDEAE: *petals when present free from one another, rarely united.*

RANUNCULACEAE

Stem lvs usually alternate and without stipules. Sepals usually 5 (may be coloured and petaloid), petals 0-5 or sometimes more, stamens numerous, ovary superior consisting of 1 to many usually free carpels, frt a group of achenes or follicles.

Plants in this family are mostly herbaceous and many contain an acrid juice.

The weeds of greatest importance in the family are those belonging to the genus *Ranunculus*, which includes the common buttercups. The following species may be encountered on farms:

R. acris L., **Acrid Buttercup (Meadow** or **Upright Buttercup)** (fig. 174). Perennial. Common on grassland. Stem-base somewhat thick but *not bulbous, stolons absent*. Sts much branched, hairy, hollow, a few inches to 3 ft. tall. Radical lvs *palmately segmented*. May-July. Inf cymose, fl stalks hairy, *not furrowed*. Sepals 5, free, hairy and *not reflexed*. Petals usually 5, free, yellow. Stamens numerous. Carpels numerous. Frt a group of achenes. Achenes smooth, beaked, light to dark brown with lighter border, 3 mm.

R. repens L., **Creeping Buttercup** (fig. 174). Perennial. Grassland and arable, particularly on wet soils. Differs from *R. acris* in the following respects: creeps above ground by stout stolons which root, and form new plants. Radical lvs divided into *3 main lobes*. May-August. 4-12 inches tall. Fl stalks *furrowed* and hairy. Achenes have rather larger hooked beak.

R. bulbosus L., **Bulbous Buttercup** (fig. 174). Perennial. Grassland, more particularly on *drier soils*. Less common in the north. St swollen below ground to form a *corm*. Radical lvs divided into 3 main lobes but less compact than *R. repens*. May-June. Up to 1 ft. tall. Fl stalks *furrowed*, hairy. Sepals *reflexed* during flowering. Achenes have a curved beak.

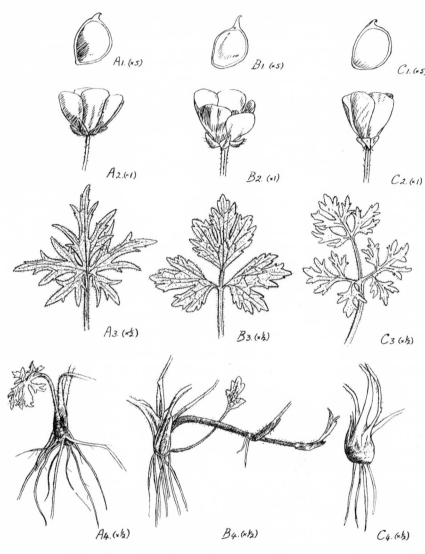

FIG. 174. Achene, flower, radical leaf, and base of plant. A1, A2, A3, A4, acrid buttercup. B1, B2, B3, B4, creeping buttercup. C1, C2, C3, C4, bulbous buttercup.

In pastures the above three species flower and seed abundantly as they are not grazed freely by livestock. If eaten in quantity in the fresh state they *may cause poisoning* of animals (p. 382) and they may reduce milk secretion and cause a bitter taint in the milk.

'Seeds' (achenes) may occur as impurities in herbage seeds (especially *R. repens*), particularly in perennial rye-grass, meadow fescue, and trefoil.

When grassland is ploughed the bulbous buttercup tends to reappear most readily, especially after shallow ploughing, because of its larger food store in the corm.

Control. Prevent seeding. Spray with MCPA or 2,4-D, preferably the former; best time spring or early summer. *R. repens* most susceptible, *R. acris* rather less, *R. bulbosus* more resistant and usually recovers after a single treatment.

R. sceleratus L., **Celery-leaved Buttercup** (fig. 175). *Annual.* Fairly common at edges of ponds and streams, in ditches and other wet places. Radical lvs rather like those of seedling celery. Sts and lvs more or less glabrous and shiny. May-September. 1-2 ft. Fls much smaller than *R. acris* (about ¼ in. diam.) and *paler yellow*. Frt oblong in outline, consists of numerous small achenes.

Very poisonous (p. 382). As it is an annual, it is readily controlled if the plants are cut down or pulled before seeds develop.

R. flammula L., **Lesser Spearwort** (fig. 175). Perennial. Wet places. Narrow, pointed, entire st lvs. June-August. About 1 ft. Fls similar to *R. acris*, but smaller (about ½ in. diam.). *Poisonous* (p. 382). *R. lingua* L., **Greater Spearwort**, a perennial in wet places, is much larger and considerably less common than *R. flammula*. *Also poisonous* (p. 382).

R. arvensis L., **Corn Buttercup (Starveacre, Staveacre, Watch Wheels)** (fig. 176). Annual. Arable, particularly in winter cereals, especially on calcareous and heavy soils. More common in the south. Lower lvs lobed or segmented, upper lvs divided into narrow segments. June-July. 1-2 ft. Fls pale yellow, smaller than *R. acris* (diam. about ⅓ in.). Frt 4-8 rather large spiny achenes. 7 mm. The hooked spines on each side of the achenes may assist distribution by animals. Achenes, sometimes known as 'watch wheels', may occur as impurities in threshed samples of cereal grain and unmilled sainfoin seed, though now less commonly than in former times.

Readily controlled with MCPA and 2,4-D. Seedlings checked by DNC and dinoseb.

R. sardous Crantz, **Hairy Buttercup,** and *R. parviflorus* L., **Small-flowered Buttercup,** are annual species, local, on arable land. Achenes papillose. Control as *R. arvensis*.

R. ficaria L., **Lesser Celandine** (fig. 176). Small perennial. Often found in pastures, but of little importance. Develops small root tubers which serve for reproduction. Lvs shiny, glabrous, cordate. March-May. Fls differ from buttercups in having only 3 sepals and 8-12 narrow petals. *Reputed to be poisonous.*

Other members of the family Ranunculaceae are:

Caltha palustris L., **Marsh Marigold** (fig. 176), which grows in wet places, and on open fields may be an indicator of bad drainage. Perennial. March-July. Fls larger than buttercups, 5 or 6 yellow petaloid sepals, petals absent,

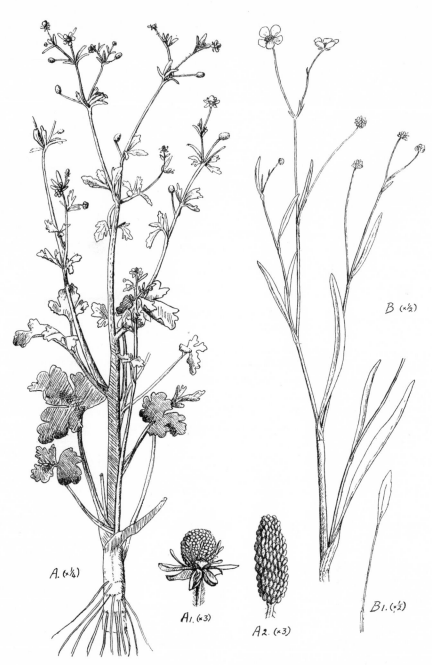

FIG. 175. A, celery-leaved buttercup; A1, flower, A2, fruit. B, lesser spearwort; B1, radical leaf.

frt a group of follicles; *poisonous. Anemone nemorosa* L., **Wood Anemone**. Perennial common in deciduous woods, about 6 in. tall, rhizomatous. Lvs palmate 3-lobed. March–May. No petals, white petaloid sepals; *poisonous. Aconitum anglicum.*, **Monkshood,** and other spp. common in gardens and occasionally wild; *poisonous. Delphinium ambiguum.*, **Larkspur,** an annual garden plant, found occasionally in arable fields in Essex and Cambridgeshire; *poisonous* (also

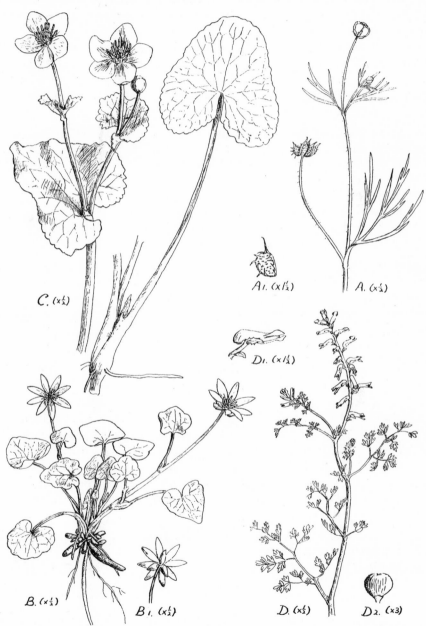

Fig. 176. A, corn buttercup; A1, achene. B, lesser celandine; B1, back of flower. C, marsh marigold. D, fumitory; D1, flower; D2, fruit.

other *Delphinium* spp.). *Helleborus* spp.: *H. foetidus* L., **Stinking Hellebore** and *H. viridis* L., **Green Hellebore,** which are uncommon, but grow wild in some localities, and *H. niger* L., **Christmas Rose,** a garden plant; all perennials and *all poisonous.*

PAPAVERACEAE (see Chapter IX)

Papaver rhoeas L., **Field Poppy** or **Corn Poppy** (fig. 177). Annual. Arable weed, common except in N. Scotland; more on soils which are not acid. Long thin tap root. Erect, branched st, 1-2 ft. Lvs pinnately divided, segments narrow. Stiff hairs on stems and lvs. June-August. Fls axillary, 2-4 in. diam., stalks hairy. Petals deep scarlet. Capsule smooth, *nearly globular.* Seed grey-brown, kidney-shaped; hexagonal surface pits; 1 mm.

Controlled by DNC; and 2,4-D ester up to flower bud stage; MCPA, 2,4-D amine and dinoseb at seedling stage only.

P. dubium L., **Long Headed Poppy,** is more common in the north than *P. rhoeas.* Fl pale red, 2-in. diam., capsule (fig. 177) more than twice as long as wide. *P. argemone* L., **Rough Long-Headed Poppy.** Common in the south on light soils, less in the north. Fl pale red, 1-2 in. diam., capsule (fig. 177) long distinctly ribbed and bristly.

Poppy seeds are very small and are produced in large numbers. They may be carried some distance by the wind. Seeds remain dormant for

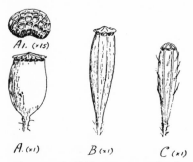

A1. (×15)

A. (×1)   *B (×1)*   *C (×1)*

FIG. 177. A, field poppy capsule; A1, seed. B, long-headed poppy capsule. C, rough long-headed poppy capsule.

many years when buried deeply in the soil, and germinate when brought to the surface again. Thus control for one season does not result in complete eradication, and ploughing of old grassland or extra deep ploughing of arable may result in the appearance of poppies on fields where they have not been seen for many years. The endosperm of the seed is rich in oil.

Powerful alkaloids, such as *morphine* and *codeine*, are present in *P. somniferum* L., **Opium Poppy.** The common British wild poppies contain small amounts of the alkaloid *rhoeadine* and the more powerful alkaloids are not present (p. 385). Poppies may be dangerous if present in very large amounts in fodder cut from short leys.

Poppies are particularly associated with cereal crops, in which they can flower and shed their seeds.

Chelidonium majus, L., **Greater Celandine.** Perennial, frequent on banks and in hedgerows near cottage gardens. Petals 4, bright yellow, ovary long and narrow. The plant contains a bright orange latex which is reputed to remove warts on external application. *Poisonous* (p. 386).

FUMARIACEAE

Fumaria officinalis L., **Fumitory** (fig. 176). Annual. Arable; more common on lighter soils. 1-3 ft., glabrous and glaucous. Lvs much divided into narrow segments. May-September. Inf long racemes, each fl shortly-stalked. Fl 2-lipped, 4 petals, pale rose-purple, upper petal spurred. Stamens 2. Ovary 1 carpel with a single ovule. Frt an ovoid nutlet, slightly rough, yellowish green, a small projection in a depression at the apex, 2 mm.

DNC (with wetter), dinoseb, CMPP and MCPA plus dicamba salts kill up to flower-bud stage, MCPA plus 2,3,6-TBA kill seedlings.

CRUCIFERAE (see Chapter IX)

Sinapis arvensis L., **Charlock (Ketlock, Kedlock, Yellows, Wild Mustard,** etc.) (fig. 178). Annual. A very common weed of arable land. Widely distributed, but especially abundant on calcareous soils and on clays and heavy loams. Slender tap root. Sts more or less branched, 6-24 in. Sts and lvs usually roughly hairy, but some plants glabrous or nearly so. Lower lvs oval or oblong, coarsely toothed and stalked, they may have a simple margin or one showing distinct lobing particularly near the base. Upper lvs simple, toothed and sessile. Infs racemes. June-July. Fl ½ in. diam., yellow. Sepals spreading. Frts siliquas with a smooth conical beak often containing a single seed at its base. Valves of frt pubescent or glabrous, with 3 faint nerves. Seeds spherical red-brown to nearly black, 1·5 mm., resemble turnip seed, but contain mustard oils and taste of mustard. May occur as an impurity in cereals and in seeds of small legumes (except wild white clover).

Most of the seeds are shed before cereal crops are cut. They can remain dormant for fifty years or more when buried deeply in the soil, and germinate when brought to the surface again. Thus ploughing up of old grassland or deeper ploughing of arable may result in the appearance of quantities of this weed. Because of the ability of the seed to remain dormant, control measures must be taken over a long period in order to eradicate the weed completely. It is very susceptible to the herbicides MCPA and 2,4-D at low rates of application, and therefore now a much less serious weed than formerly, when fields known to have a large charlock seed population in the soil were often kept as permanent grass, owing to the virtual impossibility of obtaining reasonable corn crops.

Seeding plants may cause *poisoning* of livestock (p. 385), but young plants, which may grow and be grazed in leys sown without a cover crop, are harmless.

Raphanus raphanistrum L., **Wild Radish (Runch** or **White Charlock)** (fig. 178). Annual. Arable; most abundant on non-calcareous soils. Similar to charlock but differs in the following respects: lower lvs more pinnatifid, with large rounded terminal lobe and 1-4 pairs of smaller lateral lobes; upper lvs pinnately lobed; June-September; sepals erect, petals white, lilac or pale yellow, usually with darker lilac veins; frt long and narrow, jointed, breaking when ripe into one-seeded pieces; true seeds oval or egg-shaped, grey-brown, 2·5 mm.

Sections of pods containing seed occur as an impurity in threshed cereal grain (see p. 83). MCPA, 2,4-D and DNC will kill the plant up to the beginning of flowering; dinoseb kills seedlings only. Higher concentrations of herbicides are required than for charlock.

Capsella bursa-pastoris L., **Shepherd's Purse** (fig. 179). Annual or biennial. Waste places and arable (especially in market-garden crops).

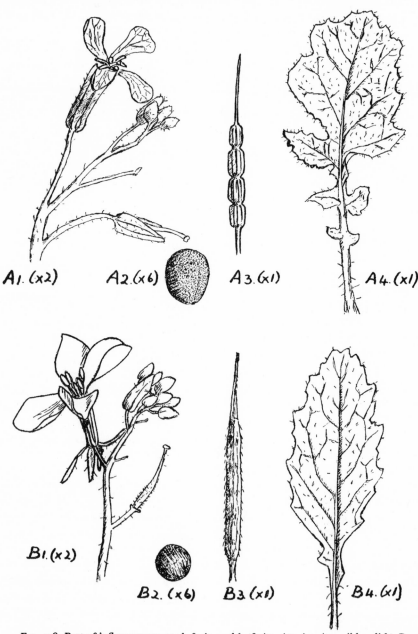

FIG. 178. Part of inflorescence, seed, fruit, and leaf. A1, A2, A3, A4, wild radish. B1, B2, B3, B4, charlock.

Thin tap root. Radical lvs form a rosette. Very variable in shape; entire, lobed or pinnatifid. Glabrous or somewhat hairy. An erect st, up to 18 in., arises from the centre of the rosette. St lvs clasp the st. Terminal and axillary racemes. Plants in flower can be found all the year round. Fls small, about 3 mm. diam., petals white. Frt a silicula, each compartment contains 10 or more seeds. Seed small, oblong, yellow to reddish brown, 1 mm. Readily controlled by selective herbicides.

Thlaspi arvense L., **Penny-cress** (fig. 179). Annual. Arable. Slender tap root. Plant glabrous. Simple st, 9-24 in. Basal lvs broadly lanceolate or obovate, upper lvs sagittate clasping the stem. May-July. Racemes short when in flower lengthen as the frts form. Fls ¼ in. diam., white. Frts almost circular with a deep notch at the apex, 5-8 seeds in each compartment. Seed oval, notched at one end, serrated concentric ridges on surface, dark reddish-brown, 2 mm., occasional in alsike seeds.

The whole plant has an unpleasant smell when crushed (it is known as 'Stinkweed' in Canada). May taint milk or butter if eaten by milking stock.

Killed at all stages of growth by low concentrations of MCPA and 2,4-D and up to flower bud stage by DNC and dinoseb.

Cardaria draba (L.), Desv. (*Lepidium draba* L.), **Hoary Pepperwort (Thanet Weed, Chalk Weed** or **Hoary Cress**) (fig. 179). Perennial, roadsides and waste places and has become a serious arable weed in some areas on most soils. Introduced to Britain from the continent early in the nineteenth century.

Vertical roots penetrate several feet, horizontal woody roots arise from them, spread extensively and produce adventitious buds from which new shoots develop. Sts stout, branched above, more or less glabrous, 1-2½ ft. Lvs alternate, lower ones stalked, upper ones clasp the stem, ovate, margin wavy with a few small teeth, surface usually (but not always) covered with short white hairs (hence 'hoary'). May-July. Inf a panicle of small flowers, corymbose. Fl white, 4-8 mm. diam. Frt more or less heart-shaped, each compartment containing one seed, style persistent. One seed only may develop resulting in an asymmetrical frt. Seed light brown or reddish-brown, egg-shaped, 2 mm.

Control. Avoid using farmyard manure which may contain seeds. Avoid carrying pieces of root on farm implements from infested to clean land (a small piece of root may produce a new patch of the weed which can later result in a serious infestation). Because of its deep and extensive root system, normal methods of cultivation are of little value. Ploughing to a depth of 15 in. followed by a bare fallow will considerably reduce. A long ley is also effective. Smother crops and thorough cultivation of root crops will help.

Winter cereals aid its spread. The discovery of the growth-regulating herbicides has considerably reduced the menace of this weed. MCPA and 2,4-D sprays are most effective. Two successive cereal crops sprayed with these herbicides gives good control providing any shoots which

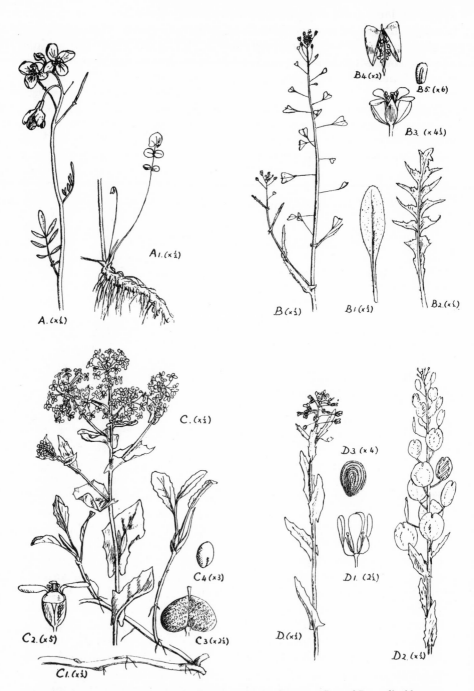

FIG. 179. A, lady's smock; A1, rhizome. B, shepherd's purse; B1 and B2, radical leaves; B3, flower; B4, fruit; B5, seed. C, hoary pepperwort; C1, creeping root; C2, flower; C3, fruit; C4, seed. D, penny-cress; D1, flower; D2, fruits; D3, seed.

appear in later crops are spot treated with the weed-killer to prevent the re-establishment of strong roots from which the weed may spread. If spraying is done at the flowering stage, MCPA and 2,4-D are equally effective, but MCPA is preferable if the crop is to be sprayed when the shoots of the weed are young.

Cardamine pratensis L., **Lady's Smock** (fig. 179). Perennial. Damp grassland throughout Britain. When abundant may indicate that the land needs draining. Radical lvs form a rosette, each lf pinnate and long-stalked; st lvs have narrow leaflets and a short stalk. Sts up to 1 ft. April-June. Raceme of lilac (occasionally white) fls. Frt a siliqua. Vegetative reproduction may occur by means of small fleshy buds formed in the axils of basal lvs. *C. hirsuta* L., **Hairy Bitter-cress.** An over-wintering annual on moist banks and waste places; becomes a troublesome weed locally. Especially common in over-wintering market-garden crops. April-September. Lvs pinnate. Fls white, small, only 4 stamens. Frt opens explosively when touched, flinging out the seeds. Seeds germinate in the autumn on cultivated land. *Coronopus squamatus* (Forsk.) Aschers, **Swine-cress (Wart-cress).** Annual. Occurring in trampled gateways and pastures, particularly in southern England. Sts prostrate, lvs pinnately cut with narrow segments. June-August. Fls fugitive, small, white. Frt broader than long, wrinkled. *C. didymus* (L.) Sm., **Lesser Swine-cress**, is an annual, introduced, occurring locally as a garden weed. *Alliaria petiolata* (Bieb.) Cavara and Grande, **Garlic Mustard (Jack-by-the-hedge).** A common hedgerow biennial with cordate lvs and white fls. This plant smells of garlic when bruised. Reputed to impart an onion flavour to milk if eaten in quantity by dairy cows. Normally animals avoid it. *Erysimum cheiranthoides* L., **Treacle Mustard**, and *Sisymbrium officinale* (L.) Scop., **Hedge Mustard**, both yellow-flowered annuals of roadsides and waste places which may become weeds of cultivated land, both readily controlled by MCPA and 2,4-D.

VIOLACEAE

Viola arvensis Murr., **Field Pansy** (fig. 180). Annual; very variable. Arable throughout Britain, more on basic or neutral soils. Shoots 6-18 in., sts angular and branched. Lvs variable, more or less oval or ovate, blunt, somewhat lobed; upper lvs narrower than lower. Large deeply toothed stipules. April-October. Fl irregular. Sepals 5 fused. Corolla about equal in size to the calyx. Petals 5, free, unequal, lower one spurred. Stamens 5; filaments broad more or less united; nectar-producing spurs project from the two lower stamens into the corolla spur. Carpels 3, united, superior. Capsule opens by 3 valves, numerous seeds on the walls of the capsule. Fls cream; sometimes the upper petal is tinged violet. Seeds light to dark brown, usually shiny more or less conical with lighter coloured caruncle at the pointed end, 2 mm. Seed slightly flattened and tends to lie on the flat side. *V. tricolor* L., **Wild Pansy,** is similar, but the corolla is larger than the sepals. Its sub-species *tricolor* occurs more on acid to neutral arable land. Fls vary in colour; whitish-purple, lilac, cream, pale yellow and golden yellow or combinations of these.

These species resist MCPA, 2,4-D, DNC and dinoseb. They are most susceptible to linuron.

CARYOPHYLLACEAE

The general characters of the weed species are: Lvs opposite, simple and entire. Nodes swollen. Inf a dichasial cyme. Fls regular. Sepals 4-5 free or united. Petals 4-5 free. Stamens 8-10. Carpels 3 or 5 united, superior, 3 or 5 styles, free-central placentation. Capsule contains numerous seeds and opens by apical teeth, usually twice as many as the styles.

Silene alba (Mill.) (*Lychnis alba* Mill.), **White Campion** (fig. 180). Short-lived perennial, On arable and leys throughout Britain. St 1-1½ ft. Lvs softly hairy, lanceolate. June-September. Fls *dioecious*. Sepals 5, united, downy. Petals white, deeply bifid. In the male fls 10 stamens. In the female fls the ovary has 5 styles, capsule opens by 10 teeth. Seeds numerous 1·5 mm., flat on one side, pale grey, covered with small peg-like warts. May be present as an impurity in badly-cleaned grass and clover seeds. Susceptible to Mecoprop.

Silene dioica (L.) Clairv. (*Lychnis dioica* L.), **Red Campion.** Common in hedgesides and open woods, may occur on cultivated land. Somewhat similar to the previous species, but with rose-coloured petals. Fls June-July. Capsule smaller and seeds purple to grey-black, 1 mm. An impurity of small legume seeds. Control, Mecoprop. Pink-flowered hybrids, *album* × *rubrum*, occur frequently.

Silene vulgaris, **Bladder Campion.** Perennial on grassy slopes, and may occur on arable land throughout Britain. Somewhat like the two preceding species, but usually glabrous. Petals white, 3 styles, capsule opens by 6 teeth, calyx becomes inflated (bladder-like) as the frt develops. Some hermaphrodite fls produced. Seeds similar to red campion, but warts more pointed. May occur in alsike and trefoil seeds. Resists MCPA and 2,4-D. Moderately susceptible to Mecoprop.

Lychnis flos-cuculi L., **Ragged Robin.** Perennial. Damp grassland and other wet places. Resembles red campion, but differs in the following respects: lvs glabrous, petals deeply 4-cleft giving the corolla a ragged appearance. Fl hermaphrodite. May-June. Capsule opens by 5 teeth.

Agrostemma githago L. (*Lychnis githago* (L.) Scop.), **Corn Cockle** (fig. 180). Annual. Arable, sandy, loamy and clay soils. Less common than in former times, as the seeds are now much more completely removed from seed corn. Strong tap root. Sts and lvs covered with white appressed hairs. St 2-4 ft. Lvs linear-lanceolate. June-August. Large fl 1½-2 in. diam. Sepals woolly, united; teeth extend beyond the petals. Petals pale reddish purple only slightly notched. Capsule opens by 5 teeth. Seed 3·5 mm. black, reddish if unripe, covered with coarse projections. The seeds germinate in the autumn as well as in the spring and therefore seedlings may be abundant in autumn-sown cereal crops. Where this is a common weed it is wise not to sow autumn cereals. Seeds may be encouraged to germinate by autumn and spring cultivations and the seedlings may then be destroyed by harrowing. Resistant to MCPA and 2,4-D. *Seeds poisonous* (p. 385).

Spergula arvensis L., **Spurrey (Dother, Tailor's Needles, Beggar-weed, Bottle Brush, Mountain Flax,** etc.) (fig. 180). Annual. Arable,

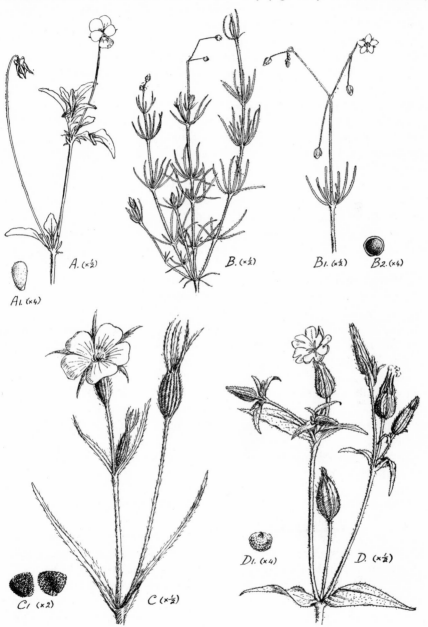

FIG. 180. A, field pansy; A1, seed. B and B1, spurrey; B2, seed. C, corn cockle; C1, seeds. D, white campion; D1, seed.

common on light soils. It grows strongly on acid soils and may swamp young crops which are growing weakly because of lime deficiency. In quantity it *may be an indicator of lime deficiency*. Slender tap root. Numerous branches from the crown. Branched sts slender, bent at the nodes, 6-18 in. tall. Lvs linear, fleshy, in pairs, but dwarf axillary shoots grow early so that there appears to be a whorl of leaves at each node. Sts and lvs often sticky. June-August. Sepals free. Petals white not forked. Styles 5. Frts turn downwards as they ripen. Numerous seeds, black with a narrow pale brown rim, 2 mm.; occasional in white clover seeds.

Regular applications of lime are usually needed in order to control this weed. It does not rapidly disappear after liming, however, as it sheds seeds early, before cereal crops are ripe. The more vigorous growth of crops after acidity has been neutralized will provide greater competition and weaken the weed. DNC kills seedlings; MCPA, 2,4-D and dinoseb are effective against young seedlings only. 2,3,6-TBA and dicamba useful.

Scleranthus annuus L., **Annual Knawel** (fig. 181). Annual or biennial. Arable, on dry sandy soils. When abundant *may indicate lime deficiency*. Sts decumbent or more or less upright, a few inches high. Lvs linear. June-September. Fls single in the forks of the st and in axillary and terminal clusters, green; *petals absent*. Frt a *one-seeded nutlet*, 2·5-3 mm., usually surrounded by the calyx. Readily reduced, after liming where necessary, by spring cultivations or by taking a root crop.

Stellaria media (L.) Vill., **Common Chickweed** (fig. 181). Annual, moist arable, especially rich land, also colonizes bare ground in grassland. Slender tap-root. Shoots 3-18 in., much branched, decumbent or ascending. Sts have a line of white hairs down one side. Lvs ovate, pointed, shiny. February-October. Inf a terminal dichasial cyme. Sepals free. Petals white, deeply bifid, shorter than the sepals. Styles 3. Capsule contains numerous seeds. Seeds small, 1 mm., reddish-brown, round to kidney-shaped, covered with rows of warty projections. May occur as an impurity in grass seeds, particularly timothy, and in white and alsike clovers.

Lambs have died after eating quantities of chickweed. It may form large indigestible lumps which ferment in the stomach. DNC, dinoseb and Mecoprop will kill young plants.

Cerastium holostoides, **Mouse-ear Chickweed** (fig. 181). Perennial. Very common on grassland and arable (a closely allied species, *C. arvense*, may also occur on dry calcareous or sandy soils). Numerous sts, procumbent at first, becoming erect, 3-15 in., upper lvs broadly lanceolate or oblong and sessile. Whole shoot covered with white hairs. April-October. Fls white, petals bifid, 5 styles, seed reddish brown, roughly triangular in outline, projections widely spaced, 0·75 mm. Seeds may be present in grass and clover seeds, particularly white clover and timothy. Young seedlings checked by MCPA, 2,4-D and Mecoprop.

CHENOPODIACEAE (see Chapter X)

Chenopodium album L., **Fat Hen (Goose-foot, Muck-weed, Lamb's-tongue)** (fig. 182). Annual. Arable; very common, most abundant and vigorous on nitrogen-rich soils. Often around manure heaps. The whole plant covered with a white meal composed of small bladder-like hairs which reflect light. Usually one main st with short branches. St tough,

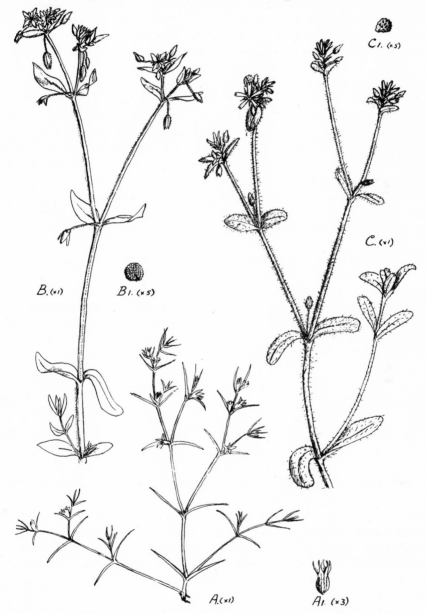

FIG. 181. A, annual knawel; A1, fruit. B, common chickweed; B1, seed. C, mouse-ear chickweed; C1, seed.

often reddish, 6-36 in. Lvs variable in shape, ovate-lanceolate and toothed, or lanceolate. July-October. Fls green, very small, produced in dense clusters at the top of the main st and on short laterals. Perianth 5 segments, joined at the base. Stamens 5. Ovary superior, one-celled, containing one ovule, two stigmas. Frt an achene loosely surrounded by the perianth. Perianth and pericarp easily rubbed off. True seed black and glossy, lens-shaped, 1·5 mm., a frequent impurity in alsike clover seeds and, less frequently, in other clovers, may also occur in Italian rye-grass, timothy, barley, oats and rye. DNC and dinoseb kill seedlings, MCPA and 2,4-D kill young plants, Desmetryne controls in kale.

Atriplex patula L., **Common Orache (Spreading Orache)** (fig. 182). Annual, arable, very common in similar situations to fat hen. Covered with white meal (more pronounced on young leaves). The plant resembles fat hen, but branches are produced early at the base; these spread out at right angles to the main st and then turn upwards. Lvs very variable, lower ones triangular to hastate, upper ones narrow, all with a few teeth. July-September. Fls unisexual, female ones have no perianth and are enclosed by 2 bracteoles which are variable in shape and size, but usually triangular and toothed, and persistent around the frt. Seeds vary in size (to 2·5 mm.) and colour; larger ones usually dull brown, smaller ones shiny and black; lens shaped, flattened vertically; may be an impurity in cereal seeds, and in red clover and lucerne. Mecoprop, 2,4-D and MCPA plus 2,3,6-TBA useful to young plant stage.

GERANIACEAE

The important weed species of this family belong to the genus *Geranium*, the general characters of which are: swollen nodes, dissected lvs with stipules, fl regular, sepals 5, petals 5, stamens 10, ovary 5 cells each with one ovule, frt 5-lobed, style projects like a beak, frt splits into 5 1-seeded sections which spring upward when ripe catapulting the seed.

The seeds of various species of cranesbill are comparable in size with clover and other small leguminous seeds and they may appear as impurities if such seeds are imperfectly cleaned.

Geranium dissectum L., **Cut-Leaved Cranesbill** (fig. 183). Annual. Arable and occasionally grassland throughout Britain. Much-branched sts, pubescent, 6-18 in. Lvs deeply dissected. May-August. Fls in pairs, ¼-½ in. diam., petals reddish-pink. Seeds oval, greyish-brown, surface distinctly pitted, 2 mm. A frequent impurity in trefoil and crimson and red clover seeds; less frequent in white clovers and lucerne, occasional in rye-grasses. MCPA and 2,4-D kill young seedlings only.

Geranium molle L., **Dove's-foot Cranesbill** (fig. 183). Annual. Arable and grassland, especially on dry soils. Smaller, less branched, more softly hairy and with less-dissected lvs than *G. dissectum*. Petals rose-purple or pink. Seeds oval or D-shaped, reddish brown, slightly rough, 1·5 mm., often enclosed in wrinkled reddish-brown pericarp. More common as an impurity in white clover seeds than in other small legumes. MCPA, 2,4-D and DNC control young seedlings only. Mecoprop more useful.

Geranium pusillum Burm., **Small-flowered Cranesbill,** is similar to *G. molle*, but covered with shorter hairs, fls pale dull lilac, petals about as long as the sepals, only 5 of the stamens have anthers, carpels smooth and pubescent. Seed D-shaped, slightly rough, reddish-brown, may be

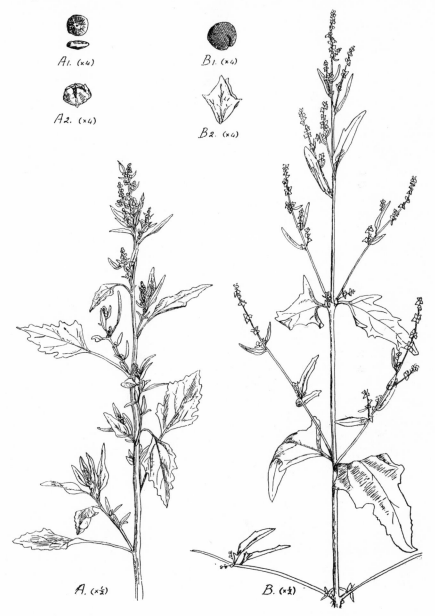

A1. (×4) *B1. (×4)*

A2. (×4)

B2. (×4)

A. (×½) *B. (×½)*

FIG. 182. A, fat hen; A1, fruits; A2, fruit in withered perianth. B, common orache; B1, fruit; B2, fruit in pair of bracteoles.

covered by *hairy*, brown, *unwrinkled* pericarp, 1·5 mm. The seed may occur as an impurity in white clover seed.

Geranium pratense L., **Meadow Cranesbill** (fig. 183). Perennial. Rather local in hedgerows and on moist grassland. Rhizomatous. St 1-4 ft. Readily recognized

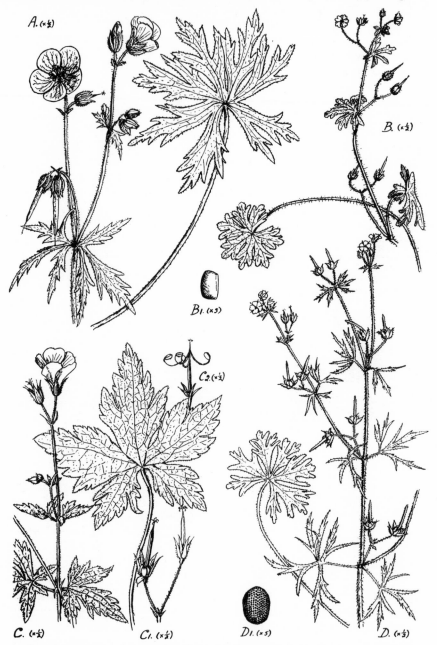

FIG. 183. A, meadow cranesbill. B, dove's-foot cranesbill; B1, seed. C, wood cranesbill; C1, fruits; C2, fruit dehiscing. D, cut-leaved cranesbill; D1, seed.

by its large purplish-blue fls up to $1\frac{1}{2}$ in. diam. June-August. Not often a serious weed. Checked by MCPA and 2,4-D only under favourable conditions.

Geranium sylvaticum L., **Wood Cranesbill** (fig. 183). Perennial. Moist woods, but also common locally in meadows in the northern parts of the British Isles. Distinguished from *G. pratense* chiefly by its less cut lvs, more dense inf and smaller purple to pink fls. June-July.

Geranium robertianum L., **Herb Robert.** A very common annual of hedgerows, damp woods and other shady places. It may spread to farmland. Sts reddish, hairy, particularly the lower part, 6-24 in. Fl pink. May-September.

LEGUMINOSAE (see Chapter XI)

Vicia hirsuta L., **Hairy Vetch** (fig. 184). Annual. Arable throughout the British Isles. Slender, hairy or glabrous, 1-3 ft., weak sts. Lvs pinnate, 4 to 8 pairs of leaflets, branched tendrils replace the top leaflets and support the plant by twining around sts of cereals, stipules lobed. May-August. Racemes of 1-6 fls. Fls small, 4-5 mm., dirty white or purplish. Pod shortly stalked, *hairy*, containing usually 2 seeds. Seeds greenish-yellow to dark brown, mottled, hilum light coloured, 2 mm. A frequent impurity in crimson clover and rye and, occasionally, in oats. Seedlings killed by MCPA and 2,4-D.

Various other species of vetch may occur on arable land, particularly cultivated vetch, *V. sativa*. Seeds of this species may be shed when a crop of vetches is grown and, as 'hard seeds' are frequent in vetches, these may remain dormant for varying periods and later germinate and grow as weeds in other crops.

Ononis repens L. (*O. arvensis* Fries.), **Rest Harrow** (fig. 184). Procumbent perennial spreading by rhizomes. Poor dry grassland. Sts 1-2 ft., root at the nodes, usually hairy, woody, branched. Lvs three leaflets or one only, hairy, large stipules. June-September. Fls pink, single in the axils of the lvs. Pod shorter than calyx. Plants often sticky; odour unpleasant. Another species of rest harrow, *O. spinosa*, is more erect, without rhizomes, sts usually spiny, pods longer than the calyx. It occurs on poor, often acid, soils as a grassland weed in England and Wales. These species decrease when the fertility of the land is improved and better herbage and increased grazing encouraged.

Genista tinctoria L., **Dyer's Greenweed** (fig. 184). Perennial shrubby plant on rough pastures in England and Wales, especially on clay. Sts 1-2 ft., smooth, green, spineless. Lvs small, $\frac{1}{2}$-1 in., oblong-lanceolate. July-September. Long racemes of large yellow fls. Flat glabrous pod. Stock do not normally eat the plant, but it is reputed to make milk bitter if eaten by milk animals. Formerly used for the production of a yellow dye. Control by grubbing out isolated clumps, burning plants when dry, improving the fertility of the land and encouraging better herbage.

Ulex europaeus L., **Gorse (Furze, Whin).** A spiny shrub, up to 6 ft. Poor pastures, downland, upland pastures and moors, usually on lighter less calcareous soils. February-June and August-September. Fls yellow. Black pods, open explosively when ripe flinging out the seeds.

Other species flower at different times of the year:

Ulex gallii Planch., **Dwarf Furze,** July-September, and *Ulex minor* Roth., **Small Furze**, July-November.

Control by grubbing out isolated bushes, cutting and burning more

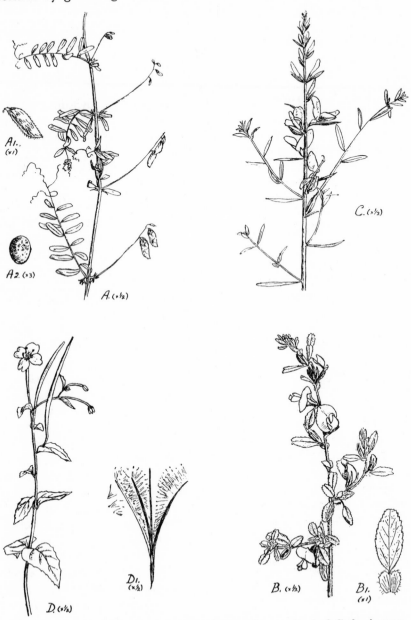

FIG. 184. A, hairy vetch; A1, pod; A2, seed. B, rest-harrow; B1, leaf. C, dyer's green-weed. D, broad-leaved willowherb; D1, fruit dehiscing.

extensive infestations at the end of July, apply basic slag and sow wild white clover seeds. Stock will graze the tender young shoots which may grow later.

Good control of top growth can be obtained by spraying 2,4,5-T ester over the bushes in July or August. On farmland the killed tops should be burnt and the land improved as above.

Sarothamnus scoparius (L.) Wimmer (*Cytisus scoparius* L.), **Broom.** A bushy plant, 2-6 ft., on poor dry pastures, commons, etc. Long, slender green stems without spines, small narrow lvs, simple or with 3 leaflets. May-June. Fls yellow, 1 in., in racemes. Pod black when ripe. The plant contains the poisonous alkaloids *cytisine* and *sparteine* in very small quantities, but it is unlikely to be eaten in sufficient quantity to be harmful to livestock.

Control by grubbing out isolated bushes, cutting and burning more extensive infestations and improving the fertility of the land as for gorse. Top growth can be controlled by spraying 2,4-D ester over the bushes in July or August.

ROSACEAE (see Chapter XII)

Potentilla anserina L., **Silverweed** (fig. 185). Perennial. Roadsides, waste places, damp grassland, occasionally on arable land. Creeps by long stolons. Lvs pinnate, deeply toothed, covered beneath and sometimes above with silvery down. June-August. Fls solitary on long stalks. Sepals 5 plus epicalyx 5, petals 5, yellow, stamens numerous, several carpels. Frt a group of achenes. Leaves readily eaten by geese. MCPA and 2,4-D check only under favourable conditions.

Potentilla reptans L., **Creeping Cinquefoil** (fig. 185). Perennial. Roadsides, waste places and occasionally on grassland. Creeps by stolons. Lvs palmate with 5 leaflets. June-August. Fls solitary, somewhat resembling those of silverweed. Frt a group of achenes. MCPA and 2,4-D check only under favourable conditions.

Filipendula ulmaria (L.) Maxim (*Spiraea ulmaria* L.), **Meadow-sweet** (fig. 185). Perennial. Wet places, ditches, swamps, near rivers and in badly drained grassland. Short rhizomes. Lvs pinnate with smaller lobes between the larger ones. Lflts irregularly toothed, terminal lflt divided into 3 lobes. Lvs whitish beneath. Sts up to 3 ft., furrowed, reddish, stiff. June-September. Fls very small, in large panicles, strongly scented. Sepals 5. Petals usually 5, cream. Stamens numerous. Carpels 6-10. Frt a group of follicles (follicles spirally twisted when ripe). Control by improving drainage, frequent cutting, application of fertilizers. MCPA and 2,4-D check only under favourable conditions.

Alchemilla vulgaris L., **Lady's Mantle** (fig. 185). Small perennial varying from 3 to 12 in. Moist grassland. Thick woody rootstock. Lvs palmatifid. June-August. Fls very small and green, in loose panicles. Not usually a serious weed.

Aphanes arvensis L. (*Alchemilla arvensis* (L.) Scop.), **Parsley Piert (Field Lady's Mantle)** (fig. 185). A very small annual, 2-5 in. Arable, dry soils.

Hairy, usually much branched. Lvs fan-shaped, 3-lobed. May-August. Fls green, very minute, in axillary clusters. Sometimes abundant, but not usually very troublesome. Resists growth-regulators but susceptible to DNC.

Rubus spp., **Brambles or Blackberries.** Woody plants which occur commonly on neglected grassland. Top growth can be controlled by

FIG. 185. A and A1, parsley piert, $\times\frac{1}{2}$. B, lady's mantle, $\times\frac{1}{2}$; B1, flower, $\times 3$. C, meadow-sweet, $\times\frac{1}{2}$. D, silverweed, $\times\frac{1}{2}$; D1, back of flower, $\times\frac{1}{2}$. E, leaf of creeping cinquefoil, $\times\frac{1}{2}$.

spraying with 2,4,5-T ester in July or August. Repeat treatment may be necessary in the following year. Grubbing out isolated bushes, burning extensive infestations, associated where necessary with spraying, followed by the application of fertilizers, will help to restore grazing.

ONAGRACEAE

The common weed species are the **Willowherbs**, which have the following general characteristics: creeping rootstock, 4 sepals, 4 petals, 4+4 stamens, inferior ovary, pod-like capsule splitting longitudinally into 4 parts, numerous hairy seeds. They are not of very great importance as farm weeds.

Epilobium montanum L., **Broad-leaved Willowherb** (fig. 184). A slender perennial, probably the commonest species. May be a pest in gardens and occasionally on arable land. Almost glabrous. Sts reddish, 6-18 in. Lvs broadly lanceolate. June-July. Fls rose-purple. MCPA and 2,4-D check mature plants only under favourable conditions.

Other species are: *Epilobium parviflorum* Schreb, **Small-flowered Hairy Willowherb.** A perennial common in moist situations, 1-3 ft. Purplish-rose fls. July-August. *E. hirsutum* L., **Great Hairy Willowherb (Codlins and Cream).** Perennial. Common in ditches and by streams, 3-5 ft. Deep rose-coloured fls. July-August. *Chamaenerion angustifolium* (L.) Scop. (*E. angustifolium* L.), **Rosebay Willowherb (Fireweed).** Perennial, 2-5 ft. Common in margins of woods and clearings. Quickly appearing in cities on bombed sites and sites of fires. Purplish-rose fls. July-September.

UMBELLIFERAE (see Chapter XII)

Scandix pecten-veneris L., **Shepherd's Needle (Venus' Comb)** (fig. 186). Annual. Arable, light chalky soils particularly, but also on calcareous clays. Erect st, 6-18 in., branched, ridged. Lvs bipinnate. Umbels usually in pairs. June-July. Fls white. Frts 2 1-seeded portions separating when ripe, slightly rough, ridged longitudinally, dark brown to black (ridges lighter), a long apical beak, 1-2 in.; the whole resembles a broad needle or the tooth of a comb. The half-frts with the beak broken off may be present in threshed cereals, which therefore require extra cleaning. DNC and dinoseb kill young plants, MCPA and 2,4-D control seedlings only.

Daucus carota L., **Wild Carrot** (fig. 186). Annual or biennial, grassland and arable, particularly near the coast and on chalky soils. Somewhat like cultivated carrot, but with thinner, hard roots. Sts 1-2 ft., hairy, branched, ridged. Lvs pinnately compound with narrow segments. June-August. Inf bears bracts and bracteoles. Fls white, sometimes purplish in the centre of the umbels. Frts ridged and spiny 2-3·5 mm. As the fruits develop the partial umbels turn inwards, the whole umbel taking on a 'bird's-nest' appearance. The seeds, usually with the spines rubbed off, were at one time a serious impurity in red clover and lucerne seeds, but their occurrence is now less common, as they are more thoroughly removed by modern seed-cleaning machinery. MCPA and 2,4-D will give some check in the seedling stage only.

Oenanthe crocata L., **Hemlock Water Dropwort** (fig. 186). Perennial. Swampy places, ditches, edges of ponds; more common in the south and west of Britain. Large tuberous roots. St 2-5 ft., grooved, hollow. The juice in the stem turns yellow on exposure to the air. Lvs bi- to tripinnate. Large compound umbels of white fls. June-July. Frt cylindrical,

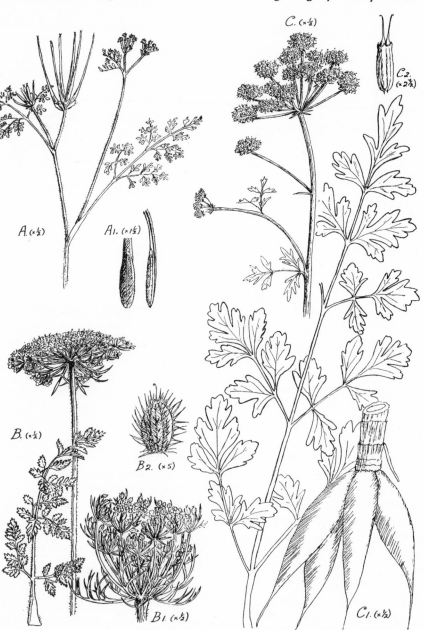

FIG. 186. A, shepherd's needle; A1, half-fruits (beak not shown in full). B, wild carrot; B1, fruiting head; B2, half-fruit. C, hemlock water dropwort; C1, tuberous roots; C2, fruit.

slightly grooved, 5 mm. The plant tastes sweet, but is *very poisonous* (see p. 382).

Conium maculatum L., **Hemlock** (fig. 187). Biennial. Damp situations, hedge-sides, open woods, by streams, etc. Strong characteristic odour when bruised. Sts *smooth*, shiny, with *purple blotches*, 2-4 ft. Lvs bi- to tri-pinnate. June-July. Large umbels with small bracts and bracteoles. Fls white. Half-frt has 5 wavy ridges, 3-4 mm. The plant is *very poisonous* (see p. 382). It is also reputed to reduce milk secretion and to give an unpleasant taint to milk, if eaten by dairy animals.

As it is a biennial it can readily be eradicated by cutting or pulling before seeding.

Cicuta virosa L., **Cowbane** (fig. 187). Perennial, wet places, ditches, marshes and edges of ponds, local. Tuberous roots. St furrowed, hollow, 2-4 ft. Lvs bi- to tri-pinnate with long, narrow segments. Compound umbels flat-topped. July-August. Fls small; white, notched petals. Half-frt has 5 flattened ridges, it is shorter than broad, 2 mm.

Very poisonous (see p. 383). Control by digging out the roots, which should be removed if livestock are liable to gain access to them.

Aethusa cynapium L., **Fool's Parsley** (fig. 187). Annual. Arable; locally a troublesome weed. Thick tap-root. Sts 1-2 ft., hollow, ribbed, branched. Lvs somewhat like parsley. July-August. Compound umbels, white flowers, long drooping bracteoles. Half-frt oval, 5 prominent ribs, pale greenish yellow, 2 orange or reddish curved stripes on the flat side, 4 mm.

Reputed to be *poisonous* (see p. 385).

Conopodium majus (Gouan) Lor. and Barr (*C. denudatum* Koch), **Pignut (Earthnut)** (fig. 187). Perennial. Common in poor grassland, except on chalk. Underground a thick tuber, brown or purplish, producing a single slender shoot 1-2 ft. high. Lvs few, finely divided; umbels small. May-July. Fls white. Most frequent in poor swards, where there is little competition. Considerably reduced when more vigorous herbage species are encouraged to compete with it. Resistant to growth regulator herbicides.

Aegopodium podagraria L., **Goutweed (Ground Elder, Bishop's Weed, Herb Gerard)**, is frequent as a weed in gardens, where it was once cultivated as a pot-herb; also roadsides and waste places near gardens, less commonly on arable land. Glabrous perennial, extensive rhizomes. Sts hollow and ridged, 1-3 ft. Radical lvs twice trifoliate; leaflets large, ovate, dentate. Stem lvs with 3 leaflets. May-July. Fls white. Resistant to 2,4,5-T and 2,3,6-TBA give some control.

The following are common hedgerow weeds which may encroach on grass-land:

Anthriscus sylvestris (L.) Bernh., **Smooth Chervil (Cow Parsley, Keck)**. Biennial or perennial. Ridged hollow sts, 2-3 ft. Lvs bi- to tri-pinnate. Lvs and bases of sts hairy. Compound umbels of small white fls. April-June. Frts *smooth*, 5 mm. *Control:* regular cutting and prevention of seeding. Not readily controlled by growth regulator herbicides.

Chaerophyllum temulentum., **Rough Chervil**. Biennial. Similar to *Anthriscus sylvestris*, but rather smaller and differing in its *solid* st., which is rough, *purple-spotted* or *completely purple* and hairy. It fls later, June-August. Frts *ridged*, often purple, narrow towards the top, 5 mm. *Control:* regular cutting before seeding.

Heracleum sphondylium L., **Hogweed (Cow Parsnip).** Large biennial or perennial. Sts hollow and ridged, 3-6 ft. Lvs pinnate with broad segments, large inflated sheathing bases to the leaf petioles. Sts and lvs roughly hairy.

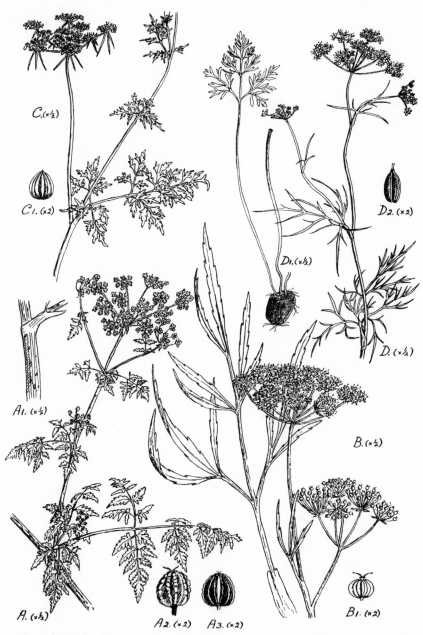

FIG. 187. A, hemlock; A1, stem; A2, fruit (green); A3, fruit (dry). B, cowbane; B1, fruit .C, fool's parsley; C1, half-fruit. D, pignut; D1, tuber and radical leaf; D2, fruit.

Weeds: Special

July-August. Fls white or pinkish. Frts flat (rather like parsnip), 8 mm. *Control:* regular cutting well before seeding. M.C.P.A. and 2,4-D check only under favourable conditions.

CUCURBITACEAE

Bryonia dioica Jacq., **White Bryony** (fig. 188). Perennial climbing plant common in hedgerows in England and Wales, but not in Scotland and Ireland. Climbs by long tendrils. Lvs 5-lobed, light green. May-September. Dioecious. Fls small greenish white. Berries red, 6-8 mm., in clusters. Roots very thick and fleshy. *Poisonous* (see p. 387).

EUPHORBIACEAE

Mercurialis perennis L., **Dog's Mercury** (fig. 188). Perennial spreading by rhizomes. Edges of woods, hedgerows and shaded places. Pubescent. Erect sts, 6-18 in. Lvs opposite, ovate-lanceolate. March-April. Dioecious. Fls very small, green, on axillary spikes, male spikes long, female spikes much shorter. Frt roundish, 2-celled, each cell containing 1 seed, 7 mm. *Poisonous* (see p. 386). A somewhat similar species, *M. annua* L., **Annual Mercury**, is also *poisonous*. It is an annual, hairless and much less common than *M. perennis*. If eaten by dairy animals, both species may reduce milk secretion and the milk may be bluish.

Euphorbia spp., **Spurges.** Several species of spurge occur on arable land. The plants are light green in colour. Several small male fls are associated with each female fl and below the group is a pair of large bracts. Capsules 3-lobed, each lobe containing 1 seed. Sts contain an irritant milky juice. The species more commonly found are:

Euphorbia peplus L., **Petty Spurge** (fig. 188). Annual, 6-12 in. Branched sts. Oval to obovate lvs. July-November. 3-rayed umbels of greenish fls. Leafy bracts ovate. *Poisonous* (see p. 385).

E. exigua L., **Dwarf Spurge**. Annual, 6-12 in. June-October. 3-5-rayed umbels. Narrower lvs and bracts. *Poisonous.*

E. helioscopia L., **Sun Spurge**. Annual, 6-18 in. Single sts. Obovate lvs rounded at the tip. June-October. Umbels 5-rayed, bracts a golden-green colour. *Poisonous.* MCPA and 2,4-D check seedlings only.

POLYGONACEAE (see Chapter XII)

1. *Polygonum*. Perianth 5, usually equal, segments. Stamens 5-8. Styles 2-3. Nut often triangular in section.

Polygonum aviculare L., **Knotgrass (Knotweed)** (fig. 189). Annual. Arable; common throughout Britain. Numerous long, thin reddish sts, often prostrate, but tending to be upright when growing in a tall crop. Lvs elliptical or lanceolate, bluish-green. Silvery, membranous, sheathing stipules. July-October. Fls pink or white, 1-6 in axils of lvs. Frt triangular, reddish-brown, 2·5 mm. Perianth often still present in 'seed' samples. The 'seeds' occur as an impurity in cereals and in red clover and lucerne seeds.

431

2,4-D ester gives good control of seedlings; MCPA checks seedlings; DNC and dinoseb kill very young seedlings only.

Polygonum bistorta L., **Snake-root (Bistort, Snakeweed)** (fig. 189). Perennial. In some districts in the northern part of the country a troublesome

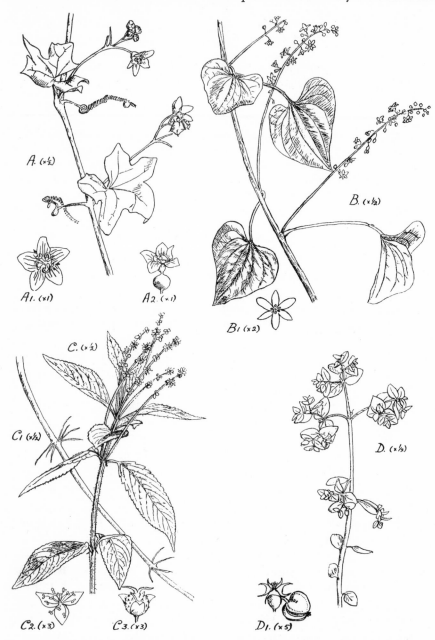

FIG. 188. A, white bryony; A1, male flower; A2, female flower. B, black bryony; B1, flower. C, dog's mercury (male plant); C1, rhizome; C2, male flower; C3, female flower. D, petty spurge; D1, male and female flowers.

weed in damp grassland. Local. Stout, much-branched rhizomes. St upright, 1-2 ft. Lvs oblong or ovate-lanceolate. Basal lvs on long stalks about twice the length of the blade, st lvs have very short stalks, sheathing stipules very long. June-August. Fls very small, pink or (rarely) white, in dense, terminal, spike-like racemes which are 1½-2 in. long. Control may involve draining the land; application of fertilizers to

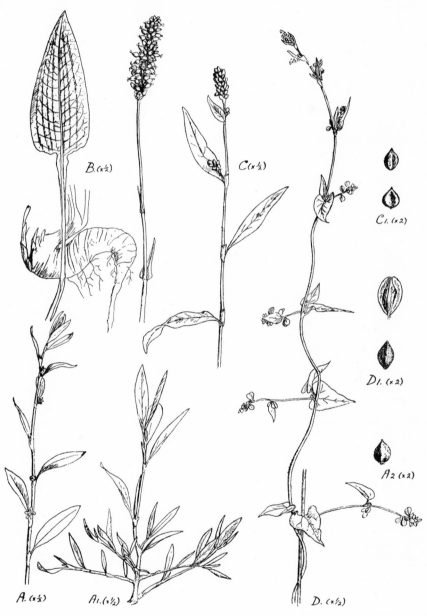

B.(x½)   C.(x½)

C1. (x2)

D1. (x2)

A2 (x2)

A. (x¼)   A1.(x½)   D. (x½)

Fig. 189. A and A1, knotgrass; A2, fruit. B, Snake-root leaf, rhizome, and inflorescence. C, redshank; C1, fruits. D, black bindweed; D1, fruit with and without perianth.

improve the herbage and frequent cutting and close grazing will help. Resists growth regulator herbicides.

Polygonum persicaria L., **Redshank (Persicaria, Lakeweed, Willow-weed, Crab Grass, Smart Weed,** etc.) (fig. 189). Annual, very common on arable land. Sts 1-2 ft., glabrous or slightly hairy, spreading and branched, reddish above. Lvs lanceolate, sometimes woolly beneath, usually some have a blackish blotch on the upper surface. July-October. Infs dense terminal spikes. Fls small, pink. Frt blunt, 3-sided, black, with shiny concave sides, some are less angular and more oval in transverse section, 2 mm. May occur as an impurity in cereal seed samples. The perianth often persists around the frt in 'seed' samples. 2,4-D ester and MCPA plus dicamba salts kill seedlings.

The land form of *P. amphibium* occurs locally as a difficult garden weed of clay soils. It resembles *P. persicaria* in appearance and, like that species, is known as **Lakeweed;** it differs in its perennial habit and creeping rhizomes. Fls are rarely produced.

Polygonum convolvulus L., **Black Bindweed** (fig. 189). Annual. Common on arable land. Twining, branched sts somewhat angular, 1-4 ft. Sts and lvs rather like *Convolvulus arvensis* (see p. 439), but lvs more heart-shaped or sagittate and fls small and green in loose axillary or terminal clusters. July-September. Persistent perianth slightly winged around the frt. Frt dull black, 3-sided, 3·5 mm. A common impurity of cereal seeds, and may be found in beet and mangel. MCPA plus dicamba, 2,4-D ester and Dichlorprop salt kill.

2. *Rumex*. Perianth 6 lobes, the 3 inner lobes larger. Stamens 6. Styles 3. Nut triangular in section, enclosed by the perianth.

Rumex acetosella L., **Sheep's Sorrel** (fig. 190). Perennial. Grassland and arable on poor sandy soils, *growing abundantly and strongly on lime-deficient land.* Branched, horizontal creeping rhizomes producing new shoots. Sts slender, much-branched, 6-20 in. Lower lvs linear to hastate, with lobes at the base pointing outwards or upwards, long petioles. Upper lvs narrow and stalked. May-August. Fls dioecious, small, in clusters on a branched panicle, often reddish. The whole plant becomes red in the late summer. Frt triangular in section, yellowish-brown or reddish-brown, often surrounded by the perianth in seed samples, 1 mm. A frequent impurity in grass seeds and in white, alsike and crimson clovers; also occurs in red clovers and lucerne. An *'injurious' weed seed* under the Seeds Regulations (see Chapter VII). Application of lime is often needed to assist control. MCPA and 2,4-D will kill young seedlings and under favourable conditions will check older plants.

Rumex acetosa L., **Common Sorrel** (fig. 190). Perennial, grassland, *on most soils*. Much larger than the previous species and not an 'indicator' of soil acidity. Sts arise from a thick rhizome. St 1-2 ft. Lower lvs stalked, sagittate, basal lobes point backwards, upper lvs clasp the stem. May-August. Fls dioecious, perianth usually reddish. Frt triangular in section, dark reddish-brown, shiny, 1·5-2 mm. *An 'injurious' weed seed* under the Seeds Regulations, but the seeds are not in fact very commonly found as an impurity of farm seeds. MCPA and 2,4-D check perennial growth only under favourable conditions.

The sorrels contain acid oxalates, and if eaten in quantity they may cause illness or death of livestock. Both species may cause a reduction of milk secretion and render the cream difficult to churn or clot.

Docks. Several species of *Rumex* commonly known as docks may be encountered. The most frequent are: *R. crispus* L., **Curled Dock**, and *R. obtusifolius* L., **Broad-leaved Dock** (fig. 190). They are perennials of arable and grassland. In each case thick tap-roots are produced by plants grown from seed. As a result of arable farming operations, the tap-roots are broken up. Adventitious buds arise on pieces of broken root and give rise to new plants.

R. crispus has narrow lvs with undulating or crinkled edges. It flowers June-October. *R. obtusifolius* has broader lvs with rather less undulating edges; the radical lvs are cordate at the base. It flowers July-September.

The frts of these two docks are shiny, chestnut-brown to dark-brown, 1·5-2 mm. The perianth is persistent around the frt, and aids distribution by wind by means of its flattened lobes. In *R. obtusifolius* the edges of the perianth lobes bear pointed projections. The frts of *R. crispus* are rather smaller and more flask-shaped, more rounded at the base than those of *R. obtusifolius*. The frts, particularly those of *R. crispus*, occur fairly regularly as impurities in seeds of almost all cereals, grasses and legumes. *They are scheduled as 'injurious'* under the Seeds Regulations (see Chapter VII).

Seedlings and young shoots growing from bits of root in arable crops are severely checked or killed by MCPA and 2,4-D. Large plants of *R. crispus* in grassland are checked and may, under favourable conditions, be killed by these materials, but *R. obtusifolius* is resistant to them. The control of these two species is the subject of legislation (see p. 370).

URTICACEAE

Urtica urens L., **Annual Nettle (Small Nettle)** (fig. 191). Arable, more particularly on light soils. Sts more or less 4-sided or ridged, 3-18 in. Lvs opposite, ovate, toothed. Stinging hairs. June-September. Fls in axillary clusters, monoecious, male and female fls in the same cluster. Perianth green, 4-lobed. Male fls with 4 stamens, female with 1 carpel containing a single ovule, 1 stigma. Frt a small achene, greenish-yellow, 2 mm.; may be an impurity in timothy seeds. 2,4-D, Mecoprop, Dichlorprop and MCPA plus 2,3,6 TBA kill young plants.

Urtica dioica L., **Common Nettle (Greater Stinging Nettle).** Perennial. Hedge-sides, woods, near buildings and in clumps in grass fields on most soils, but especially prolific on good land. Extensive creeping sts at or just below the soil surface. St 2-4 ft. Lvs ovate or cordate, toothed. Stinging hairs. June-September. Usually dioecious. Frt oval, pointed at each end, yellow-green, 1 mm., part of the perianth often present in seed samples.

This species is reputed to be an indicator of nitrogen-rich soils. It spreads rapidly, however, where there is a loose surface covering. This

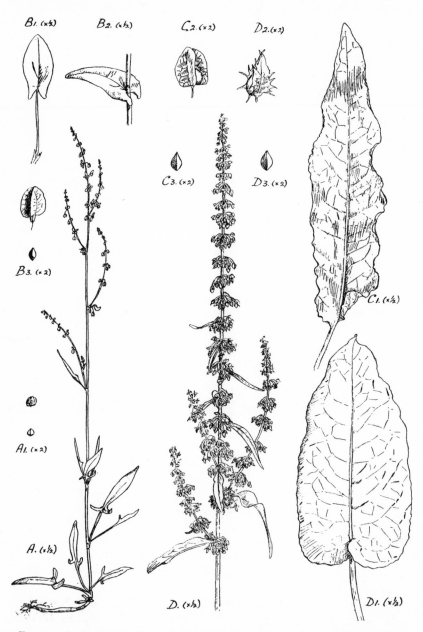

FIG. 190. A, sheep's sorrel; A1, fruit with and without perianth. B1, common sorrel radical leaf; B2, stem leaf; B3, fruit with and without perianth. C1, curled dock leaf; C2 and C3, fruit with and without perianth. D, broad-leaved dock; D1, leaf; D2 and D3, fruit with and without perianth.

covering may be fallen leaves in hedgerows or manure around a dung-heap or, on the other hand, it may be less nutritious matter, such as building rubble or road-making chippings. A means of eradication of clumps of nettles in pastures is to encourage cattle to tread them and consolidate the surface layers of soil, thus killing off the runners. This can be achieved by placing a feeding trough where cattle, in feeding, will tread the nettles. Alternatively, a salt lick placed in the clump of nettles may encourage the desired treading.

Mecoprop and 2,4,5-T most effective, 2,4-D rather less. Spray at flowering stage and again in autumn. Repeated spraying may be necessary.

II. METACHLAMYDEAE: *petals united to form a tube, rarely free or absent.*

PRIMULACEAE

Regular flowers, 5 united sepals, 5 united petals, 5 stamens epipetalous, long style with knobbed stigma, single-celled ovary with numerous ovules, free-central placentation, capsule dehiscing by apical teeth or a lid.

Anagallis arvensis L., **Scarlet Pimpernel (Poor Man's Weather Glass** or **Shepherd's Weather Glass)** (fig. 191). Annual. Arable. Sts procumbent, 6-10 in. Lvs opposite, sessile, ovate to lanceolate, dotted with black glands beneath. May-October. Single flowers in leaf axils, long stalked. Petals scarlet, united at the base only. Frt a small globular capsule opening by a lid. Seed very irregular, roughly pyramidal, surface pitted, reddish-sepia to black, 1 mm., may occur as an impurity in seeds of alsike and white clovers. Rarely sufficiently abundant to cause trouble as a weed. *Poisonous* (see p. 385). Readily killed by DNC and dinoseb; MCPA and 2,4-D kill seedlings only. Dicamba better.

Primula veris L., **Cowslip.** Perennial with a short rhizome. May be abundant in grassland on moist, calcareous loams. Lvs radical, wrinkled, ovate-oblong. April-June. Numerous yellow fls in a simple umbel. The plant is finely hairy. Reduced by manuring combined with close grazing and regular cutting.

BORAGINACEAE (see Chapter XIII)

Lithospermum arvense L., **Corn Gromwell** (fig. 191). Annual. Arable, most soils. St erect, 12-18 in. Basal lvs stalked, narrow, obtuse. Upper lvs, lanceolate. May-July. Fls creamy-white, small, $\frac{1}{3}$ in. diam. Nutlets grey, pear-shaped, somewhat angular, surface warty, 2·5-3 mm.

Readily killed by DNC and dinoseb; MCPA and 2,4-D kill seedlings only.

Echium vulgare L., **Viper's Bugloss.** Biennial. Grassy places, waste land; sometimes plentiful on arable, especially calcareous and light soils. St roughly hairy, 1-3 ft. Lvs lanceolate or oblong. June-August. Fls reddish in the bud, becoming bright blue. Nutlets dark brown, angular, pear-shaped with two smooth flat surfaces and one curved and covered with rough warts, 3·5 mm.

Often associated with the lucerne crop, which favours its biennial habit. The newly-sown crop offers little competition in its first year, and in the second year the tall weed can compete with the crop.

MCPA and 2,4-D check seedlings in cereals.

Anchusa arvensis (L.) Bieb. (*Lycopsis arvensis* L.), **Bugloss** (fig. 191). Annual or biennial. Arable, chalky and light sandy soils. Erect branched

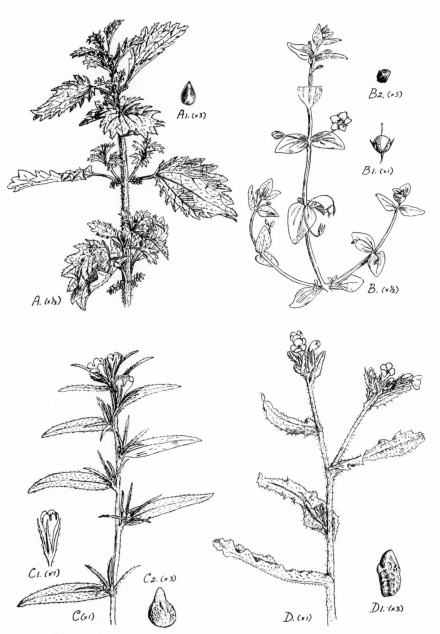

FIG. 191. A, annual nettle; A1, achene. B, scarlet pimpernel; B1, capsule; B2, seed. C, corn gromwell; C1, flower; C2, nutlet. D, bugloss; D1, nutlet.

sts, 6-18 in. Stiff, spreading, hairs. Lower lvs stalked, lanceolate, upper lvs sessile. June-July. Inf terminal curved cymes. Corolla bright blue with white scales at the throat. Nutlets netted, ovoid, dull, light to dark brown, 4 mm.

Myosotis arvensis (L.) Hill, **Common Forget-me-not.** Annual or biennial. Arable. Sts branched, 6-18 in., pubescent. Lower lvs form a rosette stalked, oblong. Upper lvs sessile oblong-lanceolate. Cymes close at flowering but elongating later. May-September. Corolla bright blue, tube shorter than calyx. Nutlets shiny, black, ovate, pointed at one end, somewhat flattened, about 1·5 mm.; may occur in seeds of timothy and, less frequently, in rye-grasses and meadow fescue. Killed by dinoseb up to flower-bud stage, MCPA and 2,4-D control seedlings.

CONVOLVULACEAE

Usually twining, herbaceous. Fls axillary single or in clusters. Sepals 5 (or 4), free. Corolla funnel-shaped or bell-shaped, 5 or 4 united petals. Stamens 5 or 4. Carpels 2 united, superior, 2 stigmas. Frt a capsule, 2 cells each containing 1 to 2 seeds.

Convolvulus arvensis L., **Field** or **Corn Bindweed (Cornbine)** (fig. 192). Perennial. Arable; almost all soils, especially those of a lighter nature. Stout rhizomes penetrate 6 ft. or more into the soil; produce widely spreading branches which give rise to new shoots. Plants are regenerated from broken pieces of rhizome. Sts slender, trailing, or climbing by twisting spirally around the sts of other plants. Lvs variable, more or less hastate, not typically sagittate, as in black bindweed, *Polygonum convolvulus*. June-September. Fls 1-3 in lf axils. Fl pink (sometimes white), funnel-shaped. Seed warty, dark brown to nearly black, 3-sided flask-shaped, two sides flattened, one rounded, angles rounded off, 3 to 4·5 mm.; may be an impurity in mangel, beet and barley seeds.

A very troublesome weed which may pull down cereal stems. Where the weed is abundant, prolonged drying of sheaves may be necessary in order to dry out the weed before stacking.

Very difficult to control because of the depth of the rhizomes. The more shallow rhizomes can be brought to the surface by deep ploughing and cultivating, and then be collected and burnt. Frequent root crops which can be cultivated to destroy the shoots and so exhaust the food store in the rhizomes, and also to prevent seeding, will help. Spraying plants in stubbles, two or three weeks after harvest, with growth regulators may help if ploughing is delayed for two weeks after spraying; 2,4-D more effective than MCPA.

Calystegia sepium (L.) Roem and Schult (*Convolvulus sepium*), **Hedge Bindweed (Large Bindweed, Bellbine)**. Perennial. Similar to the previous species, but larger, and found chiefly climbing in hedges. Not often abundant on farmland, but frequently found in gardens. June-September. Fls white (occasionally pink), calyx enclosed by large bracteoles. More common in the southern part of the country than in the north. Under favourable conditions MCPA and 2,4-D will control.

Cuscuta spp., **Dodder.** The genus *Cuscuta* consists of annual *parasitic plants*, devoid of chlorophyll, which twine around the stems and leaf stalks of host plants and send suckers (haustoria) into them. Union is effected between the vascular tissues of the suckers and of the host plant, and the dodder becomes completely parasitic upon the host.

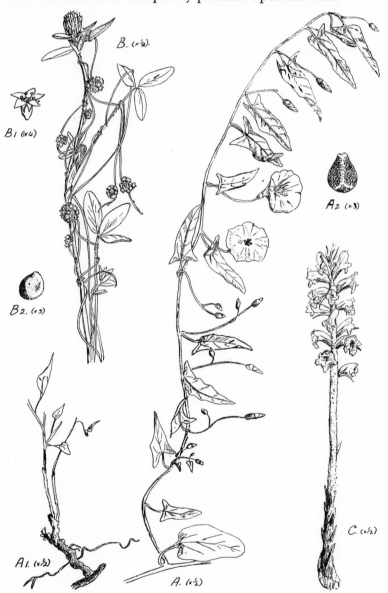

FIG. 192. A, corn bindweed; A1, rhizome; A2, seed. B, dodder on red clover; B1, flower; B2, seed. C, lesser broomrape.

There are about 100 species in various parts of the world. Among plants which may be parasitized by various species of dodder are clovers, lucerne, field beans, vetches, hops, vines, linseed and flax, hemp, carrots, potatoes, beet, gorse, nettle and heather (*Calluna*).

Cuscuta epithymum (L.) Murr., **Common Dodder,** occurs on various plants, including thyme, gorse and heather. A form of this species, formerly known as *C. trifolii* (fig. 192), occurs as a parasite on small legumes, most often on red clover and lucerne, but it is now rare in Britain on these crops as a result of the improved cleaning of seeds of clover, other small legumes and timothy, in which the seed may occur as an impurity (see Seeds Regulations, Chapter VII).

The plant has a slender, pinkish st, small scale-lvs. July-September. Axillary clusters of small, sessile, pinkish, bell-shaped fls. Capsule 2-celled, each cell containing 2 seeds. Seeds more or less spherical, but somewhat angular, dull, grey, brown or yellowish-brown, rough surface, 1-2 mm. Embryo coiled and threadlike; no cotyledons. A single thin root and a slender st produced on germination. If the st contacts a suitable host it twines around it and sends suckers into it. If the parasite fails to find a suitable host before all the food stored in the seed has been used it will die, as no further growth is possible, owing to the absence of photosynthesis.

When a seedling has successfully parasitized a host, its root dies and the parasite loses its connection with the soil. Once established on red clover, or other suitable host, the dodder will grow rapidly, covering the plant, branching and spreading to neighbouring plants. The host plants are considerably weakened and may, occasionally, be killed. If patches of this parasite are seen, the affected plants should be burnt. This should be done on the spot in order to avoid dropping pieces of the dodder stem in other parts of the field, where they may start new patches of infestation.

The species of dodder which parasitizes linseed and flax, *C. epilinum* Weihe, has yellowish fls and yellow-brown seeds.

Dodder seeds can be separated from smooth seeds, such as clovers, by mixing the seed thoroughly with fine iron filings and then passing the seed in a thin layer under a magnet, which picks out the dodder seeds because the filings adhere to the rough surface of the seeds.

SOLANACEAE (see Chapter XIII)

Atropa belladonna L., **Deadly Nightshade** (figs. 193, 194). Perennial in woods and thickets, also near ruined buildings and in hedgerows, especially on calcareous soils; *rather rare*, but more common locally. Thick, slightly creeping, root. Sts branched, 2-5 ft. Lvs alternate or in unequal pairs, oval and pointed, somewhat downy, up to 7 or 8 in. long. June-August. Fls axillary, single, bell-shaped, dull purple, about 1 in. long. Berries black, shiny, round and flattened, $\frac{1}{2}$-$\frac{3}{4}$ in. diam., 2-celled, containing many seeds. *Very poisonous* (see p. 386).

Solanum dulcamara L., **Woody Nightshade (Bittersweet)** (figs. 193, 194). Often mistakenly called deadly nightshade. Perennial. Scrambling in hedgerows and in shaded and damp situations; *common* throughout Britain. Thick, creeping root-stock. Sts somewhat woody, 2-5 ft. Lvs variable in shape, ovate, hastate or with 3 lflts. June-September. Lateral cymes of bright purple fls with conspicuous yellow anthers, rotate not bell-shaped. Berries much smaller than *Atropa*, scarlet, egg-shaped, many-seeded. The st when tasted is at first bitter, but the after-taste is sweet, hence the name bittersweet. *Poisonous* (see p. 386).

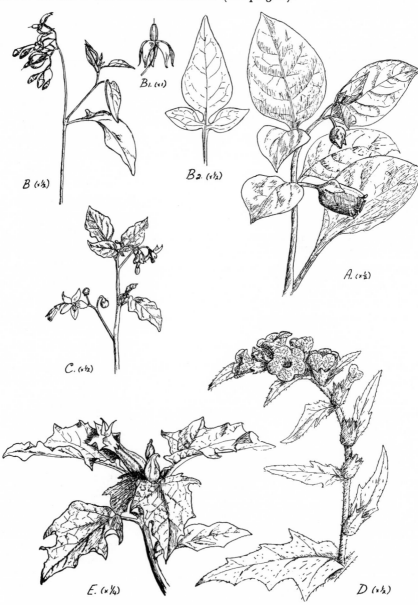

Fig. 193. A, deadly nightshade. B, woody nightshade; B1, flower; B2, leaf. C, black nightshade. D, henbane. E, thorn apple.

Solanum nigrum L., **Black Nightshade** (figs. 193, 194). Annual, arable, common in England, but local in Wales, Scotland and Ireland. Sts branched, 6-24 in. Lvs ovate. July-September. Fls small, white, rotate; berries black, globular. *Poisonous* (see p. 385). Seeds germinate late and

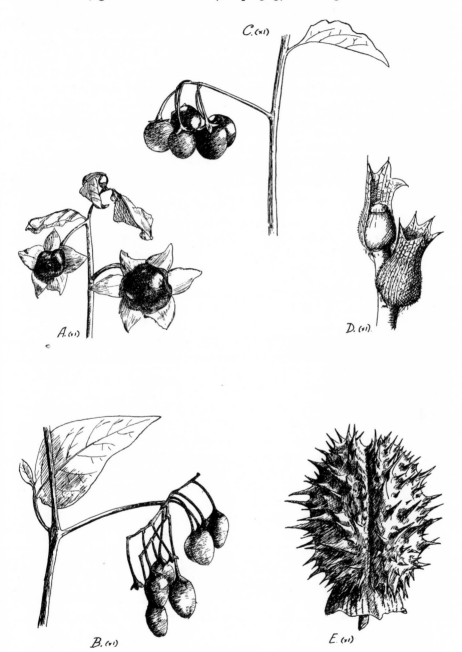

FIG. 194. A, deadly nightshade berries. B, woody nightshade berries. C, black nightshade berries. D, henbane capsule. E, thorn apple capsule.

443

thus escape early cultivations. MCPA, 2,4-D, check young seedlings only.

Hyoscyamus niger L., **Henbane** (figs. 193, 194). Annual or biennial. Casually scattered throughout Britain, chiefly on sandy soils, waste places, near old buildings, occasionally in farmyards. The plant has a strong unpleasant smell and is viscid (sticky). Sts hairy, 1-2 ft. Basal lvs stalked, ovate, st lvs sessile or clasping the stem, lobed or toothed. June-August. Fls funnel-shaped, dirty yellow usually with purple veins, anthers purple. Frt enclosed in the enlarged calyx, a capsule opening by a lid and containing numerous seeds. *Poisonous* (see p. 386). Reputed to reduce milk secretion and to taint milk.

Datura stramonium L., **Thorn Apple** (figs. 193, 194). Annual. Casual in waste places and occasionally on arable land in southern England. Erect branched sts, 1-3 ft. or more. Lvs ovate coarsely toothed. July-October. Fls very large, upright, white, funnel-shaped. Frt a capsule covered with long sharp prickles, rather like a horse-chestnut frt, but containing numerous rough black seeds. Seed 3 mm. *Poisonous* (see p. 386).

SCROPHULARIACEAE

Calyx 5 (usually), persistent. Corolla 4 or 5 petals, united, often two-lipped, but sometimes regular or nearly so. Stamens 2 or 4 (rarely 5), epipetalous. Ovary 2-celled. Frt a capsule, usually many-seeded.

Digitalis purpurea L., **Foxglove.** Biennial, copses, banks, hedgerows, on acid soils. In the first year a rosette of large ovate to lanceolate lvs. In the second year sts 2-5 ft., infl a raceme of many large fls. Corolla roughly bell-shaped, 5 petals forming a long tube, purple. Stamens 4. Large capsule. *Poisonous* (see p. 383). The poison is cumulative and may be taken in small quantity for some time before harmful effects occur. The drug digitalis, used in the treatment of heart complaints, is prepared from foxglove leaves (*D. purpurea* and *D. lanata*).

Veronica spp. **The Speedwells.** Well-known weeds with opposite lvs and small blue (occasionally white or pinkish) flowers. Calyx of 4 lobes. Corolla 4-lobed, the upper lobe being the largest, tube very short. Stamens 2. Capsule often compressed at the sides and containing few seeds. The annual species which occur on arable land are more important, as weeds, than the perennial grassland species.

Veronica chamaedrys L., **Germander Speedwell** (fig. 195). *Perennial.* Hedgerows and old grassland. Sts 6-9 in., *two lines of long white hairs* on opposite sides. Lvs ovate-cordate, toothed, hairy. May-August. *Axillary racemes.* Fls bright blue. Capsule obcordate, *shorter than sepals.* MCPA and 2,4-D check only under favourable conditions.

V. officinalis L., **Common Speedwell** (fig. 195). *Perennial.* Grassland, heaths, open woods, particularly dry soils. Sts *hairy all round.* Lvs obovate or oblong. Fls *lilac*, in axillary racemes. Capsule obovate or obcordate, *longer than the sepals.*

V. persica Poir (*V. Buxbaumii*), **Buxbaum's Speedwell** (fig. 195). *Annual.* Common on arable land. Decumbent hairy sts. Lvs triangular-ovate.

Fls all the year round. Fls *single* axillary, bright blue, the lower lobe often pale, stalks longer than the lvs. Capsule 2-lobed, keeled, ciliate. Seed pale-to-orange-yellow, obovate-oval, irregularly corrugated, hollow on one side, 1·2 mm.

Other *annual* arable species, each with *single* axillary fls, are: *V. agrestis* L., **Field Speedwell** (fig. 195). Fls pale blue the lower part very pale or white, lvs longer than broad, more regularly toothed. *V. hederifolia* L., **Ivy-leaved Speedwell** (fig. 195). Lvs thick with broad lobes. April-August. Fl lilac-blue. *Capsule not compressed. V. polita* Fries., **Grey Speedwell.** Lvs dull green, ovate coarsely toothed. Fls all the year round. Fl stalk not longer than the lvs. Petals usually uniform bright blue.

The speedwells of arable land are most readily killed by DNC. Dinoseb will kill young plants; MCPA and 2,4-D are usually not useful after the early seedling stage.

Rhinanthus minor L., **Yellow Rattle** (fig. 196). Annual. Most common in old grassland where it is allowed to run to seed each year. Sub-species or forms exist on damp soils, dry soils, calcareous soils, etc. A *hemiparasite* on the roots of grasses. St 4-sided, 6-18 in. Lvs opposite, lanceolate or linear, toothed. May-July. Terminal leafy spikes of yellow fls. Inflated calyx, 4 small teeth. Corolla upper lip longer, marked with blue or purple. Capsule flat, 2 valved, containing a few flat seeds. Ripe frts rattle when shaken. The testa is flattened to form a wing around the seed and aids wind dispersal. Seed 4 mm. Easily eradicated by grazing with sheep in spring and early summer or by cutting hay before the seed forms. Repeat for a second year. MCPA and 2,4-D check seedlings only.

Other *hemiparasitic* members of this family are: *Euphrasia officinalis* L., **Eyebright** (fig. 196). Annual. Grassland and heaths, 2-6 in. July-September. Corolla white or lilac, yellow spot and purple veins on lower lip. A number of sub-species occur, very variable. *Odontites verna* (Bell) Dum., **Red Bartsia** (fig. 196). Annual. Grassland. Up to 12in. June-September. One-sided terminal spike, purple-pink fls. *Pedicularis palustris* L., **Red Rattle.** Annual. Wet heaths and meadows, 6-18 in. May-September. Fls purplish-pink. *Pedicularis sylvatica* L., **Lousewort** (fig. 196). Perennial. Marshy land, 3-6 in. Fls pink, April-July.

OROBANCHACEAE

Orobanche minor Sm., **Lesser Broomrape** (fig. 192). A *total parasite* occasionally found in clover leys. The plant has no chlorophyll and is parasitic upon clovers, chiefly red clovers, and on sainfoin, lucerne and some other herbaceous leguminous plants. Swollen st below ground bearing membranous scale-lvs. Attached by suckers (haustoria) to the roots of a host plant. Simple st, 6-12 in., brownish, bearing scale-lvs and glandular hairs. June-September. Inf a long terminal spike. Fls yellowish-brown tinged with purple. Corolla 2-lipped. Capsule opens by 2 valves, contains abundant very minute black seeds. Seeds wind-distributed; they germinate only when in contact with the roots of a suitable host. The seed may lie dormant for a number of years. The host may be obviously

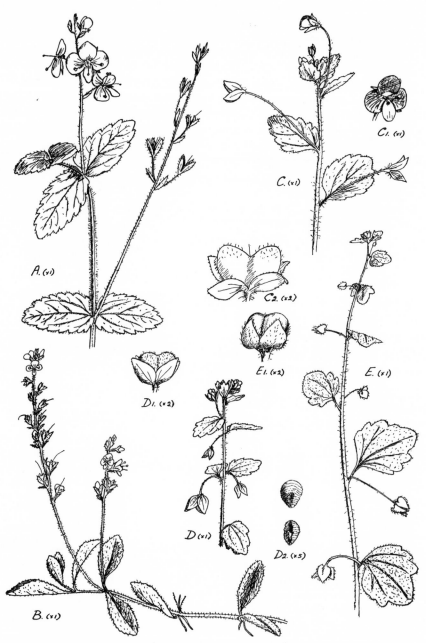

FIG. 195. A, germander speedwell. B, common speedwell. C, Buxbaum's speedwell; C1, flower; C2, capsule. D, field speedwell; D1, capsule; D2, seeds. E, ivy-leaved speedwell; E1, capsule.

weakened by the presence of the parasite. Control by prevention of seeding.

Other species of broomrape may be encountered as parasites on various host species, such as yarrow, ivy, thistles, greater knapweed, broom, gorse and carrot, but these are of little or no agricultural importance.

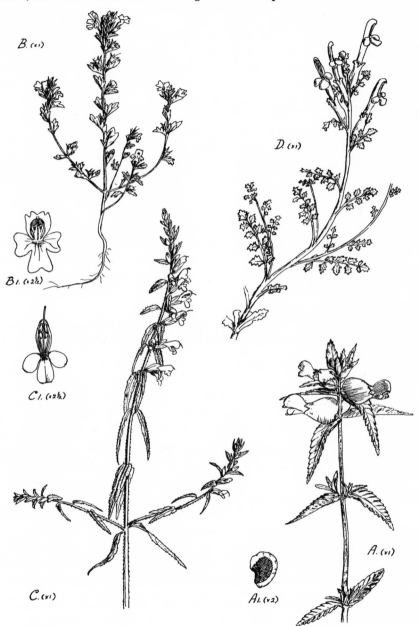

Fig. 196. A, yellow rattle; A1, seed. B, eyebright; B1, flower. C, red bartsia; C1, flower. D, lousewort.

447

LABIATAE

Square sts, opposite lvs. Fls single, or in axillary clusters with the appearance of whorls. Sepals 5, united. Corolla 2-lipped, 4 or 5 lobed. Stamens 2 or 2+2, epipetalous. Ovary 4-lobed, consisting of 2 united carpels each with a secondary division, each cell containing one ovule. Frt splits into 4 nutlets. Nutlets have two flattened sides and one rounded.

Lamium purpureum L., **Red Deadnettle** (fig. 197). Annual. Arable. Hairy. Sts branching from the base, 4-18 in., often purplish at the base. Serrated lf, tip obtuse. March-October. Whorls of fls close together. Fls pink-purple. Nutlets pear-shaped, 3-angled, greyish-brown, with scattered small white spots, 2 mm. or more.
MCPA and 2,4-D check young seedlings only.

Lamium amplexicaule L., **Henbit** (fig. 197). Annual. Arable, especially on light, dry soils. Hairy. Sts branching at the base. 2-10 in. Lvs lobed, rounded at the tip, upper ones sessile. April-August. Whorls of fls widely separated. Fls pink-purple. Nutlets narrow oval, pointed at one end, 3-angled, greyish or brownish, surface covered with small white pimples, about 2 mm.
Killed by MCPA up to flower bud stage; 2,4-D kills seedlings only.

Galeopsis tetrahit L., **Common Hemp-nettle.** Annual. Arable. St hairy, especially below the nodes, 1-2 ft. Lvs ovate-lanceolate, hairy. Calyx hairy, veins prominent. Corolla white, pink or purple, with dark markings, lower lip broad. Nutlets pear-shaped, brown, mottled, 3 mm., occasionally an impurity in oat seed.
Killed up to flower bud stage by DNC and dinoseb, seedlings killed by MCPA, but only checked by 2,4-D.

Other annual species of *Galeopsis* which may be found on arable land are: *G. bifida* (fig. 197), in which the lower lip of the corolla is convex and deeply notched, and *G. speciosa*, **Large-flowered Hemp-nettle**, which is usually larger and has a pale yellow corolla with a violet lower lip; it occurs especially on peaty soils.

Mentha arvensis L., **Corn Mint** (fig. 197). Perennial, rhizomatous, common in arable in some areas throughout Britain, mainly on damp soils. Strong smell of mint. Variable. Hairy. Sts simple or branched, 6-18 in. Lvs variable from lanceolate to rounded, tip obtuse. August-October. Corolla only slightly 2-lipped, lilac. Nutlets smooth, nearly ovoid, coming to a point at the base where there are 2 lighter-coloured scars of attachment with a ridge between them, 1 mm.
Difficult to control because the deep, fragile rhizomes are not readily cultivated out. MCPA and 2,4-D check only under favourable conditions.

Stachys arvensis L., **Field Woundwort** (fig. 198). Annual. Arable, non-calcareous soils. Branched sts, 3-12 in. Lvs ovate, tip obtuse. April-November. Fls in axillary whorls, pale purple. Nutlets smooth, slightly angular, dark brown or black, 1·5 mm. *S. palustris* L., **Marsh Woundwort.** A large

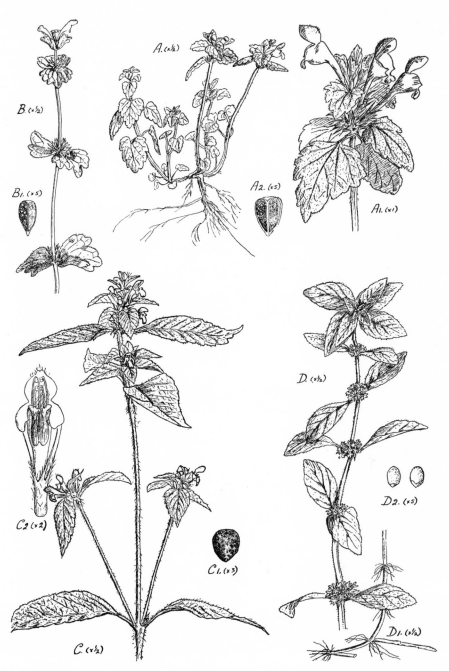

FIG. 197. A, red deadnettle; A1, inflorescence; A2, nutlet. B, henbit; B1, nutlet. C, hemp-nettle; C1, nutlet; C2, flower (*G. bifida*). D, corn mint; D1, rhizome; D2, nutlet.

449

perennial rhizomatous species found on wet permanent grassland; also appears occasionally on arable land.

A common hedgerow weed of the same genus is *S. sylvatica* L., **Hedge Wound-wort,** which is larger than *S. arvensis* and perennial, with long rhizomes and dark reddish-purple fls. It has an unpleasant odour.

Glechoma hederacea L., **Ground Ivy** (fig. 198). Perennial. Old grassland, woods,

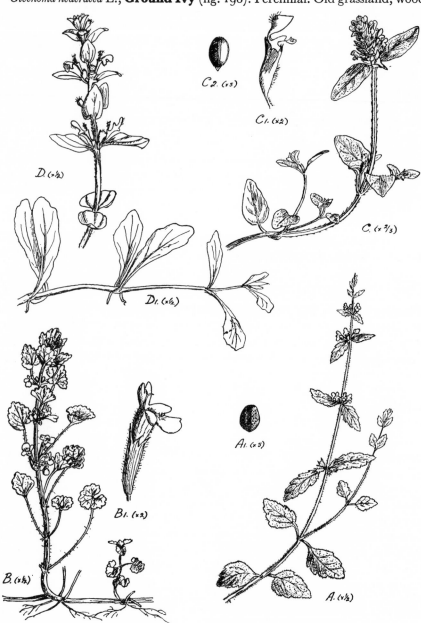

FIG. 198. A, field woundwort; A1, nutlet. B, ground ivy; B1, flower. C, self-heal; C1, flower; C2, nutlet. D and D1, Bugle.

waste places, and occasionally arable, damp heavier soils. Stoloniferous. Sts simple, 6-12 in., hairy. Lvs reniform with a crenate margin, long-stalked. March-May. Fls violet. Said to have caused poisoning of horses. Not usually a serious farm weed.

Prunella vulgaris L., **Self-heal** (fig. 198). Perennial. Often abundant in poor grassland on most soils; particularly vigorous on damp soils. Short rhizomes. St slightly hairy, 3-9 in. Lvs minutely hairy, some are toothed. June-September. Fls violet. Nutlets oval with a white basal point, glossy, brown with darker vertical lines, 1·75 mm. A frequent impurity in wild white clover seeds; also occurring, though less frequently, in red clover, alsike clover, lucerne, other white clovers, timothy and crested dog's-tail seeds.

Frequently killed by MCPA or 2,4-D, but a second application may be necessary.

Ajuga reptans L., **Bugle** (fig. 198). Perennial. Damp grassland. Short rhizomes. Long leafy stolons. Sts simple, slightly hairy, 6-12 in. Basal lvs form a rosette, upper lvs ovate, sessile. May-July. Fls blue. Inf longish, 2-8 in. Resistant to MCPA and 2,4-D. Improved drainage will help to destroy.

PLANTAGINACEAE

Lvs form a rosette or tuft. Flowering sts leafless, terminate in a close spike. Fls regular. Sepals 4. Corolla small membranous, 4-lobed. Stamens 4, long-stalked. Ovary superior 1-4-celled. Frt a capsule (opening by a lid in *Plantago*).

Plantago major L., **Broad-leaved Plantain** (fig. 199). Perennial. Arable, and colonizing exposed soil around gateways, in grass fields and on farm roads; very common. Broad lvs. May-September. Capsule 8-16-seeded. Seed irregular and variable in shape, angular, one side with ridges radiating from the scar, dull brown, 1 mm., may occur as an impurity in seeds of small legumes and timothy. Readily killed by MCPA and 2,4-D.

Plantago media L., **Hoary Plantain**. Perennial. Grassland; more on neutral and calcareous soils. Lvs broad, very downy, lying very close to the ground, petioles very short or absent. June-October. Fls scented, lilac bracts and stamens, capsule 4-seeded. Very susceptible to MCPA and 2,4-D.

Plantago lanceolata L., **Ribwort Plantain (Ribgrass)** (fig. 199). Perennial. Grassland. Lvs more or less lanceolate, more upright than the two previous species. Inf ovoid or cylindrical, short. May-October. Capsule 2-seeded. Seed brown, shiny, boat-shaped with a hollow along one side. 2-2·5 mm., a frequent impurity in seeds of red clover and lucerne, also occurs, but less frequently, in seeds of other legumes and of grasses. Readily killed by MCPA or 2,4-D.

This species is *sometimes sown*, for grazing, in seeds mixtures or in a herb-strip mixture. It is readily eaten by farm livestock and is rich in minerals. It is unsuitable for hay, as the thick leaves dry slowly and the hay may mould readily.

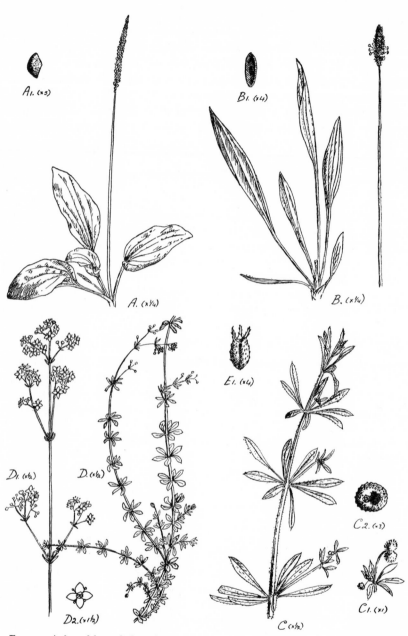

FIG. 199. A, broad-leaved plantain; A1, seed. B, ribwort plantain; B1, seed. C, cleavers; C1, fruit; C2, half-fruit (bristles rubbed off). D and D1, heath bedstraw; D2, flower. E1, field madder, half-fruit.

RUBIACEAE

Angular sts. Lvs in whorls. Fls small, in terminal or axillary panicles. Calyx absent or 4-6 teeth. Petals 4-5 united. Stamens 4-5. Ovary 2-celled, 2 styles. Frt 2 one-seeded lobes.

Galium aparine L., **Cleavers (Goosegrass, Herrif)** (fig. 199). Annual. Hedgerows; a very common and important weed of corn crops. Weak branched sts, angles bearing downward pointing prickles. Lvs 6-8 in a whorl, linear-lanceolate. June-August. Fls white. Frt splits into 2 dry 1-seeded rounded portions, covered with hooked bristles, grey, a circular pit on one side of the half frts. Half-frt 3 mm.; the bristles may be rubbed off in seed samples. One of the commonest impurities in cereal seeds; also occurs in crimson clover and sainfoin.

DNC and dinoseb kill young plants; Mecoprop gives good control.

Other common members of the genus *Galium* are: *G. Saxatile* L., **Heath Bedstraw** (fig. 199). Perennial. Grassland, heaths, soil often acid. Glabrous, 4-6 in., prostrate. June-August. Fls white in a loose terminal panicle. *G. verum* L., **Lady's Bedstraw.** Perennial on dry banks and pastures. Weak sts, 1-2 ft. lvs linear. June-September. Terminal panicles of yellow fls. *G. cruciata* (L.) Scop., **Crosswort.** Perennial, hedgerows, slender sts, 1-1½ ft., only 4 lvs in each whorl, ovate. April-June. Fls yellow, in axillary clusters. *G. mollugo* L., **Hedge Bedstraw.** Perennial. Hedgerows. Sts much branched, 1-4 ft. July-August. Fls white, in long terminal panicles.

Sherardia arvensis L., **Field Madder.** Annual, often abundant on arable land, particularly on calcareous and neutral soils. Reddish roots. Numerous spreading, much-branched sts, nearly prostrate, up to 18 in. Lvs obovate-lanceolate, pointed, in whorls of 4 to 6 (4 at the basal nodes). April-October. Fls lilac, sessile in terminal clusters with leafy bracts below, corolla funnel-shaped, 4-lobed. Frt crowned with enlarged sepal points (4-6), splits in two when ripe. Half-frt ('seed') (fig. 199) somewhat egg-shaped with a broad furrow down the inner side, crowned with the sepal points (usually 3), covered with fine white hairs, grey to dark brown, 2-3·5 mm., a frequent impurity of trefoil and crimson clover; also occurs, but less frequently, in seeds of other small legumes and in rye-grasses, meadow fescue and crested dog's-tail.

COMPOSITAE (see Chapter XIII)

(*a*) *Tubiflorae*. In this group tubular florets are present. The species dealt with first usually have an outer whorl of ligulate florets and a disk of tubular florets. The species dealt with later have tubular florets only.

The **Mayweeds** and **Chamomiles.** This group includes a number of annual or biennial weeds of arable land, all commonly called 'Mayweeds', with daisy-like flower heads of white ligulate and yellow tubular florets, finely divided leaves and achenes without a pappus.

Anthemis cotula L., **Stinking Mayweed.** Particularly on heavy soils. *Strong, unpleasant odour.* Acrid; may blister hands when handled. Sts branched from base, 1-2 ft., slightly hairy. Lvs tripinnate with narrow hair-like segments. July-September. Fl heads ½-1 in. diam., solitary on rather short stalks. Achenes light brown or grey, 10 warty ridges, 2 mm., may occur as an impurity in alsike and white clover seeds.
MCPA plus 2,3,6-TBA, DNC and dinoseb kill seedlings.

Anthemis arvensis L., **Corn Chamomile** (fig. 200). More on calcareous soils. *Little scent.* St downy, much branched above and below. Lvs hairy. Less divided and with shorter segments than *A. cotula.* June-July. Fl heads ¾-1¼ in. diam., solitary on rather long stalks. Achenes straw-coloured, ridges not warty, 2 mm., may occur as an impurity in seeds of rye-grasses and meadow fescues. Control as for *A. cotula.*

Tripleurospermum maritimum (L.) Koch Ssp *inodorum* (L.) Hyl, **Scentless Mayweed** (fig. 200). Common on all soils. *Little scent.* Sts glabrous, erect, angular, branching above, 1-2 ft. Lf segments fine and hair-like. July-October. Fl heads solitary, large, up to 2 in. diam. Achenes dark brown or black with 3 whitish ribs on the inner face and 2 dark glands at the top of the outer face, collared at the apex, 2 mm. May occur in timothy seeds and, less commonly, in rye-grasses. DNC kills young plants; Mecoprop, MCPA plus, 2,3,6-TBA and dinoseb check or kill seedlings.

Matricaria recutita L., **Wild Chamomile** (fig. 200). More on sandy and loamy soils. *Scent resembles ripe apples.* June-July. Fl heads smaller (½-¾ in. diam.) and more numerous than in the previous species. Receptacle elongated and hollow later. Achenes slender, pale grey, with 4 or 5 white ribs, about 1 mm., obliquely truncate. DNC, dinoseb and MCPA plus 2,3,6 TBA check or kill seedlings.

Matricaria matricarioides (Less.)Porter, **Rayless Mayweed** (fig. 200). Most common in gateways, farm roads, stackyards, etc. *Strong odour of pineapple.* Recognized by the absence of white ligulate florets. June-July. Achene resembles previous species, but slightly larger and with a small rim at the top. Introduced in the nineteenth century, rare before 1900, now extremely common. Seeds spread by wheels, feet, etc.

The *Anthemis* spp. and *Matricaria* spp. may cause unpleasant taints in milk and reduce milk secretion, if eaten by dairy animals.

Chrysanthemum leucanthemum L., **Ox-eye Daisy (Moon-daisy, Marguerite)** (fig. 201). Perennial. Poorly managed and infertile grassland. Thin, branched root-stock grows obliquely. St simple or slightly branched, 9-24 in. Lvs irregularly toothed. Radical lvs obovate-spathulate, st lvs narrower, wavy at the margins, clasping the st. Terminal fl heads, ray florets white, disk yellow. June-July. No pappus. Achenes black with

10 grey ribs, 2 mm., may be an impurity in seeds of timothy and crested dog's-tail. In mass the 'seed' appears silvery. Checked by MCPA and 2,4-D only under favourable conditions. Reduced by grazing with sheep in spring and early summer, cutting to prevent seeding, associated with improvement of fertility by application of the necessary fertilizers.

This sp. may taint milk and butter if eaten in quantity.

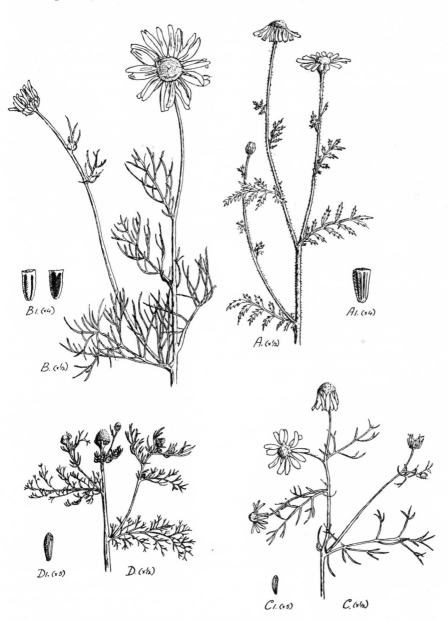

Fig. 200. A, corn chamomile; A1, achene. B, scentless mayweed; B1, achenes. C, wild chamomile; C1, achene. D, rayless mayweed; D1, achene.

455

Chrysanthemum segetum L., **Corn Marigold** (fig. 201). Annual, Arable, common in some areas on *acid soils*. St branched, 1-1½ ft. Lvs slightly fleshy, coarsely toothed or lobed, tending to clasp the stem. June-September. Fls golden yellow, ray florets few and broad. No pappus. Achenes yellow-grey, 10 rounded ribs, those from disk florets cylindrical, those from ray florets with 2 narrow wings, 2·5 mm. Seeds may lie dormant in the soil for some years. Application of lime may be necessary to assist control. DNC (with a wetter) kills young plants; dinoseb kills seedlings only; MCPA and 2,4-D are ineffective.

Bellis perennis L., **Daisy.** Perennial. Often abundant in lawns and over-grazed fields. Succeeds there because its lvs form a flat rosette on the soil surface and so escape mowing and grazing. Fibrous roots arising from a short, erect root-stock. Lvs spathulate. Ray florets white, sometimes pink-tipped, disk yellow. March-October. No pappus. Under favourable conditions, MCPA and 2,4-D give good control.

Tussilago farfara L., **Coltsfoot (Clay-weed)** (fig. 201). Perennial. Arable and waste places, widespread but often associated with wet clay soil and badly-drained patches in arable fields. Rhizomes penetrate up to 3 ft. or more, horizontal branches produce new shoots. Lvs radical, cordate, slightly toothed, woolly beneath, appear later than the fls. Fls March-April. Fl sts bear scale-lvs. Ray and disk florets yellow. Pappus sessile. Achene very slender, cylindrical, yellow to reddish-brown, shiny, with many longitudinal ribs, 3·5 mm.

Control very difficult; frequent cutting of lvs to starve out the rhizomes, early cutting of fls to prevent seeding, often improvement of drainage needed. MCPA plus 2,3,6-TBA and 2,4,5-T severely check. ditions.

Petasites hybridus (L.) Gaertn., **Butterbur.** Perennial common in damp grassland and near streams. Stout, branched rhizomes. Lvs resemble colts-foot, but more rounded and larger when mature (up to 30 in. wide). Fls March-May, before the lvs. Fl sts 6-30 in., covered with scales. Large panicles of small fl heads, fls pale purple, dioecious. *P. fragrans*, **Winter Heliotrope,** a rhizomatous garden escape, flowering January-March, occurs as a weed on banks, waste places and banks of streams.

Senecio vulgaris L., **Groundsel** (fig. 201). Annual. Arable and waste places, most soils. Fibrous roots. Sts erect, succulent, 6-12 in. Fls all the year round. Fl heads in corymbose clusters. Florets yellow, ray florets inconspicuous or absent. Pappus sessile. Achenes narrow, grey-brown, ribbed, about 2·5 mm. Reputed to be *poisonous*. DNC and dinoseb kill young plants, MCPA and 2,4-D seedlings only. Susceptible to dicamba.

Senecio jacobaea L., **Ragwort (Ragweed, Staggerweed,** etc.) (fig. 202). Biennial or short-lived perennial. One of the most common weeds of grassland, particularly on drier soils. Short, thick tap-root with stout laterals. In the first year of growth a rosette of lvs is formed near the surface of the soil. Lvs pinnatifid, of ragged appearance. Flowering sts

usually produced in the second year and the plant dies after seeding.
Sts 2-4 ft. June-October. Each fl-head like a small yellow daisy, numerous
fl-heads massed together in a flat-topped compound corymb. Pappus
sessile. Achenes cylindrical, pale brown, 2 mm., ribbed; a few short

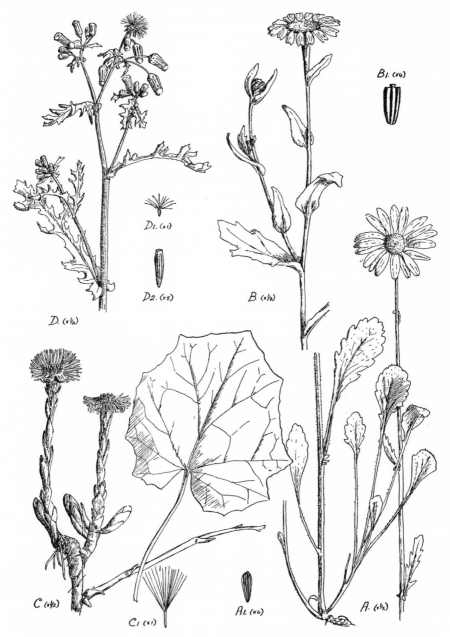

FIG. 201. A, ox-eye daisy; A1, achene. B, corn marigold; B1, achene. C, coltsfoot,
including portion of rhizome; C1, fruit. D, groundsel; D1, fruit (complete); D2, achene
(pappus removed).

457

white hairs on the ribs. Plants often attacked by caterpillars of the cinnabar moth which may defoliate them. *Poisonous* (see p. 383). This weed is probably responsible for more cases of illness and death of farm animals than all other poisonous plants together. The poisons are cumulative, and small amounts of the plant eaten over a long period may ultimately have serious effects. Grazing by sheep in spring and early summer, when the shoots are short, is often recommended as an effective means of control, but sheep have been killed by it, and great care is needed. Hay containing ragwort is a frequent cause of poisoning. *Control* by cutting the upright stems, or hand pulling after rain. This should be done at the fl-bud stage. Plants cut when in flower ripen seed if left lying on the ground; they should be burnt to prevent this and also to prevent them from being picked up and eaten by animals. Ragwort can be killed by spraying in June or early July with MCPA or 2,4-D. After spraying, animals should be kept off the field for a time as they are particularly liable to eat wilting plants. For complete control, further spraying may be needed in order to kill plants which develop from seeds or from old roots after the first application. For legislation relating to the control of this weed, see p. 370.

S. aquaticus Hill, **Marsh Ragwort.** Biennial. Occurs on marshes and wet grassland. Resembles *S. jacobaea*, but shorter, st lvs less cut and the terminal lobe always the largest, fl heads larger and fewer and more openly arranged. Contains poisonous alkaloids.

S. squalidus L., **Oxford Ragwort.** Common in waste places, on walls, bombed sites, railway embankments, etc. Thought to have escaped from the Oxford Botanic Garden in the eighteenth century; now widespread. Usually annual, shorter than *S. jacobaea*, involucre bracts dark-tipped, fl heads about the same size as *S. jacobaea*, but more openly arranged. Contains poisonous alkaloids.

Achillea millefolium L., **Yarrow (Milfoil)** (fig. 202). Perennial. Aromatic when bruised. Common in pastures, especially on dry soils, hedgesides and waste places. Extensive creeping rhizomes. St 6-18 in., little branched, furrowed. Lvs long oblong, much divided into very fine segments. Radical lvs long-stalked, st lvs sessile. July-August. Fl-heads massed together in a terminal corymb. Fl heads small with about 6 ray florets, white (sometimes pink). No pappus. Achenes oblong, flat, white-grey (silvery in bulk), fine longitudinal lines, 1·5-2 mm.

Yarrow is *sometimes sown* in seeds mixtures or herb-strip mixtures for grazing. The seed-rate should be kept low, otherwise the plant may become too abundant by reason of its creeping habit. It should not be sown on fields intended for mowing, as the flowering sts become woody. In pastures it must be well grazed, otherwise flowering sts are formed, and these are rejected by livestock. If eaten in excessive amounts by dairy cows, it may taint the milk. Sometimes persists in arable if ploughing and cultivations are not carefully done. Moderately susceptible to MCPA plus 2,3,6-TBA.

Gnaphalium uliginosum L., **Marsh Cudweed** (fig. 206). Annual. Arable, particularly damp, sandy, acid soils. St decumbent or ascending, 3-6 in., much-branched, cottony. Lvs narrow. Small fl heads in terminal clusters surrounded by lvs which overtop the clusters. Florets yellowish. July-September.

Chrysanthemum vulgare., **Tansy** (fig. 202). Perennial. Roadsides, hedgerows and waste places. Strong, unpleasant odour. Creeping root-stock. Sts 1-3 ft.,

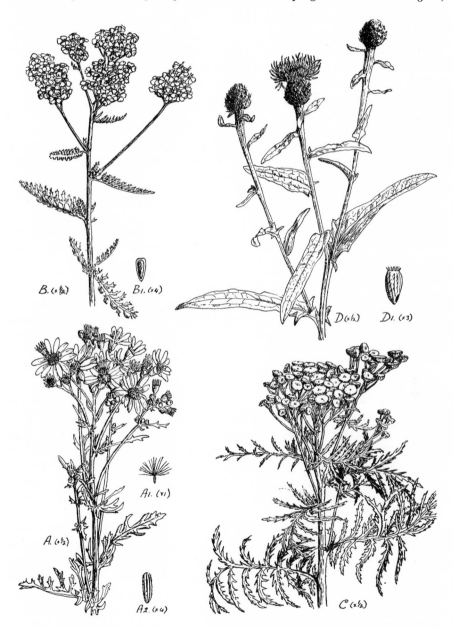

FIG. 202. A, ragwort; A1, fruit (complete); A2, achene (pappus removed). B, yarrow; B1, achene. C, tansy. D, lesser knapweed; D1, achene.

becoming rather woody. Lvs pinnate with deeply-divided lobes. July-September. Fls golden yellow, ray florets absent.

May taint milk if eaten in quantity by milking animals; its unpleasant smell and taste make grazing unlikely, however.

Centaurea nigra L., **Lesser Knapweed (Common Knapweed, Hard-heads)** (fig. 202). Perennial. Hedge-sides and old grassland. Thick, branched rhizome. Sts rigid, branched, grooved, 6-30 in. Lvs hairy. Basal lvs stalked, st lvs sessile, lower lvs oval to lanceolate, lobed or toothed, upper lvs entire or toothed near the base only, narrowing and tapering. June-October. *Florets all tubular*, purple, in hard globular heads. Involucre bracts hairy, dark brown. Achenes pale brown, 3 mm., pappus short bristles. MCPA and 2,4-D kill top growth; rhizomes killed under favourable conditions.

C. scabiosa L., **Greater Knapweed,** is a larger-flowered species with a longer pappus, found on dry grassland, roadsides, banks, cliffs, etc., especially on calcareous soils. Rare in Scotland. More resistant to MCPA and 2,4-D.

Centaurea cyanus L., **Cornflower (Bluebottle).** Annual, once very common in corn fields because of inefficient cleaning of seed-grain, now occasional in arable land. Sts branched, slender, 1-2½ ft. Lvs sessile, with a few grey woolly hairs, linear-lanceolate, lower ones with a few teeth or notches. June-August. Outer florets bright blue, central ones purplish. Achenes silvery-grey, slightly hairy, 3 mm., pappus reddish. DNC kills young plants, MCPA and 2,4-D kill seedlings only.

Cirsium arvense (L.) Scop. (*Carduus arvensis*), **Creeping Thistle** (fig. 203). *Perennial;* very common. Arable and grassland; most soils. Vertical roots from which arise extensive horizontal creeping roots. On the roots adventitious buds develop and give rise to new shoots. The plant sends up new shoots each year. Smooth sts, 1-3 ft., *without wings or spines*. Lvs more or less glabrous, spiny around the margin. July-September. Fl heads smaller and more numerous than in *C. vulgare*. Fls pale purple (occasionally whitish). *Florets all tubular*. Fls on some plants have aborted ovaries and fail to fruit. On other plants the stamens are aborted; these plants produce seed. Fls have a strong scent of honey and attract insects which carry out pollination. Pappus often blows away leaving the fruit in the flower-head. Achenes dark brown, smooth, 2·5-3·5 mm. May be an impurity in seeds of perennial rye-grass, cocksfoot, timothy, crested dog's-tail and alsike clover.

A very troublesome weed on farms, spreading extensively in grassland and growing from broken pieces of root in arable. In either case shoots growing over a relatively large area may all be of one sex, having originated from broken roots of a single plant on arable land, or arising from the creeping roots of a single plant in grassland. If male, no seed will be produced, and if female, seed will form only provided there are male plants at hand to supply pollen.

Contrary to popular belief, seeds, when formed, will germinate, but seedlings are not often seen. On arable land small shoots which may be mistaken for seedlings can be traced down in the soil to broken pieces of root (also the absence of cotyledons indicates that they are not seedlings).

Control. In grassland cutting each time the plants reach the flower bud stage, if continued over three years, will eventually exhaust the food supply in the roots and kill the plants. MCPA and 2,4-D, applied at the

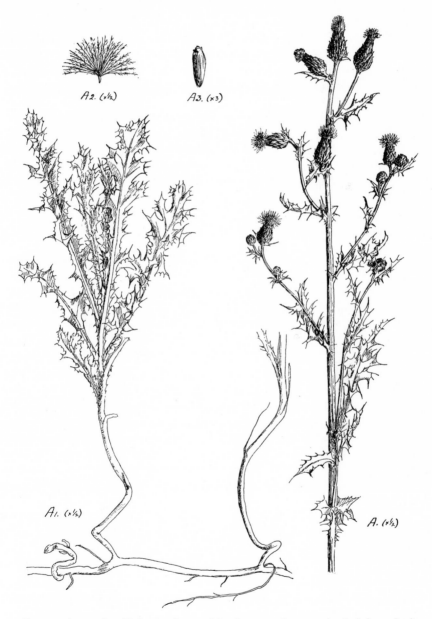

A2. (×½)   *A3. (×3)*

A1. (×½)   *A. (×½)*

FIG. 203. A, creeping thistle; A1, shoots arising from creeping root; A2, fruit (complete); A3, achene (pappus removed).

flower bud stage, will give considerable control, but for complete eradication further sprayings may be needed. On arable land spraying cereals with these weed-killers should be delayed as long as possible, so that the thistles are well grown before being sprayed. Legislation relating to the control of this weed is dealt with on p. 370.

Cirsium acaulon (L.) Scop., **Stemless** (or **Dwarf**) **Thistle**. *Perennial*, local in England, especially on closely grazed calcareous pastures. Short thick taproot. Small rosettes of lvs close to the ground. A single sessile fl head produced at the centre of the rosette. July–September. Florets bright reddish-purple. A very difficult weed to control, as its low growth makes effective cutting almost impossible. May be killed by MCPA and 2,4-D under favourable conditions, but repeated applications may be needed.

Cirsium vulgare (Savi) Ten. (*Carduus lanceolatus*), **Spear Thistle** (fig. 204). *Biennial*. Grassland; almost all soils. Deep tap-root. Rosette of lvs on the soil surface in the first year. Lvs lanceolate, deeply lobed, hairy, stiff spines around the margin. Fl stems produced in the second year, 2–4 ft., hairy, *winged and spiny*. July–October. Fl heads erect, few, single or 2 or 3 together, larger than *C. arvense*. Florets all tubular, pale reddish-purple. Achenes smooth, pale yellow, 3 to 4 mm. Pappus often blows away, leaving the frt behind. Control by spudding first-year rosettes and cutting in the early flower bud stage in the second year. MCPA and 2,4-D often kill, but more than one application may be needed to kill all plants. Control of this weed is the subject of legislation (see p. 370).

Cirsium palustre (L.) Scop., **Marsh Thistle** (fig. 204). *Biennial*. Wet grassland, ditches, etc. Fibrous roots. Rosette of lvs on the soil surface in the first year. Fl sts produced in the second year, 2–5 ft., soft, hairy, with spiny wings. Lvs dull green, *often with a purplish tinge*, spiny. Involucres practically spineless, purplish. Fl heads small, in leafy clusters. Florets dark purplish-crimson. July–September. Achenes smooth, fawn, 3 mm. Control as *C. vulgare*, plus improvement of drainage.

Carduus nutans L., **Musk Thistle**. *Biennial*. Pastures and arable, calcareous soils. More or less cottony. St 1–4 ft. with spiny wings, except just below the fl heads. Lvs deeply divided, margins spiny. June–September. Fl heads single, 1–2 in. diam., *drooping*. Florets red-purple, involucre cottony. Achenes fawn, fine transverse wrinkles, 3·5 mm.

May be abundant in new lucerne leys. In the year in which the lucerne is sown the crop offers little competition to the young thistle plants, which form surface rosettes of lvs. In the second year the tall thistle plants can compete with the lucerne. Methods of control as *C. vulgare*.

(*b*) *Liguliflorae*. In this group all the florets are ligulate and the plants contain a milky juice (latex).

Taraxacum officinale Weber, **Dandelion** (fig. 205). Perennial. Grassland. Thick deep taproot. Lvs radical, close to the ground, variously toothed. March–October. Flowering sts unbranched, smooth and without bracts.

Outer bracts of involucre long and narrow, spreading or reflexed. Florets yellow. Achenes yellow-brown, 3·5 mm. Pappus borne on a beak. Not controlled by hoeing or spudding, as adventitious shoots arise from the tap-root after cutting. Often killed by MCPA or 2,4-D if applied when

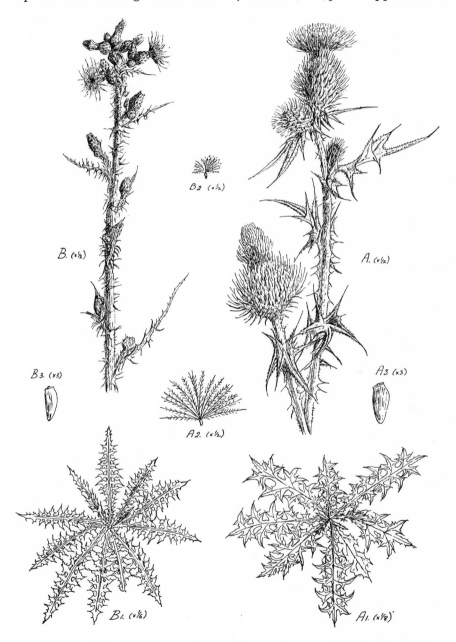

Fig. 204. A, spear thistle; A1, rosette of leaves; A2, fruit (complete); A3, achene (pappus removed). B, marsh thistle; B1, rosette of leaves; B2, fruit (complete); B3, achene (pappus removed).

463

growth is vigorous, but repeated applications may be necessary for complete eradication; 2,4-D is rather better than MCPA for this weed.

Hypochaeris radicata L., **Cat's-ear** (fig. 205). Perennial. Grassland, especially where heavily grazed; almost all soils. Short, thick, erect rootstock with fleshy roots. Lvs form a rosette close to the soil, oblong-lanceolate, margin toothed or lobed, rough hairy surface. June-September. Fl heads about 1 in. diam., resemble dandelion, but borne at the end of branched stalks bearing small bracts. Fls yellow. Flng shoots about 1 ft. Achenes orange to dark brown, rough with short projections, 5 mm., at least the inner ones beaked, beak up to 5 mm., pappus hairs in 2 rows, inner feathery outer simple. May occur as an impurity in seeds of rye-grasses, meadow fescue and crested dog's-tail.

Readily killed by MCPA and 2,4-D.

Leontodon hispidus L., **Rough Hawkbit** (fig. 205). Perennial. Old grassland, especially dry calcareous soils. Erect, branched root-stock, each branch turning upwards to produce a rosette of lvs on the soil surface. Lvs oblanceolate, toothed or lobed, hairy. From each rosette a single unbranched flowering shoot arises bearing a single fl head, 6-16 in. Fl heads 1½ in. diam. Fls yellow. June-September. Whole plant covered with rough hairs. Pappus dirty white. Achenes pale brown, longitudinal ribs bear short projections, about 7 mm., not beaked. 'Seeds' of *Leontodon* spp. occur in samples of crested dog's-tail and, more rarely, in rye-grasses.

Hieracium pilosella L., **Mouse-ear Hawkweed** (fig. 205). Perennial. Dry pastures. Long slender rhizomes. Numerous stolons above ground. Whole plant softly hairy. Fl sts 2-8 in., without scales. May-August. Single fl heads, 1 in. diam. Florets pale yellow. Pappus brownish. Achenes purplish-black, 2 mm., not beaked nor narrowed. Control as cat's-ear.

The genus *Hieracium* (Hawkweeds) contains a large number of weed species, of which this is one of the commonest.

A closely-related genus *Crepis* (Hawk's-beards) in which the pappus is usually white, also contains several common weed species. The achenes of *C. capillaris* (L.) Wallr. (*C. virens*), **Smooth Hawk's-beard,** are frequent impurities in seeds of crested dog's-tail and may also occur in rye-grasses. They are short bent spindle-shaped with 10 longitudinal ribs, greyish or light brown, no beak, 2 mm. MCPA and 2,4-D are effective against *Crepis spp.* under favourable conditions.

Lapsana communis L., **Nipplewort.** Annual, common, waste places, hedgerows, gardens, cultivated farm land. Sts branched, 1-3 ft. Lvs more or less lobed and toothed. Fl heads numerous, ¼ in. diam. Florets pale yellow. Achenes curved, narrow club-shaped, with numerous vertical ridges, pale brown, 3-4 mm., *no pappus*, a common impurity in crested dog's-tail seed, and may also occur in rye-grasses, timothy and meadow fescue. Control by preventing seeding. Control, MCPA plus dicamba.

Sonchus oleraceus L., **Common** (or **Annual**) **Sow·Thistle (Milk Thistle)** (fig. 206). Annual. Arable, gardens and horticultural crops, waste places. Long *tap-root*. Erect glabrous, branched, sts 1-4 ft. Lvs toothed, upper ones clasping the st, *pointed auricles*. June-August. Fl heads in cymose panicles. Fl yellow. Involucre bracts *smooth* or with a few stiff hairs. Achenes yellow-brown, 3 longitudinal ribs on each side, transversely ridged between the ribs, 3 mm. MCPA, 2,4-D and dinoseb kill seedlings.

Sonchus asper (L.) Hill, **Spiny Sow Thistle.** Annual. Arable and waste places. Resembles *S. oleracea*, but lvs have *curled and spiny margins, rounded auricles*, and are usually glossy above, and its fls are usually a *deeper yellow*. Achenes similar, but smooth between the ribs. MCPA, 2,4-D and dinoseb kill seedlings.

Sonchus arvensis L., **Corn** (or **Perennial**) **Sow Thistle** (fig. 206). Perennial. Arable and waste places. Strong creeping *rhizomes*. St 3-4 ft. Stem lvs clasping, *auricles rounded*. July-October. Numerous fl heads in a corymb. Fl heads much larger than *S. oleraceus*. Flowering branches and involucre bracts *covered with yellowish glandular hairs*. Florets yellow. Achenes dark brown, narrow with 5 ribs on each side, 3·5 mm. MCPA and 2,4-D will kill small seedlings and check top growth of larger plants. Prevention of seeding and frequent cutting to exhaust the rhizomes are important in the control of this weed. Two or three successive root crops with thorough cultivations and hoeing will often exhaust established plants. Where land is heavily infested sowing the land down to a long ley may prove effective because, unlike creeping thistle, this weed does not grow well in grassland.

Seeds of *Sonchus* species may be found as impurities in grass seeds, and *S. asper* may occur in sainfoin.

MONOCOTYLEDONS

LILIACEAE (see Chapter XIV)

Allium vineale L., **Wild Onion (Crow Garlic)** (fig. 207). Arable and grassland, particularly troublesome in some localities in eastern England and the south Midlands. Grows from bulbs which produce daughter bulbs, or offsets, freely. Lvs cylindrical, hollow and pointed. June-July. Flowering sts 1-3 ft. Fls in lax terminal umbels, reddish or greenish-white. Seed rarely produced in Britain. Among the fls, or entirely replacing them, small bulbs, or bulbils, are produced. The bulbils are fleshy, white or yellowish-green, often tinged with purple, and about the size of a wheat grain. When ripe they may be shed to reproduce the species. If they are harvested with wheat the threshed grain may contain bulbils as a serious impurity. Samples of wheat containing bulbils are undesirable for milling, firstly because a garlic flavour may be imparted to the flour and, secondly, because they clog the rollers of the mill and render the surface sticky. The presence of bulbils also renders wheat unsuitable for seed purposes. Such samples might result in the introduction of this very serious weed to fields where it did not exist before.

If a plant is dug up after it has flowered it will be found to have produced offset bulbs, usually 1 large *major offset* and 2 or 3 smaller *minor offsets*, the latter being darker-coloured and with a tougher outer covering. Plants which have not produced a flowering stalk develop a large bulb at their base. This is more symmetrical than the major offsets and is called a *terminal bulb*; it may be associated with 1 or 2 minor offsets.

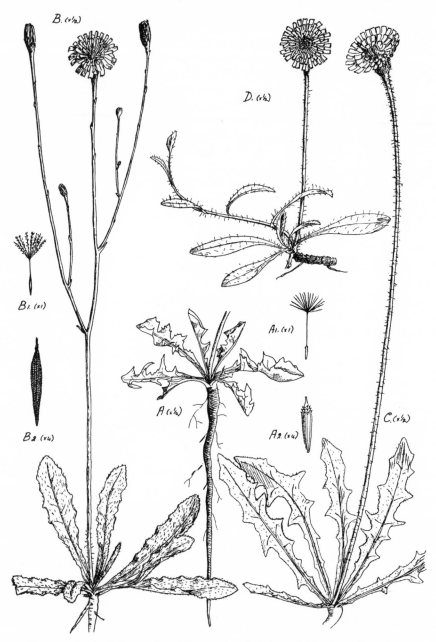

Fig. 205. A, dandelion root and leaves; A1, fruit (complete); A2, achene (pappus removed). B, cat's ear; B1, fruit (complete); B2, achene (pappus removed). C, rough hawkbit. D, mouse-ear hawkweed.

In the soil in an infested field in early September there will be the following types of reproductive body: terminal bulbs, major offsets, minor offsets and bulbils. These develop as follows:

(*a*) *Terminal bulbs* and *major offsets* usually sprout between September and November.

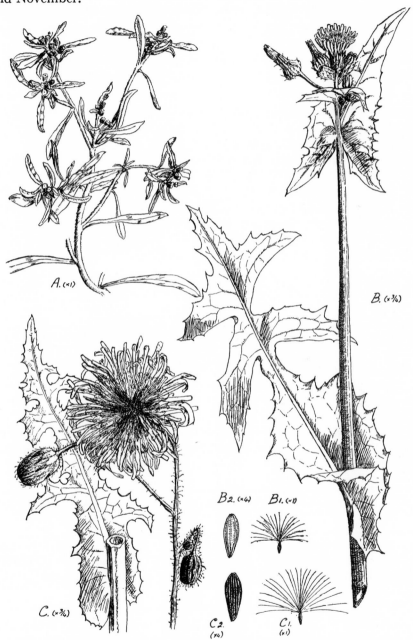

Fɪɢ. 206. A, marsh cudweed. B, common sow thistle; B1, fruit (complete); B2, achene (pappus removed). C, corn sow thistle; C1, fruit (complete); C2, achene (pappus removed).

467

(*b*) *Bulbils* rarely sprout before November and some may remain dormant until the spring.

(*c*) *Minor offsets* remain dormant at least until the end of August of the following year and many remain dormant for two years or more. The maximum period of dormancy may be as much as six years.

Control. This depends upon (i) disturbing the bulbs as much as possible after they have sprouted and used up their food reserves, and before new food reserves have been laid down in new bulbs; (ii) prevention of minor offset formation; and (iii) elimination of bulbil production.

The following system has been used successfully:

1. Take a rotation of spring crops covering six years. Do not reduce this period because plants cannot be seen in the later years. Dormant minor offsets are likely still to be present in the soil, and these must be eradicated when they eventually sprout.

2. Do not plough before November.

3. Cultivate thoroughly from the beginning of March onwards to destroy every growing plant.

4. Take root crops twice in the first three years of the rotation so that the strongest bulbs can be eradicated during row cultivations, leaving mainly dormant minor offsets to be eliminated when they sprout in succeeding years.

Where slight infestation occurs it is worthwhile to dig out the plants in order to prevent an increase of this weed. Care should be taken to remove all bulbs, including offsets. Pulling is not advisable, as the offsets are liable to break away and to be left in the ground.

Where wild onion occurs in pastures it is advisable to keep milking animals off the field, as the weed, which is readily eaten by cows, may produce an onion taint in the milk. Badly infested fields are best reserved for non-milking stock. It is possible that wild onion may taint meat; therefore it is advisable to remove animals from infested pastures a fortnight or so before slaughter.

Control of the weed in pastures is difficult. In small areas digging out by hand would be effective providing care is taken to remove all the offsets from the soil. Bad infestations may necessitate ploughing up the land and cleaning by a rotation, as above, before reseeding.

Allium ursinum L., **Ramsons (Broad-leaved Garlic)** (fig. 207). A weed with an onion odour and taste, fairly common in many localities throughout Britain. Damp woods and hedgerows, particularly on limestone. Grows from a narrow bulb. Lvs broad, elliptical, pointed. Infl a simple umbel of white fls on long pedicels, without bulbils. April-June. May taint milk if eaten by milking animals. Meat may also be tainted if the plant is eaten in quantity shortly before slaughter.

Colchicum autumnale L., **Meadow Saffron (Autumn Crocus)** (fig. 207) A weed of old grassland, rather local, but often occurring in some quantity, particularly on basic and neutral soils. Large corm with brown outer scales. Fl August-October. At this time no lvs are present above ground.

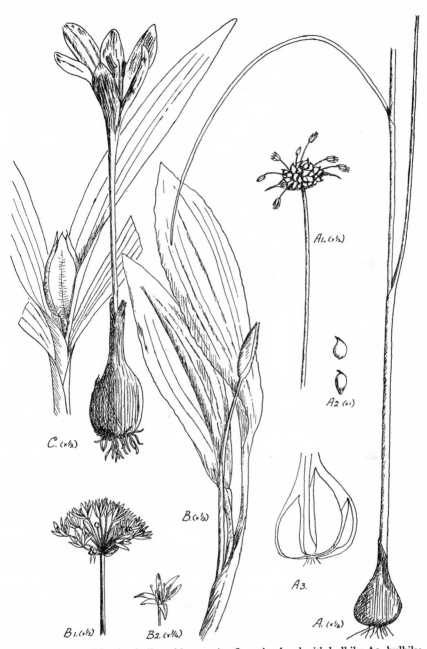

Fig. 207. A, wild onion bulb and leaves; A1, flowering head with bulbils; A2, bulbils; A3, diagram showing formation of a major and two minor offsets. B, ramsons, leaves and bud of inflorescence; B1, inflorescence; B2, flower. C, meadow saffron, corm with flower, and fruit among leaves.

The fls resemble those of the garden crocus in appearance, but not in details of structure; one or more arise from each corm, pale purple or white, long corolla tube leading down to the ovary, which is underground. The fertilized ovary remains underground until the following spring, when it is raised above ground along with the leaves. Lvs long, lanceolate, dark green. Frt a capsule, many-seeded. *Poisonous* (see p. 383). In the field animals normally avoid it, but, as records of fatalities show, this is not always the case. The poison may be secreted in milk and young animals and humans have been poisoned through consuming such milk.

Control. In small areas the corms may be dug out. Repeated defoliation, by cutting or pulling, when the leaves are just fully grown, will exhaust the food store in the corms and kill the plants, if continued for two or three years. Lvs should be removed and not left where they may be eaten by animals.

DIOSCOREACEAE

Tamus communis L., **Black Bryony** (fig. 188). Perennial, growing over hedges and in woods. Tall twining sts, 10 ft. or more, grow from a large, irregular tuber. Lvs long-stalked, cordate, very shiny. May-June. Plants dioecious. Fls small yellow-green, in axillary racemes. Frts pale red berries, 12 mm. *Poisonous* (see p. 387). Controlled by digging out the tubers.

JUNCACEAE

Fls small, floral structure resembles *Liliaceae*, but wind-pollinated.

(A) *Juncus*, **Rushes.** Glabrous plants. Lvs usually not flat and grass-like. Capsule many-seeded.

(B) *Luzula*, **Woodrushes.** Hairy plants. Flat grass-like leaves. Capsule 3-seeded.

Common Rushes. Fls in clusters small, greenish or brownish, star-shaped, 6 perianth lobes in 2 whorls, 6 stamens, 3 feathery stigmas, many seeded capsule. Sts simple, pointed, containing pith. Lvs, if present, usually rounded, resembling the sts. The rushes of agricultural interest are perennials, either tufted or with deep and extensively spreading rhizomes.

Juncus effusus L., **Common Rush** (fig. 208). Perennial. Impoverished damp grassland, more especially on acid soils. Shortly creeping but producing dense tufts of shoots. Rounded leafless sts, 2-3 ft., smooth. June-August. Panicle of fls, lateral, about 4-6 in. below the tip of the st. Seeds very small spindle-shaped, orange-yellow.

Juncus conglomeratus L., **Soft Rush.** Similar to *J. effusus* and usually occurring with that species, more restricted to acid soils, weaker and in smaller tufts. Sts ridged, particularly below the fls. Infl more compact and fls earlier than *J. effusus*. May-July.

J. effusus and *J. conglomeratus* were formerly classified as varieties of *J. communis*.

Juncus inflexus L., **Hard Rush.** Perennial. Damp grassland on heavy basic and neutral soils. Matted rhizomes. Dense tufts. Rigid sts, deeply ridged, 1-2½ ft. Lvs reduced to brown scales. July-August. Panicles loose, lateral.

Juncus articulatus L., **Jointed Rush (Sprit)** (fig. 208). Creeping

FIG. 208. A, common rush; A1, capsule. B, jointed rush; B1, inflorescence; B2, capsule. C, field woodrush; C1, capsule.

perennial. Wet pastures and moors, particularly on acid soils. Slender rhizomes. Sts slender in tufts, 2-3 ft. Cylindrical lvs with cross partitions which make them feel knotted or jointed. Panicles loose, almost terminal. June-August.

Although a few species of rush may grow under dry conditions, most species occur where the soil is damp. Even though water may not stand on the surface, the deeper layers of soil will be wet. Frequently the soil is also sour, and usually deficient of phosphate and potash.

For control of rushes drainage will often be the first consideration. Lime, when necessary to reduce acidity, and fertilizers, particularly phosphates and potash, to encourage better herbage. Frequent and systematic cutting will eventually exhaust the food in the underground parts. Before lime and fertilizers are applied it may be worthwhile to open up the soil with spiked harrows. After fertilizers have been provided a renovating mixture may be sown. This should contain ample wild white clover.

Sprays and dusts containing MCPA have been used successfully to kill *J. effusus* (other species generally resistant). Apply just before flowering and cut the rushes four weeks later.

On suitable land, after draining, if needed, plough up, apply lime and fertilizers and re-seed direct or preferably after a pioneer crop or one or two arable crops. After ploughing, many seedling rushes will grow, but these will be prevented from becoming established by arable cropping or by obtaining a dense grass sward. Seeds of rushes may lie dormant in the soil for upwards of sixty years and germinate when a suitable seed-bed is provided.

Luzula spp., **Woodrushes.** So named because of the common occurrence of species in woods and shady places. Some species, however, occur in open fields and on heaths. *Luzula campestris* (L.) DC., **Field Woodrush** (fig. 208), is very common on dry grassland. Perennial, loosely tufted. Creeping branched rhizomes. Sts 4-12 in. Lvs grass-like bearing long white hairs. Fls star-shaped, chestnut brown, 3-6 in terminal stalked or sessile clusters. March-June. Capsule containing 3 seeds. Improvement of fertility and encouragement of stronger herbage species will result in reduction of this species.

IRIDACEAE

The irises or flags occur in this family. They are of little agricultural interest apart from the fact that they *may cause poisoning* if eaten in quantity by livestock (see p. 387). A common wild species is *Iris pseudacorus* L., **Yellow Flag,** a rhizomatous perennial, in wet places, especially marshes. Broad sword-shaped lvs. May-July. Fls bright yellow, ovary inferior. Capsule opens by 3 valves.

ARACEAE

Arum maculatum L., **Wild Arum (Lords-and-Ladies, Cuckoo-pint)** (fig. 209). Perennial. Hedge-sides and shady places. White tuberous root. Lvs arrow-shaped, glabrous, shiny, *net-veined*, may bear dark purple spots. May-June.

472

Fls at the base of a long, fleshy axis (spadix), the upper part of which is usually purple, enclosed within a large pale-green sheath (spathe). Sheath sometimes purple-spotted. Fls small, unisexual, in two groups, the upper male and the lower female. Above each group are hair-like structures (abortive flowers). Frts bright red berries, 5 mm. Sheath dies as the berries ripen. *Poisonous* (see

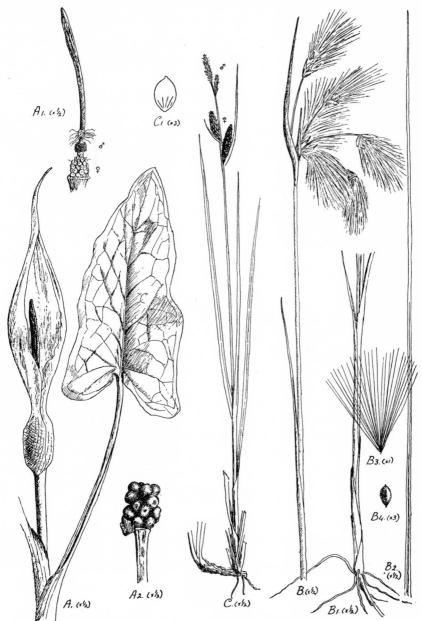

Fig. 209. A, wild arum; A1, flowers on spadix; A2, fruit. B and B1, common cotton-grass; B2, part of leaf; B3, nut and hair-like perianth; B4, nut (hairs removed). C, common sedge; C1, fruit.

p. 387). It is harmless when dried and in former days a starchy substitute for sago was prepared from the baked roots.

CYPERACEAE

Eriophorum spp., **Cotton-grasses.** Perennials possessing rhizomes. Wet boggy land, boggy moors. Leafy sts remain green in the winter. Perianth numerous bristles which elongate and become cottony later, 3 stamens, 3 stigmas, frt a dark brown 3-cornered nut.

Eriophorum angustifolium Honck., **Common Cotton-grass** (fig. 209). Extensively creeping rhizomes. Sts about 12 inches, smooth, solid. May-June. 3-7 terminal clusters of fls.

Eriophorum vaginatum L., **Harestail Cotton-grass.** More tufted, with many sts. A single terminal fl cluster. April-May. On rather drier, peaty soils.

In the north, cotton-grasses are known as 'Draw-moss', and they are of value on hill grazings for sheep early in the year when the stems may be drawn through the snow (hence the name).

Carex spp., **Sedges.** Perennials possessing rhizomes. Sts usually triangular in transverse section. Grass-like lvs in 3 ranks. Inf may consist of a single terminal spike or, in addition, there may be one to several lateral spikes, sessile or on branches. Usually monoecious, male and female fls variously arranged in the infl but usually the upper spikes or the upper parts of spikes consist of male fls, lower spikes or lower parts of spikes consist of female fls. Spikelets one-flowered with a single glume. Male fls 3 stamens. Female fls contain an ovary with 3 stigmas (2 in some species). Ovary enclosed in a bottle-shaped sac. Frt a small nut enclosed within the sac.

Carex nigra (L.) Reich., **Common Sedge** (fig. 209). Slightly creeping perennial, beside water and on wet grassland on acid soils. Sts 1-2 ft. May-July. One or two male spikes at the top of the inf and, usually, 2 or 3 female spikes below. Spikes sessile.

Many sedge species are found in wet places, some rooted in the beds of rivers or streams, others in ditches and boggy places, but some species are adapted to dry conditions. For example, *Carex flacca* Schreb, **Carnation-grass,** is found in dry, calcareous grassland. Its common name is due to its bluish-green glaucous lvs, somewhat like those of carnations. Several other sedge species have similar lvs and are popularly known as 'Carnation-grass'. Some may occur in wet, others in dry, situations.

Carex species are resistant to MCPA and 2,4-D. Control is possible by improvement of drainage, where needed, followed by liming, if necessary, application of fertilizers and improved management.

GRAMINEAE

Weed grasses are included in Chapter XVI, wild oats in Chapter XV.

PTERIDOPHYTA

Plants with separate, alternating, spore-producing and sexual generations.

POLYPODIACEAE

Pteridium aquilinum (L.) Kuhn, **Bracken** (fig. 210). Perennial. Very common on moors, upland pastures, heaths, margins of woods, mainly on light acid soils. Not on limestone or on swampy soils.

This weed has spread into and reduced the grazing value of many square miles of hill pasture. Its spread is said to be aided by stocking only with sheep. The thick cover of slowly rotting fronds prevents the growth of species useful for grazing. Animals may be poisoned through eating it in quantity, and further losses occur through fly-struck sheep hiding in the bracken.

Much-branched rhizomes spread horizontally 6-18 in. below the soil surface. Solitary fronds arise at intervals along the rhizomes and appear above the ground in spring. At first the fronds are rolled up and covered with brown scales. Fronds reach a height of 2 to 6 ft., tri-pinnate, broadly triangular in shape. Sporangia are produced on the underside of the frond all round the margin of the segments. They are protected by a thin scale or indusium and by the reflexed margin of the frond. Sporangia ripen in July and August, burst and shed the spores. Each spore which settles in a sheltered, moist, well-ventilated situation may give rise, on the soil surface, to a small shield-shaped sexual plant (prothallus), about $\frac{1}{4}$ in. across, which in turn produces a small bracken plant. A single frond can produce about 300,000,000 spores, but few ultimately produce a new plant.

Poisoning of cattle and horses has been attributed to bracken (see p. 383). It is said to be more likely to cause trouble if eaten just before it begins to wither. Bracken contains *thiaminase*, an enzyme which can destroy Vitamin B1. The symptoms of bracken poisoning in horses are typical of Vitamin B1 deficiency. In cattle Vitamin B1 deficiency does not appear to be responsible, and the cause of poisoning is not known. Small quantities of hydrocyanic acid have been found in young bracken, and tannic acid is present in mature fronds, but neither of these appears to be responsible for the symptoms produced.

In order to safeguard against the risk of poisoning, animals should be removed to other grazing for a short period after three weeks or so on bracken-infested land.

Bracken may impart a bitter taint to milk, butter and cheese and reduce milk secretion.

Control. Where it is possible to plough the infested land the most effective means of control of the bracken, and improvement of the grazing, is to plough, and eventually to re-seed, the land. Ploughing should be done between the end of June and early August. Plough as deeply as possible (10 in. or more) in order to disturb the deep rhizomes. In order to bury the top growth as completely as possible, plough a wide furrow completely inverted. Obtain a tilth by means of heavy disks working in the direction of the seams. Work in a good dressing of lime during disking. Apply nitrogenous and phosphatic fertilizers and, on a well consolidated seed-bed, sow a pioneer crop such as a mixture of rape and Italian rye-grass. The mixture should be grazed heavily with sheep or cattle in autumn and early winter. In December remove the stock and disk the land in order to aerate the soil and allow frost to penetrate. In the spring obtain a good tilth by further disking and harrowing. Re-seed with a suitable long-ley seeds mixture, or, where the fertility of the soil is low, take a further pioneer crop or a crop of oats, rye or potatoes before finally reseeding.

Where ploughing is impracticable, control can be obtained by *repeated* destruction of the fronds *each time a new crop is produced* at the expense of the food stored in the rhizomes, and *before the fronds reach maturity* and commence to replenish the food stores. Destruction of the fronds may be achieved by cutting, bruising or slashing. There are various machines suitable for these operations (where these machines can work, ploughing would usually be possible), and, on small areas, hand scything is most effective. Bracken should be attacked just before the fronds have completely unrolled and again about three weeks later. Control will be achieved only if this is repeated for at least three successive years. In conjunction with this treatment soil conditions should be improved by application of lime and phosphates and the herbage quality improved by sowing seeds of better herbage species, particularly wild white clover. The treated land will benefit from the increased stocking which then becomes possible. Stocking with cattle in addition to sheep is useful as repeated trampling by cattle helps to limit the growth of new fronds which may appear.

In order to maintain an improved sward, periodical applications of phosphates are required, and lime will be needed at intervals to prevent the soil from returning to the acid state suitable for the growth of bracken.

Extensive trials on the control of bracken by herbicides have been conducted in recent years but to date none can be recommended for large-scale control.

EQUISETACEAE

Equisetum arvense L., **Common Horsetail (Toad Pipe)** (fig. 210). Perennial. Very common in hedge-sides, waste places, cultivated ground, and occasionally on grassland. In grassland it is often not very conspicuous among other herbage and may escape notice. Underground sts penetrate about 3 ft. into the soil and produce long branches in all directions. Plants spread extensively by means of these rhizomes. In early spring brownish-white, unbranched, hollow, reproductive shoots appear. These terminate in cone-like structures which bear sporangia on their scales. The sporangia contain numerous spores which are ripe in April, when the sporangia burst and the spores are liberated. (As with bracken,

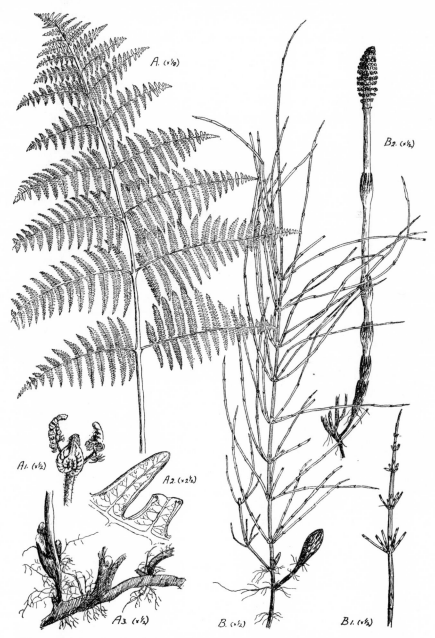

FIG. 210. A, bracken frond; A1, young frond; A2, back of part of frond; A3, rhizome. B, common horsetail, piece of rhizome with vegetative shoot and developing reproductive shoot; B1, young vegetative shoot; B2, reproductive shoot.

the spores, under suitable conditions, give rise to small sexual plants or prothalli on which a fertilization process occurs which results in the formation of a new spore-bearing plant or sporophyte.) After the spores have been shed, the fertile shoots die down. The vegetative shoots, which appear rather later than the reproductive shoots, are erect, slender, and harsh to the touch. They bear numerous slender, simple, branches in whorls of up to 12. The lvs consist of whorls of small scales with blackish tips.

Other species of this genus which are fairly common in Britain are *E. palustre* L., **Marsh Horsetail,** on wet marshy ground; *E. fluviatile* L., **Water Horsetail,** in shallow water at the edges of lakes, ponds and in ditches; *E. sylvaticum* L., **Wood Horsetail,** in damp woods on acid soils and on moors.

There is much evidence to suggest that some species, including *E. arvense*, *E. palustre* and *E. sylvaticum*, are *poisonous* to livestock (see p. 383). The effects on horses appear to be due to vitamin B1 deficiency caused by the enzyme *thiaminase* which is present in the plants (see bracken). Other factors may be involved in the poisoning of cattle, possibly alkaloids, such as *palustrine*, which have been found in some species.

Equisetum is most likely to be consumed by animals when it is present in hay. In the field cattle usually graze around it and avoid eating the plants. Samples vary in their toxicity, but on the basis of the evidence available it is well to avoid feeding hay containing much horsetail, and where it is abundant in pastures to take steps to eliminate it.

Control. Drainage may be a necessary preliminary, followed by liming. Repeated cutting of the vegetative shoots before they are fully grown will weaken the plant, but cutting for several years may be needed before complete exhaustion of the rhizomes is achieved. Cutting of the spore-bearing shoots may also be important to prevent the establishment of new plants.

MCPA and 2,4-D will kill aerial shoots, but regrowth often occurs from the rhizomes. Repeated spraying may finally kill the plants. Spraying should be done when the shoots are just fully grown. Spraying treatment should be associated with improvement of fertility, in order to encourage better herbage. As creeping buttercup is often present with these species, MCPA, which is more effective than 2,4-D against the buttercup, may be preferable.

Chapter XX

WEED SEEDLINGS

A SELECTION of seedlings, mainly of arable weeds, is described and illustrated on the following pages. Descriptions are given briefly, as most of the characteristics needed for identification are shown in the figures. Unless stated otherwise the figures are natural size.

RANUNCULACEAE

Ranunculus repens, **Creeping Buttercup.** Long white radicle. Adventitious roots arise early just below the soil surface. Cots oval, smooth, stalked. First lvs radical, toothed, petiole long and sparsely hairy.

Ranunculus arvensis, **Corn Buttercup.** Roots similar to preceding species. Cots oval, stalks broad, dull pale green. First true lvs radical, broad wedge-shaped with broad teeth at the apex. Later lvs more deeply divided into three segments, toothed. All lvs stalked and smooth.

FUMARIACEAE

Fumaria officinalis, **Fumitory.** Thin fibrous roots. Cots linear-lanceolate, pointed, smooth, grass-green. First true lvs deeply divided. Later radical lvs with three sub-divided lobes.

PAPAVERACEAE

Papaver rhoeas, **Field Poppy.** Thin fibrous root. Cots linear, smooth, grass-green. First true lvs oval. Later radical lvs with a few lobes.

CRUCIFERAE

Capsella bursa-pastoris, **Shepherd's Purse.** Fibrous root branching early. Cots small, oval, smooth, shortly-stalked. First true lvs oval, undivided, stalked, slightly hairy. Later radical lvs pinnately lobed (depth of indentation very variable), stalked, slightly hairy, forming a rosette.

FIG. 211. A and A1, Creeping Buttercup, two stages. B, Corn Buttercup. C, Fumitory. C1, cotyledon. D and D1, Field Poppy, two stages. D2, cotyledon. E, Shepherd's Purse. E1, cotyledon.

CRUCIFERAE (*contd.*)

Sinapis arvensis, **Charlock.** Cots heart-shaped, one larger than the other, on long broad stalks grooved above (more rounded at the base and shorter-stalked than the next species). First true or 'rough' lvs long oval (cf. common turnip, in which they are more rounded), toothed, dark green, hairy and rough to the touch; very variable in the amount of lobing; in some seedlings the margin is simple, in others it is lobed to various degrees. Stem elongates early and is usually hairy.

Raphanus raphanistrum, **Wild Radish.** Cots about equal, heart-shaped, lighter green and with more pointed base and longer stalked than the preceding species. First true lvs rough and hairy, spathulate, lobed and toothed, the lower part deeply lobed.

Cardaria draba, **Hoary Pepperwort.** Cots narrow oval, narrowing to a stalk, grey-green, fleshy. First true lvs small, broadly oval. Later lvs oval-ovate, may have slightly irregular margins, long petiole grooved above. Third and later lvs with sparse shiny white hairs.

Thlaspi arvense, **Penny-cress.** Hypocotyl white. Cots oblong, rather thick, stalk rather long and slender. First true lvs long-oval, with slightly irregular margins, stalked. Pungent odour when crushed, and unpleasant flavour.

VIOLACEAE

Viola arvensis, **Field Pansy.** Cots variable, oval to lanceolate, broader at base, stalk about the same length as the blade, smooth, pale green. First true lvs broadly ovate with bluntly toothed margins, light green, smooth, long-stalked. Stalks broad and channelled above.

Fig. 212. A, Charlock. A1, cotyledon. B, Wild Radish. C, Hoary Pepperwort. C1, cotyledon. D, Penny-cress. D1, cotyledon. E, Field Pansy. E1, cotyledon.

CARYOPHYLLACEAE

Cerastium holostoides, **Mouse-ear Chickweed.** Thread-like transparent root. Cots ovate-lanceolate, with broad stalk. Stem elongates early, bears lvs in opposite pairs. First lvs lanceolate, stalked, bases united to form a cup around the stem. Stem and lvs hairy.

Stellaria media, **Common Chickweed.** Very slender root. Cots lanceolate, long-stalked, smooth, light green. Stem elongates early. Lvs in opposite pairs, lanceolate, stalked, light green, a line of hairs on the edges of the leaf stalks.

Silene alba, **White Campion.** Cots ovate, smooth, yellow-green with transparent granules on the surface. True lvs broadly lanceolate, pale green, hairy, slightly sticky, in opposite pairs.

Agrostemma githago, **Corn Cockle.** Cots slightly unequal, long-oval to lanceolate, rather thick, smooth, bases united to form a cup, dull light green, soon becoming horizontal, enlarging considerably as seedling develops. First true lvs radical, opposite pairs, lanceolate, narrow towards the base but not stalked, hairy.

Scleranthus annuus, **Annual Knawel.** Very small. Cots long and narrow but flat, light green. First lvs linear, pointed, smooth, fleshy, in opposite pairs. Branches arise early from the axils of radical lvs.

Spergula arvensis, **Spurrey.** Cots linear, cylindrical, fleshy, smooth, shining, light green, small at first but increasing considerably in size. First lvs similar to cots. As the stem elongates the lvs appear to be in whorls.

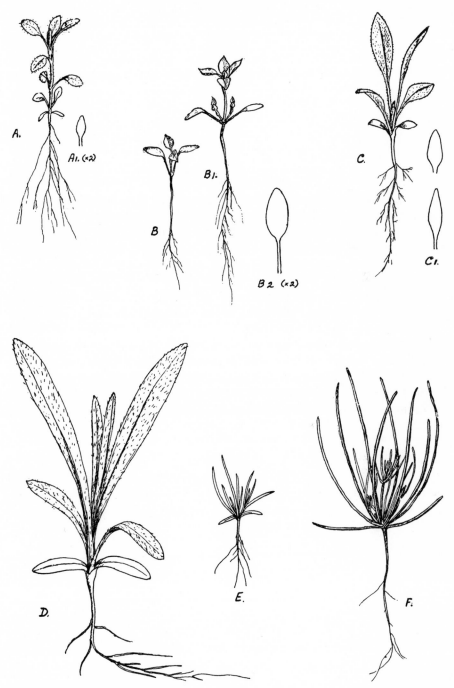

FIG. 213. A, Mouse-ear Chickweed. A1, cotyledon. B and B1, Common Chickweed, two stages. B2, cotyledon. C, White Campion. C1, two shapes of cotyledon. D, Corn Cockle. E, Annual Knawel. F, Spurrey.

CHENOPODIACEAE

Atriplex patula, **Common Orache (Spreading Orache).** Cots smooth, strap-shaped, fleshy, tapering gradually to the base but not stalked. First lvs long oval, covered with 'mealy' granules. Later lvs with two large teeth near the base of the leaf blade (hastate) and small irregular teeth along the margins. Branches arise early at the lower nodes.

Chenopodium album, **Fat Hen.** Hypocotyl often reddish near the base. Cots strap-shaped, fleshy, very shortly stalked, silvery above, red beneath. First lvs wedge-shaped, later ones nearly oval but broader at the base, 'mealy'. Young lvs often pinkish.

GERANIACEAE

Geranium molle, **Dove's-foot Cranesbill.** Cots kidney-shaped, the two lobes differing in size, long-stalked, hairy. First lvs radical, nearly round in outline but deeply lobed, hairy, long-stalked, stalks very hairy with reddish base.

LEGUMINOSAE

Vicia hirsuta, **Hairy Vetch.** Cots remain below the soil (hypogeal germination). Thin stem. First two or three lvs compound with two pairs of leaflets, more leaflets on the later lvs, small pointed stipules, rudimentary tendril at apex of leaf.

486

FIG. 214. A and A1. Common Orache, two stages. A2, cotyledon. B and B1, Fat Hen, two stages. B2, cotyledon. C, Dove's-foot Cranesbill. D, Hairy Vetch.

ROSACEAE

Potentilla anserina, **Silverweed.** Thin thread-like root, but as the seedling develops adventitious roots form at the base of the plant. Cots oval, short-stalked, smooth. Hypocotyl and stalks of cots tinged reddish-purple. First lf toothed, second lf three-lobed and toothed, later lvs pinnate. All lvs radical, dark green above with a few white hairs, covered with silvery down beneath.

Aphanes arvensis, **Parsley Piert.** Very small. Cots roundish-oval, stalked. First lf three-lobed. Later lvs deeply three-lobed, lobes toothed. Lvs hairy, whitish beneath, stalked. Lf stalks and underside of cots may be pinkish.

UMBELLIFERAE

Scandix pecten-veneris, **Shepherd's Needle.** Hypocotyl white at base and reddish or brown above. Cots linear, becoming very long, smooth, light green, well-defined mid-rib. First lvs bipinnate, the lobes deeply divided; long, grooved, slightly hairy petioles.

Aethusa cynapium, **Fool's Parsley.** Hypocotyl reddish above. Cots narrow-lanceolate, blunt, three-veined, stalked. First lvs three-lobed, each lobe on the first lf with three or more rounded teeth and on subsequent lvs more numerous teeth, long petioles, dark green. Seedling resembles parsley.

EUPHORBIACEAE

Euphorbia peplus, **Petty Spurge.** Long, slender hypocotyl brownish above. Cots long-oval, somewhat shiny beneath, light green, stalked. Stem elongates early bearing first lvs. First lvs in opposite pairs, oval, tending to roll upwards about the mid-rib, light green, slightly pinkish, with short petioles. Branches arise early from the axils of the cotyledons.

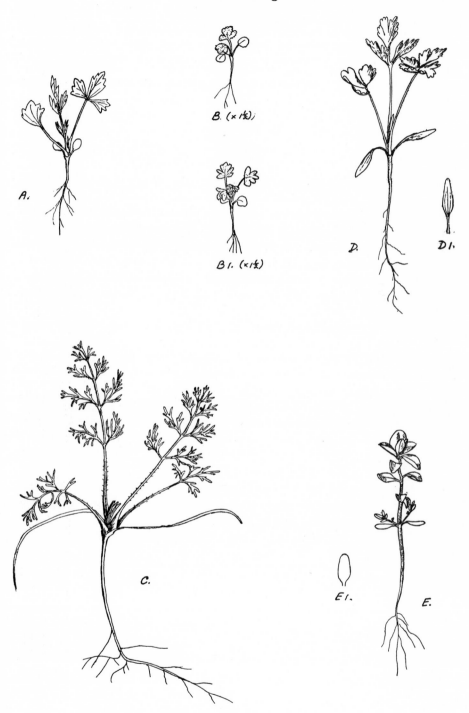

FIG. 215. A, Silverweed. B and B1, Parsley Piert, two stages. C, Shepherd's Needle. D, Fool's Parsley. D1, cotyledon. E, Petty Spurge. E1, cotyledon.

POLYGONACEAE

Polygonum persicaria, **Redshank.** Tough root. Hypocotyl often tinged reddish-brown. Cots long-oval to lanceolate, shortly stalked. Stem elongates early. Lvs lanceolate, smooth or with a few hairs on upper surface, dull green tinged red, often with a dark purplish patch on upper surface. Stipules united into a membranous cylindrical stem sheath. Stems reddish.

Polygonum convolvulus, **Black Bindweed.** Hypocotyl red. Cots narrow-lanceolate. True lvs heart-shaped, with long petioles, bluish-green. Membranous sheathing stipules.

Polygonum aviculare, **Knotgrass.** Thin, tough root. Cots linear, bases united to form a cup, whitish bloom on surface. Stem elongates early, slender, tough. Early lvs oval-lanceolate, bluish-green with a powdery bloom, membranous sheathing stipules. Branches appear early from the lower nodes. Stems reddish.

Rumex obtusifolius, **Broad-leaved Dock.** Cots long-oval to lanceolate, stalks fairly long, often pinkish. First lvs radical, roundish-ovate, slightly cordate at the base, dark green, may be tinged bright red, margins wavy, petiole long, stipules form a sheath around the st.

Rumex crispus, **Curled Dock,** is similar, but with lanceolate first lvs.

Rumex acetosella, **Sheep's Sorrel.** Hypocotyl reddish above. Cots long-oval, may be tinged red, narrowing at base to a short stalk. First lvs nearly oval to lanceolate, shortly stalked, dull green with bloom on surface. Later lvs with two projections at base of blade (hastate). Small membranous stipules form a tube round the stem. Sour taste.

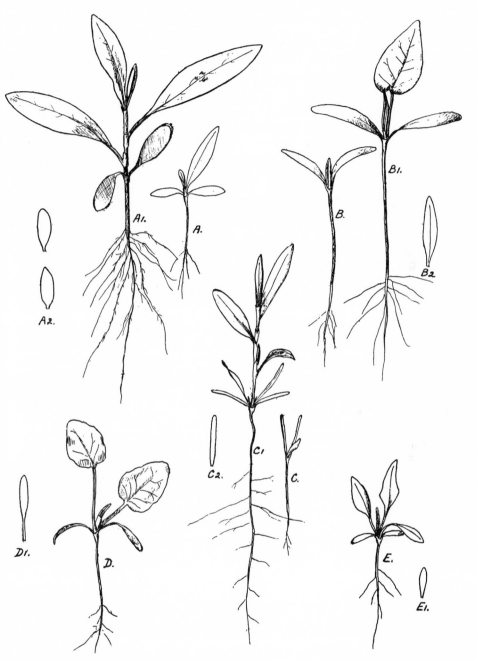

FIG. 216. A and A1, Redshank, two stages. A2, two shapes of cotyledon. B and B1, Black Bindweed, two stages. B2, cotyledon. C and C1, Knotgrass, two stages. C2, cotyledon. D, Broad-leaved Dock. D1, cotyledon. E, Sheep's Sorrel. E1, cotyledon.

URTICACEAE

Urtica urens, **Annual Nettle.** Hypocotyl light brownish-green. Cots squarish to oval, notched at the apex, stalks short at first but elongating later. Stem four-sided, elongates early. First lvs in opposite pairs, ovate, coarsely toothed; sparse stinging hairs. Branches arise early from basal nodes.

BORAGINACEAE

Myosotis arvensis, **Common Forget-me-not.** Hypocotyl fairly stout and short. Cots nearly circular, hairy on upper surface, very shortly stalked. First lvs radical, very hairy, long-oval but narrow towards the base, petiole short and broad.

Lithospermum arvense, **Corn Gromwell.** Hypocotyl whitish at base, pale green above, hairy. Cots broad-oval, slightly notched apex, distinct mid-rib, short broad stalk, hairy. Stem elongates early. First lvs long-spathulate, broadest towards the apex, covered with soft hairs, dark green.

Anchusa arvensis, **Bugloss.** Hypocotyl pale green. Cots large, oval, pointed, pale green, rough short hairs on upper surface, stalk broad, about ¼ of total length of cot. First lvs oval to oblanceolate, wavy edges, a few small teeth, stiff hairs on both surfaces with swollen bases giving warty appearance. Mid-rib very distinct.

PRIMULACEAE

Anagallis arvensis, **Scarlet Pimpernel.** Hypocotyl frequently reddish. Cots small, ovate-lanceolate, with broad stalk, may have a few dark spots on under surface. First lvs ovate, sessile, in opposite pairs, dark green, smooth, black dots on under surface. Stem four-sided. Branches early.

CONVOLVULACEAE

Convolvulus arvensis, **Field Bindweed.** Hypocotyl frequently dull red above. Cots nearly circular with indented apex, leaf-like, dark green, stalked, stalks reddish tinged, grooved above. Cots increase considerably in size as seedling develops. Stem elongates early bearing the first lvs. First lvs dull green, hastate, alternate, with long petioles. Stem angular, beginning to twine early. Branches arise early at the base.

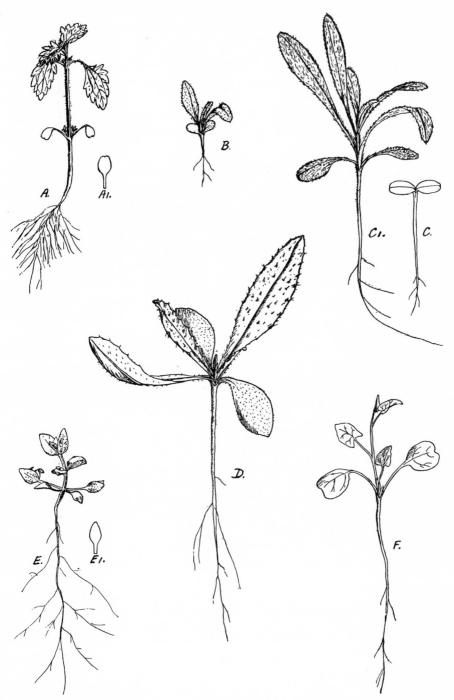

Fig. 217. A, Annual Nettle. A1, cotyledon. B, Common Forget-me-not. C and C1, Corn Gromwell, two stages. D, Bugloss. E, Scarlet Pimpernel. E1, cotyledon. F, Field Bindweed.

493

SOLANACEAE

Datura stramonium, **Thorn Apple.** Hypocotyl often purplish. Cots long-lanceolate, shortly stalked. First lvs lanceolate, margins wavy. Later lvs coarsely toothed. Unpleasant odour when bruised.

Solanum nigrum, **Black Nightshade.** Hypocotyl hairy. Cots slightly unequal, very small at first enlarging later, lanceolate, downy, light green, shortly stalked. Stem elongates early bearing first lvs. First lvs ovate, short hairs on both surfaces, alternate.

SCROPHULARIACEAE

Veronica hederifolia, **Ivy-leaved Speedwell.** Slender branched root. Cots nearly oval, narrow towards the apex, enlarging and stalks elongating later. Stem grows early bearing the first lvs. First lvs three-lobed, later ones five-lobed, hairy, in opposite pairs in seedling stage, alternating above later. Branches arise at base early.

LABIATAE

Galeopsis tetrahit, **Hemp-nettle.** Hypocotyl red. Cots broadly oval auricled at base, stalks hairy. Stem elongates early bearing first lvs. First lvs in opposite pairs, ovate-lanceolate, hairy, coarsely toothed.

Lamium purpureum, **Red Deadnettle.** Cots oval, auricled at base, a very small tooth in a shallow depression at the apex, stalked. Stem elongates early bearing the first lvs in opposite pairs. First lvs heart-shaped, coarsely toothed, hairy.

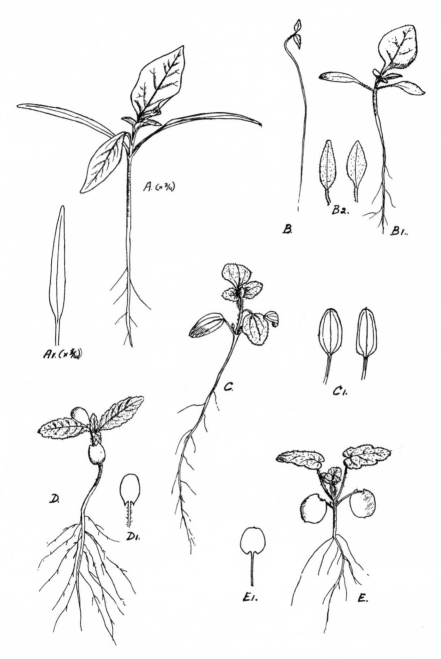

Fɪɢ. 218. A, Thorn Apple. Aɪ, cotyledon. B and Bɪ, Black Nightshade, two stages. B2, two shapes of cotyledon. C, Ivy-leaved Speedwell. Cɪ, two shapes of cotyledon. D, Hemp-nettle. Dɪ, cotyledon. E, Red Deadnettle. Eɪ, cotyledon.

RUBIACEAE

Galium aparine, **Cleavers.** Hypocotyl blotched brownish-purple above. Cots oval, notched at the apex, smooth, becoming leaf-like, stalk short at first elongating later as the cots enlarge. Stem elongates early, four-angled, bearing lanceolate hairy lvs in whorls. Lvs end in a short spine. Lf edges and stem angles with strong hooked hairs. The seedling branches early from the base.

PLANTAGINACEAE

Plantago major, **Broad-leaved Plantain.** Very short hypocotyl. Cots linear to lanceolate, withering early. Lvs radical, oval, hairy above.

Plantago lanceolata, **Ribwort Plantain.** Very short hypocotyl. Cots linear, long, fleshy. Lvs radical, long lanceolate, web of hairs at the base.

COMPOSITAE

Tripleurospermum maritimum, **Scentless Mayweed.** Hypocotyl short. Cots small, oval, rather thick. First lvs radical, first pair very small and *showing little lobing,* later ones deeply lobed.

The seedlings of *Matricaria recutita,* Wild Chamomile, are similar. In *Anthemis arvensis,* Corn Chamomile, and *Anthemis cotula,* Stinking Mayweed, the first lvs are *deeply lobed.* The odour of the bruised seedlings may also assist in identification (see descriptions of the mature plants).

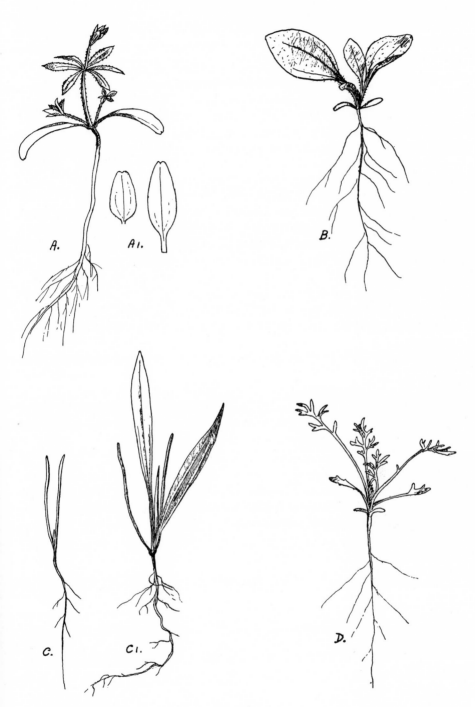

FIG. 219. A, Cleavers. A1, two shapes of cotyledon. B, Broad-leaved Plantain. C and C1, Ribwort Plantain, two stages. D, Scentless Mayweed.

497

COMPOSITAE (*contd.*)

Tussilago farfara, **Coltsfoot.** Very small. Hypocotyl light green or whitish, tinged red. Cots small, narrow-spathulate, fleshy, stalked. Lvs radical. First lvs nearly heart-shaped, whitish beneath, a few teeth on the margins, petioles varying in length. Lf blade and petiole tinged reddish. Later lvs more irregular in outline. Small shoots which may be mistaken for seedlings, but without cotyledons, may be found in spring growing from pieces of old rhizome.

Senecio vulgare, **Groundsel.** Hypocotyl stout, tinged pink. Cots long-oval or lanceolate, under surface often tinged purple, stalks deeply grooved on upper surface. Lvs alternate, oval, smooth, margin toothed, petiole grooved above and slightly hairy. Stem elongates later, succulent, angular.

Cirsium arvense, **Creeping Thistle.** Hypocotyl short and thick. Cots oval, fleshy, smooth, not stalked, united at the base. First lvs small, spathulate, with an irregular spiny margin, bristly surface hairs, surrounded by a soft web of hairs in the bud. Stem develops later covered with hairs. Small shoots without cots frequently found. These grow from pieces of old root.

Cirsium vulgare, **Spear Thistle.** As above, but cots shortly stalked later, lf margin toothed and spiny, petioles winged and longer in relation to the lf blade than in the preceding species. Rosette of lvs remains on the soil surface, the stem normally being produced in the second season.

Sonchus oleraceus, **Common Sow Thistle.** Hypocotyl short. Cots spathulate, short-stalked, may be tinged reddish beneath. First lvs radical. First lf oval, entire; second lf with a few marginal teeth; third and later lvs with numerous marginal teeth and somewhat lobed towards the base of the blade, long petiole conspicuously winged.

Sonchus asper, **Spiny Sow Thistle.** Cots as above. Lvs more rounded, less lobed or not lobed, dark green.

Chrysanthemum segetum, **Corn Marigold.** Hypocotyl slender, whitish. Cots oval to spathulate, narrowing towards the base but not stalked. First lvs in opposite pairs, long and narrow, entire or with one or two lateral lobes. Later lvs have more numerous lobes. Lvs smooth, pale green.

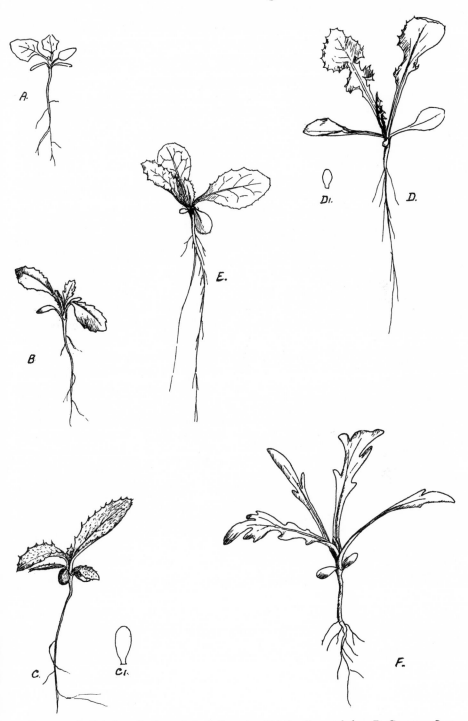

FIG. 220. A, Coltsfoot. B, Groundsel. C, Creeping Thistle. C1, cotyledon. D, Common Sow Thistle. D1, cotyledon. E. Spiny Sow Thistle. F, Corn Marigold.

BOOKS FOR FURTHER READING

Bates, G. H. *Weed Control*, 1948, Spon.

Bentham and Hooker's *Handbook of the British Flora*, rev. A. B. Rendle, 1945, L. Reeve & Co.

Brenchley, W. *Weeds of Farm Land*, 1920, Longmans, Green.

British Weed Control Conference. *Proceedings*, 1953 and succeeding years, London.

Clapham, A. R., Tutin, T. G., and Warburg, E. F. *Flora of the British Isles*, 1962, Camb. U.P.

Evans, S. G. *Weed Destruction*, 1962, Blackwell.

Forsyth, A. A. *British Poisonous Plants*, Min. of Ag. Bull. 161, 1954, H.M.S.O.

Garner, R. J. *Veterinary Toxicology*, 1957, Ballière, Tindall and Cox.

Klingman, G. C. *Weed Control as a Science*, 1961, John Wiley, N.Y.

Kummer, A. P. *Weed Seedlings*, 1951, Univ. of Chicago Press.

Long, H. C. *Poisonous Plants on the Farm*, Min. of Ag. Bull. 75, 1938, H.M.S.O.

—— *Weeds of Arable Land*, Min. of Ag. Bull. 108, 1938, H.M.S.O.

—— *Weeds of Grassland*, Min. of Ag. Bull. 41, 1932, H.M.S.O.

Mercer, S. P. *Farm and Garden Seeds*, 1958, Crosby Lockwood.

Muenscher, W. C. *Weeds*, 1955, Macmillan, N.Y.

Parkinson, S. T., and Smith, G. *Impurities of Agricultural Seed*, reprinted, slightly abridged, as *Weed Seeds as Impurities of Agricultural Seed*, Y.F.C. booklet.

Prime, C. T., and Deacock, R. J. *The Shorter British Flora*, 1948, Methuen.

Robbins, W. W., Crafts, A. S., and Raynor, R. N. *Weed Control*, 1952, McGraw Hill.

Weed Control Handbooks, British Weed Control Council. (New herbicides are constantly being introduced, and reference should therefore be made to the current handbook.)

Whyte, R. O. (ed.). *The Control of Weeds*, Herbage Publications Series, Bull. 27, 1940, Imp. Bureau of Pasture and Forage Crops, Aberystwyth.

Also various Min. of Ag. leaflets and the journals *Weed Abstracts* and *Weed Research*.

Section Four

DISEASES OF FARM CROPS

Chapter XXI

INTRODUCTION AND FUNGI: GENERAL

THE study of plant diseases in general is known as *plant pathology* or *phytopathology* (*phyton*, plant).

In plants, disease may manifest itself in diverse ways. There may be a general lack of well-being, which may finally result in the death of the plant, or symptoms may be more local, affecting only certain organs or zones of tissue. Disease may result in the death, or *necrosis*, of areas of tissue. When these areas are small and restricted, and necrosis does not spread from them, they are known as *local lesions*. Disease may produce other readily recognizable symptoms such as warty outgrowths, scabs or other malformations, variegations or internal rots.

Disease may occur in single plants or small groups of plants only, or it may spread rapidly through a crop, causing considerable loss of yield and financial loss to the farmer. In some cases extensive losses may occur through the development of disease after the crop has been harvested, e.g. various rots occurring in potatoes during storage.

When a disease spreads widely and affects many plants within a short period of time it is usually said to be *epidemic*. The term epidemic, however, is strictly applicable only to diseases of humans (*epi*, upon; *demos*, the people), and the correct term in relation to plants is *epiphytotic*, but this term is not commonly used.

Diseases bring about reduction in crop yield in various ways. They may affect root development and so restrict the growth of the plant, as in the case of club root disease of Brassicas. They may attack the leaves and thus cause reduction of the photosynthetic area, as in the case of rusts and mildews of cereals. The reduction in photosynthesis causes less food to be available for development of the grain, in the cases quoted, and may result in the development of poor crops of shrunken grain. Again, disease may directly attack the part of the crop which is of economic importance and render it useless, e.g. the smut diseases of cereals which destroy the grain and dry rot of potatoes which causes rotting of tubers in storage.

Some diseases cause their damage to the plant in more ways than one, for example potato blight kills part or the whole of the foliage, thus reducing photosynthesis and restricting tuber formation and, in addition, it may attack the tubers causing them to rot.

CAUSES OF DISEASE IN PLANTS

Plants may become unhealthy through many and varied causes. Insects and other forms of animal life, such as eelworms, may be responsible for the destruction or weakening of plants. The environment in which it is growing may be such that the plant cannot develop normally. Too little light may lead to etiolation of the shoots and general weakening of the plant. Deficiency of water may result in wilting and restricted growth. Nutritional disorders may result from deficiency or excess of essential food elements. Ill-health may also be caused by environmental conditions, such as frost, high temperature, inadequate drainage, drift from chemical sprays used in neighbouring fields, chemical fumes from industrial plant, etc.

Considerable losses often result through diseases caused by parasitic fungi and by viruses. Some plant diseases are also caused by bacteria and by a group of organisms called *Actinomycetes*, which bear resemblances both to the fungi and the bacteria.

In the following chapters we will deal first with diseases caused by living organisms, i.e. fungi, actinomycetes and bacteria. Diseases caused by viruses, which have some properties of living organisms and some of non-living matter, will be considered next, and, finally, nutritional disorders, other environmental troubles and diseases of unknown cause.

Since fungi are of very great importance as agents of disease, we must first consider the nature of these organisms in some detail.

THE FUNGI: GENERAL

The study of fungi is known as mycology (*mykos*, a mushroom; *logos*, science), and one who specializes in this science is called a mycologist.

Although the fungi cause few diseases in animals (e.g. ringworm), they are the cause of many and varied diseases in crops of all kinds.

Fungi are plants which are entirely devoid of chlorophyll, and therefore cannot carry out the process of photosynthesis. Being thus unable to manufacture carbohydrates, they must obtain the whole of their food from some external source.

Some fungi obtain their food from the living cells of plants or animals; such species are known as *parasites*. Others live entirely on the dead tissues of plants and animals; these species are termed *saprophytes*. Examples of saprophytic fungi are the well-known moulds which appear on jam, bread and cheese. Larger saprophytic fungi are the mushrooms. Saprophytic fungi are numerous in the soil, where they help to break down plant and animal remains and to render them available, ultimately, for the growth of higher plants. They are therefore of considerable importance in connection with the growth of crops in healthy soil.

Parasitic fungi may be divided into two main groups: (*a*) *obligate parasites,* and (*b*) *facultative parasites. Obligate parasites* can only develop in association with the living tissues of a host (i.e. the plant or animal which they parasitize). Examples of such species are the fungi which cause the 'rust' diseases of crops and the powdery mildews. *Facultative parasites* are those species which parasitize plants, but which are also able to live saprophytically on dead organic matter. The *Botrytis* species which cause the disease chocolate spot in field beans are examples of this type of parasite, as they readily adapt themselves to a saprophytic existence.

Some of the lower fungi consist of a multinucleate protoplasmic mass without a containing cell wall, known as a *plasmodium*. Other fungi, like the yeasts, consist of single minute cells. Most fungi, however, are composed essentially of slender filaments known as *hyphae*. The hyphae are made up of elongated tubular cells containing cytoplasm, nuclei and cell

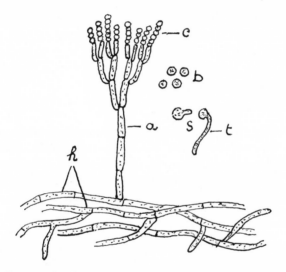

FIG. 221. Portion of *Penicillium* sp, a common type of mould species of which may develop on leather stored in damp conditions and also in some types of cheese; hyphae *h* forming part of a mycelium. The erect hypha *a* bears spores (conidia *c*) in chains at the tips of the branches. *b* individual spores. *s* spore germinating to produce a germ tube *t* from which a new mycelium will develop × 500.

sap. These tubular cells may be continuous without any cross walls—these are *aseptate* hyphae; or they may be subdivided by cross walls, and are then known as *septate* hyphae.

The hyphae elongate by growth at their tips, and they give off branches. The mass of branched hyphae is known as a *mycelium*. In some fungi the hyphae may become woven into a dense mass which, when examined under the microscope, has the appearance of a tissue (therefore named *pseudoparenchyma*). Such a mass of hyphae is termed a *stroma* (plural, *stromata*). In some highly developed fungi large numbers of hyphae may be massed together in this way to form complex structures such as the fructification of the mushroom. Some fungi, at some stage in their development, produce solid masses of hyphae containing stored food and covered with a protective layer. These structures are called *sclerotia*; they enable the fungus to withstand adverse conditions and to persist until more favourable conditions prevail. Sclerotia are met with in *Claviceps purpurea* (p. 549), which causes the disease ergot of rye and other members of the Gramineae, and in *Sclerotinia trifoliorum* the fungus causing clover rot. In some species of fungi long, branched, root-like masses of hyphae called *rhizomorphs* are produced. These spread out exploring fresh areas for food. In the dry-rot fungus, *Merulius lacrymans*, which causes the rotting of woodwork, the rhizomorphs may even pass through the mortar of walls before reaching fresh woodwork on the other side. The rhizomorphs of the fungus *Armillaria mellea*, which parasitizes many trees, look like purplish-black leather boot laces. Their colour is lighter before exposure to air. They have a tough exterior and are much-branched.

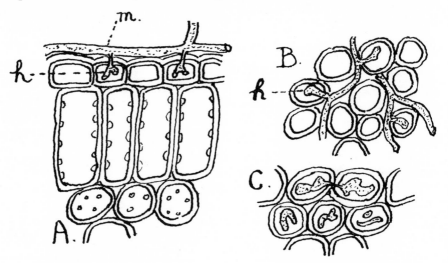

Fig. 222. A: *m*, superficial hypha; *h*, haustorium penetrating an epidermal cell. B, intercellular hyphae; *h*, haustorium. C, intracellular hyphae.

By means of the rhizomorphs this fungus can spread underground from one tree to another.

Some parasitic fungi merely grow on the surface of the host, absorbing food from the surface cells. Others penetrate more deeply into the tissues of the host. These may spread within the internal tissues by growing between the cells, in which case they are said to be *inter-cellular* parasites, or by piercing through the cell walls and developing within the cells of the host, in which case they are described as *intra-cellular* parasites. The inter-cellular fungi obtain their food by sending small branches or *haustoria* into the cells of the host, whilst intra-cellular fungi obtain their food directly from the cells in which they are growing. To aid penetration of cells the tips of the hyphae of some fungi produce enzymes which can dissolve the cellulose walls of the host cells to enable the hyphae to enter.

Mycorrhiza. The association of a fungus with a higher plant is not always harmful to the latter. Indeed, some fungi and higher plants appear to have formed an association which is of mutual benefit (symbiosis). When the young roots of many forest trees are examined they are found to be densely clothed with fungal hyphae. This association of fungus and root is called a *mycorrhiza*. In most forest trees in which this occurs the hyphae grow inwards *between* the cells of the root, whereas in some plants, such as orchids and heaths, the hyphae penetrate *into* and develop within the cells of the roots. The former is known as an *ectotrophic* mycorrhiza, whilst the latter is an *endotrophic* mycorrhiza.

In a mycorrhizal partnership the fungus probably benefits chiefly by obtaining a supply of carbohydrates from the higher plant, whilst the higher plant benefits by gaining nitrogenous and other materials which have been obtained by the fungus from the organic matter in the soil. In the case of many forest trees and some other plants, under natural conditions, the mycorrhiza is indispensable. Such plants are usually those growing on soils deficient in suitable inorganic nitrogenous substances, which can be absorbed directly by the plant, but rich in organic matter (such as decaying leaves) from which the fungi may obtain nitrogenous materials and render them available to the higher plant. It is possible that the host plant may benefit in other ways from the association. For example, it has been suggested that in some cases the fungus may supply growth-promoting substances.

Mycorrhizal fungi have been found on the roots of a wide range of crop plants, such as sugar-cane, oats, wheat, rye-grasses, coffee, tea, rubber, strawberry and orange. In some cases proof that they are present under normal conditions is lacking, and there is little evidence that they are necessary for the normal growth of the crop. There is no doubt, however, that mycorrhizal associations are of great importance to some plants, such as the forest trees and orchids mentioned above.

REPRODUCTION IN THE FUNGI

Unlike the flowering plants, fungi do not produce seeds containing an embryo and quantities of stored food. They reproduce by means of less complex bodies known as *spores*. Two main types of spores are recognized, those produced asexually and those produced after a sexual process, i.e. the combination of nuclei of different parentage, has taken place.

The sexual method of reproduction is often complicated and difficult to follow. Essentially it is comparable with that of flowering plants in that reduction division occurs before the formation of sex nuclei (gametes), giving rise to the haploid condition, and fertilization is brought about by the fusion of pairs of haploid nuclei, at some stage, to produce the diploid condition. As in higher plants, the process results in new combinations of genes, which may give rise to new races of the particular fungus with new morphological and/or physiological characteristics.

In some species of fungi both sexual reproduction and reproduction by asexual spores occur; in some species asexual spores are not known, whilst in others the sexual phase has not been observed.

Considerable diversity exists in the mode of production and in the structure of spores. The main types are mentioned below:

(A) *Asexual Reproduction*

(i) *Conidia.* These are spores abstricted from the tips of hyphae either singly or in chains. The hyphae bearing conidia are known as *conidiophores*. Conidiophores may be formed singly or in loose clusters, or they may be aggregated together in a cushion-like mass (an *acervulus*) or produced within a flask-shaped structure open at the mouth (a *pycnidium*).

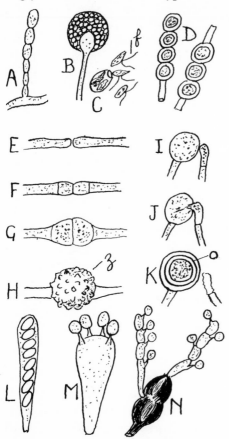

(ii) *Sporangiospores* produced by the division of the protoplasm inside specialized cells called *sporangia* (singular, *sporangium*). The sporangia may be borne on a simple or branched hypha known as a *sporangiophore*. The spores, when released, may each be covered by a cell wall, or they may be naked pieces of protoplasm equipped with fine hair-like processes, known as *flagella* (or *cilia*), the vibration of which causes the spores to move about in water. Such motile spores are known as *zoospores*.

(iii) *Chlamydospores:* these are thick-walled spores produced by the division of part or the whole of a hypha. They are often capable of remaining dormant for long periods when conditions are unfavourable for development.

Fig. 223. Reproductive bodies of fungi. A, conidia in a single chain. B, a sporangium containing spores. C, zoospores escaping from a sporangium, *f* flagellum. D, chlamydospores. E, F, G, H, stages in the production of a zygospore *z*. I, J, K, stages in the production of an oospore *o*. L, an ascus containing ascospores. M, basidium bearing 4 basidiospores. N, basidiospores of a rust fungus, borne on a short hypha of 4 cells the promycelium (basidium).

(B) *Sexual Reproduction*

(i) *Zygospores:* these are produced by some of the lower fungi. They result from a sexual fusion between two similar cells, between which differentiation of male and female is impossible.

Often zygospores are relatively large thick-walled structures capable of remaining dormant when conditions are unfavourable for development.

(ii) *Oospores*, produced by the union of male and female sex cells. In this case differentiation of sex functions of the uniting cells is possible.

Oospores are encountered only in certain of the lower fungi. They are often thick-walled and capable of remaining dormant for long periods.

(iii) *Asci* (found in the group of fungi called the *Ascomycetes*). These are sac-like or club-shaped cells which represent the *perfect* or diploid phase of the fungus as fusion of nuclei occurs at some stage in their development. Within each ascus usually eight ascospores are produced. Reduction division occurs during the formation of these so that the ascospores are haploid.

In most of the parasitic species which produce asci the ascospores are forcibly shot from the asci for some considerable distance. They may then be taken along by air currents and distributed still more widely.

(iv) *Basidia* (found in the *Basidiomycetes*). These are often more or less club-shaped cells; they represent the perfect or diploid phase, fusion of nuclei having occurred at some stage before or during their development. They give rise to *basidiospores*, during the formation of which reduction division occurs. The basidiospores are usually attached externally to the basidium by short stalks or *sterigmata* (singular, *sterigma*) and usually four are produced on each basidium. Basidiospores are also known as *sporidia*.

The basidiospores, when ripe, are shot only a very short distance from the sterigmata, and they then fall freely unless taken up by air currents. In this way they may fall freely between the downwardly-directed gills of the mushroom and other gill fungi or through the downwardly-directed pores of the bracket fungi and other species.

In the Basidiomycetes, the class of fungi producing basidia, the details of reproduction show considerable variation from one group of species to another.

GERMINATION OF SPORES

Spores which are not protected by a thick outer coat, or within a specialized protective fruiting body, are usually produced in large numbers in the spring and summer. Such spores normally germinate quickly, under suitable conditions of moisture and temperature. When they germinate they usually produce one or more thread-like hyphae or germ-tubes. If there is a suitable, and sufficient, supply of food available the germ-tube will continue to grow to produce a mycelium.

Thick-walled spores, and those protected by other means, are usually produced in the late summer and autumn and remain dormant during the winter. On germination they may produce a mycelium, but in some cases they develop in other ways, as will be seen later.

TYPES OF FUNGI

Fungi are classified largely on the basis of the type of spore-producing organs they possess. There are four main classes:

(i) The *Phycomycetes*, in which sporangia are produced at some stage in the life cycle. In this group the hyphae, when present, are aseptate.

(ii) The *Ascomycetes*, which produce asci containing ascospores. The hyphae are septate in this group.

(iii) The *Basidiomycetes*, in which basidia bearing basidiospores are produced. Again the hyphae are septate.

(iv) The *Deuteromycetes* or *Fungi Imperfecti*, a miscellaneous class in which are grouped species for which the perfect or sexual stage is not known. If spores are produced they are conidia. Some so-called species in this class may merely be phases in the life cycle of fungi classified under other names.

In order to illustrate the basic differences between the first three classes we will consider the means of spore production in some common fungus species:

(A) *Mucor mucedo*. **The Common Pin Mould of Bread.** This mould develops readily on damp bread. Fig. 224 illustrates the structure of the

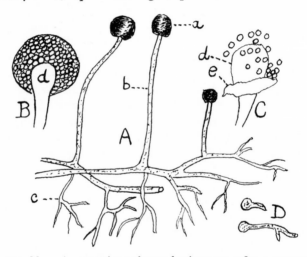

Fig. 224. *Mucor*. A, vegetative and reproductive parts, × 60: *a*, sporangium; *b*, sporangiophore; *c*, vegetative hyphae which penetrate into the food and absorb nutrients. B, sporangium in section showing spores: *d*, columella. C, sporangium after bursting and releasing its spores, *d*, columella; *e*, torn remains of outer wall. D, spores germinating.

fungus. Aseptate, branched hyphae ramify in the surface layers of the bread and, after a time, branches grow upwards into the air. These branches develop a swollen tip like a black pin-head. The swollen head is the *sporangium* which is cut off from the stalk, or *sporangiophore*, by a transverse wall. The contents of the sporangium divide up into numerous spores. As the sporangium develops the transverse wall is forced upwards within it forming the *columella*. As the spores ripen the columella increases in size, pressing them against the wall of the sporangium. The sporangium wall finally ruptures and the spores are released.

The spores, being very small and light, are readily carried away by air currents. If a spore falls on to bread which is moist, and at a suitable temperature, it will germinate producing a germ tube which ultimately extends and branches to form a new mycelium.

Under certain circumstances hyphae of two different strains of a *Mucor* species may conjugate to produce a large thick-walled *zygospore*. Conjugation does not take place between hyphae derived from the same spore or between hyphae of the same strain. The process of conjugation is comparable with a sexual fusion, but the hyphae are similar in appearance and activity, and male and female cannot therefore be distinguished. The zygospore is able to withstand adverse conditions, such as drought or extremes of cold and heat, and remains dormant whilst conditions are unfavourable. Later it may germinate to produce a sporangium.

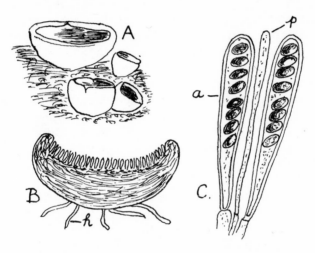

FIG. 225. *Peziza vesiculosa*. A, apothecia, × ½. B, longitudinal section of an apothecium showing asci and paraphyses on its upper surface, *h*, absorptive hypha. C: *a*, an ascus containing 8 ascospores; *p*, a paraphysis.

Mucor with its sporangia and aseptate hyphae belongs to the *Phycomycetes*. Those members of this class which produce zygospores belong to a sub-class known as the *Zygomycetes*.

(B) *Peziza vesiculosa*. Fig. 225 illustrates the appearance and structure of *Peziza vesiculosa*, a common cup-fungus which can be found growing on the ground in gardens and waste places or on manure heaps, rotting leaves, etc., from spring to autumn. Hyphae are present in the soil or rotting material from which food is absorbed. The fruiting-body (fructification) is at first closed but becomes open and cup-shaped as it ripens. It is fleshy and brittle, a pale greyish-brown colour, and about 2 in. in diameter when expanded. It consists of masses of hyphae. On the upper surface of the cup the apices of most of the hyphae form club-shaped asci each containing eight oval ascospores. Between the asci, on the surface of the cup, are hair-like hyphae known as *paraphyses*. The asci and paraphyses can be seen readily if a portion of the upper surface of the cup is teased out in water, on a microscope slide, and examined under the microscope.

Another common species of *Peziza* which may be encountered is *P. aurantia.* This is found in summer and autumn on the ground in woods and on paths. Its bright orange fructifications are up to 4 in. diameter when expanded.

These species belong to the *Ascomycetes.* In this class there are usually eight spores in each ascus, but occasionally fewer, and in a few cases sixteen or thirty-two, or more, spores may be present. The ascospores are often oval in shape, but in some species they may be rounded or elongated or linear.

In *Peziza* the fructification is known as an *apothecium.* This term is applied to the fruiting bodies which are open and cup-shaped, saucer-shaped or flat, and bear the asci exposed on the upper surface.

In some Ascomycetes the asci are enclosed in a flask-shaped fructification, known as a *perithecium,* which opens to the outside by a mouth or *ostiole* in the neck. In yet other species the asci are completely enclosed within a fruiting body known as a *cleistocarp,* which usually breaks open irregularly when ripe. The production of cleistocarps is typical of the powdery mildews, e.g. the very common powdery mildew of wheat.

A cleistocarp is frequently called a perithecium also, and the type described above as a perithecium may be referred to as an *ostiolate perithecium* to distinguish it from the completely closed perithecium or cleistocarp.

When ripe, ascospores are often forcibly shot out of the asci to a considerable distance. When they are present in a flask-shaped perithecium they may be released through the ostiole in drops of sugary fluid.

(C) *Saccharomyces* spp., **Yeasts.** The yeasts form a rather special group within the Ascomycetes. They are not very typical of that class as a whole, but are included in it because of their method of spore formation. Yeasts are described here chiefly on account of their special interest in connection with the utilization of barley and wheat crops in brewing and baking respectively.

There are many different species of yeast, of which the best-known is brewer's yeast, *Saccharomyces cerevisiae.*

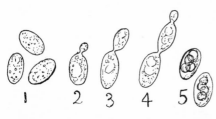

Fig. 226. A common yeast, *Saccharomyces cerevisiae.* 1, individual cells. 2, 3, and 4, cells reproducing by budding. 5, cells containing spores, × 750. (Percival.)

Yeast plants are microscopic and when examined under a microscope they are seen to consist of single round to oval cells. There are no hyphae, but under some conditions the cells may become somewhat elongated so that they then bear some resemblance to hyphae. Each yeast cell contains cytoplasm and a single nucleus. The nucleus is open in structure because a vacuole is contained within it.

510

When growing under suitable conditions the yeast cells reproduce by budding. The budded cells may remain together in chains, but they readily separate into single cells when disturbed. In solutions of sugars, e.g. malt extract, kept at a suitable temperature, budding occurs freely.

Under adverse conditions, e.g. when food supplies are inadequate, the contents of the yeast cell round off, forming from one to four spores (in some species eight spores may be formed). In some yeasts spore-formation is preceded by a sexual fusion (conjugation) between two cells. When spores are formed the original cell becomes a simple form of ascus. When the outer wall disintegrates the spores escape and each spore, under suitable conditions, can develop as a new yeast plant. The spores are able to resist adverse conditions such as desiccation or frost.

Yeast produces an enzyme *zymase* which can ferment sugar solutions to produce alcohol and carbon dioxide. For this reason, it is important in the production of alcoholic beverages and in bread-baking. Some species of yeast commonly grow on the outer surface of certain fruits, such as the grape, and watery extracts from these fruits ferment readily. In order to obtain quick fermentation of malt extracts it is necessary to add yeast to the sugary solution. During the beer-brewing process fermentation is rapid and repeated budding of the yeast cells occurs, so that considerably increased amounts of yeast are removed at the end of the process. The carbon dioxide escapes through the liquor in the form of bubbles and contributes to the froth on beers.

In the baking process sugars produced from the starch of the wheat grain dissolve in water in the dough and are fermented by the added yeast if the dough is kept warm before being placed in the oven. The fermentation produces carbon dioxide which is held in the form of bubbles within a sticky dough and causes the bread to rise. When baked, such bread has an open texture. The alcohol produced by fermentation evaporates during the baking process.

(D) *Agaricus (Psalliota) campestris*, **The Field Mushroom.** The field mushroom is a well-known saprophytic fungus. The mycelium develops in the soil, and, when conditions are favourable, fructifications are produced above ground. The fructification consists of a stalk or *stipe*, bearing a cap or *pileus* at its apex. Beneath the pileus a large number of *lamellae* or *gills* radiate from the centre. In the young mushroom the gills are covered by a membrane called the *velum*. This tears as the cap enlarges leaving a ring of tissue, the *annulus*, around the stipe. The fructification is composed of large numbers of hyphae compacted together to form *pseudoparenchyma*.

The spores are produced on the surface of the gills. A vertical section through a gill reveals, under the microscope, that the spores are borne on short stalks or *sterigmata* at the top of club-shaped *basidia* which are the apical cells of hyphae. In the field mushroom there are four spores to each basidium, but in some cultivated mushrooms two only are produced. Between the basidia there are infertile hyphae known as *paraphyses.* The basidia and paraphyses form a layer known as the *hymenium*, beneath which there is the *sub-hymenium* and a layer of hyphae in the middle of the gill known as the *trama*. Lateral branches from the trama produce the sub-hymenium and the hymenium.

The spores, when liberated, are shot for a short distance from the sterigmata and then fall vertically between the gills; they may then be carried away by air currents. Spores which eventually fall on suitable

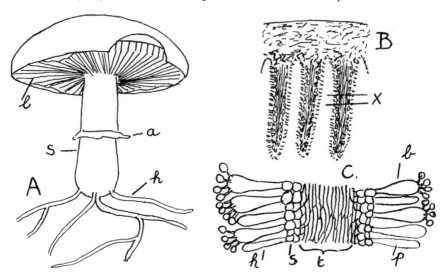

Fig. 227. Field mushroom. A: *h*, absorptive hyphae; *s*, stipe; *a*, annulus; *l*, lamellae or gills; a portion of the cap has been cut away to show a section through the gills. B, three gills in longitudinal section. C, the portion × enlarged; b, basidium bearing basidio-spores; *p*, paraphysis; *h*, hymenium; *s*, sub-hymenium; *t*, trama.

nutrient material may, if moisture and temperature conditions are suitable, develop to produce a new mycelium.

The mushroom *spawn* which is purchased by would-be growers of mushrooms consists of compressed organic matter in which mycelium of the mushroom has been developed. The mycelium is able to remain dormant for a long period in the dried, compressed organic matter, but it is desirable that the spawn should be used within a year. The spawn is broken up and mixed with large quantities of organic matter in which, under suitable conditions, the mycelium will spread and eventually produce a crop of mushrooms.

The mushroom, with its basidia and basidiospores, is classified within the third main class of fungi, the *Basidiomycetes*. Many, but not all, members of this class possess large complex fruiting bodies, comparable with the mushroom, e.g. the bracket-fungi, some of which are parasites of trees, and the honey fungus (*Armillaria mellea*), which attacks and kills trees, its honey-coloured mushroom-like fructifications appearing in clusters at the bases of trees and on infected stumps left in the ground.

SUMMARY OF CLASSIFICATION OF THE FUNGI

The table given below summarizes the main classes of fungi and provides examples of diseases caused by fungi in each class. Each class of fungi is subdivided into sub-classes which are further subdivided into families. The detailed classification of the fungi, however, is a subject for the specialist and will not be pursued further here.

FUNGI

PHYCOMYCETES. *Vegetative mycelium aseptate or absent.*
Spores usually in sporangia.
> Club root of Brassicas; powdery scab of potatoes; wart disease of potatoes; potato blight; downy mildews of sugar-beet, crucifers, hops and many other species.

ASCOMYCETES: *Mycelium usually profuse and septate. Asci formed.*
> Powdery mildews of cereals, grasses, hops and many other species. Clover rot; chocolate spot of beans; ergot of grasses and cereals; take-all and whiteheads of cereals; seedling blight and leaf spot of oats; leaf stripe of barley.

BASIDIOMYCETES: *Mycelium profuse and septate. Basidia formed.*
> Smut diseases of cereals and many other species; rust diseases of cereals and many other species.

DEUTEROMYCETES OR FUNGI IMPERFECTI: *Sporangia, asci and basidia absent so far as is known. Spores, when present, are conidia.*
> Skin spot of potatoes; dry rot of potatoes; eyespot of cereals.

In addition to the true fungi mentioned above, a group of organisms known as the *Myxomycetes* are sometimes referred to as *Slime Fungi*. The Myxomycetes do not develop a mycelium, but consist of naked masses of protoplasm. They are mainly saprophytic on vegetable debris, such as leaf mould, compost heaps, fallen twigs and logs. The protoplasmic mass is capable of *amoeboid movement*, i.e. movement by a streaming action similar to that of the primitive animal organism *Amoeba*. The organisms causing the diseases club root of cruciferous plants and powdery scab of potatoes are sometimes included in this group, but in recent times they have come to be regarded as true fungi and placed in the group of lower fungi, the Phycomycetes.

COMPARATIVE SIZES OF DISEASE-CAUSING FUNGI

Before proceeding to consider fungi as agents of disease it would be well to emphasize that most disease-causing fungi are relatively small. A microscope is necessary in order to observe single spores, and often the fructifications themselves cannot be observed readily without its aid. With a few exceptions fungus spores are considerably larger than bacteria, however, and truly gigantic in comparison with virus particles, as

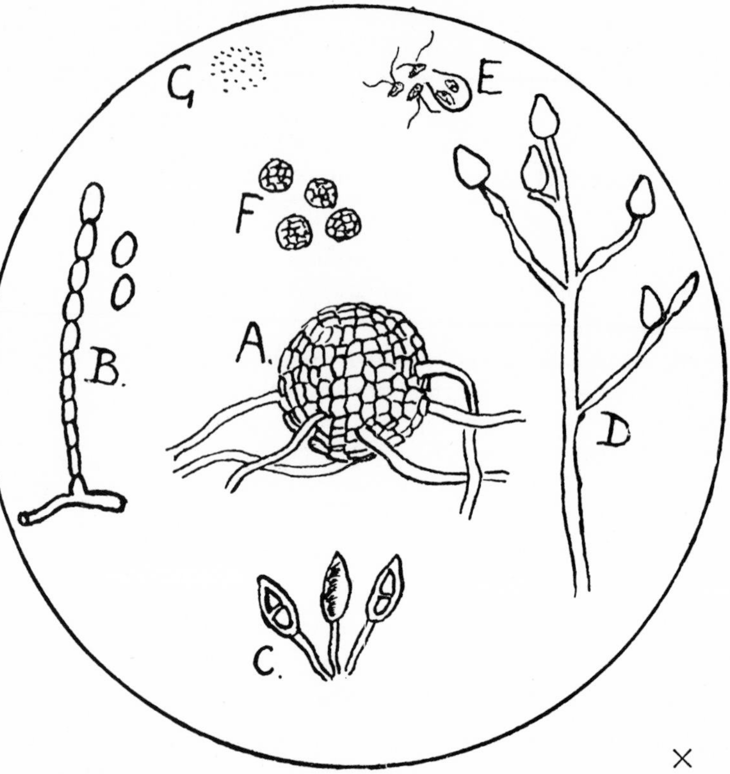

Fig. 228. Relative sizes of disease organisms. The outer circle represents the dimensions of the full stop × enlarged by 200 diameters. The disease organisms within the circle are magnified to the same degree. A, a cleistocarp of the powdery mildew of wheat fungus. B, conidia of the same fungus. C, teleutospores of the black rust of wheat fungus. D, sporangia of potato blight fungus. E, the same releasing zoospores. F, brand spores of bunt of wheat. G, fairly large bacteria.

will be seen later. The standard of measurement used in relation to fungus spores and bacteria is the *micron*, which is 0·001 mm. (usually expressed as 1 μ).

Reference to fig. 228 will provide some idea of the magnitude of some of the fungal organisms concerned with common plant diseases.

Chapter XXII

FUNGAL DISEASES: TRANSMISSION AND CONTROL

TRANSMISSION OF FUNGAL DISEASES

PLANT diseases caused by fungi are spread most usually by means of spores, although in a few cases infection occurs by other means—for example, take-all disease of cereals may be initiated by fungal hyphae present in crop remains in the soil.

Spores are usually produced in very large numbers. An idea of the prolificacy of fungi may be obtained from the figures calculated for spore production in the common mushroom: it has been estimated that a large mushroom may produce as many as 10,000,000,000 spores. In the case of the disease of wheat known as bunt (see p. 556), a single bunt ball may contain 4,000,000 or more spores.

Although the fungi are, in most cases, very prolific in spore production, few of the spores succeed in establishing themselves in conditions suitable for growth and development. For example, most of the mushroom spores eventually shrivel up and die, and comparatively few find suitable organic matter and the correct temperature and moisture conditions for germination and production of a mycelium. Similarly, many spores of the disease-causing fungi fail to bring about infection, but the very abundance of the spores makes it probable that some will encounter suitable host plants in which they may produce disease.

In many cases spores which are released into the air have a very short life. Spores which are not protected by a thick cell wall must reach a suitable host on which they can grow within a comparatively short time after release, otherwise they die. Short-lived spores usually remain alive rather longer under moist conditions than under dry conditions.

Other spores are provided with thick cell walls (e.g. brand spores of bunt of wheat) or are contained within protective cells (e.g. the resting spores of wart disease of potato), and are able to remain viable for much longer periods of time.

Fungal diseases may be transmitted in various ways. In some cases they are transmitted in the soil. In other cases transmission is by spores carried in the air by the wind. Rain splashes falling on diseased plants may take up spores and carry them to healthy plants within a limited area around the infected plant. If the drops of rain are caught up by the wind they may carry spores over a much wider area. In some cases transmission occurs by means of contaminated or infected seed. More rarely, other agents, such as insects, are involved in the transmission of disease from diseased to healthy plants. Diseases may be transported from one geographical area to another in diseased plants or seeds. With the increased speed of transport it is also possible that viable spores may be carried great distances from one country to another particularly by aircraft.

Soil-borne Diseases. These may remain in the soil of an infected field for a long period. They may persist in various ways. (*a*) As dormant spores, e.g. wart disease of potato. (*b*) As mycelium growing on crop remains, e.g. take-all of cereals. (*c*) In the form of sclerotia, as in the case of clover rot. (*d*) By infecting *alternative hosts* among the weeds. In this way the disease is enabled to persist until a suitable host crop is grown on the field. For example, take-all of cereals may persist on the roots of certain weed grasses, and club-root of cruciferous crops persists on the roots of cruciferous weeds such as charlock.

When the soil of a field is infected with spores, sclerotia or mycelium of disease organisms, there is a danger of the disease being transmitted to healthy land through the transfer of soil from one field to another. Such transfer may occur on implements or boots, on the feet of livestock, or on soil adhering to potato tubers used for seed, or the roots of plants transplanted from one field to another, for example.

Air-borne Diseases. Spores released into the air or shaken from the plant by wind or rain may, since they are so small, be caught up by air currents and carried some distance. Some may eventually fall on to a suitable host plant, which they may parasitize. Usually when spores fall on to the host plant a moist surface is important so that they may begin growth and penetrate the host quickly. In some cases when the spores are motile, e.g. the zoospores of potato blight fungus, a moist surface enables the spores to move over the surface of the plant before they begin to develop and cause infection.

Some spores which are effectively protected against desiccation may be transmitted very considerable distances in the air. For example, the uredospores of the black rust of wheat may be carried from the southern states of America to infect wheat crops hundreds of miles to the north. Such spores may be carried at a considerable height in the air, being taken up by air currents and deposited later on distant crops. Collection of fungus spores by aeroplanes has demonstrated their presence in considerable numbers at great heights above the earth.

Seed-borne Diseases. Seed-borne diseases may be present in the form of spores adhering to the outside of the seed, as in bunt of wheat, in which case the seed is said to be *contaminated*. They may be present within the tissues of the seed in the form of mycelium, as in loose smut of wheat, when the seed is said to be *infected*. Some diseases are carried in the form of pycnidia, containing spores, embedded in the outer tissues of the seed, as for example in leaf spot of celery.

Insect-borne Diseases. In a few cases insects may act as agents in the spread of plant diseases. An example of this occurs in the disease ergot of rye, in which spores are extruded in sugary fluid by infected flowers and may be carried by visiting insects to healthy flowers. Similarly, spores of some rot-causing diseases of fruit may be carried by wasps from diseased to healthy fruit. Insects are of considerably more importance in connection with the transmission of virus diseases (see Chapter XXVIII).

INFECTION OF THE HOST PLANT

The germ tubes produced by the spores of disease-producing fungi may enter plants in various ways. Some enter through natural openings such as the stomata or the lenticels; others are capable of penetrating cuticle and growing through or between the cells of the epidermis; others penetrate only through wounds in the surface layers of the plant—in damaged roots, tubers or branches, for example.

HOST RELATIONS OF THE FUNGI

A particular species of parasitic fungus usually confines its attack to a limited range of host species. Some species are very restricted in their host relationships—for example, the bunt fungus, *Tilletia caries*, usually attacks wheat only, but occasionally it also attacks rye. Other fungus species have a wider, though still limited, range, as in the case of the fungus *Plasmodiophora brassicae*, which causes the disease club-root or finger and toe in several different species, all, however, within the family Cruciferae. The fungus has been found to penetrate the roots of some non-cruciferous plants, but clubbed roots are not produced.

Often numerous physiological races of a particular fungus species exist, and these may vary in their virulence. Some races may readily infect a wide range of varieties of a particular crop species whilst others may be incapable of infecting some varieties but capable of infecting others. In other words, crop varieties may show immunity, or marked resistance, to some races of a particular parasitic species. For example, a number of physiological races exist in the fungus *Puccinia striiformis*, cause of yellow rust of wheat, and some wheat varieties show greater resistance to this disease in certain regions than in others, because of differences in the geographical distribution of the various races. The variety Desprez 80, for example, was much more heavily attacked by yellow rust in the south of England than in the north, and it is thought probable that this was due to the distribution of races 2 and 3 of the rust fungus, which are more or less restricted to the southern half of the country. The existence of different physiological races of the various disease fungi is a complicating factor in the work of the plant-breeder (see Chapter IV).

Most species of parasitic fungi require only one host plant for the completion of their full development; such fungi are said to be *autoecious*. In some cases, however, the fungus attacks two different host species at different stages of its life cycle—for example, *Puccinia graminis*, which causes black rust of wheat, spends part of its life cycle as a parasite of wheat and part as a parasite of the common barberry (*Berberis vulgaris*). The wheat and the barberry are known as *alternate hosts*, and the fungus is said to be *heteroecious*.

CONTROL OF FUNGAL DISEASES

The control of fungal diseases in farm crops depends largely on prevention rather than cure. Once a crop has fallen victim to a fungal disease it is usually impossible or impracticable to cure the infected plants. The fungus mycelium will, in most cases, have penetrated into the inner tissues of the plant, and to prevent further spread of the disease all infected tissues of all infected plants would have to be removed and destroyed. Whilst this is possible when dealing with trees, where infected branches may be cut off and destroyed, it is not practicable with herbaceous farm crops.

Immune or Resistant Varieties. The best method of prevention of disease is to grow immune or resistant crop varieties. Such varieties are not always available or, if available in some cases, they possess other characteristics which detract from their economic value. The breeding of crop varieties immune or resistant to the major diseases, and with good economic characteristics, is a problem which occupies the attention of plant-breeders all over the world. Attention of breeders is devoted chiefly to diseases which cannot be controlled easily and cheaply by other means.

In some cases good immune or resistant varieties are already available, for example varieties of potato immune to wart disease and wheat varieties resistant to yellow rust (see also p. 61).

Destruction of Infected Material. Many plant diseases start their attack from infected plant material from previous crops. It is therefore desirable, where possible, to destroy diseased plant remains by fire or deep burial, so that they may not remain as a source of infection for succeeding crops.

The destruction, by means of chemical sprays, of the haulm of potato crops infected with blight, in order to prevent infection of the tubers at lifting time (see p. 538), may also be mentioned under this heading.

In the case of perennial plants, such as fruit trees and hops, the cutting away and burning of infected parts may prevent disease from spreading to other parts of the plant and to other plants.

Extension of Rotation. In the case of soil-borne diseases, an extension of the rotation, during which susceptible crops are kept off the field *and susceptible weeds are controlled*, will often result in the fungus being starved out, providing the land is rested from the susceptible crop for a sufficient length of time. The length of rest required will vary with the various soil-borne diseases.

Elimination of Alternate Hosts. When dealing with heteroecious fungi, which require an alternate host in order to complete their life cycle, the eradication of the alternate host will assist in the control of the disease. For this reason, in countries where black rust of wheat is prevalent, steps are taken to eradicate, and prevent the planting of, the common barberry which may act as the alternate host for this disease. In some countries, however, this method of control is not fully effective against black rust (see p. 563).

Provision of Favourable Growth Conditions. In many cases a well-nourished, vigorous crop may be less liable to disease than a poorly developed one. A vigorous crop, if attacked by certain diseases, may 'grow away' from the disease and show little reduction of yield. Some diseases, however, are more liable to spread in well-developed crops—for example, 'winter proud' crops of wheat and red clover are more liable to severe attack by powdery mildew and clover rot respectively.

The ability of a crop to resist disease may depend to some extent on soil conditions. Good drainage will encourage a stronger crop by assisting root development. The presence of adequate amounts of lime is also important in maintaining a healthy crop. Lime, in addition, may have an adverse effect upon disease-producing soil fungi, as in the case of clubroot disease of Brassicas. On the other hand, lime may encourage certain disease organisms, as in the case of common scab of potato. Adequate amounts of phosphate and potash are important in producing strong, disease-resistant plants. Excessive amounts of nitrogenous fertilizers result in sappy growth and may render a crop more liable to severe damage if attacked by a fungus disease.

Lighter seeding will give fewer but stronger plants, as a result of the reduced competition for nutrients and light, and often reduce damage by particular diseases (e.g. take-all of wheat and barley). Reduction of competition by weeds may also have a similar beneficial effect.

The Use of Fungicides. Substances which will kill fungal disease organisms, known as *fungicides*, are of considerable value, providing they can be used without damage to the plant or seed.

Air-borne spores which settle on the aerial parts of a crop can be killed before they are able to infect the crop if they can be brought into contact with one of these substances. When the probable time of attack of a particular disease is predictable it may be possible, before the attack is expected, to cover the crop plants with fungicidal material, either in the form of a spray or a dust, so that when the spores fall on to the plants they are killed.

A fungicide for use on growing crops must not damage the crop to which it is applied. It should form an even film over the whole of the exposed, susceptible parts of the plant, and should persist upon the plant, and so afford protection, for a reasonable length of time.

The increase in financial yield to be expected from the crop, as a result of the use of a fungicide, must be sufficient to justify the financial outlay involved in its application. Thus, in Britain, spraying or dusting on the field scale is a worthwhile proposition in some areas, and in certain seasons, in connection with the potato crop. It is also economic with orchard crops, hops and certain seed crops such as celery. In some cases, although the use of fungicides may give control of particular diseases their use is not practical; for example, although prevention of black rust of wheat may be obtained by dusting crops several times with sulphur, in countries where the disease commonly occurs, it is not very practicable on the large scale. In Britain severe attacks of black rust are too infrequent to warrant consideration of this method.

For some crops, more especially horticultural crops, suitable insecticides may be combined with fungicides in a single spray. *Spreading agents* may sometimes be added to sprays to help to ensure an even spread, instead of the formation of globules of liquid, on the surface of the plants. These spreaders are usually soaps or soap-like substances, and sprays containing them are more readily washed off the crop, which is a disadvantage where long-continued protection of the crop is desired. Substances known as *stickers* (e.g. drying oils or Bentonite, a sodium clay) may also be added to some sprays. These increase the adhesive power of the spray but they may reduce its fungicidal value.

For seed disinfection, where spores are already present on the surface of the seed, it is necessary to coat the seed thoroughly with a suitable fungicide. In order to be effective the fungicide must usually be retained on the surface of the seed until such time as the fungus spores germinate preparatory to infecting the germinating seed.

Copper Fungicides. Many sprays and dusts commonly used on standing crops contain copper compounds which have good fungicidal properties.

The value of a mixture of copper sulphate and lime, in the control of fungal diseases, was first realized in 1882, although copper sulphate had been used previously in attempts to control diseases. It was in that year that Millardet, a professor at the University of Bordeaux, noted that grape vines, near the roadside, which had been smeared with a paste consisting of copper sulphate and lime, as a protection against pilferers, remained healthy whilst untreated vines lost their leaves early through attack by mildew.

As a result of subsequent work by Millardet and his associates, *Bordeaux mixture* became recognized as a valuable fungicide. They realized that, for large-scale use, the mixture was more easily applied in the form of a spray (i.e. mixed with water) than as the original paste, and it is in this form that it has been most widely used since that time.

In Britain, Bordeaux mixture has been used most extensively, on farms, for spraying against potato blight. It is also used as a protection against many other plant diseases, such as blight of tomatoes, common on outdoor crops and caused by the same fungus as potato blight (*Phytophthora infestans*), downy mildew of hops, leaf spot of celery and certain fungus diseases of fruit trees.

Various proportions of copper sulphate and lime have been used. It is most important that the ratio of copper sulphate to lime should be kept low, since excessive amounts of copper sulphate result in a scorching of the foliage.

The following is a suitable formula for a potato spray:

> 10 lb. powdered bluestone (crystalline copper sulphate)
> $12\frac{1}{2}$ lb. fresh hydrated lime
> 100 gall. water

This is the amount most usually used for spraying an acre of potatoes, but as the plants become larger the rate may be increased to 120 gall. of the above mixture per acre. To prepare the spray a stock solution of bluestone may be made in a wooden tub (bluestone corrodes metal containers), using 2 lb. of the powder for each gallon of water. The bluestone will dissolve more readily in warm water. When the Bordeaux mixture is required about 60 gall. of water are run into the spray tank. The $12\frac{1}{2}$ lb. of hydrated lime is than sprinkled into the tank and stirred thoroughly. Still stirring thoroughly, 5 gall. of the stock solution of bluestone is added. When thoroughly mixed, cold water is added to make up to 100 gall., and the spray, after stirring, is ready for use. The spray should be used within twenty-four hours of mixing.

Another fungicide known as *Burgundy mixture* was popular when finely powdered hydrated lime was difficult to obtain. In this mixture $12\frac{1}{2}$ lb. of washing soda is substituted for the lime in the Bordeaux mixture formula. Burgundy mixture is almost as effective as Bordeaux mixture, but there is a greater risk of scorching the foliage.

Bordeaux mixture is still one of the most effective copper fungicides. It adheres well to the foliage and is not readily washed off by rain, it is relatively cheap, and it is safe to handle. It has the disadvantage of being relatively difficult to prepare, as compared with some of the more modern spraying materials, and copper sulphate is corrosive to machine parts of iron and zinc. In addition, Bordeaux mixture badly scorches some fruit trees when used in orchards. Under dry conditions it may have a toxic effect on potatoes, resulting in scorching and early death of the foliage and consequent reduction of crop. For this reason in dry areas in the United States the organo-sulphur compounds *nabam* and *zineb* have largely replaced Bordeaux mixture for spraying potato crops.

Many proprietary copper spraying materials are now on the market, and have proved popular because of the ease of preparation of the spray. These have to a considerable extent replaced home-made Bordeaux mixture in Britain. In addition to Bordeaux-type mixtures, proprietary sprays containing either cuprous oxide or copper oxychloride have proved effective.

Whilst Bordeaux and Burgundy sprays can only be applied in high volume (around 100 gall. per acre), low-volume spraying of cuprous oxide suspensions, by means of an atomizer sprayer, is effective. As only about one-tenth of the above amount of water is needed, this method has obvious advantages. Low volume is essential for aerial spraying.

Copper fungicides are also available in the form of dusts. These have the advantage of not requiring a supply of water for their application. They are easier to apply, and lighter machinery than is needed for high-volume spraying can be used with less damage to the crop. On the other hand, they are less effective than sprays and are readily washed off the crop by a heavy shower of rain shortly after dusting. Where dusts are used, they must usually be applied more frequently than the comparable sprays.

521

A copper fungicide widely used by nurserymen is Cheshunt Compound, which was devised at the Cheshunt Glasshouse Experimental Station, particularly for the control of damping-off of tomatoes, a fungal disease which attacks seedlings and persists in the soil. The mixture consists of copper sulphate and ammonium carbonate, and in solution it is watered on to the soil. The solution will kill the damping-off fungi and certain other fungi in the soil, without injuring growing plants. Copper fungicides, such as Peronox, watered into the soil at half the strength used for spraying potato crops against blight, are also very effective for this purpose.

Mercury Fungicides. Certain compounds containing mercury possess a high fungicidal value. Corrosive sublimate (mercuric chloride) and calomel (mercurous chloride) are both effective in protecting Brassicas from club-root disease when applied around the roots. Corrosive sublimate, which is soluble in water, is quick-acting and provides protection for a short time, whilst calomel, which is relatively insoluble, acts more slowly, but provides protection for a longer period. Corrosive sublimate must be handled with care, as it is very poisonous.

Much more important is the use of organo-mercury compounds in the form of dusts, for dressing seeds, particularly cereals, against seed-borne diseases. Several proprietary seed dressings, of proved value, containing organo-mercury compounds are on the market, and their development has proved to be an important advance in the fight against seed-borne diseases.

Disease organisms which are present on the outside of seeds may usually be controlled by dressing the seed with a suitable fungicide which will kill the spores, or the mycelium they produce, before infection of the plant occurs. Before the introduction of the organo-mercury dusts, copper sulphate solution and formalin were both used for dressing (or 'pickling') cereal seed against seed-borne diseases. Whilst both these substances have fungicidal properties, their use has certain drawbacks. Both are wet methods, and the grain must be dried quickly after application of the fungicide, and sown as soon as possible, otherwise there is a marked risk of impairing the germination of the seed. Copper sulphate is suitable for wheat only, but formalin can also be used successfully on barley, oats and rye.

Dry seed dressing by means of fungicidal dusts has now largely replaced these older wet methods. Many of these proprietary dry seed dressings are based on organo-mercury compounds.

In order to obtain maximum control of disease by seed dressings, it is essential that all the seed should be thoroughly covered by the dressing. Thorough mixing of the seed and the dust is therefore important, and a fungicide, to be effective, should adhere firmly to the seed.

For dressing seed grain on the farm various machines are obtainable. The most effective types are those which tip the grain over and over and so obtain a complete mixing of the grain and the fungicide. An old butter churn can be converted into an effective seed-dresser by fitting baffles inside so that the grain and dust are thoroughly mixed when the churn is rotated. The gravity type of machine is rather less effective in providing complete disinfection. In this type the grain is poured in at the top and mixed with the dust by trickling over internal baffles before coming out at the bottom. The old methods of shaking grain and dust in a sack or of dusting the grain on the barn floor are usually not very efficient, as the dust is likely to be unevenly distributed, some grain receiving too much and some too little. Usually, for a small extra charge, ready-dressed seed can be supplied by seed merchants.

The grain should be dry and otherwise in good condition when treated, otherwise the embryos may be killed or abnormal seedlings may be produced on germination.

After dressing with organo-mercury fungicides, the grain can be kept for some time without deterioration if stored under dry, cool conditions. Often surplus dressed seed can be stored under these conditions until the following year if necessary. As a precaution, however, it is desirable to obtain a germination test of the seed if it has been stored, after dressing, for more than three months.

It should be noted that organo-mercurials are highly poisonous to humans and to animals. It is essential for men working with these substances to take precautions against inhaling the dust, and to wash their hands carefully before handling food. Surplus dressed grain should not be fed to livestock, including poultry, until it has been washed to remove the dressing. After washing, it is advisable, as a further precaution, to mix the grain with other feeding-stuffs to reduce the amount which is likely to be eaten at once.

Organo-mercurial seed dressings are marketed under various trade names, and they should be used in accordance with the instructions supplied by the manufacturer.

Some seed fungicides combine organo-mercury compounds with benzene hexachloride or other organic compounds which are useful in the prevention of wireworm attack on the crop.

The cereal diseases controlled by organo-mercury dusts include bunt of wheat and rye, covered smut of barley, loose smut and covered smut of oats, leaf stripe of barley and leaf spot or seedling blight of oats. *The loose smut diseases of wheat and barley are not controlled by seed disinfection by chemical dusts*, as the fungus in each case is present deep in the tissues of the grain, and not accessible to the chemical. These two diseases may be controlled by the hot-water treatment described later.

Organo-mercurials suitable for treatment against seed-borne diseases of sugar-beet, mangel, flax, grass and clover seeds are also available. Under some conditions, valuable results have been obtained by the use of organo-mercury dusts on seeds of beans, peas, cabbage and other vegetables.

Organo-mercurials which are effective in the form of foliage sprays have also been introduced, and, in the form of dips, organo-mercurials are used for the disinfection of seed potatoes, against dry rot and skin spot, immediately after lifting.

Sulphur Fungicides. Finely ground sulphur, colloidal sulphur and lime-sulphur (which contains polysulphides of calcium) provide effective control of some fungal diseases. They may be applied in the form of dusts or sprays and are widely used in orchards, hop gardens, vineyards, and on small fruit such as strawberries and gooseberries. They are less important on the general farm in Britain.

Certain organo-sulphur compounds are valuable fungicides. For example, the dry seed dressing *Thiram* (TMTD) is widely used for dressing flax seed to prevent seed-borne diseases. It has also proved of value as a dressing for pea seeds and other vegetable seeds. The dressed seeds are also protected from attack, in the early stages of growth, by certain soil-borne fungi which might cause the death of the seedlings.

Other organo-sulphur compounds have shown high fungicidal properties. In this group compounds commonly known as *Nabam* (Dithane D-14), *Zineb* (Dithane Z-78), *Ferbam* (Fermate) and *Ziram* (Zerlate) are used as foliage sprays.

Other Fungicides. Certain other chemicals are of value in relation to the prevention of plant diseases. Formalin, once widely used as a seed disinfectant, is valuable for the disinfection of soil and is frequently used by horticulturalists for the treatment of potting soil and seed-beds. Disinfectants containing cresylic acid are used, diluted with water, for sterilizing glasshouse soils. Dusts containing chlorinated nitrobenzene are useful for the treatment of seed potatoes to prevent dry-rot.

Many other chemicals are known to have high fungicidal properties, and research continues in an endeavour to obtain useful fungicides which are practical and cheap and have no harmful effects upon the crops or seeds to which they are applied.

Some advance in the development of *systemic* fungicides is possible in the future. A systemic fungicide is one which can be absorbed by plants and distributed, internally, throughout the plant to provide protection against an attack by fungus organisms. The term 'fungicide', in this case, is not too apt, as protection may be achieved as a result of some influence of the substance upon the physiology or the anatomy of the plant, and not by a direct lethal effect of the substance on the fungus.

Such substances must not harm the plant, or those who eat the plant, and their effect must not be short-lived. Systemic fungicides (or bactericides) which could be applied to the soil for absorption by the roots of crops would be most convenient. Such substances must not decompose quickly in the soil. Other possible means of application are as foliage sprays or, in the case of trees and other large plants, by injection.

A substance related to the plant growth-promoting substances, 2:4:6-trichlorphenoxyacetic acid, has given promising control of the chocolate spot fungus, *Botrytis fabae*, when applied to the roots of broad beans.

Another organic substance, griseofulvin (an antibiotic), has given good control of several plant diseases, including mildew of cereals (*Erysiphe graminis*) and early blight of tomato (*Alternaria solani*). Unfortunately, this substance decomposes rapidly in the soil.

Heat Treatment. Seed-borne diseases which are present deep in the tissues of the seed, and cannot be controlled by seed disinfectant dusts, may sometimes be controlled by treatment of the seed with warm water. This method is effective with loose smut of wheat and loose smut of barley, for example.

The treatment is a rather delicate operation, as the temperature of the water and the period of immersion of the seed must be such that the fungus mycelium is killed, but the embryo of the seed is not adversely affected.

In treating wheat for the prevention of loose smut, the grain is first soaked for four hours in cold water, and then immersed for ten minutes in water kept at a temperature of not less than 52° C., but not more than 54° C. Above 54° C. germination of the grain may be affected, and below 52° C. the fungal hyphae are not killed. Thus the effective margin is not very great, and considerable care is necessary in order to carry out this method of seed treatment satisfactorily. After treatment, the grain must be dried. Some seed merchants have installed the necessary equipment for the warm-water treatment of wheat and barley against loose smuts, and are able to supply treated seed.

The warm-water treatment of seed is also used for controlling canker (*Phoma lingam*) of cauliflower, broccoli and other Brassicas, and it has proved effective also for celery leaf spot (*Septoria apii* and *S. apii-graveolentis*).

Heat treatment is successful, in some cases, in controlling fungal diseases in tissues other than seeds—for example, the warm-water treatment of runners of mint has been used successfully in controlling mint rust (*Puccinia menthae*). Heat treatment for the control of certain virus diseases is dealt with later (see p. 581).

Heat treatment for the disinfection of glasshouse soil, seed-bed and potting soil is widely used by horticulturalists. In this case heat is provided in the form of steam.

Production of Disease-free Seeds. In the case of seed-borne diseases which are not easily and cheaply controlled by treatment of the seed before sowing, the best means of disease prevention is the production of seeds from healthy crops.

The various seed crop inspection schemes are designed, in part, to ensure freedom from seed-borne diseases (see Chapter VI).

In the case of the seed potato crop inspection schemes, freedom from virus diseases, which can be carried in the 'seed' tubers, is of prime importance.

Agricultural Botany

LEGISLATION IN RELATION TO PLANT DISEASES

In many countries, regulations exist which are designed (*a*) to safeguard against the introduction and spread of diseases from other countries, and (*b*) to prevent the spread of certain resident diseases within the country.

The legislation in Britain takes the form of *Orders*, issued by the Ministry of Agriculture and the Department of Agriculture for Scotland, under the general cover of *Acts* of Parliament known as *The Destructive Insects and Pests Acts, 1877-1927.*

(*a*) In order to prevent the introduction and spread of diseases from abroad, the *Importation of Plants Order, 1947*, has as its purpose the prevention of importation of unhealthy plants or parts of plants. *The Importation of Forest Trees (Prohibition Order), 1949*, is an attempt to prevent the introduction of certain diseases of forest trees.

(*b*) Should parasites gain access to the country, the *Destructive Insects and Pests Order, 1933*, may be brought into action. This order permits steps to be taken to prevent the spread of non-indigenous pests and parasitic diseases which may be found in the country.

(*c*) Orders designed to prevent the spread of diseases already established in the country are:

The Sale of Diseased Plants Orders, 1927-52, which make it an offence to sell, or to offer for sale, plants substantially affected by certain diseases and pests (the diseases include club root of Brassicas, American gooseberry mildew and fruit tree cankers), or potato tubers or narcissus plants or bulbs which are *visibly* unfit for planting because of any disease or pest attack.

The Wart Disease of Potatoes Order, 1941 (see p. 534).

The Silver Leaf Order, 1923, relating to the silver-leaf disease of apple and plum trees.

The Progressive Verticillium Wilt of Hops Order, 1947.

The Sale of Strawberry Plants and Blackcurrant Bushes Order, 1946, which prohibits the sale of strawberry runners and blackcurrant bushes (except under licence) unless they are of stocks which have been certified ('certified' plants are produced under health certification schemes).

INTERNATIONAL CO-OPERATION IN THE CONTROL OF PLANT DISEASES*

The need for international co-operation in combating plant diseases and pests has long been realized, and various efforts have been made toward that end. A major advance in this field was the signing, in 1951, of the International Plant Protection Convention, which was sponsored by the Food and Agriculture Organization of United Nations (F.A.O.).

The Convention aims at the regulation, on phytosanitary grounds of the movement of plants and plant products from one country to another. In the Convention provision was made for regional organizations to co-ordinate plant disease and pest control activities between countries in the same geographical area. The European Plant Protection Organization (E.P.P.O.), which had come into being a little earlier, was recognized by F.A.O. for this purpose.

* Moore, W. C., 'The Development of International Co-operation in Crop Protection', *Ann. Appl. Biol.*, **42**, 67-72, 1955 and Wilkins, V. E., 'International Co-operation in Action', *Ann. Appl. Biol.*, **42**, 73-5, 1955.

Chapter XXIII

DISEASES CAUSED BY PHYCOMYCETES

(Vegetative mycelium aseptate or absent. Sporangia usually produced.)

CLUB-ROOT OF BRASSICAS, *Plasmodiophora brassicae* Woron.

The fungus which causes the disease club-root, or finger and toe, does not possess a mycelium, but consists of a naked mass of protoplasm which possesses many nuclei (a *plasmodium*).

Plasmodiophora brassicae attacks a wide range of species within the family Cruciferae. The crops most commonly affected are turnip, swede, rape,

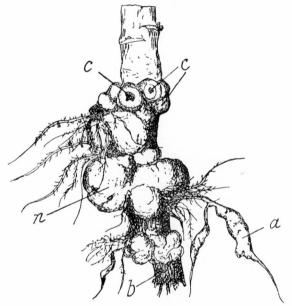

FIG. 229. Club root on cabbage. *a*, infected lateral root. *b*, decaying portion of primary root. *n*, clubbed area of main root. *c*, galls caused by the root gall weevil, cut open to show hollow interior. (Percival.)

cabbage, Brussels sprout and mustard. Weed species, including charlock, wild radish and shepherd's purse, may also be attacked. The disease is favoured by acid soil conditions, and is therefore more common on soils in which the lime content is low.

Symptoms and Cause. Plants are usually stunted and may look sickly. Where early infection occurs the plants may die when young, but some persist in a weakened condition. Wilting, and yellowing of the foliage, are often the first symptoms noticed, but when these are observed the disease has often reached an advanced stage in the roots.

527

When infected plants are dug up, the roots are found to be swollen and deformed. When the swelling is largely confined to the tap-root, which has become club-like, the disease is aptly termed 'club-root'. When lateral roots show most swelling the name *finger and toe* is often applied to the disease.

It should be noted that rounded, gall-like swellings on the roots and stem bases of Cruciferous plants may be caused by the root gall weevil, a common pest. These swellings can be distinguished by the fact that when cut across they are found to be hollow, and they may still contain a small white larva of the weevil.

When the swollen roots of club-root-infected plants are cut across, the tissues are seen to have a mottled or marbled appearance. A microscope section will show that the swelling of the root is due to division and enlargement of many of the parenchyma cells to form masses of so-called *giant cells*. These giant cells contain the plasmodia of the fungus. The plasmodia eventually divide to produce large numbers of resting spores, within the giant cells. When the diseased tissues decay and disintegrate the resting spores eventually pass into the soil. In the soil the spores may germinate immediately, but some remain dormant and still capable of germination for from three to six years.

On germination each resting spore produces a single zoospore which possesses two unequal flagella, by means of which it may move about in

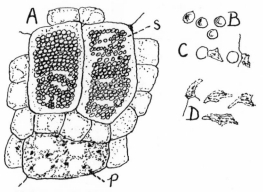

FIG. 230. Club root; A, Section of clubbed tissue: *p*, plasmodium in a giant cell *s* spores. C, spores releasing a single zoospore. D, zoospores changed into myxamoebae.

the soil water. After a time the flagella disappear, and the spore moves in an amoeboid manner (i.e. the protoplasm flows along over the surface of soil particles or roots); it is then known as a *myxamoeba*. Many of the amoeboid spores perish, but some which contact roots of suitable cruciferous plants penetrate, probably via root hairs, into the cortical cells of the root. In the root cells the fungus grows rapidly, producing a plasmodium which penetrates surrounding cells. The infected cells and the neighbouring cells divide and grow rapidly to produce the gall-like deformities of the roots.

The fungus has been found to penetrate the roots of certain non-cruciferous plants, but clubbed roots are not developed and the fungus does not seem to reach the resting stage.

Control Measures

1. The most important step toward the eradication of club-root from land in which it has become established is the application of lime. The causal fungus is favoured by acid soil conditions, and application of lime renders conditions less favourable for its development and persistence. The lime should be applied soon after the removal of an infected crop and well worked into the soil. The best forms of lime for this purpose are freshly slaked burnt lime, hydrated lime or quicklime which, applied in a finely divided state, are more effective than chalk, ground limestone or carbonate of lime.

In soil which is heavily contaminated with the disease organisms, even very heavy applications of lime may not be effective, and in addition such heavy dressings may result in other troubles (see pp. 600, 601).

2. The crop should be fed to livestock in such a way as to avoid carrying the disease to other fields. Feed the crop on the spot or on permanent grassland. Manure produced by animals which have fed on the diseased plants should be used for permanent grassland.

3. Where crops such as cabbage, cauliflower, etc., are to be grown from transplanted plants, only healthy plants should be used. Any purchased plants should be obtained from a reliable source. Under the *Sale of Diseased Plants (Amendment) Order, 1941*, plants which are substantially affected by this disease may not be sold for planting purposes.

4. Temporary protection of a crop grown from transplants may be obtained by treatment of the roots of the plants with calomel (mercurous chloride). For treatment of a large number of plants a calomel paste is most suitable. This can be prepared by mixing 1 lb. of 4 per cent. calomel dust with $\frac{1}{3}$ pint of water. This amount is sufficient for treating 100 plants. The mixing should be done in a wooden or earthenware container. The roots are dipped in the paste and the plants then planted out. Another method, suitable for gardeners, is to sprinkle a teaspoonful of the dust around in each dibble hole as the plants are planted out.

There are also some organic fungicides on the market which are claimed to be effective in the control of club-root.

5. As living spores may persist in the soil for several years, the period varying according to environmental conditions, it is advisable to avoid growing susceptible crops on infected land for as long a period as possible. During this period every effort should be made to keep down cruciferous weeds which may act as hosts for the disease organism and, if uncontrolled, enable it to persist indefinitely.

6. As the presence of excessive moisture in the soil appears to encourage infection, attention to the drainage of the land may be important.

7. Immunity to club-root has not been found among the Brassicas commonly grown on farms, but a few varieties of swedes and turnips possess a considerable degree of resistance. Notable among these are the swede varieties produced in Denmark known as *Bangholm Studsgaard* and *Bangholm Herning*. Resistant varieties of turnip are the Aberdeenshire purple-top variety *The Bruce* and the green-top variety *Wallace*. On healthy land in Britain native strains of swede are usually grown, as they give better yields here than the Danish resistant varieties.

Marrow-stem kale is normally fairly resistant, as are some strains of kohlrabi, but there are no varieties of cabbage, cauliflower, broccoli or Brussels sprout which show much resistance.

POWDERY SCAB OF POTATOES, *Spongospora subterranea* (Wallr.) Lagerh.

The fungus which causes this disease, *Spongospora subterranea*, like the club-root fungus, produces a plasmodium and no hyphae are developed.

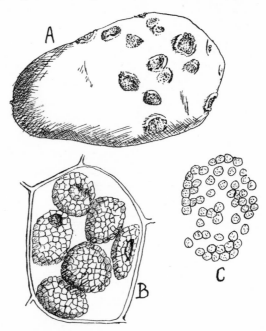

Fig. 231. Powdery scab of potato. A, infected tuber. B, cell of scabbed tissue containing spore balls. C, spore ball breaking up into individual spores.

The disease is not of great economic importance in Britain, but severe attacks occur at times, particularly in the west and north of the country. It is always more severe in a wet season and in wet soils.

Symptoms and Cause. The fungus attacks the underground parts of the potato plant, causing small warty nodules on the roots and typical powdery scabs on the tubers. Before the scabs develop on the tubers more or less circular pimples form, and as the tubers mature the skin over the pimples cracks and tears, exposing the light, powdery mass forming the scab. A rim of skin often remains around the perimeter of the scab. The scabs may be isolated or crowded together. The pimples are caused by the rapid division of cells infected by the plasmodium of the fungus. After a time the plasmodium changes to produce within the infected cells *spore-balls*, which consist of large numbers of spores loosely packed into roughly spherical aggregates

As the scabs mature the infected cells disintegrate, and the spore-balls are released as a snuff-like powder. Some spore-balls are shed into the soil, and some remain on the tubers. Thus the disease may be soil-borne or 'seed'-borne.

The spores may lie dormant until the following spring. They eventually burst, each spore releasing a single, naked, amoeboid spore which is able to move about in the soil. Young tubers are infected, probably through the lenticels, and new plasmodia develop in the surface tissues beneath the skin of the tuber. The resting spores may remain dormant for three years or more, so that there is danger of infection of any potato crop grown within that period. Infected tubers used as 'seed' may introduce the disease to fresh land.

The fungus may form small galls on the roots of tomato plants. It does not attack any native weeds, but infection of the roots of some foreign weed species of *Solanum* has been achieved experimentally.

Two other forms of the disease have been described, but they are not often encountered: the *canker* form in which the tubers are usually malformed and the tissues are deeply attacked, cankerous wounds appear and large numbers of spore-balls are released; the *tumour* form, which may develop on tubers in the clamp and takes the form of warty tumours and may be confused with wart disease. The tumours are, however, usually smoother and less corrugated on the surface, and they eventually collapse, leaving a raised scar.

Control Measures

1. As the fungus can survive in the soil for three years or more, potatoes should be kept off an infected field for at least four years.

2. Moisture encourages the disease, therefore improvement of drainage may assist in its control.

3. If infected land must be used for potatoes, the amount of disease in the soil can be greatly reduced by the application of sulphur to the soil, at the rate of from 3-6 cwt. per acre.

4. Infected tubers should be boiled before being fed to pigs, in order to avoid the risk of living spores being returned to the land in the manure. Tubers should not be thrown on manure and compost heaps for the same reason.

5. Infected 'seed' should not be planted. The sale of seed substantially attacked is prohibited under the *Sale of Diseased Plants Orders, 1927-52*.

6. There are no varieties of potato which are very resistant to this disease.

WART DISEASE OF POTATOES, *Synchytrium endobioticum* (Schilb.) Perc.

This disease at one time provided a serious threat to potato-growers in Great Britain, but in modern times, as a result of legislative control under the *Destructive Insects and Pests Acts* and the breeding and increased use of immune varieties, it is no longer of much economic importance.

The disease was first recorded in Hungary in 1896, but it is possible that it existed in Britain and elsewhere before that date. Outbreaks of the disease have occurred in every county of England and Wales, but

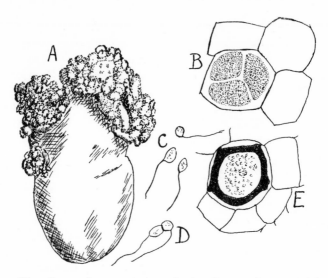

FIG. 232. Wart disease of potato. A, warted tuber. B, wart tissue containing a sorus showing 3 summer sporangia. C, zoospores. D, zoospores conjugating. E, wart tissue containing a thick-walled winter sporangium.

losses have been most serious in the north-west and the west Midlands, and in south and mid-Scotland.

The realization of the potentialities of the disease led to the search for immune varieties which took place in Britain in the early years of the twentieth century, and eventually to the breeding of modern immune varieties (see p. 75).

The disease does not attack any species other than potato under natural conditions, but several other members of the family Solanaceae, such as tomato, woody nightshade, black nightshade and henbane, have been infected experimentally.

Symptoms and Cause. The disease attacks the tubers and sometimes also the rhizomes and stems of the potato plant in the field, but it does not appear to attack the roots.

The warts normally appear on the tubers during the growing season, but they may develop during storage. They appear as grey-brown or brownish-black excrescences, with an irregular surface like lumps of cauliflower. They normally grow out from the eyes, but a badly diseased tuber may be warted all over. The warts are somewhat soft, and later they turn black and rot, leaving infected material in the soil. Some tubers on an infected plant may not be affected.

Infected tubers which develop warts after clamping may pass on the disease to other tubers in contact with them if the conditions inside the clamp are moist.

The fungus *Synchytrium endobioticum* does not form a mycelium. The presence of the fungus within infected cells of a tuber causes adjacent cells to divide abnormally, thus producing warts. Within infected cells during the summer so-called *summer sporangia* are formed in groups, or *sori*. These sporangia are thin-walled, and when the walls rupture they liberate into the soil masses of *zoospores*, each bearing a single flagellum. The zoospores, which are able to move about in the soil water, infect other tubers, penetrating the epidermis of the eyes. Repeated crops of summer sporangia, which liberate zoospores, are produced during the summer as further infections develop.

As the season advances some of the zoospores in the soil unite in pairs. Each cell so produced, on infecting potato tissues, ultimately gives rise to a thick-walled *resting sporangium*. Most resting sporangia are produced toward the autumn, but both summer sporangia and resting sporangia may be found in the same wart tissue, the former produced as a result of infection by single zoospores and the latter as a result of infection by the cells produced by the primitive sexual fusion of pairs of zoospores.

Resting sporangia are liberated into the soil, by the rotting of the wart tissue, and here they may remain dormant for many years. Persistence of these resting sporangia in the soil for from nine to twelve years has been recorded, and it is possible that they may persist considerably longer under some conditions.

When viable sporangia are present in the soil, any non-immune variety of potato, which may be planted, may be infected as a result of the germination of the resting sporangia. On germination the sporangia burst open releasing numerous zoospores which may then infect the new crop and thus start the life cycle over again.

Resting sporangia in the soil may be spread from field to field by soil adhering to the feet of humans, animals or birds, or to tractors, carts, implements, etc.

Control Measures

The modern means of prevention of this disease is to grow immune varieties. The majority of modern varieties are immune to strains of the fungus normally found in Britain. Immunity in most cases is due to hypersensitivity which causes infected cells to die quickly, and thus prevent further development of the fungus.

A few non-immune varieties are still in cultivation, the best known being the popular quality potato King Edward. Others in this group are Arran Chief, British Queen, Duke of York, Eclipse, Epicure, Ninety-fold, Sharpe's Express and Up-to-date.

Although the breeding of immune varieties appears to have solved the problem of wart disease, continuous vigilance is necessary, as many varieties regarded as immune to wart disease are now known to have succumbed to new races of *Synchytrium endobioticum*. These races are not yet established in Britain, but if such races become common wart disease may again become a serious problem.

The *Wart Disease of Potatoes Order, 1941*, provides for certain action in the event of an outbreak of the disease. The main requirements of the order are:

1. The occupier of land on which wart disease appears must report the outbreak to the Ministry of Agriculture.

2. Diseased tubers must be burnt or, if fed to pigs, must be boiled thoroughly. Other diseased parts of plants must be burnt.

3. Visibly diseased tubers may not be sold for any purpose, and tubers from diseased crops may not be sold for seed purposes.

4. Only approved immune varieties may be planted on land on which the disease has occurred at any time.

Note. Woody proliferations closely resembling wart disease may sometimes be formed on tubers on which the eyes have been killed through some cause or other. These usually occur at the heel end of the tuber.

POTATO BLIGHT, *Phytophthora infestans* (Mont) de Bary

Potato blight is one of the most destructive plant diseases in Britain. It was first recorded in Europe in 1840. In 1845-6 its attack was so severe that considerable losses of crops occurred in European countries and famine resulted in Ireland, where potatoes were the chief food of the poor; there 1,000,000 died and 1,500,000 emigrated.

The disease still occurs frequently, the intensity of attack varying from season to season, and normally being less severe in dry summers. In damp, muggy weather the disease usually spreads rapidly. The intensity of attack also varies with varieties of potato. For example, King Edward suffers severely and the tops are usually killed relatively rapidly, whilst with Majestic under similar conditions the disease progresses less rapidly, and Pentland Dell shows considerable resistance to attack.

The popular impression that the tops may be killed, in very susceptible varieties, almost overnight is, however, far from correct. In the variety King Edward, in a season which was favourable for the spread of blight, Cox* found that two weeks passed between the first observation of blight in a particular crop and the presence of 5 per cent. blight on the haulm, after that stage, death of the haulm proceeded much more rapidly (fig. 233).

The killing of the haulm cuts down photosynthesis and therefore

* Cox, A. E., 'Effect of Blight on Yields of Maincrop Potatoes', *Agriculture*, LXII, 1955, 138-41.

reduces the yield of tubers. It has been suggested that useful tuber growth ceases when the amount of damage to the haulm has reached 75 per cent.

Symptoms and Cause. Infected plants exhibit dark brown, necrotic patches on the leaves. On the underside of the leaves a white mould will be seen around the borders of the necrotic areas. Under conditions favourable for the development of the disease the patches spread, until the whole of the leaf is killed, and the stem may also die. Necrosis usually starts at the tips and edges of the leaflets; the infected areas first become dark green and water-soaked before necrosis develops.

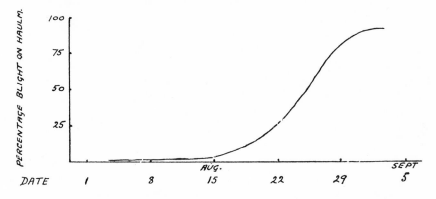

Fig. 233. Progress of blight in an unsprayed crop of King Edwards, near Colchester, 1954. After Cox, from *Agriculture* by permission of the Controller of H.M. Stationery Office.

The fungus *Phytophthora infestans* is present in infected leaves, in the form of an intercellular mycelium which spreads among the internal tissues of the leaf, causing infected areas ultimately to die. The fungus produces hyphae which grow out through the stomata of the leaf to form branched sporangiophores. Lemon-shaped sporangia are produced singly, either terminally or laterally, on the branches of the sporangiophores. These sporangia are carried to other plants, mainly by air currents or rain splashes, where they cause new infections.

Normally under moist conditions the sporangia burst to liberate a small number of zoospores, each possessing two flagella. By means of their flagella the zoospores propel themselves over the moist surfaces of potato leaves. Eventually they lose their flagella and put out germ tubes, which penetrate into the leaf. Under unfavourable conditions the sporangium may not liberate zoospores, but may germinate directly producing a germ tube which can penetrate the leaf, causing infection. In this case the sporangium behaves as a conidium.

Infection of the leaf can take place through any part of the epidermis, directly through the cuticle and epidermis or via the stomata. When the germ tubes have penetrated into the leaf they grow to produce a mycelium, with haustoria penetrating the leaf cells. The infected cells soon die and the mycelium spreads into fresh tissue. Once the disease has appeared in a crop it soon progresses through the crop if the weather is damp and muggy.

The fungus does not grow down within the plant to infect the tubers. Tuber infection is brought about by spores which fall from the leaves and are washed into the soil by rain, or, alternatively, the tubers may be infected at lifting time if the crop is lifted when the disease is still

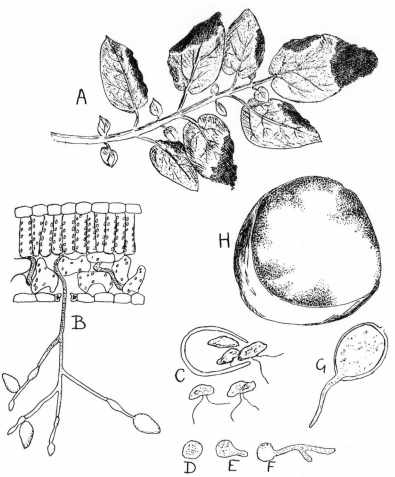

Fig. 234. Potato blight. A, underside of an infected leaf. B, section of a portion of a potato leaf showing a sporangiophore growing out through a stoma. C, sporangium releasing zoospores. D, E, F, stages in the germination of a zoospore. G, sporangium behaving as a conidium and producing a germ tube. H, section through an infected tuber.

active on the haulm. The tubers are infected through the eyes, lenticels or wounds, and the mycelium develops in the tissue just below the skin, gradually spreading inwards to the deeper tissues of the tuber. The infected cells are killed and turn brown. The discoloured areas, if intensive, are visible through the skin. Infected tubers remain firm unless secondary rots, due to invasion by other fungi and bacteria, occur.

When infected tubers are stored, the disease may progress within them, but it does not normally spread to healthy tubers during storage to any appreciable extent if they are stored dry and in well-ventilated clamps. If the atmosphere of the clamp is damp, however, secondary infections by other organisms, fungi and bacteria, often leads to a wet-rot of the blighted tubers. When such rotting occurs, the temperature inside the clamp rises and very severe rotting develops. If the bulk of the tubers have been infected before clamping the secondary wet-rots may cause the clamp to collapse.

The disease persists over winter in infected tubers, and these provide the source of infection for the succeeding crop. Blighted tubers left in the ground ('ground-keepers') will give rise to blighted shoots. Diseased tubers left around clamps, or blighted tubers present in the 'seed' planted for the new crop, may also be responsible for the start of a new attack. Seed tubers which are blighted usually sprout prematurely and produce weak sprouts. Shoots produced from tubers from any of the above sources will give rise to crops of spores early in the summer; these may carry the disease to the new potato crop. There is little evidence that the fungus normally persists in the soil in the form of mycelium or resting spores. Although oospore formation has been recorded, it has not been demonstrated that this is a regular feature in the life cycle of the fungus in the field.

The conditions under which blight is likely to spread in the field are now known, and it is possible to issue blight warnings indicating the probability of the occurrence of the disease. Such warnings are sent out by the Ministry of Agriculture through the British Broadcasting Corporation and the Press.

Blight is most likely to develop when the temperature is not less than 50° F. (10° C.) and the humidity is high (above 75 per cent.) for at least two successive days (i.e. forty-eight hours).

Control Measures

1. To protect the crop against infection, spray with a copper spray, such as Bordeaux mixture or one of the approved proprietary sprays. Where it is difficult to obtain a sufficient supply of water, low-volume spraying with cuprous oxide sprays or dusting with fungicides containing copper compounds can be satisfactory; in either case lighter machinery can be used than is needed for high-volume spraying of ordinary copper sprays, and consequently less damage to the crop is likely.

The dusts are not quite so effective as wet sprays, as they wash off readily if heavy rain arrives soon after dusting, and also it is more difficult to obtain a complete coverage of the haulm.

Machines which will produce jets of spray both above and below the foliage are usually recommended, so that both sides of the leaves may be protected by the fungicide. Spraying should be done when the weather is as dry as possible, so that the spray may dry and form a protective

s 537

covering. It should not be done in hot sunshine. Dusting should be done early in the day, when dew is still on the leaves, to dissolve the dust.

In most districts only main crops are sprayed, but in the west second earlies may also benefit from spraying. Normally, spraying should commence before the disease has arrived on a crop, but a crop which has just begun to show symptoms on a few plants, if sprayed immediately, may be saved from rapid spread of the disease.

For efficient protection, two applications of spray are normally necessary, the second about three weeks after the first, but in the south-west of England a third spraying may be advisable in seasons when blight is prevalent. Where copper dusts are used, four or more dustings at fortnightly intervals may be necessary.

In inland districts and in the north, where blight attacks later and is usually less severe, routine spraying may not be economic. In areas where severe attacks occur early in the season, yield increases of around 2-3 tons of healthy tubers per acre may frequently result from the preservation of the green foliage by spraying. Such gains over unsprayed crops may be obtained in seasons when 75 per cent. of the haulm would be killed by blight early in the season (see above). In seasons in which the 75 per cent. stage is not reached until near the end of the growing season any possible gain in yield would be offset by a loss due to damage to the foliage caused by spraying machinery passing through the crop. Thus in seasons when blight attacks early, spraying is an economic proposition. When blight does not become epidemic until late in the season, protective spraying is not economic. Thus in areas where routine spraying is normally practised the most economic method may be to give a first spraying before the plants meet in the rows and to delay subsequent spraying until blight warnings are given or the disease is known to be in the district.

2. The crop should be earthed-up efficiently, so that tubers are well covered with soil and not near the surface, where they may be readily infected. A steep firm ridge, which is not hollow at the base of the haulm, is desirable.

3. If a crop is attacked by blight, infection of the tubers is most likely to occur when spores are scattered as the crop is lifted. Digging should be delayed until the haulm has been quite dead for a fortnight, during which time the spores will perish and little harm should result.

Where lifting cannot be delayed, and when the haulm does not die off early, it is extremely advisable to 'burn off' the tops by means of a chemical spray, and so kill the spores. A solution of 10 to 15 per cent. sulphuric acid (brown oil of vitriol, B.O.V.) at 100 gall. per acre is most effective for this purpose. Tar-acid compounds, proprietary tar-oil sprays, and some newer herbicides such as diquat, may also be used. After destruction of the haulm with sulphuric acid, lifting of the crop should be delayed for at least a week, and longer delays are advised by the manufacturers of some chemical sprays. Burning-off the haulm makes the lifting of the crop an easier operation, which is an additional advantage. Machines designed for shredding the haulm in order to facilitate lifting of the crop are useful for the destruction of blighted haulm, providing the digging is delayed for at least two weeks after shredding in order to allow the haulm and the spores to die.

On small areas—in gardens, for example—the tops could be cut off and removed some days before the crop is dug.

4. All diseased haulm and diseased tubers should be destroyed. It is important that diseased tubers should not remain on the site of a clamp or riddle until the following season, when they may provide a source of new infection of crops.

5. Most probably in the future the best means of avoiding blight will be to grow resistant or immune varieties. The problem of breeding blight-resistant varieties is complicated by the existence of various races of *Phytophthora infestans*. Some varieties which are highly resistant to the common races have been produced by plant-breeders, but these have shown other defects which detract from their value to the commercial grower. Thus, the problem still remains to obtain sufficient varieties of high quality possessing the power to resist blight.

DOWNY MILDEW OF SUGAR-BEET, *Peronospora farinosa* (Fr.) Fr. (*P. schachtii* Fuckel)

In the genus *Peronospora* the sporangia do not produce zoospores, but germinate to produce a germ tube, thus they function as conidia.

Downy mildew is fairly common on sugar-beet in the Midlands and East Anglia, but it is rarer in the north of the British Isles. It attacks also the related crops, mangel, garden-beet, and sea-kale beet; wild beet (*Beta maritima*) also is very susceptible. The related weed fat hen (*Chenopodium album*) suffers from a downy mildew, but this does not infect the foregoing plants, nor is the downy mildew of beet infectious to fat hen.

Damp weather favours the spread of the disease. It is usually first noticed after singling the crop, but younger seedlings may be attacked.

Symptoms and Cause. The fungus develops in the tissues of the parts of the plant above ground, usually infecting the growing point and the young leaves. The infected leaves are thickened, and become puckered and brittle. Older leaves may also be infected, sometimes only the lower parts of the leaf showing signs of the disease. The infected leaves become covered with a downy growth of the fungus, which gives them a purplish and later a buff-grey colour. Conidia are produced singly on branched hyphae arising from this downy mould. Mild and humid conditions favour the production of conidia, which are usually more abundant on the underside of the leaf.

The infected leaves eventually die, and necrosis may spread down from them to the crown of the beet, killing the plant. Usually, however, further leaves develop from axillary buds. When the middle leaves and the growing point have been killed, and necrosis of the central part of the crown has occurred, the condition may be confused with heart-rot (see p. 601). The older leaves which were not infected early in the season may become yellow, giving an appearance which may be confused with virus yellows disease (p. 593).

The disease is spread in the field by conidia, and plants at various stages of disease may be seen in a single crop during the summer. Early infection may cause losses in yield of washed roots of around 2 tons per acre, and a reduction of 1 to 2 per cent. in sugar content. Infected plants which still retain their leaves at lifting time are difficult to pull, because the leaf stalks are brittle and break easily.

In beets grown for seed the disease may kill the plant, or cause a stunting of the flowering shoots; many flowers develop abnormally and fail to produce seed.

Resting spores (*oospores*) may be formed in diseased tissues, but their importance in carrying over the disease from one season to the next is doubted.

The chief source of infection appears to be infected roots or plants of susceptible crops which have been left lying about from the previous year. Near the coast infection may spread from the wild beet. As infected plants begin to sprout in the spring conidia are rapidly produced, and may then infect the new season's crop.

Another host which may carry the fungus over the winter is the steckling crop, of any of the susceptible group, being grown for seed production. For example, a crop of stecklings of sugar-beet near an infected root crop may become diseased. These stecklings, when planted out in the following spring, become a source of infection for the new root crops in the neighbourhood.

Control

1. Avoid, as far as possible, leaving roots around the farm from one season to the next.

2. It is best to raise steckling crops in districts remote from the commercial root crops, so that the stecklings do not become infected from the root crop, and are therefore healthy when brought to the seed-growing districts of East Anglia and the east Midlands for planting out for seed production.

This system is also valuable in attempting to reduce the incidence of virus diseases of sugar-beet (see p. 595).

Where stecklings are raised in the root-growing areas, infection of the plants may be prevented by repeated sprayings with Bordeaux mixture. Any stecklings which show the disease at transplanting time should be destroyed. If the disease appears later in odd stecklings, they should be cut down and buried on the spot. Diseased plants should not be carried from the field, as this involves the risk of scattering spores in the crop.

DOWNY MILDEW OF BRASSICAS, ETC., *Peronospora parasitica* (Fr.) Tul.

This disease attacks Brassicas, wallflowers and many other cultivated and wild plants of the order Cruciferae.

The fungus appears as a greyish-white mould, which produces conidia, found on the leaves of Brassicas especially on the underside. It may kill the leaves. It may be found on old adult leaves, and it may attack the curds of cauliflowers, but the disease is most troublesome in connection with young Brassicas raised in frames. Very moist conditions favour the disease. Protection can be obtained by dusting the plants with lime-sulphur after watering. Spraying young plants before infection with Bordeaux mixture or a suitable organic fungicide also gives good results. After an attack, all crop refuse which may contain oospores should be destroyed, and soil in frames should be disinfected before further use. Cruciferous weeds must also be controlled.

Diseases Caused by Phycomycetes

DOWNY MILDEW OF HOP, *Pseudoperonospora humuli* (Miyabe & Tak.) G. W. Wilson

Although close to *Peronospora*, the genus *Pseudoperonospora* differs in producing sporangia which give rise to zoospores.

In England this disease is serious only in seasons when July and August are abnormally wet.

Early infection of the hop cones renders them of little use for brewing, and many are shed prematurely. Late infection causes little damage, and has little effect on their value for brewing.

The fungus persists in the rootstock of infected plants of both wild and cultivated hops, infecting the new shoots in successive years.

Symptoms and Cause. From infected root-stocks, stunted and thickened shoots, known as 'basal spikes', arise in the spring. They bear small, brittle leaves

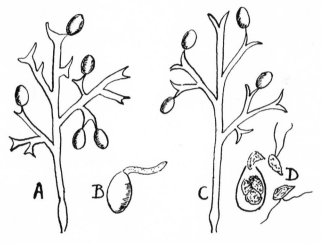

FIG. 235. A, conidiophore of *Peronospora farinosa* × 260. B, conidium germinating. C, sporangiophore of *Pseudoperonospora humuli.* × 140. D, sporangium releasing zoospores.

close together. The upper surface of the leaves is silvery-grey in appearance, and on the undersurface branched sporangiophores grow out through the stomata. The mass of sporangiophores is violet-black in colour. Later in the season the apical portions of shoots several feet high may show similar symptoms ('terminal spikes'). Lateral buds on tall bines may also be infected and produce 'lateral spikes'.

The sporangia are oval in shape. If they fall on a moist surface, they give rise to four to twelve zoospores, each with two flagella. Zoospores spread the disease rapidly in a wet season, infecting leaves and cones. On the leaves brown spots are produced, whilst the cones turn brown and may become deformed or be shed. Infected leaves turn brown and shrivel early.

Oospores are formed in the autumn in infected tissues. They are spherical, smooth and light brown in colour. The oospores persist through the winter in dead leaves, stems and cone scales. In the spring they may germinate to produce sporangiophores, which bear large sporangia producing zoospores which can infect new growth. Some oospores may remain dormant in the soil for several years.

Control Measures

1. Deformed, infected spikes should be cut off and destroyed, and after an attack all diseased material should be removed and burnt. As the disease may spread from wild hops, these should be eliminated in the vicinity of hop gardens.

2. Spraying with Bordeaux mixture, or an appropriate proprietary copper spray, provides good protection.*

3. Potash is said to increase resistance to the disease, and phosphates and nitrogenous fertilizers to favour the disease.

4. There are no immune varieties, but some resistance is shown by some varieties such as Sunshine, Fillpocket, and some strains of Fuggle.

5. Care should be taken to ensure that new sets are not obtained from an infected garden.

* For details of spraying programme, see *Diseases of Fruit and Hops*, by H. Wormald.

Chapter XXIV

DISEASES CAUSED BY ASCOMYCETES

(Mycelium usually profuse and septate, Asci formed.)

POWDERY MILDEW OF CEREALS AND GRASSES, *Erysiphe graminis* DC

This disease is found on wheat, barley, oats and rye, and on most grasses. There are a number of specialised races of the causal fungus each usually restricted to its own host species so that, for example, a badly infected crop of wheat would be unlikely to infect a neighbouring barley or oat crop.

Although the cereal varieties show various degrees of resistance, there are no varieties which are immune to the disease.

Symptoms and Cause. On wheat, greyish-white mats of mycelium appear on the lower leaf sheaths and on the leaf blades. In some seasons they may also be seen on the chaff. The mats may be small, or the infected plants may be extensively covered by the fungus and severely infected leaves may die early. Later the mats turn brown.

The disease may become extensive in a crop at any time between May and August, but it may frequently be found affecting winter wheat in the seedling stage in late autumn and early winter, especially in a mild season. Because severe early attacks kill the leaves, and so cut down photosynthesis, the growth of the crop is restricted and the yield of grain considerably reduced. The grain may also be badly shrunken. When crops are attacked later in the season the disease may not produce any marked effect on the appearance of the grain and the crop may yield well.

The mycelium grows on the surface, sending haustoria into the epidermis. It does not penetrate into the inner tissues of the host.

If a little of the mould is examined under the microscope early in the season, whilst it is still whitish in colour, numerous chains of conidia, budded off from branches of the mycelium, will be observed. These conidia spread the infection in the crop. The disease spreads most rapidly under dry, rather than wet, conditions, although some moisture is needed for the germination of the conidia, which bring about the actual infection.

Later, when the mats have become dark in colour, relatively large black cleistocarps (or perithecia) are found resting among the hyphae of the mycelium. The cleistocarps possess short appendages. Each cleistocarp contains from nine to thirty asci. Cleistocarps may overwinter in remains of the crop, but most of them burst open in the autumn, liberating their asci. Each ascus produces eight oval ascospores, which may develop whilst the asci are still contained in the cleistocarp or later, after the asci are released. The ascospores may carry the disease to the young plants

543

of the autumn-sown crops and to self-sown wheat plants (in barley it is doubtful whether the asci play any part in the spread of the disease).

In the spring mats of mycelium are present on the winter wheat and on self-sown plants which have remained over winter. From these, conidia spread the disease to other crops. This is probably the main means of dissemination of the disease in the spring, rather than by over-wintering cleistocarps. In a mild winter, conidia produced in the autumn

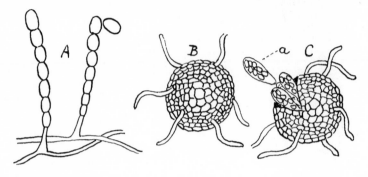

FIG. 236. Powdery mildew of cereals. A, conidia. B, a cleistocarp. C, cleistocarp bursting and releasing the asci: *a*, ascus.

may remain alive on winter crops and self-sown plants in sheltered places, and help to spread the disease in the spring.

The disease is usually most severe when the spring and early summer are dry, after a mild winter which has enabled the disease to persist and develop. In a wet spring, crops usually grow away from the disease, and suffer little harm, but a spring-sown crop growing alongside an infected winter crop may suffer severely, as plants are attacked when still quite small.

A thick crop, resulting from heavy seeding or excessive use of nitrogenous fertilizers, is liable to suffer severely.

Control Measures

1. Avoid too heavy seed rates.

2. Avoid excessive use of nitrogenous fertilizers.

3. Where a crop is thick, thorough harrowing or grazing by sheep in the spring may help.

4. Early ploughing of stubble, where infected self-sown plants may be present, will reduce sources of infection.

5. Early sowing of spring-sown cereals considerably reduces losses through mildew.

6. Repeated spraying with lime sulphur provides effective protection, but this is not practicable on the farm scale owing to mechanical damage to the crop.

7. Breeding for resistance to this disease is making good progress and, when available, resistant varieties may be sown.

Diseases Caused by Ascomycetes

POWDERY MILDEW OF HOP (OR HOP MOULD), *Sphaerotheca humuli* (DC) Burr.

In some seasons powdery mildew, which affects the leaves and young cones of the hop, causes serious losses. The infected cones are rendered useless for brewing.

Symptoms and Cause. The mildew is first seen in May or June on the surface of young leaves and stems. White patches of mycelium appear and become powdery as masses of conidia are produced. The mycelium is superficial, penetrating only into the epidermal cells.

Conidia are produced in chains. They are spread by wind and rain splashes, and produce secondary infections of leaves and young flowers.

The young female flowers are infected at the 'burr' stage. Conidia fall on to the stigmas, and hyphae grow from them into the flower tissues. Further development of the flower may be prevented or deformed cones produced. Infection of the cones can also occur through the scales, but where the scales only are infected, further development of the flowers is not prevented.

The disease spreads most rapidly under moist, warm weather conditions.

Later, black cleistocarps with long brown appendages are formed on the leaves and cones. At this stage the disease is known as 'red mould', owing to the foxy-red discoloration of the scales. The cleistocarps are thick-walled, and each contains a single elliptical ascus containing eight elliptical ascospores. The cleistocarps pass the winter on old bines, or in fallen leaves or cone scales. In the spring the ascospores, which are ejected violently into the air, may infect the new growth of the bines. Leaf spots may appear about five days after infection in a wet season, whilst, under dry conditions, three weeks may elapse before spotting appears. The spots are at first small, raised blisters which, within a day or so, give rise to the patches of mycelium on which conidia are formed.

Control Measures. Considerable control is usually obtained by dusting the bines with sulphur, commencing early in May, to provide protection against infection by ascospores, and repeating dustings at fortnightly intervals until the hops are nearly mature. Any infected lower leaves should be stripped off and destroyed to reduce the risk of further spread of the disease.

Badly mildewed material should be removed and burnt and wild hops growing in the vicinity of hop gardens eradicated.

Avoid excessive applications of nitrogenous fertilizers, as these encourage sappy growth which is more liable to become diseased.

Some varieties, such as Sunshine, are immune to the disease.

CLOVER ROT, *Sclerotinia trifoliorum* Erikss.

This disease most frequently attacks broad red clovers, but late-flowering red clovers are also susceptible, whilst white clovers and alsike are fairly resistant. Trefoil is sometimes affected, and newly-sown crops of lucerne and sainfoin may be attacked. Peas can be infected by inoculation with ascospores, but as the crop is normally sown in March it escapes the disease in the field. Vetches are occasionally attacked.

Field beans may be attacked by the same fungus, but normally it is the variety *Sclerotinia trifoliorum* var. *fabae* which causes disease in beans.

Clover rot is particularly frequent on chalky soils, and is most likely to be serious when the growth of clover is thick in the autumn. It spreads readily in a thick crop during a mild winter, and is therefore likely to be most severe when a wet autumn is followed by a mild winter.

Land on which clover dies off readily is sometimes said to be 'clover sick'. Clover sickness may be due to this fungal disease, but it may result from other causes, such as the presence in the soil of the eelworm, *Ditylenchus dipsaci*.

Symptoms and Cause. In a red clover crop, symptoms of this disease are first noticed in October and November when the leaves become peppered with small brown dots. Later the leaves die, turning dark brown. The dying leaves become covered with a thin layer of white mycelium. Mycelium, growing along the ground from diseased plants, may spread the disease to neighbouring plants during the autumn and winter.

In damp, muggy weather the parts of infected plants above the ground may be completely killed. The root remains alive for a time, but may

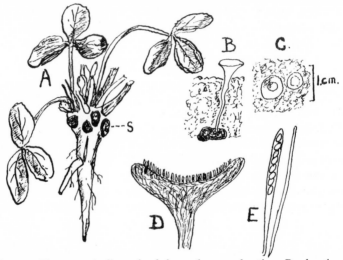

FIG. 237. Clover rot. A, diseased red clover plant; *s*, sclerotium. B, sclerotium germinated to produce an apothecium. C, apothecia seen from above on the surface of the soil. D, longitudinal section through an apothecium, showing asci on the upper surface. E, an ascus and paraphysis.

also eventually die. If the weather is cold and frosty, the disease does not progress so rapidly and the infected plants may not be completely killed and may send up fresh shoots in the spring.

On infected plants, sclerotia are formed chiefly at the top of the root near the soil surface. They may also be produced either inside or on the surface of infected stems. The sclerotia are produced chiefly in the spring, but frequently earlier. They are at first white or grey, turning black as they mature. They vary from the size of a pin-head to that of a pea. The sclerotia are left in the soil when the plant rots, and remain dormant throughout the summer.

In the autumn, sclerotia in the soil germinate, to produce small yellow-brown saucer- or funnel-shaped apothecia, which appear above the surface of the soil. Apothecia are not formed if the sclerotia are buried deeper than about 2 in. in the soil. On the upper surface of the apothecia large numbers of club-shaped asci are formed, each containing eight elliptical ascospores. The ascospores are shot violently into the air from the asci, and are dispersed by air currents to infect the stem and leaves of new plants. There is some evidence that infection, by means of ascospores, may spread to neighbouring fields.

Sclerotia may lie dormant in the soil for a number of years, and remain as a danger to susceptible crops during that time. Some arable weeds are susceptible to infection, and certain weeds, such as sow thistle, have been found to produce sclerotia which may provide a source of infection for crop plants.

Sclerotia may be harvested with the stems of clover plants which have not been killed by the disease. In this way, in crops cut for seed, small sclerotia may be introduced into samples of seed.

Control Measures

1. After an attack of clover rot, the land should be rested from susceptible crops for a number of years. On badly contaminated land, a period of from eight to twelve years' rest from such crops may be necessary before the sclerotia are completely eliminated. During this period, weeds should be controlled to prevent the possibility of the fungus persisting on weed hosts. Red clovers and field beans should be avoided. Peas may be grown without much risk. Sainfoin, alsike and white clovers may be substituted for the more susceptible crops, but as these are sometimes attacked it is best to avoid them.

Where the disease is present, red clover sown under wheat after a bean crop may suffer severely as two susceptible crops in succession occupy the land. It is a common belief among farmers that red clover is often difficult to grow after a bean crop. Clover rot may be the cause of this.*

2. Remove excess growth of the clover in the autumn by cutting or allowing sheep to graze off the strong growth in September and October.

3. Avoid excessive use of nitrogenous fertilizers. A crop adequately supplied with phosphate and potash will be more robust and less likely to suffer severely.

4. On loose soils, consolidation by rolling, where possible, in the autumn may assist clovers to resist attack. This is suggested by the fact that in infected crops the clovers are often more persistent on the headlands where consolidation occurs.

* Field beans (*Vicia faba*) are normally attacked by the variety *fabae*, but there is evidence to suggest that they may be attacked by the clover rot form of *Sclerotinia trifoliorum*, and also that var. *fabae* may be able to attack clovers. It is therefore undesirable to grow field beans or the susceptible clovers on land contaminated by either of these.

In beans the disease is first noticed about mid-March to early April, when plants begin to die. Plants may die, at various stages of growth, right up to harvest time.

The infection starts at about soil level, and the mycelium grows upwards and downwards inside the plant ultimately causing it to wither and die. Plants in an advanced stage of infection readily come away from the soil when pulled up. Sclerotia may be found attached to the root or inside the hollow stems.

5. Where the disease is known to be present in old clover leys, deep ploughing before October will prevent many sclerotia from germinating.

6. Seed should not be harvested from infected crops.

CHOCOLATE SPOT OF BEANS, *Botrytis* species

Chocolate spot occurs on field beans and broad beans (*Vicia faba*) in most seasons, but it is only in certain seasons that it causes severe damage to plants with resulting loss in yield.

Winter-sown beans are more likely to be attacked than spring-sown, and in most seasons the characteristic chocolate-coloured blotches appear upon the leaves of a winter crop from December onwards.

Symptoms and Cause. The disease occurs in two forms:

(*a*) *Non-aggressive*, in which the only symptoms are the numerous chocolate-coloured blotches on the leaves and stems, and sometimes on the pods and seed coats. This is the more common form of the disease. It has little apparent effect on the vigour and productivity of the crop.

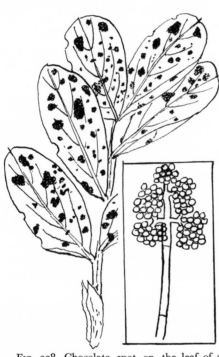

FIG. 238. Chocolate spot on the leaf of a field bean. Inset: conidiophore bearing bunches of conidia, × 330.

(*b*) *Aggressive*, in which the leaves are extensively destroyed and the crop may be rendered useless. The disease is most likely to become aggressive in seasons when late spring frosts are followed by very wet weather conditions in June and July. It is more frequent in the west of the country.

The disease is caused by two closely related species, *Botrytis cinerea* Fr. and *Botrytis fabae* Sard. Although these fungi are members of the Ascomycetes, asci do not appear to play any part in connection with this disease. The fungi live as saprophytes upon decaying vegetation, and there produce abundant conidia in clusters on branched conidiophores. Sclerotia are also produced and these, on germination, also give rise to conidiophores.

Infection of the bean crop occurs by means of conidia from the above sources. Each chocolate-coloured blotch is the result of an individual infection by a conidium. Infection occurs when the atmosphere is humid and the leaves moist. For the aggressive form to develop, the humidity must remain high. High summer temperatures appear to restrict the progress of the disease. A crop damaged by frost in the winter is liable to suffer severely. Crops grown on soils deficient in potash are often more severely affected than crops adequately nourished.

In the non-aggressive form, the mycelium does not usually penetrate beyond the epidermis of the infected area, but when the disease becomes aggressive it penetrates and grows extensively in the inner tissues of the leaf. Crops of conidia are produced on leaves which have been killed, by the fungus or by frost, and these bring about further infection of leaves.

Control Measures. Little can be done after the crop has been infected. If chocolate spot is feared, the risk of severe damage may be reduced by sowing a spring crop rather than a winter one, and ensuring an adequate potash supply in the soil.

Heavy seed rates should be avoided, as thick crops are especially liable to severe infection.

Debris from an infected crop, in which the fungi may persist and provide a source of infection, should be burnt.

ERGOT OF CEREALS AND GRASSES, *Claviceps purpurea* (Fr.) Tul.

Ergot is a disease which attacks cereals and grasses. In the cereals it is most often seen on rye, but it may occur occasionally on wheat, especially Rivet, and on barley and oats. It is found on a wide range of grasses, and occurs fairly frequently on rye-grasses. As rye is not a major crop in Britain, ergot is not of great economic importance here, although occasionally severe attacks have occurred on wheat.

Symptoms and Cause. The disease, in rye, is most apparent as the ears ripen, when, in place of some of the grains, large elongated black or purplish sclerotia are produced and protrude between the chaff. The sclerotia vary in size up to about $\frac{3}{4}$ in. in length. They consist of a hard, compact mass of mycelium, by means of which the fungus is able to remain dormant. In an infected ear, some of the spikelets around those producing sclerotia are sterile, owing to infection by the fungus.

When ripe, the sclerotia may fall to the ground, or may be harvested with the crop. Some of those harvested may remain in the grain sample after threshing, and in this way may be returned to the land among seed sown for the next crop.

In the summer, sclerotia which are on or near the surface of the soil germinate to produce bodies which look like small drum-sticks. The spherical head of one of these is called a *perithecial stroma*. It contains numerous perithecia below its surface. From one to fifty perithecial stromata may be produced by a single sclerotium. Each perithecium within the stroma contains a number of club-shaped asci, each containing eight linear ascospores about as long as the ascus. The ascospores are liberated through an aperture at the apex of the perithecium, and pass out into the air. They are liberated at about the time at which the rye crop is coming into flower. Ascospores are carried by wind, rain-splashes or insects to the flowers, where they germinate and infect the ovaries by way of the stigmas. About a week after infection, a sugary fluid, known as 'honey-dew', exudes from the florets. This contains large numbers of minute conidia which are carried to other florets by insects or rain-splashes, and so cause further infection.

After the production of 'honey-dew' the infected ovary gradually swells and hardens as the fungus becomes converted into a sclerotium, thus completing the life cycle.

The sclerotia or ergots are of medicinal value, and are grown for this

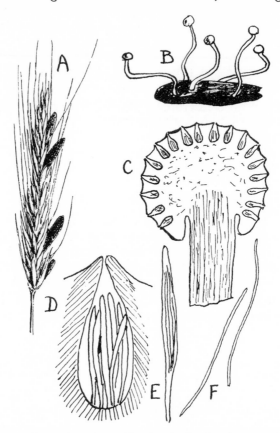

Fig. 239. Ergot. A, rye ear with sclerotia. B, sclerotium germinated. C, longitudinal section of a perithecial stroma. D, perithecium containing asci. E, an ascus containing linear ascospores. F, ascospores.

purpose on crops of rye, which are sprayed with an ascospore suspension in order to produce infection.

Ergots are dangerous in crops grown for food. If taken in quantity, in rye bread in the case of humans, or in feeding-stuffs by animals, they may cause a serious malady known as *ergotism*. Ergot poisoning or ergotism may result in a gangrenous condition, or it may affect the nervous system, producing a convulsive disorder. Both these forms are known to occur on the continent, but in Britain, in modern times, ergotism in humans is rare.

Ergot is said to cause abortion in animals and, in view of this, it may be advisable to avoid feeding hay containing ergot to pregnant animals.

Control Measures

1. Sow clean seed free from ergots.

2. After an attack, deep ploughing will bury ergots which have been shed and prevent their germination.

3. Avoid rye, for two or three years, in a field where the disease has occurred. This rest should be sufficient, as the ergots normally remain viable for about one year only.

4. Ergots may be separated from grain samples by immersing the grain in a saturated solution of common salt. The ergots float and may be removed. The grain must then be washed immediately with water.

With modern machinery, much contaminated grain can be satisfactorily cleaned without recourse to the above method. Small ergots can be riddled out and larger ones may be removed by air draughts (owing to their comparative lightness).

TAKE-ALL AND WHITEHEADS OF CEREALS, *Ophiobolus graminis* (Sacc.) Sacc.

This is a serious disease which attacks wheat and barley and some grasses such as couch, species of *Holcus* and *Agrostis*. It is most frequent on light, naturally alkaline soils, and on soils which have been limed heavily.

Ophiobolus graminis does not usually attack oats, but a variety, *Ophiobolus graminis* var. *avenae* Turner, which occurs in Wales, Scotland and parts of Northern Ireland, often does so, and this variety is also capable of infecting wheat and barley.

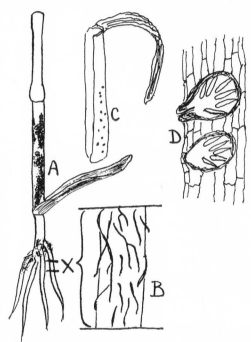

FIG. 240. Take-all on wheat. A, black mycelial patches at the base of the straw. B, runner hyphae on a portion of root. C, leaf-sheath showing perithecia. D, section of part of the leaf-sheath showing perithecia containing asci.

Symptoms and Cause. The two common names of the disease refer to different phases of its attack. At the seedling stage the young plants may be killed completely, hence the name 'take-all'. The name 'whiteheads' refers to the appearance of the ears in plants which have been attacked later, or less severely. The plants ripen early, and the ears at this phase are bleached in appearance, and often do not contain any grain. Under damp conditions the infected ears may be covered with a black mould, but this is due to secondary invasion by saprophytic fungi of other species.

In the whiteheads stage, if the leaf-sheaths at the base of the plant are removed, a smutty coating of mycelium is found on the straw. The roots are greyish-brown and invested with fairly thick brown 'runner hyphae' of the fungus. Infected roots appear stunted and break off easily.

Late in the season perithecia are formed in the outer leaf-sheaths near the base of the plants. These normally mature on the stubbles, but in wet weather they may ripen earlier. The perithecia are embedded in the tissues of the leaf-sheath. They are roughly pear-shaped, the neck protruding from the surface of the leaf-sheath. An opening, the *ostiole*, at the top of the neck, leads to the interior of the perithecium in which are produced numerous club-shaped asci each containing eight long, narrow and twisted ascospores. The ascospores, when ripe, are ejected through the ostiole in a sticky mass.

The importance of the ascospores in propagating the disease is not clear. It is possible that infection may occur when they reach the soil, but investigations suggest that mycelium, on root and stubble remains, and on the roots of susceptible grasses, is probably the chief agent of infection.

Within the crop, the disease spreads from plant to plant by the growth of mycelium from the roots of infected plants to those of healthy plants which are in contact with them. It spreads most rapidly in loose soils, and is usually more common in seasons in which the rainfall is high in spring and early summer.

Infected roots may be destroyed, but plants may recover as a result of the production of new secondary roots to replace those destroyed. Deficiency of one or more of the three major nutrients, nitrogen, phosphate and potash, will curtail this power of recovery. Heavy rainfall in January, resulting in leaching of these nutrients from the soil, may reduce the power of the crop to recover.

Control Measures

1. Where a field is badly contaminated it is important to starve out the fungus. In order to do this, susceptible crops must not be grown at too frequent intervals. Susceptible weed grasses, such as Yorkshire fog, *Agrostis* and couch, should be controlled.

Temporary leys containing rye-grasses and other grasses do not appear to carry over the disease in appreciable amounts to subsequent wheat crops,* although at one time rye-grasses were suspect. Leys are therefore a useful means of resting the land from susceptible crops.

Oats may be grown except where it is known that the oat-attacking variety of the fungus (var. *avenae*) exists.

The disease is often controlled if the land is kept free from susceptible

* Glynne, Mary D., 'Soil-borne Diseases of Cereals', *Jour. Roy. Ag. Soc. of Eng.*, 1954, **115**, 41-6.

crops for one year, and it is generally controlled by two years' freedom from such crops.

2. When a susceptible crop is to be sown, a firm seed-bed should be obtained to help to reduce the rapidity of spread of the fungus along the roots.

Drilling winter cereals in October and November, on light soils, will provide a chance for the seed-bed to become consolidated by rain early in the autumn.

3. A spring-sown crop usually shows less tendency than an autumn-sown crop to suffer severely.

4. Good manuring, and particularly an adequate supply of phosphate to encourage root development, is important in assisting the crop to resist attack. Where nitrogenous manures are required, sulphate of ammonia, which will not increase the alkalinity of the soil, is preferable to other fertilizers. On soils containing adequate phosphate and potash, addition of nitrogenous fertilizers will help to reduce the severity of the disease.

5. A system which has enabled a succession of spring-sown wheat and barley crops to be grown with little trouble through take-all involves undersowing the cereal in spring with trefoil or rye-grass, which is ploughed in in the autumn to provide nutrients for the cereal sown in the following spring.

6. Light seeding tends to reduce losses caused by take-all, as each plant then has more nutrients to enable it to produce extra roots to replace those damaged by the disease, and also to produce additional tillers.

7. After an attack, the stubble should be ploughed early to prevent maturation of the ascospores and to speed up the rotting of the stubble.

8. So far, no very resistant varieties are available.

SEEDLING BLIGHT AND LEAF-SPOT OF OATS, *Pyrenophora avenae* Ito & Kuribay

(The conidial stage of the causal fungus is known by the name *Helminthosporium avenae* Eidam. The fungus rarely produces ascospores.)

The two common names of the disease refer to two different phases in its development.

The disease is seed-borne and is found throughout Britain, although it is usually most serious in cold, wet, northern and western parts of the country. Seed grown in these areas may carry the disease to southern and eastern districts.

Symptoms and Cause. On the seed, the fungus is present as spores on the surface or as mycelium in the husk and seed coat.

When the seed is sown, infection of the coleoptile occurs as the seed germinates. One or two very narrow, brown stripes appear along the length of the coleoptile. The whole seedling may be killed before the plumule has emerged above the soil; considerable losses may occur at this stage.

When the plumule survives and green leaves are produced, the first leaf becomes infected from the coleoptile and the fungus works inwards, infecting the first four leaves successively.

The first leaf to emerge is usually twisted and has a yellow tip and small yellowish-green spots along its surface. The spots become elongated and join to form a yellowish-green stripe. The second and third leaves develop similar stripes. The stripes turn brown or reddish-brown. On the fourth leaf the attack may be less severe and small brown patches may be formed instead of stripes.

From the fifth leaf, up to the appearance of the green ear, the plant shows no further symptoms. For this reason the early symptoms have been named 'seedling blight'.

During April and early May conidiophores grow out from the epidermis in the brown areas of the diseased leaves, and on these conidia are produced, each consisting, usually, of from four to nine cells. These conidia are carried by the wind and may infect neighbouring crops. They infect the later-formed leaves, in which symptoms begin to appear in June. These secondary infections result in the appearance of scattered pale spots, which enlarge to form round or elongated blotches, which become brown in colour, with a yellow or reddish-brown or purple margin. A further crop of conidia is produced on these infected areas, and these carry the disease to further leaves and to the ears.

Fig. 241. Conidia of *Pyrenophora avenae*, × 300.

Conidia are blown on to the developing seed. Some germinate to produce a resting mycelium whilst others remain dormant. The dormant spores may remain viable until sowing time, but the main source of infection of the seedlings is the mycelium which develops in the husk and seed coat.

Moist atmospheric conditions favour the development of the secondary phase and dry ones retard it. Usually the secondary infections (leaf-spot phase) have little effect on yield of grain, but, as they result in infection of the grain, they are most serious if the grain is intended for seed.

Control Measures. Disinfection of the seed with an approved organo-mercurial dust is effective in controlling this disease. This should be a routine operation, particularly when the seed has been grown in the wetter northern and western districts.

All existing varieties of oats are more or less susceptible to this disease.

LEAF STRIPE OF BARLEY, *Pyrenophora graminea* Ito & Kuribay (Conidial stage =*Helminthosporium gramineum* Rabenh.)

This disease occurs throughout Britain. It is seed-borne and is similar in many respects to the seedling blight and leaf-spot disease of oats.

The disease is present on the grain as conidia, and as mycelium in the husk and seed coat. The coleoptile is infected as the seed germinates, and from the coleoptile the fungus works inwards infecting successive leaves.

Unlike the seedling blight of oats, infection does not stop at the fourth leaf. Each leaf is infected, and as it expands vertical pale stripes are seen on the leaf blade. As the disease develops the stripes fuse to form continuous or somewhat broken streaks from base to tip of the leaf blade. These streaks usually turn brown and the whole leaf gradually dies. Infection may pass into the nodes of the stem, which becomes discoloured. Often the infected plant is stunted.

The ear is often infected before it emerges, by hyphae from the uppermost leaf. In infected ears some or all of the grain may fail to develop. In some plants the growing point may be killed off, and as a result the ear fails to develop. In some the ear may fail to emerge following infection of the top internode of the stem.

Conidia are produced in grey-black spots on the old striped areas. They consist usually of from one to seven cells. Conidia may produce secondary infections of leaves and grain, but these do not appear to be very frequent.

Winter barley is more liable to suffer severely than spring-sown, and six-rowed barleys show greater susceptibility than two-rowed.

Control Measures. Effective control can be obtained by dressing the seed grain with an approved organo-mercury fungicide.

In order to avoid infection from diseased stubble, barley should not be grown for a second year after an attack of this disease. The fungus is able to persist for a year or more on the decaying stubble, and infection from this source could occur, even when the seed has been disinfected.

Chapter XXV

DISEASES CAUSED BY BASIDIOMYCETES

(Mycelium profuse and septate; basidia formed.)

BUNT OR STINKING SMUT OF WHEAT, *Tilletia caries* (DC) Tul.

Bunt or stinking smut is largely confined to wheat, but it has also been known to attack rye. There are several races of the fungus with different reactions to different wheat varieties.

Before the widespread adoption of fungicidal dressing of wheat seed grain, bunt was very common in wheat crops, often affecting 20 to 50

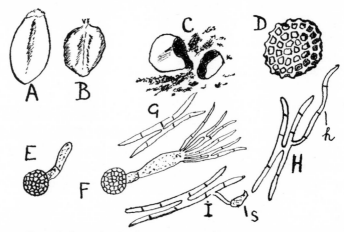

FIG. 242. Bunt of wheat. A, a healthy wheat grain. B, a bunt ball. C, bunt ball broken open and releasing a black mass of brand spores. D, brand spore. E, brand spore germinating to produce a promycelium. F, promycelium (basidium) bearing primary sporidia, some united in pairs. G, united primary sporidia. H, ditto, germinating to produce a germ tube; *h*. I, ditto, germinating to produce secondary sporidium (*s*).

per cent. of the ears. As a result of seed disinfection the disease has now become uncommon.

Symptoms and Cause. The disease is difficult to recognize readily in the standing crop. As the ear emerges from the leaf sheath, on an infected plant, it is rather narrower than a healthy ear and a bluish-green colour. Later, when the ears ripen, the chaff is pushed apart by the infected grains, which are mis-shapen, often shorter, and plumper than normal grains. As a result the ear has a 'staring' appearance. The grain is readily broken open and contains a black, somewhat greasy, mass of spores, which has a fishy smell (hence the name stinking smut).

Usually, on an infected plant, all the ears and the whole of the grain of each ear will be bunted. The bunted grains, or 'butts', do not break open in the field so that the ear does not assume the smutty appearance characteristic of loose smut.

The butts (or bunt balls) are broken usually during threshing, although some may be broken during harvest. In the threshing box, spores from the broken butts are scattered, in their millions, and adhere to healthy grains, especially to the hairy tuft at the stigma end of the grain. Healthy grain is thus contaminated.

The spores, termed *brand spores*, are thick-walled with a reticulate outer surface. These brand spores remain dormant until the seed grain is sown. They then germinate, as the seed germinates, producing a short, thick germ tube at the apex of which are formed sickle-shaped basidiospores (or primary sporidia) some of which fuse in pairs giving a typical 'H' formation (see fig. 242). From the paired basidiospores, hyphae develop which may infect the germinating seed direct or, more often, give rise to secondary sporidia which are responsible for infection.

The young seedling is infected by penetration of hyphae into the coleoptile. The mycelium then develops inside the young shoot, where hyphae work their way to the growing point. Thus as the stem elongates the mycelium is present in the terminal growing point and hyphae penetrate into the young carpels as they develop. The mycelium is thus present in the young ear, and as this grows the hyphae divide in the carpels to produce the masses of brand spores. A single bunt ball may contain from 1 to 4 million or more spores.

Control Measures. The modern method of control is by disinfection of the seed grain with a suitable fungicide, such as one of the organomercury dusts (see p. 522). The grain should be dry when dressed and, if stored after dressing, should be kept under dry, cool conditions. Under such conditions, grain may be kept for several months without injury.

LOOSE SMUT OF WHEAT, *Ustilago nuda* (Jens) Rostr. (*U. tritici* (Pers.) Rostr.)

This smut differs from bunt of wheat in that it is noticed as soon as the ears emerge from the leaf sheaths. The ear disintegrates, the ovaries breaking open and releasing millions of brand spores. These spores are smaller than those of bunt and have a smooth surface. The mass is light and powdery. The spores are blown about in the field and infect flowers of healthy ears. The brand spores produce germ tubes and infect the ovaries directly without first producing any other type of spore (cf. bunt of wheat). For long it has been thought that infection occurred via the stigma, but the work of Batts at Cambridge suggests that infection normally occurs through the surface of the pericarp.* This infection in the field, during the development of the grain, results in the formation of mycelium inside grains without affecting their development. The infected grain will therefore be threshed with healthy grain, and in the threshed sample the infected grains are not detected. It should be noted

* Batts, C. C. V., 'Observations on the Infection of Wheat by Loose Smut' (*Ustilago Tritici* (Pers.) Rostr.), *Trans. of the Brit. Mycological Soc.*, Vol. 38, 1955, 465-74.

that these grains are *infected*, because the disease is already established in their tissues, whilst in the case of bunt the grains are only *contaminated*, the disease organisms being present only on the outside of the grain.

When the infected grain is sown the mycelium keeps pace with the development of the young plant, and before the ear has emerged from the leaf sheath mycelium has infected the ovaries and divided to produce a loose, powdery mass of spores. Until the smutted ears emerge there is no obvious effect of the disease upon the plant.

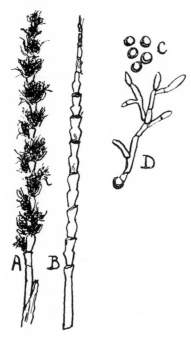

FIG. 243. Loose smut of wheat. A, smutted ear. B, rachis after the ear has disintegrated. C, brand spores. D, brand spore germinating.

The causal fungus is indistinguishable morphologically from that causing loose smut of barley and it is considered to be a variety or special form of that fungus, *U. nuda*, although formerly regarded as a distinct species *U. tritici*.

Control Measures. Because the fungus is present inside the grain, disinfection with fungicidal dusts is not effective.

The warm water treatment (see p. 525) provides effective control. Owing to the difficulty of this treatment it is better to avoid loose smut by sowing seed only from crops in which the disease was not present. The field inspection scheme for cereal seeds (see Chapter VI) helps to provide such healthy seed. Even in a crop in which smutted heads were not visible, however, some infection of the seed may have occurred through spores blown from neighbouring crops.

Breeding for resistance to loose smut is a major problem. The problem is complicated by the existence of several physiological races of the fungus. Some modern varieties are relatively susceptible to attack, e.g. Hybrid 46 and Cappelle, whilst others show a considerably higher degree of resistance, e.g. Rothwell Perdix, Champlein and Thor.

COVERED SMUT OF BARLEY, *Ustilago hordei* (Pers.) Lagerh.

This disease resembles bunt of wheat and, like that disease, it can be controlled by organo-mercurial seed dressings. Serious attacks do not often occur in Britain now.

LOOSE SMUT OF BARLEY, *Ustilago nuda* (Jens) Rostr.

In recent years this disease has become increasingly common in Britain. Some degree of infection is frequently seen, particularly in Scandinavian varieties, which are generally more susceptible than English varieties. Its life cycle resembles that of loose smut of wheat, and it can be controlled by similar means.

For the warm-water treatment, the grain is first soaked in cold water for four hours, and then in water at 49° C. for five minutes, followed by water at 51° C. for ten minutes.

As in the case of loose smut of wheat, the most practical means of control is to obtain seed from disease-free crops.

SMUTS OF OATS

Oat crops also suffer from a covered smut, *U. hordei* (*U. kolleri* Wille), and a loose smut, *U. avenae* (Pers.) Jens. As the spores of the covered smut do not always remain enclosed until harvest-time, the two smuts are often rather difficult to distinguish in the field. The loose smut is much more common. Fortunately, the loose smut does not penetrate deeply into the seed grain, and a reasonable degree of control can be obtained by disinfection of the grain with organo-mercurial dusts. Covered smut is also controlled by this means.

The causal fungus of covered smut of oats, formerly known as *U. kolleri*, is indistinguishable morphologically from *U. hordei*, which causes covered smut of barley, and is considered to be a special form of that fungus.

THE RUSTS OR UREDINALES

Rust diseases, caused by fungi belonging to the family *Uredinales*, are very common. Different species of this family attack a wide range of plants including cereals, grasses, beet and mangel, flax, leeks, plums, gooseberries, roses, antirrhinums, carnations and mint. All rusts are obligate parasites, and they produce a septate intercellular mycelium.

The causal fungi have somewhat complicated life histories, and some of them, e.g. *Puccinia graminis* (which causes black rust of wheat) are *heteroecious*, i.e. requiring two host species in order to complete their life cycle. Others, like the fungus causing flax rust, are *autoecious*, i.e. requiring only one host species during their life cycle.

The complications of the life cycle of a heteroecious rust are well exemplified by the black rust of wheat.

Puccinia graminis Pers., **Black Rust (or Stem Rust) of Wheat**

Several varieties of the fungus *P. graminis* exist. These cannot readily be distinguished from one another, but slight morphological differences do exist, for example slight constant differences in the size of the uredospores occur between one variety and another. Wheat is attacked by the variety *tritici*, and other cereals, oats, barley and rye and various grasses, are attacked by particular varieties of the fungus.

Within most varieties there exist numerous physiological races which are distinguishable only by their effect upon particular varieties of the host species. The races of the variety which produces black rust of wheat vary in their virulence in relation to different wheat varieties. Some varieties are readily attacked by a particular race whilst other varieties may show resistance to that race. Over 200 races of this variety of the fungus have been recorded, but these have been identified mainly in America and few exist in Britain.

The existence of numerous races of the fungus complicates the problem of the plant-breeder, in attempting to breed resistant varieties (see p. 62).

The black rust of wheat, in most seasons, is of minor importance in Britain, but from the world point of view it is one of the major diseases, one which is responsible for considerable annual loss of yield in the large wheat-growing areas of the world. The effects on the yield of grain are produced largely by a reduction of the green area of the plant and the eventual killing of the leaves which result in a reduction of photosynthesis. Plants are not usually killed completely, and the grain is not infected, but reduced carbohydrate production results in a lower yield of shrivelled grains.

In order to complete its life cycle, the fungus requires the common barberry (*Berberis vulgaris*), or certain other related species, as an alternate host, but under some circumstances (see below) black rust is able to appear in wheat crops year after year even in the absence of the barberry. In Britain the disease occurs regularly in S.W. Wales, where the barberry plant is common in hedgerows. In other parts of the country it is met with only occasionally. Usually it develops late in the season, and the amount of damage to the crop is not great. In some seasons the disease attacks with greater severity and causes marked reduction of yields of grain. For example, in 1955 severe attacks were experienced in S.W. England, and crops which early in the season promised to yield around 30 cwt. of grain per acre were reduced to yields of around 6 cwt. of shrivelled grain.

Symptoms and Cause. Towards the end of July and early in August elongated rusty brown pustules appear between the veins, on the leaf blades and, more particularly, on the leaf sheaths and stems of the wheat plants. These consist of masses of *uredospores* bursting through the epidermis. The uredospores are fairly thick-walled cells, oval in shape, attached singly to the tips of hyphae. They are dispersed by wind and rain-splashes and infect further wheat plants. The uredospores germinate on the damp surfaces of leaves or stems, and their germ tubes enter the plant through the stomata. The mycelium which is produced within the plant gives rise to further pustules within about a week, and a new crop of uredospores is thus produced.

As the wheat ripens the pustules become black. When this occurs, a new type of spore is being produced, namely the *teleutospores*. Teleutospores and uredospores may be found together in the same pustules. Teleutospores or winter spores are two-celled, more elongated than the uredospores, and with much thicker walls. The wall is particularly thick towards the apex of the spore. These spores are dark brown in colour. They remain attached to the straw and may lie dormant until the following spring, or, several winters may elapse before they ultimately germinate. On germination each cell of the teleutospore gives rise to a hypha

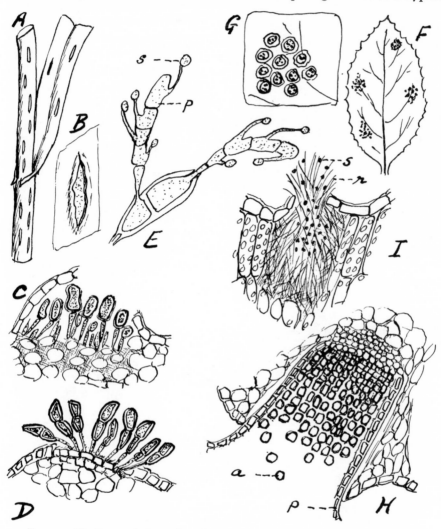

Fig. 244. Black rust of wheat. A, sori on stem, leaf-sheath and leaf-blade. B, sorus showing splitting of the epidermis. C, uredospores in section of a sorus. D, section of a sorus showing teleutospores. E, teleutospore germinated: *p*, promycelium (basidium); *s*, sporidium (basidiospore). F, barberry leaf (lower surface), showing aecidia. G, group of aecidia enlarged. H, section through an aecidium: *p*, peridium, *a*, aecidiospore. I, section through a spermogonium: *r*, receptive hyphae; *s*, spermatia.

consisting usually of four cells (the basidium or promycelium) from which small *basidiospores* (or *sporidia*) are abstricted, one basidiospore from each cell of the basidial hypha.

The basidiospores are wind-disseminated, and they infect the leaves of the alternate host, the common barberry, in spring. Penetration of the germ tube occurs directly through the cuticle. Soon after infection orange-yellow patches appear on the underside of the barberry leaves. These patches or *sori* measure up to about ½ in. in diameter and consist of numerous cup-like sections called *aecidia* or *cluster cups*. Each aecidium originates below the epidermis of the leaf and is at first surrounded by a membrane, the *peridium*. Eventually the epidermis and the peridium are ruptured, and the typical aecidium, bordered by the torn tissues of the peridium, is seen. Within the cup is an orange-yellow mass of *aecidio-spores*. The aecidiospores are budded off in chains from the tips of fertile hyphae. They are single-celled and thin-walled. Their formation is preceded by a sexual process which is described below.

In microscope sections of the leaf small flask-shaped structures, called *spermogonia*, can be seen, chiefly in the upper mesophyll of the leaf. Mature spermogonia may be seen in leaf sections before the aecidiospores develop, and they play an important role in the complete development of the aecidiospores. The spermogonia contain masses of hair-like hyphae. Some of the hyphae project from an opening of the spermogonium, on the upper surface of the leaf; these are termed *receptive hyphae*. Within the spermogonia large numbers of cells named *spermatia* are budded off from the tips of the hyphae. The spermatia are extremely minute, and they are exuded in drops of sugary fluid from the mouth (ostiole) of the spermogonium. It has been shown that two kinds of spermogonium are produced in the barberry; these may be named '+' and '−' types. The two types result from separate infections of the leaf by '+' and '−' basidiospores (two basidiospores on a basidial hypha of the teleutospore are '+' and two '−'). When spermatia of the '+' type are carried to the receptive hyphae of the '−' type (usually by insects) they fuse with the hyphae. Similarly fusions occur between '−' spermatia and '+' hyphae. Such fusions occur before the aecidiospores develop. Similar fusions may also occur between '+' and '−' hyphae in the region of the aecidia initials. It seems likely that the development of the aecidio-spores depends upon one or other of these types of sexual fusion taking place. This sexual phase is of considerable importance because it may result in new gene combinations and thus in new races of the fungus.

The aecidiospores are able to germinate immediately, but they are not able to infect the barberry. They must be carried, usually by wind, to wheat plants, which they infect. In this way the wheat crop becomes infected in the spring and the life cycle of the fungus is completed.

The above is the normal life cycle for the disease in Britain; uredo-spores, which can infect wheat directly, are normally killed off by low winter temperatures and infection of the new wheat crop comes from the barberry by means of aecidiospores. There is evidence to suggest, however, that wheat crops may be infected in the summer by uredospores which have been carried by winds from Southern Europe and North Africa.

In North America, where the wheat-growing areas cover a wide range of latitude, although infection can occur via the barberry, it also occurs as a result of uredospores being blown from more advanced crops in another area. In North Mexico and the southern states of America the autumn-sown wheat crop is well advanced by the spring when wheat is being sown in Canada, and between these two regions from north to south there are crops at successive stages of development. The disease is carried by wind-borne uredospores from more advanced crops in the south to less advanced crops farther north. In this way crops are infected in succession until finally the disease reaches the northern wheat-growing areas of Canada. Again, the rust may be carried as uredospores from the north to newly-sown crops in the south in the autumn. In Australia the fungus persists from one season to the next in form of uredospores in mild areas, and the barberry is not important. In India where wheat is grown as a winter crop in the plains the uredospores are killed off in the hot summer, but the fungus persists on self-sown wheat in the cooler foot-hills whence uredospores are carried to the next crop in the plains. Thus in countries where large quantities of uredospores are brought to newly-sown crops early in their life the disease appears annually, without the aid of the barberry, and in some seasons may assume devastating proportions.

Control Measures

1. Dusts of sulphur and of copper compounds are highly toxic to rust spores and wheat crops dusted repeatedly with these materials can be protected from attack. Such dusting may be useful for small plots, but it is not very practicable on a wide scale.

2. The elimination of the common barberry is an important step toward the control of the disease, and in some countries where black rust is prevalent campaigns have been organized for the eradication, and prevention of planting, of this species. In some countries these campaigns have been supported by legislation. For example, laws compelling the eradication of barberry bushes were passed in Connecticut in 1726 and in Massachusetts in 1755, many years before the significance of the barberry as an alternate host of the fungus was appreciated. Where infection can occur from season to season by means of uredospores, the barberry is less important and its eradication gives less control of the disease than in northern European countries in which infection normally occurs via the barberry. Eradication does, however, eliminate the sexual phase of the fungus and reduce the possibility of new races arising.

3. The most promising means of control is through the breeding of immune or highly resistant varieties of wheat. Resistance or immunity, in some varieties, has been shown to be due to the fact that when infection occurs the mycelium kills the surrounding tissue and is therefore unable to make any further growth. This is known as *hypersensitivity*.

Marked resistance to races of black rust has been found in varieties of *Triticum durum* and *T. dicoccum*, and these have been used by breeders to introduce resistance into more valuable bread wheats. Breeding for resistance to this disease is most important in countries, such as Canada and U.S.A., where the disease is a serious problem. The task of breeding resistant or immune varieties is complicated by the existence of numerous races of the fungus, and by the fact that new races may arise from time to time, either as a result of the sexual phase on the barberry, or as mutations which may occur in the uredo-stage. Thus there is always the possibility of a new race arising which may be able to devastate varieties which were highly resistant to all previously existing races. Some new races have arisen which can attack *T. durum* and *T. dicoccum* and varieties derived from them, consequently wheats which were formerly resistant have been devastated in North America. Thus the search for resistant material, for use in breeding new varieties, must continue.

YELLOW RUST OF WHEAT, *Puccinia striiformis* Westend. (*P. glumarum*).

In Britain yellow rust of wheat is more common than black rust. It is frequently to be found in wheat crops. Usually it does not cause severe injury to the crop, but in some seasons heavy infection may occur and severe losses result. The grain is not infected, but the reduction in photosynthesis caused by heavy attack on the green parts of the plant may result in reduced yields of shrivelled grain. It is only about once in ten years that the disease becomes sufficiently serious to result in a reduction of yield of grain of more than an estimated 5 to 10 per cent.

Over fifty races of the fungus are known, and distinct races attack barley, rye and certain grasses, such as cocksfoot and couch. Several physiological races attack wheat, and these vary in their virulence in relation to different varieties of wheat.

Symptoms and Cause. The disease appears earlier than black rust. Lemon-yellow to orange pustules, arranged in parallel lines, appear in the spring, chiefly on the leaf blades, but they may also occur on the leaf sheaths and later on the stems and ears. These pustules contain uredospores which infect further wheat plants.

In a severe attack the leaves may be killed off early, and as a result the grain produced will be small and shrivelled.

As the wheat matures teleutospores are produced, in black sori, chiefly on the stem and leaf sheaths and to a lesser extent on the leaf blades. The teleutospores, unlike those of black rust, do not break through the epidermis. If released the teleutospores are able to germinate in the autumn and produce basidiospores. So far as is known, this fungus does not infect any alternate host and the teleutospores, and the basidiospores which they produce, appear to have no function in the life cycle of the fungus.

Infection from one crop to the next occurs by means of uredospores. The uredospores are able to withstand several degrees of frost and so persist through the winter. Autumn-sown wheat may be infected soon after germination by means of uredospores from infected green tillers growing in stubbles left after harvest. In the new crop the disease may become visible on the leaves from January onward, but usually it is not very abundant until May.

Normally the disease spreads most rapidly in a wet, cool summer, and is checked in a hot season, but different races of the fungus appear

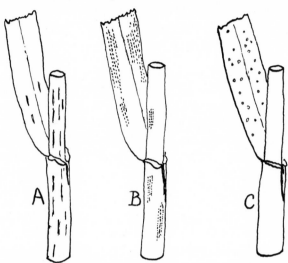

FIG. 245. Comparison of sori of wheat rusts. A, black rust. B, yellow rust. C, brown rust.

to vary in their optimum moisture and temperature requirements. Lush growth of the crop favours the spread of the disease; excessive use of nitrogenous fertilizers should therefore be avoided. An adequate supply of potash appears to produce some degree of resistance. Susceptible varieties of wheat grown after a crop of clover or other legume may suffer severely owing to the nitrogenous matter added to the soil by legumes and the depletion of the soil, by them, of phosphates and potash.

Resistance to yellow rust is inherited in a Mendelian manner, resistance being a recessive character. Resistant varieties can be bred and many modern varieties show a considerable degree of resistance to particular races of the fungus. Good resistance is shown in Britain by Hybrid 46, Rothwell Perdix and Elite Lepeuple, rather less by Champlein, Flamingo, Kloka and Opal, still less by Cappelle, Maris Widgeon and Jufy I.

Some varieties are more resistant to races of the fungus existing in one part of the country than to those in other parts of the country. Similarly, varieties which may be resistant to yellow rust in their country of origin may prove susceptible when taken to another country, where they meet other races of the fungus.

BROWN RUST OF WHEAT, *Puccinia triticina* Erikss.

This disease is not normally serious in Britain, as it attacks the crop late in the season and little damage is done. Sori are usually confined to the leaf blades and rarely occur on the leaf sheaths or stems. The pustules of uredospores are produced in clusters, or scattered over the surface of the leaf, and not in rows or lines, as in yellow rust. They are at first orange in colour, but soon turn brown. The fungus may be heteroecious. The aecidial stage has been recorded in U.S.A. on the meadow rue (*Thalictrum flavum*), but no alternate host is known in Britain, where the fungus appears to persist from year to year by means of uredospores which survive until late autumn or early winter and are thus able to infect autumn-sown crops.

CROWN RUST OF OATS, *Puccinia coronata* Corda

This disease occurs most severely in Wales and S.W. England. In a heavy attack, the foliage becomes golden-yellow with uredospores in June and July, and indifferently-filled ears and low yields result. The alternate host of the causal fungus is the buckthorn (*Rhamnus catharticus*). Some varieties of *Avena sativa* and *A. byzantina* show marked resistance and these are being used at Aberystwyth in breeding new resistant oat varieties.

Other cereal rusts which normally do little damage in Britain are BROWN RUST OF BARLEY, *P. hordei*. Otth., which has no known alternate host in Britain, but elsewhere the aecidial stage has been recorded on the Star of Bethlehem (*Ornithogalum umbellatum*), and BROWN RUST OF RYE, *P. dispersa*. Erikss & Henn, alternate host, species of *Anchusa*.

In addition to the genus *Puccinia*, there are several other genera containing rust fungi of economic importance—for example, *Uromyces*, in which the teleutospores are stalked and unicellular, contains the BEET AND MANGEL RUST, *Uromyces betae*, and the BROAD BEAN RUST, *U. fabae*; *Melampsora*, which has sessile unicellular teleutospores, includes the FLAX RUST, *M, lini*; *Phragmidium*, in which the teleutospores are stalked and consist of several cells, includes the RASPBERRY RUST, *P. rubi-idaei*, and the ROSE RUST, *P. mucronatum*.

Chapter XXVI

DISEASES CAUSED BY DEUTEROMYCETES (*FUNGI IMPERFECTI*)

(Sporangia, asci and basidia absent, so far as is known. Spores, when present, are conidia.)

SKIN SPOT OF POTATO, *Oospora pustulans* Owen & Wakef.

This disease attacks tubers in storage. As it affects their ability to sprout, its chief importance is in connection with seed potatoes.

Symptoms and Cause. Diseased tubers may be more or less unsightly in appearance, but often disease symptoms are not very noticeable, especially on thick-skinned varieties. Spots appear on the surface of the tubers. In some varieties these consist of small, round depressions, with a slightly raised centre, brown or black in colour. In other varieties the spots take the form of numerous small pimples, not surrounded by a depressed area, and the same colour as the rest of the skin of the tuber when dry, but darker when wet. The spots may be scattered, or large numbers may join together, so that extensive areas are disfigured. Often the eyes of the tubers are destroyed.

The disease does not spread extensively into the flesh, and, apart from the spotting and the killing of the eyes the tuber appears quite healthy. Such tubers may be planted in a sample of unchitted seed, but where seed has been chitted before planting, the absence of sprouts will often betray the presence of the disease.

Skin spot is believed to be contracted from the soil, but it does not develop on the tubers until some time after the crop has been lifted and stored. The form in which the fungus exists in the soil and its method of infection of the tubers are not clearly understood. It can persist in the soil for many years between potato crops.

In the diseased tubers narrow septate hyphae grow between the cells of the infected tissues. After a few days' storage in a damp atmosphere, conidiophores bearing chains of cylindrical or oblong conidia are formed at the surface of the spots. The disease makes less progress if the seed tubers are boxed and sprouted under dry, light, well-ventilated conditions. Boxing should be done as soon after lifting as possible, and the seed should not be clamped. Under damp, badly-ventilated, clamp conditions the disease makes more progress, and on many tubers the buds are likely to be killed.

Control Measures

1. Seed tubers should not be clamped, but should be boxed and sprouted under light, dry, airy conditions. Besides restricting the severity

of attack by the fungus, this also ensures that unsprouted tubers, in which the eyes have been killed, may be detected and rejected for planting.

2. Avoid planting diseased tubers which have failed to sprout, or have produced weak sprouts. This will reduce the risk of gaps in the rows and also of the return of the disease organisms to the land.

3. The development of the disease on seed potatoes may be reduced by dipping them, immediately after the crop has been lifted, in an organo-mercury fungicidal dip for one minute (see Dry-rot of Potato, later).

DRY-ROT OF POTATO, *Fusarium caeruleum* (Lib.) Sacc.

Dry-rot disease appears in potato tubers during storage. It frequently causes heavy losses in seed potatoes. Infected tubers may be obviously unfit for planting, but slightly infected tubers may inadvertently be planted, with the result that gaps may appear in the rows as a consequence of these tubers rotting in the ground.

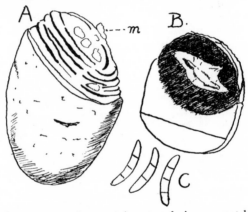

FIG. 246. Dry rot of potato. A, external view: *m*, patch of mycelium. B, tuber cut across in the diseased region, showing internal rotting and cavity containing mycelium. C, conidia.

The disease is more common in early varieties, such as Arran Pilot, Sharpe's Express, Ninetyfold, Catriona, Ulster Ensign, Ulster Premier and Arran Comet, but Home Guard and Epicure are fairly resistant. Maincrop varieties are normally more resistant than earlies, but Majestic and Redskin are moderately susceptible and the once-popular variety Doon Star is very susceptible.

Symptoms and Cause. Dry-rot may be caused by several different species of *Fusarium*. *F. caeruleum* is the most usual cause in Britain.

The disease usually develops during storage of the tubers, and may often be seen from December onwards in seed potatoes which have been boxed for sprouting. In the more susceptible varieties up to 50 per cent. of the tubers may develop the rot and be rendered useless for seed.

At first a darker-coloured, slightly sunken patch appears on the surface of the tuber. As the tissues below this patch shrink, the skin becomes wrinkled in concentric rings. Patches of mycelium burst through the skin and appear on the surface. These patches of mould may be white, pink or blue in colour. When the tuber is cut across in the diseased area, the tissue below the wrinkled area is found to be brown and shrunken and to contain cavities. The cavities contain fluffy mycelium, white, pink or blue in colour. The rot extends deeply into the tuber, which becomes hard and shrinks considerably. Unless there is a secondary infection by other rot-producing organisms, the rot remains dry.

On the patches of mycelium on the surface of the tuber, branched conidiophores are produced, these bear banana-shaped conidia. The conidia consist of from one to four cells, the four-celled type being most numerous. Occasionally in these mycelial patches, thick-walled chlamydospores are also formed. These are spherical in shape, smooth-walled and of a bluish colour.

The fungus causing the disease is present in the soil in the field and contamination of the tubers occurs before lifting. The fungus gains entry to the tuber, usually through cracks or wounds, and possibly through lenticels. The actual infection probably occurs largely after the crop has been lifted. The rotting then develops, and becomes apparent, some time after lifting.

The disease spreads from tuber to tuber by means of spores, during storage, but only damaged tubers are infected readily. When infection of a seed potato tuber occurs late, the tuber may bear sprouts at planting time, but it is liable to rot further after planting and leave a gap in the row.

Control Measures. As the main channel of infection is through cracks and bruises on the tubers, it is of prime importance that seed potatoes should be lifted, riddled and subsequently handled in such a way as to prevent excessive damage to the tubers.

The skin of the tubers will be more mature and less likely to suffer damage if the haulm is burnt off by means of sulphuric acid or some other suitable chemical spray some time before lifting the crop.

At harvest the speed and depth of the machine should be regulated to prevent excessive bruising. Harrowings, in which there is likely to be more damage, should be kept separate from the rest of the crop, and not used for seed.

During riddling, much damage is often done to tubers by the common type of riddle. For seed potatoes, hand-grading, with precautions to avoid rough handling, or the use of special rubber-coated screens on reciprocating riddles, are advised. If riddling can be delayed until two weeks or less before planting, the disease is less likely to develop.

During handling before and after transport, sacks of seed should not be dropped heavily. Re-dressing of seed, which has already been graded by the grower, should be avoided, as this involves further damage and inoculation during riddling, and also because the susceptibility of tubers increases progressively during the storage period. Seed which is boxed for sprouting should be handled carefully, and filled boxes moved about with care.

Seed of susceptible varieties should be stored in sprouting boxes in a well-ventilated and well-lighted building. Such a building should be cool, but the temperature should be kept above freezing-point in cold weather. The disease develops most rapidly in a moist atmosphere and at temperatures of about 60° F.

Protection of seed potatoes, from dry rot, can be obtained by use of fungicides in two ways:

(1) By dipping the seed, for not less than one minute, in a solution of an appropriate organo-mercurial fungicide. This must be done immediately after the crop is lifted. The seed must be carefully dried after treatment. As the fungicide is very poisonous, only tubers to be used for seed should be dipped. Any spare seed which has been dipped should not be used for human or animal food.

(2) A more practical treatment is to dust the tubers, immediately after lifting, with a fungicide containing tetrachloronitrobenzene. The seed should then be clamped for at least four weeks, as this treatment depends upon the fungicide volatilizing slowly and the vapour being held in contact with the tubers. As the fungicide markedly retards sprouting, the seed should be removed from the clamp, after treatment, and set up in boxes for sprouting for at least six weeks before planting time. Tubers treated with the dust may safely be used for feeding to animals if not required for seed.

VERTICILLIUM WILT OF HOP

This disease is caused usually by *Verticillium albo-atrum* Reinke & Berth, but more rarely by *V. dahliae* Kleb. It causes the leaves to turn yellow and die early, often affecting the regions between the veins first. The lower leaves of the bine are first affected and the woody tissues of the bine turn brown; starting at the base of the bine, this discoloration may eventually extend throughout its length. The symptoms appear usually about the time the hops are reaching maturity.

The disease takes two forms, *fluctuating* and *progressive*. The fluctuating form does not spread quickly and usually affects few bines; it fluctuates in amount from year to year. The *progressive* form, caused by a more virulent race of the fungus, spreads rapidly from plant to plant, usually killing them, the patches of dead plants increasing in size year by year. The disease spreads by spores produced on the dead bines. It is therefore important to grub out diseased plants and their immediate neighbours and to burn them on the spot. Sterilization of the soil with formalin is also recommended. Care is necessary to prevent the spread of the disease on implements, boots, etc., or by planting cuttings obtained from diseased gardens. Cuttings should be obtained from gardens certified as being free from the disease. Outbreaks of progressive verticillium wilt disease must be notified to the Ministry of Agriculture (see p. 526). Progress is being made at Wye College, Kent, in breeding varieties resistant to this disease.

Diseases Caused by Deuteromycetes (Fungi Imperfecti)

EYESPOT OF CEREALS, *Cercosperella herpotrichoides* Fron.

Wheat and barley are the crops most usually attacked by this disease. Oats and rye are more resistant, but appreciable infection may occur occasionally. Winter wheat and barley crops suffer most severely, spring-sown crops usually being infected too late for the disease to cause much damage.

Eyespot was first recognized in Britain in 1935, but there is little doubt that it existed before that time, and was a common cause of lodging of wheat and barley crops. It is to be found throughout the country, but more particularly in districts where wheat and barley are frequent crops.

Losses of up to 50 per cent. in yield of grain may result from a severe attack.

Symptoms and Cause. Young plants are infected in the autumn and early spring. Infection is brought about by spores of the fungus, usually produced on bits of diseased stubble of previous crops which have been left on the surface of the soil. Self-sown plants of wheat and barley may also play some part in producing spores which may infect the new crop, as may farmyard manure containing infected straw. Infection of the outer leaf sheaths of young plants occurs near the soil level, and the fungus grows inwards through successive leaf sheaths.

On infected plants brown-bordered, elliptical lesions appear on the leaf sheaths and occasionally on the leaf blades. These are the so-called 'eyespots'. In the centre of the eyespot a small dark patch of mycelium develops. Conidia are produced freely by this until about the middle of April. These conidia may infect further plants.

Under moist mild weather conditions the fungus may invade the young shoots so rapidly as to kill the plant or some of its tillers, thus resulting in a thin stand. Normally, the fungus progresses less rapidly, and tillers are not killed, but the fungus eventually works inwards, through successive leaf sheaths, to infect the straw near its base. Eyespots develop on the straw in the infected region. These may be observed, on the lower part of the straw, by pulling away the leaf sheaths. When the straw is split open in the region of the eye spot, a fluffy grey mycelium may often be found within.

Frequently the straw kinks in the region of the eyespot and falls over. The lodged straws lie in all directions among the upright ones, thus producing the condition commonly known as 'straggling' or 'scrawling'. In a badly infected crop, lodging may become severe throughout the crop.

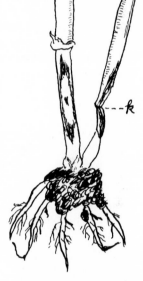

FIG. 247. Eyespot on wheat straw. *k*, straw twisting and bending in the region of the eyespot.

On some infected plants thin white ears may be formed. Such ears produce a few small shrivelled grains. Ears of this type may be confused with ears affected by take-all or white-heads (see p. 551).

Moist growing conditions and lush growth favour development of eyespot. It is more liable to appear on heavy and rich land. On fertile land, however, where the attack develops on young plants, new tillers may be produced, replacing those killed by the disease. This helps to reduce potential losses in yield.

571

Control Measures

1. Rest the land from susceptible crops. Often two years' rest from wheat and barley is sufficient, but a longer rest may be necessary. Where possible, lengthening of the period between susceptible crops by means of leys is useful, as the fungus does not persist in the grasses.

2. Avoid heavy seed rates.

3. Choose short-strawed varieties which are less likely to lodge, and manure them well. Dressings of nitrogenous fertilizers help the crop to resist the effects of the disease and to give higher yields of grain. It should be remembered, however, that heavy nitrogenous dressings may themselves result in lodging of weak-strawed varieties.

4. Spring-sown or late autumn-sown varieties are less likely to suffer severely.

5. Spraying with sulphuric acid in early March, before the fungus has penetrated into the inner regions of the shoot, is valuable. This reduces the amount of eyespot which develops in the straw, and the amount of lodging later. The spray suitable for this purpose is $12\frac{1}{2}$ per cent., by volume, of B.O.V. (brown oil of vitriol) at 100 gall. per acre. The spray will also kill or check many weeds.

6. Control sources of infection. Thorough ploughing under of old stubbles and self-sown plants of wheat and barley, as soon as possible, will help. Also the application of dung made from diseased straw to land shortly to be used for susceptible crops should be avoided.

7. The varieties Cappelle Desprez and Maris Widgeon are highly resistant. These varieties may be attacked to some degree but they are likely to stand well and little decrease in yield will result. They may help to perpetuate the disease however and are not a substitute for other crops which assist in starving out the fungus.

Note. The above disease should not be confused with 'sharp eyespot' of wheat, barley and oats, which is caused by *Corticium solani*. Sharp eyespot is less frequent in most parts of Britain, but is common in the south-west. The eyespot lesions of this disease may be present over several inches upwards from the base of the stem. The spots have a more clearly defined, but more irregular, margin than those of eyespot. The pale inner part of the lesions may bear spots of fawn or purple, instead of black, mycelium.

LEAF BLOTCH, *Rhynchosporium secalis*

This disease is causing some concern as a result of heavy attacks on barley particularly in the southern part of the country. It also attacks rye and certain grasses. Light grey blotches with dark brown margins develop on the leaves. Two-celled beaked conidia are produced on these patches in May and June. In severe cases leaves may be killed completely thus causing considerable loss of yield. The disease is most severe in cool damp conditions. The fungus over-winters as dormant mycelium in leaves and chaff. The disease may also be seed-borne but seed treatment does not control it. Crop rotation may help to reduce it.

Chapter XXVII

ACTINOMYCETES AND BACTERIA AS DISEASE AGENTS

THE ACTINOMYCETES

THE Actinomycetes show relationships to both the fungi and the bacteria and, whilst included in the bacteria by some authorities, they are regarded by others as a distinctive group of the plant kingdom. Most species consist of very narrow branched and septate hyphae. They produce spores, often in chains, formed by the division of hyphae from the tip backwards.

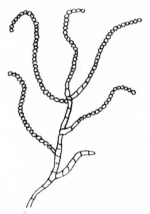

Various species of this group cause diseases in plants, animals, and humans, and members of the group are commonly present as saprophytes in the soil. The best known of the British plant diseases caused by this group is the common scab of potato.

COMMON SCAB OF POTATO, *Streptomyces scabies* (Thax.) Waksman and Henrici (*Actinomyces scabies* (Thax.) Güssow)

This is one of the most frequent diseases of potato tubers, particularly in soils of low humus content. It occurs most often on light gravelly or sandy soils, especially where the soil is

FIG. 248. Hypha and spores of an actinomycete.

naturally alkaline or where lime has recently been applied. Dry seasons favour its development. The disease renders the tubers unattractive and difficult to dispose of for human food, there may be considerable waste in peeling the tubers, and also their keeping quality may be lowered.

Symptoms and Cause. Irregular, loose, corky patches develop on the tuber. These may appear as isolated scabs, but frequently the scabbed areas run together and in extreme cases all, or most, of the tuber may be covered by the rough corky tissue. The infection is usually limited to the surface layers of the tuber. When the tubers are mature, and after lifting, scabs cease to develop.

The scabs are caused by various species of Streptomyces, of which *S. scabies* is the chief. These organisms are present in the soil, and they infect the developing tubers via the lenticels. In the infected areas small brown spots are formed. These increase in size, and the skin ruptures and the typical scabs are formed. Various forms of scab have been described, and these have been attributed to various species of Streptomyces.

573

Control Measures

1. In order to reduce the incidence of common scab in soils where the organic matter content is low, attempts should be made to increase this by ploughing in green crops, such as mustard, rye or tares. On a small scale, in gardens, the application of grass cuttings, spent hops or similar material in the furrows at planting time may help.

Fig. 249. Common scab of potato.

The influence of green manuring, though often favourable, is not always so, and the conditions under which it may be beneficial are not clearly understood. An old theory was that the scab organism lived on the humus instead of attacking the tubers, but it is now thought that green manuring may lead to the development of large populations of other organisms which are antagonistic to the scab organism.

2. Application of alkaline materials, such as lime, ashes and soot, should be avoided. Sulphate of ammonia and superphosphate should be used in preference to other nitrogenous and phosphatic fertilizers, respectively.

3. All scabbed tubers should be removed from the field and diseased material should not be returned to the land.

4. On land which has produced badly scabbed crops a long rest from potatoes of up to seven years may help, but this is not very practicable on many farms.

5. Some varieties are more susceptible than others. Owing to the possibility of infection being caused by several different species of Streptomyces, and the possibility of the existence of physiological races of each, it is difficult to give recommendations which would be generally applicable. Where severe attacks of common scab are experienced, growers would be well advised to try a few different varieties in order to discover which are most suited to the land in question. Varieties which may suffer severely are Ulster Premier, Craigs Royal, Majestic, Ulster Tarn, and Record. A greater degree of resistance may be shown by Arran Pilot, Maris Peer, King Edward and Pentland Dell.

THE BACTERIA (SCHIZOMYCETES)

The bacteria resemble fungi in their mode of nutrition. They do not contain chlorophyll, and they may obtain their food from living tissues, i.e. as parasites, or from non-living organic material, i.e. as saprophytes. Apart from this similarity, they differ from fungi in many respects. The bacteria are extremely minute, even in comparison with the spores of most fungi. Approximate average measurements are 1μ by 3μ for the rod-shaped types and 1μ diameter for spherical forms. They are usually single cells, which may be spherical, rod-shaped, comma-shaped or spiral. A typical nucleus is usually absent from these cells. They multiply by transverse division of the single cell into two separate individuals (hence the name Schizomycetes, or fission fungi). Numbers of distinct individuals may remain loosely joined to one another in chains, or clusters, or solid masses, but each grows and divides as a distinct unit. Under favourable conditions, multiplication occurs very rapidly, and within about twenty minutes of its formation one bacterium will split into two individuals. Some bacteria are provided with one or more flagella, by means of which they are motile in water and other liquids. Bacteria may produce thick-walled resting spores, usually one in each cell (*endospores*). Formation of spores is, however, extremely rare in the bacteria which cause plant diseases.

As primary agents of disease in agricultural crops, the bacteria are much less important than the fungi; they do, however, often invade tissue severely damaged through some other cause, and set up rotting of the tissue. For example, potato tubers damaged by blight may be invaded by bacteria which set up a wet-rot; roots of Brassicas damaged by club-root may be further rotted by bacteria as may parts of plants damaged by frost, insects, etc. In these cases bacteria are secondary causes of damage, begun by some other primary agent. Some serious diseases are, however, caused by bacteria. For example, bacterial diseases of fruit trees, tomatoes and ornamental plants occur in Britain, where also the water-mark disease of cricket-bat willows causes serious loss. Among important bacterial diseases in other countries are the black arm disease of cotton and the gumming disease of sugar-cane. Three examples of bacterial diseases of crop plants which may be encountered on farms in Britain are given below:

SOFT-ROT OF TURNIPS, SWEDES, ETC., *Erwinia carotovora* (*Bacterium carotovorum*)

Soft-rot is one of the most common bacterial diseases of plants. *E. carotovora* attacks a wide range of species, causing soft-rots of the fleshy parts of the storage organs. Among the crops affected are turnip, swede, potato, carrot, parsnip, onion, celery, cabbage and broccoli. It also occurs in the bulbs of hyacinths, the corms of arum lilies, the rhizomes of irises and the fruit of tomatoes.

The bacterium is rod-shaped, motile and non-sporing. It gains entry to plants through small wounds caused during thinning, weeding or hoeing, or by insects, slugs, etc. In turnips and swedes, infection may occur at any stage of growth. Some seedlings may be killed off if infected early. In larger plants the interior of the 'root' is converted into a white, pasty, rotten mass. The leaves may wilt, turn yellow and die, and the whole plant may disintegrate. In some plants the 'root', though rotting, may remain intact externally and the leaves may appear normal. The bacteria live, and multiply, in the intercellular spaces where they secrete an enzyme which dissolves the middle lamella of the cells.

Control Measures. As the disease appears to spread more readily in wet parts of fields, drainage should be rectified. Damage to the crop during thinning, weeding and hoeing should be avoided as much as possible. The use of excessive amounts of nitrogenous manures, which favour the development of sappy growth, should be avoided.

BLACK LEG OF POTATO, *Erwinia atroseptica* (*B. carotovorum*)

This disease is also known as basal stem rot. It is not usually serious or epidemic in the growing crop, but often occurs in isolated plants. As it spreads among tubers during storage, it may cause serious losses in the clamp. It is more common in the northern than in the southern parts of Britain.

Symptoms and Cause. Symptoms may appear in the crop at any stage of growth. Infected plants usually bear stiffer stems with more upright shoots. The upper leaves may have a metallic lustre and the leaf margins may curl inwards. The affected shoots are jet black at soil level and the discoloration continues down to the old tuber. Some shoots on the plant may not be affected. The leaves of infected shoots turn yellow, wilt and die early.

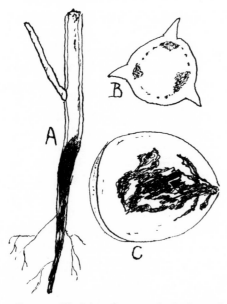

FIG. 250. Black leg of potato. A, the base of a shoot showing external blackening. B, transverse section of the stem above the blackened zone showing discoloration of the vascular bundles. C, section of tuber showing rotting extending inwards from the heel.

A transverse section of an infected stem shows a brown discoloration of the vascular tissue, which is most apparent in the three main vascular tracts. The discoloration extends right up the stem, above the externally blackened zones. The disease passes, internally, along the rhizomes and infects the new tubers through the heel. Infected tubers will be seen to have a brown discoloration or metallic lustre externally in the infected region.

When the tuber is split longitudinally through the heel, a brown rot is seen extending inwards from the heel to the internal tissues. The disease does not appear to spread in the soil to any extent, except under very wet conditions.

In the clamp, infected tubers become completely rotten and a wet mass oozes out, spreading bacteria over healthy tubers. The bacteria enter the sound tubers through cracks or wounds in the skin, or through lenticels, and further rotting occurs. The rot spreads most rapidly under wet, badly ventilated, storage conditions.

Under the certification schemes for seed potatoes, the presence of this disease in the crop may prevent the issue of a certificate.

Control Measures

1. Seed should not be saved from infected crops, as slightly diseased tubers may be planted and give rise to diseased plants.

2. Although infection via the soil seems rare, except under very wet soil conditions, it may be a wise precaution to avoid planting cut and damaged tubers in fields where the disease has occurred. Tubers cut for seed should be prepared well in advance, so that suberization of the cut surface may be complete before planting. As the disease may be transmitted on the knife it would be best to avoid cutting seed in which the presence of the disease is suspected.

3. Damage to tubers at lifting and at all stages before storage should be reduced to a minimum.

4. Tubers showing any sign of disease should not be clamped. In order to avoid losses if infected tubers are inadvertently clamped, clamps should be dry and well-ventilated.

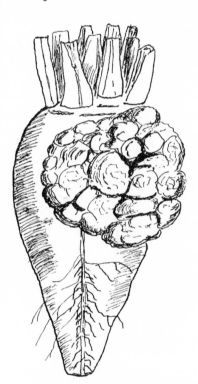

Fig. 251. Crown gall on sugar-beet.

CROWN GALL, *Agrobacterium tumefaciens* (*B. tumefaciens*)

This disease occurs on sugar-beet and mangels, tomatoes, hops, roses and fruit trees, such as apple and many other species. In sugar-beet and mangel crops it may occur on a few plants, but the number attacked is usually not serious, and the disease is of little importance in relation to these crops.

577

Symptoms and Causes. The bacterium causing the disease is short-rod-shaped, motile and non-sporing. Numerous strains exist, varying in their ability to infect different host plants. Infection of the 'roots' of sugar-beet and mangel occurs from the soil through wounds or cracks. In the infected region vigorous growth and division of cells takes place and galls are produced. The galls are more or less rounded, and vary in size from that of a pea to that of a man's fist, or even larger. They are usually produced near the crown of the storage organ. Infected plants are usually stunted, and the sugar content of the storage organ is low.

The disease develops more readily on alkaline than on acid soils, and is therefore favoured by the alkaline soil conditions which are desirable for sugar-beet.

Control Measures. Since infection occurs through wounds and abrasions, care should be taken to avoid excessive damage to the 'roots' during singling and hoeing.

Chapter XXVIII

VIRUS DISEASES

THE word 'virus' means, literally, a poison, and in this sense it has long been in use. It is only in modern times that the term has been applied to a particular type of disease-causing agent.

Viruses are extremely minute. They cannot be seen with the most powerful microscope, using ordinary light, but some have been photographed with the aid of the electron microscope. The standard of measurement used for virus particles is the millimicron, which is a millionth of a millimetre (0·000001 mm.), expressed as 1mμ.

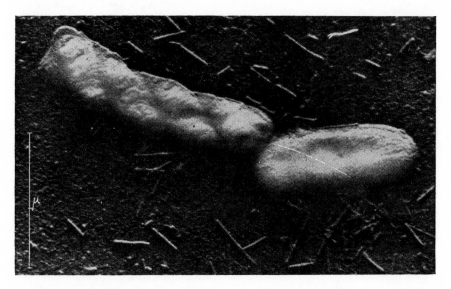

FIG. 252. Rod-shaped particles of tobacco mosaic virus surrounding two rod-shaped bacteria. Photographed by means of an electron microscope, × 36,500.
    Note. The rod-shaped virus particles tend to stick together, end to end, forming longer rods. The particles of many of the viruses which have been photographed are spherical in shape.

(By permission of Dr. R. Reed, University of Leeds.)

In the living cells of suitable hosts viruses have the power to multiply. Whether they reproduce themselves, or induce the host cells to produce further virus, is an open question.

All types of living organisms, from the lowly bacteria to man, are attacked by viruses. In animals they are the cause of numerous diseases —for example, foot-and-mouth disease of cattle, swine fever and virus pneumonia of pigs, fowl-pest of poultry, myxomatosis of rabbits and distemper of dogs. Viruses are also responsible for several ailments of humans,

579

such as, influenza, measles, mumps, small pox, chickenpox, yellow fever and infantile paralysis (poliomyelitis).

In plants, viruses may cause severe losses as a result of the disease conditions they produce. On the other hand, the presence of a particular virus in a plant may cause little obvious disturbance of the normal growth of the plant. In some cases rather decorative effects are produced by the presence of a virus in a plant, as in the case of the condition known as

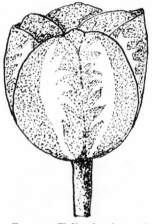

FIG. 253. Tulip showing variegation resulting from virus infection.

'break' in tulips, in which the petals show streaked or feathered variegations. There is evidence that tulips showing this effect were specially prized when they were first observed in western Europe towards the end of the sixteenth century, and permanent records of their existence are to be found in the paintings of Dutch artists of the late sixteenth and early seventeenth centuries. In the eighteenth century Van Osten claimed that the condition could be induced in a 'whole-colour' tulip by grafting into it a piece of the bulb of a 'broken' tulip. It was not until many years later that it was realized that the condition was the result of virus infection, and that, in grafting the infected tissue to the healthy plant, the virus was being transmitted. Similar breaking of petal colour may often be seen in other flowers. It occurs fairly frequently in wallflowers which have been infected with the cabbage black ring-spot virus.

Viruses are a much more serious matter in relation to such crops as the potato. Towards the end of the eighteenth century the degeneration of potato stocks, when grown year after year in the lowland parts of the country, began to cause a good deal of concern among growers. It was thought at the time that degeneration was due to continued vegetative propagation by means of tubers, and that, in order to maintain vigour, it was necessary to raise new stocks from true seed at frequent intervals. It is now recognized that this degeneration is due to the presence of various viruses, some of which produce well-known disease symptoms.

An important step in the study of viruses was taken in 1892 when Iwanowski, in Russia, showed that the sap extracted from tobacco plants showing symptoms of mosaic disease could cause mosaic to appear when injected into a healthy plant, even after the sap had been passed through porcelain filters which would prevent the passage of bacteria. He also demonstrated that the infective material multiplied in the new host plant, and that the infective matter in the sap was resistant to drying and to alcohol. Thus it was shown that the disease was caused by something invisible, smaller than bacteria, having the power to multiply in the host, and able to retain its infective properties even after treatment which would kill bacteria. Since that time filters have been found which will hold back viruses, and calculations of the size of some virus particles have been made on the basis of the size of filter pore which will just prevent their passage.

In 1935 Stanley in the United States isolated from the juice extracted from mosaic-diseased tobacco plants a substance, described as a crystalline protein, which had the infective properties of the virus, and which retained these properties even when diluted very considerably. Viruses have since been shown to consist of particles made up of protein molecules surrounding a central core of nucleic acid and known as nucleoproteins. Compounds of this type are constituents of normal healthy cells but in the case of the viruses the nucleic acid is of an aberrant type. It now seems clear that the infective property of viruses is concerned with the nucleic acid and not with the protein. These aberrant forms of nucleic acid create a disturbance of the nucleic acid synthesis of the host which results in secondary effects on the protein metabolism and thus results in the creation of further virus particles. Thus the living cells of a host are necessary to the multiplication of viruses and, unlike bacteria, they do not reproduce readily in non-living culture media.

TRANSMISSION OF VIRUSES

Viruses normally spread within an infected plant until all parts of the plant are infected; the virus is then said to be *systemic*. Usually the true seed escapes infection and therefore most viruses are not transmitted to the new plants produced from the seed. There are a few exceptions to this, the best known being mosaic of the bean (*Phaseolus vulgaris*), which is carried by a proportion of the seeds produced by an infected plant. There is also evidence to suggest that mosaic of tomato is transmitted in the seed.

Because of the systemic nature of viruses, they are transmitted by all the various means of vegetative reproduction, such as bulbs, corms, runners, rhizomes, stem tubers, root tubers, cuttings, budding and grafting. New plants produced from diseased plants, by any of these methods, will also be diseased.

Recent work suggests that some viruses may be destroyed by submitting infected plants, or parts of plants, for a time to temperatures about 37° C. In this way they may be freed from virus, and in the case of some vegetatively propagated plants, new healthy clones may then be built up.

Plant viruses are most frequently transmitted from plant to plant, in the field, by insects, which are referred to as *vectors*. The insects most usually involved are sap-sucking species which feed on the sap of infected plants and later, when feeding on healthy plants, inject virus-infected saliva into their tissues. The insects most often concerned are the aphids, but leaf-hoppers (*Jassidae*) and thrips are also concerned with the transmission of certain viruses. Turnip yellow mosaic virus is transmitted by flea-beetles, which are biting insects. Transmission by biting insects, however, is not common.

An aphid possesses a tube-like proboscis which pierces into the tissues of the plant. A little saliva is injected into the plant cells and is then sucked up again with the cell sap. If an aphid feeds on an infected plant, some of the virus will be sucked up with the sap, and at subsequent feeding periods saliva carrying the virus may be injected into the cells of a healthy plant, and so bring about infection. In the few cases of virus transmission by biting insects, infection appears to be associated with regurgitation, which occurs during feeding.

Sometimes an incubation period is necessary before the insect which has absorbed a particular virus can infect healthy plants. In some cases, e.g. sugar-beet yellows and potato leaf roll, the virus is persistent in the insect, which remains infective for a long period, without again feeding on a diseased plant. In others, e.g. sugar-beet mosaic and potato virus Y, the virus is non-persistent and the vector soon loses its ability to infect without feeding again on diseased plants. It has been proved that at least some viruses multiply within their insect vectors.

Some viruses are transmitted by contact between diseased and healthy plants, as when leaves are blown against one another by the wind or shaken together by passage of implements or men. Transmission of potato virus X and tobacco mosaic virus takes place in this way. It is possible that transmission of sap occurs as a result of minute abrasions or broken hairs on the surfaces of the leaves. In crops which are subjected to much handling by workers, viruses which are transmissible by contact may be transferred from diseased to healthy plants on the fingers of workers. Tomato mosaic (caused by the tobacco mosaic virus) may be spread from plant to plant in this way. The disease may also be spread on knives used in pruning the trusses. It is therefore important that, after contact with diseased plants, hands and implements should be thoroughly washed before healthy plants are dealt with. This virus is often present, in an active state, in cured tobacco, and can be transmitted to tomato plants from the fingers of smokers. It is therefore desirable that smokers should wash their hands thoroughly before handling tomato plants, and should not smoke whilst working with the crop. The tobacco mosaic virus can retain its infective powers outside the living plant for very long periods. Tobacco cured more than fifty years previously has been found to retain some virulence. Most viruses lose their infective powers considerably earlier than this, and many cease to be infective quite soon after removal from the living host cells.

Inoculation, by rubbing infected sap on healthy leaves, is often used for the transmission of certain viruses in the course of experimental work. In order to obtain infection in difficult cases, some slightly rough material, such as fine carborundum powder, may be rubbed gently on the leaf with the sap.

Experimentally, viruses which cannot be transmitted by other means are sometimes transmitted by grafting. A portion of a diseased plant is grafted to a healthy host. If the graft takes the virus is transmitted. This can usually be done only between fairly closely related plants. The plant parasite dodder can also transmit viruses from one host plant to another.

In a few cases it has been found that viruses may be soil-borne. Transmission may occur from infected plant remains or via soil fungi or nematodes may be the vectors. Nematodes may remain infective for periods greater than 30 days after feeding on infected material.

SYMPTOMS OF VIRUS DISEASES

The symptoms produced by viruses are very varied. Frequently they involve a reduction of chlorophyll formation which results in pale areas appearing in the leaves. This may result in mottling, or a mosaic effect, or in distinct chlorotic areas. A curling or puckering of the leaves may occur. Sometimes necrosis of the diseased tissues results, and in some cases the whole plant may die. More often, the plant continues to grow in a weakened condition. In the case of perennial plants, new shoots produced in successive years show symptoms of the disease.

Symptoms caused by a particular virus often vary when the virus is present in different host species. Different varieties of the same host species may also show differences of symptoms. For example, there is a certain amount of variety in the symptoms produced by the leaf-roll virus in different potato varieties.

Some viruses infect certain host plants, and multiply within them, without producing any readily observed symptoms. Such host plants, which are said to be *tolerant* of the virus, are known as *carriers* and, although not obviously diseased, they may serve as a source of infection to other plants in which the virus may produce disease symptoms.

Plants may be infected by more than one virus. Often the symptoms produced by a combination of viruses differ from those produced by any one of the viruses singly. Two viruses to which a plant is tolerant when each is present singly may produce severe disease symptoms when present together (see crinkle of potato). Thus a further disadvantage of tolerance to viruses is that a plant when infected by a virus to which it is normally tolerant may become severely diseased if it is already infected with another virus to which it is tolerant.

Some plants, when infected with certain viruses, react by the formation of necrotic areas around the point of infection. In these necrotic areas (local lesions) the virus is confined and prevented from spreading to the rest of the plant. Such plants are said to be *hypersensitive* to the particular virus. Hypersensitivity may take another form, in which the infected plant is rapidly killed. In this case the diseased plant and the virus it contains are eliminated together. In crops in the field both these forms of hypersensitivity will restrict the spread of the virus, from the infected plants to other plants. Crop varieties showing hypersensitivity are said to be *field immune* to the particular virus.

STRAINS OF VIRUSES

Many viruses exist in the form of a number of different 'strains' or 'variants'. Often some strains of a particular virus are more virulent than others. The strains may arise by some process comparable with mutation in plants. The existence of various strains, and the possibility of the appearance of new ones, complicate the problems of plant-breeders in their attempts to obtain resistant crop varieties (see p. 62).

The presence of a weak strain of a virus in a plant may protect it from damage by a more virulent strain. For example, in potatoes it has been found that when a weak strain of virus X is present a more virulent strain does not multiply.

IDENTIFICATION OF VIRUSES

Many viruses produce different symptoms in different varieties of a host species. Some are able to produce disease in more than one species of plant and often different symptoms are produced in the various host species. Thus, it will be clear that some means of identifying viruses is necessary. Since it is impossible to see viruses by the ordinary microscope, or to produce cultures on artificial media, as can be done with bacteria and some fungi, other means of identification are necessary.

Identification may be achieved by means of the symptoms produced on certain standard *indicator plants*. The most widely-used indicator plant is the tobacco which is susceptible to infection by a wide range of plant viruses. When infected by a particular virus, the tobacco plant will produce characteristic symptoms, such as local lesions varying in size, shape, colour, etc., clearing of the veins, mottling of the younger leaves, and so on, by means of which the virus may be identified. Some other indicator plants, which are used in this way, are *Nicotiana glutinosa*, thornapple (*Datura stramonium*), tomato, cucumber and French bean.

Another aid to identification of some plant viruses depends upon the fact that when plant viruses are injected into suitable experimental animals the animal reacts by producing antibodies. A few days after injection a little blood may be taken from the animal and from it an antiserum can be obtained. When the antiserum is mixed with the virus from which it was produced a precipitate forms. All strains of the particular virus will produce a precipitate with the antiserum, but other plant viruses will not do so. Thus, if an unknown virus is tested with the antiserum of a known virus and a precipitate is obtained, the unknown can be identified as a strain of the known. By the same means the presence of a particular virus in plant organs may be demonstrated. For example, by use of the appropriate antisera, tests can be made for the presence of various viruses in potato tubers, and this is of considerable value in speeding up the work of producing virus-free stocks. The use of antisera, whilst of great value in relation to some plant viruses, is somewhat restricted by the fact that it has been found impossible, so far, to produce antisera for many viruses.

Rabbits are usually used for the production of antisera, but other animals such as horses, guinea pigs and fowls have also been used.

THE OCCURRENCE AND CONTROL OF VIRUS DISEASES

Virus diseases are extremely numerous and are found in most crop and weed species. About 200 distinct disease-causing viruses are known and new ones are still being discovered. Mosaic and variegation effects, caused by viruses, may often be seen in wild plants, such as dandelion and docks. Virus diseases cause serious degeneration of strawberry and raspberry stocks, and the hop plant may suffer as a result of infection by a number of different viruses. Several virus diseases occur in tomatoes; of these, mosaic, streak and spotted wilt are examples. Many virus diseases of vegetables and root crops of all kinds are known. Examples which may occur on farms are cabbage black ring-spot, cabbage mosaic, mosaic of cauliflower and broccoli, mosaic of turnip and swede, pea mosaic and the several virus diseases of potato and sugar-beet. Among virus diseases occurring in important crops in other countries are mosaic and other virus diseases of sugar-cane, phloem necrosis of tea, rosette of groundnuts, leaf-curl of cotton, swollen-shoot disease of cocoa, and bunchy-top of banana. In a book of this nature it is not possible to deal with many virus diseases in detail. The common virus diseases of potato and sugar-beet, some of which are of considerable economic importance, will be considered in some detail, in order to illustrate some of the characteristics of virus diseases and methods for their control.

The general methods involved in the control of virus diseases may be summarized as follows:

1. The control of sources of infection.

2. The control of insect vectors, if practicable.

3. Care in handling plants, in cases where the virus can be spread by contact.

4. Planting virus-free stocks of vegetatively propagated plants, e.g. potatoes, hops, strawberries, raspberries, etc.

5. Sowing virus-free seed, in the case of the few seed-borne viruses.

6. Producing new clones from parts of plants in which virus has been destroyed by heat treatment or from apical meristems which are virus-free.

7. Growing immune, resistant or hypersensitive varieties when possible.

VIRUS DISEASES OF POTATO

LEAF-ROLL

This disease is one of the chief causes of degeneration of potato stocks when they are grown repeatedly in the lowland areas of England. In recent years, as a result of the more widespread use of certified seed (see p. 84), plants showing this disease have become less common in field crops, but they may frequently be seen in cottage gardens in crops which have been grown from stocks kept for seed year after year.

The virus is spread by aphids, chiefly the peach aphid, *Myzus persicae*. Winged forms of the insect are capable of carrying the virus some distance from infected to healthy crops, and wingless forms, which crawl from plant to plant within the crop, disseminate the virus among surrounding plants after feeding on a diseased plant. Aphids must feed on infected plants for some time, and twenty-four hours must elapse before they become infective. Once an aphid is infective with this virus it remains so for a long period, often until its death. The disease may also be transmitted by aphids to tomato, woody nightshade and thornapple.

If the potato plant is infected early in the season, the leaflets of *the young upper leaves* roll upwards, but the older leaves are not affected. This stage is known as *primary leaf-roll*. Although the older leaves do not show rolling symptoms, the virus is carried to all parts of the plant, and consequently the tubers will be infected. If infection of the plant occurs in the later stages of growth, there may be no rolling of the leaflets at all, but the tubers will be infected.

When infected tubers are planted in the following and subsequent years they give rise to plants in which the leaflets of *the lower, older leaves* are rolled upwards, and possibly the upper leaves will also show some upward curling. This condition is known as *secondary leaf-roll*. Usually the rolled leaves are paler in colour, thicker, and harsh to the touch. The shoots produce a characteristic rattle when shaken. In the infected shoots part of the phloem breaks down (known as *phloem necrosis*) and starch accumulates in the leaves. Infected tubers are usually indistinguishable from healthy ones, but in one or two varieties, such as Golden Wonder and Catriona, a necrosis of the phloem occurs, which appears as brown streaks and spots in the tissues. This condition is known as *net necrosis*.

Considerable variation in the extent of the leaf symptoms occurs in different varieties of potato. In the varieties Up-to-date and Great Scot, only slight rolling of the lowermost leaves occurs, whilst the variety Craigs Defiance is severely affected. In King Edward fairly pronounced rolling occurs, and usually this is accompanied by a pink coloration of the lower surface of the leaves. Plants showing secondary leaf-roll are usually lacking in vigour and may be markedly stunted. Often the lower leaves turn brown at the margins and in the intervenal regions towards the end of the season. These latter symptoms may be confused with the symptoms of potash deficiency.

Leaf-roll results in the production of a smaller number of tubers and often, but not always the tubers are mainly small ones. Because of the tendency for small tubers to be produced, a relatively high proportion of diseased to healthy tubers is likely to be selected when a crop containing diseased and healthy plants is riddled for seed.

In the warmer, drier areas of the country the aphid *Myzus persicae* is usually abundant and the winged forms move freely. In such areas rapid spread of leaf-roll occurs, resulting in the subsequent rapid degeneration of potato stocks. In cool, moist areas where the wind velocity is frequently high, as in the seed-growing areas of Scotland and certain hilly districts in England and Wales, aphids are less common and move about less readily. In such areas stocks of potatoes can be grown with a high degree of freedom from leaf-roll, and it is in such areas that certified crops with a high standard of health are produced for seed purposes.

FIG. 254. *Left:* leaf roll of potato. *Right:* underside of a potato leaf showing early symptoms of leaf drop streak. (By courtesy of the Director, Rothamsted Experimental Station.)

Some varieties show a higher degree of resistance to leaf-roll in the field than others. For example, Ulster Chieftain, Craigs Alliance and Dr. McIntosh are very susceptible, whilst Home Guard, Ulster Prince, Craigs Royal, Arran Viking are less frequently infected and in King Edward, Pentland Crown and Ulster Tarn resistance is greater.

LEAF-DROP STREAK AND RUGOSE MOSAIC (SEVERE MOSAIC), *Potato Virus Y*

The virus known as potato virus Y is another potential cause of severe losses in the potato crop, but, as with leaf-roll, losses have been considerably reduced by the increased use, by farmers, of certified seed. Virus Y is disseminated in the field by aphids, chiefly *Myzus persicae*. The insect vector can transmit the virus immediately after feeding on an infected leaf, but it loses its infectivity within a few hours and must again feed on an infected plant if its infectivity is to be restored.

The symptoms of infection by this virus differ somewhat in different

Fig. 255. *Above:* leaf drop streak; leaves dying and hanging from the stem. *Below:* shoots of King Edward showing rugose mosaic, *left*, and a healthy shoot *right*. (From Min. of Ag. Advisory Leaflet, No. 139. By permission of the Controller of H.M. Stationery Office.)

varieties. In the year of infection in most varieties, such as Majestic and Arran Banner, a condition known as *Leaf-drop Streak* develops. Shortly after infection the upper leaves become mottled, and on the lower leaves a necrosis develops in the form of black streaks along the underside of the veins. The necrosis later spreads throughout the blades of the leaflets and the petioles, and the leaves may fall off or remain hanging from the stem by a thread of tissue. The youngest leaves at the top of the stem, although mottled, do not die in this way, but remain, as a tuft, at the top of the shoot. Some varieties, such as Kerr's Pink and Arran Pilot, do not show the leaf drop streak symptoms, and Sharpe's Express develops the dark streaks only.

Tubers saved for seed from infected plants give rise to plants with quite different symptoms. The plants are stunted, with mottled and crinkled leaves, and without the leaf-drop streak symptoms. The stems become weak, as the plant gets older, and tend to lie on the ground. Only a few small tubers are produced. This phase of the disease is known as *rugose* (i.e. Rough) *mosaic*; it is a severe mosaic. Some varieties are more susceptible than others. For example, Arran Pilot, Arran Comet, Craigs Royal are very susceptible, whilst Ulster Chieftain, Ulster Dale and Majestic are only moderately so, and Pentland Beauty, Pentland Crown and Ulster Tarn show good resistance.

Virus Y can also infect cabbage, kale, Brussels sprout, garden pea, red clover and common bindweed. Other members of the potato family (Solanaceae) are also susceptible. These plants include tomato, woody nightshade, black nightshade and henbane. Such plants may provide a source of infection for the potato crop, as well as in some cases, such as cabbage and kale, providing a means for the overwintering of the insect vectors.

MOTTLE OR MILD (OR SIMPLE) MOSAIC, *Virus X*

Until recently potato Virus X was the most widely distributed of all potato viruses. The majority of stocks of many commercial varieties were infected with it. It was quite common in Scottish seed stocks, and in some varieties it was difficult or impossible to find plants which were free from virus X. New stocks of old varieties free from virus X are now being produced by research stations and supplied to seed-growers, so that the annual losses through this virus should be considerably reduced.

In most varieties the symptoms of infection are a faint mottling of the leaves, and a slight crinkling of the edges of the leaflets. Other varieties, although infected, show no very obvious symptoms. In spite of lack of obvious symptoms of infection, however, it has been estimated that infected crops may yield 2 to 4 tons per acre less than healthy ones.

In some varieties, such as King Edward, Arran Crest, Craigs Defiance and Epicure, quite marked symptoms appear when young plants are artificially inoculated with this virus. In these varieties the leaves are not mottled, but necrotic areas arise on the uppermost leaf, and later the growing points and shoots are killed. The shoots die from the apex downwards. This reaction is known as *top necrosis*. In the field the disease does not spread in these varieties and is rarely seen. The disease is apparently so lethal that if infection does occur, under field conditions, the whole plant is killed or the tissues are killed off at the spots of infection, and the virus, being shut off from the rest of the plant by dead tissue, fails to spread. This *field immunity* due to hypersensitivity is a valuable characteristic.

There are a number of strains of virus X some of which are more virulent than others. Evidence suggests that environment can have a pronounced effect on the severity of the symptoms produced by a particular strain.

Virus X is not spread by aphids nor, so far as is known, by any other insect vector. It can be transmitted by the leaves of diseased plants rubbing against those of a healthy plant. This probably occurs in the field with the help of wind. There may be some other means of transmission as yet unknown. One suggestion is that contact of underground parts, between diseased and healthy plants, may bring about infection.

Mild mosaic symptoms may be caused in some varieties by other viruses, such as virus A. Several varieties of potato are hypersensitive to virus A and therefore field-immune. Unlike virus X, virus A is transmitted by aphids.

Frequently viruses X and Y occur together in the same plant. This association usually produces a severe mosaic, with symptoms similar to those of rugose mosaic caused by virus Y alone in the year after primary infection with that virus.

CRINKLE, *Virus X* plus *Virus A*

The disease known as crinkle is caused by the presence of virus X together with virus A in the same plant. The symptoms produced by the two viruses in combination vary somewhat according to the variety of potato. Usually the plants are dwarfed and there is a pronounced puckering of the leaves, which may curve downwards at the edges. Diffuse, slightly yellowish areas occur all over the leaf. Later the yellow areas change to a rusty brown colour. The leaves are brittle and easily injured. This disease is also classed as a 'severe mosaic'.

The disease develops when virus A is carried, by aphids, to plants already infected with virus X. Varieties which are hypersensitive, and therefore field-immune, to either virus never develop this disease in the field. Examples of such varieties are Arran Crest, Epicure, Great Scot, Craigs Defiance, Craigs Royal and Kerr's Pink.

PARACRINKLE, *Virus E*

This virus is of interest, but of little economic importance. It is present in all plants of the variety King Edward, in which it causes no disease symptoms. It does not spread in the field to other varieties, but it may be transmitted to them artificially by grafting. When thus transmitted, to some varieties, the virus causes the severe symptoms known as paracrinkle.

Other viruses of the potato crop are known, some of little importance in Britain. For example, virus G produces a condition, known as *Aucuba mosaic*, in which the leaves become spotted or blotched with bright yellow, like the leaves of the variegated laurel species, *Aucuba japonica*. The disease is not common, and it does not appear to spread to any extent under field conditions. Recent work in Holland has demonstrated the probable importance of a virus known as virus S, which is present in stocks of many European varieties of potato. Usually the virus produces no very obvious symptoms, but losses of up to 15 per cent. have been estimated for crops infected with this virus. Like virus X, it is probably transmitted by contact, no insect vector having yet been discovered.

THE CONTROL OF VIRUS DISEASES OF POTATO

As plants cannot readily be cured once they are infected with viruses, methods which aim at preventing infection must be utilized. In the case of viruses which are disseminated by insects, the control of the insect vectors would be of value, and developments along these lines are discussed later. Production of healthy crops at present depends largely upon (*a*) the production of healthy stocks for the seed-grower, and (*b*) the multiplication of these stocks under conditions which do not favour the spread of viruses, so that the ware producer may be ensured a supply of healthy seed.

It is essential for breeders of potato varieties to take all precautions to prevent infection of their stocks (see p. 76). When valuable new seedlings have been obtained, it is necessary to multiply the stock under conditions where viruses will not spread, until supplies are sufficient to pass on to seed-growers for further multiplication under the Potato Seed Certification schemes (see p. 84). It is important to maintain nucleus stocks in a virus-free condition so that seed-growers may always be ensured a source of supply of superlatively healthy seed. In the case of many of the older varieties, entirely virus-free stocks are difficult or impossible to find. At Cambridge and elsewhere, testing is carried out with the object of obtaining virus-free tubers which can be used for building up virus-free nucleus stocks. Some stocks which have been produced in this way are maintained in Northern Ireland and Scotland.

Virus-tested seed (V.T.S.) is obtained from certified crops grown from tubers obtained from single plants which had been leaf-sampled throughout and found to be free from Virus X; it is used to produce Foundation seed (F.S.) which can then be used for 'SS' seed production. The Potato Seed Certification schemes have already been outlined in an earlier section of this book (see Chapter VI). The highest grades of seed are produced in areas where aphids are not common and winged forms do not move about freely. The winged forms of the peach aphid, *M. persicae*, fly most readily when the temperature is above 18° C. (65°F.), the relative humidity less than 70 per cent. and the velocity of the wind less than five miles an hour. Thus low temperatures, high humidity and high winds prevent the migration of winged forms to crops on which they may start infection. Such conditions prevail in regions, usually at high altitudes, in Scotland, Ireland, parts of England, chiefly in the north and west, and in Wales. In some areas these conditions may prevail at low altitudes, particularly near the coast, and it is likely that a high standard of health could be maintained in potato stocks in such areas.

Certification of seed stocks provides some guarantee against the presence of the readily observable virus diseases, but even in the highest grade of seed, i.e. that having the 'SS' Certificate, a mild form of virus X could be widespread in the sample. By the use of the new clones free from virus X which have been produced in recent years, seed which is free from this virus may be produced and national losses through virus X reduced.

Commercial ware growers often purchase just sufficient high-grade certified seed to produce the seed for their ware crop of the following year. This latter 'once-grown' seed can be very satisfactory if a little care is taken in its production. The high-grade certified seed should be planted as far away as possible from crops which are not grown from fresh, certified seed. These crops may be severely infected and serve as a source of infection of the healthy crop. Tubers left in the soil from previous crops may produce diseased plants from which virus infection may be carried to the crop. It is therefore important to plant the new seed on land free from such groundkeepers and, as a policy, to prevent groundkeepers, as far as possible, on other fields. In northern and western areas where aphids are less common, healthy home-grown seed may often be produced, from an original certified stock, for a number of years especially if it is possible to rogue out any plants showing virus symptoms. Roguing should be done early, before the plants meet in the rows. Firstly, because plants infected with virus X will be removed before they can infect their neighbours through contact between their foliage, secondly, because aphids will not yet be very active, and thirdly, because the diseased plants will not have formed tubers which might by chance be left in the ground and later harvested with the crop. In other areas, where aphids are common, it is doubtful whether roguing is economically worthwhile. In such districts it is a good policy to use certified seed every year.

Rapid deterioration of a healthy stock may result from growing the crop in close proximity to a source of infestation by aphids. The aphid *M. persicae* lays its eggs in crevices in peach and apricot trees where they pass the winter. *Aphis rhamni*, which can disseminate potato virus Y, overwinters, in the form of eggs, on buckthorn bushes which are often present in hedges. In seed-growing districts these plants should be avoided. More important is the overwintering of the insects themselves which occurs particularly on Brassica crops on farms and in gardens, on plants in glasshouses, and in mangel clamps where roots carrying leaves bearing aphids have been clamped. Healthy seed for further seed production should not be planted close to such sources of aphids. Aphids may also persist in chitting houses and may sometimes be seen there on the sprouts of seed potatoes set out in boxes. Viruses may be spread by these aphids which, after feeding on sprouts of diseased tubers, may carry the virus to healthy sprouts. Where aphids are present in a chitting-house they may be destroyed by fumigation of the house with nicotine.

Experiments by research workers at Rothamsted suggest that spraying the potato crop with contact or systematic insecticides in order to control the aphids possesses economic possibilities. Spraying started soon after the plants come through and continued at fortnightly intervals will stop or reduce the spread of aphid-carried viruses. In this way a farmer may keep his certified stock healthy for a longer period so that less frequent purchase of new seed stocks will be necessary. For the later sprayings the insecticide may be incorporated in the anti-blight spray.*

Control of virus disease through the breeding of immune varieties is a possibility of the future. Some of the problems involved in this work have been discussed earlier (see Chapter V). Field immunity to the Mild Mosaic type viruses X and A can be bred into new varieties, and in Craigs Defiance field immunity to four such viruses X, A, B and C has been obtained. The problem is more difficult in relation to leaf-roll and virus Y. In the case of leaf-roll, although some varieties are more susceptible than others, no immune or hypersensitive varieties are known. It is possible that breeding will produce varieties showing greater resistance, and that some form of immunity may be discovered, possibly in wild species. The problem is some way from solution also in the case of virus Y. Some varieties on the continent and in America are claimed to be highly resistant, and resistance may also be found in some wild species. Having discovered suitable breeding material it will still remain for the breeder to combine good commercial characteristics with resistance to viruses, in order to satisfy the needs of the farmer.

VIRUS DISEASES OF SUGAR-BEET

Two virus diseases are common in the sugar-beet crop in Britain— namely, *virus yellows* and *mosaic*. The viruses causing these diseases may also attack other forms of *Beta vulgaris*, such as mangel, sugar-mangel, fodder-beet, garden beet, spinach beet and seakale beet. The wild beet (*B. maritima*) may also be affected, as may some members of the genus *Chenopodium*, such as fat hen.

VIRUS YELLOWS. This disease is of considerable economic importance. It can be found in most areas where sugar-beet crops are grown, but it is often particularly severe in the Eastern Counties where sugar-beet and mangel are also grown for seed.

In a root crop the disease is more serious when infection occurs early in the season. Severe infection at this time may result in the reduction of sugar-yield to about half. Infection late in the season is less serious. Severe infection of seed crops may result in a reduction in seed-yield of 30 to 50 per cent.

The virus is transmitted by aphids, chiefly the peach aphid *Myzus persicae*,

* Broadbent, L., and Burt, P., 'The Control of Potato Virus Diseases by Insecticides', *The Agr. Rev.*, **1**, 60-2, June, 1955.

and, to a much smaller extent, by the black bean aphid, *Aphis fabae*. After feeding on diseased plants, the insects remain infective for a long time without further visits to such plants.

In the root crop the symptoms of the disease are largely confined to the outer leaves of the plant. The most obvious symptom consists of yellowing between the veins of the leaves. In addition, the leaves are thicker and less pliable than healthy leaves. They rattle when shaken and break

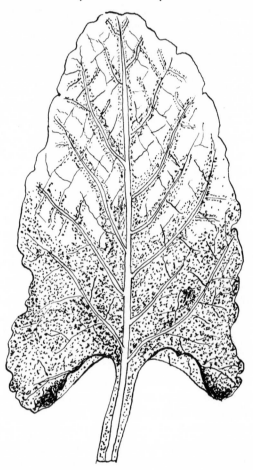

FIG. 256. Virus yellows of sugar-beet. Showing yellowing at the top of the leaf spreading between the main veins the sides of which remain green.

easily, with a characteristic crackle, when crushed in the hand. The yellowing usually begins in the upper part of the leaves, at the tips and margins, and spreads downwards and inwards between the veins. Characteristically it is a bright orange-yellow colour, but in odd plants, and more generally in some varieties, it may be reddish or rusty brown. The infected leaves show less tendency to flag in warm dry weather. As the season progresses necrosis occurs in the yellow areas which die early.

594

MOSAIC. This disease is less serious than virus yellows and usually not so frequent in crops as that disease. The virus is transmitted by *M. persicae* and *A. fabae*. The insects do not remain infective for very long, after feeding on an infected plant, and they must again feed on such a plant if they are to become infective again.

The symptoms of the disease consist of a light and dark green mottling of the leaves which is more readily observed in the younger central leaves. The effects of this disease on the crop as a whole are normally not very serious.

Control of Virus Diseases of Sugar Beet. Since virus yellows and mosaic are not carried by the seeds the seedlings produced by them are free from these diseases. Infection of the new crop must take place from some external source. Control of the diseases is therefore concerned with the reduction of the sources of virus infection, from which aphids may obtain the virus, together with any practical means of reducing aphid infestation of the crop. Infestation of the root crop in spring, by aphids, may come from peach trees, brassica crops, glasshouses, etc., but these aphids must first feed on infected plants before they become infective. Aphids may overwinter on mangels in and around clamps or on beet or mangel stecklings. From these the aphids may have picked up viruses which they may transfer directly to the new root crop. Infected roots left in fields may also provide a source of virus from which aphids may carry disease to the new crop.

The chief lines of attack on these diseases involve.

(1) Thorough cleaning up of fields after a susceptible crop, so that diseased plants are not left to grow in the following season.

(2) Clearing up the site of mangel clamps so that sprouting mangels, which may be diseased, are not left around where aphids may feed on them. Clamp sites should be cleared and ploughed by the end of March.

(3) Growing stecklings, for the seed crop, in areas where aphids are not abundant and where beet and mangel root crops are not common. Such areas are those suitable for growing certified stocks of seed potatoes. Stecklings produced in these areas may then be planted out for seed production in the seed-growing areas of the Eastern Counties, with little risk of infection being transferred from them to the root crop.

If stecklings are raised from seed in the root-growing districts, they may escape infection from the root crop if the seed is sown in late August after the aphids have left the root crop. Protection of the steckling beds by early and repeated sprayings of an insecticide, such as nicotine, to kill the aphids, may help.

If stecklings are infected, they should not be planted out in the spring, but should be burnt. They will not only yield poorly, but will also provide a source of virus for the root crop.

(4) Early sowing of the root crop, so that plants are well established before aphids become active. This may encourage bolting, so that 'non-bolting' strains are desirable for this purpose.

(5) Obtaining a good plant population with no gaps in the rows. Each aphid can only infect a limited group of plants, and a high plant population may ensure that a good proportion of the crop may escape infection. Isolated plants in a gappy crop appear to attract the winged aphids, which alight and start infection of the crop.

(6) Spraying the crop as a protection against aphids is an economic practice in some seasons and spray warnings are issued by the sugar beet factories so that spraying may be done when it will be most effective. The protection afforded by the spray must cover as long a period as possible and for this purpose approved systemic sprays are most useful.

Chapter XXIX

NON-PARASITIC DISEASES

(A) *Nutritional Disorders*. For healthy growth it is necessary for plants to be able to obtain adequate amounts of certain chemical elements from the soil (mineral elements). Largely on the basis of results of experiments in which plants were grown with their roots in solutions of various salts, seven mineral elements were originally considered to be essential for plant growth. These so-called 'essential elements' were nitrogen, phosphorus, potassium, sulphur, calcium, magnesium and iron. It is now known that certain other elements, although absorbed in relatively small quantities, are also important for the healthy growth of plants. The elements now considered essential may be divided roughly into two groups: *major elements*, which are required by plants in relatively large amounts; and *trace elements*, which are utilized in much smaller amounts. Trace elements are sometimes spoken of as *minor elements*, but this name may be misleading, as it suggests that they are of minor importance in plant nutrition, whereas in fact all these elements are essential in providing a proper balance for healthy growth. An inadequate supply of any one of them in a form which may be absorbed by the roots, can be the limiting factor to healthy development of the plant. In the following account, therefore, the term essential element is used to include both major and trace elements.

The essential elements are as follows:

Major Elements. Nitrogen, phosphorus, potassium, calcium, sulphur and magnesium.

Trace Elements. Iron, boron, manganese, copper, zinc and molybdenum.

Some plants also absorb other elements, such as sodium, chlorine and silicon. Such elements may produce beneficial effects on certain plants, but there is no proof that they are essential, as a rule, for normal plant growth.

The essential elements must be present in the soil in a form in which they are available for absorption by the root hairs of plants. Under certain circumstances, essential elements, although present in the soil, may be unavailable because they are not present in such a form. For example, heavy dressings of lime may render boron unavailable, and as a result certain crops may suffer severely from boron deficiency. It is also important that a correct balance of the essential elements should be available to the plant. Excessive amounts of one element may upset the balance and render supplies of the other elements inadequate, with the result that symptoms of disease appear in the crop. Ill-health may also be produced by excess of certain elements, which, absorbed in too great amount, may interfere with cell metabolism. Thus disorders may be produced either by deficiencies or by excesses of particular elements.

Deficiency of any of the essential elements gives rise to certain 'disease' symptoms, which are fairly well defined for a particular crop. But deficiency symptoms show considerable variety as between one type of crop and another. With experience it is possible, to some extent, to distinguish between the symptoms produced in crops in the field by deficiencies of some of the essential elements. Exact diagnosis, by visual symptoms, is often difficult, however, and requires considerable experience and familiarity with the particular type of deficiency. Potash deficiency usually causes marginal scorch of leaves, but marginal scorch may result in some crops from deficiency of other elements, such as phosphorus or boron, and from other causes. Similarly, yellow, reddish or orange tints often appear as symptoms of nitrogen deficiency, but in some crops deficiency of other elements, such as magnesium, may produce similar tints.

Suspected deficiencies of some of the major elements, such as phosphorus and potassium, can readily be checked by soil analysis. Suspected deficiencies of trace elements cannot be checked in this way. In order to check a diagnosis in such cases, tests may be performed on tissues from suspected plants, and from healthy plants for comparison. Or a check may sometimes be possible by observations of the effects of spraying over the plant a dilute solution containing a suitable compound of the element suspected to be deficient.

Some of the nutritional disorders which are likely to occur in crops in Britain are briefly summarized below.

Nitrogen Deficiency. Plants require nitrogenous materials from the soil in relatively large amounts, and consequently soils frequently become deficient in these materials, and symptoms of this deficiency are often seen on farms. Plants suffering from inadequate absorption of this element show reduced growth and produce smaller leaves, which are paler green. The leaves may develop yellow, reddish or orange tints. In Brassica crops, the older leaves become tinted. Sugar-beet and mangels show stunted growth and pallor of the leaves. Cereals tiller badly in the absence of adequate nitrogen supplies.

Phosphorus Deficiency. Phosphorus is frequently present in soils in amounts inadequate for healthy plant growth, and therefore plants showing symptoms of this deficiency are not difficult to find. In the absence of adequate supplies of this element, the development of the root system is restricted. The leaves show a tendency to become bluish-green and lack lustre. If tints develop in the leaves, they are more usually purplish than red or yellow: sometimes a dull bronzing occurs. The leaf margins may become necrotic, producing a scorched appearance. The whole plant will usually be stunted, few lateral shoots develop, and the leaves may shed prematurely.

Potassium Deficiency. Application of fertilizers containing potassium is frequently required on farmland in Britain. Crops such as potatoes and sugar-beet make heavy demands on the potassic fertilizers in the soil, and these crops often show signs of deficiency of potassium. Potassium is important in the nutrition of plants because it plays a part in enabling the manufacture of carbohydrates by the plant. In consequence, plants which manufacture and store large quantities of carbohydrate are most severely affected by deficiency of the element. Production of tubers, fruits and grain is severely affected. Root and shoot development are restricted and the leaves are bluish-green, sometimes with a chlorosis between the veins. Frequently in dicotyledons the margins and tips of the leaves become scorched. In potatoes the upper surfaces of the leaves become distinctly bronzed and necrotic areas develop on the underside; later, scorching of the tips and margins of the leaflets develops. The tops die early and, as a result, yield of tubers is low. In clovers, necrotic spots appear on the margins of the leaves and these are followed by marginal scorch. Cereals are stunted, but they tiller freely. The leaves are bluish-green, though sometimes

FIG. 257. Potash deficiency. Marginal necrosis on leaf of field bean.

slight chlorosis may develop, and the tips and margins frequently turn brown. Few ears are produced, and small yields of undersized grain result. Apart from these growth limitations, deficiency of potash also renders plants less resistant to many diseases. Potash deficiency is more likely to develop frequently on sandy soils than on clay soils.

Calcium Deficiency. Root development is usually restricted by shortage of calcium. Leaf symptoms, which develop particularly in young leaves, include chlorosis around the margins. The leaf margins may be irregular in outline and they may curl upwards. Later marginal scorching may occur. Calcium deficiency symptoms may appear in plants growing on acid soils, but frequently symptoms which appear on such soils are a result of acidity rather than calcium deficiency.

Magnesium Deficiency. On farmland magnesium deficiency is not frequent in Britain; it may occur in acid, light, sandy soils. A common symptom of the deficiency is chlorosis of the leaves. Production of chlorophyll is reduced because magnesium is an element which enters into the composition of chlorophyll. Various brilliant tints may develop, dark brown necrotic patches may form between the veins, and the leaves fall early. Usually symptoms show in the older leaves first. The deficiency may be corrected by application of magnesium limestone or dolomite or by a dressing of magnesium sulphate (usually 1 to 2 cwt. per acre, but sometimes heavier applications are needed).

Iron Deficiency. Iron is important in the manufacture of chlorophyll by plants, in which it plays a catalytic role. For this reason, deficiency of iron is associated with chlorosis of the leaves. In contrast with the chlorosis produced by magnesium deficiency, it affects the young leaves first. Symptoms of iron deficiency may arise occasionally in this country on naturally calcareous soils or soils which have been limed excessively. For this reason, the symptoms are sometimes called *lime-induced chlorosis*. Iron deficiency is most often seen in fruit trees growing on chalk soils in Kent. Cabbages, kales and other Brassica crops show a marbling of the leaves. Cereals and other farm crops are not often affected. Application of iron salts to the soil is not successful in overcoming the deficiency, as iron is rapidly rendered unavailable in highly calcareous soils. The usual treatment for fruit trees is to introduce tablets containing iron salts into holes bored in the trunks of the trees.

Manganese Deficiency. This deficiency occurs here and there in Britain, most frequently in the Eastern Counties of England, usually on alkaline peat soils. On other soils excessive dressings of lime, which render manganese unavailable to the plant, may result in the appearance of manganese-deficiency symptoms in crops. Considerable variety in the symptoms resulting from manganese deficiency is found in different crops. Usually the leaves become chlorotic. The symptoms are fairly striking in the potato, in which the young upper leaves are pale and rows of small brown-black spots, running parallel to the veins, develop. In some crops certain named 'diseases' are caused by manganese deficiency. Some of these are:

1. SPECKLED YELLOWS OF SUGAR-BEET AND MANGEL. This condition bears some similarity to mosaic disease, with which it might be confused. In this case, however, the leaves are more upright and appear more triangular in shape, owing to the upward rolling of their margins. The tissue between the veins shows a mosaic of light and darker areas. Brownish spots may appear between the veins; these become necrotic and fall out.

2. GREY SPECK OR GREY LEAF OF OATS. Grey or buff spots or streaks develop on the lower part of the lamina of the older leaves of young plants. These areas coalesce and the affected areas turn brown and necrotic. The upper part of the leaf blade hangs down, but may remain green. The whole plant may eventually die or, if it recovers, few panicles and little grain may be produced.

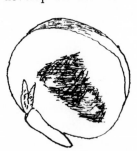

FIG. 258. Marsh spot. Pea split open to show the inner surface of a cotyledon.

3. MARSH SPOT OF PEAS. The most notable symptom of the deficiency in peas is the brown marking which appears on the inner surface of the cotyledons of the seed. This can be observed if the skin is removed and the cotyledons separated. The mark may be small or quite extensive.

In severe cases the tissue may become shrivelled and collapse, leaving a hollow in the middle of the seed. Because this condition was at one time frequent in peas grown in the Romney Marsh area, it became known by the name of 'Marsh' spot. Usually there are no other symptoms in the plant, and the deficiency is only detected when the seeds are split open. If the deficiency is extreme, there may be some chlorosis of the leaves.

Control of Manganese Deficiency. The application of ¼ cwt. per acre of manganese sulphate at seeding-time is sometimes useful. On alkaline soils this is not very effective, because here the deficiency is due to the locking up of manganese in a form unavailable to the plant, and any manganese applied to the soil may be rendered unavailable. A more effective method is to spray the crop with manganese sulphate solution. This is the only reliable method for peas, for which spraying should usually be done towards the end of flowering or, if practicable, at mid-flowering and again seven days later.* 5 lb. of manganese sulphate per acre, applied in a high volume or low volume spray, is used for peas.

Boron Deficiency. High alkalinity and water shortage increase the likelihood of boron deficiency. Thus it is most often met with on soils which are naturally calcareous, or which have been over-limed, and on dry sandy and gravelly soils. Diverse conditions are produced by boron deficiency in different crops. The following are a few of the better-known examples:

1. HEART-ROT OF SUGAR-BEET AND MANGEL. The young, innermost leaves are weak and eventually die. A rot develops at the centre of the crown and proceeds downwards into the storage organ. When the 'root' is cut horizontally in two, discoloration of the vascular tissues may be observed, in addition to the central rotting from the crown. The older leaves wilt and may become yellow and wither. The symptoms may be confused with those of advanced stages of the disease downy mildew (*Peronospora farinosa*).

2. BROWN HEART OR RAAN OF TURNIP AND SWEDE. There may be no external symptoms in these crops, but when the storage organ is cut across, the centre is found to be brown and water-soaked. Affected roots usually become woody and unpalatable.

3. BROWNING OR HOLLOW STEM OF CAULIFLOWER. Brown areas appear in the pith of the stem and branches of the curd. Hollows later develop in these areas. The curd itself may develop a rusty-brown discoloration on the surface. The young leaves may be distorted and the epidermis of stems and petioles becomes rough.

4. CRACKED STEM OF CELERY. The leaf stalks crack above the veins, and the broken tissues curl back and turn brown. The leaves show a brown mottling and the young heart leaves may die.

Control of Boron Deficiency. The deficiency can usually be corrected by the application of borax to the soil at the rate of 20 lb. per acre. Borax is often mixed with fertilizers for this purpose. On soils liable to suffer

* Sharp, W. O., and Blunt, C. F., 'Control of Marsh Spot of Peas', *Farmer and Stockbreeder*, May 17th, 1955, 53-5.

from boron deficiency, care should be taken to avoid excessive application of lime, which may render the boron in the soil unavailable to the plant.

Excesses of Mineral Elements

Excessively high concentrations of mineral salts in solution in the soil may result in plasmolysis and death of root hairs, and ultimately in the

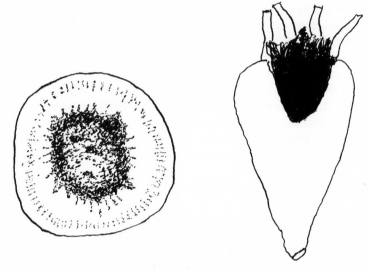

Fig. 259. Boron deficiency. *Left:* transverse section of a swede showing symptoms of brown heart. *Right:* longitudinal section of a sugar-beet showing heart rot.

death of the plant. Where concentrations of solutes are not sufficiently high to affect the plant in this way, other adverse effects may be produced by the presence of a particular element in excess of the amount required for a correct balance of mineral nutrients.

In modern farming, heavy applications of nitrogenous fertilizers are often made. This can often be done with advantage, providing a good balance is maintained between nitrogen and other elements. From a practical point of view, phosphate and potash fertilizers are most likely to be needed to maintain such a balance. Excess nitrogen results in dark green, lush growth which may render the crop more susceptible to certain diseases. Flowering and seed production may be delayed. Cereals lodge more readily. Symptoms of deficiency of some other essential element may appear as a result of the upset in the balance of available nutrients.

Excess of manganese may result in symptoms of iron deficiency. Other trace elements such as boron may be extremely toxic to plants when present in excessive amounts. Thus care is needed, when attempting to rectify deficiencies, in order to avoid excessive applications of the remedy.

(B) *Soil Acidity.* Acidity of the soil may cause poor growth or failure of crops. Most of our crops can grow under slightly acid conditions, but as acidity increases, the growth of some crops is restricted or prevented. Acidity may prevent the development of seedlings in extreme cases. If the seedlings develop the plants produced will have a restricted root system and the shoots will be stunted and yellow. Effects of lime deficiency may be those of calcium deficiency, but more often it is the acidity of the soil which has the most devastating effect on the plant. In order to correct the acidity, much larger dressings of lime are required than would be necessary to satisfy the demands of the crop for the element calcium, which is not absorbed in very large amounts.

Usually fields are not uniformly sour, and the crop will appear patchy, having failed completely or become markedly stunted, in some areas which are very acid, whilst developing more normally in other, less acid areas. Failures due to acidity are more likely to be encountered in crops, such as red clover, sugar-beet, mangel and barley, which are not tolerant of a very high degree of acidity. In rye, potatoes and oats, which are least sensitive to acidity, crop failures from this cause are less likely to occur. Often an abundance of certain weeds such as spurrey, sheep's sorrel and corn marigold, will provide further evidence of soil acidity.

(C) *Other Non-parasitic Causes of Ill-health.* Flooding or waterlogging of land may have serious effects on crops. Where the spaces between the soil particles are filled with water, air is excluded. All the crop plants grown on farms in this country depend upon a supply of air in the soil for respiration by their roots. When air is excluded, root growth is restricted, and if the soil remains waterlogged for a long period the plants die off. Waterlogging also interferes with bacterial activity in the soil, and nitrification is limited. For this reason, plants growing in patches which have been waterlogged may show signs of nitrogen deficiency.

A good seed-bed is important for healthy growth of crops. In addition to free drainage, the compactness of the soil is important. Roots growing in soil which is too loose may be restricted in their growth and restricted growth of the plant as a whole will result.

Excessive competition with weeds for light, air, moisture and mineral substances will result in weakening of the crop. Competition for the mineral elements may result in the appearance of symptoms of deficiency of elements which are in short supply in the soil. Most usually, symptoms of nitrogen deficiency appear for this reason.

Occasionally plants growing in a humid atmosphere which restricts transpiration may accumulate water in their tissues and cell division may occur, resulting in the development of swellings. Where these swellings are extensive the condition is known as *oedema* or *dropsy*.

On dry soils and under prolonged dry atmospheric conditions plants may wilt. If wilting is prolonged, death may occur.

Frost may kill off young green shoots. Blackening of the shoots of winter beans or of early-planted potatoes, for example, as a result of frost, is not uncommon. Freezing results in the formation of ice crystals in the intercellular spaces and the withdrawal of water from the cells. This may result in dehydration of the protoplasm and death of the cells. At low temperatures starch contained in plant organs is converted into sugars; thus stored potatoes become sweet as a result of freezing. The tubers may later become soft, owing to the breaking down of cells, and rotting by invading organisms may follow. Sometimes the effects of damage by frost early in the life of a plant may not become apparent until some time later. For example, wheat plants affected by frost may show little sign of damage until after the ears appear; these may produce little grain and they may also be distorted.

Excessively high temperatures, which are unlikely under field conditions in Britain, may also result in the death of plants.

Brown spots and streaks which may be seen on the leaves of crops, particularly cereals, may have been caused by fertilizers applied as top dressings. Such fertilizers have not been quickly washed into the soil, but have dissolved slowly and created a strong solution, causing plasmolysis in the area of the leaf on which the particles have fallen.

Drift from weed-killers used in neighbouring cereal crops may have drastic effects on broad-leaved crops (Dicotyledons), particularly in the case of the 'hormone' type weed-killers. Effects similar to those produced on the susceptible broad-leaved weeds may result (see p. 400).

Potatoes in storage may become blackened internally, producing a condition known as *black heart*, which is caused by restriction of oxygen

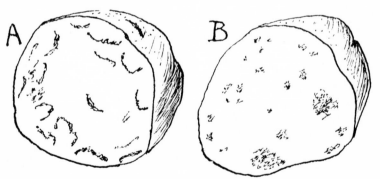

Fig. 260. A, Spraing. Potato tuber cut across showing typical brown markings. B, Rust spot. Tuber cut across to show rust spots in the tissues.

supply and increase of carbon dioxide, resulting from imperfect ventilation of the store.

Smoke and fumes from industries may cause ill-health or death of crop plants. This is usually due to the presence of sulphur dioxide.

Finally, in some cases 'diseased' conditions may result from causes as yet unknown. Such conditions are exemplified by *rust spot* of potato tubers, in which rusty brown spots occur in the internal tissues and *spraing*, which also affects potatoes, appearing as irregular curved brown markings inside the tubers.

BOOKS FOR FURTHER READING

Bawden, F. C. *Plant Diseases*, 1948, Nelson.

—— *Plant Viruses and Virus Diseases*, 1964, The Ronald Press Co., New York.

British Mycological Society, Plant Pathology Committee, *List of Common British Plant Diseases*, 1944, Camb. Univ. Press.

Brooks, F. T. *Plant Diseases*, 1953, Oxford Univ. Press.

Butler, Sir E. J., and Jones, S. G. *Plant Pathology*, 1949, Macmillan, London.

Dowson, W. J. *Manual of Bacterial Plant Diseases*, 1949, Adam and Chas. Black, London.

—— *Plant Diseases Due to Bacteria*, 1957, Cambridge.

De Ong, E. R. *Insect, Fungus and Weed Control*, 1953, Thames and Hudson.

Green, D. E. *Diseases of Vegetables*, 1946, Macmillan, London.

Heald, F. D. *Manual of Plant Diseases*, 1953, McGraw-Hill.

Holmes, E. *Practical Plant Protection*, 1955, Constable.

Large, E. C. *The Advance of the Fungi*, 1940, Jonathan Cape, London.

Martin, H. (Editor). *Insecticide and Fungicide Handbook for Crop Protection*, 1963, Blackwell.

McKay, R. *Potato Diseases*, 1955, Dublin.

Ministry of Agriculture and Fisheries Bulletins:
  No. 129. *Cereal Diseases*, by W. C. Moore and F. Joan Moore.
  No. 123. *Diseases of Vegetables*, by L. Ogilvie.
  No. 142. *Sugar Beet Diseases*, by R. Hull.

Ministry of Agriculture and Fisheries Leaflets (numerous).

Sampson, K., and Western, J. H. *Diseases of British Grasses and Herbage Legumes*, 1954, Camb. Univ. Press.

Smith, K. M. *Beyond the Microscope*, 1952, Penguin Books, Ltd.

—— *Plant Viruses*, 1960, Methuen.

—— *Recent Advances in the Study of Viruses*, 2nd Ed., 1951, J. & A. Churchill, Ltd.

—— *A Textbook of Plant Virus Diseases*, 1957, J. & A. Churchill.

—— *The Virus, Life's Enemy*, 1948, Camb. Univ. Press.

—— *Virus Diseases of Farm and Garden Crops*, 1945, Littlebury & Co., Worcester.

Wallace, T. *The Diagnosis of Mineral Deficiences in Plants by Visual Symptoms*, 3rd Ed., 1962, H.M.S.O., London.

Weston, W. A. R. D., and Taylor, R. E. *The Plant in Health and Disease*, 1948, Crosby Lockwood.

Whitehead, T., McIntosh, T. P., and Findley, W. M. *The Potato in Health and Disease*, 1953, Oliver and Boyd, Edinburgh and London.

Wormald, H. *Diseases of Fruit and Hops*, 1955, Crosby Lockwood.

Also the following journals dealing with original research: *Annals of Applied Biology; Journal of Applied Bacteriology; Journal of Agricultural Research; Journal of Agricultural Science; Phytopathology; Plant Pathology; The Review of Applied Mycology; Transactions of the British Mycological Society.*

APPENDIX I

GLOSSARY

Words which are explained in the text when first used are not listed here.

Achene: a small, dry, one-seeded indehiscent fruit.

Actinomorphic: symmetrical about more than one diameter; regular.

Adnate: united with another part of a different kind.

Adventitious: out of the ordinary course; applied, for example, to roots arising from a stem or buds arising from a root.

Anatropous ovule: inverted so that the funicle and micropyle are adjacent.

Androecium: the stamens considered as a whole; the male part of the flower.

Annual: completing its life cycle within a year.

Anterior: facing outwards away from the axis, usually towards the bract.

Anther: the part of a stamen which contains pollen.

Apetalous: without petals.

Apical: at the apex.

Apocarpous ovary: with the carpels free from one another.

Appressed: pressed flat and close to an organ.

Ascending: curving upwards.

Axil of leaf: the angle between the leaf and stem.

Axillary: arising in the axil of a leaf or bract.

Beak of a fruit: a narrow prolongation.

Berry: a fleshy fruit without a hard layer of pericarp around the seeds, usually with several seeds.

Biennial: completing its life within two years and flowering in the second year only.

Bifid: deeply divided in two.

Blade of a leaf: the flat part or lamina.

Bract: a leafy structure beneath a flower or group of flowers.

Bracteole: a secondary bract, as on the pedicel of a flower.

Bulb: a swollen underground bud with fleshy scales and/or leaf bases on a short stem.

Calyx: the sepals considered as a whole.

Cambium: a layer of cells dividing to produce phloem externally and xylem internally. See also *cork cambium.*

Capitate: having a rounded head.

Capsule: a dry dehiscent fruit derived from two or more united carpels.

Carpel: one of the units composing the gynaecium (or pistil) and containing one or more ovules.

Caruncle: a warty or fleshy outgrowth from the surface of a seed, near the micropyle.

Cauline leaves: borne on an aerial stem.

Caryopsis: a dry one-seeded fruit with the pericarp and testa fused together.

Chlorenchyma: tissue containing chlorophyll.

Chlorophyll: the green pigment of plants, concerned with photosynthesis.

Ciliate: (i) having cilia or flagella, (ii) having a marginal fringe of long hairs.

Cleistogamous flowers: not opening, pollination taking place within the closed flower.

Collenchyma: tissue consisting of cells with walls strengthened by layers of cellulose, with the thickening mainly at the corners.

Compound leaves: composed of two or more separate leaflets.

Connate: united with another part of the same kind.

Cork cambium: a layer of cells which divides to produce cork cells.

Corm: a rounded, swollen, fleshy underground stem, outwardly resembling a bulb, but solid.

Corolla: the petals considered as a whole.

Cortex: the tissue between the epidermis (or the piliferous layer of roots) and the endodermis or starch sheath.

607

Cotyledon(s): the first leaf (leaves) of a seed forming part of the embryo.

Culm: the aerial stem of a grass or sedge.

Cuneate: triangular and attached at the point; of leaf bases.

Cytoplasm: the protoplasm other than the nucleus.

Deciduous: falling off, usually when mature.

Decumbent: lying on the ground but ascending at the end.

Decurrent leaf: having the base prolonged down the stem often in the form of wings or projections.

Decussate leaves: in pairs, opposite, each pair at right angles to the succeeding pair.

Dehiscent: opening to shed seeds (or spores).

Diam.: an abbreviation of diameter.

Diarch: having two strands of xylem.

Dioecious: having male and female flowers on different plants.

Dissected: deeply cut into narrow lobes.

Distichous: in two opposite vertical ranks.

Drupe: a fruit with the outer part fleshy and the seed enclosed in a woody layer of pericarp.

Emarginate: with a shallow notch at the apex.

Endodermis: a single layer of cells between the cortex and the vascular tissue.

Endosperm: food-storing tissue formed after fertilization outside the embryo of a seed.

Ephemeral: short-lived.

Epicalyx: a whorl of sepal-like lobes close to the calyx.

Epidermis: the outer layer of cells.

Epigeal: above ground; in epigeal germination the cotyledons appear above the soil.

Epipetalous: attached to the petals.

Exstipulate: without stipules.

Extravaginal: outside the sheath.

Extrorse anthers: opening towards the outside of the flower.

Filament: the stalk of a stamen.

Flexuous: wavy.

Follicle: a dry several-seeded fruit formed from one carpel and dehiscing along the inner side.

Fructification: a general term for a structure bearing spores or containing seeds.

Fruit: the ripened gynaecium (pistil) containing the seeds. Some so-called fruits include additional parts such as the succulent receptacle in strawberry.

Funicle: the stalk of an ovule.

Gamopetalous: having the petals united.

Gamosepalous: having the sepals united.

Geniculate: bent abruptly or 'kneed'.

Glabrous: not hairy.

Glaucous: of a pale bluish-green, often somewhat waxy, appearance.

Gynaecium: the female part of a flower including the ovary or ovaries and the style(s) and stigma(s).

Habit: the general form of growth of a plant.

Habitat: the place in which a plant grows, plus the external factors associated with that place which affect the growth of the plant.

Halophyte: a plant which can grow in soil containing appreciable amounts of common salt.

Hemiparasite: obtaining part of its food from a host plant.

Herbaceous: not woody; of plants dying down to ground level in winter.

Hermaphrodite: having both male and female parts.

Hexamerous: floral parts in sixes.

Hilum: of a seed, the scar left by the stalk (funicle).

Hirsute: with rather long, rough hairs.

Hispid: bearing stiff hairs.

Hoary: covered with very short hairs which produce a whitish appearance.

Hypocotyl: the part of the axis between the root and the cotyledons.

Hypogeal: below ground; in hypogeal germination the cotyledons remain below the ground.

Imbricating: overlapping; like the tiles on a roof.

Indehiscent: not opening to release seeds or spores.

Indigenous: native, not introduced from elsewhere.

Inflorescence: a group of flowers on a common axis.

Internode: the part of the stem between two successive nodes.

Intravaginal: within the sheath.

Introrse anthers: opening towards the centre of the flower.

Involucre: one or more whorls of bracts usually below a compact inflorescence (as in Compositae).

Irregular: not symmetrical about more than one diameter (zygomorphic).

Lamina: of a leaf; the flat part or blade.

Lateral: at the side.

Latex: a milky juice.

Legume: a dry fruit derived from a single carpel and splitting along both sutures.

Lignified: bearing deposits of the woody material lignin.

Ligulate: strap-shaped. Also used to indicate possession of a ligule.

Loculicidal capsule: dehiscing down the middle of each compartment (loculus), between the partitions.

Loculus: a compartment, as in an ovary.

Lomentum: a dry fruit, usually elongated, which breaks transversely into one-seeded portions.

Lyrate: pinnatifid, but having a large terminal lobe and smaller laterals.

Mericarp: a one-seeded portion of a fruit, produced by the ripe fruit breaking into pieces.

Meristematic tissue: undifferentiated cells which divide to produce further cells.

Micropyle: the minute opening in the testa of an ovule through which the pollen tube enters; often visible in the resulting seed.

Monoecious: having separate male and female flowers on the same plant.

Mucronate: provided with a minute point.

Node: the part of a stem from which a leaf arises.

Nucellus: a mass of cells within an ovule and surrounding the embryo sac.

Nut: a fruit containing a single seed and having a woody pericarp; usually derived from a syncarpous ovary.

Nutlet: a small nut, also used for a small nut-like portion of a schizocarpic fruit (Labiatae and Boraginaceae).

Ob-: reversed, e.g. obovate = ovate but attached by the narrow end instead of by the broad end (see fig. 261).

Obtuse: blunt at the tip.

Orthotropous ovule: upright, with the micropyle and funicle at opposite ends.

Ovary: the part of the gynaecium containing the ovules.

Ovoid: shaped like an egg in three dimensions.

Ovule: a structure containing an embryo sac and, after fertilization, developing into a seed.

Papillose: covered with papillae (pimple-like projections).

Pappus: a ring of hairs or scales at the top of a fruit. A hairy pappus often assists in wind dispersal of the fruit.

Parenchyma: a tissue consisting of living cells with uniform thin cellulose walls.

Pedicel: a flower stalk.

Peduncle: an inflorescence stalk.

Pentamerous flower: having the parts in fives.

Perennial: persisting for more than two years.

Perfect flower: having both male and female parts.

Perianth: the part of a flower external to the stamens, including petals and sepals when both present.

Perianth segment: a separate leaf of the perianth, usually used when petals and sepals cannot be distinguished.

Pericarp: the fruit wall, enclosing the seed(s); derived from the carpel or ovary wall.

Pericycle: a layer of non-conducting tissue one or more cells thick at the periphery of the vascular tissue.

Periderm: a protective layer on the outside of parts of some plants, consisting chiefly of cork and cork cambium.

Perisperm: a food-storing tissue in some seeds, derived from the nucellus.

Persistent: not shed when mature.

Petaloid: resembling petals, often coloured.

Petals: the inner whorl of the perianth, often brightly coloured.

Petiole: the leaf stalk.

Phloem: tissue containing sieve tubes in which elaborated foods are translocated.

Pistil: the female part of the flower (gynaecium).

Pistillate: having female parts only.

Pith: the tissue (usually parenchyma) central to the vascular tissue.

Placenta: the place within the ovary at which the ovules are attached.

Placentation: the arrangement of the placentae and the ovules.

Plumule: the embryo shoot in a seed.

Polygamous: having unisexual and hermaphrodite flowers on the same or on different plants.

Polypetalous: having petals free from one another.

Posterior: of floral parts; facing towards the axis.

Prickle: a sharply pointed outgrowth of the surface of a plant organ.

Procumbent stem: lying loosely on the surface of the ground.

Prostrate stem: lying fairly close to the ground.

Protandrous: stamens dehiscing before the stigmas are receptive.

Protogynous: stigmas receptive before the stamens dehisce.

Protoxylem: the first-formed elements of the primary xylem.

Pubescent: bearing short, soft hairs.

Pyxidium: a capsule which dehisces by a circular slit causing the upper part to form a cap which falls off.

Radical: arising from soil-level.

Radicle: the embryo root in the seed.

Receptacle: the portion of the axis to which the floral parts are attached. Also used for the enlarged part of the peduncle to which the florets are attached in the Compositae and Dipsacaceae.

Reflexed: turned sharply backwards or downwards.

Regular: symmetrical about more than one diameter (actinomorphic).

Reniform: kidney-shaped.

Reticulate: forming a network or having a network of surface ridges or markings.

Rhizomatous: having rhizomes.

Rhizome: a more or less elongated underground stem.

Root tuber or tuberous root: a short swollen root storing food.

Rotate corolla: flat, plate-like, not tubular or bell-shaped.

Rugose: having a wrinkled surface.

Runner: a long prostrate stem rooting at the apex and producing a new plant which later becomes detached from the parent.

Scarious: of leaves or bracts, thin dry membranous.

Schizocarp: a dry syncarpous fruit breaking up when ripe into one-seeded indehiscent portions.

Sclerenchyma: strengthening tissue with lignified cell walls.

Secondary xylem and *secondary phloem:* produced from cells derived from the cambium.

Sepaloid: resembling sepals.

Sepals: the outer whorl of floral lobes, usually green.

Septicidal capsule: dehiscing along the partitions (septa).

Septum: a partition, e.g. the wall between neighbouring compartments of an ovary.

Sessile: not stalked.

Shrub: a short much-branched woody plant.

Sieve tubes: tubular cells with perforated transverse walls, present in the phloem and forming a longitudinal system for the translocation of elaborated foods.

Silicula: a short broad pod divided into two compartments by a thin septum and dehiscing when mature by the separation of the two valves formed by the pericarp.

Siliqua. a fruit similar to a silicula but long and narrow.

Simple: of a single piece, not compound.

Solitary flower or flower head: borne singly.

Sp.: an abbreviation of *species* (plural Spp.).

Spathulate or *spatulate:* spatula-shaped, like the handle of a spoon.

Spine: a stiff sharply-pointed structure, a modified branch, petiole, stipule or peduncle.

Ssp.: an abbreviation of *sub-species*.

Staminate: having male parts (stamens) only.

Staminode: a rudimentary or imperfectly developed stamen.

Stellate: star-shaped.

Stigma: the part of the gynaecium which receives the pollen.

Stipules: outgrowths at the base of a leaf.

Stolon: a slender stem, above ground, which becomes prostrate and roots where the nodes touch the soil.

Stoloniferous: having stolons.

Style: a more or less elongated outgrowth of the gynaecium bearing the stigma.

Stylopodium: the enlarged base of a style; as in the Umbelliferae.

Subulate: awl-shaped, narrowing from the base to a sharp point.

Succulent: soft, thick and juicy.

Suture: the line of union of two parts; in fruits dehiscence may take place along a suture.

Syncarpous: consisting of two or more united carpels.

Tap-root: a well-developed vertical main root bearing lateral roots.

Tendril: a slender organ which helps to support a plant by twining around neighbouring stems and other suitable objects. May be a modified stem, leaf or leaflet.

Terminal: at the end of, terminating.

Testa: the outer covering of a seed.

Thorn: a modified shoot, leaf or part of a leaf which is woody and sharp-pointed.

Tracheid: an elongated, lignified, water-conducting cell with pointed end walls (see xylem).

Trifid: deeply divided into three.

Trifoliate: having three leaves or leaflets.

Truncate: appearing to be cut off abruptly.

Tuber: a short, swollen underground stem storing food. See also *root tuber.*

Unilocular: having one compartment only.

Unisexual: of one sex only.

Var.: an abbreviation of variety.

Vascular bundles: strands of food- and water-conducting tissue, containing xylem and phloem.

Viscid: sticky.

Versatile: with the anther so attached to the filament that it turns freely.

Vessels: tubular structures in plants in which water is translocated, part of the xylem.

Whorl: three or more structures of the same type arising at the same level.

Xerophyte: a plant adapted to dry conditions.

Xylem: wood; containing vessels and/or tracheids, fibres and xylem parenchyma.

Zygomorphic: not symmetrical about more than one diameter, irregular.

Zygote: the product of the union of two gametes.

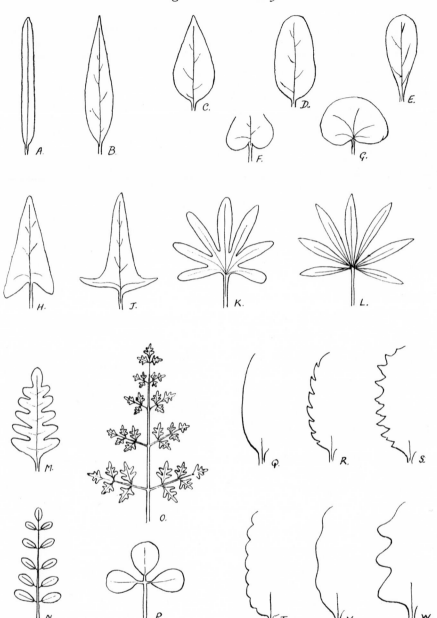

Fig. 261

LEAF SHAPES

Leaf Shapes: A, linear; B, lanceolate; C, ovate; D, oblong (or oval); E, spathulate; F, cordate base; G, reniform; H, sagittate; J, hastate; K, palmatifid; L, palmate; M, pinnatifid; N, pinnate; O, bipinnate with pinnatifid leaflets; P, trifoliate.

Leaf Margins: Q, entire; R, serrate; S, dentate; T, crenate; V, sinuate; W, pinnately lobed.

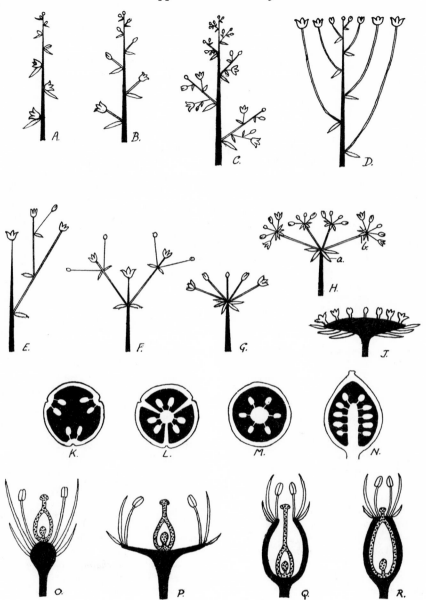

FIG. 262

Types of Inflorescence: A, spike; B, raceme; C, panicle; D, corymb (corymbose raceme); E, monochasial cyme; F, dichasial cyme; G, simple umbel; H, compound umbel: (*a*) bract, (*b*) bracteole; J, capitulum.

Types of Placentation: K, Parietal (T.S.); L, axile (T.S.); M, free central (T.S.); N, free central (L.S.).

Types of Flower Structure, showing position of gynaecium (stippled) in relation to the rest of the floral parts (pedicel and receptacle shown in black): O, hypogynous; P, perigynous; Q, perigynous; R, epigynous (receptacle and pericarp fused).

APPENDIX II

DERIVATIONS OF PLANT NAMES

Gk. = Greek; Lat. = Latin

A. Names of Genera

Achillea: named after Achilles.

Aconitum: the classical name.

Aegilops: classical name for a kind of wild oat.

Aegopodium: Gk., goat foot, refers to the shape of the leaf.

Aethusa: from the Gk. word meaning glistening, refers to leaves.

Agave: Gk., noble.

Agropyron: Gk., field wheat.

Agrostemma: Gk., field wreath.

Agrostis: Gk., field.

Aira: Gk. name for a grass.

Ajuga: Lat., unyoked, the calyx not two-lipped.

Alchemilla: of Arabic origin, refers to alchemy.

Alliaria: Lat., from *Allium*, garlic.

Allium: Lat., garlic.

Alopecurus: Gk., fox tail.

Ammophila: Gk., sand-loving.

Anagallis: Gk., delightful.

Anemone: from the Gk. *anemos*, wind.

Anthoxanthum : Gk., yellow flower.

Anthriscus: ancient Roman name.

Apium: ancient Gk. name.

Arachis: from *Arachidna*, an early name of a seed-burying clover.

Armoracia: ancient name of the horse radish.

Arum: a Gk. plant-name derived from the Arabic *ar*, fire; refers to the burning taste.

Arundo: Lat., a reed.

Asparagus: old Gk. name.

Atriplex: ancient Lat. name.

Atropa: Lat., *Atropos*, one of the Fates who cuts the thread of life.

Avena: old Lat. name.

Bambusa: from the Malayan name.

Bellis: Lat. *bellus*, pretty.

Beta: classical name.

Brachypodium: Gk., short stalk.

Brassica: ancient name for cabbage.

Briza: Gk., *brizo*, to nod, refers to the movement of the panicles.

Bromus: Gk., food.

Bryonia: Gk., to sprout, refers to annual sprouting from the tuber.

Calamagrostis: Gk., *calamas*, a reed, *agrostis*, a grass.

Caltha: Lat. name for a marigold.

Calystegia: probably from the Gk. *kalyx*, calyx or cup, *stego*, covering; refers to the bracts enclosing the calyx.

Cannabis: ancient Gk. name.

Capsella: Lat. *capsula*, a small box.

Cardamine: Gk. *kardia*, the heart, *damao*, to subdue; refers to use as a heart sedative.

Cardaria: Gk. *kardia*, the heart; refers to the heart-shaped fruit of *C. draba*.

Carduus: old Lat. name.

Centaurea: old Gk. name for a plant which was reputed to have healed a wound in the foot of a centaur.

Cerastium: Gk., horn; refers to the shape of the capsule.

Ceratonia: Gk. a horn, from the shape of the pod.

Chaerophyllum: Gk. *chairo*, to please, *phullon*, leaf; refers to the scent.

Chelidonium: from the Gk. for a swallow; refers to the time of flowering.

Chenopodium: Gk., goose foot; refers to the shape of the leaf of some species.

Chrysanthemum: Gk., golden flower.

Cichorium: Arabic name.

Cicuta: Lat. name for hemlock.

Cirsium: Gk. name of a species of thistle.

Colchicum: Colchis on the Black Sea.

Conium: the Gk. name.

Conopodium: Gk., cone foot, from the shape of the stylopodium.

614

Convolvulus: Lat. *convolvo,* to entwine.

Coriandrum: the classical name.

Coronopus: Gk., crow feet; refers to deeply cleft leaves.

Crataegus: Gk., strength; refers to the wood.

Crepis: from the Gk. word for a shoe.

Cuscuta: from the Gk. to entangle.

Cydonia: Cydon (now Canea) in Crete.

Cynara: Gk., like a dog's tooth; refers to involucre spines.

Cynodon: Gk., dog tooth; may refer to the rows of tooth-like spikelets.

Cynosurus: Gk., dog's tail.

Dactylis: Gk., refers to fingers.

Datura: Indian name.

Daucus: old Gk. name.

Delphinium: Gk. *delphis,* dolphin; refers to the shape of the flower.

Deschampsia: after Des Longchamps, a French naturalist.

Digitalis: Lat., finger of a glove.

Dipsacus: Gk., thirst; water collects in the leaf bases of some species.

Echium: Gk. *echis,* viper.

Epilobium: Gk., upon the pod.

Equisetum: Lat. *equus,* horse, *seta,* bristle.

Erysimum: from the Gk., to blister.

Euphorbia: Euphorbus, physician to Juba, King of Mauretania.

Euphrasia: from the Gk., meaning to gladden, from its old use for improving eyesight.

Faba: Lat. name for bean.

Fagopyrum: Gk., beech wheat.

Festuca: ancient Lat. name for a blade of grass.

Filipendula: Lat., hanging thread; refers to the thread-like attachments of the root tubers of some species.

Foeniculum: Lat. *foenum,* hay; probably refers to the narrow leaf-segments.

Fragaria: Lat., fragrance.

Fumaria: Lat. *fumus,* smoke; refers to the smell of the roots.

Galeopsis: Gk., weasel-like.

Galium: Gk. *gala,* milk; some species were used to curdle milk.

Gastridium: Gk., a small pouch.

Genista: old Lat. name.

Geranium: from the Gk. for a crane.

Glechoma: old Gk. name.

Glyceria: from the Gk. for sweet.

Glycine: Gk., sweet.

Gnaphalium: from the Gk. for wool.

Helianthus: Gk. *helios,* the sun, *anthos,* a flower.

Helleborus: old Gk. name of one of the species.

Heracleum: refers to the god Hercules.

Hieracium: Gk. *hierax,* a hawk.

Holcus: classical name for a grass.

Hordeum: old Lat. name for barley.

Humulus: Lat. *humus,* the ground; if not supported, it runs along the ground.

Hyoscyamus: Gk. name for a poisonous plant.

Hypochaeris: ancient classical name.

Iris: Gk., the rainbow.

Isatis: Gk. name for some dye-producing plant.

Juncus: Lat. *jungo,* to bind or tie, from the use for binding.

Koeleria: Koeler, a German botanist.

Lactuca: Lat. *lac,* milk; refers to the latex.

Lamium: from the Gk. word for throat.

Lapsana: ancient classical name.

Lathyrus: Gk. name for some leguminous plant.

Leersia: after a German botanist, J. D. Leers (1727-74).

Leontodon: Gk. *leon,* lion, *odous,* a tooth.

Lepidium: Gk., little scale; refers to the fruits.

Linum: the Lat. name for flax.

Lithospermum: Gk., stone seed.

Lolium: Lat. name for darnel.

Lotus: classical name for some clover species.

Lupinus: Lat. *lupus,* wolf; some species were supposed to destroy the soil.

Luzula: Lat. *luciola,* a glow-worm.

Lychnis: from the Gk. for a flame; refers to the colour of the flowers of some species.

Lycopersicon: Gk., wolf peach; may relate to the fact that the fruit was at one time thought to be poisonous.

Lycopsis: Gk., wolf face.

Malus: classical name for an apple tree.

Manihot: Brazilian name.

Matricaria: Lat. *mater,* mother, from its former medicinal use by women.

Medicago: Medea, where lucerne was supposed to have originated.

Melandrium: Lat. name of the plant.

Melilotus: honey lotus, from the scent.

Mentha: ancient Gk. name.

Mercurialis: after the god Mercury.

Milium: Lat., millet.

Molinia: Molina, a Chilean botanist.

Musa: named after the physician to the first Roman Emperor Octavius Augustus.

Nardus: Gk. *nardos,* spikenard; the tufted growth resembles that plant.

Nepeta: old Lat. name.

Nicotiana: after Nicot, a French Ambassador in Portugal, who obtained seeds of tobacco.

Nasturtium: nasus tortus, twisted nose; refers to pungent properties.

Odontites: Gk. *odous,* tooth.

Oenanthe: Gk., wine flower, from the scent.

Onobrychis: Gk., asses' food.

Ononis: old Gk. name.

Ornithopus: Gk., bird foot.

Orobanche: Gk. *orobos,* vetch, *anchein,* to strangle.

Oryza: from the Arabic name.

Panicum: old Lat. name.

Pastinaca: Lat. *pastus,* food.

Pedicularis: Lat. *pediculus,* louse.

Pennisetum: Lat., feather-bristle.

Petasites: Gk. *petasos,* a broad-brimmed hat; refers to the leaves.

Petroselinum: Lat. *petra,* a rock, *selinon,* parsley.

Phalaris: Gk. *phalaros,* shining; refers to the seeds.

Phaseolus: ancient name of some bean or vetch.

Phleum: old Gk. name for some other plant.

Pimpinella: ancient name.

Pisum: classical name.

Plantago: old Lat. name.

Poa: Gk., grass or fodder.

Polygonum: Gk., many-kneed; refers to the numerous enlarged nodes.

Potentilla: Lat. *potens,* powerful, medicinally.

Poterium: from the Gk. for drinking cup; refers to the use of the leaves in cooling drink.

Primula: Lat. *primus,* first; refers to early flowers.

Prunella: brunella, *braune,* German for a throat disease which *Prunella* was supposed to relieve.

Prunus: Lat. name for the plum tree.

Psamma: from the Gk. for sand.

Pteridium: from the Gk. name for ferns.

Puccinellia: after Professor Puccinelli, an Italian botanist (1808-50).

Pyrus: old Lat. name for the pear.

Ranunculus: Lat., a little frog; refers to the fact that many species grow in wet places.

Raphanus: Gk. *raphanos,* appearing quickly; refers to rapid germination.

Rheum: old Gk. name from *Rha,* the Volga, from which area rhubarb was obtained.

Rhinanthus: Gk. *rin,* snout, *anthos,* flower.

Rubus: Lat. *ruber,* red; refers to the colour of the fruits of some species.

Rumex: Lat. name.

Sanguisorba: Lat., blood-stopping.

Sarothamnus: from the Gk. for a broom.

Scandix: Gk. name for another species.

Scleranthus: Gk., hard-flower.

Scorzonera: old French *scorzon,* a serpent; formerly used for snake-bites.

Secale: old Lat. name of some grain.

Senecio: Lat. *senex,* old man; probably refers to the white pappus.

Setaria: Lat. *seta,* a bristle.

Sherardia: after W. Sherard, an English botanist.

Sieglingia: named after Professor Siegling (1800).

Silene: Gk. *sialon,* saliva; a sticky secretion is produced by some species.

Sinapis: old Lat. name for mustard
Sisymbrium: a Gk. plant-name.
Solanum: Lat. *solamen,* quieting; refers to its sedative properties.
Sonchus: ancient classical name.
Sorghum: from the Italian name.
Spartina: from the Gk. word for cord.
Spergula: Lat., to scatter, from the scattering of the seeds.
Spinacea: Lat. *spina;* refers to the spiny fruits.
Stachys: from the Gk. for a spike, the inflorescence.
Stellaria: Lat., star.
Symphytum: Gk., to grow together; refers to the supposed healing properties.

Tamus: an old name.
Tanacetum: possibly from the Gk. for immortal; refers to long-lived flowers.
Taraxacum: from an old Arabic name.
Tetragonia: Gk., four-angled fruit.

Thlaspi: old Gk. name.
Tragopogon: Gk., goat's beard.
Trifolium: Lat., three-lobed leaves.
Trigonella: Lat., a little triangle.
Triodia: Gk., three-toothed.
Trisetum: Lat., three bristles.
Triticum: Lat. name for wheat.
Tussilago: Gk. *tussis,* a cough; refers to its use in medicines.

Ulex: possibly from the Celtic *uile-ex,* all prickles.
Urtica: Lat. *uro,* to burn.

Veronica: after St. Veronica.
Vicia: Lat. *vincire,* wind round.
Viola: old Lat. name.
Vulpia: Lat. *vulpes,* fox, from the long awns.

Zea: old Gk. name for some other cereal.

B. Specific Names

Specific names are usually adjectives the gender of which agrees with that of the generic name. Thus, in association with different generic names, we may have *sativus,* masculine, *sativa,* feminine, and *sativum,* neuter; *arvensis,* masculine or feminine, and *arvense,* neuter; *ruber,* masculine, *rubra,* feminine, and *rubrum,* neuter. Adjectives ending in *-ens,* such as *procumbens,* remain the same in each gender.

Where substantive names (nouns) are used, they are given their own termination, e.g. *Achillea millefolium.* Such names are often printed with an initial capital, thus, *Achillea Millefolium, Allium Cepa,* etc. They are often old generic names.

acaule: without a stem.
acephalus: without a head.
acetosellus: sourish.
acetosus: acid.
acris: acrid, biting, sharp.
aestivus: summer.
agrestis: rural, rustic.
agriocrithon: agrion, wild; *crith,* barley.
albus: white.
alexandrinus: of Alexandria.
altissimus: tall.
amplexicaulis: clasping the stem.
ananassus: resembling the pineapple (*Ananas*).
angustifolius: narrow-leaved.
annuus: annual.
anserina: pertaining to geese.
aparine: adhering.
aquilinus: aquiline, curved like an eagle's beak.

arabicus: Arabian.
arenarius: of sandy places.
articulatus: articulated, jointed.
arundinaceus: reed-like.
arvensis: growing in cultivated fields.
asper: rough, as with hairs or projections.
avium: of birds.

baccatus: berried.
belladonna: Italian, beautiful lady, from the use of the juice in beautifying the eyes.
biennis: biennial.
bistortus: twisted twice.
botrytis: clustered, racemose.
brevis: short.
bulbosus: bulbous.
bullatus: puckered, wrinkled.

caeruleus: sky-blue.
caespitosus: tufted.
campestris: of fields or plains.
canariensis: of the Canary Islands.
caninum: pertaining to dogs.
capillaris: fine as a hair.
capitatus: headed.
cardunculus: from *carduus*, a thistle.
carinatus: keeled.
caulorapa: stem turnip.
cepa: Lat. for onion.
cerasus: cherry-bearing.
chamaedrys: on the ground and an oak; refers to the habit of the plant and the shape of the leaves.
chiloensis: of Chile.
chinensis: of China.
cinerariifolius: leaves like *Cineraria*.
cinerea: ash-coloured.
coccineus: scarlet.
communis: growing in colonies; sometimes used in the sense of common or usual.
commutatus: changing or changed.
compactus: compact, dense.
compressus: compressed, flattened.
convolvulus: entwined, wound together.
corniculatus: having a little horn.
coronatus: crowned.
cotulus: cup-like.
crispus: crisped, curled.
crista-galli: cock's-comb.
cristatus: crested.
crocatus: saffron, yellow.
cruciatus: cross-like.
cucubalis: pigeon's crop.
cyanus: dark blue.
cynanthus: blue-flowered.

demissus, weak, humble.
denticulatus: denticulate, slightly toothed.
dicoccus: with two grains or berries.
didymus: growing in pairs.
dioicus: dioecious.
discolor: of two colours.
dissectus: dissected, deeply cut.
distichus: in two ranks.
diurna: of the day.
domesticus: domesticated.
draba: old name of a cress.
dubium: doubtful.
dulcamara: bitter-sweet.
dulcis: sweet.
duriusculus: somewhat hard or rough.
durus: hard.

echinatus: prickly, bristly.
effusus: very loosely-spreading.
elatior: taller.
elatius: taller.
epilinum: upon *Linum* (flax or linseed).
epithymum: upon thyme.
erectus: erect.
esculentus: edible.
europaeus: European.
exiguus: small, slender.
expansus: expanded.

falcatus: sickle-shaped.
fallax: false.
farfara: from the old Latin name of colts-foot.
fatuus: foolish, simple, unsavoury, useless.
ficarius: fig-like, refers to the leaves.
fistulosus: fistular, hollow-cylindrical.
flaccus: flaccid, flabby, soft.
flammula: an old generic name.
flavescens: yellowish.
flavus: yellow.
flexuosus: flexuose, wavy.
fluitans: floating.
foenum-graecum: Greek hay.
foetidus: fetid, bad-smelling.
fruticans: shrubby.
fullonum: of fullers.

gallicus: of France or Gaul.
gemmiferus: bearing buds.
geniculatus: geniculate, jointed.
glomeratus: clumped, shaped like a ball.
glutinosus: gluey, sticky.
gracilis: slender.
gramineus: grass-like.
graveolens: strongly-smelling.

hastatus: hastate, halberd-shaped.
hederaceus: of the ivy (*Hedera*).
helioscopius: turning towards the sun.
hexastichus: in six ranks.
hirsutus: hirsute, hairy.
hispanicus: of Spain.
hispidus: hispid, bristly.
hortensis: of gardens.
hyemalis: of winter.
hypogeus: beneath the ground.

idaeus: Mount Ida, Asia Minor.
incarnatus: flesh-coloured.

inermis: unarmed, without awns, thorns or spines.
inflatus: inflated.
inflexus: hard, rigid.
intybus: Latin name for chicory.

Jacobaea: of St. James; refers to time of flowering, St. James' day, July 25th.

lanatus: woolly.
lanceolatus: lance-shaped.
latifolius: broad-leaved.
leucanthus: white-flowered.
ligulatus: ligulate, strap-shaped.
linguus: tongue-shaped.
ludovicianus: of St. Louis.
lupulinus: like a hop.
lupulus: lupus, wolf, from its tenacious clinging.
luteus: yellowish.

macranthus: large-flowered.
macrocarpus: large-fruited.
maculatus: spotted.
major: greater.
majus: greater.
maritimus: maritime, of the sea.
maximus: largest.
medius: medium, intermediate.
melongena: a kind of melon.
micranthus: small-flowered.
microcarpus: small-fruited.
microphyllus: small-leaved.
millefolius: thousand-leaved.
minor: smaller.
minus: smaller.
mollis: soft.
mollugo: soft, tender.
monococcus: with one grain or berry.
monogynus: having one carpel.
montanus: of the mountains.
multiflorus: many-flowered.
muralis: of walls.
myosuroides: like the tail of a mouse.
myurus: mouse-tail.

napellus: little turnip, refers to the tuberous root.
napus: classical name for turnip.
neglectus: neglected; not recognized earlier.
nemoralis: growing in woods or groves.

nemorosus: growing in groves.
niger: black.
nigricans: turning black.
nodosus: having swollen nodes.
nudifloris: naked-flowered.
nudus: nude, naked.
nutans: nodding.

obtusifolius: obtuse-leaved, blunt-tipped.
odoratus: aromatic, fragrant.
officinalis: officinal, used in medicine.
oleiferus: oil-producing.
oleraceus: garden vegetable; leaves used in cooking.
orientalis: Oriental, Eastern.
ovinus: pertaining to sheep.
oxyacanthus: sharp-spined.

pallidus: pale.
palmatus: palmate.
palustris: growing in marshes.
parviflorus: having small flowers.
patens: spreading.
patulus: spreading, stretched out.
pectinatus: comb-like.
peplus: classical name for a species of spurge.
peregrinus: foreign, exotic.
perennis: perennial.
perpusillus: extremely small.
persicarius: peach-like.
persicus: of Persia.
petiolatus: having a leaf-stalk (petiole).
pilosellus: finely-woolly.
pinnatus: pinnate.
podagraria: foot chain; refers to its use for gout.
politus: polished.
polonicus: Polish.
polyacanthus: many-spined.
polyanthus: many-flowered.
porrifolius: leek-leaved.
porrum: Lat. name for leek.
praecox: precocious, early.
pratensis: growing in meadows.
procumbens: procumbent.
prostratus: prostrate, lying flat.
pubescens: pubescent, downy.
pungens: pungent.
pusillus: very small.

radicans: rooting.
ramosus: branched.

619

rapa: old Lat. name for turnip.
raphanistrum: old generic name.
reflexus: reflexed, bent back.
repens: creeping.
reptans: creeping.
resupinatus: upside down.
rhaponticum: rha, rhubarb, *Pontus,* an area bordering on the Black Sea.
rhoeas: ancient name for corn poppy.
rostratus: beaked.
ruber: red.
rubescens: becoming red.
rugosus: wrinkled.

saccharum: of sugar.
sanguineus: blood-red.
saponarius: soapy.
sativus: cultivated.
sceleratus: cursed.
schoenoprasum: Gk., rush-leek.
scoparius: broom-like, having numerous thin branches.
secalinus: rye-like.
segetum: growing in cornfields.
sepium: of hedges or fences.
serotinus: late, late-flowering.
serratus: serrated.
sessilis: sessile, stalkless.
setosus: full of bristles.
somniferus: causing sleep.
speciosus: showy.
sphondylium: an old generic name.
spinosus: full of spines.
spontaneus: originating of itself.
squalidus: squalid, filthy, stiff.
squamosus: full of small scales.
squarrosus: spreading at the tips.
stellatus: star-like.
sterilis: sterile, infertile.
stoloniferus: having stolons.
stramonium: ancient name for thorn apple.
strictus: upright, erect, inflexible, tight.
strigosus: having stiff bristles.

suaveolens: sweetly-scented.
supina: lying back.
sylvaticus: forest-loving.
sylvestris: growing in woods or forests.

tardus: late.
tartaricus: of Tartary, central Asia.
temulentus: drunken.
tenuifolius: slender-leaved.
tenuis: slender.
textilis: related to textiles.
tinctorius: pertaining to dyers.
tomentosus: densely-woolly.
tremulus: trembling, quivering.
tricolor: three-coloured.
trifurcatus: three-forked.
trivialis: common, ordinary.
tuberosus: having tubers.
turgidus: turgid, full.

uliginosus: growing in marshes.
unioloides: like *Uniola,* another genus of grasses.
urens: stinging, burning.
ursinus: pertaining to bears.
usitatissimus: in most common use.

vaginatus: sheathed.
variabilis: variable.
vavilovi: after N. I. Vavilov, a Russian scientist (1886-1942).
ventricosus: bellied.
veris: true, genuine.
vernus: vernal, of the spring.
versicolor: variously coloured.
viciifolius: vetch-leaved.
vineale: of vineyards.
virens: green.
viridis: green.
vulgaris: vulgar, common.
vulnerarius: healing wounds.
vulpinus: of the fox.

INDEX

Chief references are indicated in black type. Technical terms which may be used frequently are indexed only for the page on which they are explained (for other technical terms, see *Glossary*).

621

x